SCHAUM'S OUTLINE OF

THEORY AND PROBLEMS

of

MICROPROCESSOR
FUNDAMENTALS

Second Edition

•

by

ROGER L. TOKHEIM, M.S.

Chairman, Department of Industrial Education
Henry Sibley High School
Mendota Heights, Minnesota

SCHAUM'S OUTLINE SERIES

McGRAW-HILL PUBLISHING COMPANY

New York   St. Louis   San Francisco   Auckland   Bogotá   Caracas
Hamburg   Lisbon   London   Madrid   Mexico   Milan   Montreal
New Delhi   Oklahoma City   Paris   San Juan   São Paulo
Singapore   Sydney   Tokyo   Toronto

ROGER L. TOKHEIM holds B.S. and M.S. degrees from St. Cloud State University and an Ed.S. degree from the University of Wisconsin–Stout. He is the author of *Digital Electronics* and its companion, *Activities Manual for Digital Electronics*, *Schaum's Outline of Theory and Problems of Digital Principles*, *Electronics and Microcomputer Circuits— 146 Practical Projects*, and numerous other instructional materials on science and technology. An experienced educator at the secondary and college levels, he is presently an instructor of industrial education and computer science at Henry Sibley High School, Mendota Heights, Minnesota.

Schaum's Outline of Theory and Problems of
MICROPROCESSOR FUNDAMENTALS

2 3 4 5 6 7 8 9 0 SHP SHP   9 4 3 2 1 0

ISBN 0-07-064999-5

Sponsoring Editor, John Aliano
Production Supervisor, Leroy Young
Project Supervision, The Total Book

Library of Congress Cataloging-in-Publication Data

Tokheim, Roger L.
    Schaum's outline of theory and problems of microprocessor
fundamentals / by Roger L. Tokheim. -- 2nd ed.
        p.   cm. -- (Schaum's outline series)
    Includes index.
    ISBN 0-07-064999-5
    1. Microprocessors.   2. Microprocessors--Problems, exercises, etc.
I. Title.
QA76.5.T559   1990
004. 16'076--dc19   88-7923
                                                                    CIP

Preface

The electronics student or specialist of tomorrow must have a knowledge of microprocessors and microprocessor-based systems. This will include knowledge not only of microcomputer hardware but of software as well. Microprocessors are the basis for an exciting new breed of intelligent devices. Microprocessors are found in diverse products: from children's toys to automobiles, from microcomputers to home appliances, from industrial robots and machinery to home entertainment equipment. Because of programmable devices called microprocessors, the development of intelligent machines is expected to accelerate in the future.

The second edition of *Schaum's Outline of Microprocessor Fundamentals* provides the reader with the basic topics customarily covered in a first course in microprocessors. The Schaum's Outline philosophy of concentrating on typical problems encountered while studying any subject is supported in this outline by the use of over 1100 solved and supplementary problems dealing with microprocessors and microcomputers. Complete solutions accompany most of the problems in this book.

The second edition of *Schaum's Outline of Microprocessor Fundamentals* contains most of the same topics which made the first edition a great success. Several additions were made in the second edition which reflect new training practices, technological changes, and suggestions from students and instructors. Two chapters covering the 8-bit 6502/65C02 microprocessor were added giving hardware and programming details. By popular demand, a chapter surveying selected 16- and 32-bit microprocessors was also added. Included are the Intel 8086, 8088, 80186, 80188, 80286, and 80386 16- and 32-bit processors. Also included are the Motorola 68000, 68008, 68010, 68012, 68020, and 68030 microprocessors. Finally, the Western Design Center 65802 and 65816 16-bit microprocessors are surveyed.

The topics outlined in this book were carefully selected to coincide with courses taught at the upper high school, vocational-technical, community college, and beginning college level. Many of the most widely used vocational-technical level textbooks and lab manuals on microprocessors and microcomputers were analyzed. The topics and problems included in this Schaum's Outline are similar to those encountered most frequently in these standard books. Program segments listed in this Outline were carefully checked for accuracy on typical inexpensive microcomputer trainers. Some of these trainers are available from Intel Corporation, Heath/Zenith, and Lab-Volt Systems.

The second edition of *Schaum's Outline of Microprocessor Fundamentals* begins with a short introduction to computers. Next, background information on numbers, computer codes, and computer arithmetic is presented along with a brief review of basic digital devices. Commercial microprocessor-based systems are very complex. Because of this a simplified generic microprocessor is used to introduce microcomputer fundamentals, the microprocessor, programming the microprocessor, and interfacing the microprocessor. The register and instructions sets of the generic microprocessor are subsets of the 8080/8085 MPU. Next, three of the most popular 8-bit microprocessors are covered in some detail. The microprocessor units described are the Intel 8080/8085, the Motorola 6800, and the 6502/65C02. Two chapters are dedicated to each microprocessor. The final chapter briefly surveys other more complex 16- and 32-bit microprocessors from Intel, Motorola, and Western Design Center.

Appreciation is extended to McGraw-Hill's John Aliano for his assistance and patience. My gratitude to engineering student Darrell Klotzbach for his fine research efforts, meticulous proofreading, and careful checking of many of the programs in this book. Special thanks to my family, Caroline, Dan, and Marshall for their help, patience, and encouragement.

ROGER L. TOKHEIM

Contents

Chapter 1

Introduction to Computers

1.1 INTRODUCTION

Computers have been in general use since the 1950s. Formerly, digital computers were large, expensive machines used by governments and large businesses. The size and shape of the digital computer has changed in the past owing to a new device called the microprocessor. The *microprocessor* is an IC (integrated circuit) that contains much of the processing capabilities of a large computer. The microprocessor is a small but extremely complex LSI (large-scale-integration) device that is programmable. Computers use a stored program. Smaller computers, called *microcomputers*, also use the *stored-program* concept. A microcomputer contains a microprocessor and at least some form of semiconductor memory.

Large, expensive computers are usually *general-purpose* units. They are typically reprogrammed and used for many jobs. *Dedicated computers* are becoming very common because of the use of the small, inexpensive microprocessor. A dedicated computer is programmed for and performs only a few tasks, as in toys, thermostats, automobiles, and appliances.

1.2 COMPUTER ORGANIZATION

The traditional sections of a digital computer are shown in Fig. 1-1. The basic computer system consists of five units: the *input* unit, the *control* and *arithmetic* units (contained in the CPU, or central processing unit), the *memory* unit, and the *output* unit. This organization of functional parts may be called the *architecture* of the computer.

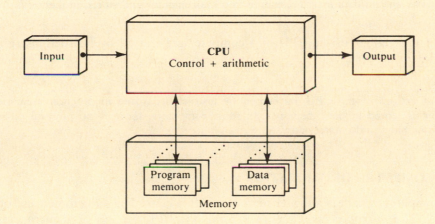

Fig. 1-1 General organization of a computer

The physical units shown in boxes in Fig. 1-1 are referred to as *hardware*. To be useful, the *program memory* must tell the CPU what to do. Preparing the list of *instructions* is called *programming*. The list of instructions is a *program* and is stored either temporarily or permanently in the program memory. These programs manipulate information called *data*. *Software* is a general term used to cover all programs. If software is stored permanently in program memory, it is sometimes called *firmware*.

Briefly, the computer works in the following manner. Both program and data are fed into the CPU and are transferred to their respective memory locations. The CPU reads the first instruction from program memory and executes it. Instructions may be as simple as ADD two numbers,

1

MOVE data, INPUT or OUTPUT data, or JUMP to a different place in the program. After the data manipulations are complete, the results are transferred to the output of the computer. Again, most actions of the CPU are caused by the instructions stored in program memory.

SOLVED PROBLEMS

1.1 List five functional sections of a digital computer.

Solution:

The five functional sections of a computer are shown in Fig. 1-1 as the input, control, arithmetic, memory, and output units. CPU is a general term for the unit that includes the control and arithmetic units as well as several other units.

1.2 The actual electronic units such as those symbolized by the boxes in Fig. 1-1 are referred to as _____, while the programs instructing the computer what to do are called software.

Solution:

The actual physical electronic units in a computer are referred to as hardware.

1.3 A person called a programmer writes a list of _____ which is called a program.

Solution:

A programmer writes a list of instructions which is called a program.

1.4 List the two types of information that are input and stored in the memory of a computer.

Solution:

A program and data must be entered into the computer and stored in memory.

1.5 Most of the actions of the CPU in a computer are caused by instructions stored in _____ memory.

Solution:

Most actions of the CPU are caused by instructions stored in program memory. Data to be processed is stored in data memory. In some computers, there is no physical difference between program memory and data memory.

1.3 MICROCOMPUTER ORGANIZATION

A microcomputer system is a digital computer. It is classed as a *micro* because of its small size and low cost. The *microprocessor* generally forms the CPU section of a microcomputer system. The organization of a typical microcomputer is diagramed in Fig. 1-2. The microcomputer contains all five basic sections of a computer: (1) the *input* unit, (2) the *control* and (3) *arithmetic* units contained within the microprocessor, (4) the *memory* unit, and (5) the *output* unit.

The microprocessor controls all the units of the system using the *control lines* shown at the left in Fig. 1-2. Besides the control lines, the *address bus* (16 parallel conductors) selects a certain memory location, input port, or output port. The *data bus* (eight parallel conductors) on the right is a *two-way path* for transferring data in and out of the microprocessor unit. It is important to note that the microprocessor unit (MPU) can send data to or receive data from the memory using the data bus.

If a program is stored permanently, it is usually placed in a memory device called a *read-only memory* (ROM). The ROM (rhymes with "mom") is usually a permanently programmed memory

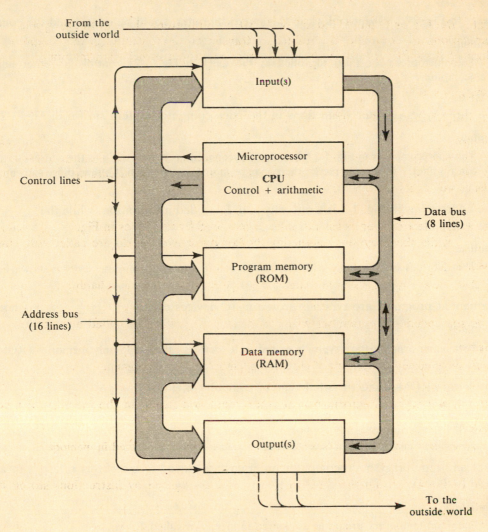

Fig. 1-2 Typical microcomputer organization

chip in IC form. Temporary data memory is usually stored in an IC device called a *read/write memory* (RWM). In common practice, the read/write memory is referred to as a *random-access memory*, or *RAM* (rhymes with "jam"). Microcomputer user programs that are of a temporary nature are also stored in the RAM section of memory along with data. The RAM and ROM sections of memory are shown separate in Fig. 1-2 because they are usually separate ICs.

The system shown in Fig. 1-2 represents the general organization of a microcomputer. Most microcomputers would have these minimum features plus several more. For clarity, it is customary on block diagrams to omit the necessary power supply, clock, and some feedback lines to the microprocessor unit.

SOLVED PROBLEMS

1.6   The CPU of a microcomputer is an IC called a _____.

   Solution:

   The CPU of a microcomputer is generally an IC called a microprocessor. With some designs several IC chips are needed to perform the job of the CPU.

1.7   Refer to Fig. 1-2.   Which block in this microcomputer would be considered the *control* unit?

Solution:

The microprocessor (also identified as the CPU in Fig. 1-2) controls all other units in the microcomputer.

1.8   List three types of interconnections in the microcomputer system shown in Fig. 1-2.

Solution:

The microcomputer in Fig. 1-2 labels the interconnections between ICs as the address bus, data bus, and control lines.   In actual practice there may be more lines between ICs than those shown in Fig. 1-2.

1.9   The address bus in Fig. 1-2 is a one-way path for coded information, while the _____ bus is a two-way path.

Solution:

The data bus is a two-way path for information in the microcomputer system shown in Fig. 1-2.

1.10   Permanent programs are typically stored in IC devices called _____-_____ memories.

Solution:

Permanent programs are typically stored in IC devices called read-only memories (ROMs).

1.11   The letters ROM stand for what type of computer memory?

Solution:

ROM stands for read-only memory.

1.12   Data and temporary microcomputer programs are stored in memories referred to as _____ (RAM, ROM).

Solution:

Data and temporary programs are stored in memories called RAM.

1.13   Microcomputer RAM data storage is _____ (permanent, temporary).

Solution:

RAM storage is temporary.

1.14   The place information enters or leaves a computer is called a _____ (port, slot).

Solution:

Information enters or leaves a computer system through places called ports.

1.4 MICROCOMPUTER OPERATION

As an example of microcomputer operation refer to Fig. 1-3.   In this example the following procedure is illustrated:

1.   Press the A key on the keyboard.
2.   Store the letter A in memory.
3.   Print the letter A on the screen of the cathode-ray tube (CRT) monitor.

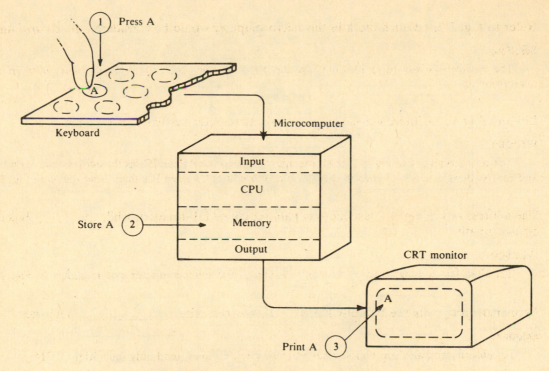

Fig. 1-3 Typical microcomputer operation

The input-store-output procedure outlined in Fig. 1-3 is a typical microcomputer system operation. The electronic hardware used in a system like that in Fig. 1-3 is quite complicated. However, the transfer of data within the system will help explain the use of the different units within the microcomputer.

The more detailed diagram in Fig. 1-4 will aid understanding of the typical microcomputer input-store-output procedure. First, look carefully at the *contents* section of the program memory in Fig. 1-4. Note that instructions have already been loaded into the first six memory locations. From Fig. 1-4, it is determined that the instructions currently listed in the program memory are:

1. INPUT data from input port 1.
2. STORE data from port 1 in data memory location 200.
3. OUTPUT data to output port 10.

Note that there are only three instructions in the above program. It appears that there are six instructions in the program memory in Fig. 1-4. The reason for this is that instructions are usually broken into parts. The first part of instruction 1 above was to INPUT data. The second part tells from where the data comes (from port 1). The first *action* part of the instruction is called the *operation* and the second part the *operand*. The operation and operand are located in separate memory locations in the program memory in Fig. 1-4. For the first instruction in Fig. 1-4, program memory location 100 holds the INPUT operation while memory location 101 holds the operand (port 1) telling from where information will be input.

Two new sections have been identified inside the microprocessor in Fig. 1-4. These two sections are called *registers*. These special registers are the *accumulator* and the *instruction register*.

The sequence of events happening within the microcomputer in the input-store-output example in Fig. 1-3 is outlined in Fig. 1-4. The flow of instructions and data will be followed by keying on the circled numbers in the diagram. Remember that *the microprocessor (MPU) is the center of all data transfers and operations*. Refer to Fig. 1-4 for all steps below.

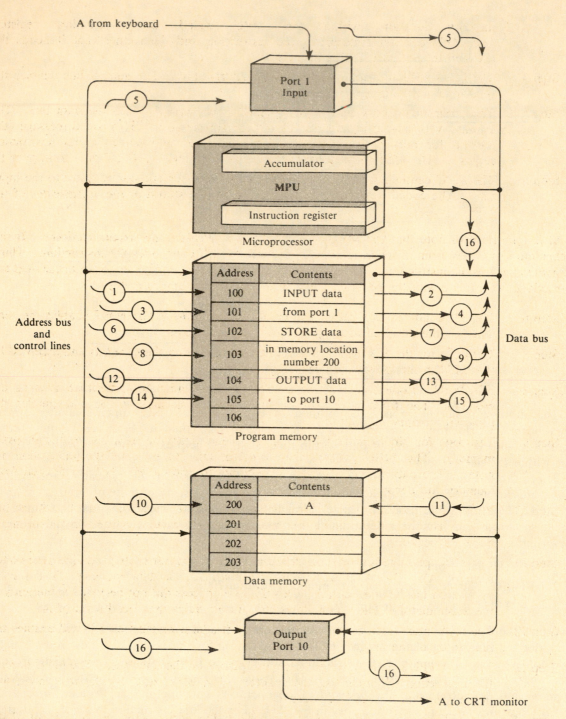

Fig. 1-4 Step-by-step operation of a microcomputer as it executes the instructions in program memory

Step 1   The MPU sends out address 100 on the address bus.   A control line *enables* (turns on) the *read* input on the program memory IC (to read means to copy information from a memory location).   This step is symbolized on Fig. 1-4 by the encircled 1.

Step 2   The program memory reads out the first instruction (INPUT data) on the data bus, and the MPU accepts this coded message.   The instruction is placed in a special memory location within the MPU called the instruction register. The MPU *decodes* (interprets) the instruction and determines that it needs the operand to the INPUT data instruction.

Step 3   The MPU sends out address 101 on the address bus. The control line enables the read input of the program memory.

Step 4   The program memory places the operand (from port 1) onto the data bus. The operand was located at address 101 in program memory. This coded message (the address for port 1) is accepted off the data bus and placed in the instruction register. The MPU now decodes the entire instruction (INPUT data from port 1).

Step 5   The MPU causes port 1 to open using the address bus and control lines to the input unit. The coded form for A is transferred to and stored in the *accumulator* of the MPU.

It is important to note that the MPU always follows a *fetch-decode-execute sequence*. It first fetches the instruction from program memory. Second, the MPU decodes the instruction. Third, the MPU executes the instruction. Try to notice this fetch-decode-execute sequence in the next two instructions. Continue with the program listed in the program memory in Fig. 1-4.

Step 6   The MPU addresses location 102 on the address bus. The MPU enables the read input on the program memory using the control lines.

Step 7   The code for the STORE data instruction is read onto the data bus and accepted by the MPU in the instruction register.

Step 8   The MPU decodes the STORE data instruction and determines that it needs the operand. The MPU addresses the next memory location (103) and enables the program memory read input.

Step 9   The code for "in memory location 200" is placed on the data bus by the program memory. The MPU accepts this operand and stores it in the instruction register. The entire "STORE data in memory location 200" has been fetched from memory and decoded.

Step 10   The execute process now starts. The MPU sends out address 200 on the address bus and enables the *write* input of the data memory (to write means to copy data into a memory location).

Step 11   The MPU puts the information stored in the accumulator on the data bus (the coded form of A). The A is written into location 200 in data memory. The second instruction has been executed. This STORE process did not destroy the contents of the accumulator. The accumulator still also contains the coded form of A.

Step 12   The MPU must fetch the next instruction. It addresses location 104 and enables the read input of the program memory.

Step 13   The "OUTPUT data" instruction code is placed on the data bus. The MPU accepts the instruction in the instruction register. The MPU decodes the instruction and determines that it needs an operand.

Step 14   The MPU places address 105 on the address bus and enables the read input of the program memory.

Step 15   The program memory puts the code for the operand "to port 10" on the data bus. The MPU accepts this code in the instruction register.

Step 16   The MPU decodes the entire instruction "OUTPUT data to port 10." The MPU activates port 10 using the address bus and control lines to the output unit. The MPU places the code for the A (still stored in the accumulator) on the data bus. The A is transmitted out of port 10 to the CRT monitor.

Most microprocessors transfer information in a fashion similar to the one detailed in Fig. 1-4.   The greatest variations are probably in the input and output sections.   Several more steps may be required to get the input and output sections to operate properly.

It is important to notice that the MPU is the center of and controls all operations.   The MPU follows the fetch-decode-execute sequence.   The actual operations of the microprocessor, however, are dictated by the instructions listed in program memory.

SOLVED PROBLEMS

1.15   The list of instructions executed by a microcomputer is called a _____.

Solution:

The list of instructions executed by a microcomputer is called a program.

1.16   Most microcomputer instructions consist of two parts called the operation and the _____.

Solution:

Most instructions consist of two parts called the operation and the operand.

1.17   Microcomputer instructions in program memory are generally performed in _____ (consecutive, random) order.

Solution:

Instructions in program memory are *generally* performed in consecutive order.   Later, special *branch* instructions will be introduced that make the MPU jump to other than the next consecutively numbered instruction.   They are never performed in random order.

1.18   Refer to Fig. 1-4.   After executing the "OUTPUT data to port 10" instruction, the MPU would point to address location _____ in program memory for the next instruction.

Solution:

After executing the "OUTPUT data to port 10" instruction in Fig. 1-4, the MPU would point to address location 106 in program memory for the next instruction.   Program memory location 106 is blank in Fig. 1-4, so the action of the MPU would be unpredictable.   A WAIT or HALT instruction would probably be placed here so that the action of the computer could be predicted.

1.19   Refer to Fig. 1-4.   A microcomputer instruction such as "STORE data in memory location 201" would result in the transfer of data from the MPU to location 201 in _____ memory.

Solution:

An instruction such as "STORE data in memory location 201" would result in the transfer of data from the MPU to location 201 in data memory.

1.20   Refer to Fig. 1-4.   A microcomputer instruction such as "STORE data in memory location 202" would result in the transfer of data from the MPU's _____ (accumulator, instruction register) to address location _____ in RAM.

Solution:

An instruction such as "STORE data in memory location 202" would result in the transfer of data from the MPU's accumulator to address location 202 in RAM.   This data would then be contained in both RAM memory location 202 and the MPU's accumulator.   The contents of the accumulator are not destroyed when data is stored.

1.21   The _____ (read, write) process occurs when data is copied from a memory location.

Solution:

   The read process occurs when data is copied from a memory location.

1.22   Placing data into a storage location is a process called _____ (reading, writing) into memory.

Solution:

   Putting data into a storage location is a process called writing into memory.

1.23   For each instruction in program memory, the MPU goes through a _____-_____-_____ sequence.

Solution:

   For each instruction in program memory, the MPU goes through a fetch-decode-execute sequence. Some books call this the *locate-read-interpret-execute cycle.*

1.24   Refer to Fig. 1-4. After step 16, when the instruction "OUTPUT data to port 10" is complete, what data is contained in the accumulator of the MPU?

Solution:

   The accumulator still contains the code for A. Reading data from a register or memory location only copies the information that is there and does not destroy the data.

1.25   Refer to Fig. 1-4. After step 16, do the instructions in memory locations 100 through 105 still exist?

Solution:

   Yes. Reading instructions does not destroy the contents of that memory location.

Supplementary Problems

1.26   In electronics, the letters IC stand for _____ _____.   *Ans.*   integrated circuit

1.27   In electronics, the letters LSI stand for _____-_____ _____.   *Ans.*   large-scale integration

1.28   In computers, the letters CPU stand for _____ _____ _____.   *Ans.*   central processing unit

1.29   An LSI IC that has most of the capabilities of a computer's CPU is called a _____.
Ans.   microprocessor

1.30   In microcomputers, the letters MPU stand for _____ _____.   *Ans.*   microprocessor unit

1.31   Microcomputers that perform only one or two tasks are said to be _____ (general-purpose, dedicated) computers.   *Ans.*   dedicated

1.32   A classical computer organization would probably list what five major units?
Ans.   input, control, arithmetic, memory, output

1.33   A list of computer instructions is classified as _____ (hardware, software).   *Ans.*   software

1.34   Information that is manipulated within a computer is called _____ (data, numerical information).
Ans.   data

1.35   A person who writes lists of instructions for a computer is called a _____.   _Ans_.   programmer

1.36   Permanent storage of a program inside a microcomputer would probably be done in a _____ (RAM, ROM).   _Ans_.   ROM

1.37   The _____ (RAM, ROM) is an IC device widely used in microcomputers as a read/write memory.
Ans.   RAM

1.38   Refer to Fig. 1-2.   The instructions stored in the program memory would be _____ (permanent, temporary).   _Ans_.   permanent (stored in ROM)

1.39   Refer to Fig. 1-4.   After step 16 is complete, the MPU will attempt the _____ (decode, fetch, execute) procedure.   _Ans_.   fetch

1.40   Refer to Fig. 1-4.   The MPU accesses a specific memory location by using the _____ bus.
Ans.   address

1.41   Refer to Fig. 1-4.   Coded information is transferred from the MPU's accumulator to a storage location in data memory using the _____ bus.   _Ans_.   data

1.42   If the MPU fetched and decoded an instruction saying "STORE data in memory location 205," the data would come from the _____.   _Ans_.   accumulator (within the MPU)

1.43   A microcomputer contains at least an input unit, an output unit, an MPU, and a program and data _____.   _Ans_.   memory

1.44   A temporary read/write memory is designated by either the three letters RWM or _____.
Ans.   RAM

Chapter 2

Numbers, Computer Codes, and Arithmetic

2.1 BINARY NUMBERS

Digital computers use *binary numbers*. The binary, or *base 2*, number system uses only the digits 0 and 1. These *binary digits* are called *bits*. In the computer's electronic circuits a 0 bit is usually represented by a LOW voltage, whereas a 1 bit corresponds to a HIGH voltage.

Human beings are trained to understand the *decimal number system*. The decimal, or *base 10*, system has 10 digits (0–9). The decimal number system also has a *place value* characteristic. For instance, Fig. 2-1a shows that the decimal number 1327 equals one 1000 plus three 100s plus two 10s plus seven 1s ($1000 + 300 + 20 + 7 = 1327$).

The binary number system also has a place value characteristic. The decimal value for the first four binary places is shown in Fig. 2-1b. The binary number 1001 (say one, zero, zero, one) is then

Powers of 10	10^3	10^2	10^1	10^0
Place value	1000s	100s	10s	1s
Decimal	**1**	**3**	**2**	**7**
Decimal	1000 +	300 +	20 +	7 = 1327

(*a*) Place values in a decimal number

Powers of 2	2^3	2^2	2^1	2^0
Place value	8s	4s	2s	1s
	MSB			LSB
Binary	**1**	**0**	**0**	**1**
Decimal	8 +	0 +	0 +	1 = 9

(*b*) Place values in a binary number

Decimal		Binary				Decimal		Binary			
10s	1s	8s	4s	2s	1s	10s	1s	8s	4s	2s	1s
	0				0		8	1	0	0	0
	1				1		9	1	0	0	1
	2			1	0	1	0	1	0	1	0
	3			1	1	1	1	1	0	1	1
	4		1	0	0	1	2	1	1	0	0
	5		1	0	1	1	3	1	1	0	1
	6		1	1	0	1	4	1	1	1	0
	7		1	1	1	1	5	1	1	1	1

(*c*) Decimal and binary equivalents

Fig. 2-1

converted to its decimal equivalent of 9. The 1s bit of the binary number in Fig. 2-1b is called the *least significant bit* (LSB), whereas the 8s bit is labeled the *most significant bit* (MSB).

The binary equivalents for the decimal numbers from 0 through 15 are shown in Fig. 2-1c. Persons working with computers memorize at least these binary numbers.

Convert the binary number 10110110 (say one, zero, one, one, zero, one, one, zero) to its decimal equivalent. The procedure is shown in Fig. 2-2a. For each 1 bit in the binary number, the decimal place value is written below. The decimals are then added ($128 + 32 + 16 + 4 + 2 = 182$), yielding 182. The small *subscripts* in Fig. 2-2b are used to note the base (sometimes called the radix) of the number. The number 10110110_2 is then a binary, or base 2, number. The number 182_{10} is then a decimal, or base 10, number.

Powers of 2	2^7	2^6	2^5	2^4	2^3	2^2	2^1	2^0
Place value	128s	64s	32s	16s	8s	4s	2s	1s

Binary	1	0	1	1	0	1	1	0	
Decimal	128	+	32	+ 16	+	4	+ 2	=	182

(*a*) Binary-to-decimal conversion

$$10110110_2 = 182_{10}$$

(*b*) Subscripts designate the base of the number

Fig. 2-2

Convert the decimal number 155 to a binary number. Figure 2-3 shows a procedure for making this conversion. The decimal number 155 is first divided by 2, leaving a quotient of 77 with a remainder of 1. This remainder becomes the least significant bit (LSB) of the binary number and is transferred to this position in Fig. 2-3. The quotient (77) is then transferred as shown by the arrow and becomes the next dividend. The quotients are repeatedly divided by 2 until the quotient becomes 0 with a remainder of 1. This is shown in the second-to-last line in Fig. 2-3. The bottom line shows the result of the conversion as $155_{10} = 10011011_2$.

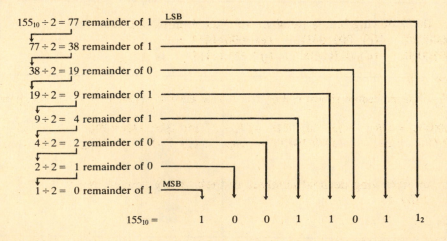

Fig. 2-3

SOLVED PROBLEMS

2.1 Most human beings understand the decimal number system, whereas digital computers use the base 2, or _____, number system.

Solution:

Digital computers use the base 2, or binary, number system containing only the digits 0 and 1.

2.2 The term *bit* means _____ _____ when dealing with binary numbers.

Solution:

Bit means binary digit.

2.3 The number 100_{10} is a base _____ number.

Solution:

The number 100_{10} is a base 10 number, as indicated by the subscript 10 after the number.

2.4 Write the base 2 number one, one, zero, zero using a subscript.

Solution:

1100_2.

2.5 The letters MSB mean _____ _____ _____ when dealing with binary numbers.

Solution:

The letters MSB mean most significant bit. In the number 1000_2, the 1 is the MSB.

2.6 From memory, convert the following binary numbers to their decimal equivalents:
(a) 0001   (b) 0101   (c) 1000   (d) 1011   (e) 1111   (f) 0111

Solution:

Refer to Fig. 2-1c. These binary numbers are to be memorized. The decimal equivalents to the binary numbers are as follows:
(a) $0001_2 = 1_{10}$ (c) $1000_2 = 8_{10}$ (e) $1111_2 = 15_{10}$
(b) $0101_2 = 5_{10}$ (d) $1011_2 = 11_{10}$ (f) $0111_2 = 7_{10}$

2.7 Convert the following binary numbers to their decimal equivalents:
(a) 10000000   (c) 00110011   (e) 00011111
(b) 00010000   (d) 01100100   (f) 11111111

Solution:

Follow the procedure shown in Fig. 2-1b. The decimal equivalents to the binary numbers are as follows:
(a) $10000000_2 = 128_{10}$ (c) $00110011_2 = 51_{10}$ (e) $00011111_2 = 31_{10}$
(b) $00010000_2 = 16_{10}$ (d) $01100100_2 = 100_{10}$ (f) $11111111_2 = 255_{10}$

2.8 Convert the following decimal numbers to their binary equivalents:
(a) 39   (b) 48

Solution:

Follow the procedure shown in Fig. 2-3. The binary equivalents to the decimal numbers are as follows:

(a)
$$39_{10} \div 2 = 19 \text{ remainder of 1 (LSB)}$$
$$19 \div 2 = 9 \text{ remainder of 1}$$
$$9 \div 2 = 4 \text{ remainder of 1}$$
$$4 \div 2 = 2 \text{ remainder of 0}$$
$$2 \div 2 = 1 \text{ remainder of 0}$$
$$1 \div 2 = 0 \text{ remainder of 1 (MSB)}$$
$$39_{10} = 100111_2$$

(b)
$$48_{10} \div 2 = 24 \text{ remainder of 0 (LSB)}$$
$$24 \div 2 = 12 \text{ remainder of 0}$$
$$12 \div 2 = 6 \text{ remainder of 0}$$
$$6 \div 2 = 3 \text{ remainder of 0}$$
$$3 \div 2 = 1 \text{ remainder of 1}$$
$$1 \div 2 = 0 \text{ remainder of 1(MSB)}$$
$$48_{10} = 110000_2$$

2.2 HEXADECIMAL NUMBERS

A typical microcomputer memory location might hold the binary number 10011110.   This long string of 0s and 1s is hard to remember and difficult to enter on a keyboard.   The number 10011110_2 could be converted to a decimal number.   Upon conversion it is found that 10011110_2 equals 158_{10}.   This conversion process takes too long.   Most microcomputer systems use *hexadecimal notation* to simplify remembering and entering binary numbers such as 10011110.

The hexadecimal, or base 16, number system uses the 16 symbols 0 through 9, A, B, C, D, E, and F.   Decimal, hexadecimal, and binary equivalents are shown in Fig. 2-4.

Decimal	Hexadecimal	Binary			
		8s	4s	2s	1s
0	0	0	0	0	0
1	1	0	0	0	1
2	2	0	0	1	0
3	3	0	0	1	1
4	4	0	1	0	0
5	5	0	1	0	1
6	6	0	1	1	0
7	7	0	1	1	1
8	8	1	0	0	0
9	9	1	0	0	1
10	A	1	0	1	0
11	B	1	0	1	1
12	C	1	1	0	0
13	D	1	1	0	1
14	E	1	1	1	0
15	F	1	1	1	1

Fig. 2-4 Counting in decimal, hexadecimal, and binary number systems

Note from Fig. 2-4 that each hexadecimal symbol can represent a unique combination of 4 bits. The binary number 10011110 could then be represented as 9E in hexadecimal. That is, the 1001 part of the binary number equals 9, according to Fig. 2-4, and the 1110 part of the binary number equals E in hexadecimal. Therefore 10011110_2 equals $9E_{16}$. Remember that the subscripts give the base of the number.

Convert the binary number 111010 to hexadecimal (hex). Start at the LSB and divide the binary number into groups of 4 bits each, as shown in Fig. 2-5a. Then replace each 4-bit group with its equivalent hex digit. The 1010_2 equals A in hex (see Fig. 2-4). The 0011_2 equals 3 in hex. Therefore 111010_2 equals $3A_{16}$.

	4-bit group	4-bit group				
Binary	0011	1010		Hexadecimal	7	F
	↓	↓			↓	↓
Hexadecimal	3	A		Binary	0111	1111

(a) Binary-to-hexadecimal conversion   (b) Hexadecimal-to-binary conversion

Fig. 2-5

Convert the hexadecimal number 7F to its binary equivalent. Figure 2-5b shows that each hex digit is replaced with its 4-bit binary equivalent. In this example, binary 0111 is substituted for hex 7 and 1111_2 replaces F_{16}. Therefore $7F_{16}$ equals 1111111_2.

Hexadecimal notation is widely used to represent binary numbers. Persons who use hexadecimal notation must memorize the table shown in Fig. 2-4.

Convert the hexadecimal number 2C6E to its decimal equivalent. The procedure is shown in Fig. 2-6a. The place values for the first four hexadecimal digits are shown as 4096, 256, 16, and 1. The hex number contains fourteen (E_{16}) 1s, six 16s, twelve (C_{16}) 256s, and two 4096s. Each place value is multiplied and the products are added to yield $11,374_{10}$.

Powers of 16	16^3	16^2	16^1	16^0
Place value	4096s	256s	16s	1s

Hexadecimal	2	C	6	E
	↓	↓	↓	↓
	4096	256	16	1
	×2	×12	×6	×14
Decimal	8192 +	3072 +	96 +	14 = $11,374_{10}$

(a) Hexadecimal-to-decimal conversion

$15,797_{10} \div 16 = 987$ remainder of $5_{10} = 5_{16}$ LSD

$987 \div 16 = 61$ remainder of $11_{10} = B_{16}$

$61 \div 16 = 3$ remainder of $13_{10} = D_{16}$

$3 \div 16 = 0$ remainder of $3_{10} = 3_{16}$ MSD

$15,797_{10} =$ 3   D   B 5_{16}

(b) Decimal-to-hexadecimal conversion

Fig. 2-6

Convert the decimal number 15,797 to its hexadecimal equivalent. The procedure is shown in Fig. 2-6*b*. The first line shows $15,797_{10}$ being divided by 16, giving a quotient of 987_{10} with a remainder of 5_{10}. The remainder is then converted to its hexadecimal equivalent. Therefore 5_{10} equals 5_{16}. The hex remainder (5_{16}) becomes the least significant digit (LSD) in the hexadecimal number. The first quotient (987) becomes the dividend in the second line and is divided by 16. The second quotient is 61 with a remainder of 11_{10}, or hexadecimal B. Line 3 shows 61 divided by 16, yielding a quotient of 3 with a remainder of 13_{10}, or D_{16}. The fourth line in Fig. 2-6*b* shows the dividend (3) being divided by 16, yielding a quotient of 0 with a remainder of 3_{10}, or 3_{16}. When the quotient becomes 0, as in line 4, the calculation is complete. The 3_{16} is the most significant digit (MSD). The procedure shown in Fig. 2-6*b* converts the decimal number 15,797 to its hex equivalent of $3DB5_{16}$.

SOLVED PROBLEMS

2.9 Hexadecimal notation is widely used in microcomputer work as a "shorthand" method of representing _____ (binary, decimal) numbers.

> **Solution:**
>
> Hexadecimal notation is widely used to represent binary numbers.

2.10 The hexadecimal number system is sometimes called the base _____ system.

> **Solution:**
>
> The hexadecimal number system is sometimes called the base 16 system owing to its use of 16 unique symbols.

2.11 Convert the following hexadecimal numbers to their binary equivalents:
(*a*) C   (*c*) F   (*e*) 1A
(*b*) 6   (*d*) E2   (*f*) 3D

> **Solution:**
>
> Using the table in Fig. 2-4, follow the procedure shown in Fig. 2-5*b*. The binary equivalents for the hexadecimal numbers are as follows:
> (*a*) $C_{16} = 1100_2$ (*c*) $F_{16} = 1111_2$ (*e*) $1A_{16} = 00011010_2$
> (*b*) $6_{16} = 0110_2$ (*d*) $E2_{16} = 11100010_2$ (*f*) $3D_{16} = 00111101_2$

2.12 Convert the following binary numbers to their hexadecimal equivalents:
(*a*) 1001   (*c*) 1101   (*e*) 10000000
(*b*) 1100   (*d*) 1111   (*f*) 01111110

> **Solution:**
>
> Using the table in Fig. 2-4, follow the procedure shown in Fig. 2-5*a*. The hexadecimal equivalents for the binary numbers are as follows:
> (*a*) $1001_2 = 9_{16}$ (*c*) $1101_2 = D_{16}$ (*e*) $10000000_2 = 80_{16}$
> (*b*) $1100_2 = C_{16}$ (*d*) $1111_2 = F_{16}$ (*f*) $01111110_2 = 7E_{16}$

2.13 Convert the following hexadecimal numbers to their decimal equivalents:
(*a*) 7E   (*b*) DB   (*c*) 12A3   (*d*) 34CF

> **Solution:**
>
> Using the table in Fig. 2-4, follow the procedure shown in Fig. 2-6*a*. The decimal equivalents to the hexadecimal numbers are as follows:
> (*a*) $7E_{16} = (16 \times 7) + (1 \times 14) = 126_{10}$

(b) $DB_{16} = (16 \times 13) + (1 \times 11) = 219_{10}$
(c) $12A3_{16} = (4096 \times 1) + (256 \times 2) + (16 \times 10) + (1 \times 3) = 4771_{10}$
(d) $34CF_{16} = (4096 \times 3) + (256 \times 4) + (16 \times 12) + (1 \times 15) = 13{,}519_{10}$

2.14 $48{,}373_{10} = $ _____ $_{16}$

Solution:

Using the table in Fig. 2-4, follow the procedure shown in Fig. 2-6b.

$$48{,}373_{10} \div 16 = 3023 \text{ remainder of } 5_{10} = 5_{16} \text{ (LSD)}$$
$$3023 \div 16 = \ 188 \text{ remainder of } 15_{10} = F_{16}$$
$$188 \div 16 = \ \ 11 \text{ remainder of } 12_{10} = C_{16}$$
$$11 \div 16 = \ \ \ \ 0 \text{ remainder of } 11_{10} = B_{16} \text{ (MSD)}$$
$$48{,}373_{10} = BCF5_{16}$$

2.3   BCD NUMBERS

Pure binary numbers are represented by hexadecimal notation owing to the ease of conversion. However, binary-to-decimal conversion is quite difficult. In calculators, games, and digital instruments, where there are frequent user inputs and outputs in decimal, a special code is used to represent these decimal numbers. This code is called the *BCD (binary-coded-decimal) code*. Decimal and BCD equivalents are shown in the table in Fig 2-7a. Technically, this table details the *8421 BCD code*. The 8421 part of the name gives the place values for the 4 bits in the BCD code. Other BCD codes are also used, such as the 5421 BCD code and the excess-3 code.

	BCD			
Decimal	8s	4s	2s	1s
0	0	0	0	0
1	0	0	0	1
2	0	0	1	0
3	0	0	1	1
4	0	1	0	0
5	0	1	0	1
6	0	1	1	0
7	0	1	1	1
8	1	0	0	0
9	1	0	0	1

(a)   The 8421 BCD code

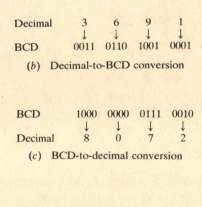

Decimal   3   6   9   1
              ↓   ↓   ↓   ↓
BCD   0011   0110   1001   0001

(b)   Decimal-to-BCD conversion

BCD   1000   0000   0111   0010
              ↓   ↓   ↓   ↓
Decimal   8   0   7   2

(c)   BCD-to-decimal conversion

Fig. 2-7

Convert the decimal number 3691 to its 8421 BCD equivalent. The procedure is shown in Fig. 2-7b. Each decimal digit is translated directly to its 4-bit BCD equivalent. This example shows that 3691_{10} equals $0011\ 0110\ 1001\ 0001_{BCD}$.

Convert the BCD number 1000 0000 0111 0010 to its decimal equivalent. The procedure is detailed in Fig. 2-7c. Each 4-bit group is translated directly to its decimal equivalent. This example shows that $1000\,0000\,0111\,0010_{BCD}$ equals 8072_{10}.

Microprocessors add pure binary numbers. However, many microprocessors do have special instructions for changing the result of additions into BCD notation. The BCD number is then easily interpreted as a decimal number using the simple procedures shown in Fig. 2-7b and c.

SOLVED PROBLEMS

2.15 The letters BCD stand for _____-_____ _____.

> **Solution:**
>
> BCD stands for binary-coded decimal.

2.16 The most common BCD notation is the _____ (5421, 8421) code.

> **Solution:**
>
> The most common BCD notation is the 8421 code.

2.17 Convert the following decimal numbers to their 8421 BCD equivalents:
(a) 39   (c) 40   (e) 82
(b) 65   (d) 17   (f) 99

> **Solution:**
>
> Follow the procedure shown in Fig. 2-7b. The BCD equivalents for the decimal numbers are as follows:
> (a) $39_{10} = 0011\,1001_{BCD}$ (c) $40_{10} = 0100\,0000_{BCD}$ (e) $82_{10} = 1000\,0010_{BCD}$
> (b) $65_{10} = 0110\,0101_{BCD}$ (d) $17_{10} = 0001\,0111_{BCD}$ (f) $99_{10} = 1001\,1001_{BCD}$

2.18 Convert the following 8421 BCD numbers to their decimal equivalents:
(a) 1000 0000   (c) 1001 0010   (e) 0100 0011
(b) 0000 0001   (d) 0111 0110   (f) 0101 0101

> **Solution:**
>
> Follow the procedure shown in Fig. 2-7c. The decimal equivalents for the BCD numbers are as follows:
> (a) $1000\,0000_{BCD} = 80_{10}$ (c) $1001\,0010_{BCD} = 92_{10}$ (e) $0100\,0011_{BCD} = 43_{10}$
> (b) $0000\,0001_{BCD} = 1_{10}$ (d) $0111\,0110_{BCD} = 76_{10}$ (f) $0101\,0101_{BCD} = 55_{10}$

2.4 BINARY ARITHMETIC

Adding, subtracting, or multiplying binary numbers is performed in a manner similar to decimal arithmetic. Most microprocessors have instructions for adding and subtracting binary numbers. More advanced microprocessors even have multiply and divide instructions, i.e., the 8086, 8088, 80286, 80386, and 68000.

The simple rules for binary addition are shown in Fig. 2-8a. The first two rules on the left are obvious. The third rule shows that binary $1 + 1 = 10$ with the most significant 1 being *carried out* to the next higher place. The fourth rule shows binary $1 + 1 + 1 = 11$. Here the augend, addend, and carry in are all 1s. The result is a sum of 1 with a carry out of 1.

Add the binary numbers 00111011 and 00101010. This problem is illustrated in Fig. 2-8b. Check your understanding of this procedure. The decimal equivalents to the binary numbers are shown for convenience at the right. The sum of 00111011 and 00101010 is shown in Fig. 2-8b as 01100101_2.

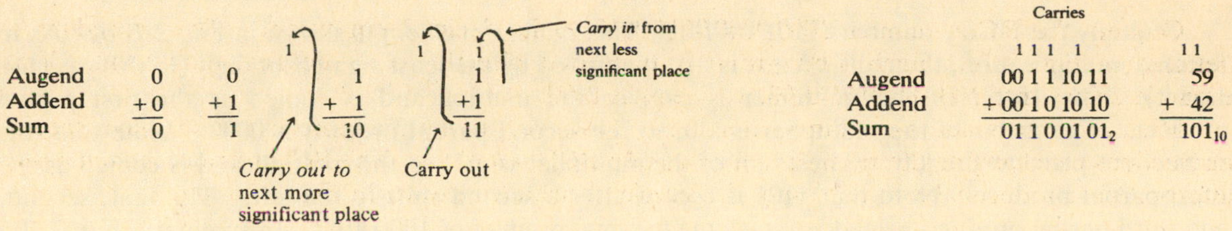

				Carry in from next less significant place		Carries 1 1 1 1	1 1
Augend	0	0	1	1	Augend	00 1 1 10 11	59
Addend	+0	+1	+1	+1	Addend	+00 1 0 10 10	+42
Sum	0	1	10	11	Sum	01 1 0 01 01$_2$	101$_{10}$

Carry out to next more significant place   Carry out

(a)   Rules for binary addition   (b)   Binary addition problem

Fig. 2-8

The rules for binary subtraction are shown in Fig. 2-9a. The first three rules are the same as in decimal subtraction. The last rule requires a *borrow* from the next more significant place (the 2s place). With the borrow, the minuend becomes binary 10 and the subtrahend is 1 with a difference of 1.

Minuend	0	1	1	$\overset{0}{\cancel{1}}$ 0		0 $\overset{1}{\cancel{0}}$ $\overset{10}{\cancel{0}}$ $\overset{10}{\cancel{1}}$ 0 1 0 1	$\overset{7}{\cancel{8}}\overset{1}{5}$
Subtrahend	−0	−1	−0	−1		−0 0 1 1 1 0 0 1	−5 7
Difference	0	0	1	1		0 0 0 1 1 1 0 0$_2$	2 8$_{10}$

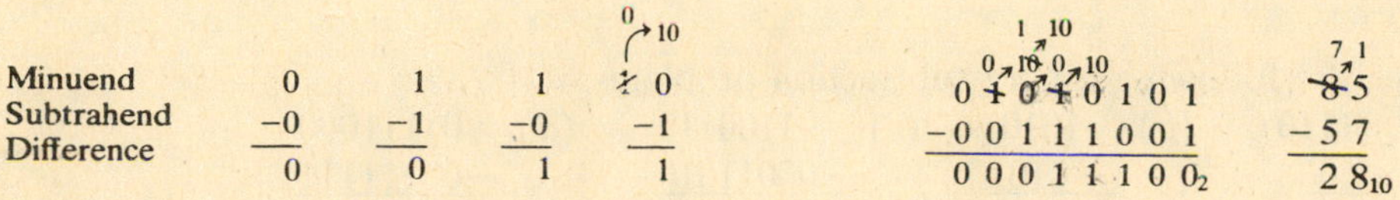

(a)   Rules for binary subtraction   (b)   Binary subtraction problem

Fig. 2-9

Subtract the binary number 00111001 from 01010101. This sample problem is detailed in Fig. 2-9b. The 1s, 2s, and 4s columns of the binary subtraction problem are quite simple to follow using the first three rules from Fig. 2-9a. The 8s column shows a 1 being subtracted from 0. A 1 is borrowed from the 16s column. Now 1 is subtracted from 10$_2$, yielding a difference of 1 according to the fourth rule in Fig. 2-9a. After the borrow, the 16s column shows 1 subtracted from the new minuend of 0. Based on rule 4, a 1 must be borrowed from the next more significant place (from the 32s place). The 32s place minuend is 0. The 32s place must then borrow from the 64s place where there is a 1. The 32s place borrows from the 64s place. Finally, the 16s place can borrow from the 32s place. The minuend in the 16s place is then 10$_2$, and the subtrahend is 1, with a difference of 1. The 32s place now shows 1 − 1 yielding a difference of 0. The 64s place shows 0 − 0 yielding a difference of 0. The 128s place shows 0 − 0 also yielding a difference of 0. In summary, the sample problem in Fig. 2-9b shows binary 00111001 subtracted from 01010101$_2$ yielding a difference of 00011100$_2$. The problem is also shown in decimal form at the right.

The rules for binary multiplication are shown in Fig. 2-10a. The first two rules need no explanation. The multiplier is 1 in the latter two rules. When the multiplier is 1 in binary multiplication, the *multiplicand is copied* as the product. When the multiplier is 0, the product is always 0.

Multiplicand	0	1	0	1	Multiplicand	1101	13
Multiplier	×0	×0	×1	×1	Multiplier	× 101	×5
Product	0	0	0	1	First partial product	1101	65$_{10}$
					Second partial product	0000	
					Third partial product	1101	
					Final product	1000001$_2$	

(a)   Rules for binary multiplication   (b)   Binary multiplication problem

Fig. 2-10

Multiply the binary numbers 1101 by 101. This sample problem is shown in Fig. 2-10b. As in decimal multiplication, the multiplicand is first multiplied by the least significant digit (in this case the 1s bit). The 1s bit of the multiplier is a 1, so the multiplicand is copied as the first partial product. The 2s bit of the multiplier is a 0, so the second partial product is 0000. Note that it is *shifted* one place to the left. The 4s bit of the multiplier is a 1, so the multiplicand is copied as the third partial product. Note that 1101 is copied after a second shift to the left. The first, second, and third partial products are added, yielding the final product of 1000001_2. In summary, Fig. 2-10b shows that $1101_2 \times 101_2 = 1000001_2$ or that $13_{10} \times 5_{10} = 65_{10}$.

SOLVED PROBLEMS

2.19   Solve the following binary addition problems:

     (a)   1010   (b)   1101   (c)   01011011   (d)   00111111
           +0101   +0101   +00001111   +00011111

Solution:

     Refer to Fig. 2-8. The binary sums for the problems are as follows:
     (a) 1111   (b) 10010   (c) 01101010   (d) 01011110

2.20   Solve the following binary subtraction problems:

     (a)   1110   (b)   1010   (c)   01100110   (d)   01111000
           −1000   − 0101   −00011010   −00111111

Solution:

     Refer to Fig. 2-9. The binary differences for the problems are as follows:
     (a) 0110   (b) 0101   (c) 01001100   (d) 00111001

2.21   The top number in a multiplication problem is called the _____, while the bottom number is called the multiplier and the answer is called the _____.

Solution:

     The top number in a multiplication problem is called the multiplicand, while the bottom number is called the multiplier and the answer is called the product.

2.22   Solve the following binary multiplication problems:

     (a) 1001   (b)   1101   (c) 1111   (d)   1110
        ×11   ×1001   ×101   ×1110

Solution:

     Refer to Fig. 2-10. The binary products for the problems are as follows:
     (a) 11011   (b) 1110101   (c) 1001011   (d) 11000100

2.5   TWOS COMPLEMENT NOTATION

Generally binary numbers are used inside computers. Sometimes, however, a special code called *2s complement notation* is used when *signed numbers* are required. This system simplifies computer circuitry.

A typical register, or storage location, inside a microprocessor might look like the one in Fig. 2-11a. This register has space for 8 bits of data. The bit positions are numbered from 7 through 0. Binary place values are shown across the bottom of the register. Bit 7 would be the 128s place, bit 6 the 64s place, etc.

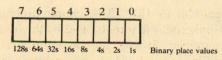

(a) Labeling storage locations in an 8-bit register

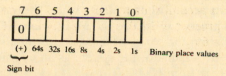

(b) Positive numbers identified by a 0 in the sign bit location in the register

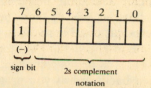

(c) Negative numbers identified by a 1 in the sign bit location in the register

Fig. 2-11

The typical organization of an 8-bit register used for storing *signed numbers* is shown in Fig. 2-11*b* and *c*. Bit 7 in both registers is the *sign bit*. The sign bit tells whether the number is (+) positive or (−) negative. A 0 in the sign bit position means the number is positive, whereas a 1 in bit position 7 indicates a negative number.

If the signed number is positive as in Fig. 2-11*b*, the remaining memory locations (6–0) hold a 7-bit binary number. For instance, if the register in Fig. 2-11*b* were to hold 01000001, it would

Decimal	Representation of signed numbers	
+127	0111 1111	Positive numbers
⋮	⋮	represented
+8	0000 1000	the same as in
+7	0000 0111	straight binary
+6	0000 0110	
+5	0000 0101	
+4	0000 0100	
+3	0000 0011	
+2	0000 0010	
+1	0000 0001	
+0	0000 0000	
−1	1111 1111	Negative numbers
−2	1111 1110	represented in 2s
−3	1111 1101	complement form
−4	1111 1100	
−5	1111 1011	
−6	1111 1010	
−7	1111 1001	
−8	1111 1000	
⋮	⋮	
−128	1000 0000	

Fig. 2-12 Signed decimal numbers and their equivalent 2s complement notations

mean decimal +65 (positive sign bit + 64 + 1).   If the register in Fig. 2-11*b* held 01111111, it would equal $+127_{10}$ (positive sign bit + 64 + 32 + 16 + 8 + 4 + 2 + 1).   This is the highest positive number that could be represented in this 8-bit register.

If the signed number is *negative* as in Fig. 2-11*c*, the register would hold the *2s complement form* of that number.   The table in Fig. 2-12 shows the 2s complement notation for both positive and negative numbers.   Note that the positive numbers have a 0 as the MSB, while the rest of the number corresponds to a binary number.   Negative numbers have a 1 as the MSB.   Look at the +0 line of the table in Fig. 2-12.   The 2s complement notation for +0 is 00000000.   In the line below, note that 11111111 is the 2s complement notation for −1.   Think of the system as an odometer that is being turned backward as you progress down the chart from 00000000 to 11111111.

What would be the 2s complement notation for −9?   The steps for making this conversion are outlined in Fig. 2-13*a*.   The steps are:

Step 1   List the unsigned decimal number.   Write 9 in this example.

Step 2   Convert the decimal to a binary number.   Write the binary number 00001001 in this example.

Step 3   Complement each bit forming the *1s complement*.   Write 11110110 as the 1s complement in this example.

Step 4   Add 1 to the 1s complement number.   In this example add 1 to 11110110.

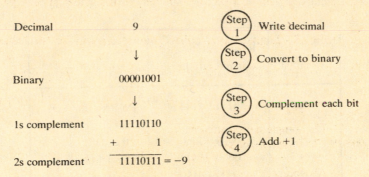

(*a*)   Forming the 2s complement of a negative number

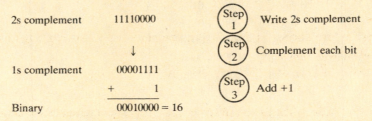

(*b*)   Finding the decimal equivalent for a 2s complement number

Fig. 2-13

The result is the 2s complement notation for the negative of the decimal number.   In the example in Fig. 2-13*a*, −9 equals 11110111 in 2s complement form.   Note that the sign bit (11110111) is 1, which means this is a negative number.

What is the equivalent decimal value for the 2s complement number 11110000?   The procedure for making this conversion is detailed in Fig. 2-13*b*.   The procedure of complementing and adding 1 is the same used for converting from binary to 2s complement.   The procedure in Fig. 2-13*b* shows each bit of the 2s complement number being changed, forming the 1s complement.   A 1 is then added to the 1s complement number, forming the binary number 00010000, which is equal to 16. This means that the 2s complement notation 11110000 equals -16_{10}. The 16 must be negative because the sign bit (MSB) of the 2s complement number is a 1.

SOLVED PROBLEMS

2.23 When signed numbers are stored in an 8-bit microprocessor register, the MSB (bit 7) is called the _____ bit.

Solution:

When signed numbers are stored in an 8-bit microprocessor register, the MSB (bit 7) is called the sign bit.

2.24 Determine whether the following 2s complement notations stand for positive or negative numbers.
(*a*) 01110000   (*b*) 11001111   (*c*) 10001111   (*d*) 01010101

Solution:

(*a*) Twos complement 01110000 is a positive number because the sign bit equals 0.
(*b*) Twos complement 11001111 is a negative number because the sign bit equals 1.
(*c*) Twos complement 10001111 is a negative number because the sign bit equals 1.
(*d*) Twos complement 01010101 is a positive number because the sign bit equals 0.

2.25 Using the table in Fig. 2-12, give the 2s complement notation for the following signed decimal numbers:
(*a*) +1   (*b*) +5   (*c*) +127   (*d*) −1   (*e*) −2   (*f*) −128

Solution:

Refer to Fig. 2-12.
(*a*) +1 = 00000001 (2s complement notation)
(*b*) +5 = 00000101 (2s complement notation)
(*c*) +127 = 01111111 (2s complement notation)
(*d*) −1 = 11111111 (2s complement notation)
(*e*) −2 = 11111110 (2s complement notation)
(*f*) −128 = 10000000 (2s complement notation)

2.26 Using the procedure shown in Fig. 2-13*a*, translate the following signed decimal numbers to their 2s complement form:
(*a*) −10   (*b*) −21   (*c*) −34   (*d*) −96

Solution:

Refer to Fig. 2-13*a*. The 2s complement notations for the signed decimal numbers are as follows:
(*a*) First step (convert decimal to binary): $10_{10} = 00001010_2$
       Second step (complement): $00001010_2 \rightarrow 11110101$
       Third step (add 1): 11110101 + 1 = 11110110 (2s complement) = -10_{10}
(*b*) First step (convert decimal to binary): $21_{10} = 00010101_2$
       Second step (complement): $00010101_2 \rightarrow 11101010$
       Third step (add 1): 11101010 + 1 = 11101011 (2s complement) = -21_{10}
(*c*) First step (convert decimal to binary): $34_{10} = 00100010_2$
       Second step (complement): $00100010_2 \rightarrow 11011101$
       Third step (add 1): 11011101 + 1 = 11011110 (2s complement) = -34_{10}
(*d*) First step (convert decimal to binary): $96_{10} = 01100000_2$
       Second step (complement): $01100000_2 \rightarrow 10011111$
       Third step (add 1): 10011111 + 1 = 10100000 (2s complement) = -96_{10}

2.27   Twos complement and _____ (BCD, binary) bit patterns are the same for *positive* decimal numbers.

     Solution:

        Twos complement and binary bit patterns are the same for positive decimal numbers.

2.28   Using the procedure shown in Fig. 2-13b, translate the following 2s complement notations to their signed decimal equivalents:

     (a) 11111011   (b) 00001111   (c) 10001111   (d) 01110111

     Solution:

        The signed decimal equivalents of the 2s complement notations are as follows

(a) 11111011 (2s complement) $= -5_{10}$

     $11111011 \xrightarrow{\text{complement}} 00000100$

$$\begin{array}{r} + 1 \\ \hline 00000101 = 5 \end{array}$$

(b) 00001111 (2s complement) $= +15$

(c) 10001111 (2s complement) $= -113$

     $10001111 \xrightarrow{\text{complement}} 01110000$

$$\begin{array}{r} + 1 \\ \hline 01110001 = 113 \end{array}$$

(d) 01110111 (2s complement) $= +119$

2.6   TWOS COMPLEMENT ARITHMETIC

     A microprocessor can use 2s complement numbers because it can *complement*, *increment* (add $+1$ to a number), and *add* binary numbers. Microprocessors do not have subtract circuitry. Instead they use an adder and 2s complement numbers to perform subtraction.

     Add the signed decimal numbers $+5$ and $+3$. The process is shown for both decimals and 2s complement numbers in Fig. 2-14a. From the table in Fig. 2-12 it is found that $+5$ equals 00000101 in 2s complement notation, whereas $+3 = 00000011$. The 2s complement numbers 00000101 and 00000011 are then added like regular binary numbers, yielding the 2s complement sum of 00001000. The sum 00001000 equals $+8_{10}$.

Augend	(+5)	00000101
Addend	+ (+3)	+ 00000011
Sum	(+8)	00001000

(a)   2s complement addition problem

Augend	(+3)	00000011
Addend	+ (−8)	+ 11111000
Sum	(−5)	11111011

(c)   2s complement addition problem

Augend	(+7)	00000111
Addend	+ (−3)	+ 11111101
Sum	(+4)	⟨1⟩00000100

         Discard
         overflow

(b)   2s complement addition problem

Augend	(−2)	11111110
Addend	+ (−5)	+ 11111011
Sum	(−7)	⟨1⟩11111001

         Discard
         overflow

(d)   2s complement addition problem

Fig. 2-14

     Add the signed decimal numbers $+7$ and -3. The procedure using both decimal and 2s complement numbers is shown in Fig. 2-14b. From the table in Fig. 2-12 it is found that $+7 = 00000111$ and $-3 = 11111101$ in 2s complement notation. The 2s complement numbers of 00000111 and 11111101 are then added as if they were regular binary numbers, yielding the sum of 100000100. The MSB is an overflow carry from the 8-bit register and is discarded. This leaves the 2s complement sum of 00000100, or $+4_{10}$.

     Add the signed decimal numbers $+3$ and -8. The procedure is detailed in Fig. 2-14c. From the table in Fig. 2-12 it is found that $+3 = 00000011$ and $-8 = 11111000$ in 2s complement notation. The 2s complement numbers of 00000011 and 11111000 are added as if they were regular binary numbers, yielding a sum of 11111011. Again from Fig. 2-12 it is determined that the 2s complement sum of 11111011 equals -5_{10}.

Add decimal -2 and -5. The procedure is detailed in Fig. 2-14d. From the table in Fig. 2-12 it is found that in 2s complement notation $-2 = 11111110$ and $-5 = 11111011$. The 2s complement numbers 11111110 and 11111011 are then added as if they were regular binary numbers. The sum is 111111001. The MSB is an overflow carry from the 8-bit register and is discarded. The sum of 2s complement numbers 11111110 and 11111011 is then 11111001 (2s complement). Using Fig. 2-12 it is determined that the 2s complement sum of 11111001 equals -7_{10}.

Subtract the decimal signed number $+5$ from $+8$. The procedure is outlined in Fig. 2-15a. The minuend ($+8$) equals 00001000. The subtrahend is $+5$, or 00000101. The 00000101 must be converted to its 2s complement form (complement and add 1), yielding 11111011. The "minuend" of 00001000 is added to the 2s complement of the subtrahend 11111011 as if they were binary numbers. The sum equals 100000011. The MSB is an overflow carry from the register and is discarded, leaving the sum of 00000011. From the table in Fig. 2-12 it is determined that the 2s complement sum of 00000011 equals $+3_{10}$. Note that to subtract, the subtrahend is converted to its 2s complement form and then added to the minuend. *By using 2s complement representation and an adder, the microprocessor can perform subtraction.*

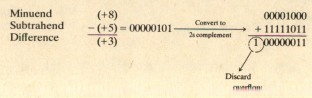

(a) 2s complement subtraction problem using addition

Minuend   (+2)   00000010
Subtrahend $-(+6)$ = 00000110 —Convert to 2s complement→ + 11111010
Difference   (−4)   11111100

(b) 2s complement subtraction problem using addition

Fig. 2-15

Subtract the larger decimal number $+6$ from $+2$. The procedure is shown in Fig. 2-15b. The minuend of $+2$ equals 00000010 (2s complement). The subtrahend of $+6$ equals 00000110. This subtrahend is converted to its 2s complement form (complement and add 1), yielding 11111010. The 2s complement numbers 00000010 and 11111010 are then added as if they were binary numbers, yielding a sum of 11111100. From the table in Fig. 2-12 it is determined that the 2s complement sum of 11111100 equals -4_{10}.

SOLVED PROBLEMS

2.29 Add the following signed decimals using 2s complement numbers:

(a)   (+7)   (b)   (+31)
    + (+1)   + (+26)

Solution:

Follow the procedure shown in Fig. 2-14a. The sums of the additions are as follows:

(a)   (+7)   00000111   (b)   (+31)   00011111
    + (+1)   + 00000001   + (+26) + 00011010
    (+8) = 00001000 (2s complement)   (+57) = 00111001 (2s complement)

2.30 Add the following signed decimals using 2s complement numbers:

(*a*)   (+8)   (*b*)   (+89)
       + (−5)   + (−46)

Solution:

Follow the procedure shown in Fig. 2-14*b*.   The sums of the additions are as follows:

(*a*)   (+8)   00001000   (*b*)   (+89)   01011001
       + (−5)   + 11111011   + (−46)   + 11010010
       (+3) = ①00000011   (2s complement)   (+43) = ①00101011   (2s complement)

          discard overflow   discard overflow

2.31 Add the following signed decimals using 2s complement numbers:

(*a*)   (+1)   (*b*)   (+20)
       + (−6)   + (−60)

Solution:

Follow the procedure shown in Fig. 2-14*c*.   The sums of the additions are as follows:

(*a*)   (+1)   00000001   (*b*)   (+20)   00010100
       + (−6)   + 11111010   + (−60)   + 11000100
       (−5) =   11111011   (2s complement)   (−40) =   11011000   (2s complement)

2.32 Add the following signed decimals using 2s complement numbers:

(*a*)   (−3)   (*b*)   (−13)
       + (−4)   + (−41)

Solution:

Follow the procedure shown in Fig. 2-14*d*.   The sums of the additions are as follows:

(*a*)   (−3)   11111101   (*b*)   (−13)   11110011
       + (−4)   + 11111100   + (−41)   + 11010111
       (−7) = ①11111001   (2s complement)   (−54) = ①11001010   (2s complement)

          discard overflow   discard overflow

2.33 Subtract the following signed decimals using 2s complement numbers:

(*a*)   (+7)   (*b*)   (+113)
       − (+2)   − (+50)

Solution:

Follow the procedure shown in Fig. 2-15*a*.   The results of the subtraction problems are as follows:

(*a*)   (+7)   00000111
             − (+2) = 00000010 ──2s complement and add──▶ + 11111110
                     (+5) =   ①00000101   (2s complement)

                                                  discard overflow

(*b*)   (+113)   01110001
             − (+50) 00110010 ──2s complement and add──▶ + 11001110
                     (+63)   ①00111111   (2s complement)

                                                  discard overflow

2.34 Subtract the following signed decimals using 2s complement numbers:

(a)   (+3)   (b)   (+12)
    −(+8)   −(+63)

Solution:

Follow the procedure shown in Fig. 2-15b. The results of the subtraction problems are as follows:

(a)

$$
\begin{array}{ccc}
(+3) & & 00000011 \\
\underline{-\ (+8)} = 00001000 & \xrightarrow[\text{and add}]{\text{2s complement}} & \underline{+\ 11111000} \\
(-5) = & & +\ 11111011 \quad \text{(2s complement)}
\end{array}
$$

(b)

$$
\begin{array}{ccc}
(+12) & & 00001100 \\
\underline{-\ (+63)} = 00111111 & \xrightarrow[\text{and add}]{\text{2s complement}} & \underline{+\ 11000001} \\
(-51) = & & 11001101 \quad \text{(2s complement)}
\end{array}
$$

2.7 BIT GROUPING

A single binary digit is called a *bit*. Four bits grouped together are called a *nibble*. Eight bits grouped together form a *byte* (rhymes with "light").

A very important characteristic of any microprocessor is the size of the accumulator. Simple microprocessors commonly use 8-bit accumulators. The *word size* of the microprocessor is then 8 bits. In this case 1 byte makes up a word. Microprocessors have word lengths of 4, 8, 16, or even 32 bits. A 16-bit microprocessor then has a word length of 2 bytes, or 16 binary digits. A *word* is a group of bits that is processed as a single number or instruction by the microprocessor. An 8-bit microprocessor transfers and stores all data in 8-bit groups via eight parallel conductors called the data bus.

The contents of an 8-bit microcomputer's memory might look like the one in Fig. 2-16a. Note that each address location (labeled contents) holds an 8-bit group of information. Each byte is called a *memory word* since the microprocessor is an 8-bit unit. Each memory word has a specific meaning when it is fetched to and decoded by the microprocessor. The binary contents of memory in Fig. 2-16a could stand for one of the following:

1. a binary number
2. a signed binary number
3. a BCD number
4. a character (a letter of the alphabet)
5. an instruction
6. a memory address
7. an input or output port address

Consider the top memory location (01100100_2) in Fig. 2-16a. The contents of this memory location are 11011011. This memory word could be interpreted as follows:

1. as a binary number—$11011011_2 = 219_{10}$.
2. as a signed binary number—11011011 (2s complement) $= -37_{10}$.
3. as a BCD number—this could not be a binary-coded-decimal number because neither 1101 or 1011 is a BCD code.
4. as a character—this would not stand for any ASCII (ASCII is a popular special alphanumeric code) character.
5. as an instruction—11011011 = the INPUT instruction for the popular Intel 8080/8085 microprocessor.

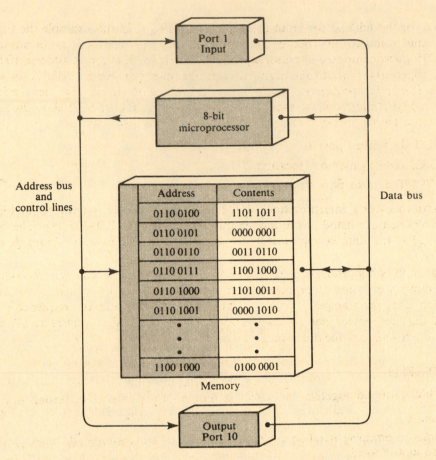

(a) Typical binary memory contents in a microcomputer

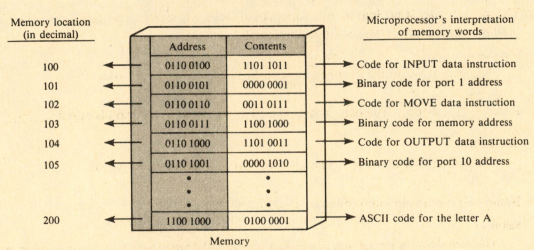

(b) The microprocessor's interpretations of the contents of memory

Fig. 2-16

6. as a memory address—$11011011_2 = DB_{16}$ = memory location 219_{10}.

7. as an address for an input or output port—11011011_2 = port 219_{10}.

The top memory word in Fig. 2-16a could be the binary number for 219_{10}, the signed binary number for -37_{10}, the 8085 microprocessor's instruction for INPUT, the address for memory location DB_{16}, or the address for input or output port 219_{10}. In this example the top memory word (11011011) could stand for any one of five different locations, instructions, or amounts.

If the 8085 microcomputer operator started the program counter at address 100_{10} (01100100_2), then the microprocessor would fetch and decode the memory word 11011011 as an INPUT data instruction. The microprocessor would then continue down to the next address of 101_{10} (01100101_2). The contents of the memory in Fig. 2-16a are the same as those in Fig. 1-4. Recall that the program shown in Fig. 1-4 performed the following instructions:

1. INPUT data from port 1.
2. STORE data in memory location 200.
3. OUTPUT data to port 10.

The microprocessor's interpretation of the memory contents is detailed in Fig. 2-16b. The program instructions are listed in the top six memory locations ($100-105_{10}$). The bottom memory location (200_{10}) is the data storage location. In this case ASCII for the letter A is stored in this memory location.

In summary, it is important to note that bits are grouped into words in microcomputers. These program memory words are interpreted by the microprocessor in sequence *one at a time*. It is important for the programmer to know how the microprocessor sequences and interprets data. Each microprocessor has its own unique instruction codes; however, all microprocessors sequence through memory locations in a similar manner.

SOLVED PROBLEMS

2.35 Four bits grouped together are called a nibble, whereas an 8-bit group is called a _____.

Solution:

An 8-bit grouping is called a byte. Under special circumstances this 8-bit group might also be referred to as a word.

2.36 The _____ size is an important characteristic of a microprocessor and has to do with the number of bits transferred and processed as a group.

Solution:

Word size is one of the most important characteristics of a microprocessor.

2.37 Refer to Fig. 2-16a. The byte of data stored in any memory location is called a _____ word.

Solution:

The byte of data stored in any memory location is called a memory word.

2.38 Name seven possible interpretations of an 8-bit memory word.

Solution:

The contents of a storage location in memory could be interpreted as a binary number, a signed binary number (2s complement notation), a BCD number, a character, an instruction, a memory address, and an input or output port address.

2.39 Refer to Fig. 2-16b. How is the memory word (00000001) at address 101_{10} interpreted by the microprocessor?

Solution:

Refer to Fig. 2-16b. The microprocessor fetches the memory word (00000001) expecting it will tell from *what port* to input data. The memory word tells the microprocessor to input data from port 1.

2.40   Refer to Fig. 2-16*b*.   How is the memory word (00110111) at address 102_{10} interpreted by the microprocessor?

Solution:

Refer to Fig. 2-16*b*.   The microprocessor fetches the memory word (00110111) expecting it will be a new instruction.   The word 00110111 is decoded by the microprocessor to mean MOVE data from the accumulator to the storage location whose address is given in the next memory location.

2.41   The codes used for instructions are the same for all microprocessors, and therefore a program written for an Intel microprocessor will work on a Motorola unit (true or false).

Solution:

False.   Each microprocessor has its own unique instruction code.

Character	ASCII	Character	ASCII
Space	010 0000	A	100 0001
!	010 0001	B	100 0010
"	010 0010	C	100 0011
#	010 0011	D	100 0100
$	010 0100	E	100 0101
%	010 0101	F	100 0110
&	010 0110	G	100 0111
'	010 0111	H	100 1000
(	010 1000	I	100 1001
)	010 1001	J	100 1010
*	010 1010	K	100 1011
+	010 1011	L	100 1100
,	010 1100	M	100 1101
-	010 1101	N	100 1110
.	010 1110	O	100 1111
/	010 1111	P	101 0000
0	011 0000	Q	101 0001
1	011 0001	R	101 0010
2	011 0010	S	101 0011
3	011 0011	T	101 0100
4	011 0100	U	101 0101
5	011 0101	V	101 0110
6	011 0110	W	101 0111
7	011 0111	X	101 1000
8	011 1000	Y	101 1001
9	011 1001	Z	101 1010

Fig. 2-17   Partial list of the ASCII character set

2.8 ALPHANUMERIC CODES

Codes that contain both alphabetic characters and numbers are needed when microcomputers communicate with devices such as a teletype or CRT (cathode-ray tube) terminal. These codes are called *alphanumeric codes*.

The most commonly used alphanumeric code in microcomputer systems is the *American Standard Code for Information Interchange* or ASCII (pronounced "ask-ee"). A partial listing of the 7-bit code is shown in Fig. 2-17. This listing contains 7-bit codes for numbers, capital letters, and punctuation marks. The full code also has codes for lowercase letters and control characters.

SOLVED PROBLEMS

2.42 Binary codes that represent both numbers and letters are called _____ codes.

Solution:

Alphanumeric codes are used to represent both numbers and letters.

2.43 The ASCII representation of the number 0 is 011 0000. The number 9 is represented in ASCII by _____ (7 bits).

Solution:

Refer to Fig. 2-17. The number 9 is represented in ASCII by 011 1001.

2.44 Masking out the three most significant bits in the ASCII representation of 0 through 9 will leave the _____ equivalent of that number.

Solution:

Refer to Fig. 2-17. Masking out the three most significant bits in the ASCII representation of 0 through 9 will leave the binary or BCD equivalent of that number.

Supplementary Problems

2.45 From memory, convert the following binary numbers to their decimal equivalents:
(*a*) 0000   (*b*) 0010   (*c*) 0011   (*d*) 0111   (*e*) 1001   (*f*) 1100
Ans. (*a*) 0   (*b*) 2   (*c*) 3   (*d*) 7   (*e*) 9   (*f*) 12

2.46 $01101001_2 = $ _____$_{10}$ *Ans.* 105_{10}

2.47 $60_{10} = $ _____$_2$ *Ans.* 111100_2

2.48 The binary number 10011100 is represented as 9C in _____ notation.   *Ans.* hexadecimal

2.49 $8D_{16} = $ _____$_2$ *Ans.* 10001101_2

2.50 $01011111_2 = $ _____$_{16}$ *Ans.* $5F_{16}$

2.51 $3C_{16} = $ _____$_{10}$ *Ans.* 60_{10}

2.52 $90_{10} = $ _____$_{16}$ *Ans.* $5A_{16}$

2.53 $92_{10} = $ _____$_{BCD}$ *Ans.* $1001\,0010_{BCD}$

2.54 $1000\,0110_{BCD} = $ _____$_{10}$ *Ans.* 86_{10}

2.55   Solve the following binary addition problems:
    (*a*) 11000011 (*b*) 01101110
        $+\,00111100$ $+\,00111101$
    Ans.   (*a*) 11111111_2 (*b*) 10101011_2

2.56 $11011000_2 - 00110011_2 = $ _____$_2$ *Ans.* 10100101_2

2.57 $1001_2 \times 1101_2 = $ _____$_2$ *Ans.* 1110101_2

2.58   When positive and negative numbers are stored in a microprocessor register, if the sign bit (MSB) is 1, the number is _____ (negative, positive).   *Ans.*   negative

2.59   The 2s complement notation 01111110 represents a _____ (negative, positive) number.
    Ans.   positive

2.60   Translate the following signed decimal numbers to their 8-bit 2s complement form:
    (*a*) $+12$ (*b*) -12 *Ans.*   (*a*) 00001100 (2s complement)   (*b*) 11110100 (2s complement)

2.61   Translate the following 2s complement numbers to their signed decimal equivalents:
    (*a*) 01110100 (*b*) 11011101 *Ans.*   (*a*) $+116_{10}$ (*b*) -35_{10}

2.62   Add the following signed decimals using 8-bit 2s complement numbers:
    (*a*) $(+13)$ (*b*) $(+17)$ (*c*) (-6)
       $+\,(+8)$ $+\,(-8)$ $+(-14)$
    Ans.   (*a*) 00010101 (2s complement)   (*b*) 00001001 (2s complement)
          (*c*) 11101100 (2s complement)

2.63   Subtract the following signed decimals using 8-bit 2s complement numbers:
    (*a*) $(+13)$ (*b*) $(+19)$
       $-\,(+5)$ $-\,(+29)$
    Ans.   (*a*) 00001000 (2s complement)   (*b*) 11110110 (2s complement)

2.64   A byte is a group that contains _____ bits.   *Ans.*   8

2.65   A nibble is a group that contains _____ bits.   *Ans.*   4

2.66   The most popular word size for simple microprocessors is _____ (8,48) bits.   *Ans.*   8

2.67   Refer to Fig. 2-16*a*. This is a basic block diagram of a _____ (microcomputer, microprocessor).
    Ans.   microcomputer

2.68   Refer to Fig. 2-16*b*. How is memory word (11010011) at address 104_{10} interpreted by the microprocessor?
    Ans.   Refer to Fig. 2-16*b*. The microprocessor fetches the memory word (11010011) expecting it will be a new instruction. The word (11010011) is decoded by the microprocessor to mean OUTPUT data from the accumulator to the output port number given in the next memory location.

2.69   The letters ASCII stand for _____.   *Ans.*   American Standard Code for Information Interchange

2.70   A(n) _____ code would probably be used to translate from a typewriter keyboard input device to a microcomputer system.   *Ans.*   alphanumeric or ASCII

Chapter 3

Basic Digital Devices

3.1 LOGIC GATES

Circuits used to process digital signals are called *logic gates*. *Logic symbols* are used to identify these circuits. The seven gates that are the fundamental logic elements in digital systems are illustrated in Fig. 3-1.

The names of the seven logic elements are given in the left column in Fig. 3-1. Standard graphic logic symbols are illustrated in the second column. The third column shows the exact action (output) of the circuit with given inputs. In the truth table, a 0 means a LOW voltage level whereas a 1 means a HIGH voltage level. The right column in Fig. 3-1 gives the *Boolean expression* for each logic element. Boolean expressions are a type of "shorthand" used to represent a logic function.

Logic function	Logic gate symbol	Truth table	Boolean expression
Inverter	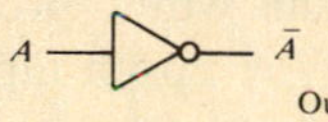	Input A / Output $\bar{A}$: 0 → 1 1 → 0	$A = \bar{A}$
AND NAND	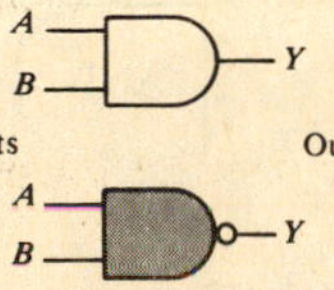	Inputs B A / Outputs AND NAND: 0 0 → 0 1 0 1 → 0 1 1 0 → 0 1 1 1 → 1 0	$A \cdot B = Y$ $\overline{A \cdot B} = Y$
OR NOR	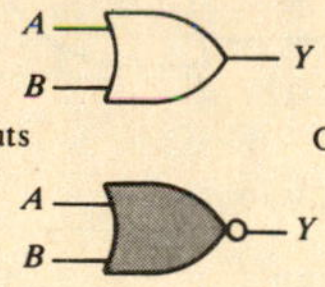	Inputs B A / Outputs OR NOR: 0 0 → 0 1 0 1 → 1 0 1 0 → 1 0 1 1 → 1 0	$A + B = Y$ $\overline{A + B} = Y$
Exclusive OR Exclusive NOR	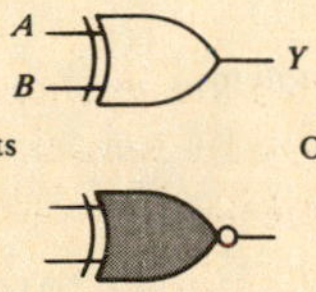	Inputs B A / Outputs XOR XNOR: 0 0 → 0 1 0 1 → 1 0 1 0 → 1 0 1 1 → 0 1	$A \oplus B = Y$ $\overline{A \oplus B} = Y$

Fig. 3-1 The seven logic functions compared

Notice that each logic symbol in Fig. 3-1 has a distinctive shape. A few manufacturers are beginning to use rectangular symbols for all logic devices. These new logic symbols are based on the untried standard (IEEE Standard 91-1984) developed by the Institute of Electrical and Electronics Engineers. For now, however, all workers in this area will recognize the distinctively shaped logic symbols drawn in Fig. 3-1.

The example in Fig. 3-2 gives some practice in using the information on logic gates. What are the outputs of the inverter (sometimes called a NOT gate) in Fig. 3-2 with pulse a at the input? According to the second line of the truth table in Fig. 3-1, the output would be 0, or opposite the input. When pulse b (a 0, or LOW) reaches the input of the inverter, the output would go HIGH, or to a 1. Input pulse c would produce a LOW output, whereas pulse d would produce a HIGH output. The process of inverting is also called *complementing* or *negating*. The Boolean expression for complementing is $A = \bar{A}$ (read as A complemented equals not A or A not). The overbar reads as *not* and is used to invert or complement the variable or expression beneath.

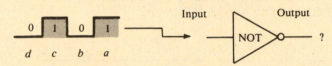

Fig. 3-2 Inverter problem

Another example is shown in Fig. 3-3a. A 2-input AND gate is shown. The input pulses at a are 0 and 1. According to the truth table in Fig. 3-1, this would produce a LOW, or 0 output. The pulses a, b, and c would all produce LOW outputs. When both inputs to the AND gate are HIGH (see pulse d in Fig. 3-3a), the output will go HIGH, or to 1.

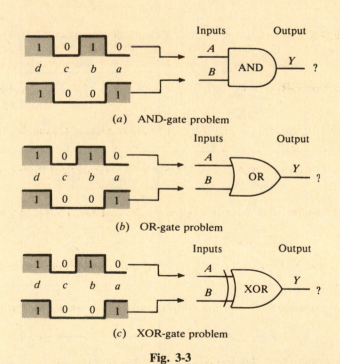

(a) AND-gate problem

(b) OR-gate problem

(c) XOR-gate problem

Fig. 3-3

Consider the problem shown in Fig. 3-3b. Here the nibbles 1010 (at input A) and 1001 (at input B) are being ORed together. The output nibble would be determined using the OR truth table in Fig. 3-1. The output nibble would be 1011 as a result of ORing 1010 with 1001. Note that first the pulses at a are ORed, then the pulses at b, etc.

What is the output nibble after 1010 and 1001 are exclusively ORed (XORed) together as in Fig. 3-3c? Using the XOR truth table in Fig. 3-1, it is determined that the result of XORing 1010 with 1001 is 0011.

Microprocessors can perform logical operations. Typically a microprocessor will have NOT (complement or negate), AND, OR, and XOR instructions. These instructions operate on groups of bits similar to the logic gates in Figs. 3-2 and 3-3.

SOLVED PROBLEMS

3.1   List the names of seven logic functions.

Solution:

Refer to Fig. 3-1. The seven logic functions are named NOT (inverter), AND, NAND, OR, NOR, exclusive OR (XOR), and exclusive NOR (XNOR).

3.2   List the names of four logic functions that can commonly be performed by single microprocessor instructions.

Solution:

Many microprocessors have instructions that perform the NOT, AND, OR, and XOR logic functions.

3.3   If a microprocessor ANDed 1100 with 1011, the output nibble would be _____.

Solution:

Refer to the AND truth table in Fig. 3-1. The output result of ANDing 1100 with 1011 would be 1000.

3.4   If a microprocessor ORed 0011 with 1000, the output nibble would be _____.

Solution:

Refer to the OR truth table in Fig. 3-1. The output result of ORing 0011 with 1000 would be 1011.

3.5   If a microprocessor complemented (NOTed) 1001, the output nibble would be _____.

Solution:

Refer to the inverter truth table in Fig. 3-1. The output result of complementing 1001 would be 0110.

3.6   If a microprocessor XORed 0011 with 0110, the output nibble would be _____.

Solution:

Refer to the exclusive-OR truth table in Fig. 3-1. The output result of XORing 0011 with 0110 would be 0101.

3.7   Describe the outputs from the NAND gate shown in Fig. 3-4.

Solution:

Refer to the NAND truth table in Fig. 3-1. The output pulses in Fig. 3-4 would be as follows:
pulse $a = 1$ pulse $c = 1$
pulse $b = 0$ pulse $d = 1$

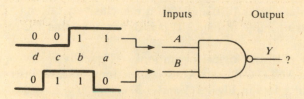

Fig. 3-4 Pulse-train problem

3.8   Describe the outputs from the XNOR gate shown in Fig. 3-5.

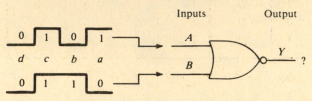

Fig. 3-5   Pulse-train problem

Solution:

Refer to the exclusive-NOR truth table in Fig. 3-1.   The output pulses in Fig. 3-5 would be as follows:

pulse $a = 0$ pulse $c = 1$
pulse $b = 0$ pulse $d = 1$

3.2 COMBINING LOGIC GATES

Digital systems are composed of combinations of logic gates.   Logic gate combinations can be described by a truth table, Boolean expression, or a logic-symbol diagram.

Consider the truth table illustrated in Fig. 3-6a.   This truth table shows all of the possible combinations of the four inputs (D, C, B, and A).   Note that only the combination 1010 will produce a 1, or HIGH output.   An equivalent Boolean expression for this truth table is listed to the right of the table in Fig. 3-6a.   The inputs are ANDed, forming the Boolean expression $D \cdot \bar{C} \cdot B \cdot \bar{A} = Y$ (read as D AND not C AND B AND not A equals output Y).

A logic-symbol diagram is developed from the Boolean expression.   Such a procedure is diagramed in Fig. 3-6b.   Inputs A and C must be complemented using an inverter.   A 4-input AND gate is being used at the output.

A commonly used simplified version of the same logic-symbol diagram is shown in Fig. 3-6c.   In this diagram the inverters are shown as *invert bubbles*.   These invert bubbles may also be considered as *active LOW inputs*.   In other words, to activate the AND gate in Fig. 3-6c, input A and C must be LOW while B and D must be HIGH.   Because inputs B and D must be HIGH to activate the AND gate, they are considered *active HIGH inputs*.

Consider the truth table in Fig. 3-7a.   Two input combinations will produce a 1, or HIGH output.   The Boolean expression for this truth table then becomes $D \cdot \bar{C} \cdot \bar{B} \cdot \bar{A} + D \cdot C \cdot \bar{B} \cdot A = Y$ (read as D AND not C AND not B AND not A ORed with D AND C AND not B AND A equals output Y).

The Boolean expression is next converted into a logic-symbol diagram.   This procedure is illustrated in Fig. 3-7b.   Note that this type of Boolean expression creates an AND-OR pattern of logic gates, with the OR gate being nearest the output.   The pattern of this Boolean expression is called the *sum-of-products* or *minterm* form.   Minterm Boolean expressions are generated from the 1s in the output column of the truth table in the manner shown in Fig. 3-7a.

Inputs				Output	Inputs				Output
D	C	B	A	Y	D	C	B	A	Y
0	0	0	0	0	1	0	0	0	0
0	0	0	1	0	1	0	0	1	0
0	0	1	0	0	1	0	1	0	1
0	0	1	1	0	1	0	1	1	0
0	1	0	0	0	1	1	0	0	0
0	1	0	1	0	1	1	0	1	0
0	1	1	0	0	1	1	1	0	0
0	1	1	1	0	1	1	1	1	0

$\rightarrow D \cdot \bar{C} \cdot B \cdot \bar{A} = Y$

(a)   Converting truth table to equivalent Boolean expression

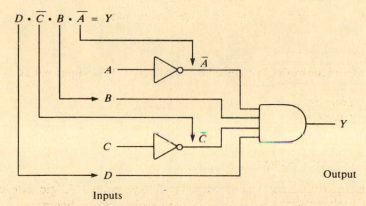

(b) Converting Boolean expression to logic-symbol diagram

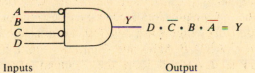

(c) Simplified logic-symbol diagram

Fig. 3-6

SOLVED PROBLEMS

3.9   Refer to Fig. 3-6c.   Inputs B and D are active _____ (HIGH, LOW) inputs, whereas inputs A and C are active _____ (HIGH, LOW) inputs.

Solution:

In Fig. 3-6c, inputs B and D are active HIGH inputs, whereas inputs A and C are active LOW inputs.   In other words, the 4-input AND gate can be activated (output goes HIGH) only when inputs A and C are LOW and inputs B and D are HIGH.

Inputs				Output	Inputs				Output	
D	C	B	A	Y	D	C	B	A	Y	
0	0	0	0	0	1	0	0	0	1	$\rightarrow D \cdot \bar{C} \cdot \bar{B} \cdot \bar{A}$
0	0	0	1	0	1	0	0	1	0	
0	0	1	0	0	1	0	1	0	0	
0	0	1	1	0	1	0	1	1	0	or
0	1	0	0	0	1	1	0	0	0	
0	1	0	1	0	1	1	0	1	1	$\rightarrow D \cdot C \cdot \bar{B} \cdot A$
0	1	1	0	0	1	1	1	0	0	
0	1	1	1	0	1	1	1	1	0	

(a) Converting truth table to equivalent minterm Boolean expression

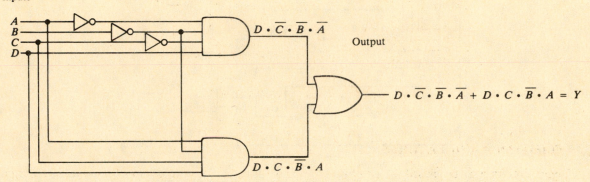

(b) Converting minterm Boolean expression into a logic-symbol diagram

Fig. 3-7

Inputs				Output	Inputs				Output
D	C	B	A	Y	D	C	B	A	Y
0	0	0	0	0	1	0	0	0	0
0	0	0	1	0	1	0	0	1	1
0	0	1	0	0	1	0	1	0	0
0	0	1	1	0	1	0	1	1	0
0	1	0	0	0	1	1	0	0	0
0	1	0	1	0	1	1	0	1	0
0	1	1	0	0	1	1	1	0	0
0	1	1	1	0	1	1	1	1	1

Fig. 3-8

3.10   Write the Boolean expression for the truth table in Fig. 3-8.

Solution:

There are two input combinations that produce a HIGH output in the truth table in Fig. 3-8.   From these combinations the minterm Boolean expression $D \cdot \bar{C} \cdot \bar{B} \cdot A + D \cdot C \cdot B \cdot A = Y$ is developed.

3.11   Draw a logic-symbol diagram of a circuit that will generate the truth table in Fig. 3-8.

Solution:

The Boolean expression for the truth table in Fig. 3-8 is $D \cdot \bar{C} \cdot \bar{B} \cdot A + D \cdot C \cdot B \cdot A = Y$.   From this expression the AND-OR logic-symbol diagram shown in Fig. 3-9 is drawn.

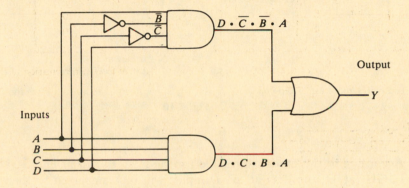

Fig. 3-9   Logic diagram solution

3.3   FLIP-FLOPS AND LATCHES

Logic circuits may be classified into two large categories.   The first group is *combinational logic circuits*, which are composed of gates.   The second group is *sequential logic circuits*, which include devices called flip-flops.   Flip-flops are interconnected to form sequential logic circuits for data storage, timing, counting, and sequencing.   Flip-flops have an extremely valuable *memory characteristic*.   A flip-flop will "remember" its inputs even after the inputs are removed.   A logic gate, however, will not "remember" its output state after the inputs are removed.

The logic symbol for the common *D flip-flop* (also called the *data flip-flop*) is diagramed in Fig. 3-10a.   The logic symbol shows two inputs labeled D (for data) and CK (for clock).   Flip-flops usually have complementary outputs labeled Q and $\bar{Q}$ (not Q).   The Q output is the most often used and is considered the *normal* output.   The $\bar{Q}$ output is called the *complementary* or inverted output of the flip-flop.   The $>$ on the CK input of the D logic symbol denotes that this flip-flop transfers data from input to output on the positive-going edge ($\uparrow$) of the clock pulse.

The modes of operation for the D flip-flop are shown in the left column of the table in Fig. 3-10b.   To *set* the flip-flop means to load a 1 into the normal (Q) output.   The first line of the truth table in Fig. 3-10b shows that placing a 1 at the D input and pulsing the CK (clock) input once causes output Q to be set to 1.   The second line shows the flip-flop being reset.   To *reset* means to clear the Q output to 0.   To *hold* means to store the output data.   When the flip-flop is in the hold mode, changes in the logic state at the data input will cause no change in the outputs.   The hold condition illustrates the memory characteristic of the D flip-flop.   Note that setting and resetting is with respect to output Q.

Consider the logic symbol illustrated in Fig. 3-11a of a *4-bit transparent latch*.   Each latch (flip-flop) inside the symbol is a storage or memory device.   Think of the 4-bit latch as containing four D flip-flops with their clock inputs connected to the enable (E) input shown on the symbol in

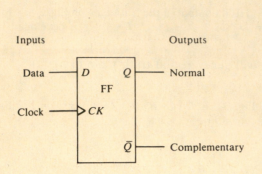

Mode of operation	Inputs		Outputs	
	D	CK	Q	$\bar{Q}$
Set	1	↑	1	0
Reset	0	↑	0	1
Hold	X	No clock pulse	Same as before	

0 = LOW
1 = HIGH
X = irrelevant
↑ = LOW-to-HIGH transition of the clock pulse

(a) Logic symbol for D flip-flop

(b) Mode-truth table for D flip-flop

Fig. 3-10

Fig. 3-11a.   According to the mode-truth table for the latch shown in Fig. 3-11b, when the enable (E) input is HIGH (at 1), the data at the D inputs will be transferred to their respective outputs (Q_0–Q_3).   The 4-bit word arrives in parallel form (as opposed to serial form) and is also output in parallel form.   This is called parallel-in and parallel-out.   The latch storage device is but one application of a flip-flop.

The JK flip-flop is probably the most widely used in sequential logic circuits owing to its adaptability.   A logic symbol for a typical JK flip-flop is illustrated in Fig. 3-12a.   The JK flip-flop has two data inputs labeled J and K plus a clock (CK) input.   The JK flip-flop also has the customary Q (normal) and $\bar{Q}$ (complementary) outputs.

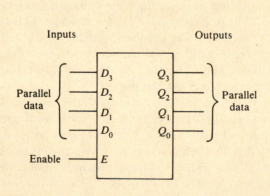

Mode of operation	Inputs		Output
	D	E	Q
Data enabled	0	1	0
	1	1	1
Data latched	X	0	Same as before

0 = LOW
1 = HIGH
X = irrelevant

(a) Logic symbol for 4-bit transparent latch

(b) Mode-truth table for latch

Fig. 3-11

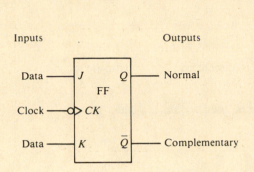

Mode of operation	Inputs			Outputs	
	J	K	CK	Q	$\bar{Q}$
Toggle	1	1	↓	Opposite state	
Set	1	0	↓	1	0
Reset	0	1	↓	0	1
Hold	0	0	↓	No change	

0 = LOW
1 = HIGH
↓ = HIGH-to-LOW transition of the clock pulse

(a) Logic symbol for JK flip-flop   (b) Mode-truth table for JK flip-flop

Fig. 3-12

A JK flip-flop has four modes of operation, which are described in Fig. 3-12b.   The *toggle mode* of operation means that on each successive clock pulse the outputs will change to their opposite logic state.   In the toggle mode, output Q of a JK flip-flop would go HIGH-LOW-HIGH-LOW, etc., on repeated clock pulses.

The truth table in Fig. 3-12b shows that the JK flip-flop will toggle when both data inputs J and K are HIGH, providing a clock pulse arrives at the CK input.   The actual toggling action takes place when the clock pulse changes from HIGH to LOW, as shown by the arrow (↓) in the truth table.

The JK flip-flop is in the *set mode* when data inputs $J = 1$ and $K = 0$.   The second line of the truth table in Fig. 3-12b shows that a HIGH-to-LOW transition of the clock pulse then sets Q to 1.   The *reset mode* (clearing Q to 0) is shown in the third line of the truth table.   The last line of the truth table in Fig. 3-12b describes the *hold mode* (do nothing mode) of the JK flip-flop.   When both data inputs (J and K) are LOW, a clock pulse at the CK input will have no effect on the outputs.

Triggering is an important characteristic of flip-flops.   Flip-flops can be classed as either *edge-triggered* or *level-triggered* devices.   The logic symbols in Figs. 3-10a and 3-12a suggest these flip-flops are edge-triggered by the small > (greater than) symbol next to the clock input.   The D flip-flop is triggered on the L-to-H (LOW-to-HIGH) transition of the clock pulse.   This is shown in the truth table and on the logic symbol (no bubble on the CK input implies it takes a 1 to activate the clock).   The D flip-flop is also called a *positive-edge-triggered* flip-flop because it is the positive-going edge of the clock pulse that triggers the flip-flop.

The JK flip-flop is a *negative-edge-triggered* flip-flop.   This is shown both in the truth table and on the logic symbol in Fig. 3-12.   The bubble at the CK input of the JK flip-flop logic symbol implies that it takes a LOW to activate the clock.   Because the JK flip-flop is edge-triggered, it actually takes a H-to-L (HIGH-to-LOW) transition (negative-going) of the clock pulse to trigger the flip-flop.

The 4-bit transparent latch illustrated in Fig. 3-11 is a level-triggered device.   This means that when the enable input (similar to the CK inputs on flip-flops) in HIGH, any binary data at the inputs (D_3-D_0) will appear immediately at the outputs (Q_3-Q_0).   For this reason the latch is said to be transparent.

SOLVED PROBLEMS

3.12   Sequential logic circuits contain devices called _____.

Solution:

   Sequential logic circuits contain flip-flops.

3.13   A memory characteristic used for storing data is typical of _____ (flip-flops, gates).

Solution:

   Flip-flops have a memory characteristic and can be used for storing data.

3.14   A D flip-flop is also called a _____ flip-flop.

   A D flip-flop is also called a data flip-flop.   It is also sometimes called a delay flip-flop.

3.15   The normal output of a flip-flop is the _____ (Q, $\bar{Q}$) output.

Solution:

   The normal output of a flip-flop is the Q output.   The $\bar{Q}$ output is the inverted, or complementary, output.

3.16   List the three modes of operation for the D flip-flop shown in Fig. 3-10.

Solution:

   Refer to the mode-truth table in Fig. 3-10b.   The D flip-flop can operate in the set, reset, or hold modes.

3.17   List the mode of operation of the D flip-flop during each of the five clock pulses in Fig. 3-13.

Solution:

   Refer to the mode-truth table in Fig. 3-10b.   Based on this table, the modes of the D flip-flop during each pulse in Fig. 3-13 are as follows:
   pulse a = set mode   pulse d = set mode
   pulse b = reset mode   pulse e = reset mode
   time period c (no pulse) = hold mode

3.18   List the binary outputs at the normal output (Q) of the D flip-flop in Fig. 3-13 after each of the clock pulses.

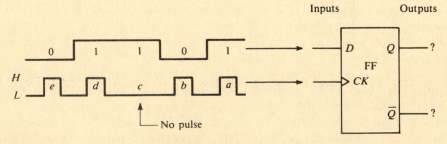

Fig. 3-13 D flip-flop problem

Solution:

   Refer to the mode-truth table in Fig. 3-10*b*.   The binary outputs at *Q* of the *D* flip-flop from Fig. 3-13 are as follows:

after pulse *a* = 1   after pulse *d* = 1
after pulse *b* = 0   after pulse *e* = 0
time period *c* (no pulse) = 0 (same as after pulse *b*)

3.19   A latch is a _____ (counting, storage) device.

Solution:

   The prime function of a latch is data storage.

3.20   Refer to Fig. 3-11.   The enable input of this 4-bit latch is activated by a logical _____ (0, 1).

Solution:

   Refer to the mode-truth table in Fig. 3-11*b*.   Based on the truth table, the enable input of this 4-bit latch is activated by a logical 1.

3.21   List the four modes of operation of the *JK* flip-flop in Fig. 3-12.

Solution:

   Refer to the mode-truth table in Fig. 3-12*b*.   The modes of operation of the *JK* flip-flop are toggle, set, reset, and hold.

3.22   List the mode of operation of the *JK* flip-flop during each of the clock pulses in Fig. 3-14.

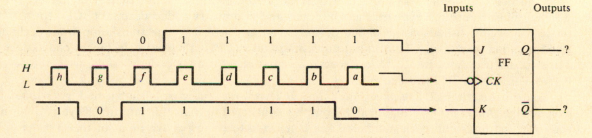

Fig. 3-14   *JK* flip-flop problem

Solution:

   Refer to the mode-truth table in Fig. 3-12*b*.   Based on this table, the modes of the *JK* flip-flop during each pulse in Fig. 3-14 are as follows:

pulse *a* = set   pulse *e* = toggle
pulse *b* = toggle   pulse *f* = reset
pulse *c* = toggle   pulse *g* = hold
pulse *d* = toggle   pulse *h* = toggle

3.23   List the binary outputs at the normal output (*Q*) of the *JK* flip-flop in Fig. 3-14 *after* each of the clock pulses.

Solution:

   Refer to the mode-truth table in Fig. 3-12*b*.   The binary outputs at *Q* of the *JK* flip-flop from Fig. 3-14 are as follows:

after pulse a = set to 1   after pulse e = toggle to 1
after pulse b = toggle to 0   after pulse f = reset to 0
after pulse c = toggle to 1   after pulse g = hold at 0
after pulse d = toggle to 0   after pulse h = toggle to 1

3.24   Refer to Fig. 3-10.   This D flip-flop is a (n) _____ (edge, level) -triggered device.

Solution:

The D flip-flop in Fig. 3-10 is an edge-triggered device.   This is shown on the logic-symbol diagram by the > symbol.   It is also shown in the truth table by the ↑ symbol, indicating that the flip-flop triggers on the L-to-H transition of the clock pulse.

3.25   Refer to Fig. 3-11.   This 4-bit latch is a(n) _____ (edge, level) -triggered device.

Solution:

The 4-bit transparent latch in Fig. 3-11 is a level-triggered device.

3.26   Refer to Fig. 3-12.   This JK flip-flop is a _____ (negative, positive) -edge-triggered device.

Solution:

The JK flip-flop in Fig. 3-12 is a negative-edge-triggered device since it triggers on the H-to-L (negative-going) transition of the clock pulse.

3.4 ENCODERS, DECODERS, AND SEVEN-SEGMENT DISPLAYS

Consider the simple block diagram of a calculator in Fig. 3-15a.   In this digital system the decimal input from the keyboard must be translated into binary-coded-decimal (BCD) form.   This process is accomplished by the digital device called an *encoder*.   The translation from decimal to BCD is called encoding.   The central processing unit's (CPU's) output is in binary-coded decimal.   The decoder translates the BCD to a special seven-segment display code.   To the user, the decoder is translating from BCD to decimal.

A logic diagram of a typical *decimal-to-BCD priority encoder* is shown in Fig. 3-15b.   The encoder has 9 *active LOW* inputs and 4 outputs connected to indicator lamps.   Keyboard wiring is shown at the left, with each numbered key connected to its respective input of the encoder.   The example in Fig. 3-15b shows that the 7 key is depressed, which *activates* (grounds) input 7 of the encoder.   This input causes a BCD output of 0111, as shown on the displays in Fig. 3-15b.   Most encoders have a *priority* feature.   This means that if two keys are pressed at the same time, the one with the highest decimal value will activate the outputs.   It is understood that power supply connections would be needed to complete the wiring of the encoder in Fig. 3-15b.   The encoder would probably be purchased as a single IC, but it could be constructed from individual logic gates.   It would take about 10 to 20 logic gates to produce this circuit.

Consider the decoder-display circuit detailed in Fig. 3-15c.   The *BCD−to−seven-segment de-coder* is translating the 0111_{BCD} into its equivalent of 7 on the seven-segment LED display.   The seven-segment LED display used in this circuit is called a common anode type because all seven LEDs (which form the seven segments) have their anodes connected to the single +5-V power source.   The seven-segment LED display in Fig. 3-15c has *active LOW* inputs, as shown by the bubbles at inputs a through g.   It takes a LOW to activate a segment on the display.   Also note that the decoder has compatible active LOW outputs.   The seven 150-Ω resistors in each line between decoder and display are limiting resistors to hold the currents to safe levels.   The example in Fig. 3-15c shows that only decoder outputs a, b, and c are activated (at logical 0).   The other outputs (d, e, f, and g) remain at a logical 1.   The display in Fig. 3-15c has only one +5-V power connection,

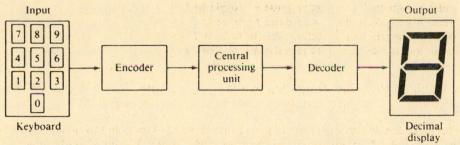

(a) Simplified block diagram of calculator circuit

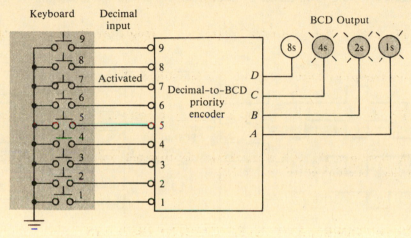

(b) Logic diagram of keyboard-encoder circuits

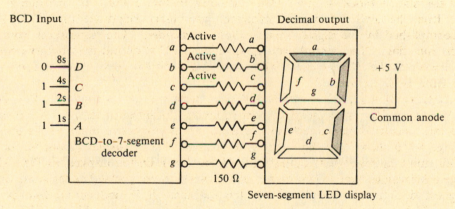

(c) Logic diagram of decoder-display circuits

Fig. 3-15

whereas the decoder would have two power connections. The decoder power connections have been omitted from the diagram. Typical real-world BCD–to–seven-segment decoders also contain inputs for *blanking* (turning all segments off) and for *lamp test* (turning all segments on).

SOLVED PROBLEMS

3.27 The encoder in Fig. 3-15b translates from a decimal keyboard to _____ (ASCII, BCD) form.

Solution:

Refer to Fig. 3-15b. This encoder translates decimal keyboard switch closures into BCD form.

3.28   The encoder in Fig. 3-15b has active _____ (HIGH, LOW) inputs.

Solution:

Refer to Fig. 3-15b. This encoder has active LOW inputs. This is represented on the logic diagram by the bubbles at the inputs to the encoder.

3.29   The decoder in Fig. 3-16 translates from binary-coded decimal to _____ (decimal, hexadecimal).

Solution:

The decoder in Fig. 3-16 translates from BCD to decimal representation on the seven-segment display.

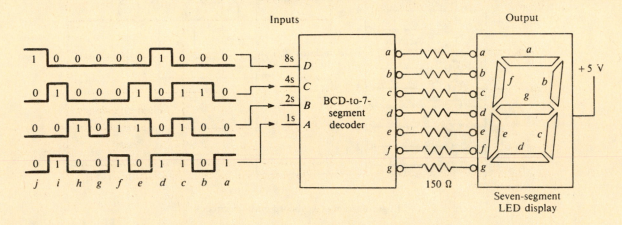

Fig. 3-16   BCD–to–seven-segment decoder problem

3.30   The decoder in Fig. 3-16 has active _____ (HIGH, LOW) inputs and active _____ (HIGH, LOW) outputs.

Solution:

The decoder in Fig. 3-16 has active HIGH inputs and active LOW outputs.

3.31   List the *decimal* indications of the seven-segment display for each input pulse in Fig. 3-16.

Solution:

The decimal outputs for the various pulses in Fig. 3-16 are as follows:

pulse $a = 1$ pulse $f = 3$
pulse $b = 4$ pulse $g = 0$
pulse $c = 7$ pulse $h = 2$
pulse $d = 9$ pulse $i = 5$
pulse $e = 6$ pulse $j = 8$

3.5 BUFFERS AND THREE-STATE DEVICES

The art of designing electronic circuitry that can translate signals from one section of a system to another is referred to as *interfacing*. In a microprocessor-based system, interfacing may take the form of buffers, multiplexers, analog-to-digital converters (ADC), digital-to-analog converters (DAC), discrete transistor drivers, and isolators (optical or relays).

In this section we will concentrate on just one interface device, the buffer. Manufacturers have designed a variety of special ICs called *buffers* to serve as interface devices in special situations. The logic symbol for a typical *noninverting bus buffer* is illustrated in Fig. 3-17a. The operation of the bus buffer is detailed in the mode-truth table in Fig. 3-17b. The bus buffer has an active LOW enable input, and the data is not inverted as it passes through the buffer. When the bus buffer is disabled, the output is permitted to "float" and has no effect on the bus line. In the disabled condition, the output of the gate does not sink or draw any current from the bus line. The bus buffer in Fig. 3-17 is said to have *three-state* (or *tristate*) *outputs*.

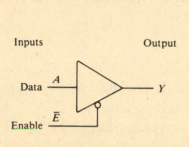

Mode of operation	Inputs		Output
	$\bar{E}$	A	Y
Enabled	0	0	0
	0	1	1
Disabled	1	0	High impedance (output voltage floats)
	1	1	

(a) Logic symbol for three-state bus buffer

(b) Mode-truth table for three-state bus buffer

Fig. 3-17

The outputs of logic devices are usually defined as either HIGH or LOW. For this reason, outputs from two logic devices cannot be wired together because if one is HIGH and the other is LOW, then the output will be undefined and the ICs may be damaged. Manufacturers have developed special ICs with three-state outputs for use when the outputs of several ICs must share a common output path or bus. Three-state devices have output states of HIGH, LOW, and a special *high-impedance state* (*high-Z state*). When the three-state device is in its high-Z state, its output is effectively disconnected or isolated from the bus.

The logic diagram for a bus transceiver is sketched in Fig. 3-18a. This *three-state bus transceiver*

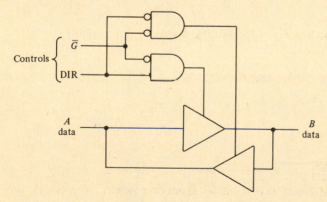

Control inputs		Operation
Enable	Direction	
$\bar{G}$	DIR	
L	L	*B* data to *A* bus
L	H	*A* data to *B* bus
H	X	Isolation (high *Z*)

H = HIGH logic level
L = LOW logic level
X = irrelevent

(a) Logic diagram for three-state bus transceiver

(b) Mode-truth table for three-state bus transceiver

Fig. 3-18

is a noninverting buffer that can send data in either direction. Such a two-way buffer would be required between the RAM and data bus and also between the microprocessor and data bus in a microcomputer system. As a practical matter, transceivers are built into RAMs and microprocessors.

The operation of the three-state bus transceiver is detailed in the truth table shown in Fig. 3-18b. The transceiver has two control inputs ($\bar{G}$ and DIR). The DIR input controls the *direction* of data flow. A HIGH at the DIR input means terminal A is the data input and terminal B is the output to the bus. A LOW at the DIR input means terminal B is the data input and terminal A is the output to the bus. A LOW at the $\bar{G}$ input to the transceiver activates the buffers and allows data to pass through. However, a HIGH at the $\bar{G}$ input disables the buffers. When disabled, the A and B terminals are *isolated* from one another.

SOLVED PROBLEMS

3.32 The output of a three-state logic device can be logical 1, logical 0, or in the high- _____ (voltage, impedance) state.

Solution:

The output of a three-state logic device can be HIGH, LOW, or in the high-impedance state.

3.33 Refer to Fig. 3-18. The transceiver is a three-state bus buffer that can pass data in _____ (either, one) direction.

Solution:

The transceiver in Fig. 3-18 can pass data in either direction (from A to B or from B to A) depending on the logic level at the DIR control.

3.34 Refer to Fig. 3-18. If the transceiver's enable control ($\bar{G}$) is HIGH, will the buffers pass data?

Solution:

No. With the transceiver's enable control HIGH, data terminals A and B are isolated and no data can pass in either direction.

3.35 The bus buffer gate in Fig. 3-19 has an active _____ (HIGH, LOW) enable input.

Solution:

The bus buffer in Fig. 3-19 has an active LOW enable input.

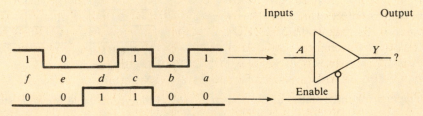

Fig. 3-19 Three-state bus buffer problem

3.36   Refer to Fig. 3-19.   List the outputs from the bus buffer gate during each of the six input pulses.

Solution:

The outputs from the bus buffer gate in Fig. 3-19 during each of the six input pulses are as follows:

during pulse $a = 1$ (gate enabled)   during pulse $d =$ high-Z state (gate disabled)

during pulse $b = 0$ (gate enabled)   during pulse $e = 0$ (gate enabled)

during pulse $c =$ high-Z state (gate disabled)   during pulse $f = 1$ (gate enabled)

3.6 SEMICONDUCTOR MEMORIES

The flip-flop, or latch, is the basic *memory cell* used in many semiconductor memories. Semiconductor memories are usually divided into two groups: *read/write memories* and *read-only memories* (ROM).   The names imply the differences between the two types of memories.   A ROM is a nonvolatile memory with its binary pattern of 0s and 1s *permanently* programmed by the manufacturer.   The read/write memory is a memory that can be easily programmed, erased, and reprogrammed by the user.   The programming is called *writing* into memory.   *Copying data from memory*, without destroying the contents, is called *reading* from memory.   The read/write memory is *most often* called a *RAM* (*random-access memory*).   Generally, the RAM's program is *volatile*, which means it will be lost if the power to the IC is turned off for even an instant.   Microcomputer systems typically contain both ROM and RAM types of semiconductor storage.   The ROM and RAM storage locations are usually in separate ICs.

Read-only memories come in four versions.   The standard ROM is programmed by the manufacturer.   The PROM (*programmable read-only memory*) can be programmed permanently by the user or distributor using special equipment.   It can be programmed only once.   The EPROM (*erasable programmable read-only memory*) can be programmed and erased by the user.   Stored data in the EPROM can be erased by shining high-intensity ultraviolet light through a special transparent window in the top of the IC.   Another erasable PROM is the EAROM (*electrically alterable read-only memory*).   The EAROM can be erased and programmed by the user with special equipment.   The EAROM is erased electrically rather than with ultraviolet light.   The ROM, PROM, EPROM, and EAROM are all considered permanent *nonvolatile* memories and do not lose their data when power to the IC is turned off.

RAMs are also subdivided into two groups.   If the read/write memory contains flip-flop-like circuits as memory cells, it is called a *static RAM* (SRAM).   A simpler form of read/write memory cell is the basis for the *dynamic RAM* (DRAM).   Because the memory cell of the dynamic RAM is based on capacitance, the cells must be refreshed hundreds of times per second.   The static RAM needs no refreshing and will hold its binary information indefinitely as long as the IC is powered.   Dynamic RAMs have the advantage of higher capacity and lower power consumption over static RAMs.

A newer semiconductor memory device is the *nonvolatile RAM* (NVRAM).   The NVRAM combines identical capacity static RAM and electrically erasable PROMs (EEPROMs).   Data can be transferred back and forth between the SRAM and EEPROMs by store and recall operations.   Data can be safely stored in the nonvolatile EEPROM when power is turned off.   When power is turned on, the data in the EEPROM is automatically recalled into the SRAM section of the nonvolatile RAM.   The concept of a nonvolatile RAM is also implemented by microcomputer manufacturers using regular RAM chips with a battery backup.

In microcomputers, RAMs are used for temporary storage of user programs and data.   ROMs are most often used to store machine language instructions that may be referred to as the *monitor program*.   The monitor program may contain unchangeable initialization routines, input/output routines, and arithmetic algorithms.

SOLVED PROBLEMS

3.37 In actual practice, the read/write memory is referred to as a _____ (RAM, ROM).

Solution:

In actual practice, the read/write memory is referred to as a RAM.

3.38 The letters RAM stand for _____-_____ _____ in digital electronics.

Solution:

The letters RAM stand for random-access memory.   In practice, semiconductor RAMs also are read/write memories.

3.39 The letters PROM stand for _____ _____-_____ _____.

Solution:

The letters PROM stand for programmable read-only memory.

3.40 The ROM and _____ (RAM, PROM) are both permanent nonvolatile storage devices.

Solution:

The ROM and PROM are both permanent nonvolatile storage devices.   The ROM is programmed by the manufacturer, while the PROM is programmed by the user.

3.41 The RAM is a _____ (nonvolatile, volatile) storage device.

Solution:

The RAM is a volatile storage device.

3.42 The letters EPROM stand for _____ _____ _____-_____ _____ in digital electronics.

Solution:

The letters EPROM stand for erasable programmable read-only memory.

3.43 The letters EAROM stand for _____ _____ _____-_____ _____.

Solution:

The letters EAROM stand for electrically alterable read-only memory.

3.44 The EPROM is considered to be a _____ (temporary, permanent) storage device.

Solution:

The EPROM is considered to be a permanent storage device.   It can be erased and reprogrammed, but only with special equipment.

3.45 Read/write memories are many times classed as either static or _____ RAMs.

Solution:

RWMs are many times classed as either static or dynamic RAMs.

3.46 The _____ (dynamic, static) RAM uses nearly standard flip-flops as memory cells.

Solution:

The static RAM uses nearly standard flip-flops as memory cells.

3.47 The _____ (dynamic, static) RAM needs its storage locations *refreshed* hundreds of times per second.

Solution:

The dynamic RAM needs its storage locations refreshed hundreds of times per second.

3.48 In a microcomputer, a PROM might be used to hold a _____ (monitor, temporary user) program.

Solution:

In a microcomputer, a PROM might be used to hold a monitor program.

3.49 The letters NVRAM stand for _____.

Solution:

The letters NVRAM stand for nonvolatile RAM.

3.50 The newer NVRAMs contains both static RAMs and _____ (DRAMs, EEPROMs).

Solution:

NVRAMs contain identical capacity SRAMs and EEPROMs.

3.7 USING RAMS AND ROMS

The organization of a RAM or ROM can be thought of as being similar to a truth table. Figure 3-20a shows one possible organization of memory locations. This table represents the organization of a 16×4 bit RAM. The table shows that data in the memory is organized into sixteen 4-bit groups referred to as words in this table. In Fig. 3-20a, most of the boxes (memory cells) are empty except word 12, which contains the stored data 0101. In actual practice, each "empty" cell would contain some pattern of 0s and 1s.

A logic symbol for a 16×4 bit RAM is illustrated in Fig. 3-20b. As diagramed, the 64-bit RAM is in the process of *writing* input data 0101 into memory location 12_{10} (1100_2). The data inputs contain the data to be stored (0101_2). Word location 12_{10} is located by setting the address inputs to 1100_2 (12_{10}). Next the two controls ($\overline{CS}$ and $\overline{WE}$) place the RAM in the *write mode* of operation. Note that the *write-enable* ($\overline{WE}$) and *chip-select* ($\overline{CS}$) inputs must be LOW for the write operation to take place. The 0101_2 is then placed in word location 12_{10}, as shown in Fig. 3-20a. The $\overline{CS}$ input control is called the memory enable by some manufacturers.

The mode-truth table for the 64-bit RAM is detailed in Fig. 3-20c. This RAM is in the *write mode* when both controls ($\overline{WE}$ and $\overline{CS}$) are LOW. During the write operation, the 4-data bits (D_4, D_3, D_2, D_1) are loaded into the memory location pointed to by the address. During the write operation, the outputs ($\bar{O}_4$, $\bar{O}_3$, $\bar{O}_2$, $\bar{O}_1$) float HIGH. With control inputs $\overline{CS} = 0$ and $\overline{WE} = 1$, the RAM is in the *read mode*. During the read mode, the complement of the data word pointed to by the address inputs appears at the outputs. The data stored in RAM is not destroyed by the read operation. In the *hold mode*, the outputs all go HIGH and no data enters from the four D inputs.

The 64-bit RAM in Fig. 3-20 is an extremely small capacity memory chip and is illustrated because of its simplicity. However, this 16×4 bit static RAM can still be purchased as a TTL (transistor-transistor logic) integrated circuit (7489 IC).

Address	Bit D	Bit C	Bit B	Bit A
Word 0				
Word 1				
Word 2				
Word 3				
Word 4				
Word 5				
Word 6				
Word 7				
Word 8				
Word 9				
Word 10				
Word 11				
Word 12	0	1	0	1
Word 13				
Word 14				
Word 15				

(a)   Organization of a 16 × 4 bit RAM

Fig. 3-20

In the last decade, great advances have been made in producing very large capacity semiconductor memories at low cost.   Common dynamic RAMs would now include 16,384 × 1; 65,536 × 1; 131,072 × 1; 1,048,576 × 1; 16,384 × 4; 65,536 × 4; and 262,144 × 4 chips. Dynamic RAM modules in even larger capacities are available.

A ROM IC would operate similarly to the RAM when it is in its *read* and *hold* modes.   A ROM comparable to the one in Fig. 3-20 would have all the inputs and outputs of the RAM *except the data inputs and the write-enable input*.   A word would be *read* from ROM by addressing a specified word location and then pulsing the *chip-select* ($\overline{CS}$) input with a LOW.

Some typical ROM IC organizations and capacities might be 512 × 4; 2048 × 8; 4096 × 8; 8192 × 8; 16,384 × 8; 65,536 × 8; and 131,072 × 8.   Some EEPROM modules come in even larger capacities.

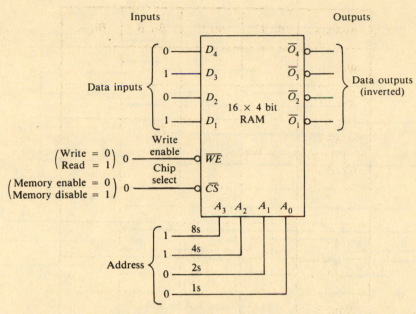

(b) Logic symbol for a 16 × 4 bit RAM

Mode of operation	Control inputs		Outputs
	$\overline{CS}$	$\overline{WE}$	$\bar{O}$
Write	0	0	Logical 1 state
Read	0	1	Complement of data stored in memory
Hold	1	X	Logical 1 state

X = irrelevant

(c) Mode-truth table for 64-bit RAM

Fig. 3-20 (*cont.*)

SOLVED PROBLEMS

3.51 The 64-bit RAM in Fig. 3-21 is in the _____ (hold, write) mode during pulse *a*, and all the outputs are therefore floating _____ (HIGH, LOW).

Solution:

During pulse *a* in Fig. 3-21, both controls ($\overline{CS}$ and $\overline{WE}$) are HIGH. The mode-select table in Fig. 3-20c indicates that this is the hold mode for the RAM and the outputs will float HIGH.

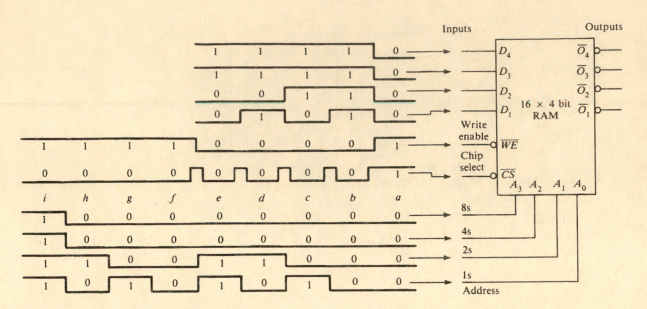

Fig. 3-21 A static RAM problem

3.52 The RAM in Fig. 3-21 is in the _____ (read, write) mode during pulses *b*, *c*, *d*, and *e*.

Solution:

During pulses *b*, *c*, *d*, and *e* in Fig. 3-21, both controls ($\overline{CS}$ and $\overline{WE}$) are LOW. The mode-select table in Fig. 3-20*c* indicates that this is the write mode for the RAM. The data from the *D* inputs is being copied into the memory location addressed by the *A* inputs during these four pulses.

3.53 The RAM in Fig. 3-21 is in the _____ (read, write) mode during pulses *f*, *g*, *h*, and *i*.

Solution:

During pulses *f*, *g*, *h*, and *i* in Fig. 3-21, $\overline{CS} = 0$ and $\overline{WE} = 1$. The mode-select table in Fig. 3-20*c* indicates that this is the read mode for the RAM. The data stored at the storage location pointed to by the address inputs will appear at the outputs in inverted form. The read operation does not destroy the contents of the RAM.

3.54 Refer to Fig. 3-21. List the address and the data stored in the RAM during the write operation in pulses *b*, *c*, *d*, and *e*.

Solution:

The storage location (address) and data stored during each write operation are as follows:
pulse *b* = address = 0000; data stored = 1111
pulse *c* = address = 0001; data stored = 1110
pulse *d* = address = 0010; data stored = 1101
pulse *e* = address = 0011; data stored = 1100

3.55 Refer to Fig. 3-21. List the address and the data appearing at the outputs of the RAM during the read operation in pulses *f*, *g*, *h*, and *i*.

Solution:

The storage location (address) and output data during each read operation are as follows:
pulse *f* = address = 0000
      data stored = 1111
      output data (inverted) = 0000

pulse g = address = 0001
      data stored = 1110
      output data (inverted) = 0001
pulse h = address = 0010
      data stored = 1101
      output data (inverted) = 0010
pulse i = address = 1111
      data stored = no data was stored at this location
      output data = unknown (the output will be unpredictable)

3.56 If the RAM illustrated in Fig. 3-21 were a ROM, what input(s) would be omitted from the logic diagram?

   Solution:

   The RAM in Fig. 3-21 could be converted to a ROM logic symbol by omitting the write-enable and 4 data inputs.   A ROM is permanently programmed by the manufacturer and has no write mode.

Supplementary Problems

3.57 If flip-flops are interconnected to form sequential logic circuits, then _____ _____ are used to form combinational logic circuits.   *Ans.* logic gates

3.58 A logic function can be described in four ways: by its name, its graphic logic symbol, its truth table, or its _____ expression.   *Ans.* Boolean

3.59 Refer to Fig. 3-22.   Describe the pulse train at output Y if this logic circuit is a 2-input OR gate.
      Ans.   pulse $a = 0$, pulse $b = 1$, pulse $c = 1$, pulse $d = 1$

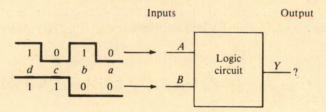

Fig. 3-22 Pulse-train problem

3.60 Refer to Fig. 3-22.   Describe the pulse train at output Y if this logic circuit is a 2-input NAND gate.
      Ans.   pulse $a = 1$, pulse $b = 1$, pulse $c = 1$, pulse $d = 0$

3.61 Refer to Fig. 3-22.   Describe the pulse train at output Y if this logic circuit is a 2-input XOR gate.
      Ans.   pulse $a = 0$, pulse $b = 1$, pulse $c = 1$, pulse $d = 0$

3.62 Microprocessors typically have which four logic instructions in their instruction set?
      Ans.   NOT (complement or negate), AND, OR, and XOR

3.63 Write the Boolean expression for the truth table shown in Fig. 3-23.
      Ans. $\bar{C} \cdot B \cdot \bar{A} + C \cdot B \cdot A = Y$

	Inputs		Output
C	B	A	Y
0	0	0	0
0	0	1	0
0	1	0	1
0	1	1	0
1	0	0	0
1	0	1	0
1	1	0	0
1	1	1	1

Fig. 3-23

3.64 Draw a logic-symbol diagram of a circuit that will generate the truth table in Fig. 3-23.
Ans. See Fig. 3-24.

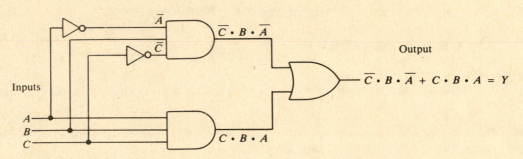

Fig. 3-24 AND-OR logic-diagram solution

3.65 To *set* a flip-flop means to load a 1 into the normal or _____ $(Q, \bar{Q})$ output.   *Ans.* Q

3.66 To *reset* a flip-flop means to load a 0 into the _____ $(Q, \bar{Q})$ output.   *Ans.* Q

3.67 When a flip-flop is called a latch, it is used as a _____ (counting, memory) device.   *Ans.* memory

3.68 List the mode of operation of the *JK* flip-flop during each of the clock pulses in Fig. 3-25.
Ans.   pulse *a* = reset   pulse *c* = toggle   pulse *e* = toggle
   pulse *b* = toggle   pulse *d* = set   pulse *f* = hold

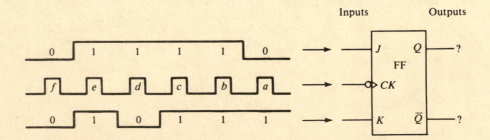

Fig. 3-25 *JK* flip-flop problem

3.69   List the binary outputs at the normal output (Q) of the *JK* flip-flop in Fig. 3-25 *after* each of the clock pulses.
    Ans.   pulse $a = 0$ pulse $c = 0$ pulse $e = 0$
                    pulse $b = 1$ pulse $d = 1$ pulse $f = 0$

3.70   Electronic code translators are commonly referred to as _____ or _____.
    Ans.   encoders, decoders

3.71   A seven-segment LED display may be driven by a device called a _____-to-seven-segment _____.
    Ans.   BCD, decoder

3.72   Refer to Fig. 3-15c.   To light LED segment d, input d of the display must be driven _____ (HIGH, LOW) by the decoder.   *Ans*.   LOW

3.73   The letters TTL stand for _____-_____ _____ in digital electronics.
    Ans.   transistor-transistor logic

3.74   When TTL or CMOS devices are connected to microcomputer bus lines, the outputs must be of the _____-_____ type.   *Ans*.   three-state

3.75   When the output of a three-state TTL device is in neither a logical 0 nor a logical 1 state but is allowed to float at the voltage level of the bus line, it is said to be in the high-_____ state.
    Ans.   impedance (Z)

3.76   List the two types of semiconductor memories typically used in microcomputer systems.
    Ans.   RAM and ROM

3.77   A ROM and _____ (PROM, RAM) are very similar in that they are both permanent-type memories.
    Ans.   PROM

3.78   Placing data into memory is called the _____ (read, write) operation.   *Ans*.   write

3.79   Copying data out of memory is called the _____ (read, write) operation,   *Ans*.   read

3.80   In common practice, the letters used to designate a read/write semiconductor memory are _____ (EPROM, RAM).   *Ans*.   RAM

3.81   Modern RAM ICs can be purchased in what two basic types?   *Ans*.   static, dynamic

3.82   Temporary user programs would be stored in _____ (EPROM, RAM) in a microcomputer.
    Ans.   RAM

3.83   What is the length of each word in a 256×4 bit RAM?   *Ans*.   4 bits long

3.84   How many *words* of data can a 32×8 bit ROM hold?   *Ans*.   32

3.85   What is the total capacity (in bits) of a 512×8 bit EAROM?   *Ans*.   4096 bits

Chapter 4

Microcomputer Fundamentals

4.1 INTRODUCTION

More than 20 companies produce a wide variety of general-purpose microprocessors. Even more companies assemble microprocessors, memories, and other components into microcomputer systems. Because of these wide variations, a generic microcomputer has been selected for study in this chapter. This universal microcomputer will have many of the characteristics of common microcomputers.

When learning about a new microprocessor, the programmer must study the following:

1. Microprocessor architecture
2. Instruction set
3. Minimal system using this microprocessor
4. Control signals
5. Pin functions

The architecture can deal with the arrangement of registers in the CPU, the number of bits in the address and data buses, etc.

The instruction set is a listing of the operations the microprocessor can perform. This includes transferring data, arithmetic and logical operations, data testing and branching instructions, and input/output operations. These instructions use a variety of addressing modes.

A schematic of a minimal system will show how other devices are connected to the microprocessor. A minimal system may contain a microprocessor, a clock, a RAM, a ROM, input/output ports, an address decoder, and a power supply. Sometimes these functions are performed by separate ICs or components; however, some microprocessor units contain most of these capabilities.

The control signals include outputs that direct other ICs (such as RAMs, ROMs, and I/O ports) when to operate. Some typical control signals might govern memory reading and writing or input/output reading and writing.

A study of each IC pin function will further detail special inputs and outputs of the microprocessor. Other pins might be power supply, clock, serial data I/O, interrupt inputs, and bus control.

4.2 SIMPLIFIED MICROCOMPUTER ARCHITECTURE

A microcomputer architecture is diagramed in Fig. 4-1. At the center of all operations is the *MPU* (microprocessor unit). The MPU needs a power supply and clock connections. The clock may be a separate circuit or may reside within the microprocessor chip. A simple MPU might have 16 address lines which form the one-way *address bus*. The MPU also has the typical 8 buffered data lines which connect to the two-way *data bus*.

The microcomputer architecture shown in Fig. 4-1 shows two types of semiconductor memory used in this system. The ROM is the permanent memory which probably contains the monitor program for the system. The ROM has address inputs along with chip-select and read-enable input lines. The ROM also has 8 buffered three-state outputs connected to the data bus. Each memory word is then 8 bits wide. Of course the ROM would also have power supply connections, although they are many times omitted from block diagrams.

The architecture in Fig. 4-1 also shows a RAM as the temporary read/write storage device. The RAM has address inputs along with chip-select and read/write-enable inputs. The RAM has 8 buffered three-state outputs connected to the data bus. This RAM inputs, outputs, and stores data as 8-bit words. RAM power supply connections are also shown.

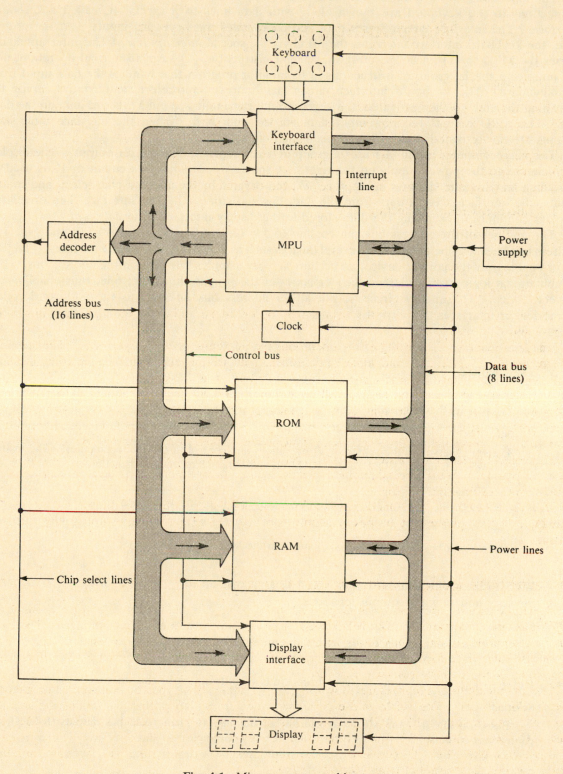

Fig. 4-1 Microcomputer architecture

The microcomputer system diagramed in Fig. 4-1 uses a keyboard as the input device. Power connections to the keyboard are shown along with data lines to a special IC called a *keyboard interface*. The interface circuit stores data and coordinates the keyboard inputs. At the proper time, the keyboard interface *interrupts* the MPU via the special *interrupt line*. This interrupt signal causes the MPU to (1) finish executing the current instruction, (2) suspend normal operation, and (3) jump to a special group of instructions in its monitor program that handles the data input from the keyboard. The keyboard interface circuit has address, chip-select, and control inputs for activating the unit. When activated, the keyboard interface unit will put keyboard data on the data bus. The MPU accepts the new input data via the data bus. When the interface three-state outputs are not activated, they return to their high-impedance state.

The microcomputer in Fig. 4-1 uses a group of seven-segment displays for output. The display is connected to the power supply on the right. A special *display interface* circuit or IC is used to store data and drive the displays in Fig. 4-1. When activated by the address, chip-select, and enable inputs, the interface accepts data from the data bus and stores it. The interface then drives the displays continuously, showing the data stored in the display interface in visual form.

The 16 lines of the address bus can contain 65,536 (2^{16}) different patterns of 0s and 1s. The address bus lines may be attached to several devices such as RAMs, ROMs, and interfaces. To turn on or enable *only* the correct device, an *address decoder* samples the data on the address bus. The combinational logic of the address decoder activates the proper chip-select line, thus enabling the correct device. To simplify circuitry, not all 16 address bus lines go to the address decoder, memories, or interfaces.

SOLVED PROBLEMS

4.1 Refer to Fig. 4-1. The _____ (MPU, RAM, ROM) serves as the center of all operations and control in the microcomputer.

Solution:

The MPU serves as the center of all operations and control in the microcomputer. The instructions, however, from the ROM and/or RAM do guide the microprocessor's actions.

4.2 Refer to Fig. 4-1. The _____ (address, data) bus is a one-way data path.

Solution:

The address bus is a one-way data path from the MPU to all devices.

4.3 With 16 lines, the address bus in Fig. 4-1 can access up to _____ (16,384, 65,536) separate memory and/or input/output locations.

Solution:

The 16-line address bus in Fig. 4-1 can access up to 65,536 (2^{16}) memory locations.

4.4 Refer to Fig. 4-1. Name at least three kinds of outputs from the microprocessor unit.

Solution:

Based on Fig. 4-1, the MPU has address bus outputs (16 lines), data bus outputs (8 lines), and control bus outputs.

4.5 Refer to Fig. 4-1. Name at least four kinds of inputs to the microprocessor unit.

Solution:

Based on Fig. 4-1, the MPU has power supply inputs, clock inputs, interrupt input(s), and data bus inputs (8 lines).

4.6   Refer to Fig. 4-1.   List at least four kinds of inputs to the ROM.

Solution:

Based on Fig. 4-1, the ROM has power supply inputs, address inputs from the address bus, a chip-select input, and a read-enable input from the control bus.

4.7   Refer to Fig. 4-1.   List the output(s) from the ROM.

Solution:

Based on Fig. 4-1, the ROM has three-state data bus outputs (8 lines).

4.8   Refer to Fig. 4-1.   List at least four kinds of inputs to the RAM.

Solution:

Based on Fig. 4-1, the RAM has power supply inputs, address inputs from the address bus, a chip-select input, read- and write-enable inputs from the control bus, and data bus inputs (8 lines).

4.9   Refer to Fig. 4-1.   List the output(s) from the RAM.

Solution:

Based on Fig. 4-1, the RAM has three-state data bus outputs (8 lines).

4.10   Refer to Fig. 4-1.   List at least five kinds of inputs to the special keyboard interface circuit.

Solution:

Based on Fig. 4-1, the keyboard interface circuit has power supply inputs, address inputs from the address bus, a chip-select input, control inputs from the control bus, and data inputs from the keyboard.

4.11   Refer to Fig. 4-1.   List at least two kinds of outputs from the keyboard interface circuit.

Solution:

Based on Fig. 4-1, the keyboard interface circuit has an interrupt output and three-state data bus outputs (8 lines).

4.12   What is the purpose of the interrupt output from the keyboard interface circuit in Fig. 4-1?

Solution:

The keyboard interface circuit in Fig. 4-1 activates the interrupt line when it is ready to send keyboard input data to the MPU.

4.13   What does the MPU do when the interrupt line in Fig. 4-1 is activated by the keyboard interface circuit?

Solution:

When the interrupt line in Fig. 4-1 is activated, the MPU does the following:
(*a*)   Completes the instruction it is currently executing
(*b*)   Suspends normal operation
(*c*)   Jumps to a special group of instructions that handles the input of data from the keyboard

4.14   Refer to Fig. 4-1.   List at least five kinds of inputs to the special display interface circuit.

Solution:

Based on Fig. 4-1, the display interface circuit has power supply inputs, address inputs from the address bus, data inputs from the 8-line data bus, a chip-select input, and control inputs from the control bus.

4.15   Refer to Fig. 4-1.   List the outputs from the special display interface circuit.

Solution:

Based on Fig. 4-1, the display interface circuit has data outputs to drive the seven-segment displays.

4.16   What is the purpose of the address decoder in Fig. 4-1?

Solution:

The address decoder in Fig. 4-1 selects and helps enable a *single* device such as keyboard interface, ROM, RAM, or display interface.

4.3   SIMPLIFIED MEMORY ORGANIZATION

Writing into or reading from a storage location is called *accessing* memory.   Generally, data storage can be classified as either sequential-access or random-access memory.   Data in a *sequential-access memory* is located by searching in serial fashion through all the storage locations.   For example, when data are stored on magnetic tape, the tape must be searched from end to end to find the appropriate data.

In a *random-access memory*, any storage location can be written into or read from in a given time (called the *access time*).   The semiconductor RAM and ROM storage devices used in microcomputers are both of the faster random-access type.

The generic microcomputer that has been studied had 16 lines in the address bus.   This is typical of many smaller microcomputers used for training.   These 16 address lines can generate a total of 65,536 (2^{16}) different combinations of 0s and 1s.   Several binary combinations are shown below the address bus in Fig. 4-2.   It is customary to represent the binary address in hexadecimal form.   As shown in Fig. 4-2, the address $0000\ 0000\ 0000\ 0000_2$ equals 0000H (0000_{16}).   Notice the use of the H to designate hexadecimal representation.   The highest address generated by the 16-line bus in Fig. 4-2 would be $1111\ 1111\ 1111\ 1111_2$ which is represented as FFFFH ($FFFF_{16}$).

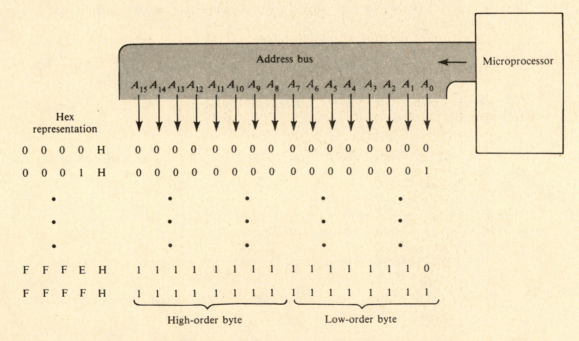

Fig. 4-2 Representation of microprocessor addresses

The diagram in Fig. 4-3 represents a microcomputer *memory map*. The 16-bit address bus from the microprocessor can generate 65,536 (10000_{16}) unique addresses. Some of these addresses are listed in hexadecimal notation in the left column in Fig. 4-3. In this particular microcomputer, the first 256 (100_{16}) locations are found in ROM. The ROM is probably a 256×8 bit ROM (256 words, each word 8 bits wide). If the address bus accesses address 0000H, the ROM will output its permanently programmed pattern of 0s and 1s (the word 11000011).

It is convenient for beginners to think of the first 256 (100_{16}) bytes or words of data in ROM in Fig. 4-3 as being on page 00H. Note that the page number is equal to the hexadecimal representation of the high-order byte of the address (see Fig. 4-2). Thus when dealing with page 00H, only the two low-order hexadecimal digits need be considered. Some microprocessors use

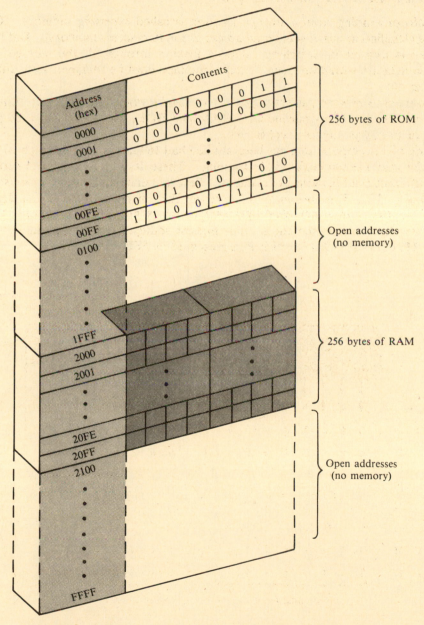

Fig. 4-3 Simplified memory map showing ROM and RAM locations

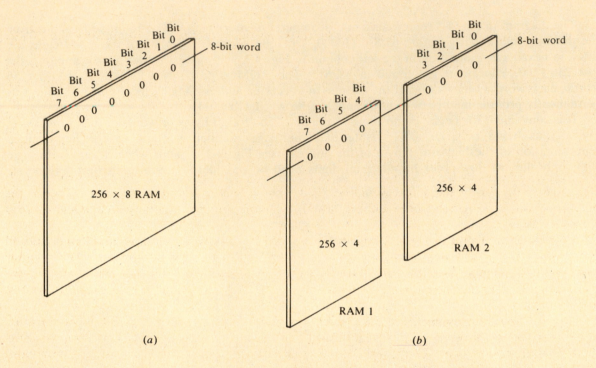

(a)   (b)

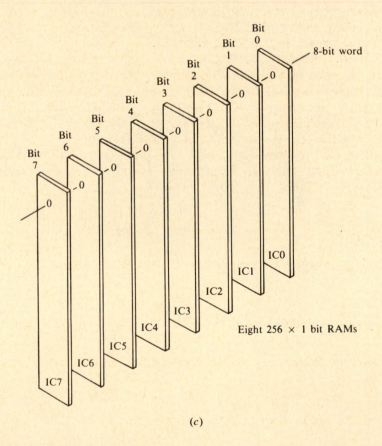

(c)

Fig. 4-4 Three methods of forming a 256×8 bit read/write memory using semiconductor RAMs

simplified instructions for accessing memory locations on the very first page of memory (i.e., 6502, 65816).

The simplified memory map in Fig. 4-3 shows that pages 01H through 1FH (addresses 0100H–1FFFH) contain no memory in this microcomputer. Accessing this open area will cause unpredictable results since neither program or data is stored here. The microcomputer's read/write memory (RAM) is located on page 20H according to the memory map in Fig. 4-3. The RAM is a 256×8 bit storage device. The designers of the microcomputer system could place the RAM on any other page. Accessing pages 21H through FFH in this microcomputer would cause unpredictable results because no storage devices are located in this open area.

If a microprocessor were to write into storage location 2000H in Fig. 4-3, the eight memory cells (bits) across the top of the RAM would be filled with 0s and 1s from the data bus. Then if the microprocessor were to read from address 2000H, the same data previously written would be read from the RAM.

Physically, the ROM in Fig. 4-3 is probably a single IC. However, RAMs are often organized differently. In Fig. 4-3, the darker storage area of the RAM is divided into halves. This suggests that the RAM storage area on page 20H is physically two separate ICs. In this example, two 256×4 bit RAMs are being used to form the 256×8 bit storage area on page 20H of this microcomputer.

Three physical arrangements of semiconductor RAM ICs are shown in Fig. 4-4. The single IC in Fig. 4-4a is organized as a 256×8 bit RAM. Two ICs are used in Fig. 4-4b to form the same 256×8 bit storage device. Here, two 256×4 bit RAMs are used to build the needed 8-bit word width. The eight RAMs shown in Fig. 4-4c also form a 256×8 bit read/write storage device.

The arrangement of ICs shown in Fig. 4-4c is very commonly used in building larger read/write memories. Commonly 1024×1; $16,384 \times 1$; $65,536 \times 1$; and $1,048,576 \times 1$ RAM ICs are used. Using the technique shown in Fig. 4-4c, eight 4096×1 bit RAMs would be needed to form a common 4096×8 bit read/write memory. Note that in such a configuration, all eight of these RAMs would be activated by the same chip-select line from the address decoder.

In a microcomputer system, the amount of memory is divided into 1K blocks. A storage capacity of 1K would *not mean exactly* 1000, but instead 1K means 2^8 or 1024 bytes of memory (1024×1). Then, 4K of storage means 4096 bytes of memory ($1024 \times 4 = 4096$). If a commercial microcomputer had 256K of memory, it actually would have 262,144 ($1024 \times 256 = 262,144$) memory locations each 8 bits wide. The memory capacities of commercial microcomputers now range from about 64K to more than 1 million (1M) bytes. A storage capacity of 1M would really mean 1,048,576 ($1024 \times 1024 = 1,048,576$) bytes of memory.

SOLVED PROBLEMS

4.17 Writing into or reading from a microcomputer memory location is called _____ (accessing, finding) memory.

   Solution:
   Writing into or reading from a memory location is called accessing memory.

4.18 Both RAMs and ROMs used in microcomputers are examples of _____ (random, sequential) -access memories.

   Solution:
   Both RAMs and ROMs are examples of random-access memories.

4.19 Refer to Fig. 4-2. If the address on the address bus were 0010 0000 0000 0000, what memory location (hexadecimal number) would be accessed by the microprocessor?

Solution:

Binary 0010 0000 0000 0000 equals 2000H. Memory location 2000H would be accessed if the address bus output were 0010 0000 0000 0000 in Fig. 4-2.

4.20 Refer to Fig. 4-3. If the microcomputer addresses memory location 0001H, the _____ (RAM, ROM) will output _ _ _ _ _ _ _ _ (8 bits).

Solution:

According to the memory map in Fig. 4-3, location 0001H accesses ROM, which outputs the permanently stored data of 00000001.

4.21 Refer to Fig. 4-3. If the microcomputer accesses memory location 2001H and if the storage device is placed in the write mode, a _____ (byte, nibble) of data from the data bus will be placed in the _____ (RAM, ROM).

Solution:

According to Fig. 4-3, storage location 2001H is in RAM and each word is 8 bits wide, which is called a byte.

4.22 Refer to Fig. 4-3. What are the output results on the data bus if the microprocessor reads storage location FFFFH?

Solution:

According to the memory map in Fig. 4-3, no memory device resides at address FFFFH, and therefore the output would be unpredictable.

4.23 The _____ (RAM, ROM) appears to be implemented using only a single IC in Fig. 4-3.

Solution:

The ROM appears to be implemented using only a single IC in Fig. 4-3. In this example the read/write memory was implemented using two 256×4 bit RAM ICs.

4.24 The RAM in Fig. 4-3 is said to reside on what page?

Solution:

The RAM in Fig. 4-3 is said to reside on page 20H of memory. The two high-order hexadecimal digits are considered the page number in this system.

4.25 Eight $16,384 \times 1$ bit RAM ICs could be arranged similarly to those in Fig. 4-4c to form a $16,384 \times 8$ bit read/write memory. This is referred to as a _____K memory.

Solution:

The $16,384 \times 8$ bit RAM would be referred to as a 16K memory. The 16K memory has 16,384 bytes or memory words.

4.26 Refer to Fig. 4-3. What is the maximum memory that can be accessed by 16 address lines?

Solution:

A 16-line address bus can access a 64K memory. The addresses range from 0000H through FFFFH, which equals $65,536_{10}$ locations. In this case the memory words are 8 bits wide; however, other systems may have 4 or 16 bits per word.

4.27 If a commercial microcomputer contains 512K of storage, it actually would have _____ memory locations each 8 bits wide.

Solution:

A microcomputer with a 512K memory would actually have 524,288 ($1024 \times 512 = 524{,}288$) bytes of memory.

4.4 INSTRUCTION SET

The group of instructions that a specific microprocessor can execute is called its *instruction set*. Microprocessor instruction sets may have as few as eight or as many as 200 basic instructions. Instruction sets are not standardized. This is due to the individualism of each manufacturer and to the differences in architecture and intended use of microprocessors.

Instructions in an instruction set can be categorized in several ways. Instructions in this chapter will be organized into the following categories:

1. Arithmetic instructions
2. Logical instructions
3. Data transfer instructions
4. Branch instructions
5. Subroutine call instructions
6. Return instructions
7. Miscellaneous instructions

A simple microprocessor instruction set would include the following *arithmetic instructions*:

1. Add
2. Subtract
3. Increment
4. Decrement
5. Compare
6. Negate

Other arithmetic instructions used by some microprocessors might include add with carry, subtract with carry/borrow, multiply, and divide operations.

The same simplified microprocessor would have the following *logical instructions*:

1. AND
2. OR
3. Exclusive OR
4. Not
5. Shift right
6. Shift left

Other logical instructions used by some microprocessors might include shift right arithmetic, rotate right, rotate left, rotate right through carry, rotate left through carry, and the test operation.

The basic microprocessor would contain variations of the following *data transfer instructions*:

1. Load
2. Store

3. Move

4. Input

5. Output

Other data transfer instructions used by some microprocessors might include exchange and various clear and set operations.

The microprocessor would contain the following *branch instructions* in its instruction set:

1. Unconditional branch

2. Branch if zero

3. Branch if not zero

4. Branch if equal

5. Branch if not equal

6. Branch if positive

7. Branch if negative

Other conditional branch instructions used by some microprocessors might depend on conditions such as greater than or less than, no carry or carry, or no overflow or overflow. The branch operations are the decision-making instructions.

A simple microprocessor would have a *subroutine call instruction* (referred to as CALL) to make the program jump to a special group of instructions which perform a specific task. All microprocessors have the unconditional call instruction, and some have conditional call instructions as well. Conditional call instructions might include call if zero, call if not zero, call if positive, call if not positive, etc.

At the end of a subroutine, the program must return to where it originally left off in the main program listing. This task is accomplished with a *return instruction*. Return instructions might include return from subroutine or return from interrupt operations. Returns are usually unconditional, but some microprocessors contain conditional return instructions.

A simplified microprocessor instruction set would include the following *miscellaneous instructions*:

1. No operation

2. Push

3. Pop

4. Wait

5. Halt

Other miscellaneous instructions might include enable interrupt, disable interrupt, break, and decimal adjust operations.

Microprocessor users encounter several ways of describing the same instruction. Several of these methods are diagramed in Fig. 4-5 for the add instruction for the Motorola 6800 microprocessor. The mame of the instruction is typically an *action verb* and is called the *operation*. In Fig. 4-5a, the operation is to add. MPU users also frequently work with abbreviated forms of the instruction called the *mnemonic*. In Fig. 4-5a, the mnemonic for this particular add operation is ADD A (note that mnemonics are capitalized). The instruction register and instruction decoding circuitry of a microprocessor understands only 0s and 1s. The *op code* is the hexadecimal representation of the 8-bit binary code that will cause the MPU to execute the instruction. In Fig. 4-5a, the op code for ADD A is $8B_{16}$ (10001011_2) for the 6800 microprocessor. The symbolic column in Fig. 4-5a shows that the contents of memory (M) are added to the contents of accumulator A in the MPU, with the arrow denoting that the sum is placed in accumulator A.

An example using the add instruction (ADD A) is diagramed in Fig. 4-5b. The contents of

Operation	Mnemonic	Op code (hex)	Symbolic (all register labels refer to contents)
Add	ADD A	8B	$A + M \rightarrow A$

(a) Summary of the add instruction

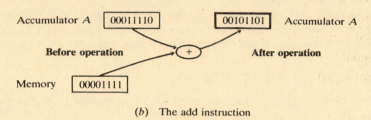

(b) The add instruction

Fig. 4-5

accumulator A (00011110_2) are added to the contents of memory (00001111_2), with the sum (00101101_2) being placed in accumulator A at the right.   Note that the contents of the memory location in Fig. 4-5b have not changed, whereas the contents of accumulator A have been changed, and now accumulator A holds the new sum.

SOLVED PROBLEMS

4.28   The group of operations that a microprocessor can perform is called its _____ _____.

Solution:

  The group of operations that a microprocessor can perform is called its instruction set.

4.29   List seven types of instructions found in a microprocessor's instruction set.

Solution:

  One grouping of instruction set operations lists the following categories: arithmetic, logical, data transfer, branch, subroutine call, return, and miscellaneous instructions.

4.30   An ADD operation is an arithmetic instruction, whereas an OR operation is classified as a _____ instruction.

Solution:

  An OR operation is classified as a logical instruction.

4.31   Shift operations are classified as _____ instructions.

Solution:

  Shift operations are classified as logical instructions.

4.32   List five basic data transfer operations found in most microprocessor instruction sets.

Solution:

  Microprocessor data transfer operations include load, store, move, input, and output instructions.

4.33 A microprocessor's decision-making operations are called the _____ instructions.

Solution:

A microprocessor's decision-making operations are called the branch instructions.

4.34 List several conditional branch operations that might be found in a microprocessor's instruction set.

Solution:

Typical microprocessor conditional branch instructions include the following: branch if zero, branch if not zero, branch if equal, branch if not equal, branch if positive, branch if negative, branch if greater than, branch if less than, branch if carry, branch if no carry, branch if overflow, and branch if no overflow.

4.35 A special group of instructions which perform a commonly used specific task in a program is called a(n) _____ (index, subroutine).

Solution:

A special group of instructions which perform a commonly used specific task in a program is called a subroutine.

4.36 What common instruction causes the microprocessor to jump to a subroutine?

Solution:

The CALL or subroutine call instruction causes the MPU to jump to a subroutine.

4.37 What instruction is placed at the end of a subroutine to guide the microprocessor back to the correct place in the main program?

Solution:

The return from subroutine (RET) instruction is placed at the end of a subroutine to cause the microprocessor to jump back to the correct place in the main program. This instruction may also restore several registers to their condition before the call subroutine operation.

4.38 List five miscellaneous operations found in the instruction sets of many microprocessors.

Solution:

Miscellaneous MPU instructions include no operation, push, pop, wait, halt, enable interrupt, disable interrupt, break, and decimal adjust operations.

4.39 Refer to Fig. 4-6a. What heading should appear above the SUB A in the chart describing the subtract instruction?

Solution:

The abbreviation SUB A is the mnemonic for subtract from accumulator A. The heading above SUB A in Fig. 4-6a should then be "Mnemonic."

4.40 The hexadecimal 80 in Fig. 4-6a is called the _____ _____.

Solution:

The 80_{16} in Fig. 4-6a is called the op code for the subtract instruction.

Operation	?	? (hex)	Symbolic (all register labels refer to contents)
Subtract	SUB A	80	$A - M \rightarrow A$

(a) Summary of the subtract instruction

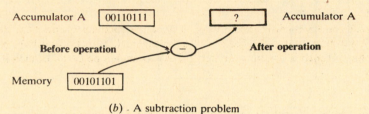

(b) - A subtraction problem

Fig. 4-6

4.41 Refer to Fig. 4-6b. The binary difference that would appear in accumulator A after the SUB A operation would be _____.

Solution:

Binary $00110111 - 00101101 = 00001010$ (decimal $55 - 45 = 10$). Accumulator A would contain the difference of 00001010_2 after the SUB A operation in Fig. 4-6b.

4.5 SIMPLIFIED CPU ORGANIZATION

The primary functioning unit of any computer system is called the *central processing unit*, or *CPU*. Many microprocessor ICs *are* the CPU of the system. It is common in computer technology to implement the program memory, data memory, input/output interfaces, address decoder, and CPU with separate ICs, as suggested in the system in Fig. 4-1. The MPU forms the central processing unit in this system.

Generally the CPU will contain storage elements called registers and computational circuitry called the arithmetic and logic unit (ALU). The CPU will also contain instruction-decoding circuitry and a control and timing section. The CPU will also have the necessary input and output connections.

The primary functions of the CPU of a microcomputer are to:

1. Fetch, decode, and execute program instructions in the proper order

2. Transfer data to and from memory and to and from the input/output sections

3. Respond to external interrupts

4. Provide overall timing and control signals for the entire system

Most microprocessor CPUs contain at least the elements diagramed in Fig. 4-7. The main sections include the various registers, the arithmetic and logic unit, the instruction decoder, the all-important control and timing section, along with inputs and outputs. Most CPUs actually contain several more special registers as well as many specialized inputs and outputs not detailed in Fig. 4-7.

The CPU's *arithmetic and logic unit (ALU)* performs operations such as add, shift/rotate, compare, increment, decrement, negate, AND, OR, XOR, complement, clear, and preset. If the ALU were directed to add using the ADD instruction, the procedure might appear to be something

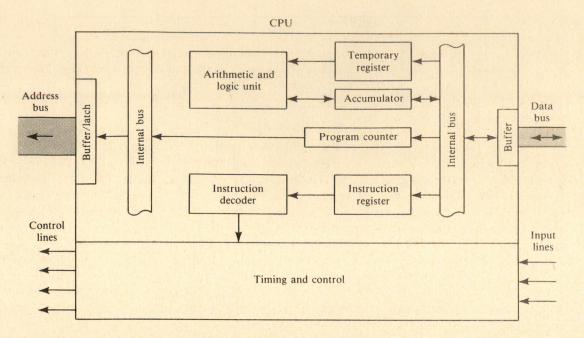

Fig. 4-7 Simplified CPU architecture

like that diagramed in Fig. 4-8a. Here the accumulator contents ($0A_{16}$) are being added to the temporary register contents (05_{16}). The sum ($0F_{16}$) is then placed back into the accumulator.

Some of the functional sections in a typical ALU are diagramed in Fig. 4-8b. The ALU contains an adder and shifter, with the results being fed back into the accumulator via the internal data bus. Of critical importance to the programmer is the *status register* located in the ALU. The

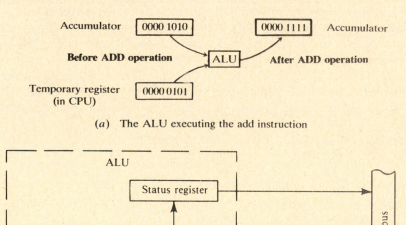

(a) The ALU executing the add instruction

(b) Organization of the ALU

Fig. 4-8

status register may also be referred to as the *condition code register* or the *flags*.   The register is really a group of individual flip-flops that can be set or reset based on the conditions created by the last ALU operation.   The individual flip-flops, or flags, include indicators for zero, negative results, carry from the MSB, etc.   The flags are used for decision making when using subsequent branching instructions.   The temporary and accumulator registers shown in Fig. 4-8*b* are many times considered to be part of the ALU.   The accumulator is typically used in most operations performed by the CPU, such as data transfers.

The *control* and *timing section* shown in Fig. 4-7 is probably the most complex section of the CPU.   It affects and sequences all events within the CPU and the entire microcomputer.   In a previous chapter it was mentioned that each program instruction can be divided into fetch, decode, and execute stages.   Each of these stages can be further subdivided into a series of tiny steps that might be referred to as a *microprogram*.   The microprogram for each instruction resides in the *instruction-decoding* section and is carried out by the control and timing section of the CPU.

A 16-bit register called a *program counter* is shown as part of the CPU in Fig. 4-7.   The program counter is responsible for keeping track of the address of the next instruction to be fetched from memory.   Because program instructions are normally performed in sequence, the program counter normally counts upward until told to do otherwise.   Many common microprocessors have a 16-bit program counter which will access 64K memory words via the address bus.   The normal sequential execution of program instructions can be altered by special branch, call, or return instructions, or interrupts which cause the program counter to jump to a number other than the next-higher address.   To run a program after a power-on sequence, the computer operator must initially set the program counter to the number of the first instruction in the program.

The *fetch-decode-execute instruction sequence* is fundamental to computer operation.   The first instruction fetched from program memory is *assumed* to be the op code for the first instruction and is placed in the *instruction register* by the CPU control section.   The op code is then interpreted by the *instruction decoder*.   The instruction decoder then directs the control and timing section to execute the specific instruction.

The CPU organization shown in Fig. 4-7 is a simplified version.   Most microprocessor CPUs contain at least several more 8-bit and 16-bit registers.   Great variation exists in microprocessors as to the number and types of registers within the CPU.

SOLVED PROBLEMS

4.42   The letters CPU stand for what part of a microcomputer system?

Solution:

The letters CPU stand for central processing unit.

4.43   Refer to Fig. 4-1.   The CPU resides within which block of this microcomputer system?

Solution:

The central processing unit resides within the MPU (microprocessor unit) block of the system shown in Fig. 4-1.

4.44   A CPU will generally contain (*a*) storage devices called _____, (*b*) computational circuitry called the _____, (*c*) _____-_____ circuitry, and (*d*) a _____ and timing section.

Solution:

A CPU will generally contain (*a*) storage devices called registers, (*b*) computational circuitry called the ALU, (*c*) instruction-decoding circuitry, and (*d*) a control and timing section.

4.45   List four primary jobs of the CPU of a microcomputer.

Solution:

Four jobs of the CPU of a microcomputer are to:
(*a*)   Fetch, decode, and execute program instructions in the proper order
(*b*)   Transfer data to and from memory and input/output sections
(*c*)   Respond to external interrupts
(*d*)   Provide overall timing and control signals for the entire system

4.46   The letters ALU stand for what part of a microcomputer?

Solution:

The letters ALU stand for arithmetic and logic unit.

4.47   Refer to Fig. 4-9. What are the binary contents of the accumulator after the AND operation?

Solution:

The binary contents of the accumulator in Fig. 4-9 after the bit-by-bit ANDing are 00000000.   The AND truth table is shown in Fig. 3-1.

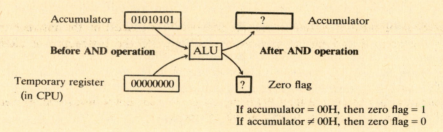

If accumulator = 00H, then zero flag = 1
If accumulator ≠ 00H, then zero flag = 0

Fig. 4-9

4.48   Refer to Fig. 4-9.   The zero flag will be _____ (set, reset) after the AND operation.

Solution:

The zero flag condition is based on the contents of the accumulator after the AND operation.   Because the accumulator equals zero, the zero flag in the status register will be set to 1 after the AND operation in Fig. 4-9.

4.49   The status register in the ALU is also called a _____ code register, and the individual flip-flops are called _____ (flags, signs).

Solution:

The status register in the ALU is called a condition code register by some manufacturers, and the individual flip-flops are many times called flags.

4.50   What major section of the CPU affects and sequences all events within the CPU and the entire microcomputer?

Solution:

The control and timing section of the CPU affects and sequences all events within the CPU and the entire microcomputer.

4.51 The register in the CPU that keeps track of the address of the next instruction to be fetched from program memory is called the _____ _____.

Solution:

The program counter keeps track of the address of the next instruction to be fetched from program memory.

4.52 The program normally increments upward, accessing program memory instructions in sequential order except when altered by what types of instructions?

Solution:

Branch, call, or return instructions, or interrupts can alter the normal incrementing of the program counter.

4.53 At the beginning of the run of a program the op code of the first instruction is placed in the _____ (accumulator, instruction register) of the CPU.

Solution:

At the beginning of the run of a program, the op code of the first instruction is placed in the instruction register of the CPU.

4.54 The section of the CPU that interprets the op code placed in the instruction register and directs the control and timing section how to execute the instruction is called the _____

_____.

Solution:

The instruction decoder of the CPU interprets the op code in the instruction register and directs the control and timing section how to execute the instruction.

4.6 MICROCOMPUTER OPERATION

Consider the simple task of adding three numbers such as $10 + 5 + 18 = 33_{10}$. A short microcomputer program could be written to perform this elementary task using the following steps:

Instruction 1   LOAD the first number (10_{10}) into the CPU.

Instruction 2   ADD the second number (5_{10}) to the first.

Instruction 3   ADD the third number (18_{10}) to the sum of the first two numbers.

Instruction 4   STORE the sum of the three numbers (33_{10}) in data memory location 2000_{16}.

After loading into program memory, the above instructions might appear like those in the memory diagramed in Fig. 4-10. Note that the first instruction of the program starts at address 0000H. The first instruction (LOAD the number 0AH) takes up 2 bytes of memory. The first byte of memory holds the *operation* part of the instruction, while the second byte holds the *operand*. The op code for the LOAD operation is given as 86H (10000110_2) for the microprocessor being used in this example. The operand 0AH (00001010_2) is the first number to be loaded into the accumulator of the microprocessor. Note in Fig. 4-10 that it is customary to represent the binary quantities in both the address and contents columns with hexadecimal notation. In the actual machine these are HIGH and LOW voltage levels.

Assume that the program is placed in the RAM block of the microcomputer illustrated in Fig. 4-1. Also assume that the microcomputer's CPU has the features detailed in Fig. 4-7. Then Fig. 4-11 details the results of each of the four operations of the LOAD-ADD-ADD-STORE program.

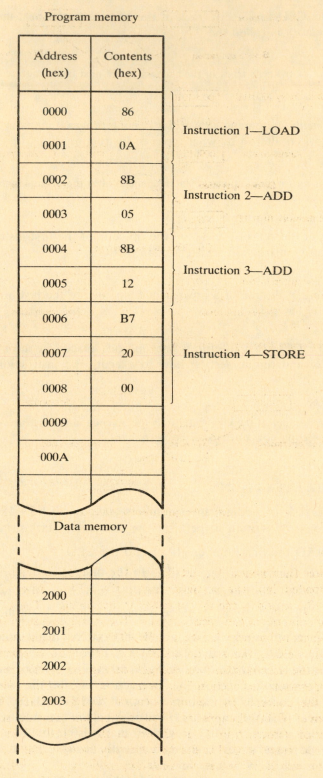

Fig. 4-10   A microcomputer program segment for adding $10 + 5 + 18$

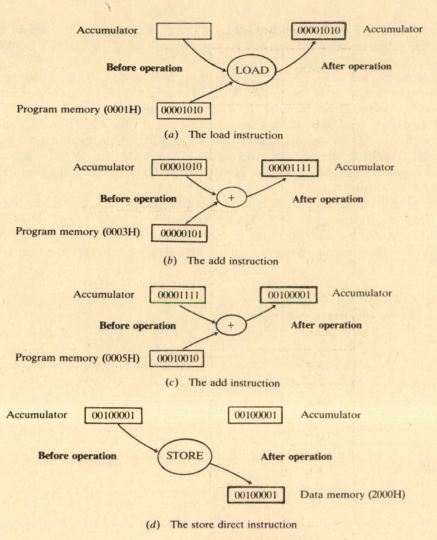

(a)   The load instruction

(b)   The add instruction

(c)   The add instruction

(d)   The store direct instruction

Fig. 4-11

The LOAD operation (instruction 1), detailed in Fig. 4-11a, shows the contents of memory location 0001H being loaded into the accumulator of the CPU. After the operation, the accumulator holds 00001010_2, which is the first number to be added. The LOAD operation writes over and erases the prior contents of the accumulator. The ADD operation (instruction 2) is shown in Fig. 4-11b. The contents of memory location 003H (00000101_2) are added to the contents of the accumulator (00001010_2), yielding the sum of 00001111_2. The sum is placed in the accumulator. Note that the number in the accumulator was changed during the ADD operation.

The second ADD operation (instruction 3) is detailed in Fig. 4-11c. The accumulated sum of 00001111_2 is added to the contents of memory location 0005H. Binary $00001111 + 00010010 = 00100001$. The final sum of 00100001_2 appears in the accumulator after the second ADD operation.

The STORE operation (instruction 4) is shown in Fig. 4-11d. The accumulator contents (00100001_2) are transferred to and stored in the data memory location 2000H. It is noteworthy that the data memory location was identified in the program memory in 2 separate bytes (location 007 and 0008H). Program memory location 0006H in Fig. 4-10 holds B7H, which is the op code for the STORE direct instruction.

Consider the fetching, decoding, and executing of the LOAD instruction at address 0000H and 0001H in program memory in Fig. 4-10. This type of LOAD instruction would probably be executed in about 2 to 6 microseconds (μs) by many microcomputers. Some of the actions that occur in the CPU, busses, control lines, and memories are detailed for just this LOAD instruction in the Fig. 4-12.

Starting at the top left in Fig. 4-12, the program counter in the CPU is initially set to the address of the first program step.   Next the 16-bit address is transferred to the address register and then on to the address bus and program memory.   To activate the program memory, the CPU sends a read signal ($R/\bar{W}$ line at 1) while the address decoder (not part of the CPU) enables the memory chip select ($\overline{CS}$) with a 0.   Next the program counter in the CPU is incremented to 0001H.   Program memory location 0000H is accessed and read onto the data bus.   The op code (86H) for the LOAD instruction is transferred to the instruction register of the CPU.   This completes the fetch op code stage of the LOAD instruction.

Next the op code (86H) which is held in the CPU instruction register is interpreted by the instruction decoder.   In this case the CPU determines that it is the *LOAD immediate instruction*, which means it will load the contents of the memory location immediately following the op code into the accumulator.   The program counter contents (0001H) are transferred to the address register,

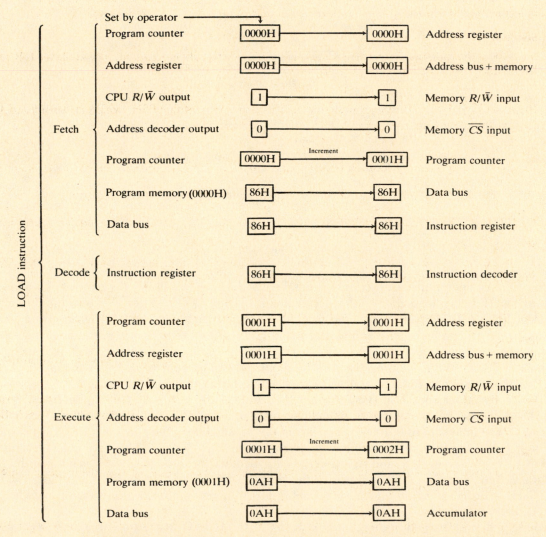

Fig. 4-12 A detailed analysis of the load immediate instruction

address bus, and memory.   The CPU generates a HIGH read pulse, which goes to the $R/\bar{W}$ input of the memory.   A LOW is applied to the $\overline{CS}$ memory input, which enables the memory.   In the line third from the bottom in Fig. 4-12, the program counter is incremented to 0002H, getting ready for the next instruction fetch.   Memory location 0001H is accessed, and the contents (0AH) are output onto the data bus and then into the CPU's accumulator.   Note that both the fetch and execute stages of this instruction were similar read memory operations except the data read from memory was transferred to a different register in the CPU.   The op code in the fetch stage is always placed in the instruction register.

SOLVED PROBLEMS

4.55 The two parts of a microprocessor instruction are called the *operation* and the _____.

Solution:

The two parts of a microprocessor instruction are called the operation and the operand.

4.56 Refer to Fig. 4-10.   When program memory location 0002H is accessed, the contents (8B) are transferred via the _____ (address, data) bus to the _____ register of the CPU.

Solution:

When the program memory location 0002H in Fig. 4-10 is accessed, the contents (8B) are transferred via the data bus to the instruction register in the CPU.

4.57 Refer to Fig. 4-10.   Program memory location 0003H contains 05H, which is considered the _____ (operand, operation) part of the instruction.

Solution:

In Fig. 4-10, memory location 0003H contains 05H, which is considered the operand part of the instruction.

4.58 A 16-bit binary number is customarily represented by _____ (a number) hexadecimal digits.

Solution:

A 16-bit binary number is customarily represented by four hexadecimal digits.   Therefore $0010\ 0000\ 0000\ 1111_2$ would be represented by 200F in hexadecimal notation.

4.59 List the three stages that the CPU cycles through when running any instruction.

Solution:

The CPU cycles through the fetch, the decode, and the execute stage when running any instruction.

4.60 Refer to Fig. 4-12.   The *fetch* stage of this instruction is basically a _____ (read, write) operation, with the memory contents ending up in the _____ (accumulator, instruction register) of the CPU.

Solution:

The fetch stage of this or any instruction is basically a read operation, with the memory contents ending up in the instruction register.

4.61 During the fetch stage of an instruction, the _____ (instruction decoder, program counter) points to the address of the op code to be accessed in memory.

Solution:

During the fetch stage of an instruction, the program counter points to the address of the op code to be accessed in memory.

4.62   Refer to Fig. 4-12.   Besides the address inputs, what two other memory inputs need to be activated to read a byte from storage?

Solution:

Based on Fig. 4-12, the $R/\overline{W}$ (read/write) input from the MPU and the $\overline{CS}$ (chip-select) inputs of memory from the address decoder need to be enabled along with the address inputs to read a byte from storage.

4.63   Refer to Fig. 4-10.   After instruction 4 is executed by the CPU, what hexadecimal number would be stored in data memory location 2000H?

Solution:

The program in Fig. 4-10 added 0AH + 05H + 12H, which totals 21H.   The sum of 21H would then be stored in data memory location 2000H.   This is also illustrated in Fig. 4-11*d*.

4.64   Refer to Fig. 4-12.   After an initial power-on sequence, the setting of the program counter is done by the _____ (address decoder, operator).

Solution:

The initial setting of the program counter is done by the operator.   The program counter is set at the program memory address of the first instruction in the program being run.   This initial program counter setting may or may not be 0000H as it was in Fig. 4-12.

Supplementary Problems

4.65   List five things that need to be studied when learning about a new microprocessor.
Ans.   architecture, instruction set, minimal system using the microprocessor, control signals, and pin functions

4.66   The 16-bit one-way bus in Fig. 4-1 is called the _____ bus.   *Ans.*   address

4.67   The 8-bit two-way bus in Fig. 4-1 is called the _____ bus.   *Ans.*   data

4.68   Refer to Fig. 4-1.   The MPU connections to the data bus are considered _____ (inputs, outputs, both inputs and outputs).   *Ans.*   both inputs and outputs

4.69   Refer to Fig. 4-2.   If the address on the address bus were 0010 0000 1000 1111, what memory location (hex number) would be accessed by the microprocessor?   *Ans.* $208F_{16}$

4.70   Refer to Fig. 4-3.   If the microcomputer accesses memory location 00FEH, the ROM will _____ (output, accept) __ __ __ __ __ __ __ __ (8 bits).   *Ans.*   output, 00100000

4.71   The ROM in Fig. 4-3 is said to reside on what page of memory?   *Ans.* 00_{16} (page zero)

4.72   Eight 4096 × 1 bit RAM ICs could be arranged similarly to those in Fig. 4-4*c* to form a 4096 × _____ bit read/write memory.   This would be referred to as a _____K memory.   *Ans.* 8, 4

4.73   The list of operations that can be performed by a microprocessor is called its _____ set.
Ans. instruction

4.74   An ADD operation is an arithmetic instruction, whereas a STORE operation is classified as a _____
_____ instruction.   *Ans.* data transfer

4.75   Branch operations are the microprocessor's _____-making instructions.   *Ans.* decision

4.76   Subroutine call instructions and _____ (arithmetic, return) instructions are always associated with
subroutines.   *Ans.* return

4.77   The computational circuitry in a CPU is referred to as the _____ (three letters).
Ans. ALU (arithmetic and logic unit)

4.78   A microcomputer's CPU typically contains a variety of temporary storage devices called _____
(registers, ROMs).   *Ans.* registers

4.79   A microcomputer's CPU contains circuitry used for interpreting instructions; this is called the _____
_____.   *Ans.* instruction decoder

4.80   A microcomputer's CPU contains a block of circuitry for sequencing events; this is called the _____
and _____ section.   *Ans.* control, timing

4.81   The microcomputer's CPU resides in a device called a(n) _____ (interface, microprocessor).
Ans. microprocessor

4.82   Refer to Fig. 4-13.   What are the binary contents of the accumulator after the OR operation?
Ans. 00111111

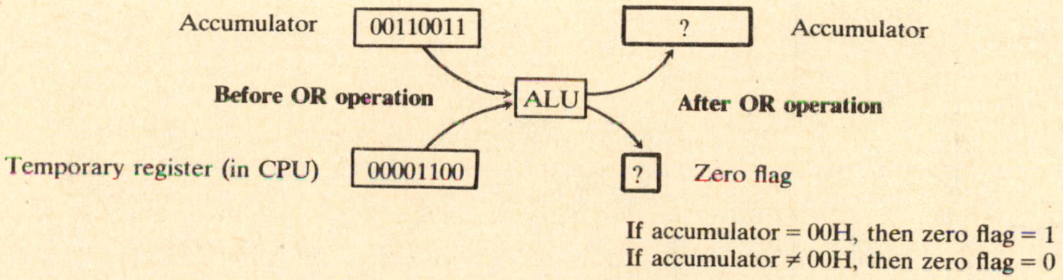

Accumulator   `00110011`   `?`   Accumulator

Before OR operation → ALU ← **After OR operation**

Temporary register (in CPU)   `00001100`   `?`   Zero flag

If accumulator = 00H, then zero flag = 1
If accumulator ≠ 00H, then zero flag = 0

Fig. 4-13   The OR instruction

4.83   Refer to Fig. 4-13.   The zero flag will be _____ (set, reset) after the OR operation.   *Ans.* reset

4.84   Flags are part of a special condition code or _____ register found in the ALU of the central processing
unit of a microcomputer.   *Ans.* status

4.85   The CPU's program counter keeps track of the _____ (address, time) of the next program instruction
to be executed.   *Ans.* address

4.86   During the fetch stage, an _____ (op code, operand) is read from program memory and transferred to
the instruction register of the CPU.   *Ans.* op code

4.87   During the decoding stage, the instruction decoder in the _____ (CPU, program memory) interprets
the op code that currently resides in the _____ (instruction, temporary) register.
Ans. CPU, instruction

Program memory

Address (hex)	Contents (hex)
0000	84
0001	00
0002	4C
0003	B7
0004	20
0005	01
0006	

Instruction 1—logical AND the operand 00H with the unknown contents of the CPU accumulator

Instruction 2—INCREMENT the accumulator

Instruction 3—STORE the contents of the accumulator in data memory location 2001H

Data memory

2000	
2001	
2002	

(a) Program segment

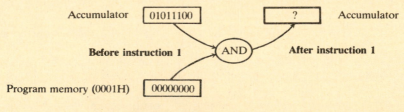

(b) The AND instruction

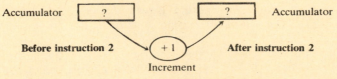

(c) The increment instruction

Fig. 4-14

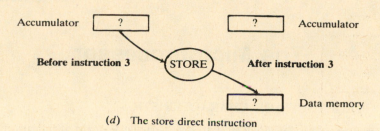

(d) The store direct instruction

Fig. 4-14

4.88   Refer to Fig. 4-14a and b.   What are the binary contents of the CPU's accumulator in Fig. 4-14b after the AND operation?   *Ans.* 00000000_2

4.89   Refer to Fig. 4-14a and c.   The binary contents of the CPU's accumulator in Fig. 4-14c after the increment operation are _____ (8 bits).   *Ans.* 00000001_2

4.90   Refer to Fig. 4-14a and d.   What is the hexadecimal address of the data memory location shown in Fig. 4-14d?   *Ans.*   2001H

4.91   Refer to Fig. 4-14a and d.   The binary contents of the data memory location shown in Fig. 4-14d after the store operation are _____ (8 bits).   *Ans.* 00000001_2

4.92   Refer to Fig. 4-14a.   What two program memory locations hold the address for the store operation?   *Ans.*   0004H and 0005H

4.93   Refer to Fig. 4-14a.   The op code for instruction 1 is _____ (hex), whereas the operand is _____ (hex).   *Ans.*   84H, 00H

4.94   Refer to Fig. 4-14a.   The op code for instruction 2 is _____, whereas the operand is _____.   *Ans.*   4CH, there is no operand for the increment instruction

4.95   Refer to Fig. 4-14a.   The op code for instruction 3 is _____, whereas the operand is _____.   *Ans.*   B7H, 2-byte operand combines to form the data memory address of 2001H

Chapter 5

The Microprocessor

5.1 COMMON MICROPROCESSOR CHARACTERISTICS

A *microprocessor* may be briefly defined as a very large-scale integration (VLSI) chip that performs the tasks of a central processing unit of a microcomputer or other automatic control system. The following is an abbreviated outline of the major characteristics shared by almost all 8- and 16-bit microprocessors. This listing serves to give the student an overview of the important characteristics of various microprocessors.

Power Connections

Microprocessors (except the 8080) require a 5-V dc regulated power supply.

Bit Size

Microprocessors are commonly classified as either 4-, 8-, 16-, or 32-bit units. The bit size of a microprocessor is sometimes referred to as its word size. The width of the accumulator register is a good clue as to the word size of a microprocessor. The 8080/8085, 6800, 6502, and Z80 are common 8-bit microprocessors. The 8086, 8088, 68000, 65816, and Z8000 are typical 16-bit MPUs. The 80386, 68020, 32000, and Z-80000 are examples of advanced 32-bit microprocessors.

Data Lines

Microprocessors transfer data or instructions between the MPU and memory (or I/O) via a bidirectional data bus. The 6800, 6502, Z80, and 8088 are processors that use 8-bit external data busses. Many 8080 family members multiplex either address or control information on the data lines part of the time.

Address Lines

Most older microprocessors (8080/8085, 6800, 6502) use 16-bit address busses which can address only 2^{16} or 64K of memory. The newer 16-bit MPUs have 16-, 20-, or 23-bit address busses. A wider address bus permits addressing of larger memories.

Control Lines

Most microprocessors would feature some or all of the following control lines:

1. Clock lines
2. Read/write lines
3. Input/output lines
4. Interrupt lines
5. Reset lines
6. Bus control lines
7. Cycle status lines

Internal Registers

Program Counter. The program counter (PC) is the register that holds the address of the next program instruction. The width of the program counter is the same as the width of the address bus. The program counter typically contains 16 bits in 8-bit microprocessors but is wider in 16- and 32-bit MPUs.

Accumulator. The accumulator is the register(s) associated with the ALU operations and sometimes I/O operations. It may be 8, 16, or 32 bits wide. The 8080/8085, 6800, and 6502 MPUs all have 8-bit accumulators. Some processors (68000 and Z8000) have only general-purpose registers that may be used as accumulators.

Status Register or Flags. The status register is available on all microprocessors. The individual bits in the register are called *flags*. The conditions of the flags are generally associated with ALU operations and are used by subsequent branch and jump instructions for decision making.

General-Purpose Registers. General-purpose registers may be used to temporarily store data or hold an address. They are not assigned a specific task. In 8-bit microprocessors, general-purpose registers cannot function as an accumulator in ALU and I/O operations. However, 16-bit MPUs usually allow general-purpose registers to be used as accumulators.

Index Register. The index register is used to hold the address of an operand when the indexed address mode is used (8080/8085, 6800, 6502, Z80, 8086). General-purpose registers are used as index registers on the Z8000 and 68000 microprocessors.

Stack Pointer Register. The stack pointer (SP) is a specialized register that keeps track of the next available memory location in the stack. The *stack* is a reserved area in RAM used for temporary storage of data, return addresses, and content of registers. The stack is used during subroutine calls and interrupts.

Addressing Modes

An *addressing mode* is the technique used to fetch the desired operand during the execution of an instruction. Individual microprocessors may not use all of the addressing modes listed below:

1. Inherent (implied) addressing mode
2. Immediate addressing mode
3. Extended or absolute addressing mode
4. Register addressing mode
5. Register indirect addressing mode
6. Index addressing mode
7. Zero page (direct) addressing mode
8. Relative addressing mode
9. Based addressing mode
10. Based index addressing mode
11. String addressing mode
12. I/O addressing mode
13. Status register addressing mode

Generally, the more modern 16-bit microprocessors have more powerful and flexible addressing modes.

SOLVED PROBLEMS

5.1   Almost all microprocessors require a _____-V dc regulated power supply.

    Solution:

        All microprocessors (except the 8080) require a 5-V dc regulated power supply.

5.2   The 8080/8085, 6800, Z80, and 6502 are all examples of _____-bit microprocessors.

    Solution:

        The 8080/8085, 6800, Z80, and 6502 are all examples of 8-bit microprocessors.   They all have 8-bit accumulators.

5.3   Most 8-bit microprocessors use _____ (8, 16)-bit data busses for transferring data and instructions to and from memory (or I/O).

    Solution:

        Most 8-bit MPUs use 8 data lines.

5.4   Most 8-bit microprocessors use _____ (8, 16, 20)-bit address busses.

    Solution:

        Most 8-bit microprocessors use 16-bit address busses.   The 16-bit bus will address 2^{16} or 64K of memory.

5.5   The _____ control line sends a message from the MPU to the RAM, telling the RAM whether the memory access is a read or a write operation.

    Solution:

        The MPU's read/write control line signals the RAM whether the memory access is a read or a write operation.

5.6   The MPU's internal register that holds the address of the next program instruction is the _____.

    Solution:

        The program counter holds the address of the next instruction in memory.

5.7   The individual bits in a microprocessor's status register are commonly called _____.

    Solution:

        The individual bits in a microprocessor's status register are commonly called flags.

5.2 DATA SHEET DESCRIPTIONS

    Literature on specific microprocessors contains several common features.   Typical data sheets contain information on IC packaging, pin diagrams, and the function of each IC pin.   The architecture of the CPU is diagramed, along with a description of the major features.   Timing diagrams appear in the literature along with the processor's instruction set.   The data sheet also diagrams typical systems using the microprocessor.

    The microprocessor is typically housed in a *40-pin dual-in-line package* integrated circuit (40-pin DIP IC).   Two such packages are illustrated in Fig. 5-1.   The 40-pin DIP in Fig. 5-1*a* is encased in

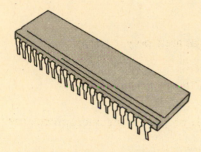

(a) Plastic 40-pin **DIP** microprocessor

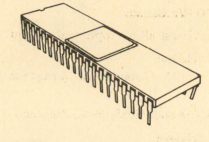

(b) Ceramic 40-pin DIP microprocessor

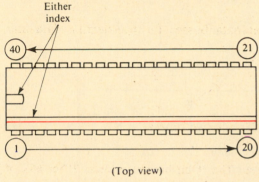

(c) Pin numbering on plastic 40-pin DIP IC

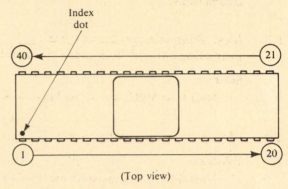

(d) Pin numbering on ceramic 40-pin DIP IC

Fig. 5-1

plastic, whereas the one in Fig. 5-1b uses a ceramic base.   The ceramic microprocessor package is suited for higher-temperature operation.   Microprocessors also commonly come in 28-, 42-, 50-, and 68-pin packages.   The larger units may be packaged in newer surface-mounted flat chip carriers.

Two methods of determining pin 1 on the 40-pin DIP IC are detailed in Fig. 5-1c and d.   Notice the center notch and the lengthwise groove which serve as index marks on the plastic DIP IC in Fig. 5-1c.   Immediately *counterclockwise* from these index marks is pin 1 of the IC.   In Fig. 5-1d, the dot at the lower left is the index mark to show which IC terminal is pin 1.   The pins are then numbered upward in a counterclockwise direction around the IC when it is viewed from the top.

A *pin diagram*, such as the one shown in Fig. 5-2a, is included on microprocessor data sheets.   The manufacturer then details the name and use of each pin on the microprocessor.   The pin diagram and brief descriptions in Fig. 5-2 are for the Intel 8080 microprocessor.   Note that pins 2, 11, 20, and 28 are power supply pins.   Pins 15 and 22 ($\phi 1$, $\phi 2$) are clock inputs from a two-phase external clock circuit.   Pins 3 through 10 of the 8080 IC are bidirectional (meaning sometimes they are inputs and other times they are outputs), based on the direction of the arrows in Fig. 5-2a.   These data pins (D_0-D_7) are the eight connections to the system's data bus.   A 16-bit system address bus would connect to the A_0 to A_{15} address outputs.   Six other outputs (*SYNC, DBIN, WAIT, $\overline{WR}$, HLDA*, and *INTE*) carry timing and control signals to other parts of the system.   Four other inputs (*READY, HOLD, INT*, and *RESET*) are control inputs gathering information from other parts of the system.   The table in Fig. 5-2b gives added details about each pin on the Intel 8080 microprocessor.

A typical data sheet might also diagram the structure of the microprocessor.   Figure 5-3a shows a block diagram of the Intel 8080 microprocessor.   The CPU diagram in Fig. 5-3a of the 8080 microprocessor shows the internal registers, including the accumulator, B and C, D and E, H and L, stack pointer, status register (flags), and several temporary registers.   The block diagram also shows the instruction register and instruction decoder, as well as the timing and control section.   The 8080 CPU diagram also shows the ALU and associated flags and decimal adjust block in Fig. 5-3a.   The 8

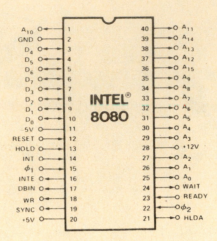

(*a*) Pin diagram for the Intel 8080 microprocessor (*Courtesy of Intel Corporation*)

Pin name	Purpose	Input or output
GND, +5 V, −5 V, +12 V	Power supply connections	Inputs
$\phi 1$, $\phi 2$	Clock signals	Inputs
D_0–D_7	Data lines	Bidirectional
A_0–A_{15}	Address lines	Outputs
SYNC	Synchronizer	Output
DBIN	Data input strobe	Output
WAIT	MPU in wait state	Output
$\overline{WR}$	Write strobe	Output
HLDA	Hold acknowledge	Output
INTE	Interrupt acknowledge	Output
READY	Data input stable	Input
HOLD	Hold request	Input
INT	Interrupt request	Input
RESET	Reset MPU	Input

(*b*) Pin functions for the Intel 8080 microprocessor

Fig. 5-2

data inputs/outputs as well as the 16-bit address outputs are buffered. The 8080 CPU also contains many internal control lines, data paths, and busses.

Some data sheets also contain a summary of the CPU registers that are of concern to the programmer. Figure 5-3*b* shows the registers of the 8080 that are used by the programmer. Note that the main register is the *A* register, or accumulator. The *B* and *C*, *D* and *E*, and *H* and *L* registers are general-purpose units. The stack pointer, program counter, and flats are specialized registers. The *HL* register pair can also be used as an address register.

Data sheets contain elaborate *timing diagrams* showing the relationship between the clock inputs and other external signals (sync, write, address outputs, data inputs/outputs, etc.) as well as internal operations. The manufacturer also includes schematics illustrating how the microprocessor is used in a *minimal system*. An 8080-based minimum system might include the microprocessor, clock, system controller, RAM, ROM, and input/output port interfaces.

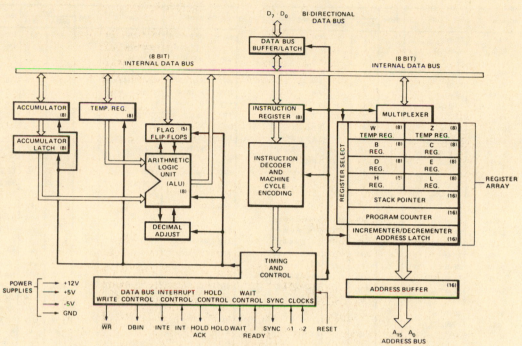

(a) Functional block diagram of the Intel 8080 microprocessor (*Courtesy of Intel Corporation*)

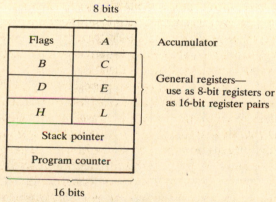

(b) Programming registers in the Intel 8080 CPU

Fig. 5-3

Manufacturer's data sheets also contain detailed information on the microprocessor's *instruction set*. The instruction set summary for Intel 8080/8085 microprocessors is shown in Fig. 5-4. The Intel 8085 is an updated version of the 8080 microprocessor and uses almost the same instruction set. The 8085 processor will be studied in greater detail in Chaps. 10 and 11.

Consider the very first 8080/8085 instruction in Fig. 5-4. The "add with carry immediate" instruction is symbolized with Intel's special mnemonic of ACI. The op code for the instruction is CEH, as shown in the second ("Code") column. The third column ("Bytes") shows how many program memory bytes are required for the instruction. The table shows that the ACI instruction requires 2 bytes of program memory space. The first location would contain the op code CEH, while the second program memory location would hold the number to be added: the data or the

Instruction		Code	Bytes	T States 8085A	T States 8080A	Machine Cycles
ACI	DATA	CE data	2	7	7	F R
ADC	REG	1000 1SSS	1	4	4	F
ADC	M	8E	1	7	7	F R
ADD	REG	1000 0SSS	1	4	4	F
ADD	M	86	1	7	7	F R
ADI	DATA	C6 data	2	7	7	F R
ANA	REG	1010 0SSS	1	4	4	F
ANA	M	A6	1	7	7	F R
ANI	DATA	E6 data	2	7	7	F R
CALL	LABEL	CD addr	3	18	17	S R R W W*
CC	LABEL	DC addr	3	9/18	11/17	S R•/S R R W W*
CM	LABEL	FC addr	3	9/18	11/17	S R•/S R R W W*
CMA		2F	1	4	4	F
CMC		3F	1	4	4	F
CMP	REG	1011 1SSS	1	4	4	F
CMP	M	BE	1	7	7	F R
CNC	LABEL	D4 addr	3	9/18	11/17	S R•/S R R W W*
CNZ	LABEL	C4 addr	3	9/18	11/17	S R•/S R R W W*
CP	LABEL	F4 addr	3	9/18	11/17	S R•/S R R W W*
CPE	LABEL	EC addr	3	9/18	11/17	S R•/S R R W W*
CPI	DATA	FE data	2	7	7	F R
CPO	LABEL	E4 addr	3	9/18	11/17	S R•/S R R W W*
CZ	LABEL	CC addr	3	9/18	11/17	S R•/S R R W W*
DAA		27	1	4	4	F
DAD	RP	00RP 1001	1	10	10	F B B
DCR	REG	00SS S101	1	4	5	F*
DCR	M	35	1	10	10	F R W
DCX	RP	00RP 1011	1	6	5	S*
DI		F3	1	4	4	F
EI		FB	1	4	4	F
HLT		76	1	5	7	F B
IN	PORT	DB data	2	10	10	F R I
INR	REG	00SS S100	1	4	5	F*
INR	M	34	1	10	10	F R W
INX	RP	00RP 0011	1	6	5	S*
JC	LABEL	DA addr	3	7/10	10	F R/F R R†
JM	LABEL	FA addr	3	7/10	10	F R/F R R†
JMP	LABEL	C3 addr	3	10	10	F R R
JNC	LABEL	D2 addr	3	7/10	10	F R/F R R†
JNZ	LABEL	C2 addr	3	7/10	10	F R/F R R†
JP	LABEL	F2 addr	3	7/10	10	F R/F R R†
JPE	LABEL	EA addr	3	7/10	10	F R/F R R†
JPO	LABEL	E2 addr	3	7/10	10	F R/F R R†
JZ	LABEL	CA addr	3	7/10	10	F R/F R R†
LDA	ADDR	3A addr	3	13	13	F R R R
LDAX	RP	000X 1010	1	7	7	F.R
LHLD	ADDR	2A addr	3	16	16	F R R R R

Instruction		Code	Bytes	T States 8085A	T States 8080A	Machine Cycles
LXI	RP,DATA16	00RP 0001 data16	3	10	10	F R R
MOV	REG,REG	01DD DSSS	1	4	5	F*
MOV	M,REG	0111 0SSS	1	7	7	F W
MOV	REG,M	01DD D110	1	7	7	F R
MVI	REG,DATA	00DD D110 data	2	7	7	F R
MVI	M,DATA	36 data	2	10	10	F R W
NOP		00	1	4	4	F
ORA	REG	1011 0SSS	1	4	4	F
ORA	M	B6	1	7	7	F R
ORI	DATA	F6 data	2	7	7	F R
OUT	PORT	D3 data	2	10	10	F R O
PCHL		E9	1	6	5	S*
POP	RP	11RP 0001	1	10	10	F R R
PUSH	RP	11RP 0101	1	12	11	S W W*
RAL		17	1	4	4	F
RAR		1F	1	4	4	F
RC		D8	1	6/12	5/11	S/S R R*
RET		C9	1	10	10	F R R
RIM (8085A only)		20	1	4	–	F
RLC		07	1	4	4	F
RM		F8	1	6/12	5/11	S/S R R*
RNC		D0	1	6/12	5/11	S/S R R*
RNZ		C0	1	6/12	5/11	S/S R R*
RP		F0	1	6/12	5/11	S/S R R*
RPE		E8	1	6/12	5/11	S/S R R*
RPO		E0	1	6/12	5/11	S/S R R*
RRC		0F	1	4	4	F
RST	N	11XX X111	1	12	11	S W W*
RZ		C8	1	6/12	5/11	S/S R R*
SBB	REG	1001 1SSS	1	4	4	F
SBB	M	9E	1	7	7	F R
SBI	DATA	DE data	2	7	7	F R
SHLD	ADDR	22 addr	3	16	16	F R R W W
SIM (8085A only)		30	1	4	–	F
SPHL		F9	1	6	5	S*
STA	ADDR	32 addr	3	13	13	F R R W
STAX	RP	000X 0010	1	7	7	F W
STC		37	1	4	4	F
SUB	REG	1001 0SSS	1	4	4	F
SUB	M	96	1	7	7	F R
SUI	DATA	D6 data	2	7	7	F R
XCHG		EB	1	4	4	F
XRA	REG	1010 1SSS	1	4	4	F
XRA	M	AE	1	7	7	F R
XRI	DATA	EE data	2	7	7	F R
XTHL		E3	1	16	18	F R R W W

Machine cycle types:

F	Four clock period instr fetch	DDD	Binary digits identifying a destination register	B = 000, C = 001, D = 010 Memory = 110
S	Six clock period instr fetch	SSS	Binary digits identifying a source register	E = 011, H = 100, L = 101 A = 111
R	Memory read	RP	Register Pair	BC = 00, HL = 10
I	I/O read			DE = 01, SP = 11
W	Memory write		*Five clock period instruction fetch with 8080A.	
O	I/O write		†The longer machine cycle sequence applies regardless of condition evaluation with 8080A.	
B	Bus idle		•An extra READ cycle (R) will occur for this condition with 8080A.	
X	Variable or optional binary digit			

Instruction set for the Intel 8080/8085 microprocessors (*Courtesy of Intel Corporation*)

Fig. 5-4

operand. The "*T* States" column shows the relative length of time it takes to execute the instruction. The right column in the table refers to the basic external operations the CPU is performing. In this case the F stands for the normal *instruction fetch* from program memory, while the R stands for a memory *read*. Instruction set summaries like the one shown in Fig. 5-4 are extremely valuable to the person who must program an 8080-based microcomputer system. Added details on each instruction are also included in the data manual.

SOLVED PROBLEMS

5.8   Name at least five things a typical microprocessor data sheet would contain.

Solution:

A typical microprocessor data sheet might contain information on IC packaging, pin diagrams, name and function of each IC pin, microprocessor's organization or architecture, timing diagrams, instruction set, and typical systems using the processor.

5.9   When viewed from the top, pin 1 is immediately _____ (clockwise, counterclokcwise) from the index mark on a DIP IC.

Solution:

See Fig. 5-1c and d.   When viewed from the top, pin 1 is immediately counterclockwise from the index mark.

5.10   Refer to Fig. 5-2.   The D_0 through D_7 pins on the 8080 IC are _____ (inputs, outputs, bidirectional) data lines which are connected to the system's data bus.

Solution:

According to Fig. 5-2, the D_0 through D_7 pins on the 8080 IC are bidirectional data lines.

5.11   Refer to Fig. 5-2.   Which single output of the 8080 microprocessor would be strobed LOW during the write operation?

Solution:

Based on Fig. 5-2b, the $\overline{WR}$ (write strobe) output would be activated by a LOW to signal a system storage device that data is to be written into memory.

5.12   Refer to Fig. 5-2.   The 8080 microprocessor uses a power unit that will supply what voltage(s)?

Solution:

Based on Fig. 5-2, the 8080 requires power supply voltages of -5, $+5$, and $+12$ V.

5.13   Refer to Fig. 5-3b.   List at least six general-use registers located in the 8080 CPU.

Solution:

Based on Fig. 5-3b, the general-purpose 8-bit registers in the 8080 CPU are the B, C, D, E, H, and L registers.   Although not labeled as such, the accumulator is also considered a general-purpose register.

5.14   Refer to Fig. 5-3a.   The program counter register contains _____ bits.

Solution:

Based on Fig. 5-3a, the program counter contains 16 bits (note the small 16 at the right in the program counter block).

5.15   The flags (status register) are most closely associated with the _____ (ALU, instruction decoder).

Solution:

The flags are most closely associated with the ALU.

5.16   Refer to Fig. 5-4.   The Intel mnemonic for the "add immediate" instruction is ADI.   The 8080 op code for the ADI instruction is _____ (hex).

Solution:

Based on Fig. 5-4, the mnemonic for the "add immediate" instruction is ADI and the 8080 op code is $C6_{16}$.

5.17   Refer to Fig. 5-4.   The ADI instruction will require the use of _____ (a number) bytes of program memory.

Solution:

Based on information in the "Bytes" column in Fig. 5-4, the ADI instruction (add immediate instruction) will require the use of 2 bytes of program memory.

5.18   Refer to Fig. 5-4.   While executing the ADI instruction, the 8080 CPU goes through an instruction fetch machine cycle and a _____ (read, write) cycle.

Solution:

Based on information in the "Machine Cycles" column of Fig. 5-4, the ADI instruction causes the CPU to go through an instruction fetch machine cycle and a read cycle.   The F in the "Machine Cycles" column stands for an instruction fetch cycle, while the R stands for the memory read cycle.

5.3   PIN DIAGRAM AND FUNCTIONS

A somewhat more complex generic microprocessor will be examined in the next few sections. This microprocessor will have many features found in real-life units.   Many of the specific output control signals have been left off the MPU for simplicity.

The pin diagram for the generic microprocessor is shown in Fig. 5-5a.   The MPU is shown housed in a 40-pin DIP.   This IC uses a +5-V power supply connected to pins 1 and 2.   Using a single +5-V power supply seems to be common in the newer microprocessor designs.

The X_1 and X_2 pins at the upper right in Fig. 5-5a are for attaching a crystal to regulate the clock frequency of the MPU.   As is the trend in newer units, the clock circuitry is built into this microprocessor chip, whereas older designs needed a separate clock generator circuit.   The *CLK* output (pin 38) is a clock signal for use as a system clock.   The frequency of the *CLK* output is probably less than that of the internal clock.

The system's address bus would connect to the IC pins labeled A_0 through A_{15} in Fig. 5-5a.   These 16 address outputs can access up to 65,536 (2^{16}) memory and/or input/output locations.

The flow of instructions and data in and out of the microprocessor passes through the pins labeled D_0 through D_7 on the IC in Fig. 5-5a.   These pins (21–28) are *bidirectional* in that they sometimes serve as inputs and other times as outputs.   Typically these data pins can also be placed in the three-state condition (high-impedance state).

Pin 30 of the IC in Fig. 5-5a is the *write control* output.   A LOW on the $\overline{WR}$ pin indicates that the data on the data bus is to be written into the selected memory or I/O location.   The *read control* output is labeled $\overline{RD}$ (pin 31) on the IC in Fig. 5-5a.   A LOW on the $\overline{RD}$ pin indicates that the selected memory or I/O device is to be read and that the data bus is available for the data transfer.   Data is read from memory or an I/O device when this signal is LOW.

Enabling the *reset* input in Fig. 5-5a causes the MPU to stop work on the current program and jump to an initializing routine.   A LOW signal appearing at the $\overline{RESET}$ input of the MPU will reset the program counter to some predetermined number, such as 0000_{16}.   Other internal CPU registers may also be reset or their contents may be changed during the reset operation.   When the $\overline{RESET}$ input goes HIGH again (disabled), the CPU will start executing instructions at the new memory

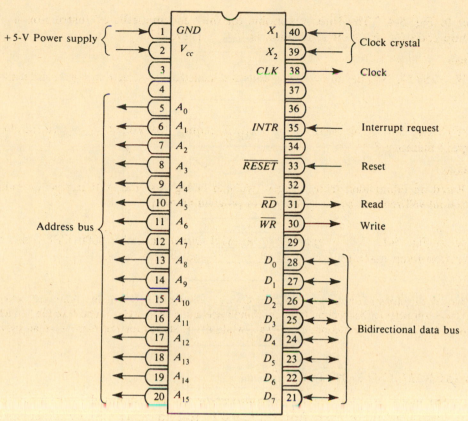

(a) Pin diagram for generic microprocessor

Pin name	Purpose	Input or output
GND, V_{cc}	Power supply connections	Inputs
X_1, X_2	Crystal connections for internal clock	Inputs
CLK	Clock signal	Output
A_0–A_{15}	Address bus	Outputs
D_0–D_7	Data bus	Bidirectional
$\overline{RD}$	Read control	Output
$\overline{WR}$	Write control	Output
$INTR$	Interrupt request	Input
$\overline{RESET}$	Reset program counter	Input

(b) Pin functions for generic microprocessor

Fig. 5-5

location 0000_{16} (or other predetermined memory location).   This memory location begins a system
initializing routine usually contained in ROM. Most microprocessor actions are in step with the
clock, and therefore they are said to be synchronous.   The $\overline{RESET}$ input to the MPU is asynchronous and may break in and stop a half-executed instruction.

    The *interrupt request* input to the microprocessor is pin 35 in Fig. 5-5*a*. The *INTR* input
responds to a HIGH from some *external* device.   Figure 5-6 will help demonstrate what happens as

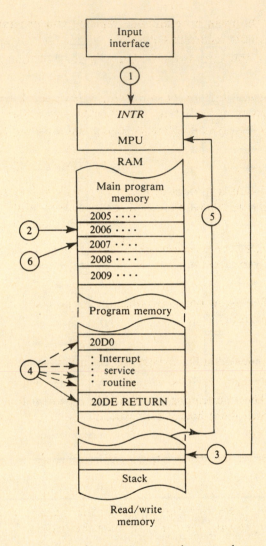

Fig. 5-6 Steps in processing an interrupt request input to the generic microprocessor

the MPU responds to the interrupt request signal.   Assume the input interface circuit in Fig. 5-6 had 8 parallel bits ready to transfer to the MPU.   The procedure can be followed by keying on the circled numbers in Fig. 5-6 as follows:

1. The input interface sends an interrupt request signal to the MPU.   See the circled 1 in Fig. 5-6.

2. The MPU completes the instruction it is executing (instruction from memory location 2006H).

3. Because control must return later to instruction 2007H, the contents of the program counter (now 2007H) and most CPU internal registers are pushed into a special area of RAM called a *stack*.   These will be returned in proper order to the CPU registers and program counter later.

4. The MPU now jumps to a predetermined address in program memory that holds the special program called the interrupt service routine (at address 20D0 in this example).   The MPU then executes the instructions in the interrupt service routine, which in this case is an input operation.   At address 20DE the MPU finds the end of the interrupt service routine and is told to return to the main program.

5.   Before returning to the main program, the register and program counter data are popped from the stack and returned to the CPU.

6.   The program counter now returns the CPU to memory location 2007H in the main program, where it continues.

The interrupt is a very useful method of permitting a peripheral device to break in and get the MPU to do something almost immediately.   Most microprocessors have one or more interrupts.   Interrupt inputs may also be called resets, restarts, maskable interrupts, or traps.

SOLVED PROBLEMS

5.19   Refer to Fig. 5-5.   This microprocessor uses a _____-V power supply and _____ (external, internal) clock circuitry with pins 39 and 40 connected to a(n) _____ (ac voltage, crystal).

   Solution:

   Based on Fig. 5-5, this microprocessor uses a +5-V power supply and internal clock circuitry with pins 39 and 40 connected to a crystal.

5.20   Refer to Fig. 5-5a.   The arrow points outward from pin 5 because this terminal is a(n) _____ (bidirectional, input, output).

   Solution:

   The arrow pointing outward in Fig. 5-5a symbolizes that this address terminal (pin 5) is an output.

5.21   Refer to Fig. 5-5a.   The line leaving pin 30 of the microprocessor is considered part of the _____ (address, control, data) bus of a microcomputer.

   Solution:

   Pin 30 in Fig. 5-5a is the write output, which is considered part of the control bus of a microcomputer.

5.22   Refer to Fig. 5-5a.   A LOW signal at pin 33 of the microprocessor would _____ (disable, enable) the reset input, causing the MPU to reset the program _____ (counter, memory) to 0000_{16}.

   Solution:

   Based on Fig. 5-5, a LOW signal at pin 33 would enable the reset input, causing the MPU to reset the program counter to 0000_{16}.   The bar over the $\overline{RESET}$ indicates that a LOW is required to enable this input.

5.23   Refer to Fig. 5-5.   The reset pin is a(n) _____ (asynchronous, synchronous) input in that it does not act in step with the clock.

   Solution:

   The reset pin on the MPU in Fig. 5-5 is an asynchronous input in that it does not act in step with the clock.

5.24   Refer to Fig. 5-5.   Data transfers are performed with _____-bit parallel words in this microprocessor.

   Solution:

   According to Fig. 5-5a, the data bus must be 8 bits wide, and therefore data transfers are performed with 8-bit parallel words.

5.25   Refer to Fig. 5-5.   An interrupt request signal is an _____ (input to, output from) the microprocessor.

   Solution:

   Based on the direction of the arrows in Fig. 5-5, an interrupt request signal is an input to the microprocessor.

5.26   An interrupt request causes the MPU to jump to and execute an interrupt _____ _____ in program memory and then return to the main program.

   Solution:

   Based on Fig. 5-6, an interrupt request causes the MPU to jump to and execute an interrupt service routine in program memory and then return to where it left off in the main program.

5.4   MICROPROCESSOR ARCHITECTURE

Almost all microprocessors contain at least the following:

1.   Arithmetic and logic unit
2.   Several registers
3.   Program counter
4.   Instruction-decoding circuitry
5.   Timing and control section
6.   Bus buffers and latches
7.   Internal busses and control lines
8.   Several control inputs and outputs

Besides these items, a microprocessor chip may also contain such functional units as:

1.   ROM storage
2.   RAM storage
3.   Serial input/output ports
4.   Internal clock circuitry
5.   Programmable timers
6.   Interrupt priority arbitration circuitry
7.   I/O communication serial to parallel interface logic
8.   Direct memory access control logic

In the last section the pin diagram and functions of a generic microprocessor were studied.   The architecture of that same MPU will be looked at in this section.   The microprocessor's internal organization, or architecture, is illustrated in Fig. 5-7.

Starting with the external connections, the MPU in Fig. 5-7 has eight bidirectional data bus connections which lead to the internal data bus.   On the left side, the MPU has 16 address bus outputs which latch addresses from the internal bus.   Control outputs are shown at the lower left; they are the write, read, and clock lines.   Two input signals are accepted by this MPU at the lower right in Fig. 5-7; they are the reset and the interrupt request lines.   This MPU has internal clock circuitry which needs only an external crystal (or capacitor in some cases) to make it operate.   The microprocessor in Fig. 5-7 is powered by a single +5-V power supply.

The functions of many of the units within the MPU in Fig. 5-7 have been examined in previous discussions.   These familiar functions are only briefly defined as follows:

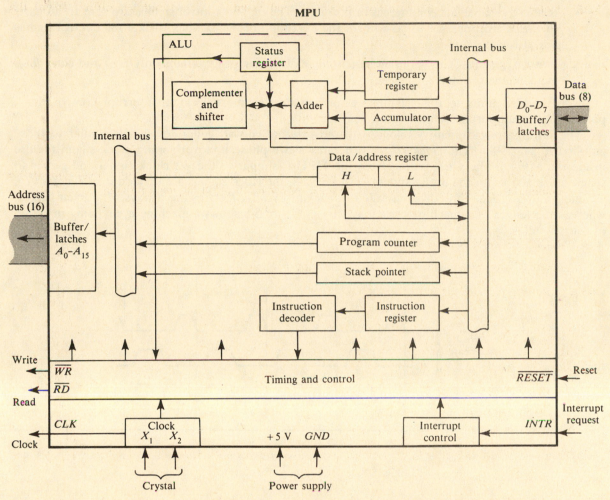

Fig. 5-7 Functional block diagram of the generic microprocessor

1. **Instruction register:** This unit is an 8-bit register that holds the first byte of an instruction (the op code).

2. **Instruction decoder:** This unit interprets the contents of the instruction register, determines the exact microprogram to be followed in executing the entire instruction, and directs the control section accordingly.

3. **Arithmetic and logic unit:** This unit performs the arithmetic, logic, and rotate operations which affect the status register (flags). The results from the ALU section are placed back into the accumulator via the internal bus. The temporary register and accumulator are many times considered part of the ALU. The flag conditions are fed back to the timing and control unit.

4. **Accumulator:** This unit is an 8-bit general-purpose register that is the focus of most arithmetic, logic, load, store, and I/O instructions.

5. **Program counter:** This unit is a 16-bit storage area that always points to the next instruction to be executed. It always contains a 16-bit address. It can be incremented or reset by the control section or modified by transfer instructions.

6. **Timing and control unit:** This section receives signals from the instruction decoder to determine the nature of the instruction to be executed. Information from the status register

is also available for conditional branching. Timing and control signals are sent to all parts of the microprocessor to coordinate the execution of instructions. External control signals are also generated.

7. Status register: The very simple generic MPU in Fig. 5-7 contains only *zero* and *carry flags* in its status register.

Newly added units to this microprocessor include the internal clock, interrupt control, stack pointer, and multipurpose data/address register.

The internal clock circuitry, along with the external crystal, generates signals similar to those graphed in Fig. 5-8. The *clock circuit* generates a two-phase nonoverlapping clock signal for use inside the MPU. The *CLK* output from the MPU is similar to the $\phi2$ clock signal and serves to synchronize actions in the entire system. In Fig. 5-8, the clock signals are divided into *T states* (T_1, T_2, etc.) and a longer time division called a *machine cycle*. *T* states are always of a given length, whereas the length of a machine cycle may vary. Figure 5-8 shows a machine cycle being made up of four *T* states.

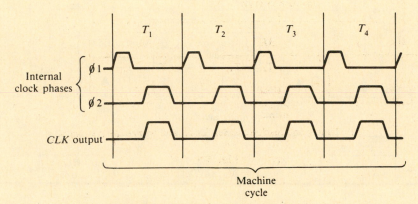

Fig. 5-8 Clock timing waveforms

The relationship between *T* states (T_1, T_2, etc.) and machine cycles (M_1, M_2, etc.) is shown in Fig. 5-9*a*. Machine cycles are associated with MPU *actions* such as read, write, fetch, or execute. In this microprocessor the *types of machine cycles* are:

1. Read (an op code fetch)

2. Read from memory or I/O

3. Write in memory or I/O

4. Execute an internal operation

The store instruction is divided into four machine cycles (M_1–M_4) in Fig. 5-9*a*. They are first, the op code fetch (read); second, the read program memory; third, another read program memory; and fourth, the write-in-memory operation. The entire combination of four actions (read, read, read, and write) is called an *instruction cycle*, as shown in Fig. 5-9*a*. Note that not all machine cycles take the same amount of time. In Fig. 5-9*a*, the first machine cycle (M_1) takes four *T* states while the other machine cycles each take only three *T* states. The entire instruction cycle for the store instruction takes 13 *T* states.

An example of the timing of an ADD immediate instruction is shown in Fig. 5-9*b*. The first machine cycle (M_1) is the op code fetch (read) operation. During T_4 of M_1 the MPU decodes the ADD instruction and decides it needs two more machine cycles to complete the instruction. The

STORE instruction
Store contents of accumulator in memory location given by the next two bytes in program memory

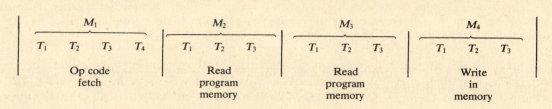

(a)   Timing and machine cycles for a store immediate instruction

ADD instruction
Add contents of accumulator to contents of next byte in program memory and leave sum in accumulator

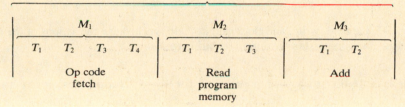

(b)   Timing and machine cycles for an add immediate instruction

Fig. 5-9

second machine cycle (M_2) reads the next byte in program memory as the operand while M_3 executes the add operation in the ALU of the microprocessor.   Observe from Fig. 5-9 that machine cycles are not all the same length, nor are instruction cycles.

The *interrupt control unit* in Fig. 5-7 will accept an interrupt signal from an external device through the *INTR* input.   It then guides the actions of the MPU via the control unit through steps 2 to 6 outlined earlier in Fig. 5-6.   In brief, it jumps to an interrupt service routine which responds to the interrupt request and when complete returns to the main program.

The *stack pointer* in Fig. 5-7 is something like a program counter in that it holds an address, decrements or increments its contents, and can be loaded with a new address.   The stack pointer is 16 bits wide in this microprocessor, so it can access 16 address lines.   The use of the stack pointer will be detailed later in Sec. 5.6.

The *data/address register* shown in Fig. 5-7 is actually two 8-bit registers that can be used separately or as a combined register pair.   The two 8-bit data/address registers are labeled H and L (for *high*-order byte and *low*-order byte).   They are usually referred to as the H register and the L register unless they are used together, and then they are called the *HL register pair*.   The H and L registers are general-purpose registers something like the accumulator in that they can be incremented, decremented, and loaded with data and they can be the source of stored data.   The *HL* register pair also can serve as an *address register* to hold the destination address for storing or the source address when loading data.   In summary, the H and L registers can be used for storing and manipulating data or they may be used for *address pointing*.   Section 5.5 will deal with the use of the data/address register.   Some microprocessors have a special register called a *data counter* that points to memory locations (used like the *HL* register pair in this unit).

SOLVED PROBLEMS

5.27 Name at least six functional units contained on most microprocessor chips.

Solution:

Most MPU chips contain at least an ALU, several registers, a program counter, instruction-decoding circuitry, a timing and control section, bus buffers and latches, internal busses and control lines, and several control inputs and outputs.

5.28 Refer to Fig. 5-7.   What functional unit is found between the data bus and the internal data bus of this microprocessor?

Solution:

A bus buffer and latches are located between the data bus and the internal data bus of the generic MPU in Fig. 5-7.

5.29 Refer to Fig. 5-7.   What three output control lines help synchronize the actions of other parts of a microprocessor-based system?

Solution:

On the MPU in Fig. 5-7, the read, write, and clock outputs help synchronize the actions of the other parts of the system.   Most microprocessors have more control signals.

5.30 The program counter is a 16-bit storage area reserved for _____ (addresses, instructions).

Solution:

The program counter is a 16-bit storage area reserved for addresses.   It always points to the address of the next instruction to be executed.

5.31 Refer to Fig. 5-7.   The read and write control signals are generated by the _____ and _____ section of the MPU.

Solution:

The read and write control signals are generated by the timing and control section of this MPU.   The timing and control section follows the directions of the instruction decoder or sometimes the interrupt control unit.

5.32 Name the four types of machine cycles used by the generic microprocessor that is being studied in this section.

Solution:

The generic microprocessor uses the following types of machine cycles: read or op code fetch, read from memory or input/output, write in memory or input/output, and execute an internal operation.

5.33 In Fig. 5-9 which takes a shorter time to execute—the add instruction or the store instruction?

Solution:

T states are always the same length.   The add instruction in Fig. 5-9 requires only 9 T states while the store instruction requires 13 T states.   Therefore, the add instruction takes a shorter time to execute.

5.34 If each T state equals 500 nanoseconds (ns), how long does it take to execute the add instruction shown in Fig. 5-9?

Solution:

The add instruction takes nine *T* states to execute according to the diagram in Fig. 5-9.   Therefore, 9×500 ns $= 4.5$ μs.   The add instruction takes 4.5 μs to execute.

5.35 Refer to Fig. 5-7.   Activating the *INTR* input causes the _____ _____ unit to direct the timing and control section to jump temporarily to an interrupt service routine in program memory.

Solution:

Activating the *INTR* input of the MPU in Fig. 5-7 causes the interrupt control unit to direct the timing and control section to jump temporarily to an interrupt service routine in program memory.

5.36 The stack pointer is something like the program counter in that it holds a _____-bit _____ (address, instruction).

Solution:

The stack pointer is something like the program counter in that it holds a 16-bit address.

5.37 Refer to Fig. 5-7.   The two storage units labeled *H* and *L* are called the _____/_____ register.

Solution:

The two storage units in Fig. 5-7 labeled *H* and *L* are called the data/address registers or general-purpose registers.

5.38 Refer to Fig. 5-7.   When the two data/address registers are linked together and used as a 16-bit storage area, they are called the _____ register pair.

Solution:

When the two data/address registers in Fig. 5-7 are linked together and used as a 16-bit storage area, they are called the *HL* register pair.

5.39 Refer to Fig. 5-7.   The data/address registers can be used for storing and manipulating data, or combined as a pair, they may be used for _____ _____ (address pointing, data selecting).

Solution:

The data/address registers in Fig. 5-7 can be used for storing and manipulating data, or combined as a pair, they may be used for address pointing.

5.5 USING THE DATA/ADDRESS REGISTER

An interesting feature of the generic microprocessor in Fig. 5-7 is the use of the *HL* register pair to address memory locations.   It is said that the *HL* register pair is being used as a *pointer* or *address pointer* when it temporarily takes over the job of the main program counter in pointing out addresses in memory or I/O.   Several very common microprocessors, such as the 8080/8085 and Z80, have registers of this type to point to addresses.   The *HL* register pair may be known as address register, data counter, pointer, or general-purpose register on other microprocessors.

Consider the simple task of adding the contents of three consecutive memory locations and storing the sum in the next memory location.   The memory contents for this problem are detailed in Fig. 5-10.   The program is loaded into memory locations 2000H to 200AH, while the three numbers to be added (0CH + 0AH + 07H) are loaded into data memory locations 2100H to 2102H.   The

Program memory

Address (hex)	Contents (hex)	
2000	3A	
2001	00	Instruction 1—LOAD accumulator
2002	21	
2003	21	
2004	01	Instruction 2—LOAD *HL* register pair
2005	21	
2006	86	Instruction 3—ADD
2007	23	Instruction 4—INCREMENT *HL* register pair
2008	86	Instruction 5—ADD
2009	23	Instruction 6—INCREMENT *HL* register pair
200A	77	Instruction 7—STORE accumulator
200B		

Data memory

2100	0C
2101	0A
2102	07
2103		← Sum
2104	
2105	

Fig. 5-10 Memory contents and instructions for a sample addition problem

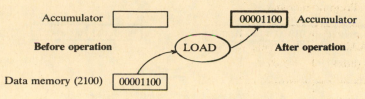

(a)   Instruction 1—load accumulator

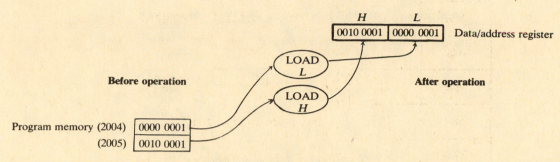

(b)   Instruction 2—load *HL* register pair

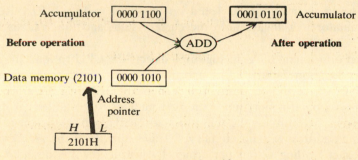

(c)   Instruction 3—add

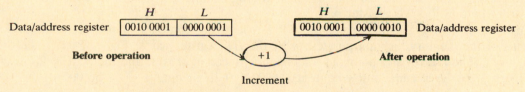

(d)   Instruction 4—increment *HL* register pair

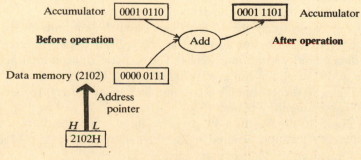

(e)   Instruction 5—add

Fig. 5-11

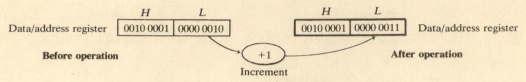

(f) Instruction 6—increment *HL* register pair

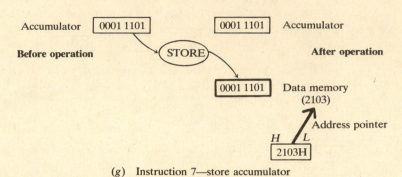

(g) Instruction 7—store accumulator

Fig. 5-11 (*cont.*)

program contains seven instructions, as listed on the right in Fig. 5-10. Remember that in this program the accumulator will always hold the current sum, and the *HL* register pair will hold an address.

The first instruction (op code 3A) in Fig. 5-10 directs the CPU to load the accumulator with the contents of memory location 2100H. The execution of this load accumulator direct instruction is detailed in Fig. 5-11*a*, where the contents of data memory location 2100H are loaded into the CPU accumulator. The accumulator now holds the first number to be added (0CH).

Instruction 2 in Fig. 5-10 directs the CPU to load 2101H into the 16-bit *HL* register pair. This location (2101H) is an address in data memory. This is the "load the *HL* register pair immediate" instruction. The exact loading action performed by instruction 2 is detailed in Fig. 5-11*b*. Note that the contents of the first program memory location (2004H) are loaded into the low-order byte (*L*) in the *HL* register. The contents of the next program memory location are loaded into the *H* or high-order byte in the *HL* register pair.

Instruction 3 in Fig. 5-10 directs the CPU to add the contents of the accumulator with the contents of the memory location pointed to by the *HL* register pair. Figure 5-11*c* details the add procedure. The *HL* register points to data memory location 2101H, and the ALU adds its contents (00001010_2) to the accumulator's contents (00001100_2), yielding a sum of 00010110_2, which is transferred back into the accumulator.

Instruction 4 in Fig. 5-10 directs the CPU to increment (add +1 to) the contents of the *HL* register pair. The incrementing action of the CPU is shown graphically in Fig. 5-11*d*. Note that only the low-order byte has changed in the *HL* register pair.

Instruction 5 in Fig. 5-10 directs the CPU to again add the contents of the accumulator to the contents of the memory location pointed to by the *HL* register pair. Figure 5-11*e* shows the *HL* register pointing to data memory location 2102H. The contents of both memory location 2102H and the accumulator are added, yielding the sum of 00011101_2, which is placed in the accumulator.

Instruction 6 in Fig. 5-10 directs the CPU to again increment the *HL* register pair. Figure 5-11*f* graphically details this incrementing action.

Instruction 7 in Fig. 5-10 directs the CPU to store the contents of the accumulator (the sum of 00011101_2) in the memory location pointed to by the *HL* register pair. Figure 5-11*g* shows the accumulator sum being stored in data memory location 2103H.

The instructions that used the *HL* register pair as a pointer (instructions 3, 5, and 7) use an addressing mode called *register indirect addressing*. Addressing modes will be covered in more detail in the next chapter.

SOLVED PROBLEMS

5.40   Another name used for the address register is _____ (data, program) counter.

Solution:

Another name used for the address register is data counter.

5.41   Refer to Fig. 5-10.   What hexadecimal sum would be transferred into data memory location 2103H after this program had been executed?

Solution:

Adding $0C + 0A + 07 = 1D_{16}$ ($12 + 10 + 7 = 29_{10}$).   The sum of $1D_{16}$ would be transferred to data memory location 2103H after the program in Fig. 5-10 was executed.

5.42   Refer to Figs. 5-10 and 5-11.   The accumulator always holds the _____ (instruction, sum), while the *HL* register pair holds a(n) _____ (address, program count).

Solution:

The accumulator in Fig. 5-10 always holds the current sum, while the *HL* register pair holds an address.   The address in the *HL* register pair is then used for pointing to memory locations.

5.43   Refer to Fig. 5-10.   When using the *HL* register pair as an address pointer as in Fig. 5-11*c*, what addressing mode is being used?

Solution:

The register indirect addressing mode is being used in instruction 3 (add instruction) in Fig. 5-10.

5.44   Refer to Fig. 5-12.   What are the hexadecimal contents of the accumulator and *HL* register pair at the beginning of this program?

Solution:

Based on information in Fig. 5-12, the accumulator contents at the beginning of the program are 00001111_2, or $0F_{16}$.   The *HL* register pair contents at the beginning of the program are $0010\ 0001\ 0000\ 0010_2$, or 2102_{16}.

5.45   What are the contents of the accumulator after the execution of instruction 1 (add instruction) in Fig. 5-12?

Solution:

See Fig. 5-13.

5.46   What are the contents of the *HL* register pair after the execution of instruction 2 (increment instruction) in Fig. 5-12?

Solution:

The *HL* register pair contents $= 2102 + 1 = 2103H$.   After instruction 2 in Fig. 5-12, the *HL* register pair contents will be 2103H.

5.47   What are the contents of the accumulator after the execution of instruction 3 (add instruction) in Fig. 5-12?

Solution:

See Fig. 5-14.

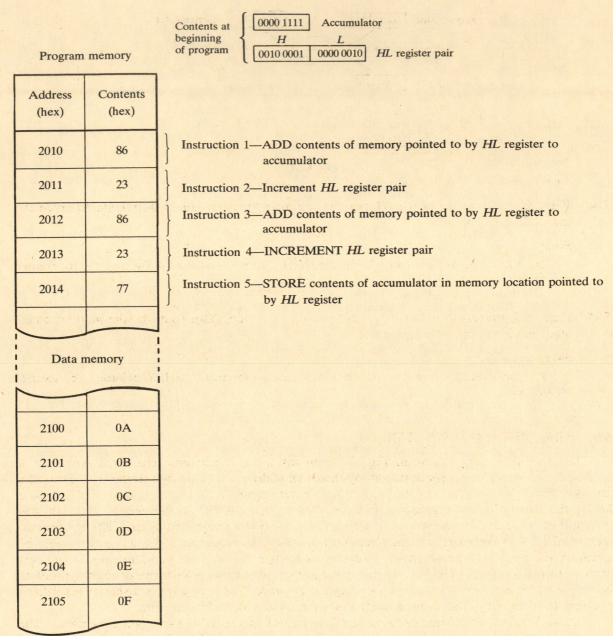

Fig. 5-12 Memory contents and instructions for an addition problem

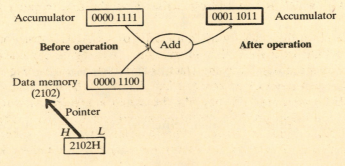

Fig. 5-13

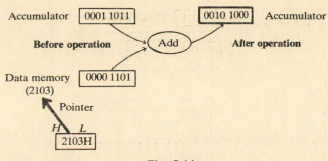

Fig. 5-14

5.48   What are the contents of the *HL* register pair after the execution of instruction 4 (increment instruction) in Fig. 5-12?

Solution:

The *HL* register pair contents = 2103 + 1 = 2104H.   After instruction 4 in Fig. 5-12, the *HL* register pair contents will be 2104H.

5.49   Refer to instruction 5 in Fig. 5-12.   Where will the accumulator contents (the sum) be stored after executing this store instruction?

Solution:

The sum (00101000_2) will be stored in data memory location 2104H, as pointed to by the *HL* register pair.

5.6   USING THE STACK POINTER

The generic microprocessor in Fig. 5-7 contains a stack pointer.   The *stack pointer* is a specialized 16-bit counter-register that always holds an address.   The address in the stack pointer is the location of a special group of storage locations in data memory referred to as the *stack*.   In some MPUs the stack may be a group of storage areas located on the microprocessor chip.   It was observed in Sec. 5.3 that when an interrupt service routine was performed by the CPU, the current data in all the CPU registers must be temporarily stored.   The contents of these registers would be stored in the stack.   Likewise, when a regular subroutine is used, the program counter contents must be stored so that the CPU can return to the proper place in program memory when the routine is complete.   The temporary storage area used is the stack.   A *subroutine* is a shorter specialized program (like multiply) that is used many times throughout the main program.

The stack in the generic microprocessor will be located in a section of read/write memory.   The programmer selects a group of locations in RAM to serve as the stack.   The stack pointer is loaded with an address *one above* the top address in the stack.   This is shown in Fig. 5-15.   The stack pointer is set to 220AH, which is one address higher than the first memory location in the stack, which is 2209H.

Data can be written into the stack by using a PUSH or a CALL instruction.   Data can be read from the stack using a POP or a RETURN instruction.   Writing on the stack is sometimes called *pushing the stack*, whereas reading from the stack is referred to as *popping the stack*.   The stack works as a sequential-access memory so that the last data in is the first data out.   This is called a *last-in–first-out*, or LIFO, memory.   It may also be called a first-in–last-out, or FILO, memory.

The PUSH instruction might produce results as shown in Fig. 5-16*a*.   The contents of the *HL* register pair are being pushed into the stack.   Note that the 2-byte *HL* register pair must be pushed into two memory locations.   The sequence of actions may be followed by keying on the circled numbers.

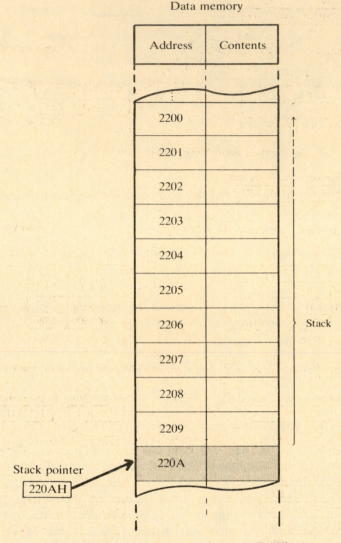

Fig. 5-15 Setting up the stack in RAM

1. The stack pointer in the CPU decrements from 220AH to 2209H.

2. The stack pointer points to storage area 2209H over the system address bus, and the high-order byte (00000000_2) is pushed into the stack.

3. The stack pointer is again decremented from 2209H to 2208H.

4. The stack pointer points to storage area 2208H over the system address bus, and the low-order byte (00001111_2) from the data/address register is stored in the stack.

Another PUSH operation is illustrated in Fig. 5-16*b*. This time, however, the contents of the accumulator and status register are being pushed into the stack. Again follow the action by keying on the circled numbers in Fig. 5-16*b*.

5. Before this operation, the stack pointer is pointing at the last entry in the stack. It is said that it is pointing at the *top of the stack*. The stack pointer is now decremented to 2207H.

6. The stack pointer addresses location 2207H in the stack, and the accumulator contents (01010101_2) are pushed onto the stack.

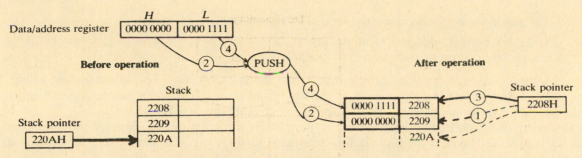

(a) Pushing data/address register contents on the stack

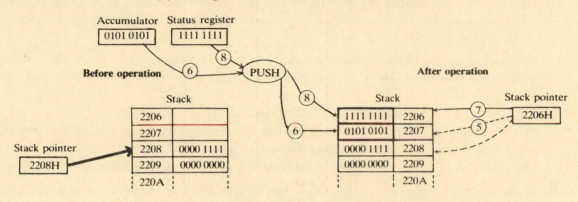

(b) Pushing the accumulator and status register contents on the stack

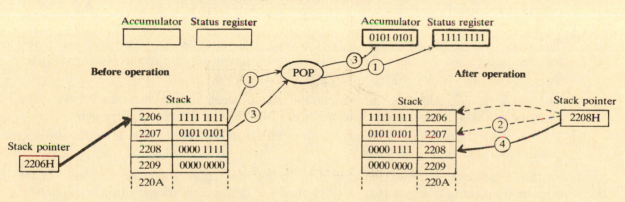

(c) Restoring accumulator and status register contents by popping from the stack

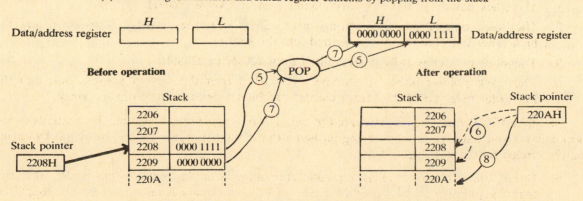

(d) Restoring data/address register contents by popping from the stack

Fig. 5-16

7. The stack pointer is decremented from 2207H to 2206H.

8. The stack pointer addresses location 2206H. The contents of the status register (11111111_2) are pushed on top of the stack.

The stack can continue to grow as more pushing onto the stack occurs. This is symbolized in Fig. 5-15 with the dashed line leading upward to the top of the stack. The stack has no definite upper limits except for those imposed by the location of other programs and RAM size.

Generally, for each PUSH there must later be a POP instruction to take data off the top of the stack. Because the stack is a LIFO (last-in–first-out) memory, the data must come off in reverse order. The unloading of the stack is detailed in Fig. 5-16c and d.

Consider the POP instruction in Fig. 5-16c. The accumulator and status register are reloaded with the data they once held. The sequence of actions in popping the stack may be followed by keying on the circled numbers in Fig. 5-16c.

1. The stack pointer addresses the top of the stack, or memory location 2206H. The contents of the status register (11111111_2) are popped off the top of the stack and returned to the ALU.

2. The stack pointer is incremented from 2206H to 2207H.

3. The stack pointer addresses location 2207H in the stack. The top of the stack is popped, and the contents are returned to the accumulator in the CPU.

4. The stack pointer is incremented to 2208H and now points at the next location to be popped.

The status register and accumulator contents have been restored to what they were before the PUSH operation in Fig. 5-16b.

The data/address register's contents are next popped from the stack in Fig. 5-16d. Again follow the sequence of actions by keying on the circled numbers in Fig. 5-16d.

5. The stack pointer addresses the top of the stack (location 2208H). The contents of this location in the stack are popped and returned to the low-order byte of the *HL* register pair.

6. The stack pointer is incremented to 2209H.

7. The stack pointer addresses the top of the stack, which is now location 2209H. The contents (00000000_2) are returned to the high-order byte of the *HL* register pair.

8. Finally, the stack pointer is incremented from 2209H to 220AH in preparation for the next push or call operation.

Popping data off the stack and restoring it to the data/address register reverses the action of the PUSH instruction executed in Fig. 5-16a. PUSH and POP instructions are used in pairs; however, there are usually many other instructions between the two instructions which change the data in the CPU registers.

The generic microprocessor pushed and popped register pairs. Some microprocessor's push and pop only 1-byte registers with a single instruction. In some MPUs, the stack pointer may point to the empty memory location one above the top of the stack instead of at the top of the stack as in the generic microprocessor. It must be remembered that the programmer originally set the stack pointer to 220AH in this example to define the location of the stack in RAM.

SOLVED PROBLEMS

5.50 The stack pointer in Fig. 5-7 is a specialized 16-bit counter-register that always holds an _____ (address, instruction op code).

   Solution:
   The stack pointer always holds an address.

5.51 The stack is a special sequential-access memory organized as a _____ (four letters) -type storage area.

Solution:

The stack is a special sequential-access memory organized as a LIFO-type storage area.

5.52 In the generic microprocessor, the _____ (designer, programmer) determines the location of the stack in RAM.

Solution:

The MPU programmer determines the location of the stack in RAM when using the generic microprocessor.

5.53 Refer to Fig. 5-15. Memory location _____ (hex number) is the first stack location that will be used during a push or call operation.

Solution:

Memory location 2209H is the first stack location that will be used in Fig. 5-15 during a push or call operation.

5.54 "Pushing the stack" refers to a _____ (read, write) operation in a LIFO memory.

Solution:

"Pushing the stack" refers to a write operation in a LIFO memory.

5.55 Refer to Fig. 5-17*a*. Step 1 shows the _____ _____ being decremented from 0009H to 0008H.

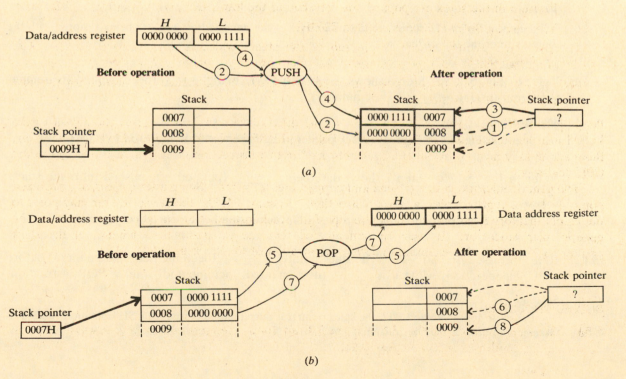

Fig. 5-17

Solution:

Step 1 in Fig. 5-17a shows the stack pointer being decremented.

5.56   Refer to Fig. 5-17a. Step 2 shows the high-order byte of the data/address register being _____ (popped, pushed) into the _____ (L register, stack).

Solution:

Step 2 in Fig. 5-17a shows the high-order byte of the data/address register being pushed into the stack.

5.57   Refer to Fig. 5-17a. Step 4 shows the low-order byte of the data/address register being pushed into stack location _____ (hex number).

Solution:

Step 4 in Fig. 5-17a shows the low-order byte of the data/address register being pushed into stack location 0007H.

5.58   Refer to Fig. 5-17b. Before the operation, the stack pointer points to the _____ (bottom, top) of the stack, which is currently 0007H.

Solution:

Before the operation in Fig. 5-17b, the stack pointer points to the top of the stack, which is currently 0007H.

5.59   Refer to Fig. 5-17b. Step 5 shows the _____ (high, low) -order byte of the data/address register being restored with the contents from the top of the _____ (stack, stack pointer).

Solution:

Step 5 in Fig. 5-17b shows the low-order byte of the data/address register being restored with the contents from the top of the stack.

5.60   Refer to Fig. 5-17b. Step 6 shows the stack pointer being _____ (decremented, incremented) from 0007H to _____ (hex number).

Solution:

Step 6 in Fig. 5-17b shows the stack pointer being incremented from 0007H to 0008H.

5.61   Refer to Fig. 5-17b. Step 7 shows data being _____ (popped off, pushed into) the stack.

Solution:

The reading action during step 7 in Fig. 5-17b shows data being popped off the stack.

5.62   Refer to Figs. 5-16 and 5-17. The stack pointer is _____ (decremented, incremented) before a PUSH operation, while it is _____ (decremented, incremented) after a POP instruction.

Solution:

Based on Figs. 5-16 and 5-17, the stack pointer is decremented before a PUSH operation, while it is incremented after a POP instruction.

Supplementary Problems

5.63 A _____ may be defined as a VLSI chip that performs the tasks of the CPU of a microcomputer.   *Ans.* microprocessor

5.64 The 8086, 8088, 68000, 65816, and Z8000 are all examples of _____-bit microprocessors.   *Ans.* 16

5.65 The 16 address lines on the 8080/8085, 6800, or 6502 microprocessors can directly address _____K of memory.   *Ans.* 64

5.66 The _____ _____ register keeps track of the top of the stack in RAM.   *Ans.* stack pointer

5.67 A manufacturer's data sheet is least likely to contain a _____ (list of programming techniques, pin diagram) for the microprocessor.   *Ans.* list of programming techniques

5.68 Refer to Fig. 5-2. The interrupt request on the 8080 microprocessor is an _____ (input, output) terminal.   *Ans.* input

5.69 Refer to Fig. 5-4. The 8080's CALL instruction has an op code of _____ (hex number), and the instruction requires _____ bytes of program memory.   *Ans.* CDH, 3

5.70 Refer to Fig. 5-5. When the $\overline{WR}$ pin is LOW, it is _____ (disabled, enabled) and the MPU is _____ (reading from, writing into) memory or input/output.   *Ans.* enabled, writing into

5.71 Refer to Fig. 5-5. Which input to the unit changes the program counter to 0000H and causes the microprocessor to begin an initializing routine?   *Ans.* reset

5.72 The typical microprocessor is most likely to contain a(n) _____ (ALU, RAM storage area).
Ans. ALU

5.73 During the first program memory read of an instruction cycle, the data coming off the data bus is transferred to the _____ (accumulator, instruction register).
Ans. instruction register (this is the op code fetch machine cycle)

5.74 The generic microprocessor has four types of machine cycles. They include the op code fetch or read cycle, a _____-from-memory cycle, a write-into-memory cycle, and an execute an internal operation cycle.   *Ans.* read

5.75 Machine and instruction cycles vary in length; however, time periods called _____ _____ are of a given length.   *Ans.* *T* states

5.76 In the generic microprocessor, which time period is shorter—an instruction cycle or a machine cycle?
Ans. machine cycle

5.77 The _____ _____ in Fig. 5-7 interprets the contents of the instruction register, decides which internal microprogram to follow, and signals the timing and control unit the procedure to be followed.
Ans. instruction decoder

5.78 The _____ (three letters) of the microprocessor in Fig. 5-7 performs the adding, subtracting, ANDing, ORing, and shifting operations.   *Ans.* ALU

5.79 The generic microprocessor contains a zero and a carry flag. These are located in the _____ (interrupt control, status register).   *Ans.* status register

5.80 The program counter and the data/address register of the generic microprocessor are alike in that both can _____ (point to memory locations, temporarily store instructions).
Ans. point to memory locations

5.81 What three units in Fig. 5-7 can point to memory locations?
Ans. program counter, stack pointer, and data/address register

5.82 Refer to Fig. 5-10, instruction 2. The *HL* register pair is loaded with _____ (an address, data) in this
program. *Ans.* an address

5.83 Refer to Figs. 5-10 and 5-11*d*. The _____ register is incremented from _____ (hex number) to
_____ (hex number) after the operation. *Ans.* data/address (or *HL*), 2101H, 2102H

5.84 Refer to Figs. 5-10 and 5-11*e*. Instruction 5 is an add _____ (immediate, register indirect) instruction.
Ans. register indirect

5.85 Refer to Figs. 5-10 and 5-11*g*. Instruction 7 is a store _____ (direct, register indirect) instruction.
Ans. register indirect

5.86 Refer to Fig. 5-17*a*. The microprocessor is _____ (popping, pushing) the stack in this diagram.
Ans. pushing

5.87 The contents of the stack pointer in Fig. 5-17*a* *after* the operation would be _____ (hex number).
Ans. 0007H

5.88 The stack is a specialized temporary _____ (random, sequential) -access memory used during _____
(push, store) and _____ (load, pop) instructions. *Ans.* sequential, push, pop

Chapter 6

Programming the Microprocessor

6.1 MACHINE AND ASSEMBLY LANGUAGES

On the most basic level, the microprocessor responds to a listing of operations that is called a *machine program*. The contents of the program memory in Fig. 6-1a represent such a program in machine code. The program starts at address 2000H with the op code 00111110_2 and ends at address 2006H with 01110110_2. Programs in this form are almost impossible for human beings to understand.

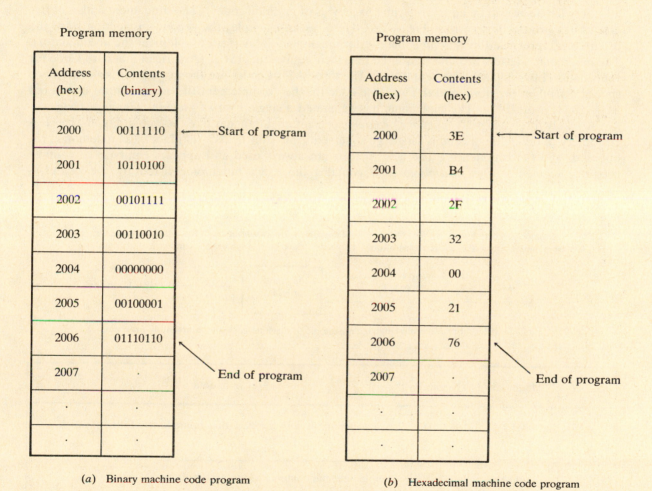

Program memory

Address (hex)	Contents (binary)	
2000	00111110	⟵——Start of program
2001	10110100	
2002	00101111	
2003	00110010	
2004	00000000	
2005	00100001	
2006	01110110	
2007	.	End of program
.	.	
.	.	

(a) Binary machine code program

Program memory

Address (hex)	Contents (hex)	
2000	3E	⟵——Start of program
2001	B4	
2002	2F	
2003	32	
2004	00	
2005	21	
2006	76	End of program
2007	.	
.	.	
.	.	

(b) Hexadecimal machine code program

Fig. 6-1

The machine program in Fig. 6-1a can be made somewhat easier to handle if the binary numbers are represented in hexadecimal notation. The same program is repeated with the contents in hexadecimal in Fig. 6-1b. The program segment shown in Fig. 6-1b is still considered to be in machine code even though the binary is represented by hexadecimal notation. Programs in this form are also very difficult to understand.

On a more human level, the program previously described in machine code might be described as follows:

1. Load the binary number (10110100) into the accumulator of the microprocessor.
2. Complement each bit of the binary number in the accumulator to form the 1s complement.
3. Store the 1s complement result in data memory location 2100_{16}.

The program segment described changes an 8-bit binary number to its equivalent 1s complement form.

The question arises: How do you get from the somewhat lengthy human language description of the program to the machine code? The answer lies in a simple programming language one step up from the machine program you observed in Fig. 6-1. An *assembly language* uses words and phrases to represent microprocessor machine codes. Generally, one phrase or statement in assembly language will be equal to from 1 to 3 bytes of machine code. The fundamental idea of this assembling process is shown in Fig. 6-2a. Here, as an example, the second instruction from the program is represented by a *unique* three-letter mnemonic CMA (for *complement the accumulator*). The mnemonic's letters are first translated into their equivalent *ASCII* (American Standard Code for Information Interchange) representation. The three ASCII codes are then evaluated, in order, by a special *assembler program*, and the machine code for the "complement the accumulator" comes out as 00101111_2, or 2FH. The mnemonic has generated a single byte of *machine language* code.

A handwritten *assembly language program* segment might appear like the one in Fig. 6-2b. It is customary to divide the assembly language statements into four fields: (1) label, (2) mnemonic, (3) operand, and (4) comments. The label field is not always used and appears empty in this simple program segment. The *mnemonic field* contains the exact mnemonic listed by the manufac-

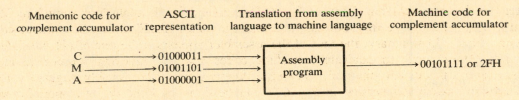

(a) Translation of assembly language mnemonic to machine code by an assembly program

Label	Mnemonic	Operand	Comments
	MVI	A, B4H	; Load accumulator with the data that immediately follows, which is B4H
	CMA		; Complement the contents of the accumulator
	STA	2100H	; Store the contents of the accumulator in memory location 2100H
	HLT		; Stop MPU

(b) Assembly language program

Fig. 6-2

Address (hex)	Contents (hex)	Label	Mnemonic	Operand	Comments
2000	3E		MVI	A,B4H	; Load accumulator with the data that immediately follows, which is B4
2001	B4				
2002	2F		CMA		; Complement the contents of the accumulator
2003	32		STA	2100H	; Store the contents of the accumulator in memory location 2100H
2004	00				
2005	21				
2006	76		HLT		; Stop MPU

(c) Combined machine and assembly language program

Fig. 6-2 (cont.)

turer. This field tells the assembly program essentially the operation to be performed. The *operand field* contains information on *registers*, *data*, or *addresses* associated with the operation. Using the information from just the mnemonic and operand fields, the assembly program can generate the correct machine language code. The assembly program may also assign program memory locations for the machine code listings. The *comment field* is *not* evaluated by the assembly program but is only reprinted. The comment field is valuable in helping understand what is happening in the program.

After the assembly program shown in Fig. 6-2b is assembled, it might look something like the program in Fig. 6-2c. Here the addresses and machine codes (listed under the contents column) have been added. In summary, the task of the assembler appears to be one of (1) translating the mnemonics and operands to equivalent machine codes and (2) assigning consecutive memory locations to each op code and operand. The task of getting from the assembly language version in Fig. 6-2b to the assembled version in Fig. 6-2c can be done by hand or by a special computer assembly program.

A program composed of symbolic statements, such as the assembly language program segment in Fig. 6-2b, is sometimes called the *source program*. After the source program has been translated (by the assembler or compiler) to its machine-coded form, it is called the *object program*. Assembly language programming is just a method for "humanizing" the operations of a microprocessor. Even higher-level languages are available (BASIC, FORTRAN, Pascal, etc.) which make the job of programming even simpler. For instance, one statement in BASIC, FORTRAN, or Pascal might be equivalent to as many as 20 to 30 machine codes. The chapter title referred to programming a microprocessor (as opposed to a microcomputer) because the chapter will deal with using the microprocessor's instruction set directly. Assembly language programming will be used because it aids understanding of the microprocessor's instruction set and operations.

SOLVED PROBLEMS

6.1 Both program segments shown in Fig. 6-1 are considered _____ (assembly, machine) programs.

Solution:

Both program segments shown in Fig. 6-1 are considered machine programs.

6.2 A(n) _____ (assembly, machine) language uses words and phrases to represent micro-processor instructions.

Solution:

An assembly language uses words and phrases to represent microprocessor instructions.

6.3 A(n) _____ (assembler, monitor) is a special computer program for translating from assembly language to machine language.

Solution:

An assembler is a special computer program for translating from assembly language to machine language.

6.4 List the typical four fields in an assembly language statement.

Solution:

See the labels at the top in Fig. 6-2b. The four fields in an assembly language statement are label, mnemonic, operand, and comments.

6.5 After the assembly program is assembled, it will contain the memory address and the _____ (BASIC, machine) code for each assembly language statement.

Solution:

See an assembled program segment in Fig. 6-2c. After the assembly program is assembled, it will contain the memory address and the machine code for each assembly language statement.

6.2 SIMPLIFIED INSTRUCTION SET

An instruction set will be presented for the generic microprocessor illustrated in Fig. 5-7. The mnemonics and op codes used are a subset of the 8080/8085 microprocessor's instruction set. The copyrighted mnemonics and op codes are used by permission of Intel Corporation. Arbitrary mnemonics were considered for the generic microprocessor. It was decided, however, that using a subset of the 8080/8085 instruction set would give the student a head start on that MPU when studying Chaps. 8 and 9. It should be mentioned that 8080/8085 programs are compatible with 8086 and 8088 systems.

A summary of registers available to the programmer in the generic microprocessor is illustrated in Fig. 6-3. At the upper right is the general-purpose 8-bit accumulator (A). At the upper left is the 8-bit status register containing the flags. In the expanded view of the status register, a carry flag (CY) is shown in the B_7 position, while the zero flag (Z) is located in the B_0 position. Bit positions 1 through 6 are not used in the status register of the simplified generic microprocessor. It is customary for real-life microprocessors to have several more flags.

On the second line down in Fig. 6-3 are the H and the L registers. These are multipurpose data/address registers. They may be used separately as general-purpose data registers or as a *register pair* (called the *HL register pair*). As a register pair they are used for address pointing.

Two dedicated 16-bit registers are located across the bottom in Fig. 6-3. The program counter (PC) points at the next instruction to be executed by the CPU. The stack pointer (SP) holds the address of the top of the stack. The stack is located in RAM in this system.

The instruction set for the generic microprocessor is divided into the same seven categories listed in Chap. 4. To review, these categories are:

1. Arithmetic instructions
2. Logical instructions

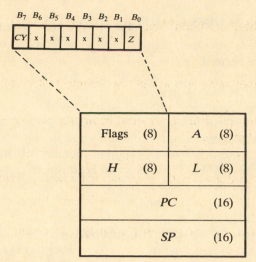

Fig. 6-3 Programming model for the generic microprocessor

3. Data transfer instructions
4. Branch instructions
5. Subroutine call instructions
6. Return instructions
7. Miscellaneous instructions

The generic MPU can execute only 67 different instructions compared with 239 in the full Intel 8085 instruction set.   To aid your study, only a single category of instructions will be considered at a time.

SOLVED PROBLEMS

6.6   The 67 operations performed by the generic microprocessor are a subset of what real-life MPU's instruction set?

Solution:

The operations performed by the generic microprocessor are a subset of the Intel 8080/8085 MPU's instruction set.   Also, 8080/8085 programs are compatible with 16-bit 8086 and 8088 systems.

6.7   Refer to Fig. 6-3.   List three 8-bit general-purpose registers in the generic microprocessor.

Solution:

The accumulator (A) and the H and L data/address registers in Fig. 6-3 are considered general-purpose storage devices in the generic microprocessor.

6.8   Refer to Fig. 6-3.   The status register in the generic microprocessor contains what two flags?

Solution:

According to Fig. 6-3, the status register of the generic microprocessor contains carry and zero flags.

6.9   Refer to Fig. 6-3.   List two dedicated 16-bit registers indirectly used by the programmer in the generic microprocessor.

Solution:

According to Fig. 6-3, the generic microprocessor contains a 16-bit program counter (PC) and a 16-bit stack pointer (SP).

6.3 INSTRUCTION SET—ARITHMETIC OPERATIONS

The *arithmetic instructions* are the first of the generic microprocessor's operations to be considered. These are summarized in Fig. 6-4. These include the add, subtract, increment, decrement, and compare instructions. Observe in Fig. 6-4 that there are four add instructions. The accumulator, identified as the A register in Fig. 6-4, holds one of the numbers to be added. Each add instruction specifies a different source for the other number to be added.

Consider the first instruction listed in the table in Fig. 6-4. The "add A immediate" instruction is a 2-byte instruction with the format shown near the right in the table. As always, the op code (C6H in this case) appears in the first byte of program memory, with the data to be added to the accumulator in the second byte. The ADI instruction is shown in diagram form in Fig. 6-5a. The immediate data in program memory (00010000_2) is added to the contents of the accumulator (00001111_2). The sum (00011111_2) is returned to the accumulator after the operation.

The second instruction in Fig. 6-4 is the "add register L to A" (mnemonic of ADD L). A sample problem using this register-to-register instruction is shown in Fig. 6-5b. The accumulator contents (00001000_2) are added to the contents of the L register (00000001_2). The sum (00001001_2) of the ADD L instruction is returned to the accumulator after the operation.

The third line in Fig. 6-4 shows the "add H to A" (mnemonic of ADD H) single-byte instruction. This is another register-to-register add instruction. A sample problem using the ADD H instruction is detailed in Fig. 6-5c. The contents of register A (00101100_2) are added to the contents of register H (00010011_2), yielding a sum of 00111111_2. The sum is deposited in the accumulator after the operation is complete.

The fourth line in Fig. 6-4 shows the "add register indirect" (mnemonic equals ADD M) single-byte instruction. Location of the data to be added to is somewhat more complicated using this *register indirect addressing mode*. A sample problem using the ADD M instruction is shown in Fig. 6-5d. The HL register pair holds a 16-bit address. The HL register pair then points to the appropriate data memory location (LOC). The contents (00000011_2) of this location are added to the contents of the accumulator (01100000_2). The sum (01100011_2) is returned to the accumulator after the add operation. Register indirect instructions use a 16-bit register (usually the HL register pair) as an address pointer.

Look again at the "add register indirect" instruction (ADD M) in Fig. 6-4. The description says "Add LOC ($H\&L$) to A" which you would read as, "add the contents of the memory location pointed to by the HL register pair to the contents of the A register." Reading across in Fig. 6-4 for the "add register indirect" instruction, you see that the addressing mode is register indirect. The unique assembly language mnemonic for this instruction is ADD M, with an op code of 86_{16}. According to the "Bytes" column in Fig. 6-4, the "add register indirect" instruction is a 1-byte instruction. The instruction format is diagramed showing the single instruction byte containing the op code for the instruction. The column second from the right in Fig. 6-4 details, in symbolic form, the operation being performed by the CPU. The symbolic statement for the ADD M instruction is rewritten in Fig. 6-6. Following the pattern used by Intel Corporation and somewhat backward from customary notation, the symbolic statement reads from right to left. On the right side of the arrow, the first operand is identified as the contents of A (accumulator). The single parentheses ( ) mean "contents of" in this notation. The + sign stands for the operation to be performed, which is addition in this case. The double parentheses (( )) denote a register indirect instruction. The $((H)(L))$ means "the contents of HL register point to the second operand's location in memory." In other words, the second operand resides in a memory location pointed to by the contents of the HL register pair. After the operation, the result is transferred to register A, or the accumulator.

The column at the far right in Fig. 6-4 lists the flags that are affected by the execution of an instruction. As an example of how flags are affected by an operation, consider adding binary 11111111 to 00000001, as shown in Fig. 6-7. The pencil-and-paper method of adding these two 8-bit

Arithmetic instructions

Description of operation	Addressing mode	Mnemonic	Op code	Bytes	Instruction format	Symbolic	Flags affected
Add A to data	Immediate	ADI	C6	2	Op code / data	$(A) \leftarrow (A) + \text{(byte 2)}$	Z, CY
Add L to A	Register	ADD L	85	1	Op code	$(A) \leftarrow (A) + (L)$	Z, CY
Add H to A	Register	ADD H	84	1	Op code	$(A) \leftarrow (A) + (H)$	Z, CY
Add LOC (H & L) to A	Register indirect	ADD M	86	1	Op code	$(A) \leftarrow (A) + ((H)(L))$	Z, CY
Subtract data from A	Immediate	SUI	D6	2	Op code / data	$(A) \leftarrow (A) - \text{(byte 2)}$	Z, CY
Subtract L from A	Register	SUB L	95	1	Op code	$(A) \leftarrow (A) - (L)$	Z, CY
Subtract H from A	Register	SUB H	94	1	Op code	$(A) \leftarrow (A) - (H)$	Z, CY
Subtract LOC (H & L) from A	Register indirect	SUB M	96	1	Op code	$(A) \leftarrow (A) - ((H)(L))$	Z, CY
Increment A	Register	INC A	3C	1	Op code	$(A) \leftarrow (A) + 1$	Z
Increment HL	Register	INX H	23	1	Op code	$(HL) \leftarrow (HL) + 1$	
Decrement A	Register	DCR A	3D	1	Op code	$(A) \leftarrow (A) - 1$	Z
Decrement HL	Register	DCX H	2B	1	Op code	$(HL) \leftarrow (HL) - 1$	
Compare A with data	Immediate	CPI	FE	2	Op code / data	$(A) - \text{(byte 2)}$	$Z = 1$ if $(A) = \text{(byte 2)}$ $CY = 1$ if $(A) < \text{(byte 2)}$
Compare A with L	Register	CMP L	BD	1	Op code	$(A) - (L)$	$Z = 1$ if $(A) = (L)$ $CY = 1$ if $(A) < (L)$
Compare A with H	Register	CMP H	BC	1	Op code	$(A) - (H)$	$Z = 1$ if $(A) = (H)$ $CY = 1$ if $(A) < (H)$
Compare A with LOC (H & L)	Register indirect	CMP M	BE	1	Op code	$(A) - ((H)(L))$	$Z = 1$ if $(A) = ((H)(L))$ $CY = 1$ if $(A) < ((H)(L))$

( ) = contents of
(( )) = register indirect addressing
+ = add
− = subtract

Fig. 6-4 Arithmetic instructions for the generic microprocessor (subset of Intel 8080/8085 instructions)

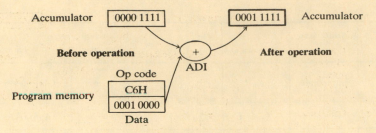

(a) The add A immediate instruction

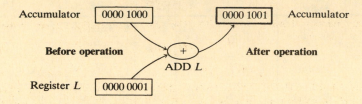

(b) The add L to A instruction

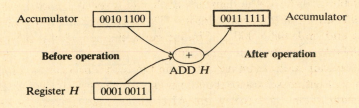

(c) The add H to A instruction

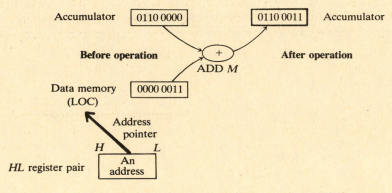

(d) The add register indirect instruction

Fig. 6-5

Result		First operand	Operation	Second operand
(A)	⟵	(A)	+	((H)(L))
Contents of register A	Transferred to	Contents of register A	Add	Contents of HL register point to operand location in memory

Fig. 6-6   Interpreting ADD—operations using the symbolic code from the instruction set table

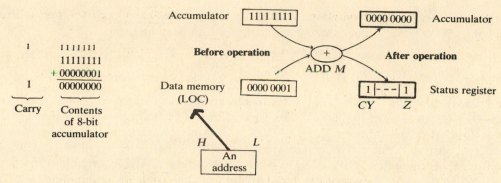

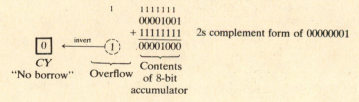

(a) Adding binary numbers showing carry   (b) The ADD *M* instruction's effect on the flags and accumulator

Fig. 6-7

numbers is shown in Fig. 6-7*a*. The same problem is shown being executed by the generic microprocessor using the ADD *M* instruction in Fig. 6-7*b*. The accumulator holds 11111111_2, while a location in data memory pointed to by the *HL* register pair holds the other number to be added (00000001_2). After the addition is complete, the accumulator holds the least significant 8 bits of the sum, which is 00000000_2. The status register's carry flag is set to 1, indicating that there was a carry from the most significant bit of the accumulator. The zero flag tests the contents of the accumulator after the operation and finds 00000000_2. Finding zero, the zero flag is set to 1, indicating that the accumulator is 00000000 after the add operation.

Next consider the four subtraction operations in the instruction set of the generic microprocessor in Fig. 6-4. Each instruction subtracts the contents of some register or memory location from the contents of the accumulator. Internally the ALU of the microprocessor does not have subtract hardware; therefore it performs subtraction by converting the subtrahend to its 2s complement form and adding.

As an example, consider the subtraction problem detailed in Fig. 6-8. Binary 00000001 is being subtracted from 00001001 (09H − 01H = 08H). The paper-and-pencil procedure is shown in Fig. 6-8*a*. To review, binary subtraction can be performed by *adding* the binary minuend to the 2s

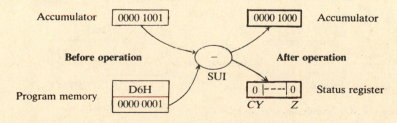

(a) Binary subtraction by converting subtrahend to 2s complement form and adding

(b) The subtract immediate instruction

Fig. 6-8

complement form of the subtrahend with the overflow being disregarded.   The subtrahend in this problem is 00000001_2, which is converted to its 2s complement form:

$$00000001 \xrightarrow{\text{complement}} 11111110 \quad \text{1s complement}$$
$$11111110 + 1 \quad = \quad 11111111 \quad \text{2s complement}$$

The 2s complement form (11111111) of the subtrahend is then added to the minuend, yielding a sum of 1 0000 1000, as seen in Fig. 6-8a.   The 1 in the most significant position of the sum is an overflow and is not part of the difference of 00001000_2.   The microprocessor uses the overflow to affect the carry (or "borrow") flag.   When subtracting, the CPU inverts the overflow, and this becomes the contents of the carry flag (CY).·   In Fig. 6-8a, the overflow of 1 is inverted and resets the carry flag to 0.   When the carry flag is reset in a subtraction problem, it means that no borrow occurred or that the minuend is larger than the subtrahend.

The "subtract immediate" instruction (mnemonic of SUI) is being used in the subtraction example in Fig. 6-8b.   The immediate data from the second byte of program memory (00000001_2) is being subtracted from the contents of the accumulator (00001001_2).   The difference of 00001000_2 is transferred to the accumulator after the subtraction.   The carry ("borrow") flag is reset to 0, indicating that no borrow occurred or that the number in the accumulator before the operation was greater than the number from memory.   The zero flag tests the accumulator contents after the subtract operation.   The accumulator contents are 00001000, which is *not zero*, so the zero flag is reset to 0.

Consider another subtraction problem where the minuend is less than the subtrahend.   The problem is to subtract binary 00000110 from the smaller 00000101 ($05H - 06H = FFH$ or -1_{10}).   The paper-and-pencil method of calculating this problem is illustrated in Fig. 6-9a.   The subtrahend is converted to its 2s complement form in a manner like this:

$$00000110 \xrightarrow{\text{complement}} 11111001 \quad \text{1s complement}$$
$$11111001 + 1 \quad = \quad 11111010 \quad \text{2s complement}$$

The minuend (00000101_2) is then added to the 2s complement form of the subtrahend (11111010), yielding a difference of 11111111.   The difference of 11111111 is the 2s complement representation

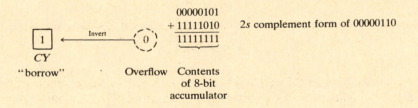

(a)   Binary subtraction showing effect of overflow on carry flag

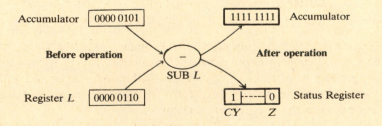

(b)   The subtract L from A instruction

Fig. 6-9

of -1_{10} as shown in Fig. 2-12.   Figure 6-9a also shows that the addition causes no overflow, or a 0 in the overflow register.   This is inverted (because of the subtraction operation), yielding a 1 in the *CY* or "borrow" flag position.   When the *CY* flag is set to 1 after a subtraction operation, it means the accumulator number is less than the number in the register or memory location.   The carry flag set to 1 implies that the number in the accumulator after the subtraction is a 2s complement representation of a negative number.   The 11111111 in the accumulator in Fig. 6-9b represents -1_{10}.

The generic microprocessor's instruction set has four *compare instructions* shown in the last four lines in Fig. 6-4.   The compare instructions subtract the memory or register contents from the accumulator contents but *do not change* the contents of either.   The *flags are affected* by the compare instructions.

The "compare register *L*" instruction is used as an example in Fig. 6-10.   Equal numbers (00010000_2) in the accumulator and *L* register are being compared by the microprocessor.   Note in Fig. 6-10a that neither the accumulator nor the *L* register changes contents after the compare operation.   However, the flags in the status register are affected.

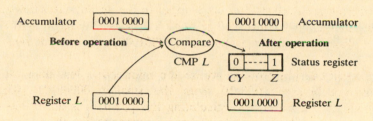

(a)   The compare *A* with *L* instruction

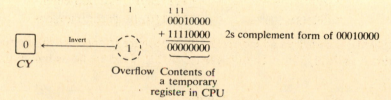

(b)   Effect on carry flag when the internal CPU binary subtraction occurs during the compare operation

Fig. 6-10

According to information in the symbolic column in Fig. 6-4, the contents of the *L* register are subtracted from the contents of the *A* register when using the "CMP *L*" instruction.   Figure 6-10b shows this process using the paper-and-pencil method.   The subtrahend (contents of the *L* register) is changed to its 2s complement form by the procedure

$$00010000 \xrightarrow{\text{complement}} 11101111 \quad \text{1s complement}$$
$$11101111 + 1 \quad = \quad 11110000 \quad \text{2s complement}$$

The minuend (00010000_2) and 2s complement subtrahend (11110000) are then added, yielding 1 0000 0000.   The least significant eight places are evaluated to see if they equal zero.   They do equal zero, so the zero flag is set to 1.   The overflow of 1 is inverted by the ALU, and the carry flag equals 0 in this example.   A reset carry flag ($CY = 0$) means that the contents of the accumulator are greater than or equal to the contents of register *L*.

In summary, the arithmetic operations that can be performed by the generic MPU are typical of what most instruction sets can perform.   Most microprocessors would have a few more arithmetic instructions and several more flags in their status registers.   The flags will be used later to affect the result of the conditional branch or jump instructions.

SOLVED PROBLEMS

6.10   Refer to Fig. 6-4.   The "subtract immediate" instruction has a mnemonic of _____ and an op code of D6H and is a _____ (number) -byte instruction.

Solution:

Based on the fifth line down in Fig. 6-4, the "subtract immediate" instruction has a mnemonic of SUI and an op code of D6H and is a 2-byte instruction.

6.11   Refer to Fig. 6-4.   To increment means to _____ (add 1 to, subtract 1 from) the contents of a register in the microprocessor.

Solution:

To increment means to add 1 to the contents of a register in the microprocessor.

6.12   Refer to Fig. 6-4.   What increment instruction *does not* affect the zero flag?

Solution:

Based on the information from Fig. 6-4, the INX *H* (increment *HL* register pair) instruction does not affect the zero flag.

6.13   The contents of the accumulator in Fig. 6-11 after the decrement operation are _____ (8 bits).

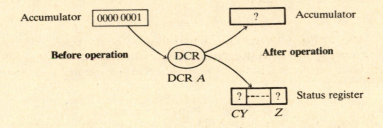

Fig. 6-11

Solution:

The DCR *A* instruction means to subtract one from the value in the accumulator, and therefore $00000001 - 1 = 00000000$.   The accumulator in Fig. 6-11 will contain 00000000 after the decrement operation.

6.14   Refer to Fig. 6-4.   The zero flag in Fig. 6-11 is _____ (reset, set) to _____ (0, 1) after the decrement operation.

Solution:

The contents of the accumulator are tested after the decrement operation and are found to be zero; therefore the zero flag in the status register in Fig. 6-11 is set to 1.

6.15   Refer to Fig. 6-4.   What is the condition of the carry flag in Fig. 6-11 after the decrement operation?

Solution:

According to Fig. 6-4, the carry flag (*CY*) is not affected by the decrement *A* operation, and therefore the condition of the carry flag in the status register is unpredictable.

6.16   Refer to Fig. 6-4.   List the contents of the accumulator and two program memory locations after the "compare immediate" operation in Fig. 6-12.

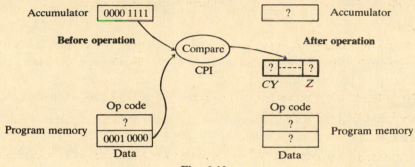

Fig. 6-12

Solution:

Compare instructions do not change the contents of the registers or memory locations compared.   Therefore, the accumulator will still contain 00001111 after the compare operation in Fig. 6-12.   The op code for the CPI instruction is FE_{16} (see from Fig. 6-4), while the immediate data in program memory will still be 00010000.

6.17   Refer to Fig. 6-4.   The zero flag in Fig. 6-12 will be _____ (reset to 0, set to 1) after the "compare immediate" operation.

Solution:

The zero flag in Fig. 6-12 will be reset to 0 after the "compare immediate" operation.   The symbolic column in Fig. 6-4 shows that the compare instruction is basically a subtraction operation with the difference being evaluated.   In this case the difference was not zero, so the zero flag was not raised or it was reset.

6.18   Refer to Fig. 6-4.   The carry flag in Fig. 6-12 will be _____ (reset to 0, set to 1) after the "compare immediate" operation.

Solution:

The carry flag in Fig. 6-12 will be set to 1 after the "compare immediate" operation because the result of the CPU's internal subtraction notes that the accumulator contents are less than the contents of the data section of program memory.   Remember that the carry flag is really a "borrow" flag when subtracting.

6.19   Refer to Fig. 6-4.   The contents of the *HL* register pair in Fig. 6-13 after the increment operation will be _____ (hex).

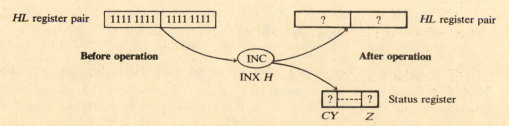

Fig. 6-13

Solution:

To increment the contents of the *HL* register pair means $1111\,1111\,1111\,1111 + 1 = 1\,0000\,0000\,0000\,0000$. The most significant 1 in the sum is carried out the left end of the *H* register. Therefore, the results in the *HL* register pair after the operation will be $0000\,0000\,0000\,0000$, or 0000_{16}.

6.20 Refer to Fig. 6-4.   What is the condition of the flags in Fig. 6-13 after the increment the *HL* register pair instruction?

Solution:

According to Fig. 6-4, the flags are not affected by the results of the increment the *HL* register pair instruction, and therefore the contents of the status register will be unpredictable.   Note that arithmetic operations on accumulator contents affect flags, whereas this operation was on the contents of the *HL* register pair.

6.21 The flags are affected by most arithmetic operations but are used by the microprocessor during execution of _____ (branch, logical) instructions.

Solution:

The flags are affected by most arithmetic operations but are used by the microprocessor during branch (conditional) instructions.

6.4 INSTRUCTION SET—LOGICAL OPERATIONS

The *logical instructions* are the second of the generic microprocessor's operations to be considered.   These are summarized in Fig. 6-14.   These include AND, OR, exclusive OR, complement (NOT), and rotate instructions.   The organization of the table in Fig. 6-14 is the same as that used for the arithmetic operations earlier.   Again, the focus of most operations is on the contents of the accumulator.   As with the arithmetic instructions, the addressing mode has to do with how and where other data is found in the microprocessor-based system.

Consider using the generic microprocessor's "AND immediate" instruction, as shown in Fig. 6-15*a*.   The contents of the accumulator (00010011) are ANDed with the second byte of data from program memory (00000001).   The numbers are ANDed bit by bit.   Based on the AND truth table in Fig. 3-1, only the least significant bit in each number is a 1; therefore the output will be 00000001.   The result of the AND operation is placed in the accumulator.   According to the last column in Fig. 6-14, all AND operations result in the carry flag being cleared to zero.   This result is also shown in Fig. 6-15*a*.   The result of ANDing is tested to determine whether it is zero.   It is not zero, and therefore the zero flag is reset to 0.   Note the use of the dot (·) in Fig. 6-14 under the symbolic column to denote the AND operation.

A second example using an AND instruction is illustrated in Fig. 6-15*b*.   Here the "AND register indirect" instruction (mnemonic of ANA *M*) is used.   The contents of the accumulator are ANDed (bit by bit) with the contents of the data memory location pointed to by the *HL* register pair.   In ANDing 00111100 with 00000001, it is found that the output result is 00000000, which ends up in the accumulator.   The carry flag is cleared based on information from Fig. 6-14.   The result in the accumulator (00000000) is tested and found to be zero; therefore the zero flag is raised or set to 1.

Look carefully at Fig. 6-15*a* and *b*.   In both examples the second operand is 00000001.   This operand is being used as a *mask*.   The 00000001 mask in Fig. 6-15*a* and *b* may be used for resetting the seven most significant bits to zero.   Or possibly, the single 1 in the 00000001 mask may be used, along with the zero flag, to test the presence of a 0 or 1 in the LSB position of the accumulator contents.   Be careful: Observe that the contents of the accumulator are changed when the AND

Logical instructions

Description of operation	Addressing mode	Mnemonic	Op code	Bytes	Instruction format	Symbolic	Flags affected
AND A with data	Immediate	ANI	E6	2	Op code / Data	$(A) \leftarrow (A) \cdot (\text{byte 2})$	Z / CY is cleared
AND A with L	Register	ANA L	A5	1	Op code	$(A) \leftarrow (A) \cdot (L)$	Z / CY is cleared
AND A with H	Register	ANA H	A4	1	Op code	$(A) \leftarrow (A) \cdot (H)$	Z / CY is cleared
AND A with LOC (H & L)	Register indirect	ANA M	A6	1	Op code	$(A) \leftarrow (A) \cdot ((H)(L))$	Z / CY is cleared
OR A with data	Immediate	ORI	F6	2	Op code / Data	$(A) \leftarrow (A) + (\text{byte 2})$	Z / CY is cleared
OR A with L	Register	ORA L	B5	1	Op code	$(A) \leftarrow (A) + (L)$	Z / CY is cleared
OR A with H	Register	ORA H	B4	1	Op code	$(A) \leftarrow (A) + (H)$	Z / CY is cleared
OR A with LOC (H & L)	Register indirect	ORA M	B6	1	Op code	$(A) \leftarrow (A) + ((H)(L))$	Z / CY is cleared
Exclusive OR A with data	Immediate	XRI	EE	2	Op code / Data	$(A) \leftarrow (A) \oplus (\text{byte 2})$	Z / CY is cleared
Exclusive OR A with A	Register	XRA A	AF	1	Op code	Clears accumulator $(A) \leftarrow (A) \oplus (A)$	$Z = 1$ / CY is cleared
Exclusive OR A with L	Register	XRA L	AD	1	Op code	$(A) \leftarrow (A) \oplus (L)$	Z / CY is cleared
Exclusive OR A with H	Register	XRA H	AC	1	Op code	$(A) \leftarrow (A) \oplus (H)$	Z / CY is cleared
Exclusive OR A with LOC (H & L)	Register indirect	XRA M	AE	1	Op code	$(A) \leftarrow (A) \oplus ((H)(L))$	Z / CY is cleared
Complement A (1s Complement)	Inherent	CMA	2F	1	Op code	$(A) \leftarrow (\bar{A})$	
Rotate A right through carry	Inherent	RAR	1F	1	Op code		CY
Rotate A left through carry	Inherent	RAL	17	1	Op code		CY

( ) = contents of
(( )) = register indirect addressing
· = AND
+ = OR
⊕ = XOR

Fig. 6-14 Logical instructions for the generic microprocessor (subset of Intel 8080/8085 instructions)

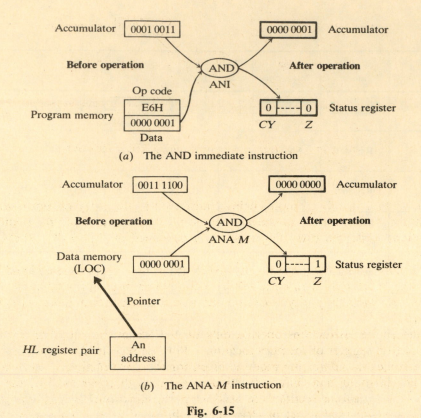

(a) The AND immediate instruction

(b) The ANA M instruction

Fig. 6-15

instructions are used.   Some microprocessors have special "bit test instructions" which AND the accumulator with a mask byte without changing the contents of the accumulator while changing flags.

The four OR instructions listed in Fig. 6-14 all OR the accumulator contents with some other memory or register location.   An example of an OR operation is shown in Fig. 6-16.   Here the accumulator contents are 11001100, while the L register holds 00001111.   The result of the OR operation is shown as 11001111.   The numbers are ORed bit-by-bit using the OR truth table found in Fig. 3-1.   The 00001111 in register L may be considered a mask that will always set the least significant 4 bits to 1111.   Notice the use of the logical OR symbol (+) in the symbolic column of Fig. 6-14.

The last two logical operations listed in the table in Fig. 6-14 are the rotate through carry instructions.   The diagrams in the symbolic column of the table show the shifting action caused by these instructions.

Consider the example in Fig. 6-17 using the rotate accumulator right through carry instruction.   The contents of the accumulator (00110001) will be rotated one position to the right with the

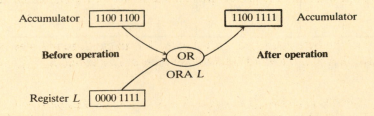

Fig. 6-16 The OR A with L instruction

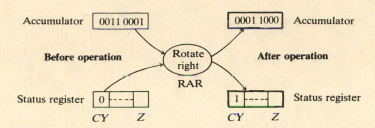

Fig. 6-17 The rotate *A* right through carry instruction

least significant bit (a 1 in this example) being transferred to the carry bit position. The present carry will enter the MSB position in the accumulator. The accumulator then contains 00011000 after the operation, while the carry flag is set to 1 as shown in Fig. 6-17. The zero flag is not affected.

With one or more rotate instructions, any given bit position could be tested and a carry flag set or reset. The carry flag could then be tested by a conditional branch instruction. Another use of rotate instructions is to test for parity. *Even parity* would be a binary number with an even number of 1s in the word.

Note that the rotate instructions operate only on the accumulator and do not have to get an operand from another register or memory location. For this reason, the addressing mode is called *inherent*, or sometimes no addressing mode is listed for these instructions. Most microprocessors have several types of rotate and shift instructions other than the ones used by the generic MPU.

In summary, the logical instructions are used for performing Boolean algebra manipulations on variables. They are also used to set or clear specific bits in a word. They may also be used for testing and comparing bits. The applications of these instructions are usually not as obvious as the add and subtract instructions.

SOLVED PROBLEMS

6.22 Refer to Fig. 6-14. The contents of the accumulator in Fig. 6-18 after the AND operation are _____ (8 bits).

Solution:

ANDing 11110011 with 10000000 bit by bit yields 10000000. The contents of the accumulator in Fig. 6-18 after the AND operation are 10000000.

6.23 Refer to Fig. 6-14. List the condition of the flags in Fig. 6-18 after the AND operation.

Solution:

Based on information in line 3 in Fig. 6-14, the carry flag will be cleared to 0. After the AND operation, the contents of the accumulator are found to be not zero; therefore the zero flag is reset to 0.

6.24 If the purpose of the byte in register *H* in Fig. 6-18 is to check to see whether the MSB in the accumulator is a 0 or a 1, the word 10000000 in register *H* is called a _____ (mask, test word).

Solution:

The word 10000000 in register *H* in Fig. 6-18 is called a mask if its purpose is to check the MSB in the accumulator to determine whether it is a 0 or a 1. Using this mask with the ANA *H* instruction, if the zero flag is 1, then the MSB of the accumulator byte is 0; if the zero flag is 0, then the MSB is 1.

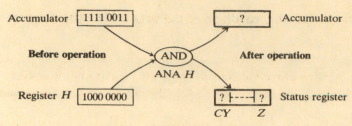

Fig. 6-18

6.25 Refer to Fig. 6-14.   When using the "OR *A* immediate" instruction (mnemonic of ORI), the operand that will be ORed with the accumulator contents comes from _____ (data, program) memory.

Solution:

The "OR *A* immediate" instruction fetches its operand from the second byte of program memory.

6.26 The + symbol used in the logic instruction table in Fig. 6-14 denotes the _____ (add, OR) operation.

Solution:

The + symbol used in the logic instruction table in Fig. 6-14 denotes the OR operation.

6.27 Refer to Fig. 6-14.   The source of the address (LOC) of the operand in data memory in Fig. 6-19 is the _____ (*HL* register pair, stack pointer).

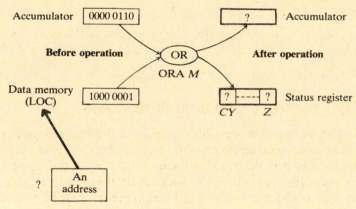

Fig. 6-19

Solution:

Based on information about the ORA *M* instruction in Fig. 6-14, the source of the address (LOC) of the operand in data memory in Fig. 6-19 is the *HL* register pair.

6.28 Refer to Fig. 6-14.   The contents of the accumulator after the OR operation in Fig. 6-19 are _____ (8 bits).

Solution:

The contents of the accumulator after the bit-by-bit ORing in Fig. 6-19 are 10000111.

6.29   Refer to Fig. 6-14.   List the condition of the flags in the status register in Fig. 6-19 after the OR operation.

Solution:

Based on information from the table in Fig. 6-14, the carry flag is cleared to 0.   The accumulator contents are not zero; therefore the zero flag is reset to 0.

6.30   Refer to Fig. 6-14.   The contents of the accumulator in Fig. 6-20 after the rotate left operation are _____ (8 bits).

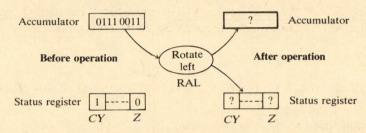

Fig. 6-20

Solution:

The action of the rotate left instruction is diagramed in the symbolic column in Fig. 6-14.   The contents of the accumulator in Fig. 6-20 after the rotate left operation are 11100111.

6.31   Refer to Fig. 6-14.   List the condition of the flags in the status register in Fig. 6-20 after the rotate left operation.

Solution:

According to Fig. 6-14, only the carry flag is affected by the rotate left instruction; therefore the zero flag remains at 0.   The carry flag is placed at 0 because the MSB in the accumulator is rotated left into the carry position.

6.5   INSTRUCTION SET—DATA TRANSFER OPERATIONS

The *data transfer instructions* are the third category of the generic microprocessor's operations to be considered.   These are summarized in Fig. 6-21.   These include the move from register to register, the load from memory, the store in memory, the input and output, and the set carry flag instructions.   Most programs contain more data transfer instructions than other types of operations.   Almost all data transfer instructions do not affect the flags in this MPU.   There are many instructions in this group, so data may be transferred from any memory location to any register or from any register to any memory location or other register.   Microprocessors with more CPU registers have more data transfer instructions.   Keep in mind that each transfer instruction will have a source of data and a destination for the data.   The addressing mode deals with how and where the source of data is found.

Consider the very first move operation listed on the table in Fig. 6-21.   Data is to be moved from register L to register A, or the accumulator.   The assembly language mnemonic (MOV A,L) first suggests the action, which is to move (MOV).   The next letter in the mnemonic (A in this example) is the *destination* of the data, whereas the last letter (L in this example) is the *source* of the data.   This seems a little backward, but it is the convention used by Intel Corporation with 8080/8085 instructions.   Some microprocessors identify the source and destination in different manners and in the opposite order.

Data transfer instructions

Description of operation	Addressing mode	Mnemonic	Op code	Bytes	Instruction format	Symbolic	Flags affected
Move L to A	Register	MOV A,L	7D	1	Op code	$(A) \leftarrow (L)$	
Move H to A	Register	MOV A,H	7C	1	Op code	$(A) \leftarrow (H)$	
Move A to L	Register	MOV L,A	6F	1	Op code	$(L) \leftarrow (A)$	
Move A to H	Register	MOV H,A	67	1	Op code	$(H) \leftarrow (A)$	
Move HL to PC	Register	PCHL	E9	1	Op code	$(PC) \leftarrow (HL)$	
Move HL to SP	Register	SPHL	F9	1	Op code	$(SP) \leftarrow (HL)$	
Load A with data	Immediate	MVI A	3E	2	Op code / Data	$(A) \leftarrow (\text{byte } 2)$	
Load L with data	Immediate	MVI L	2E	2	Op code / Data	$(L) \leftarrow (\text{byte } 2)$	
Load H with data	Immediate	MVI H	26	2	Op code / Data	$(H) \leftarrow (\text{byte } 2)$	
Load LOC (H & L) to A	Register indirect	MOV A,M	7E	1	Op code	$(A) \leftarrow ((H)(L))$	
Load HL with data	Immediate	LXI H	21	3	Op code / Low-order data / High-order data	$(L) \leftarrow (\text{byte } 2)$ $(H) \leftarrow (\text{byte } 3)$	
Load SP with data	Immediate	LXI SP	31	3	Op code / Low-order data / High-order data	$(SP) \leftarrow (\text{byte } 2+3)$	
Load HL from LOC aa	Direct	LHLD	2A	3	Op code / Low-order address / High-order address	$(L) \leftarrow ((\text{byte } 2+3))$ $(H) \leftarrow ((\text{byte } 2+3)+1)$	
Load A from LOC aa	Direct	LDA	3A	3	Op code / Low-order address / High-order address	$(A) \leftarrow ((\text{byte } 2+3))$	
Store A at LOC aa	Direct	STA	32	3	Op code / Low-order address / High-order address	$(\text{address}) \leftarrow (A)$	
Store HL at LOC aa	Direct	SHLD	22	3	Op code / Low-order address / High-order address	$(\text{address}) \leftarrow (L)$ $(\text{address}+1) \leftarrow (H)$	
Store A at LOC (H & L)	Register indirect	MOV M,A	77	1	Op code	$((H)(L)) \leftarrow (A)$	
Store L at LOC (H & L)	Register indirect	MOV M,L	75	1	Op code	$((H)(L)) \leftarrow (L)$	
Store H at LOC (H & L)	Register indirect	MOV M,H	74	1	Op code	$((H)(L)) \leftarrow (H)$	
Input to A from port at LOC a	Direct	IN	DB	2	Op code / Port address	$(A) \leftarrow \left(\text{port address}\right)$	
Output from A to port at LOC a	Direct	OUT	D3	2	Op code / Port address	$\left(\text{port address}\right) \leftarrow (A)$	
Set carry flag	Inherent	STC	37	1	Op code	$(CY) \leftarrow 1$	CY is set to 1

( ) = contents of   (( )) = register indirect addressing   PC = program counter   SP = stack pointer

Fig. 6-21 Data transfer instructions for the generic microprocessor (subset of Intel 8080/8085 instructions)

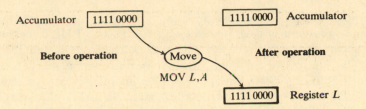

Fig. 6-22   The move *A* to *L* instruction

Consider the move operation diagramed in Fig. 6-22. The source of data is the *A* register (accumulator), while the destination is register *L*. The accumulator contents (11110000) are transferred to register *L* without any modification. The accumulator also retains this data after the move operation is complete.

A second move operation is diagramed in Fig. 6-23. Here the source of data is the 16-bit *HL* register pair, while the destination is the 16-bit stack pointer. If you look closely at the mnemonic for the "move *HL* to *SP*" instruction, it does make some sense when you remember that the destination register is listed first (*SP* in this example) while the source is listed last (*HL* in this example). The mnemonic is then SPHL for the "move *HL* to *SP*" instruction.

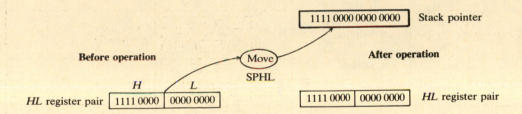

Fig. 6-23   The move *HL* to *SP* instruction

There are five "load immediate" instructions in the load category. "Load immediate" instructions are many times used to place an initial value in the microprocessor register early in the program. An example of a load instruction is detailed in Fig. 6-24. The 16-bit *HL* register pair is to be loaded with immediate data from program memory. Note in Fig. 6-21 that the "load *HL* with data" instruction requires a 3-byte instruction. The first byte is the op code (21H in this example), whereas the next 2 program memory bytes are data bytes. The second byte holds the low-order data (00000011 in this example) which is loaded into the *L* register. This is shown in Fig. 6-24. Next the third byte holds the high-order data (00111100 in this example) which is loaded into the *H* register of the *HL* register pair.

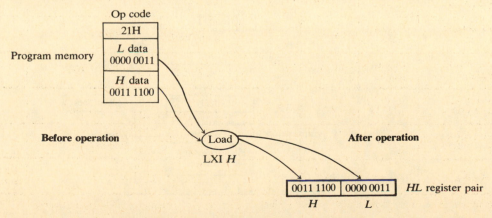

Fig. 6-24   The load *HL* immediate instruction

The next example illustrates the use of the "load *HL* direct" instruction (mnemonic of LHLD). The sample problem is diagramed in Fig. 6-25. The LHLD instruction uses the *direct addressing mode*, according to the table in Fig. 6-21. The second and third bytes of program memory are the 16-bit address of the data memory location where the data to be loaded will be found. Follow in Fig. 6-25. Start with the 3-byte instruction at the lower left in program memory. The op code for the LHLD instruction is given as 2AH. The CPU then assembles the next 2 program bytes into a 16-bit address (shown in dashed lines). This 16-bit address serves as the address pointer for finding a location (LOC) in data memory. This data memory byte is then loaded into the *L* register. The contents of the next data memory location (labeled LOC + 1 in this example) are then loaded into the *H* register.

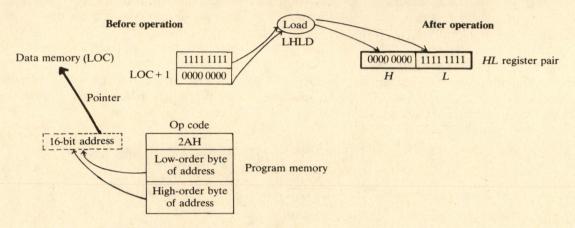

Fig. 6-25 The load *HL* direct instruction

The generic microprocessor has five store instructions, which are summarized in Fig. 6-21. Store operations are widely used for depositing results and other data in memory. Consider the sample problem shown in Fig. 6-26 using the "store *A* direct" instruction. The contents of the accumulator (register *A*) are stored in a data memory location (LOC) that is pointed to by a 16-bit address formed by the second and third bytes in the instruction. After the store operation, both the data memory location (LOC) and the accumulator hold the same data (11000000 in this example).

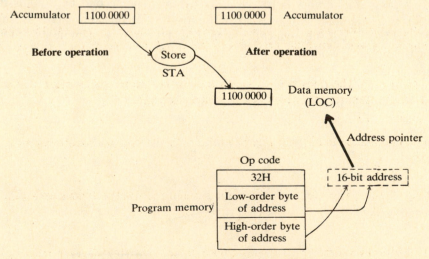

Fig. 6-26 The store *A* direct instruction

The input instruction listed on the third line from the bottom in Fig. 6-21 is similar to a load instruction. The source of the data transfer is an input port identified by an 8-bit binary number $(0–255_{10})$. The destination is the accumulator of the CPU. An example is shown in Fig. 6-27 using the input instruction. Data from the input port pointed to by the second byte in the instruction is transferred to the accumulator of the microprocessor. In this example, 00001111 is input and transferred to the accumulator from a port identified as LOC.

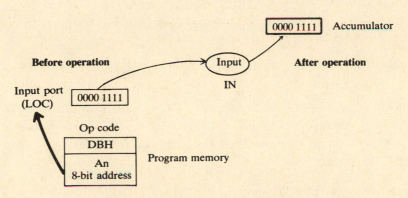

Fig. 6-27 The input direct instruction

SOLVED PROBLEMS

6.32 Refer to Fig. 6-21. During use of the MOV H,A instruction, the _____ (A, H) register is the source of data whereas the _____ (A, H) register is the destination.

Solution:

Based on information in Fig. 6-21, the A register is the source whereas the H register is the destination of data during the execution of the MOV H,A instruction.

6.33 Refer to Fig. 6-21. During use of the PCHL instruction, the _____ (HL, PC) register is the source of data whereas the 16-bit _____ _____ is the destination.

Solution:

Based on information in Fig. 6-21, the HL register is the source whereas the 16-bit program counter is the destination of data during the execution of the PCHL instruction.

6.34 Refer to Fig. 6-21. The flags are _____ (affected, not affected) by most of the data transfer operations in the generic microcomputer's instruction set.

Solution:

Based on information in the right column in Fig. 6-21, the flags are not affected by most of the data transfer operations.

6.35 Refer to Fig. 6-21. The assembly language mnemonic for the load instruction used in Fig. 6-28 is _____.

Solution:

Based on information from the table in Fig. 6-21, the assembly language mnemonic for the load instruction used in Fig. 6-28 is MVI A.

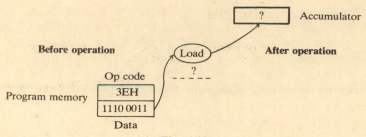

Fig. 6-28

6.36 The contents of the accumulator in Fig. 6-28 after the load operation are _____ (8 bits).

Solution:

The contents of the accumulator in Fig. 6-28 after the load operation are 11100011.

6.37 Refer to Fig. 6-21. The load operation shown in Fig. 6-28 uses _____ (direct, immediate) addressing.

Solution:

Based on information from the table in Fig. 6-21, the load operation shown in Fig. 6-28 uses immediate addressing.

6.38 Refer to Fig. 6-21. The MOV *A,M* instruction has an op code of 7EH, it uses _____ (direct, register indirect) addressing, and the source of data is a _____ (data, program) memory location pointed to by the *HL* register pair.

Solution:

Based on information from Fig. 6-21, the MOV *A,M* instruction has an op code of 7EH, it uses register indirect addressing, and the source of data is a data memory location pointed to by the *HL* register pair.

6.39 Refer to Fig. 6-21. The SHLD instruction has an op code of 22H and uses _____ (direct, immediate) addressing.

Solution:

Based on information from Fig. 6-21, the SHLD instruction has an op code of 22H and uses direct addressing.

6.40 Refer to Fig. 6-21. The "store *HL* direct" instruction (op code = 22H) is a _____ (number) -byte instruction. The last 2 bytes of the program instruction contain _____ (data, address) information.

Solution:

Based on information from Fig. 6-21, the "store *HL* direct" instruction (op code = 22H) is a 3-byte instruction. The last 2 bytes of the program instruction contain address information.

6.41 Refer to Fig. 6-21. The source of data when using the OUT instruction in Fig. 6-29 is the _____ (*A*, *H*, *L*) register.

Solution:

According to Fig. 6-21, the source of data when using the OUT instruction in Fig. 6-29 is the *A* register, which is also called the accumulator.

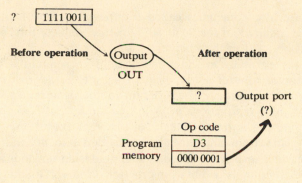

Fig. 6-29

6.42 After the output operation in Fig. 6-29, output port number _____ (hex) will contain the data _____ (8 bits).

   Solution:

   After the output operation in Fig. 6-29, output port number 01H will contain the data 11110011. The address for the output port came from the second byte of program memory.

6.6 INSTRUCTION SET—BRANCH OPERATIONS

The *branch instructions* are the fourth category of the generic microprocessor's operations to be considered. These are summarized in Fig. 6-30. Note that the description of the operations refer to these as *jump instructions*. The terms *jump* and *branch* will be considered synonymous in this chapter. Some manufacturers make a distinction between jump and branch instructions. Branch

Branch instructions

Description of operations	Addressing mode	Mnemonic	Op code	Bytes	Instruction format	Symbolic	Flags affected
Jump to LOC *aa*	Immediate	JMP	C3	3	Op code / Low-order address / High-order address	$(PC) \leftarrow$ (address)	
Jump to LOC *aa* if zero	Immediate	JZ	CA	3	Op code / Low-order address / High-order address	If zero flag = 1, then $(PC) \leftarrow$ (address)	
Jump to LOC *aa* if not zero	Immediate	JNZ	C2	3	Op code / Low-order address / High-order address	If zero flag = 0, then $(PC) \leftarrow$ (address)	
Jump to LOC *aa* if carry set	Immediate	JC	DA	3	Op code / Low-order address / High-order address	If carry flag = 1, then $(PC) \leftarrow$ (address)	
Jump to LOC *aa* if carry not set	Immediate	JNC	D2	3	Op code / Low-order address / High-order address	If carry flag = 0, then $(PC) \leftarrow$ (address)	

( ) = contents of
PC = program counter

Fig. 6-30 Branch instructions for the generic microprocessor (subset of Intel 8080/8085 instructions)

or jump operations are also sometimes called *transfer-of-control instructions*. Because the operations in Fig. 6-30 are a subset of the 8080/8085 instruction set, Intel's convention of calling these jump instructions will be used in this chapter.

The microcomputer normally executes instructions in sequential order. The generic microprocessor's 16-bit program counter always keeps track of the address of the next instruction to be fetched from memory and executed. The program counter is normally sequenced upward one count at a time. Branch or jump instructions provide one method of changing the value in the program counter, thereby altering the normal sequence of program execution.

Branch or jump instructions are typically subdivided into *unconditional jump* and *conditional jump operations*. The first instruction listed in Fig. 6-30 is an unconditional jump instruction. The "jump immediate" instruction is a 3-byte instruction used for loading a specific address into the program counter of the CPU. A sample problem using this unconditional jump instruction is shown in Fig. 6-31. Here the address 2000H is being loaded into the program counter. The address information immediately follows the op code and therefore is called immediate addressing. Note in Fig. 6-31 that the low-order part of the 16-bit address is located in the second byte in program memory, whereas the third byte holds the high-order part of the address. An instruction of this type would be used for initially setting the program counter when starting to run a new program. The unconditional branch or jump instruction can be thought of as a method of loading new address information into the program counter.

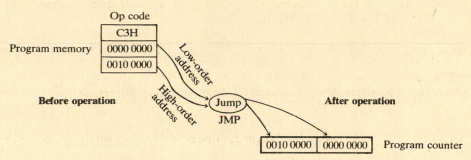

Fig. 6-31   The unconditional jump instruction

The last four branch operations detailed in Fig. 6-30 are conditional jump instructions. These instructions will cause the immediate address to be placed in the program counter *only if the condition specified is satisfied*. Otherwise the program counter will simply sequence upward. A sample problem using the "jump if zero" instruction is diagramed in Fig. 6-32. In this example, the program counter is at 2013H before the operation and will continue to sequence upward from here unless the zero flag is set to 1. The CPU evaluates the condition of the zero flag in the status

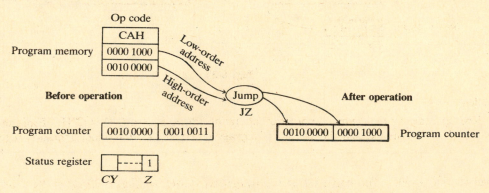

Fig. 6-32   The jump if zero instruction

register and finds it set to 1. This means that the last arithmetic or logic operation's result was a zero. The conditions are right for a jump, and the MPU loads the program counter with the new address of 2008H. The new address comes from program memory. Therefore this instruction is said to use immediate addressing. The next instruction to be executed will be the instruction at memory location 2008H and not 2013H as might have been expected. The generic microprocessor jumped to a new location in program memory. Jumps or branches can be made upward or downward in program memory. The example in Fig. 6-32 illustrates a downward jump, which is probably the most common.

Branch or jump instructions are found in almost every microprocessor program. They are valuable because of their decision-making characteristic. Branch or jump instructions are used to form program loops and branches. Looping and branching are two programming techniques you will study later in this chapter.

SOLVED PROBLEMS

6.43 Branch instructions are also referred to as _____ (leap, jump) or _____-of-control operations.

Solution:

Branch instructions are also referred to as jump or transfer-of-control operations.

6.44 It is said that _____ (logical, conditional jump) operations are decision-making instructions.

Solution:

Conditional jump operations are said to be decision-making instructions.

6.45 Refer to Fig. 6-30. The assembly language mnemonic for the jump operation diagramed in Fig. 6-33 is _____.

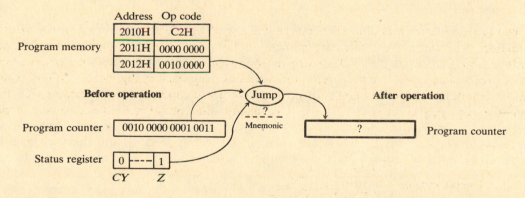

Fig. 6-33

Solution:

The op code for the "jump if not zero" operation shown in Fig. 6-33 is C2H. From the table in Fig. 6-30 it is determined that the assembly language mnemonic for this jump operation is JNZ.

6.46 Refer to Fig. 6-30. The contents of the program counter in Fig. 6-33 after the "jump if not zero" operation are _____ (hex).

Solution:

The zero flag in the status register in Fig. 6-33 is set to 1, which means that the last arithmetic or logical operation resulted in zero. The condition for a jump is *not satisfied*. The address in the second and third bytes of program memory are not loaded into the program counter. The contents of the program counter remain at 2013H, as they were before the conditional jump instruction. The next instruction to be executed is located at 2013H.

6.47 Refer to Fig. 6-30. The mnemonic for the "jump if carry" instruction in Fig. 6-34 is JC, whereas the op code is _____ (hex).

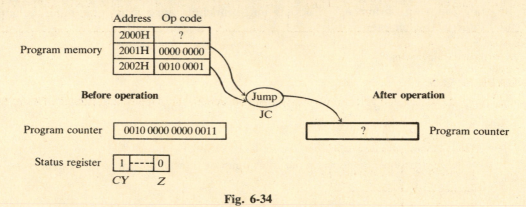

Fig. 6-34

Solution:

The mnemonic for the "jump if carry" instruction in Fig. 6-34 is JC, whereas the table in Fig. 6-30 indicates that the op code for this instruction is DAH.

6.48 The contents of the program counter after the jump operation in Fig. 6-34 will be _____ (hex).

Solution:

The carry flag is set to 1, and therefore the condition for the jump operation is satisfied. The MPU loads the new address 2100H into the program counter. The next instruction to be executed is located at 2100H in program memory.

6.7 INSTRUCTION SET—SUBROUTINE CALL AND RETURN OPERATIONS

The *subroutine call and return instructions* are the fifth category of the generic microprocessor's operations to be considered. These are summarized in Fig. 6-35. Note that the generic microprocessor has only two instructions in this group. The call and return instructions are always used in pairs.

The 3-byte call instruction is used within the main program to cause the microprocessor to jump to a subroutine. In the example shown in Fig. 6-36, the subroutine is a short group of instructions which cause a time delay of 1 s. When the MPU encounters the first call instruction at location 200DH, it finds the address for the jump in the next 2 program bytes. The address of the instruction following the call is saved in the stack (not shown in Fig. 6-36). The MPU then jumps to the start of the subroutine at location 1000H. The instructions in the 1-s time delay subroutine are performed until the CPU encounters the return instruction. The address saved in the stack (2010H) is returned to the program counter, and the MPU continues the main program where it left off when the subroutine was first called. The MPU executes the instructions in order until it encounters the second call instruction at address 2020H. The MPU saves the address of the next instruction (2023H) in the stack and jumps to the subroutine at address 1000H. Upon completing the time

Subroutine call and return instructions

Description of operation	Addressing mode	Mnemonic	Op code	Bytes	Instruction format	Symbolic	Flags affected
Call subroutine at LOC *aa*	Immediate/ register indirect	CALL	CD	3	Op code / Low-order address / High-order address	$((SP)-1) \leftarrow (PCH)$ $((SP)-2) \leftarrow (PCL)$ $(SP) \leftarrow (SP)-2$ $(PC) \leftarrow (address)$	
Return from subroutine	Register indirect	RET	C9	1	Op code	$(PCL) \leftarrow ((SP))$ $(PCH) \leftarrow ((SP)+1)$ $(SP) \leftarrow (SP)+2$	

( ) = contents of
(( )) = register indirect addressing
PC = program counter
SP = stack pointer

Fig. 6-35 Subroutine call and return instructions for the generic microprocessor (subset of Intel 8080/8085 instructions)

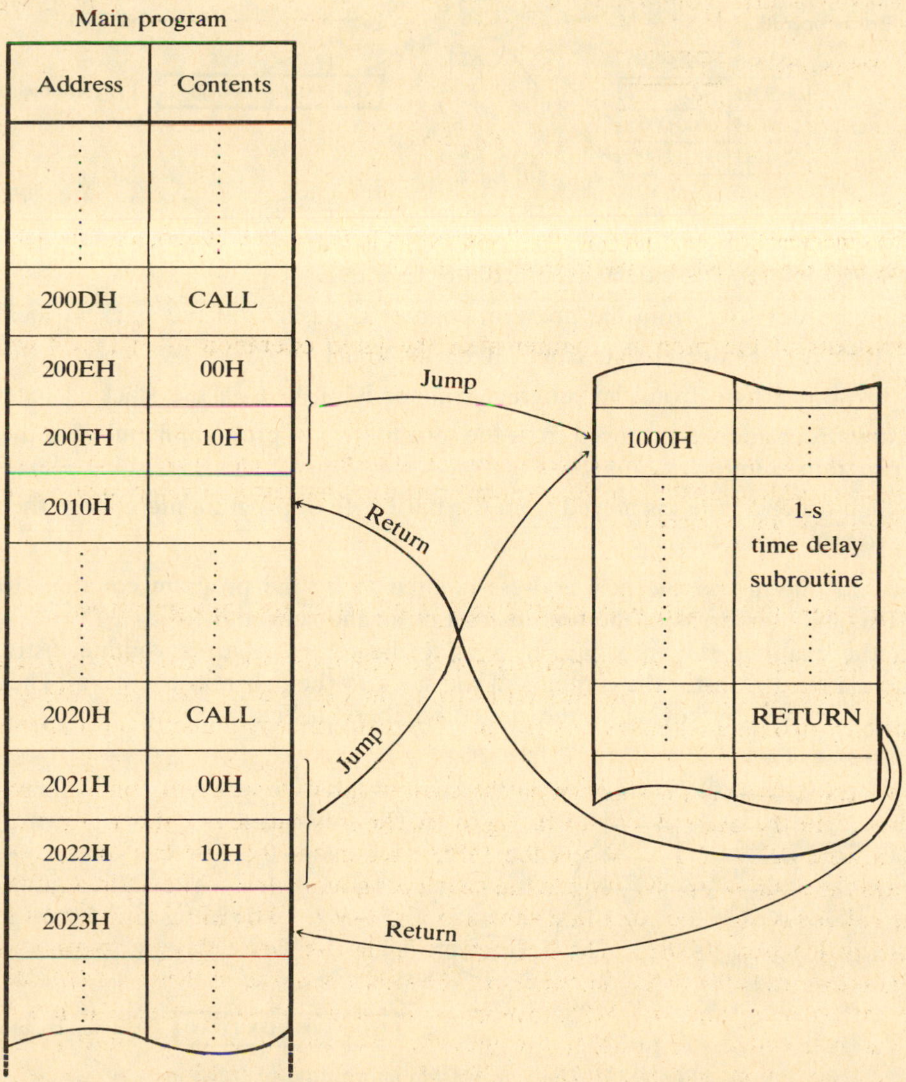

Fig. 6-36 Program flow from main program to subroutine and back using call and return instructions

delay subroutine again, the return instruction pops the address of the next main program instruction (2023H) off the stack and transfers it to the program counter. A subroutine may be used many times in the execution of a main program. The subroutine may be stored in RAM or ROM.

The *call instruction combines the functions of the push and jump operations*. Figure 6-37 details the use of the call instruction. It first pushes the current contents of the program counter on the stack. Secondly, the program counter must be loaded with a new address to perform the jump to subroutine operation. The sequence of actions may be followed by keying on the circled numbers in Fig. 6-37.

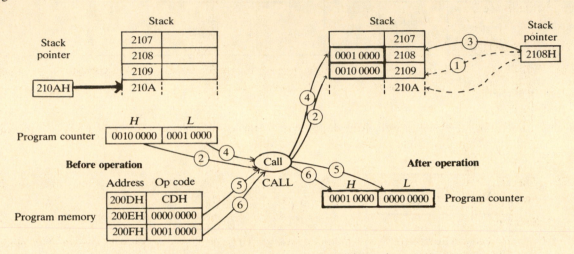

Fig. 6-37 The subroutine call instruction

1. The stack pointer decrements from 210AH to 2109H.
2. The high-order byte from the program counter is pushed on the stack at location 2109H.
3. The stack pointer decrements from 2109H to 2108H.
4. The low-order byte from the program counter is pushed on the stack at location 2108H.
5. The low-order address is moved from the second byte of program memory to the low byte of the program counter.
6. The high-order address is moved from the third byte of program memory to the high byte of the program counter.

The MPU would now go to the new address pointed to by the program counter (1000H in this example). This is the address of the first instruction in the subroutine.

Consider the example shown in Fig. 6-38 using the return from subroutine instruction. The return instruction must transfer the contents of the stack to the program counter. The sequence of actions may be followed by keying on the circled numbers in Fig. 6-38.

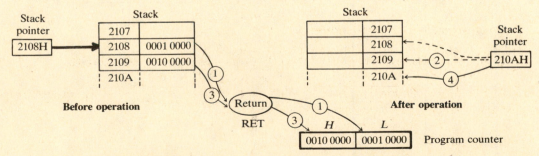

Fig. 6-38 The return from subroutine instruction

1. The top of the stack (location 2108H) is popped, with the contents being transferred to the low byte of the program counter.

2. The stack pointer is incremented from 2108H to 2109H.

3. The top of the stack (now location 2109H) is popped, with the contents being transferred to the high byte of the program counter.

4. The stack pointer is incremented from 2109H to 210AH.

The program counter now holds the 16-bit address (2010H) of the next instruction to be fetched from the program memory.

SOLVED PROBLEMS

6.49 The _____ (call, return) instruction is part of the main program, whereas the _____ (call, return) instruction comes at the end of a subroutine.

Solution:

See Fig. 6-36. The call instruction is part of the main program, whereas the return instruction comes at the end of a subroutine.

6.50 The call is a _____ (number) -byte instruction. The last 2 bytes contain the address of the first instruction in _____ (main memory, a subroutine).

Solution:

The call is a 3-byte instruction, based on the table in Fig. 6-35. The last 2 bytes contain the address of the first instruction in a subroutine.

6.51 The call operation performs the functions of both the _____ (pop, push) and the _____ (add, jump) instructions.

Solution:

The call operation performs the functions of both the push and the jump instructions.

6.52 Refer to Fig. 6-39. The contents of stack location 2109H after the call operation will be _____ (8 bits).

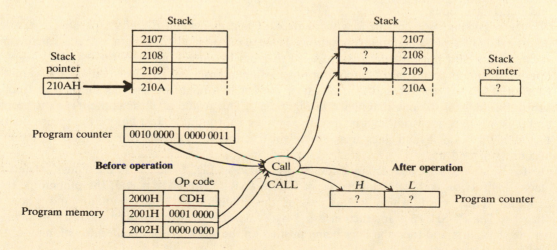

Fig. 6-39

Solution:

The contents of stack location 2109H in Fig. 6-39 after the call operation will be 00100000. The high-order byte of the program counter will be stored in the stack first, according to the table in Fig. 6-35 and the diagram in Fig. 6-37.

6.53 Refer to Fig. 6-39. The contents of stack location 2108H after the call operation will be
_____ (8 bits).

Solution:

The contents of stack location 2108H in Fig. 6-39 after the call operation will be 00000011. The low-order byte of the PC will be stored in the stack second.

6.54 Refer to Fig. 6-39. The stack pointer will contain _____ (hex) after the call operation.

Solution:

After the call operation in Fig. 6-39, the stack pointer will point at the top of the stack, which will be location 2108H.

6.55 Refer to Fig. 6-39. The contents of the program counter after the call operation will be
_____ (hex).

Solution:

The contents of the program counter after the call operation in Fig. 6-39 will be 0010H. This is the address of the first instruction in the subroutine.

6.56 Subroutine call and return instructions are almost always used _____ (in pairs, singly).

Solution:

Subroutine call and return instructions are almost always used in pairs.

6.8   INSTRUCTION SET—MISCELLANEOUS OPERATIONS

The *miscellaneous instructions* are the last category of the generic microprocessor's operations to be considered. These are summarized in Fig. 6-40. These include the push, pop, no operation, and halt instructions.

The push and pop instructions were used in Sec. 5.6 when the stack pointer and stack were discussed. The push and pop operations place data on and take data off the microcomputer's stack. Push and pop instructions are used in pairs because what goes on the stack using a push operation should be taken off with a pop instruction. Push and pop instructions are widely used in subroutines. A "push A and flags on stack" instruction might be used as the first instruction in a subroutine such as the one diagramed in Fig. 6-36. This would save the contents of the accumulator and flags so that they would not be disturbed by the subroutine. Just before the return operation in Fig. 6-36, a "pop A and flags from stack" instruction would restore the original contents of the accumulator and flags.

Consider the first instruction listed on the table in Fig. 6-40. It is the "push A and flags on stack" instruction and has a mnemonic of PUSH *PSW*. The *PSW* part of the mnemonic stands for *p*rogram *s*tatus *w*ord, which in this case is the contents of the accumulator and status register (flags). The PUSH *PSW* instruction is a 1-byte instruction, with the accumulator (A) being placed on the stack first and then the flags being pushed on the stack. For detailed functioning of the push and pop instructions, review Sec. 5.6.

The "no operation" instruction does nothing except consume 1 or 2 μs. It is a 1-byte instruction which causes only the program counter to be incremented. No other registers are

Miscellaneous instructions

Description of operation	Addressing mode	Mnemonic	Op code	Bytes	Instruction format	Symbolic	Flags affected
Push A and flags on stack	Register indirect	PUSH *PSW*	F5	1	Op code	$((SP)-1) \leftarrow (A)$ $((SP)-2) \leftarrow (\text{flags})$ $(SP) \leftarrow (SP)-2$	
Push *HL* on stack	Register indirect	PUSH *H*	E5	1	Op code	$((SP)-1) \leftarrow (H)$ $((SP)-2) \leftarrow (L)$ $(SP) \leftarrow (SP)-2$	
Pop A and flags from stack	Register indirect	POP *PSW*	F1	1	Op code	$(\text{Flags}) \leftarrow ((SP))$ $(A) \leftarrow ((SP)+1)$ $(SP) \leftarrow (SP)+2$	
Pop *HL* from stack	Register indirect	POP *H*	E1	1	Op code	$(L) \leftarrow ((SP))$ $(H) \leftarrow ((SP)+1)$ $(SP) \leftarrow (SP)+2$	
No operation	Inherent	NOP	00	1	Op code	$(PC) \leftarrow (PC)+1$	
Halt	Inherent	HLT	76	1	Op code		

( ) = contents of
(( )) = register indirect addressing
A = accumulator
SP = stack pointer

Fig. 6-40 Miscellaneous instructions for the generic microprocessor (subset of Intel 8080/8085 instructions)

affected.   The no operation instruction is used as a filler when a program statement or two are removed during debugging.   The no operation instructions then bridge between the two sections of the program so that the MPU can advance from one segment to the other.   The no operation instruction can also be used to consume time in a timing loop.

The halt instruction is used at the end of a program to stop the microprocessor from progressing through more "instructions" in program memory.   Only a reset or interrupt request input to the MPU can start the generic microprocessor when the microprocessor is in the halt mode.

SOLVED PROBLEMS

6.57   Refer to Fig. 6-40.   The PUSH *PSW* operation being used in Fig. 6-41 has an op code of
_____ (hex).

Solution:
According to the table in Fig. 6-40, the PUSH *PSW* operation has an op code of F5H.

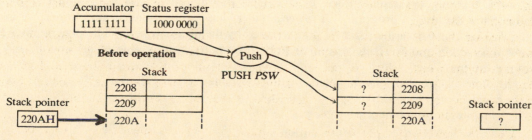

Fig. 6-41

6.58   Refer to Fig. 6-40. During the execution of the PUSH *PSW* instruction used in Fig. 6-41, the stack pointer is first _____ (decremented, incremented) and the contents of the _____ (accumulator, status register) are transferred to stack location _____ (hex).

Solution:

Use the table in Fig. 6-40 and the procedure from Fig. 5-16*b*. During the execution of the PUSH *PSW* instruction used in Fig. 6-41, the stack pointer is first decremented and the contents of the accumulator are transferred to stack location 2209H.

6.59   Refer to Fig. 6-40. List the contents of the stack pointer and stack locations 2208H and 2209H after the push operation diagramed in Fig. 6-41.

Solution:

Use the table in Fig. 6-40 and the procedure from Fig. 5-16*b* as references. After the push operation shown in Fig. 6-41, the stack pointer will point at location 2208H and will hold the contents of the status register, which are 10000000. Stack location 2209H will hold the contents of the accumulator, which are 11111111.

6.60   Refer to Fig. 6-40. If the PUSH *PSW* instruction is used to place the contents of CPU registers on the stack, then the _____ (mnemonic) instruction would be used to restore the contents of these registers.

Solution:

If the PUSH *PSW* instruction is used to place the contents of CPU registers on the stack, then the POP *PSW* instruction would be used to restore the contents of these registers.

6.61   Push and pop instructions are frequently used in pairs in _____ (resets, subroutines).

Solution:

Push and pop instructions are frequently used in pairs in subroutines.

6.62   The _____ (halt, no operation) instruction will stop the microprocessor from fetching and executing another instruction until it receives an external reset or interrupt request signal.

Solution:

The halt instruction will stop the microprocessor from fetching and executing another instruction until it receives an external reset or interrupt request signal. The halt instruction is typically placed at the end of a program.

6.9   WRITING A PROGRAM

The programmer of a microprocessor-based system must be very familiar with the instruction set. The tables in Figs. 6-4, 6-14, 6-21, 6-30, 6-35, and 6-40 detail the operations that can be performed by the generic microprocessor. The programmer must also be familiar with the registers available when writing a program. A *programming model* of the generic microprocessor is shown in Fig. 6-3. It summarizes the registers that are used by the programmer. The programmer must also be aware of the general architecture of the microcomputer and be able to understand the memory map for the unit.

The steps in program development might be summarized as follows:

1. Define and analyze the problem.
2. Draw flowchart of problem solution.

3. Write assembly language program.
4. Write or generate machine language version of program.
5. Debug the program.
6. Document the program.

Consider the simple task of writing a program for adding the contents of three consecutive memory locations and storing the sum. It is common for programmers to construct a *flowchart* or *flow diagram* of the problem. A functional flowchart for the sample problem is shown in Fig. 6-42a. The *functional flowchart* shows the general procedure of adding three numbers together and

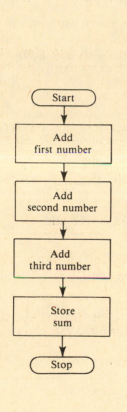

(a) Functional flowchart for adding three numbers

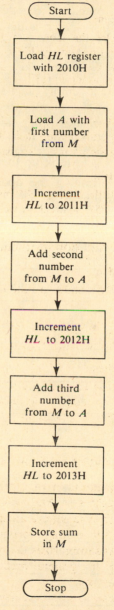

(b) Detailed flowchart

Fig. 6-42

storing the sum in memory. This flowchart lacks adequate detail for translating directly into an assembly language or machine language program segment.

A *detailed flowchart* was developed and is diagramed in Fig. 6-42*b*. In this flowchart each rectangular block corresponds to a command or microprocessor operation. The detailed flowchart is therefore dependent on the specific microprocessor system being programmed, whereas the functional flowchart could be used with any MPU.

Next, an assembly language version of the detailed flowchart is developed. Such an assembly language program segment is shown in Fig. 6-43*a*. The four typical fields—label, mnemonic, operand, and comment—are listed across the top. Carefully copied below are the *exact* mnemonics and operands for the microprocessor. Recall that the label field does not require entries. The comments are a great help in understanding the function of each instruction in the program segment. Comparing the detailed flowchart in Fig. 6-42*b* with the assembly language program listing in Fig. 6-43*a*, it is determined that each block on the flowchart has an equivalent assembly language statement. Take as an example the first rectangular block in Fig. 6-42*b*. The "load *HL* register with 2010H" in this block is equivalent to the assembly language statement "LXI *H*,2010H; Load *HL* register pair with address 2010H" from Fig. 6-43*a*.

After the assembly language version is written, the program must be translated into bit patterns understood by the microprocessor or into what is called machine code. This can be done by hand or by special computer programs called assemblers. Manual coding is done by:

1. Using the instruction set tables (Figs. 6-4, 6-14, 6-21, 6-30, 6-35, and 6-40 for the generic MPU) to look up the op codes for each mnemonic

2. Determining the operands (either data or addresses) when required by a multibyte instruction

3. Assigning sequential program memory addresses to each instruction and operand

Label	Mnemonic	Operand	Comments
	LXI	*H*,2010H	; Load *HL* register pair with address 2010H (will be used as address pointer)
	MOV	*A,M*	; Load accumulator with first number from memory location 2010H
	INX	*H*	; Increment *HL* register pair to 2011H
	ADD	*M*	; Add second number from memory location 2011H to accumulator
	INX	*H*	; Increment *HL* register pair to 2012H
	ADD	*M*	; Add third number from memory location 2012H to accumulator
	INX	*H*	; Increment *HL* register pair to 2013H
	MOV	*M,A*	; Store sum from accumulator in memory location 2013H
	HLT		; Stop MPU

(*a*)   Assembly language program for adding three numbers and storing the sum

Fig. 6-43

Address (hex)	Contents (hex)	Label	Mnemonic	Operand	Comments
2020	21		LXI	H,2010H	; Load *HL* register pair with address 2010H (will be used as address pointer)
2021	10				
2022	20				
2023	7E		MOV	A,M	; Load accumulator with first number from memory location 2010H
2024	23		INX	H	; Increment *HL* register pair to 2011H
2025	86		ADD	M	; Add second number from memory location 2011H to accumulator
2026	23		INX	H	; Increment *HL* register pair to 2012H
2027	86		ADD	M	; Add third number from memory location 2012H to accumulator
2028	23		INX	H	; Increment *HL* register pair to 2013H
2029	77		MOV	M,A	; Store sum from accumulator in memory location 2013H
202A	76		HLT		; Stop MPU

(b) Combined machine and assembly language program

Fig. 6-43 (*cont.*)

Consider our sample problem that added the contents of three consecutive memory locations and stored the sum in the fourth location.   The assembly language version is reproduced at the right in Fig. 6-43*b*.   The two left columns show the program memory addresses assigned and the hexadecimal op code or operand.   The contents represent the 8-bit words that would be stored in program memory.

Consider the first assembly language statement in Fig. 6-43*b*.   The mnemonic and operand read "LXI *H*,2010H," which must be assigned an op code and in this case two operands.   The table in Fig. 6-21 contains the needed information on this type of operation (data transfer instruction).   The "LXI *H*" mnemonic is found about halfway down the table in Fig. 6-21, and its op code is 21H.   This is written in the "Contents" column in Fig. 6-43*b*.   It is noted from the table in Fig. 6-21 that this instruction required 2 extra bytes of data.   The low-order data byte (10H in this example) is listed first at address 2021H.   The high-order data byte (20H in this example) is listed next at address 2022H.   The remainder of the assembly language mnemonics in Fig. 6-43*b* represent single-byte instructions.   The hexadecimal op codes are looked up on the appropriate instruction set table and recorded in the "Contents" column, as shown in Fig. 6-43*b*.   The program in the left columns is in machine code and can be entered into the microprocessor system.

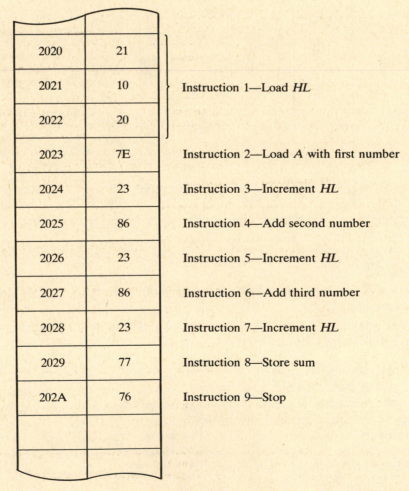

Data memory

Address (hex)	Contents (hex)	
2010	0F	
2011	09	
2012	06	
2013		←Sum

Program memory

2020	21	Instruction 1—Load *HL*
2021	10	
2022	20	
2023	7E	Instruction 2—Load *A* with first number
2024	23	Instruction 3—Increment *HL*
2025	86	Instruction 4—Add second number
2026	23	Instruction 5—Increment *HL*
2027	86	Instruction 6—Add third number
2028	23	Instruction 7—Increment *HL*
2029	77	Instruction 8—Store sum
202A	76	Instruction 9—Stop

Fig. 6-44 Memory contents and instructions for adding three numbers and storing the sum

The program is next tested for proper operation. This is called *debugging* (taking out the errors or "bugs"). The commonsense procedures used include comparing the flowchart and program, double-checking op codes, and stepping through the program at the desk with a simulated problem. Next it is common to enter the program and known data in a microprocessor system and check the answers. Several test problems are usually run.

The last step in programming is documentation. Documentation is a description of the program telling how the program should perform and how to use it and including details such as flowcharts, program listings, program and data addresses used, and comments. Documentation becomes much more complicated on large programs. Larger programs require levels of documentation such as design documents, operator manuals, and descriptive documents.

Consider the sample problem being performed by our program segment in Fig. 6-44. Here the machine code has been entered into program memory (addresses 2020–202AH). The numbers to be added (0F, 09, 06H) in our sample problem are entered in data memory locations 2010 through 2012H. See if you can follow the step-by-step operation of this program as it adds $0F + 09 + 06$, yielding a sum of 1EH. This program can actually be run on most 8080/8085-based microprocessor trainers.

Although real microcomputer programs are quite lengthy, they consist of a group of program segments similar to the example. Typically, each segment is written and tested before the entire program is put together for final testing. The sample program segment developed is only one possible way to solve the problem posed. The program that was developed is called a straight-line program in that there are no branches or jumps.

SOLVED PROBLEMS

6.63 The microprocessor system programmer must be familiar with the system architecture, MPU instruction set, system memory map, and registers in the CPU. A summary of the MPU registers available to the programmer is given in a diagram called the programming _____ (model, set).

Solution:

A summary of the MPU registers available to the programmer is given in a diagram called the programming model.

6.64 List six sequential steps in the development of a microprocessor-based system program as suggested by this section.

Solution:

The six sequential steps in program development listed in this section were define and analyze the problem, draw flowchart of problem solution, write assembly language version of program, write or generate machine language version of program, debug the program, and document the program.

6.65 A graphic representation of a problem's solution is called a _____.

Solution:

A graphic representation of a problem's solution is called a flowchart or flow diagram. Two examples are shown in Fig. 6-42.

6.66 After drawing a detailed flowchart (such as the one shown in Fig. 6-42*b*), the next programming step is to write a(n) _____ (assembly, machine) language program.

Solution:

An assembly language program is typically written after drawing a detailed flowchart.

6.67 In writing a machine language version of a program, instructions are assigned sequential program memory _____ (addresses, interrupts).

Solution:

In writing a machine language version of a program, instructions are assigned sequential program memory addresses.

6.68 In writing a machine language version of a program, the _____ (ASCII, op codes) and operands are listed in _____ (decimal, hexadecimal) form for each program location.

Solution:

In writing a machine language version of a program, the op codes and operands are listed in hexadecimal form for each program location.

6.69 What are the contents of the *HL* register pair after the execution of instruction 1 in Fig. 6-44?

Solution:

Refer to Fig. 6-43.   The contents of the *HL* register pair are 2010H after execution of instruction 1 in Fig. 6-44.

6.70 What are the contents of the accumulator after the execution of instruction 4 in Fig. 6-44?

Solution:

Adding 0F + 09 = 18H.   The contents of the accumulator after the execution of instruction 4 in Fig. 6-44 are 18H.

6.71 What are the contents of the accumulator after the execution of instruction 6 in Fig. 6-44?

Solution:

Adding 0F + 09 + 06 = 1EH.   The contents of the accumulator after the execution of instruction 6 in Fig. 6-44 are 1EH.

6.72 What are the contents of data memory location 2013H after the execution of instruction 7 in Fig. 6-44?

Solution:

The sum has *not* yet been stored in data memory location 2013H, and therefore its contents are some random bit pattern.

6.73 What are the contents of data memory location 2013H after the execution of instruction 8 in Fig. 6-44?

Solution:

The sum of 0F + 09 + 06 = 1EH is stored in data memory location 2013H after the execution of instruction 8 in Fig. 6-44.

6.74 Finding and correcting errors in a program is a process commonly called _____ (debugging, failure logging).

Solution:

Finding and correcting errors in a program is a process commonly called debugging.

6.75 The final step in writing a program is referred to as _____.

Solution:

The final step in writing a program is referred to as documentation. This might include several levels such as design documentation, an operator's manual, and descriptive documentation.

6.10 ADDRESSING MODES

Consider the microprocessor instruction to add. In the generic microprocessor it was assumed that one of the numbers to be added was located in the accumulator. However, where does the second number come from and how is the number retrieved? The many *retrieval methods* are called the *addressing modes* of the microprocessor. Each microprocessor has its own retrieval methods, or addressing modes. These must be well understood by the programmer. Addressing modes have been mentioned many times in previous sections. But because many students have difficulty with addressing modes, this section will review those used by the generic microprocessor.

The addressing modes listed in the generic microprocessor's instruction set are:

1. Inherent
2. Register
3. Immediate
4. Direct
5. Register indirect

The first two addressing modes on the list (inherent and register) deal with operands that are located within the CPU itself. The last three addressing modes (immediate, direct, and register indirect) deal with operands that are located outside the CPU in memory locations or I/O ports. These are the same addressing modes used by the Intel 8080/8085 microprocessor.

Consider an example of an *inherent instruction*. The "set carry flag" from the data transfer group in Fig. 6-21 is one such instruction. Inherent instructions such as the "set carry flag" instruction are always 1-byte instructions because further data is not required to complete the operation. All actions occur within the CPU. The action of the generic microprocessor's "set carry flag" instruction is diagrammed in Fig. 6-45a. No data or addresses need be retrieved from other CPU registers, memory locations, or I/O ports. The STC instruction sets the carry flag (*CY*) to 1 without affecting other registers or flags.

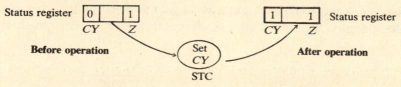

(*a*) The set carry flag instruction (inherent addressing)

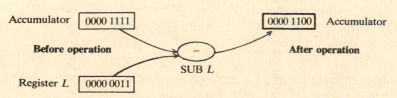

(*b*) The subtract *L* from *A* instruction (register addressing)

Fig. 6-45

In *register instructions*, the operand is retrieved from an internal CPU register. Consider the example of a register instruction. The "subtract *L* from *A*" operation from the arithmetic group in Fig. 6-4 is one such instruction. Register operations (like inherent instructions) are always 1-byte instructions because further data or addresses from outside the CPU are not required. All actions occur within the CPU. The action of the "subtract *L* from *A*" instruction is detailed in Fig. 6-45*b*. The minuend (00001111 in this example) is held in the accumulator, while the subtrahend (00000011 in this example) is contained in register *L*. After the internal subtract operation, the difference (00001100 in this example) is transferred to the accumulator.

In *immediate instructions*, the operand comes from the next byte (or sometimes the next 2 bytes) in *program memory*. The operand follows *immediately after* the op code in the instruction. Consider the example of an immediate instruction. The "load *SP* with data" from the data transfer group in Fig. 6-21 is one such instruction. From the table in Fig. 6-21 it is determined that this is a 3-byte instruction. Generally, immediate operations are specified with either 2- or 3-byte instructions. The example in Fig. 6-46 shows 2 bytes of data being retrieved from program memory and loaded into the stack pointer (*SP*). The low-order byte (01110000 in this example) is loaded first, and then the high-order byte (00000010 in this example) is loaded. Immediate mode instructions are convenient for loading initial values into CPU registers or the stack pointer.

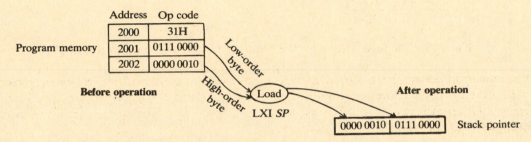

Fig. 6-46   The load stack pointer instruction (immediate addressing)

In *direct instructions*, the second and third bytes in program memory *point directly to the address* of the operand in data memory. The second and third bytes in program memory are addresses in a direct instruction, whereas they were operands in immediate addressing. Consider the example of a direct instruction. The "input to *A* from port at LOC *a*" operation from the data transfer group in Fig. 6-21 is one such instruction. From the table in Fig. 6-21 it is determined that this is a 2-byte instruction. Generally, direct operations are specified with either 2- or 3-byte instructions. The example in Fig. 6-47 shows the input port contents (11000011 in this example) being transferred to the microprocessor's accumulator. The exact input port is being pointed to by the address in the second byte of the program instruction (this address is 00001010, or 10_{10}, in this example).

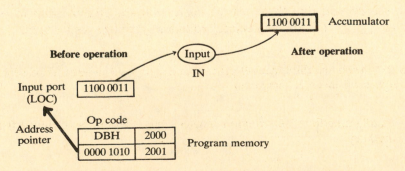

Fig. 6-47   The input instruction (direct addressing)

In *register indirect instructions*, the special *HL* register pair *points to the address* of the operand in data memory.   Consider the example of a register indirect instruction.   The "load LOC (*H* & *L*) to *A*" (mnemonic of MOV *A*,*M*) from the data transfer group in Fig. 6-21 is one such instruction.   From the table in Fig. 6-21 it is determined that this is a 1-byte instruction.   Register indirect operations are always specified by 1-byte instructions.   The example in Fig. 6-48 shows the contents of memory location 2080H (11110000 in this example) being loaded into the accumulator.   The address (2080H in this example) of the correct data memory location is pointed to by the contents of the *HL* register pair.   The *HL* register pair is called the data/address register in the generic microprocessor.   In this case the *HL* register pair is being used as an address register.

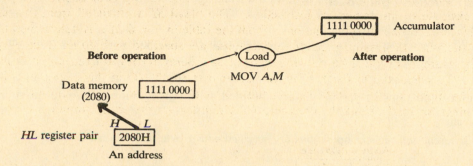

Fig. 6-48   The load *A* from memory instruction (register indirect addressing)

Other microprocessors have variations of the direct addressing mode called by such names as zero page or base page addressing, absolute addressing, present page addressing, and extended addressing.   Other modes not used by our generic microprocessor include the very popular indexed addressing and also program relative addressing.

SOLVED PROBLEMS

6.76   List the five addressing modes used by the generic microprocessor.

Solution:

The five addressing modes used by the generic microprocessor are inherent, register, immediate, direct, and register indirect.   These addressing modes are also used in the 8080/8085 microprocessor.

6.77   When using a(n) _____ (direct, inherent) instruction, no operand retrieval is required.

Solution:

When using an inherent instruction, no operand retrieval is required.

6.78   When the second and third bytes of the instruction are used to point to the address of the operand, the _____ (direct, immediate) addressing mode is being used.

Solution:

When the second and third bytes of the instruction are used to point to the address of the operand, the direct addressing mode is being used.

6.79   When an "add immediate" instruction is used, the operand is retrieved from _____ (data, program) memory.

Solution:

When an "add immediate" instruction is used, the operand is retrieved from program memory.

6.80 When a _____ (register, register indirect) instruction is used, the *HL* register pair in the CPU points to the address of the operand.

Solution:

When a register indirect instruction is used, the *HL* register pair in the CPU points to the address of the operand.

6.81 When both operands (such as the minuend and subtrahend in a subtraction problem) are located in internal CPU registers, the _____ (immediate, register) addressing mode can be used for retrieving the operands.

Solution:

When both operands are located in internal registers, the register addressing mode can be used for retrieving the operands.

6.82 Inherent and register operations are specified with _____ (number) -byte instructions.

Solution:

Inherent and register operations are specified with 1-byte instructions.

6.83 Operations using the direct addressing mode are specified with _____ (number) -byte instructions.

Solution:

Operations using the direct addressing mode are specified with 2- or 3-byte instructions.

6.84 Operations using the register indirect addressing mode are specified with _____ (number) -byte instructions.

Solution:

Operations using the register indirect addressing mode are specified with 1-byte instructions.

6.11 PROGRAM BRANCHING

Consider the simple task of deciding which of two numbers is larger and storing the larger in a specific memory location. A flowchart for solving this problem is drawn in Fig. 6-49a. Starting from the top of the flowchart, the first two rectangles represent the loading of the two numbers into the *A* (accumulator) and *L* (data) registers. The next rectangle represents the compare operation, where the contents of register *L* are subtracted from the contents of register *A*. Compare operations do not affect register contents but do affect the flags. The next diamond-shaped box in the flowchart is called a *decision symbol*. This symbolizes the decision point within the program. A question is always asked within this decision symbol. In this example the decision symbol poses the question: Is $(A) \geq (L)$? If the answer to this question is yes, the program continues downward and the contents of the *A* register are stored in memory, and then the processor is halted by the stop symbol. If, however, the answer to the question in the decision symbol is no, the program branches to the right and the contents of the *L* register are stored in memory, and then the processor is halted. The use of decision symbols in a flowchart leads to what is called branching within a program.

The assembly language version of the program to compare two numbers and place the value of the larger one in memory location 2040H is detailed in Fig. 6-49b. Note that in the program example in Fig. 6-49b, the accumulator (A) is loaded with 15_{10} while register *L* is loaded with

6_{10}. Upon comparing (the third instruction in this example), it is found that $(A) > (L)$ and therefore the carry (CY) flag is reset to 0. The jump instruction (mnemonic of JC in this example) looks at the carry flag and finds $CY = 0$. This causes the MPU to continue to the next instruction in sequence, which is to "store (A) at memory address 2040H." The higher number (0FH) is stored in memory location 2040H by the "STA" operation. Next the MPU is stopped by the halt (HLT) instruction. The last three shaded instructions in the assembly language program in Fig. 6-49b were not used in this example. In the flowchart in Fig. 6-49a, the program continued straight down the chart and did not branch to the right.

Consider the same assembly language program with the contents of the accumulator being less than the contents of register L. Such a program listing is shown in Fig. 6-49c. In this example the accumulator is loaded with 0AH (10_{10}), while register L is loaded with the larger value of 0EH (14_{10}). The compare instruction sets the CY flag to 1 because $(A) < (L)$. The "jump if carry flag is set" operation (mnemonic of JC in this example) looks at the CY flag and determines it is set to 1. The jump instruction then causes the program counter to change to the address of the location (called STORE L in this example) of the next instruction. Note that the MPU then has jumped over two instructions to where the STORE L symbolic address is listed in the label column. The MPU then executes the last three instructions, which store the contents of register L (the larger number, which is 0EH in this example) in memory location 2040H. On the flowchart in Fig. 6-49a, the program progressed to the decision symbol and then it branched to the right and down to the lower-right stop symbol.

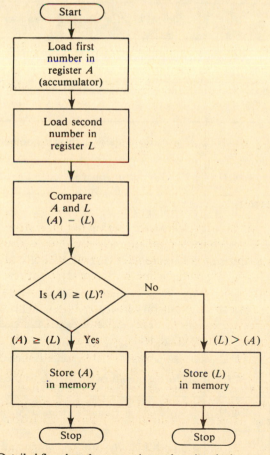

(a) Detailed flowchart for comparing and storing the larger number

Fig. 6-49

Label	Mnemonic	Operand	Comments
	MVI	$A,0FH$	; Load accumulator with first number (15_{10})
	MVI	$L,06H$	; Load register L with second number (6_{10})
	CMP	L	; Compare (A) and (L) CY flag = 1 if $A < L$
	JC	STORE L	; Jump to STORE L location if $CY = 1$ (if $A < L$); otherwise continue with next instruction
	STA	2040H	; Store (A) at memory location 2040H
	HLT		; Stop MPU after storing (A)
STORE L	MOV	A,L	; Move contents of register L to the accumulator
	STA	2040H	; Store (A) at memory location 2040H
	HLT		; Stop MPU after storing contents of register L

(b)   Assembly language program using the store A branch

Label	Mnemonic	Operand	Comments
	MVI	$A,0AH$	; Load accumulator with first number (10_{10})
	MVI	$L,0EH$	; Load accumulator with second number (14_{10})
	CMP	L	; Compare (A) and (L) CY flag = 1 if $A < L$
	JC	STORE L	; Jump to STORE L location if $CY = 1$ (if $A < L$); otherwise continue
	STA	2040H	; Store (A) at memory location 2040H
	HLT		; Stop MPU after storing (A)
STORE L	MOV	A,L	; Move contents of register L to the accumulator
	STA	2040H	; Store (A) at memory location 2040H
	HLT		; Stop MPU after storing contents of register L

(c)   Assembly language program using the store L branch

Fig. 6.49   (cont.)

Look again at the last three instructions in Fig. 6-49c. The object of these instructions was to store the contents of the L register in memory location 2040H. It was determined from the instruction set table in Fig. 6-21 that the generic microprocessor does not have an instruction for storing register L directly in memory. Therefore it was necessary to first transfer the contents of register L to A and then store A in memory. Sometimes it is found that microprocessors with limited instruction sets (like the generic MPU) are more difficult to program than units with more comprehensive instruction sets.

In summary, the branching techniques observed in the flowchart are performed by jump (sometimes called branch) instructions. Conditional branch instructions make a decision based on the condition of a particular flag in the status register. The jump instruction's use of a symbolic address was observed. The branching technique is very commonly used in most programs.

SOLVED PROBLEMS

6.85 The diamond-shaped box in Fig. 6-49a is called a _____ _____ (decision symbol, branch diamond).

Solution:

The diamond-shaped box in Fig. 6-49a is called a decision symbol.

6.86 The "compare A with L" instruction in Fig. 6-49b _____ (does, does not) change the values in the accumulator.

Solution:

Compare instructions do not change the values in the accumulator even though an internal subtraction occurs ($A - L$ in this example).

6.87 The "compare A with L" instruction in Fig. 6-49b is used to affect the _____ (CY, Z) flag in this program.

Solution:

The "compare A with L" instruction in Fig. 6-49b is used to affect the CY flag in this program. The zero (Z) flag is also affected but not subsequently tested by a branch instruction in this program.

6.88 Refer to Fig. 6-49. If the contents of the accumulator (A) and register L are equal, the carry flag is _____ (reset to 0, set to 1) by the compare instruction and the _____ ("No," "Yes") branch is taken from the decision symbol in Fig. 6-49a.

Solution:

If $(A) = (L)$ in Fig. 6-49a, the carry flag is reset to 0 by the compare instruction and the "Yes" branch is taken from the decision symbol.

6.89 Refer to Fig. 6-49. If register A contains 1AH and register L contains A5H, the jump instruction will cause the CPU to _____ (continue with the next instruction, jump to location STORE L).

Solution:

If $A = 1AH$ and $L = A5H$ in Fig. 6-49, the jump instruction will cause the CPU to jump to location STORE L. The jump is caused by the carry flag being set to 1 by the compare instruction. The compare instruction sets the carry flag to 1 because $A < L$.

6.90 Refer to Fig. 6-49b and c.   The operand following the "JC" instruction is listed as STORE L; this is called a(n) _____ (absolute, symbolic) address.

Solution:

The operand in Fig. 6-49b and c following the "JC" instruction is listed as STORE L; this is called a symbolic address when used in an assembly language program.

6.91 Jump or branch instructions are used _____ (often, seldom) in actual computer programs.

Solution:

Jump or branch instructions are used often in actual computer programs.

6.12 PROGRAM LOOPING

Microprocessors are especially useful in performing repetitive tasks.   For instance, the flowchart in Fig. 6-50 represents a program that will count from 0 to 254 (0–FEH) and output the count to an appropriate peripheral device.   This program has the characteristics of most looping programs. Starting from the top, it is customary to *initialize* registers.   In this example the accumulator (A) is cleared to 00H.   Next the accumulator contents are output to the appropriate peripheral device.   This is referred to as the *repeated process*.   Next the contents of the accumulator (A) are incremented or the count has been *modified*.   The compare and decision symbols perform the *test procedure* to determine whether the count in the accumulator has yet reached FFH.   If the answer to the question in the decision box (Is A = FFH? in this example) is no, the program branches to the left and back to the output block.   This is called the *loop*.   The program would follow the loop

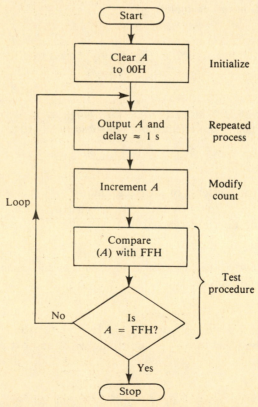

Fig. 6-50 Flowchart of the counting problem that uses program looping

254_{10} times and then exit the program to the stop symbol.   The flowchart illustrated in Fig. 6-50 represents a program that may be only 15 to 30 instructions long.   If all 255_{10} passes through the program were straight-line-programmed, the listing might be thousands of instructions long.   Program looping is a convenient method of shortening programs that have repetitive processes.

Another example of a program using the looping technique is shown in Fig. 6-51.   This program segment places the sequence of numbers 0 through 8 in sequential memory locations 2040 through 2048H.   Refer to the program flowchart in Fig. 6-51a.   The first two rectangles near the top are for initializing the *HL* register pair with 2040H and the accumulator with 00H.   The third rectangle down represents the store process that will be repeated nine times in this program.   The MPU would repeatedly store the contents of the accumulator in the memory location pointed to by the *HL* register pair.   In the first pass through, the contents of the accumulator (00H) would be stored in memory location 2040H.

The fourth and fifth rectangles down in Fig. 6-51a represent operations that modify the address in the *HL* register pair and the count in the *A* register.   As an example, during the first pass through the program, the *HL* register pair is incremented to 2041H while the accumulator is incremented to 01H.

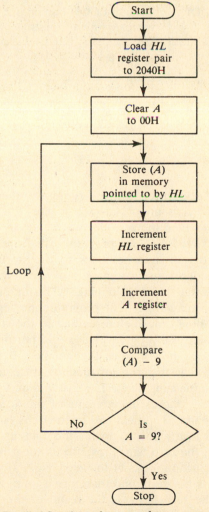

(a)   Detailed flowchart of count-and-store program

Fig. 6-51

Label	Mnemonic	Operand	Comments
	LXI	H,2040	; Load *HL* register pair with 2040H (used as an address pointer)
	XRA	A	; Clear accumulator to 00H [(A)⊕(A) = 00H in accumulator]
LOOP	MOV	M,A	; Store contents of accumulator in memory location pointed to by the *HL* register pair
	INX	H	; Increment *HL* register pair
	INR	A	; Increment the accumulator
	CPI	09H	; Compare—is (A) = 09H yet? If (A) = 09H, then the zero flag is set to 1
	JNZ	LOOP	; Jump to LOOP location if $Z = 0$ [if $(A) < 09H$]; otherwise continue with next instruction
	HLT		; Stop MPU

(b)   Assembly language version of count-and-store program

Fig. 6-51 (*cont.*)

The compare rectangle and decision symbol represent the test operations. The compare rectangle subtracts 09H from the contents of A to set or reset the zero flag. If $A < 9$, the zero flag will be reset. However if $A = 9$, then the zero flag will be set to 1. The decision symbol asks the question: Is $A = 9$? If the answer is yes, the program exits from the loop and ends. If, however, the answer is no, then the program branches back to the store instruction near the top of the diagram. Many looping procedures use compare and conditional jump instructions to test a modified count to determine when to stop looping. The modified count that is tested in this example is the contents of the accumulator. The program represented by the flowchart in Fig. 6-51*a* would repeat the store process nine times before exiting to the stop symbol.

An assembly language version of a program that would perform as specified by the flowchart is shown in Fig. 6-51*b*. The program will store the numbers 0 through 8 in sequential memory locations 2040 through 2048H. The first two instructions are equivalent to the first two blocks on the flowchart. They are for initializing the *HL* register pair to 2040H and the accumulator to 00H. The MOV *M,A* instruction stores the contents of the accumulator in the memory location pointed to by the *HL* register pair. The next two instructions (INX *H* and INR *A*) increment the *HL* and *A* registers. The CPI instruction compares the contents of *A* with the constant 09H. If register *A* contains from 0 to 8, the zero flag is reset to 0, but if register *A* contains 9, the zero flag will be set to 1. The JNZ instruction looks at the zero flag. If the zero flag = 0, the result of the internal subtraction $(A) - 09H$ is not zero, and therefore a jump is made to a location given by the symbolic address LOOP. If the zero flag = 1, the result of the internal subtraction $(A) - 09H$ is zero, and therefore the program exits the loop and continues to the next instruction. The next instruction is HLT, which stops the program.

SOLVED PROBLEMS

6.92   Program _____ (looping, modulation) is a method of shortening programs that must perform repetitive operations.

Solution:

Program looping is a method of shortening programs that must perform repetitive operations.

6.93   Refer to Fig. 6-51*a*.   The "clear *A* to 00H" rectangle represents an instruction used for _____ (initializing, testing) the contents in the accumulator.

Solution:

The "clear *A* to 00H" rectangle in Fig. 6-51*a* represents an instruction used for initializing the contents in the accumulator.

6.94   Refer to Fig. 6-51*a*.   If the contents of the accumulator are 8 in the compare block, the program _____ (loops, stops) after the decision block.

Solution:

If the contents of the accumulator in Fig. 6-51*a* are 8 in the compare block, the program loops after the decision block.   Note that the decision block asks: Is $A = 9$?   The answer is no, and therefore the program branches to the loop.

6.95   Refer to Fig. 6-51*b*.   The "CPI" operation _____ (compares, complements) the contents of the _____ (*A, HL*) register with the constant 09H.   It performs this operation by the use of an internal subtraction.

Solution:

The "CPI" operation in Fig. 6-51*b* compares the contents of the *A* register with the constant 09H.   Refer to the table in Fig. 6-4 for detailed information on the compare immediate instruction.

6.96   Refer to Fig. 6-51*b*.   If the zero flag is set to 1, the JNZ instruction will cause the MPU to _____ (continue with the next instruction, loop back to the MOV *M, A* instruction).

Solution:

If the zero flag is set to 1 in Fig. 6-51*b*, the JNZ instruction will cause the MPU to continue with the next instruction.

6.97   The looping process depends on the program causing the MPU to execute a group of operations over and over and also having the ability to _____ (change, stop) the repetitions at the correct time.

Solution:

The looping process depends on the program causing the MPU to execute a group of operations over and over and also having the ability to stop the repetitions at the correct time.   There are a few looping programs that continue in the loop until interrupted by a reset and therefore do not need the ability to exit the program by software means.

6.98   Refer to Fig. 6-51*a*. This program repeats the "store (*A*) in memory" operation nine times, and the program follows the loop path out of the diamond-shaped decision symbol _____ (number) times.

>   **Solution:**
>
>   The program in Fig. 6-51*a* repeats the "store (*A*) in memory" operation nine times while the program follows the loop path out of the diamond-shaped decision symbol only eight times. This is because one store operation already took place before the first loop.

6.13   USING SUBROUTINES

A *subroutine* is a subprogram that may be used many times in the main program or is commonly used by a programmer in many programs. A subroutine is sometimes used so often it is placed permanently in ROM. The transfer of control from the main program to the subroutine is performed by a *call* instruction. The reverse, or transfer of control from the subroutine back to the main program, is performed by a *return* instruction. The *push*, *pop*, and *load stack pointer* instructions are also typically used with subroutines.

A functional flowchart for a sample problem is shown in Fig. 6-52*a*. The task of the microprocessor system is to input two samples in the form of binary numbers and add them together and save the sum. The first three larger rectangles at the top of the flowchart suggest this procedure. Next the sum will be multiplied by a number called a scaling factor. The result of the multiplication, or product, is then stored. The sum from the third large rectangle down is now restored to the *A* register in the MPU. This sum is tested in the diamond-shaped decision block. If the sum is equal to or greater than 10H (16_{10}), the program exits to the alarm mode. If the sum is less than 10H, the program loops back and inputs new samples. This type of program might be used in industrial instrumentation where the following occur:

1. The sum of two inputs must be continuously monitored.

2. The sum must be scaled to a more appropriate value and this value stored.

3. The sum of two inputs must be checked at least each second to determine whether it is dangerously large, and if it is, the program must be exited to the alarm mode.

The program is designed to loop continuously, taking new samples each cycle. The loop is exited to the alarm mode only if a problem exists. An operator or other program would then handle the alarm procedure, symbolized in Fig. 6-52*a* with the round connector symbol.

A detailed flowchart for the same problem is drawn in Fig. 6-52*b*. On this flowchart each rectangle is equivalent to a microprocessor operation. The large shaded block, however, represents a *group* of instructions called the MULTIPLY subroutine.

An assembly language program is written based on the detailed flowchart in Fig. 6-52*b*. Each block on the flowchart corresponds to an assembly language statement. An assembly language listing for just the main program is detailed in Fig. 6-53. This listing uses only operations available from the generic microprocessor's instruction set. The actual subroutine listing for the multiply operation is not included in Fig. 6-53.

The first three assembly language statements in Fig. 6-53 initialize the stack pointer to 20C0H, the *HL* register pair to 2040H, and the accumulator (*A*) to 00H. The fourth statement adds the contents of *A* (currently 00H) to the contents of the memory location pointed to by the *HL* register pair (address 2040H). Refer to Fig. 6-54, which shows the main program, data, subroutine program, and stack memory used in this example. From Fig. 6-54, note that the contents added to *A* from location 2040H are 05H. At the end of the fourth instruction, the contents of *A* are 05H (00 + 05 = 05).

The fifth instruction of the main program in Fig. 6-53 increments the *HL* register pair. The sixth instruction adds memory location 2041H to *A*. From Fig. 6-54 it is determined that location

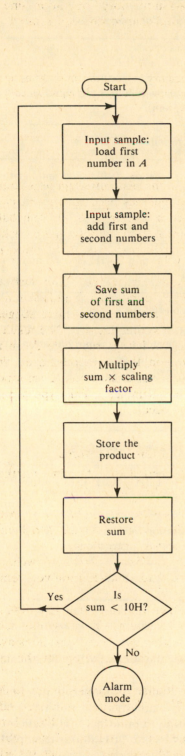

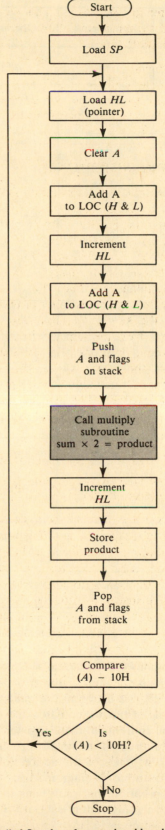

(a) Functional flowchart for instrumentation problem

(b) Detailed flowchart for sample-add-multiply-store-
      and-loop-again instrumentation problem

Fig. 6-52

Label	Mnemonic	Operand	Comments
	LXI	*SP*,20C0H	; Load stack pointer with 20C0H
START	LXI	*H*,2040H	; Load *HL* register pair with 2040H (*HL* used as address pointer in main program)
	XRA	*A*	; Clear accumulator to 00H
	ADD	*M*	; Add (*A*) to memory location 2040H (first number to be added is at 2040H)
	INX	*H*	; Increment *HL* register pair to 2041H
	ADD	*M*	; Add (*A*) to memory location 2041H (second number to be added is at 2041H)
	PUSH	*PSW*	; Push (*A*) and flags on the stack
	CALL	MULTIPLY	; Call MULTIPLY subroutine at memory location 2050H
	INX	*H*	; Increment *HL* register pair to 2042H
	MOV	*M,A*	; Store the product at memory location 2042H
	POP	*PSW*	; Pop the stack and restore (*A*) and flags
	CPI	10H	; Compare (*A*) with 10H [(*A*) − 10H] If (*A*) < 10H, then $CY = 1$; otherwise $CY = 0$
	JC	START	; Jump to START location (address 2003H) if $CY = 1$; otherwise continue to next instruction
	HLT		; Start MPU

Fig. 6-53 Assembly language version of the main instrumentation program

2041H contains 09H, whereas *A* holds 05H. The sum in *A* after the second ADD *M* instruction is 0EH. This is the sum of the two samples.

The next instruction in the main program in Fig. 6-53 is the PUSH *PSW* operation, which saves the contents of the accumulator and flags. This must be done because the next call instruction will destroy the contents of these registers when performing the multiply subroutine. The call operation stores the address of the next instruction in the main program (address 200EH in this example) in the stack, then it jumps to the address of the first instruction in the subroutine (address 2050H). This call to subroutine is diagramed in Fig. 6-54. Temporarily consider the call instruction a simple multiply operation that multiplies the contents of *A* by 2. The whole subroutine in this example then performs this multiplication: $0E \times 02 = 1CH$. The product in the accumulator upon the return from subroutine is 1CH.

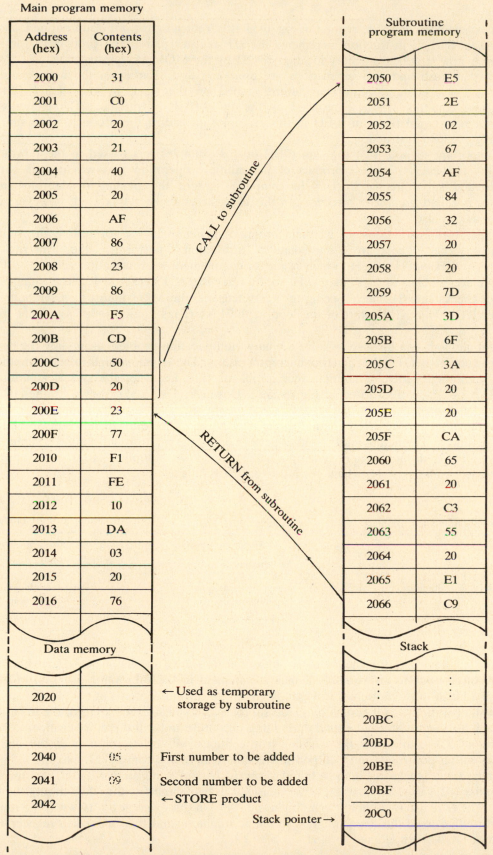

Fig. 6-54 Instrumentation problem memory contents and storage locations

The next main program instruction in Fig. 6-53 after returning from the subroutine is at address 200EH. This INX H instruction increments the HL register pair. The product of the multiply subroutine is now stored in memory location 2042H by the MOV M,A instruction.

Recall that push and pop instructions are used in pairs. Earlier in the main program the contents of the accumulator and flags were pushed on the stack by the PUSH PSW operation. These contents are now restored by the POP PSW instruction. The contents of the accumulator now equal the sum (0EH in this example) instead of the product. The sum will be tested using the next instruction.

It is important to note that the sum (0EH in this example) was passed to the subroutine for processing. However, it was a product of the multiply operation that was passed out of the subroutine and subsequently stored. In computer jargon, the passing of data to and from subroutines is called *parameter passing*. In this case the A register was used; however, memory storage areas can also be used.

The next two instructions in the main program in Fig. 6-53 are for testing the sum in the accumulator. The "compare immediate" instruction performs the internal CPU subtraction: $0EH - 10H = FEH$, which is the 2s complement representation of -2_{10}. The contents of the accumulator are less than 10H, so the carry flag (CY) is set to 1. The "jump if carry" instruction checks the CY flag. Seeing the carry flag set, the MPU jumps to a symbolic address called START. This is the start of the loop at the LXI H instruction (address 2003H from Fig. 6-54).

Several methods can be used to solve a binary multiplication problem using only the operations in the instruction set of the generic microprocessor. The most straightforward method uses repeated addition to solve a multiplication problem. For instance, the typical solution to the problem $5 \times 3 = 15_{10}$ is illustrated in Fig. 6-55a. However, Fig. 6-55b shows another method of solving the same problem using the *repeated-addition method*. Here the multiplicand is repeatedly added, the number of times being equal to the multiplier. The result of this repeated addition is then the product. The actual multiplication performed by the multiply subroutine is summarized in Fig. 6-55c. The multiplicand in the example is 0EH, while the multiplier is 02H. The multiplicand is added twice, yielding 1CH, which is considered the product.

Multiplicand   Multiplier   Product
    5 $\times$ 3 $=$ 15_{10}

Multiplier $= 3$ Product

$$\underset{\text{Multiplicand}}{\underbrace{5 + 5 + 5}} = 15_{10}$$

Multiplier $= 2$ Product

$$\underset{\text{Multiplicand}}{\underbrace{0E + 0E}} = 1C_{16}$$

(a) Decimal multiplication

(b) Repeated-addition method of multiplication

(c) Repeated-addition method of multiplication

Fig. 6-55

A detailed flowchart for the multiply subroutine is shown in Fig. 6-56. Each block in this flowchart corresponds to an assembly language statement in the subroutine program in Fig. 6-57.

The first block in the flowchart in Fig. 6-56 saves the current contents of the HL register pair by using a push operation. It is common in most subroutines to push the contents of the MPU registers on the stack because they may be used during the subroutine and will therefore change the values in the registers. Of course the HL register pair contents will be restored near the end of the subroutine with a pop operation (see pop instruction near the bottom in this example).

The next three blocks in Fig. 6-56 initialize the L, H, and A registers. The L register will hold the multiplier (02H in this example). The register will be decremented to 00H during the multiply routine. The H register will hold the multiplicand (0EH in this example). This was the sum passed to the subroutine from the main program in the accumulator and then moved to register H. The accumulator (A) is then cleared to 00H.

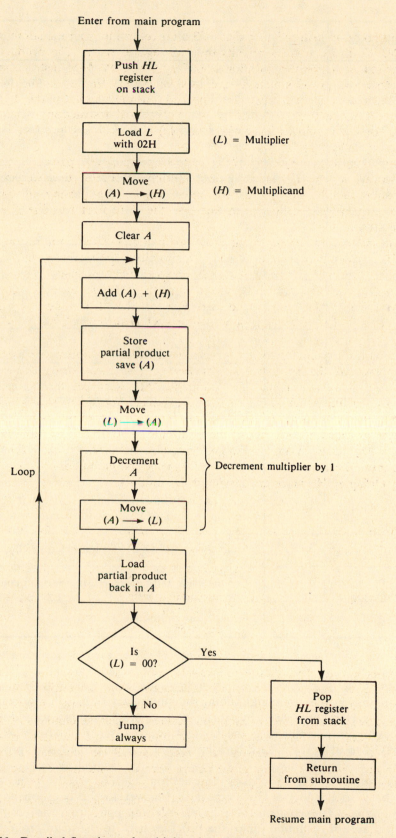

Fig. 6-56 Detailed flowchart of multiply subroutine used in instrumentation problem

Label	Mnemonic	Operand	Comments
	PUSH	H	; Push (H) and (L) registers on stack to save HL register pair contents
	MVI	L,02H	; Load register L with 02H (this is the scaling factor); 02H is the *multiplier*
	MOV	H,A	; Move (A) → (H); contents of H = *multiplicand*; save the sum in H
	XRA	A	; Clear A
LOOP	ADD	H	; Add (H) + (A); store sum in A
	STA	2020H	; Store (A) in memory location 2020H (2020H is used as temporary storage)
	MOV	A,L	; Move (L) to A
	DCR	A	; Decrement register A
	MOV	L,A	; Move (A) to L
	LDA	2020H	; Load contents of memory location 2020H in A (restore contents of A from temporary memory 2020H)
	JZ	DONE	; Jump to DONE location (address 2065H) if Z = 1 or if (L) are decremented to 00H; otherwise continue with next instruction
	JMP	LOOP	; Jump always to LOOP location (address 2055H)
DONE	POP	H	; Pop the stack and restore HL register pair contents
	RET		; Return from subroutine

Fig. 6-57 Assembly language version of multiply subroutine used in instrumentation problem

The fifth block in Fig. 6-56 represents adding the multiplicand (0EH in this example) to A. The partial product of 0EH is then saved by storing at temporary memory location 2020H while the accumulator is used for decrementing the contents of register L. After the multiplier is decremented from 02H to 01H, it is placed back in register L. Next the partial product is restored to the accumulator.

The decision symbol in Fig. 6-56 asks the question: Is (L) = 00? If the answer is no, the program jumps back to the loop. However, if the answer to the question is yes, the program branches to the right. The contents of the HL register pair are restored by the pop operation. Finally, the return operation jumps the program back to the main program. According to the diagram in Fig. 6-54, the return from subroutine is made to address 200EH in the main program.   Since the multiplier in this example is 02H, the program would pass twice through the add-store-move-decrement-move-load sequence and then exit to the main program.   Note that the final product of 1CH would be passed to the main program by remaining in the accumulator.

An assembly language listing for the multiply subroutine is detailed in Fig. 6-57.   Each assembly language statement corresponds to a block on the detailed flowchart in Fig. 6-56.   Try to follow the flow of the program in Fig. 6-57.   Refer to the flowchart for help.

In summary, when using call and return instructions, be sure to use them in pairs.   See that the proper registers are initialized and double-check the stack pointer.   Also use the push and pop instructions in pairs.   Be aware of how parameters (data) are passed to and from the subroutine.

Subroutines are widely used by programmers.   The advantages of using subroutines are:

1.   They add structure to the program which makes the program easier to understand.
2.   They make debugging easier.
3.   They shorten the program.
4.   They make writing longer programs easier and more efficient.

The disadvantage of using subroutines is that a program will run somewhat slower when subroutines are called.

SOLVED PROBLEMS

6.99   The multiply subroutine flowcharted in Fig. 6-56 used the _____ (add-and-shift, repeated-addition) method of calculating a product.

Solution:

The multiply subroutine flowcharted in Fig. 6-56 used the repeated-addition method of calculating a product.   The add-and-shift method is another more common method of multiplying using a series of adds and shifts to calculate a product.

6.100   Refer to Fig. 6-54.   What types of microprocessor instructions use the memory location called the stack?

Solution:

Call, return, push, and pop instructions all use the LIFO memory area called the stack in Fig. 6-54.

6.101   The purpose of the LXI *SP* instruction in Fig. 6-53 is to _____ (initialize, test) the stack pointer.

Solution:

The purpose of the LXI *SP* instruction in Fig. 6-53 is to initialize the stack pointer.

6.102   If the carry flag is set to 1 in Fig. 6-53, the "JC" operation will cause the MPU to fetch the _____ (HLT, LXI *H*) instruction next.

Solution:

If the carry flag is set to 1 in Fig. 6-53, the "JC" operation will cause the MPU to fetch the LXI *H* instruction next at symbolic address START.

6.103   The call instruction in Fig. 6-53 causes the contents of the _____ (*A* register, program counter) to be pushed on the stack and the program counter set to _____ (hex address).

Solution:

The call instruction in Fig. 6-53 causes the contents of the program counter to be pushed on the stack and the program counter set to 2050H. The multiply subroutine is located at address 2050H as shown in Fig. 6-54.

6.104 The POP *PSW* instruction in Fig. 6-53 pops the contents of the _____ (accumulator, program counter) and the flags from the stack and returns them to the CPU.

Solution:

The POP *PSW* instruction in Fig. 6-53 pops the contents of the accumulator and the flags from the stack and returns them to the CPU. See miscellaneous instructions chart (Fig. 6-40).

6.105 A diamond-shaped decision symbol such as the one in Fig. 6-56 is typically replaced by a _____ (compare, jump) instruction when the program is written.

Solution:

A diamond-shaped decision symbol such as the one in Fig. 6-56 is typically replaced by a jump instruction when the program is written. The assembly language program in Fig. 6-57 shows that the "JZ" or jump if zero instruction is used in this case.

6.106 During the multiply subroutine in Fig. 6-57, the value of the multiplicand is held in the _____ (H, L) register while the value of the multiplier is held in the _____ (H, L) register.

Solution:

During the multiply subroutine in Fig. 6-57, the value of the multiplicand is held in the *H* register while the value of the multiplier is held in the *L* register.

6.107 During the multiply subroutine, the contents of the _____ (H, L) register are decremented to 00H.

Solution:

During the multiply subroutine, the contents of the *L* register are decremented to 00H.

6.108 Refer to Figs. 6-53 and 6-57. The *H* and *L* registers are used as _____ _____ (address pointers, data registers) in the main program and as _____ _____ (address pointers, data registers) in the subroutine.

Solution:

Based on information in Figs. 6-53 and 6-57, the *H* and *L* registers are used as address pointers in the main program and as data registers in the multiply subroutine.

Supplementary Problems

6.109 A(n) _____ (assembly, machine) language listing is characterized by the use of hexadecimal memory addresses, op codes, and operands.   *Ans.* machine

6.110 A typical assembly language program statement is divided into four ____ (fields, segments) titled label, mnemonic, operand, and comment.   *Ans.* fields

6.111 An assembly language version is sometimes called a(n) _____ (object, source) program.
Ans. source

6.112 BASIC is considered a higher-level language because each program statement represents _____ (less, more) microprocessor machine operations than an assembly language statement.   *Ans.* more

6.113 The flags in Fig. 6-3 are part of the CPU storage device called the _____ register.   *Ans.* status

6.114 When the *H* and *L* registers are linked together as the *HL* register pair, they are usually used for _____ pointing.   *Ans.* address

6.115 The stack in the generic microprocessor system (or in an 8080/8085 system) is located in _____. *Ans.* RAM

6.116 The 16-bit register labeled *SP* in Fig. 6-3 is the _____ _____.   *Ans.* stack pointer

6.117 The 16-bit register labeled *PC* in Fig. 6-3 is the _____ _____.   *Ans.* program counter

6.118 As a general rule, microprocessor arithmetic operations _____ (do, do not) affect the flags. *Ans.* do

6.119 During a microprocessor compare instruction, only the _____ (*A*, status) register's contents are affected by the operation.   *Ans.* status (flags are affected)

6.120 Refer to Fig. 6-58. The contents of the accumulator after the ADD *L* operation will be _____ (8 bits). *Ans.* 00000001

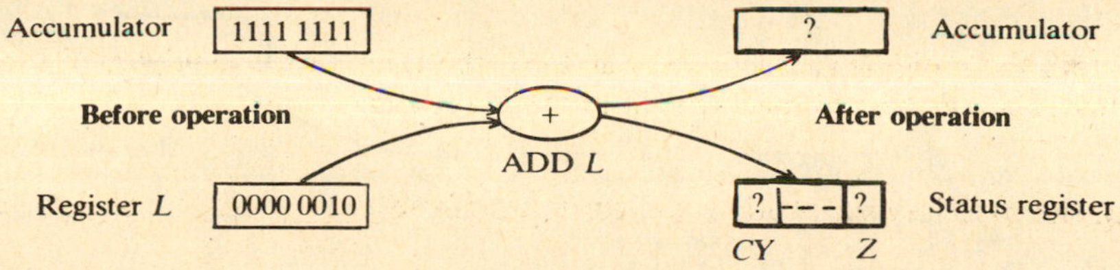

Accumulator `1111 1111`   `?` Accumulator

Before operation   +   **After operation**
                                      ADD *L*

Register *L* `0000 0010`   `?` --- `?` Status register
                                                 CY   Z

Fig. 6-58

6.121 After the ADD *L* operation in Fig. 6-58, the carry flag will be _____ (reset to 0, set to 1) while the zero flag will equal _____ (0, 1).   *Ans.* set to 1, $Z = 0$

6.122 Internally the microprocessor does not have subtract hardware; therefore it performs subtraction by converting the _____ (minuend, subtrahend) to its 2s complement form and adding. *Ans.* subtrahend

6.123 During use of a subtract instruction from the table in Fig. 6-4, a reset carry flag ($CY = 0$) means _____ (borrow, no borrow) or that the minuend is _____ (greater, less) than the subtrahend. *Ans.* no borrow, greater

6.124 Refer to Fig. 6-59. The contents of the accumulator after the SUB *H* operation will be _____ (8 bits), which is the 2s complement representation of _____ (decimal).   *Ans.* 11111110, -2_{10}

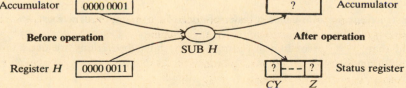

Accumulator `0000 0001`   `?` Accumulator

Before operation   −   **After operation**
                                      SUB *H*

Register *H* `0000 0011`   `?` --- `?` Status register
                                                 CY   Z

Fig. 6-59

6.125 After the SUB H operation in Fig. 6-59, the carry ("borrow") flag will be _____ (reset to 0, set to 1) while the zero flag will equal _____ (0, 1).   *Ans.*   set to 1, $Z = 0$

6.126 As a general rule, flags in the status register _____ (are, are not) affected by microprocessor logical instructions.   *Ans.*   are

6.127 The ($\cdot$) symbol used in the logical instruction table in Fig. 6-14 denotes the _____ (AND, multiply) operation.   *Ans.*   AND

6.128 Refer to Fig. 6-14.   If the MPU's accumulator = 11101110 and the carry flag = 0, what are the contents of the accumulator and carry flag after an "RAR" instruction?
Ans.   accumulator = 01110111, carry flag = 0

6.129 Almost all data transfer instructions _____ (do, do not) affect the flags in the microprocessor's status register.   *Ans.*   do not

6.130 Refer to Fig. 6-21.   When using the "MOV L, A" instruction, the _____ (A, L) register is the source of data, whereas the _____ (A, L) register is the destination.   *Ans.* A, L

6.131 Refer to Fig. 6-21.   The IN and OUT instructions use _____ (direct, inherent) addressing.
Ans.   direct

6.132 Refer to Fig. 6-21.   The "LDA" instruction used in Fig. 6-60 has an op code of _____ (hex) and uses a _____ (number) -byte instruction.   *Ans.*   3AH, 3

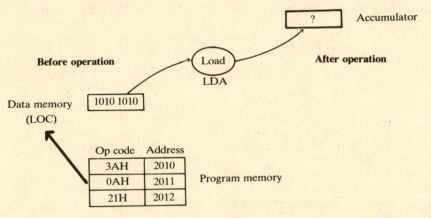

Fig. 6-60

6.133 The contents of the accumulator after the load operation in Fig. 6-60 are _____ (8 bits).
Ans.   10101010

6.134 The source of data in Fig. 6-60 was data memory location _____ (hex).   *Ans.*   210AH

6.135 Refer to Fig. 6-21.   The load operation shown in Fig. 6-60 uses _____ (direct, immediate) addressing.
Ans.   direct

6.136 Jump instructions are also called transfer-of-control or _____ instructions.   *Ans.*   branch

6.137 It is said that _____ (conditional, unconditional) jump operations are decision-making instructions.
Ans.   conditional

6.138 Jump operations affect the contents of the _____ _____ (program counter, stack pointer).
Ans.   program counter

6.139 Refer to Fig. 6-30.   The op code for the JZ instruction used in Fig. 6-61 is _____ (hex).
Ans.   CAH

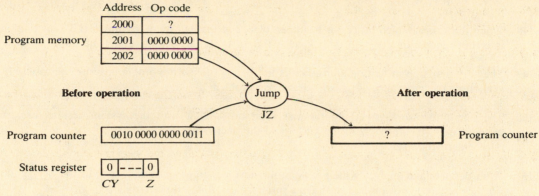

Fig. 6-61

6.140 The contents of the program counter after the operation in Fig. 6-61 will be _____ (hex).
Ans.   2003H (same as it is before operation because no jump occurs)

6.141 The generic microprocessor's _____ (call, return) instruction performs the function of both a push and a jump instruction.   *Ans*.   call

6.142 The _____ (call, return) operation is the very last instruction in a subroutine.   *Ans*.   return

6.143 Refer to Fig. 6-62.   The contents of stack location 2109H after the call operation will be _____ (8 bits).   *Ans*.   00100000 (20H)

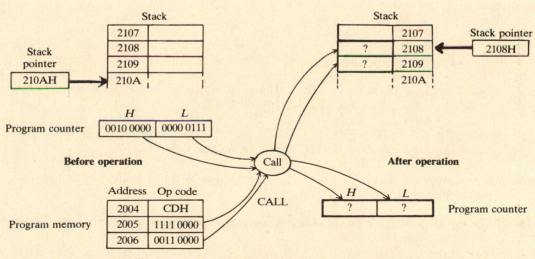

Fig. 6-62

6.144 Refer to Fig. 6-62.   The contents of stack location 2108H after the call operation will be _____ (8 bits).   *Ans*.   00000111 (07H)

6.145 Refer to Fig. 6-62.   The contents of the program counter after the call operation will be _____ (hex).
Ans.   30F0H (0011 0000 1111 0000 in binary)

6.146 Refer to Fig. 6-62.   The contents of the program counter after the call operation point to the first instruction in the _____ (stack, subroutine).   *Ans*.   subroutine

6.147 Refer to Fig. 6-40.   If the "PUSH *PSW*" instruction were used as the first instruction of a subroutine, the _____ (mnemonic) instruction would be used at the end just before the return.
Ans.   POP *PSW*

6.148 When the generic microprocessor has been placed in the halt mode by the "HLT" instruction, only an interrupt request or a _____ (clock, reset) input to the MPU can restart the unit.   *Ans.*   reset

6.149 The very first step in writing a program is to _____ (define the problem, write the assembly language version of the program).   *Ans.*   define the problem

6.150 The microprocessor system programmer must be familiar with the system architecture, the system memory map, the registers in the CPU, and the microprocessor's _____ _____ .
Ans.   instruction set

6.151 After defining and analyzing the problem, the next step in programming is to draw _____ (documentation, flowcharts) showing the problem's solution.   *Ans.*   flowcharts

6.152 Generic microprocessor operations using the immediate addressing mode are specified with _____ (number) -byte instructions.   *Ans.*   2 or 3

6.153 Refer to Fig. 6-40.   The "PUSH *H*" operation is a _____ (number) -byte instruction which uses the _____ addressing mode.   *Ans.*   1, register indirect

6.154 Refer to Fig. 6-4.   The "compare *A* with *L*" operation is a _____ (number) -byte instruction which uses the _____ addressing mode.   *Ans.*   1, register

6.155 Refer to Fig. 6-21.   The "LDA" operation is a _____ (number) -byte instruction which uses the _____ addressing mode.   *Ans.*   3, direct

6.156 A _____ (question is asked, statement of fact is made) inside a decision symbol on a programming flowchart.   *Ans.*   question is asked

6.157 A _____ (conditional branch, logical) instruction is used to perform the operation represented by the decision symbol on a flowchart.   *Ans.*   conditional branch

6.158 Many times _____ (compare, load) instructions are used in a program just before a conditional branch operation.   *Ans.*   compare

6.159 Refer to Fig. 6-51*b*.   What is the purpose of the "XRA *A*" operation in this program?
Ans.   Clear the accumulator to 00H, thereby initializing register *A*

6.160 The program _____ technique is used when repetitive tasks must be performed by a microprocessor.
Ans.   looping

6.161 Refer to Fig. 6-50.   The highest number output by this program would be _____ (hex) or _____ (decimal).   *Ans.*   FEH, 254_{10}

6.162 Commonly used microcomputer subroutines are sometimes stored permanently in _____ (RAM, ROM).   *Ans.*   ROM

6.163 The "JC" instruction tests the _____ (*CY*, *Z*) flag in the generic microprocessor.
Ans.   *CY* (carry flag)

6.164 Push and _____ (add, pop) instructions should be used in pairs.   *Ans.*   pop

6.165 Call and _____ (jump, return) instructions should be used in pairs.   *Ans.*   return

Chapter 7

Interfacing the Microprocessor

7.1 INTRODUCTION

Most microprocessors have little functional value by themselves. Most do not contain a substantial memory, and few have input and output ports which connect directly to peripheral devices. Microprocessors operate as part of a system. The interconnection, or linkage, of the parts within this system is called *interfacing*. Generally, an interface is a shared boundary between two or more devices which involves sharing information. Other considerations in interfacing include synchronization, direction of data transmission, and sometimes the adjustment of signal levels or modes.

Consider the simplified microprocessor-based system diagramed in Fig. 7-1. The interface, or linkage, between each of the devices shown and the microprocessor unit will be surveyed. Therefore, interfacing the MPU with the ROM and the RAM will be covered as well as interfacing the MPU with input/output (I/O) devices. Little detailed information will be given on specific peripheral devices. It is obvious from Fig. 7-1 that the address, data, and control busses play an important role in linking the parts of the system together. Interfacing deals with the synchronization and transmission of data to and from the MPU, and therefore software as well as hardware must be studied.

Generally, data transfers in and out of the MPU over the busses take the form of one of these activities:

1. Memory read
2. Memory write
3. I/O read
4. I/O write
5. Interrupt or reset handling

When it is said that data is input from another device, it means *input in relation to the MPU*. Likewise, an output would be output from the microprocessor unit. Generally, the microprocessor is the focus of all operations. However, some MPUs release control of the address and data busses for a time so that a peripheral device may access the main system memory directly without going through the MPU. This is called *direct memory access* (DMA).

The diagram in Fig. 7-1 suggests that the MPU, ROM, RAM, input interface adapter, and output interface adapter are separate devices. This may or may not be true depending on the specific system. It is quite common for manufacturers to produce peripheral interface adapters that are compatible with their microprocessor units. These are usually general-purpose in that they can typically be programmed to function as either an input or an output interface device. Some manufacturers integrate RAM and I/O ports or ROM and I/O ports on the same IC to decrease system component numbers. Manufacturers also produce specialized interface components in IC form. Some of these specialized components include programmable communications interfaces, programmable DMA controllers, programmable interrupt controllers, diskette controllers, synchronous data link controllers, CRT controllers, and keyboard/display controllers.

7.2 INTERFACING WITH ROM

Consider interfacing the microprocessor with a read-only memory (ROM) or programmable read-only memory (PROM). The MPU and ROM section of a system is diagramed in Fig.

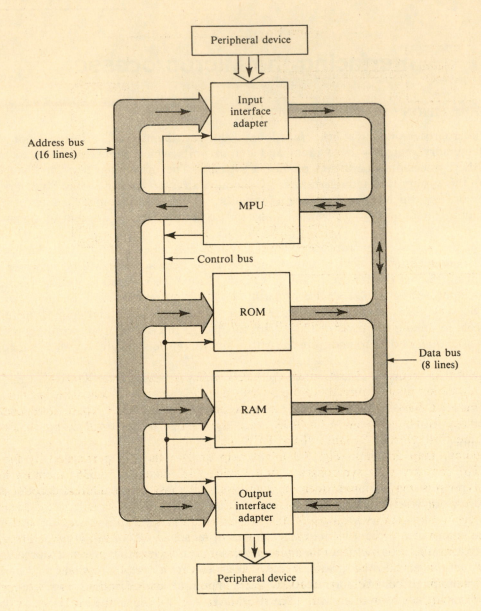

Fig. 7-1 Block diagram of microprocessor-based system

7-2. All 8 data bus lines are connected to the output terminals $(O_0 - O_7)$ of the ROM. The single read output $(\overline{RD})$ goes from the MPU to the output-enable $(\overline{OE})$ input of the ROM.

The least significant 12 bits of the address bus $(A_0 - A_{11})$ are connected to the $4K \times 8$ ROM. The ROM IC's built-in decoder can access any one of 4096 $(2^{12} = 4096)$ 8-bit read-only memory words using the 12 address inputs. The most significant 4 address lines $(A_{12} - A_{15})$ go to a combinational logic element called an address decoder. To access and read data from the ROM the MPU must:

1. Set address on address lines A_0 through A_{11}.
2. Set $\overline{OE}$ LOW using the read control line.
3. Set $\overline{CS}$ LOW using the address decoder and chip-select line.

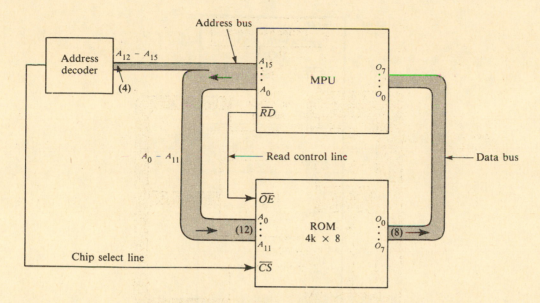

Fig. 7-2 Interfacing ROM with microprocessor

Assume the MPU wants to access memory location 0000H ($0000\,0000\,0000\,0000_2$). The least significant 12 bits are applied directly to the ROM's decoding circuitry via address lines A_0 through A_{11}. The most significant 4 bits (A_{12}–A_{15}) also are part of the address. These are decoded by an *address decoder*. If A_{12} through $A_{15} = 0000_2$, then the address decoder will output a LOW which will enable the chip-select ($\overline{CS}$) input of the ROM in Fig. 7-2.

The memory map drawn in Fig. 7-3 might help explain the job performed by the address decoder. The memory map symbolizes a unit having 64K (actually 65,536) memory locations. This memory map is divided into sixteen 4K segments. The task of the address decoder is to help the MPU access *only one* of the 4K segments at a time. If the 4 inputs to the address decoder were 0000, then segment 0 (memory locations 0000–0FFFH) would be accessed. However, if the input to the address decoder were 0001, then segment 1 (memory locations 1000–1FFFH) would be accessed, etc. In summary, the most significant 4 address lines select a segment of memory whereas the least significant 12 bits determine the specific memory location within that 4K segment.

When interfacing the MPU with ROM, the important considerations are *addressing* and *timing*. Addressing has been discussed. The diagram in Fig. 7-4 shows the MPU signals that affect the reading of an 8-bit memory word from the ROM. The top line of the timing diagram shows the address lines (A_0–A_{15}) changing to their respective logic levels. According to the circuit in Fig. 7-2, address lines A_0 through A_{11} activate the address inputs of the ROM while A_{12} through A_{15} are decoded by the address decoder activating the chip-select ($\overline{CS}$) input of the ROM. A short time later the read output ($\overline{RD}$) of the MPU enables the output enable of the ROM. Stored data is placed on the data bus and collected off the data bus by the MPU. One critical time limitation is shown in Fig. 7-4. After the address lines have settled to their respective logic levels and the $\overline{CS}$ ROM input has been activated, it takes a given amount of time to access the memory word. This is called the *read access time* and is a characteristic of the particular ROM or PROM being used. It is the time required for the internal ROM decoders to locate the correct byte in memory.

Notice the use of small circles and arrows in Fig. 7-4. These indicators are used to symbolize an important *cause-and-effect relationship* in the timing diagram. As an example, in Fig. 7-4 the H-to-L (HIGH-to-LOW) transition of the read output causes the MPU data bus pins to switch from their three-state condition to accept data off the data bus as an input. The dashed line in the data inputs line stands for a three-state or high-impedance condition. Again on the L-to-H transition of

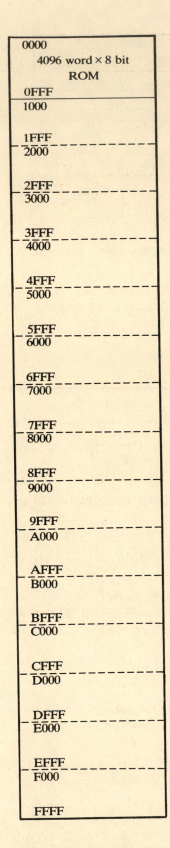

Fig. 7-3 Memory map

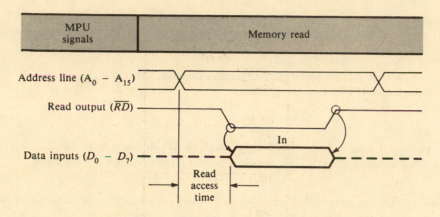

Fig. 7-4 Timing diagram—MPU signals during ROM read operation

the $\overline{RD}$ output the MPU data bus pins switch back to their three-state condition and stop accepting data off the data bus.   The timing diagram in Fig. 7-4 shows only MPU signals and does not show ROM inputs and outputs.

SOLVED PROBLEMS

7.1   The read-only memory in Fig. 7-2 can store _____ (number) words, each word being _____ (number) bits wide.

Solution:

The storage unit in Fig. 7-2 is referred to as a 4K × 8 bit ROM, which means it can store 4K (or 4096) words, each word being 8 bits wide.

7.2   A 4K ROM needs _____ (number) address inputs to decode the 4096 separate memory locations.

Solution:

According to Fig. 7-2, a 4K ROM would need 12 address inputs to decode and access the 4096 separate memory locations.

7.3   Refer to Fig. 7-2.   The most significant 4 address lines are decoded by the _____ (address, ROM) decoder.

Solution:

The most significant 4 address lines (A_{12}–A_{15}) are decoded by the address decoder.

7.4   Which segment of the memory map in Fig. 7-3 will the address decoder select if the MPU puts out $0010\,0000\,0000\,1111_2$ on the address bus?

Solution:

The most significant 4 bits (0010 in this example) are decoded by the address decoder and determine in this case that segment 2 will be accessed.   Segment 2 in Fig. 7-3 includes the 4096 memory locations numbered 2000 through 2FFFH.

7.5   Refer to Fig. 7-4.   During a memory read operation, the last MPU output to be activated is the _____ (A_0–A_{15}, $\overline{RD}$) line(s).

Solution:

Based on information in Fig. 7-4, the last MPU output to be activated is the $\overline{RD}$ line.

7.6   When the MPU's $\overline{RD}$ output goes LOW, it enables the ROM's _____ ($\overline{CS}$, $\overline{OE}$) input as well as causing the MPU's data bus pins to _____ (accept data off the data bus, go to the three-state condition).

Solution:

According to Figs. 7-2 and 7-4, when the MPU's $\overline{RD}$ output goes LOW, it enables the ROM's $\overline{OE}$ input as well as causing the MPU's data bus pins to accept data off the data bus.

7.7   The ROM's characteristic that deals with how long it takes for the address to be decoded and a specific memory location accessed is referred to as the _____ _____ time.

Solution:

The ROM's characteristic that deals with how long it takes for the address to be decoded and a specific memory location accessed is referred to as the read access time.

7.3   INTERFACING WITH RAM

Read/write storage devices are by common usage called RAMs. RAMs are usually subdivided by manufacturers into static and dynamic types. This section will deal with the static RAM, which is easier to interface than the dynamic type.

Consider the MPU and the RAM section of a system which is diagramed in Fig. 7-5. Note that the RAM is organized as a 4K (actually 4096 words) × 8 bit unit. It contains 4096 words each 8 bits wide. It is common for this large a static RAM unit to be made up of many RAM ICs. One such 4K × 8 bit memory module contains 32 static 1024 × 1 bit RAM ICs. The memory module or

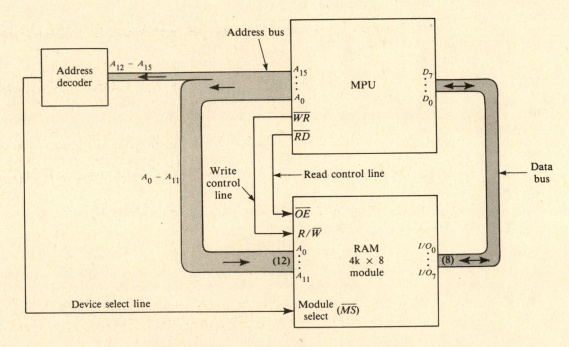

Fig. 7-5   Interfacing RAM with microprocessor

memory card also contains about 10 extra ICs for gating and buffering. This $4K \times 8$ bit RAM memory unit diagramed as a block in Fig. 7-5 is in itself a complex system.

The microprocessor-based system's memory map is again shown in Fig. 7-6. The 4K RAM memory has been added arbitrarily in the third segment down (called segment 2). As with the ROM, the address decoder in Fig. 7-5 will have the task of generating an enable signal on the device-select line. The address decoder will send a LOW pulse to the module-select ($\overline{MS}$) input to enable the RAM only when the most significant 4 address lines (A_{12}–A_{15}) equal 0010_2. As with the ROM, the decoding of the least significant 12 address lines (A_0–A_{11}) is performed by RAM decoding circuitry.

The data bus becomes a two-way 8-bit path for data read from or written into the RAM in Fig. 7-5. The least significant 12 MPU address lines go directly to the address inputs of the RAM module via the address bus. The most significant 4 MPU address lines are connected to the address decoder. The write output ($\overline{WR}$) of the MPU is connected via the write control line to the $R/\overline{W}$ input of the RAM. Note that this RAM input is a read/write input. This means that when the MPU is not enabling the write output with a LOW, the $\overline{WR}$ terminal puts out a HIGH which specifies a read operation to the RAM. The MPU's read ($\overline{RD}$) output is connected via the read control line to the output enable ($\overline{OE}$) of the RAM. A LOW on the read control line will enable the outputs of the RAM module.

The timing diagram in Fig. 7-7 shows the microprocessor and RAM signals during the read operation. The MPU's address lines are set to a valid address, and then the read output ($\overline{RD}$) goes LOW. The data bus goes from a three-state to an input condition. The MPU is ready to accept data off the data bus. The RAM's module-select ($\overline{MS}$) and output-enable ($\overline{OE}$) inputs are both driven LOW or enabled by the address decoder and the read control line from the MPU. The

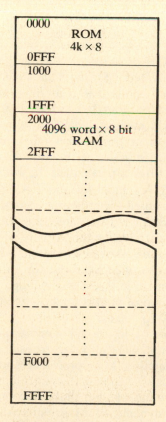

Fig. 7-6 Memory map

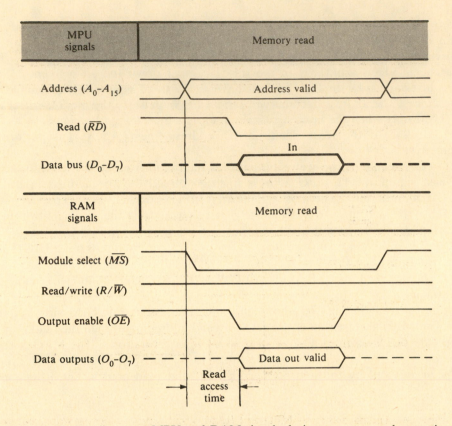

Fig. 7-7 Timing diagram—MPU and RAM signals during memory read operation

read/write ($R/\bar{W}$) input is held HIGH or in the read mode.   Shortly after the output enable ($\overline{OE}$) goes LOW, the data outputs are activated.   Stored data is placed on the data bus by the outputs of the RAM.   As on a ROM, the *read access time* is an important characteristic of the RAM.   The maximum read access time might range from 250 to 1000 ns for common static RAMs.

The timing diagram for the RAM memory write operation is shown in Fig. 7-8.   The sequence of events during the write operation first involves sending an address to the RAM and address decoder.   The address decoder in turn activates the module-select ($\overline{MS}$) input (this might be the chip-select inputs on single ICs).   After a time called the *address setup time*, the MPU write pulse ($\overline{WR}$) activates the read/write ($R/\bar{W}$) input of the RAM and places the RAM in the write mode.   The write pulse must be enabled for at least a certain minimum time called the *write pulse time* (also called the write pulse width).   At the same time the write pulse is output, the data to be written in memory is placed on the data bus by the MPU.   Shortly thereafter, the RAM accepts the data off the data bus and writes into the addressed location.   The minimum time for a write cycle is called the *write cycle time* and is identified near the top of the diagram in Fig. 7-8.   A typical minimum write cycle for a common static RAM might range from 250 to 1000 ns.   The minimum address setup time for the same group of RAMs might range from 20 to 200 ns while the minimum write pulse time might be from 180 to 750 ns.

The labeling and the numbers of inputs on commercial RAMs vary.   The output signals available from commerical microprocessors also vary considerably.   Manufacturers' data manuals must be examined carefully for details.   Microprocessor and RAM signals will not be found in combined diagrams as in Figs. 7-7 and 7-8 in manufacturers' data books.   Timing diagrams will have to be examined separately to determine whether they are compatible.   Because memory cells need refreshing every few microseconds, dynamic RAMs are more difficult to interface than static memory units.

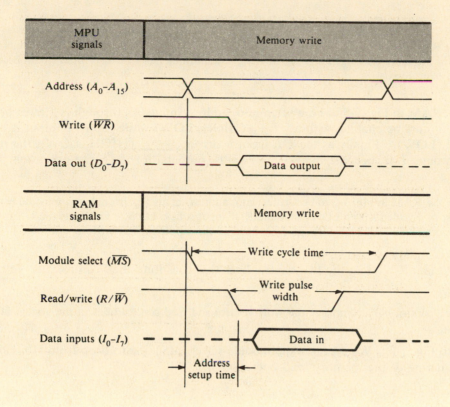

Fig. 7-8 Timing diagram—MPU and RAM signals during memory write operation

SOLVED PROBLEMS

7.8 By common usage, the RAM is functionally a _____ (read-only, read/write) storage device.

Solution:

By common usage, the RAM is functionally a read/write storage device.

7.9 Which type of RAM is easier to interface with a microprocessor—static or dynamic?

Solution:

The static RAM is the easier type to interface with a microprocessor.

7.10 Refer to Fig. 7-6. If the MPU addresses 2030H, the address decoder will select segment _____ (number) in memory. A _____ (RAM, ROM) storage device resides at this location in this system.

Solution:

If the MPU in Fig. 7-6 addresses 2030H, the address decoder will select segment 2 (0010_2) in memory. A RAM storage device resides at this location according to the memory map in Fig. 7-6.

7.11 The RAM block in Fig. 7-5 contains _____ (number) words, each word being _____ (number) bits wide. This size RAM probably consists of a _____ (group of ICs, a single IC).

Solution:

The RAM block in Fig. 7-5 contains 4K (actually 4096) words, each word being 8 bits wide. This size RAM probably consists of a group of ICs. One such memory card (printed circuit board with ICs) contains over 40 ICs.

7.12 For the RAM in Fig. 7-5 to be written into, address inputs A_0 through A_{11} must be activated, then $\overline{MS}$ must be enabled with a _____ (HIGH, LOW) while the $R/\overline{W}$ input is held _____ (HIGH, LOW). Finally as the $\overline{OE}$ input is driven _____ (HIGH, LOW), the pins labeled I/O_0 through I/O_7 become the _____ (inputs, outputs) for the write operation.

Solution:

For the RAM in Fig. 7-5 to be written into, address inputs A_0 through A_{11} must be activated, then $\overline{MS}$ must be enabled with a LOW while the $R/\overline{W}$ input is held LOW. Finally as the $\overline{OE}$ input is driven LOW, the pins labeled I/O_0 through I/O_7 become the inputs for the write operation.

7.13 Refer to Fig. 7-5. List the two control lines that constitute the "control bus" in this system.

Solution:

The "control bus" comprises the write control and read control lines in the system in Fig. 7-5.

7.14 Refer to Fig. 7-7. What causes the module-select ($\overline{MS}$) line to drop from HIGH to LOW at the beginning of the memory read operation?

Solution:

The most significant 4 bits of the address bus are decoded by the address decoder. The address decoder activates the module-select ($\overline{MS}$) line when 0010_2 is present at its inputs.

7.15 Refer to Fig. 7-7. The read access time is the time required for the stored data to reach the RAM outputs from the time a valid address first reaches the address inputs. The read access time for a typical RAM memory might be about 500 _____ (μs, ns).

Solution:

The read access time for a typical RAM memory might be about 500 ns.

7.16 During the write operation in Fig. 7-5, the D_0 through D_7 pins of the microprocessor are considered _____ (inputs, outputs) and are _____ (receiving data from, sending data to) the data bus.

Solution:

During the write operation, the D_0 through D_7 pins of the microprocessor are considered outputs and are sending data to the data bus.

7.17 Refer to Fig. 7-8. The write cycle time is _____ (longer, shorter) than the write pulse time of a RAM.

Solution:

According to Fig. 7-8, the write cycle time is longer than the write pulse time of a RAM.

7.18 Refer to Fig. 7-8. The $R/\overline{W}$ input to the RAM is driven LOW by the _____ control signal from the microprocessor.

Solution:

According to Fig. 7-5, the $\overline{WR}$ control signal from the MPU drives the $R/\overline{W}$ input of the RAM to LOW during a write operation.

7.4 INPUT/OUTPUT INTERFACING BASICS

An input or output operation is the act of transferring data to or from a selected peripheral device. The microprocessor is the focus of all operations, so an *input* will mean data flows into the MPU whereas an *output* will mean data flows out of the MPU. Those locations where data is input from or output to are usually called input or output *ports*.

From the table of data transfer instructions in Fig. 6-21, it appears that the generic microprocessor uses the IN and OUT instructions for transferring data to and from I/O ports. These data transfer instructions are illustrated in Fig. 7-9a. The output instruction is represented by the OUT mnemonic in assembly language programs, while the input instruction uses the IN mnemonic. The instruction formats for these operations are also reproduced in Fig. 7-9a showing the op code followed by a device number or port address. The byte-long port address can select one of 256 (2^8) ports. The port address comes from the least significant 8 address lines (A_0–A_7). Figure 7-9a also shows two additional output control signals added to the generic microprocessor. When using the OUT operation, a special *input/output write* ($\overline{I/O\ W}$) signal is used. The IN operation also requires the use of a special output signal called the *input/output read* ($\overline{I/O\ R}$) signal. Both of these output signals are active LOW signals and are illustrated coming from the microprocessors in Fig. 7-9a. The use of special control signals, such as the $\overline{I/O\ W}$ and $\overline{I/O\ R}$ in Fig. 7-9a, is referred to as *isolated* or *accumulator input/output*.

Data transfers using the IN and OUT instructions are classed as *program-controlled I/O*. Program instructions are controlling the transfer of data during the IN and OUT operations. Data transfers can be initiated by the peripheral device saying, "I'm ready to send or receive data." *Interrupts* are used by a peripheral device to initiate MPU action. Recall that when the MPU receives an interrupt request, it finishes the instruction it is executing and jumps to an *interrupt service routine* in program memory. This interrupt service routine might include input and output operations.

Program-controlled I/O is divided into two techniques. The isolated I/O technique was observed in Fig. 7-9a using the special IN and OUT instructions. The other technique treats the input and output locations as regular memory addresses. This technique is called *memory-mapped I/O*. With memory-mapped I/O the regular memory access instructions are used. In Fig. 7-9b the "store A direct" instruction is used to output data to an output port. Next in Fig. 7-9b the regular "load A direct" instruction is used to input data from an input port or device. From Fig. 7-9b it is determined that the address lines must be decoded and are used for selecting an exact input or output port address. The usual write ($\overline{WR}$) and read ($\overline{RD}$) control signals are also used to input or output data. Any memory access instruction can be used to input and output data using the memory-mapped I/O technique.

The memory-mapped I/O technique is probably the most common and can be used with any microprocessor. The isolated I/O technique can be used only with microprocessors that have separate IN and OUT instructions and special input/output write and read control outputs.

It is common to refer to an output as "an output to a peripheral device." In actual practice, however, the output from the microprocessor is not directly to a peripheral device but to a memory device which stores the data for the peripheral unit. This can be seen in the system diagram in Fig. 7-1. The blocks labeled "input interface adapter" and "output interface adapter" are memory devices. It is common for I/O interface adapters to also have characteristics other than memory.

An elementary output interface and peripheral device is shown in Fig. 7-10a. Note that the output indicator is a simple light-emitting diode (LED). The output interface adapter contains a *D* flip-flop. Assume that the "store A direct" instruction is being executed by the MPU and that the accumulator contains 00000001. Assuming an address of 8000H, the A_{15} line is HIGH and activates

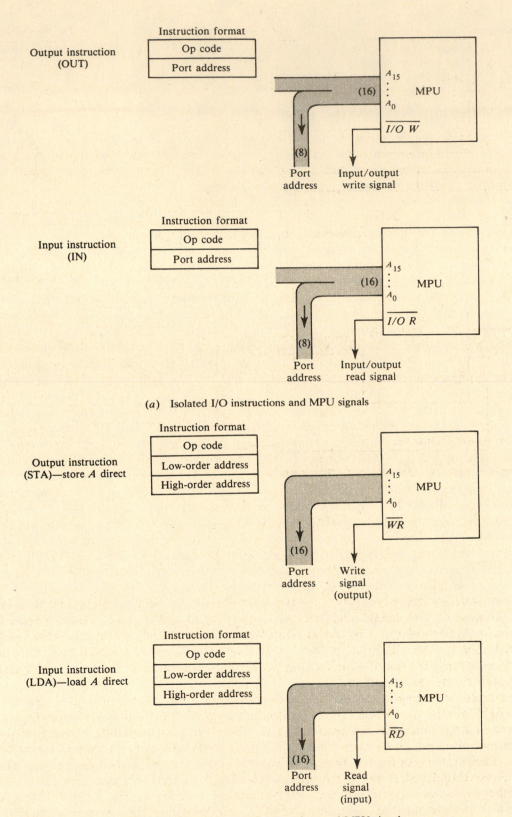

(a) Isolated I/O instructions and MPU signals

(b) Memory-mapped I/O instructions and MPU signals

Fig. 7-9

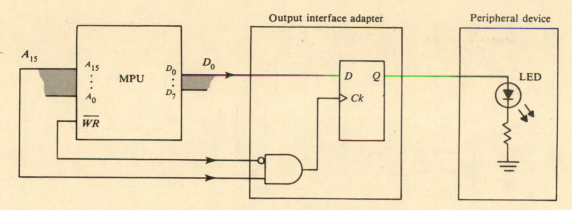

(a) Interfacing single LED output bit indicator

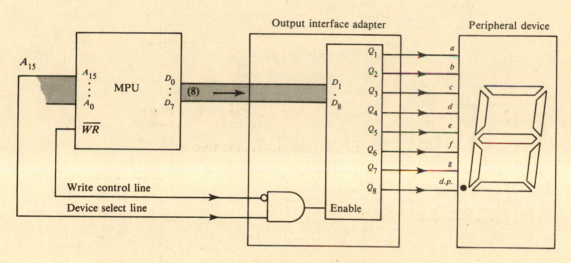

(b) Interfacing seven-segment display

Fig. 7-10

the bottom input of the AND gate. Shortly thereafter, a HIGH appears on the data bus line (D_0). The write control signal $(\overline{WR})$ goes LOW, activating the AND gate. This causes the 1 bit to be latched in the D flip-flop. The HIGH latched at output Q of the flip-flop causes the LED or bit indicator to light. The MPU then proceeds with other activities, but the output interface adapter (memory) continues to cause the LED to light. The idea illustrated for a single bit of data in Fig. 7-10a is fundamental to all outputs.

The output interfacing in Fig. 7-10b is somewhat more complicated. It transfers 8 bits of data from the MPU via the data bus to the output interface adapter. The output interface adapter stores the data in an 8-bit latch in the customary manner. Note that address line A_{15} must be HIGH while the write control output $(\overline{WR})$ must pulse LOW for a time to latch data on the seven-segment LED display. Each segment of the LED (a–g and decimal point) acts exactly like the single LED in Fig. 7-10a. A HIGH latched at any Q output of the latch will cause that segment to light.

Another elementary peripheral and interface device is shown in Fig. 7-11a. The peripheral device is a simple switch for selecting either a HIGH or LOW logic level. A single input data line is connected to the D input of the data flip-flop inside the input interface adapter. When the MPU executes an instruction such as "load A direct from memory location 8000H," the AND gate is

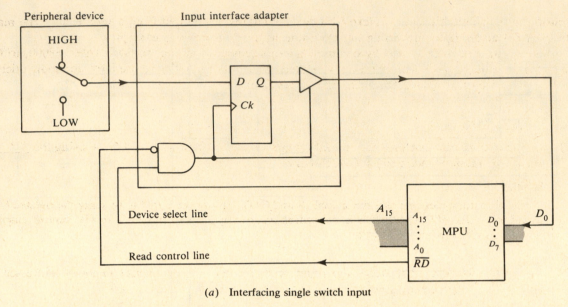

(a) Interfacing single switch input

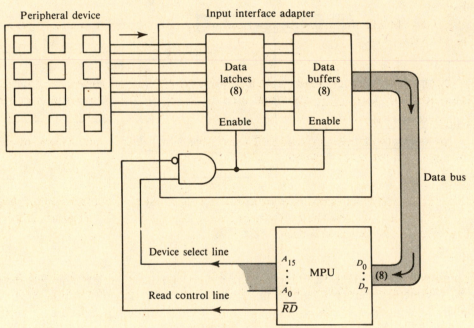

(b) Interfacing keyboard input

Fig. 7-11

activated, latching the input data.   The output buffer is enabled, permitting the data to pass through to the single data bus line (D_0). The MPU accepts the HIGH data bit from the data bus and transfers it to the accumulator.   Shortly thereafter, the AND gate is disabled, also disabling the data bus buffer.   The output of the input interface adapter is now disabled and in its high-impedance state and has no effect on other data bus transfers.

The memory-mapped input technique is being used in Fig. 7-11.   Typically, several address lines would be decoded by an address decoder to activate the device-select line.   Figure 7-11b is an extension of the single-bit input.   Here 8-bit parallel data is being input from a keyboard.   The read control ($\overline{RD}$) and simple addressing are the same as used in previous examples.

Memory-mapped I/O is used by common microprocessors such as the 6800, 6809, 68000, 6502, and 65816.   Isolated I/O (sometimes also called data channel I/O) is used by common microprocessors such as the 8080/8085, Z80, 8086, 8088, and Z8000.

SOLVED PROBLEMS

7.19 A microcomputer that uses the special IN and OUT instructions is said to be using the _____ (isolated, memory-mapped) I/O technique.

Solution:

A microcomputer that uses the special IN and OUT instructions is said to be using the isolated I/O technique.   Use of this technique is dependent on the microprocessor having special control outputs such as an I/O read and I/O write.

7.20 The I/O technique that treats the input and output ports as regular memory addresses is called _____ (isolated, memory-mapped) I/O.

Solution:

The I/O technique that treats the input and output ports as regular memory addresses is called memory-mapped I/O.

7.21 If the normal MPU memory read ($\overline{RD}$) and write ($\overline{WR}$) control outputs are connected to I/O interface adapters, the _____ (isolated, memory-mapped) I/O technique is being used.

Solution:

If the normal MPU memory read ($\overline{RD}$) and write ($\overline{WR}$) control outputs are connected to I/O interface adapters, the memory-mapped I/O technique is being used.

7.22 Data is transferred to the accumulator of the MPU in Fig. 7-11b after address line A_{15} goes _____ (HIGH, LOW) and the read control line ($\overline{RD}$) goes _____ (HIGH, LOW), which in turn enables the latches and buffers.

Solution:

Data is transferred to the accumulator of the MPU in Fig. 7-11b after address line A_{15} goes HIGH and the read control line ($\overline{RD}$) goes LOW, which in turn enables the latches and buffers.

7.23 During the input operation the MPU unit in Fig. 7-11b is probably executing the _____ (IN, LDA) instruction.

Solution:

This system is using the memory-mapped I/O technique.   With this technique the regular memory reference data transfer instructions are used.   Therefore during the input operation the MPU unit in Fig. 7-11b is probably executing the LDA (load A direct) instruction.

7.24 When the data buffers are enabled, they _____ (block, permit) passage of data from the latches to the data bus.

Solution:

When the data buffers are enabled, they permit passage of data from the latches to the data bus.

7.25   Refer to Fig. 7-11b.   To what addresses will the input interface respond?

Solution:

Anytime the most significant address line (A_{15}) is HIGH, the device-select line is activated.   This is not a practical addressing method because 32K (the bottom eight 4K segments in Fig. 7-3) will be used up by this single output device.

7.5   INTERFACING WITH PRACTICAL I/O PORTS

Manufacturers produce I/O interface circuits in IC form.   One such IC is the *Intel 8212 8-bit input/output port*.   The 8212 I/O port IC can be used as an input or output port adapter.

A microprocessor similar to the generic MPU or the Intel 8080 is shown in Fig. 7-12 interfaced with a seven-segment display using the 8212 I/O port.   The 8212 I/O port serves as the output interface adapter in this system.   The seven-segment display is the peripheral device.   The MPU is using the isolated I/O technique in this diagram.   Note that with the isolated (or accumulator) I/O technique the output device-select line is *fully decoded* from the least significant 8 address lines

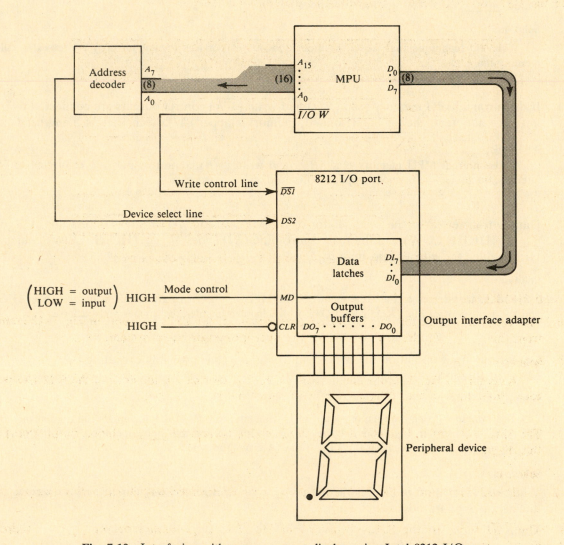

Fig. 7-12   Interfacing with seven-segment display using Intel 8212 I/O port

$(A_0 - A_7)$.   The isolated I/O technique also uses a special *input/output write* control output ($\overline{I/O\,W}$) which has been added to the MPU in Fig. 7-12.   Recall that the isolated I/O technique permits the use of only the IN and OUT instructions.

The 8212 I/O port IC is being used as an output port in Fig. 7-12.   This is determined by noting that the mode control input (*MD*) to the 8212 is HIGH.   When the *MD* input is HIGH, the 8212 is in the *output mode*.   The data bus lines from the MPU are connected to the 8 data input lines ($DI_0 - DI_7$) of the 8212 I/O port.   The 8 data out lines ($DO_0 - DO_7$) from the 8212 are connected to the inputs of the seven-segment LED display.   The 8212 I/O port does have a clear input, but it is disabled with a HIGH in this circuit.   Internally the 8212 unit has eight data latches and output buffers.   The 2 device-select inputs ($\overline{DS1}$, *DS2*) are the control inputs for the 8212 I/O port when used in this mode.   When $\overline{DS1}$ is activated by a LOW and *DS2* is activated by a HIGH, data off the data bus will be latched in the data latches and will also appear at the output pins ($DO_0 - DO_7$), thus activating the segments on the LED display.

The operation of the 8212 I/O port, while being used in the output mode, is detailed in Fig. 7-13.   Note in the timing diagram that as soon as the input control signals ($\overline{DS1}$ and *DS2*) are activated, the input data is latched in the I/O port and is available at the output pins.   In the output mode the output buffers are permanently enabled, so latched data appears at the output pins even after the $\overline{DS1}$ and *DS2* control pins return to their disabled states.

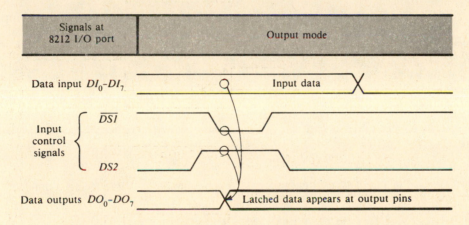

Fig. 7-13   Timing diagram—I/O port signals during output mode

SOLVED PROBLEMS

7.26   The data arriving at the DI_0 through DI_7 terminals of the 8212 I/O port in Fig. 7-12 comes from the _____ (address, data) bus of the microprocessor-based system.

Solution:

According to Fig. 7-12, the data arriving at the DI_0 through DI_7 terminals of the 8212 I/O port comes from the data bus of the microprocessor-based system.

7.27   The 8212 I/O port in Fig. 7-12 is being used as an 8-bit parallel _____ (input, output) port in this diagram.

Solution:

The 8212 I/O port in Fig. 7-12 is being used as an 8-bit parallel output port in this diagram.

7.28   The $\overline{DS1}$ input to the 8212 diagramed in Fig. 7-13 is generated by the _____ (address decoder, MPU's $\overline{I/O\,W}$ signal).

Solution:

According to Fig. 7-12, the $\overline{DS1}$ input to the 8212 I/O port is generated by the MPU's $\overline{I/O\ W}$ signal.

7.29 The $DS2$ input to the 8212 diagramed in Fig. 7-13 is generated by the _____ (address decoder, MPU's data bus).

Solution:

According to Fig. 7-12, the $DS2$ control input to the 8212 I/O port is generated by the address decoder. The least significant 8 address lines are being fully decoded in this system, which means 256 output device numbers are available.

7.30 The 8212's output buffers are permanently _____ (disabled, enabled) while the unit is in its output mode. This means that the buffers _____ (block data from, pass data to) the data outputs (DO_0–DO_7).

Solution:

The 8212's output buffers are permanently enabled while the unit is in its output mode. This means that the buffers pass data to the data outputs (DO_0–DO_7).

7.31 Refer to Fig. 7-13. Data is latched into the 8212 I/O port when both control inputs _____ and _____ are activated.

Solution:

Data is latched into the 8212 I/O port in Fig. 7-13 when both control inputs $\overline{DS1}$ and $DS2$ are activated.

7.32 The system in Fig. 7-12 uses the _____ (isolated, memory-mapped) I/O interfacing technique.

Solution:

The system in Fig. 7-12 uses the isolated, or accumulator, I/O interfacing technique.

7.6 SYNCHRONIZING I/O DATA TRANSFERS USING INTERRUPTS

To this point it was assumed that when the program directed the MPU to input from a port there was valid data available at that location. This may not be the case, however, since peripheral devices (such as a keyboard) do not act at the same speed as the MPU. For this reason several data transfer synchronizing techniques are available. These are *polling* and *interrupts*.

The polling technique is also called programmed I/O. Polling is the simplest method of synchronizing I/O and is used in smaller dedicated applications. The idea of polling is to repeatedly input and/or output data by using a *polling loop* in the program.

Assume an extremely simple MPU-based system using a single input switch and a single LED output indicator. The systems shown in Figs. 7-10a and 7-11a could be combined using a single MPU, an input switch with an input interface adapter, and an output LED with an output interface adapter. An extremely simple polling loop could be constructed to first read the input switch and then write this condition in the LED output indicator. In this example, the read-write-read-write-etc. loop would be continuous. The MPU is polling the input and updating the output every few microseconds.

More commonly the polling loop might be polling one of several I/O devices. The MPU would ask the first device if it needed service. If service was indicated by a true flag condition, the MPU would service that device. If no service was indicated by a false flag condition, the MPU would go on to a second I/O device, etc.

The system diagramed in Fig. 7-14 uses an interrupt request line to notify the microprocessor when data is ready to be transferred to the CPU.   Recall that the generic microprocessor had a single interrupt request input (*INTR*).   When activated with a HIGH, the MPU would finish the current instruction, store the current register and program counter contents on the stack, and jump to a special *interrupt service routine*.   After taking care of the interrupt, the MPU would return to executing the main program.   In this example, the interrupt service routine may be as simple as inputting and storing keyboard entries.

Consider the system in Fig. 7-14.   The microprocessor is interfaced with a keyboard using the Intel 8212 I/O port IC as the input interface adapter.   The mode control (*MD*) of the 8212 unit is LOW, which means it is operating as an input adapter.   The clear (*CLR*) input to the 8212 unit is disabled with a HIGH.   The 8-bit parallel data from the keyboard arrives at the data inputs (DI_0–DI_7) of the 8212 unit.   In this system, the *strobe input (STB) controls the data latches*, while the 8212s *device-select inputs ($\overline{DS1}$ and DS2) control the output buffers*.   The keyboard must place an 8-bit data word at the data inputs of the 8212 unit and must also produce a HIGH pulse (strobe) to latch this data into the I/O port's internal data latches.   These events are represented in Fig. 7-15 by the top three waveforms.   Again it is the HIGH strobe from the keyboard that latches data in the 8212 I/O port.

According to the lower waveform in Fig. 7-15, shortly after data is strobed into the data latches,

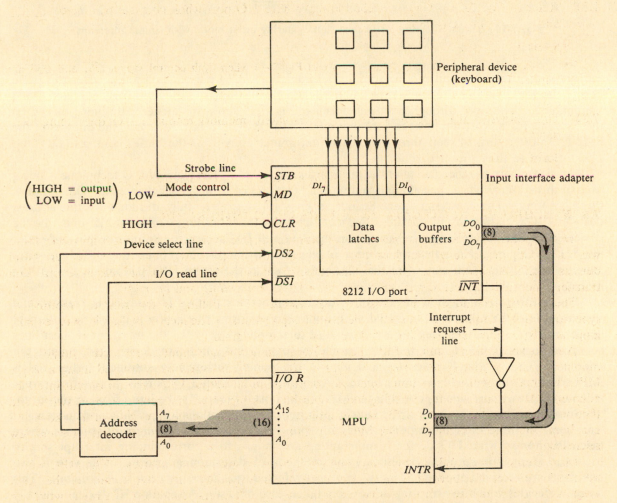

Fig. 7-14   Interfacing with keyboard using the Intel 8212 I/O port with simple interrupt

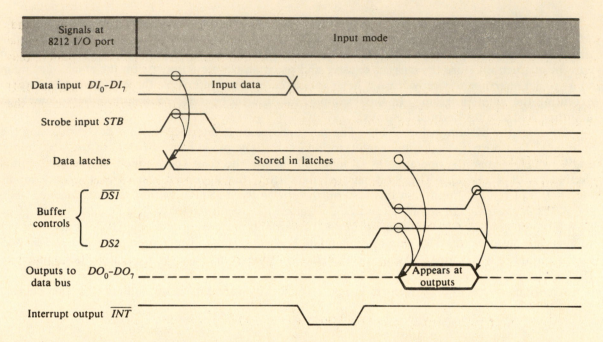

Fig. 7-15   Timing diagram—I/O port signals during input mode with simple interrupt

the circuitry of the 8212 unit produces an output interrupt ($\overline{INT}$) pulse.   Some time after this pulse gets to the MPU via the interrupt request line, the 8212 unit's output buffer controls ($\overline{DS1}$ and $DS2$) are enabled.   The third through sixth waveforms in Fig. 7-15 show the latched data being placed on the data bus for a short time by the 8212 unit's $\overline{DS1}$ and $DS2$ controls.   Note that the outputs of the 8212 I/O port return to their three-state condition immediately after the buffer controls ($\overline{DS1}$ and $DS2$) return to their disabled state.

Consider again the interfacing of the keyboard in Fig. 7-14.   The isolated I/O technique is being used in this system.   The special input/output read ($\overline{I/O\ R}$) control signal activates the $\overline{DS1}$ input of the 8212 unit.   The least significant 8 address lines (A_0-A_7) are fully decoded by the address decoder.   The output of the address decoder activates the $DS2$ input of the 8212 unit via the device-select line.   Recall that in this system the $\overline{DS1}$ and $DS2$ inputs control the output buffers of the 8212 I/O port.   Note that an inverter is placed in the interrupt request line.   This inverter matches the active LOW output of the 8212 unit's $\overline{INT}$ to the active HIGH input on the MPU's *INTR*.

The interrupt is a method of informing the microprocessor that an I/O device is "ready" and action needs to be taken.   The special subroutine that performs this action is called the interrupt service routine.   If several devices are capable of interrupting the MPU, the interrupt request lines could be logically ORed and the CPU would have to "find" the I/O device that caused the interrupt.   The "finding" process would involve the polling technique mentioned earlier and is referred to as the *polled-interrupt* scheme.   Associated with each I/O port in a polled-interrupt scheme is a *status port* whose code tells the MPU if the port is "ready" to be input from or output to.

Some microprocessors have several interrupt inputs and instructions for enabling and disabling at least some of these interrupt inputs.   Many microprocessors use *vectored-interrupt* schemes where the MPU knows what I/O device is interrupting and jumps to a corresponding interrupt service routine.   Many microprocessors also contain methods of determining priority of service if two interrupts are received at once.   This is sometimes referred to as *interrupt priority arbitration*.   This circuitry decides which interrupting device gets taken care of first.   A separate IC device is usually required to perform this task.   The Intel 8259 priority interrupt control unit is one such element.

The advantages of polling over interrupts are that polling requires less interfacing hardware and, because it is under program control, it is synchronous. The disadvantages of the polling technique are that it requires extensive software, wastes MPU time, and if many devices must be polled, may take a lot of time to respond to an I/O device in need of service.

The advantages of interrupts over polling are their fast response time, their better use of MPU time, and their need for less software. The disadvantages are their asynchronous operation and the need for more extensive interfacing hardware.

SOLVED PROBLEMS

7.33 An interrupt request is initiated by a(n) _____ (I/O device, program instruction).

Solution:

An interrupt request is initiated by an I/O device.

7.34 An interrupt request is sent to the MPU when an I/O port is _____ (not ready, ready) for service.

Solution:

An interrupt request is sent to the MPU when an I/O port is ready for service.

7.35 Refer to Fig. 7-14. The 8212 I/O port is operating in its _____ (input, output) mode in this circuit.

Solution:

The 8212 I/O port in Fig. 7-14 is operating in its input mode in this circuit. The LOW at the mode input (MD) places this I/O port in the input mode.

7.36 Refer to Fig. 7-14. For keyboard data to be latched into the internal data latches of the 8212 unit, the _____ (clear, strobe) input must be pulsed _____ (HIGH, LOW). This pulse comes from the _____ (keyboard, MPU) in this system.

Solution:

For keyboard data to be latched into the internal data latches of the 8212 unit in Fig. 7-14, the strobe input must be pulsed HIGH. This pulse comes from the keyboard in this system.

7.37 Upon execution of the IN (input) instruction, the MPU in Fig. 7-14 causes the I/O read line to go _____ (HIGH, LOW) and the device-select line to go _____ (HIGH, LOW). This in turn enables the _____ (data latches, output buffers) in the 8212 I/O port.

Solution:

Upon execution of the IN (input) instruction, the MPU in Fig. 7-14 causes the I/O read line to go LOW and the device-select line to go HIGH. This in turn enables the output buffers in the 8212 I/O port.

7.38 Polling is sometimes referred to as _____ I/O.

Solution:

Polling is sometimes referred to as programmed I/O.

7.39 List the advantages and disadvantages of interrupts over polling as an I/O synchronizing technique.

Solution:

The advantages of using interrupts are that they respond quickly to the I/O devices need for service, make better use of the MPU's time, and use less software. The disadvantages of using interrupts are their asynchronous nature and the need for more extensive interfacing hardware.

7.7 ADDRESS DECODING

A simple microprocessor-based system is shown in Fig. 7-16. Data can be input via the keyboard and output on a single seven-segment display. The control and data-select lines are all shown. The input and output interface adapters are Intel 8212 I/O ports. Synchronization of data transfer from the input interface adapter is accomplished by using a simple interrupt. The system uses the memory-mapped I/O technique, thereby treating the I/O ports as memory locations. Each of the individual interfaces has been examined in previous sections. This section will investigate the address decoding circuitry that might be used in such a system.

The system diagram in Fig. 7-16 shows the most significant 4 address lines (A_{12}–A_{15}) forming the input to the address decoder. The task of the address decoder in this system is to:

1. Generate a LOW output for the ROM device-select line when the most significant 4 address lines equal 0000_2

2. Generate a LOW output for the RAM device-select line when the most significant 4 address lines equal 0010_2

3. Generate a HIGH output for the output interface adapter's device-select line when the most significant 4 address lines equal 1000_2

4. Generate a HIGH output for the input interface adapter's device-select line when the most significant 4 address lines equal 1001_2

A memory map of the system is shown in Fig. 7-17. The 4096 storage locations in ROM will be located in segment 0 or addresses 0000 through 0FFFH. The segment number in this case is the hexadecimal equivalent of the 0000_2 that generated the ROM device-select signal. Another 4096 addresses are located in segment 2 of the memory map in Fig. 7-17. This 4K of memory is RAM. The output port is allocated addresses in segment 8 of the memory map while the input port uses segment 9. Note that any of the 4096 addresses from 8000 through 8FFFH will activate the single output interface adapter. This is true because only 4 of the 16 address lines are decoded. This is referred to as *partial address decoding* and works fine if no other output devices need to be added that have addresses in segment 8. In like manner, any of the 4096 addresses from 9000 to 9FFFH will activate the single input interface adapter in this system. Again, this is true because the address bus is only partially decoded.

One simple solution to the address decoding problem in this system is shown in Fig. 7-18. A 1-of-16 decoder IC and two inverters are used to decode the most significant 4 address lines (A_{12}–A_{15}). Recall that the decoder (also called a demultiplexer) acts something like a rotary switch, activating only one output (0–15) at a time. The output activated in the 1-of-16 decoder depends on which select lines (S_0–S_3) are enabled. Therefore if the select lines equal 0000, then output 0 is activated with a LOW. Figure 7-18 shows that decoder output 0 feeds the device-select line for the ROM and selects segment 0 of the memory map. If the decoder select lines equal 0010 ($S_3 = 0$, $S_2 = 0$, $S_1 = 1$, $S_0 = 0$), output 2 of the 1-of-16 decoder is activated with a LOW. Output 2 is used to enable the device-select line to the RAM.

If the most significant 4 address lines in Fig. 7-18 were at 1000_2, then output 8 of the decoder would be activated with a LOW. An inverter complements this output to be compatible with the necessary HIGH pulse needed to activate the output interface adapter's device-select line. Likewise a 1001_2 at the select inputs of the 1-of-16 decoder will enable the input interface adapter's device-select line with a HIGH pulse. The unused outputs could be employed for adding more peripheral devices or memory devices at a later time.

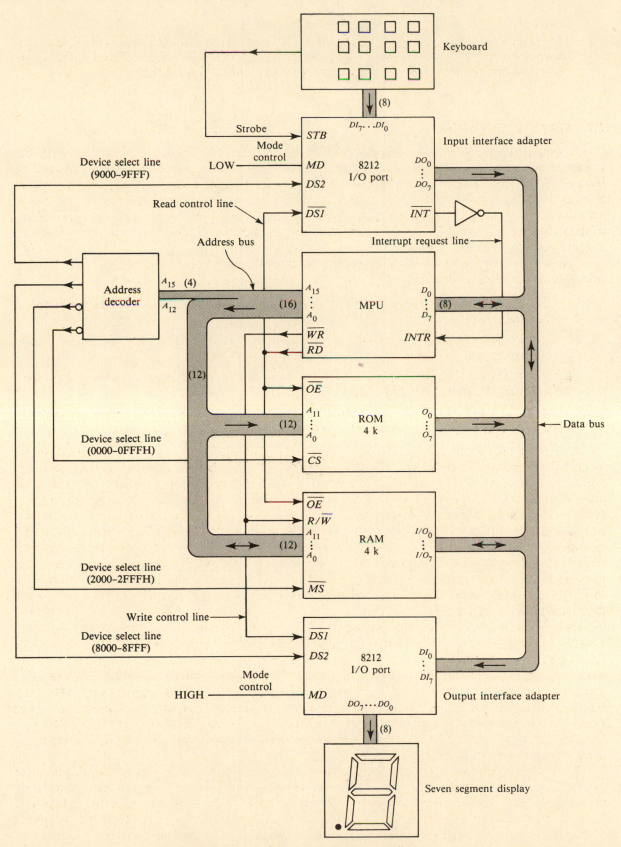

Fig. 7-16 Microprocessor-based system diagram

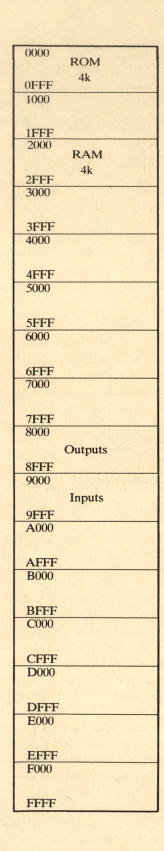

Fig. 7-17 Memory map for microprocessor-based system

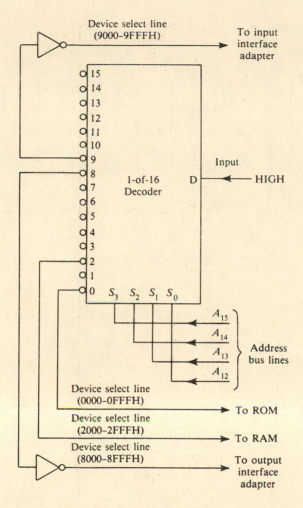

Fig. 7-18   Using the 1-of-16 decoder as an address decoder

The ROM and RAM addresses in Fig. 7-16 are *fully decoded*. Full decoding means that all 16 address lines are decoded, and therefore all possible addresses can be accessed. The I/O port addresses, however, are only partially decoded. For instance, the instruction "LDA, 9000H" would input data from the keyboard which is referred to as memory location 9000H. Also consider the instruction "LDA, 9FFFH." This instruction directs the CPU to load data into the accumulator from location 9FFFH, which in this case will also access the same keyboard data. To identify *a memory-mapped* I/O port with a *unique* hexadecimal number, the 16-bit address bus must be fully decoded.

Full address decoding schemes for the input and output interface adapters are shown in Fig. 7-19. Figure 7-19a shows all 16 address lines entering the address decoder. Only when the address is 8000H will the NOR gate output a HIGH device-select signal to the output interface adapter. All other possible combinations of the 16 inputs will yield a LOW output, which disables the device-select line and the output interface adapter.

Full address decoding for the input interface adapter is illustrated in Fig. 7-19b. The unique address of 9000H is the only one that will cause the NOR-gate output to go HIGH, thereby activating the input interface adapter via the device-select line. Any other combination of 0s and 1s will cause a LOW output from the address decoder, which disables the input interface adapter.

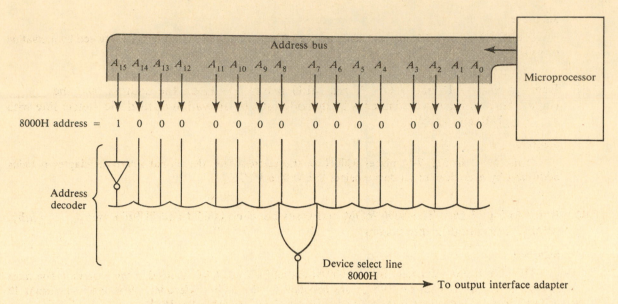

(a) Logic diagram for fully decoding output device at address 8000H

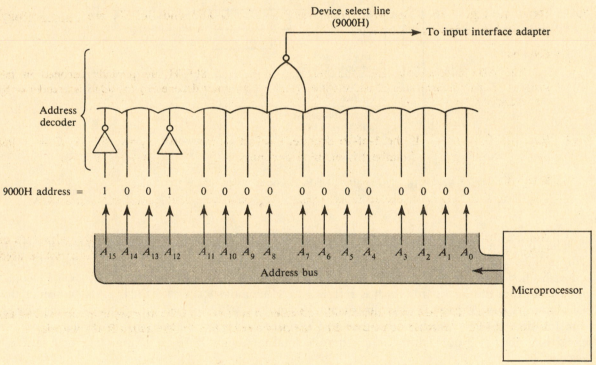

(b) Logic diagram for fully decoding input device at address 9000H

Fig. 7-19

SOLVED PROBLEMS

7.40 Refer to Figs. 7-16 and 7-17. If the MPU places 0300H on the address bus, the _____ (RAM, ROM) is being addressed by activation of its device-select line with a _____ (HIGH, LOW).

Solution:

If the MPU in Fig. 7-16 places 0300H on the address bus, the ROM is being addressed by activation of its device-select line with a LOW.

7.41 Refer to Figs. 7-16 and 7-17. If the MPU places 8300H on the address bus, the _____ (input, output) interface adapter is being addressed by activation of its device-select line with a _____ (HIGH, LOW).

Solution:

If the MPU in Fig. 7-16 places 8300H on the address bus, the output interface adapter is being addressed by activation of its device-select line with a HIGH.

7.42 Refer to Fig. 7-16. The 4096 ROM addresses between 0000H and 0FFFH are _____ (fully, partially) decoded in this system.

Solution:

The 4096 ROM addresses between 0000H and 0FFFH are fully decoded in this system. The most significant 4 address lines (A_{12}–A_{15}) are decoded by the address decoder. The least significant 12 address lines (A_0–A_{11}) are decoded by an address decoder within the ROM.

7.43 Refer to Fig. 7-16. The 4096 addresses between 8000H and 8FFFH are _____ (fully, partially) decoded in this system.

Solution:

The 4096 addresses in Fig. 7-16 between 8000H and 8FFFH are partially decoded in this system. The least significant 12 address lines (A_0–A_{11}) are not decoded by the address decoder or by the output device.

7.44 Refer to Fig. 7-18. If the 1-of-16 decoder's select inputs equal $S_3 = 1$, $S_2 = 1$, $S_1 = 1$, and $S_0 = 0$, output _____ (number) is enabled and puts out a _____ (HIGH, LOW).

Solution:

If the 1-of-16 decoder's select inputs equal 1110, output 14 is enabled and puts out a LOW.

7.45 Assume another 4K RAM were to be added to the system in Fig. 7-16 with the addresses of 1000H to 1FFFH. Output _____ (number) of the 1-of-16 decoder in Fig. 7-18 could be used to drive the device-select line for this added 4K RAM module.

Solution:

If another 4K RAM were added with addresses in segment 1 of the memory map, output 1 of the decoder in Fig. 7-18 could be used to drive the device-select line for the added RAM module.

Supplementary Problems

7.46 Interconnection, or linkage, of parts within a microprocessor-based system is called _____.
Ans. interfacing

7.47 An interface is a shared boundary between two devices which involves sharing _____ (information, storage). *Ans.* information

7.48   Other considerations in interfacing include the direction of data transmission and _____ (matrixing, synchronization).   *Ans.* synchronization

7.49   The three interconnections or data paths in a microprocessor-based system include the data bus, the _____ bus, and the _____ bus.   *Ans.* address, control

7.50   When an MPU releases control of the data and address busses so that a peripheral device can access the main system memory without going through the CPU, it is called _____ _____ _____, or DMA.   *Ans.* direct memory access

7.51   Refer to Fig. 7-2.   The address bus is _____ (fully, partially) decoded in this system.   *Ans.* fully

7.52   Refer to Fig. 7-2.   After addressing, a _____ (HIGH, LOW) at both the $\overline{CS}$ and $\overline{OE}$ inputs to the ROM will cause a memory _____ (read, write) operation to be executed.   *Ans.* LOW, read

7.53   Refer to Fig. 7-4.   The small circles and arrows stand for a cause-and-_____ relationship on timing diagrams.   *Ans.* effect

7.54   Refer to Fig. 7-2.   The outputs of the ROM (O_0–O_7) are in the _____ (HIGH, high-impedance) state when the storage unit is not being accessed.   *Ans.* high-impedance

7.55   If the write control line in Fig. 7-5 is LOW, the RAM is placed in the _____ (read, write) mode.   *Ans.* write

7.56   The read control line in Fig. 7-5 enables the RAM's _____ input with a _____ (HIGH, LOW).   *Ans.* $\overline{OE}$ (output-enable), LOW

7.57   During the read operation in Fig. 7-5, the D_0 through D_7 pins of the microprocessor are considered _____ (inputs, outputs) and are _____ (receiving data from, sending data to) the data bus.   *Ans.* inputs, receiving data from

7.58   Special IN (input) and OUT (output) instructions are used if the _____ (isolated, memory-mapped) I/O technique is employed.   *Ans.* isolated

7.59   The output interface adapter in Fig. 7-10*b* contains a gate and an 8-bit _____ for storing output data.   *Ans.* latch (or data latch)

7.60   The triangular device inside the input interface adapter in Fig. 7-11*a* is an output _____.   *Ans.* buffer (or three-state buffer)

7.61   The system in Fig. 7-12 is using the _____ (isolated, memory-mapped) I/O technique.   *Ans.* isolated

7.62   The 8212's output buffers are _____ (enabled by $\overline{DS1}$, permanently enabled) in the system diagramed in Fig. 7-12.   *Ans.* permanently enabled

7.63   The system in Fig. 7-14 uses an _____ to notify the microprocessor when data is ready to be transferred to the CPU.   *Ans.* interrupt (or interrupt request)

7.64   In Fig. 7-14, an interrupt is generated by the _____ (input interface adapter, MPU) _____ (before, after) the 8212's strobe input latches data in the data latches.   *Ans.* input interface adapter, after

7.65   Upon receiving the interrupt request in Fig. 7-14, the MPU completes the current instruction, stores the current register and program counter contents in stack, and jumps to a short program called the _____ _____ _____.   *Ans.* interrupt service routine

7.66 _____ is a technique by which each I/O device is periodically sampled to determine whether it is "ready" and needs servicing.   *Ans.* Polling

7.67 Refer to Fig. 7-16.   The input peripheral device in this system is the _____.   *Ans.* keyboard

7.68 Refer to Fig. 7-16.   The _____ (output interface adapter, RAM) latches output data and holds it at the inputs of the seven-segment display.   *Ans.* output interface adapter

7.69 Refer to Fig. 7-16.   Synchronization of data transfer from the input interface adapter in this system is accomplished by using a _____ (polled-interrupt, simple interrupt) scheme.
Ans. simple interrupt

7.70 Refer to Fig. 7-16.   The ROM and RAM addresses are _____ (fully, partially) decoded in this system.
Ans. fully

7.71 Refer to Fig. 7-16.   The input and output port addresses are _____ (fully, partially) decoded in this system.   *Ans.* partially

Chapter 8

The Intel 8080/8085 Microprocessor

8.1 INTRODUCTION

The very first microprocessor was introduced by Intel Corporation in 1971. Intel introduced the 4-bit 4004 and the 8-bit 8008 in that year. In 1974, Intel introduced the 8080 microprocessor, which handles 8-bit data words and has a 16-bit address line and a 16-bit stack pointer. The Intel 8085 microprocessor is an enhancement of the 8080 unit. It integrates the clock, system control, and interrupt prioritization within the microprocessor IC, thereby reducing the number of ICs used in most systems. The 8085 also operates on a single +5-V power supply. The 8085 MPU uses all the same instructions as the 8080, thereby making them program compatible. The 8085 microprocessor does add two instructions to take advantage of some of its added hardware capabilities.

The generic microprocessor introduced in earlier chapters was a simplified version of the Intel 8080/8085 MPU. Having become familiar with the generic microprocessor, most students will have little difficulty learning about the 8085 MPU. The 8085 MPU will have more internal registers, many more possible instructions, more control signals, and a few different features compared with the generic microprocessor.

One trend in the evolution of microprocessors has been to integrate more functions into fewer ICs. A simple microprocessor-based system may well have needed in excess of 20 ICs only a short time ago. The system shown in Fig. 8-1 contains only three ICs. The MPU is the Intel 8085 shown controlling the system bus and two other special peripheral interface ICs.

The specially designed peripheral interface chips shown in block form in Fig. 8-1 are the Intel 8155 and 8355 ICs. The 8155 device contains 2048 bits of static RAM organized as a 256×8 bit memory. This unit also contains three I/O ports and a timer. Two of the I/Os are 8-bit general-purpose ports. The remaining 6-bit unit can be used as an input port, as an output port, or as a control signal path for the two 8-bit ports. The 8155 is programmable and also contains a status register and a 14-bit timer-counter.

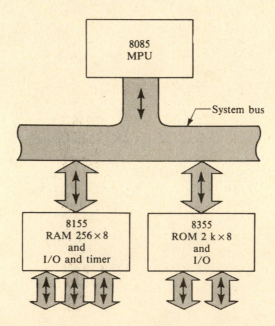

Fig. 8-1 Block diagram of simple 8085 system using special interface chips

The other chip shown in the block diagram in Fig. 8-1 is the 8355 peripheral interface IC.   The 8355 device contains 16,384 bits of ROM organized as a 2048×8 bit memory.   The 8355 also contains two general-purpose 8-bit I/O ports.

The 8080/8085 and its 16-bit and 32-bit relatives have become some of the most widely used general-purpose microprocessors in the world.   Relatives of the 8080/8085 microprocessor by Intel include the 8086, 8088, 80186, 80188, 80286, and 80386.   Several of these chips were selected to serve as the CPU in popular IBM microcomputers.

8.2   THE 8085 PIN DIAGRAM AND FUNCTIONS

The Intel 8085 8-bit microprocessor is housed in a 40-pin dual-in-line package (DIP).   The *pinout diagram* for the 8085 MPU is reproduced in Fig. 8-2a.   In Fig. 8-2b is a chart summarizing the pin names and descriptions.   Manufacturer's literature may specify an 8085 or 8085A microprocessor.   The 8085A unit is a slight revision of the original 8085 microprocessor.   Later revisions include the higher-speed upgrades such as the 8085A-2, 8085AH, 8085AH-2, and 8085AH-1.

The generic microprocessor used 16 pins for address lines and eight pins for data bus connections.   With the added functions of the 8085, the 40-pin DIP did not have enough pins for all the inputs and outputs.   For that reason, the manufacturer uses pins 12 through 19 as dual-purpose address/data bus lines ($AD_0 - AD_7$).   The unit is said to have an 8-bit *multiplexed address/data bus*.   The least significant 8 address lines share pins with the 8 data bus lines.   To multiplex means to first select one and then another, etc.   Therefore, to multiplex the address/data bus means to first use the bus to send an address and next to send or receive data via the same bus.   The 8085 has a special signal for informing the peripherals when the address/data bus is sending an address and when the bus is functioning as a data bus.   This special signal is called the *address latch enable* (ALE) control signal.   Note that the address/data bus pins are bidirectional or may be three-stated (also called tristated).   The ALE pin is a control output.

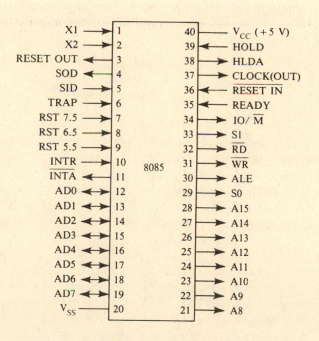

(a) Pin diagram of 8085 MPU

Fig. 8-2

Pin name	Description	Type
AD0—AD7	Address/Data bus	Bidirectional, tristate
A8—A15	Address bus	Output, tristate
ALE	Address latch enable	Output*
$\overline{RD}$	Read control	Output, tristate
$\overline{WR}$	Write control	Output, tristate
IO/$\overline{M}$	I/O or memory indicator	Output, tristate
S0, S1	Bus state indicators	Output
READY	Wait state request	Input
SID	Serial data input	Input
SOD	Serial data output	Output
HOLD	Hold request	Input
HLDA	Hold acknowledge	Output
INTR	Interrupt request	Input
TRAP	Nonmaskable interrupt request	Input
RST 5.5	Hardware vectored	Input
RST 6.5	interrupt requests	Input
RST 7.5		Input
$\overline{INTA}$	Interrupt acknowledge	Output
$\overline{RESET IN}$	System reset	Input
RESET OUT	Peripherals reset	Output
X1, X2	Crystal or RC connections	Input
CLK	Clock signal	Output
V_{CC}, V_{SS}	Power, ground	

*This output is tristate on the 8085, but not on the 8085A.

(b) Pin names and functions

Fig. 8-2 (cont.)

The 8085, like the generic microprocessor, has a total of 16 address lines.   The most significant 8 address lines are connected to pins A_8 through A_{15} in Fig. 8-2.   These connect directly to the address bus as in the generic microprocessor.   These pins are outputs or can be three-stated.   Other pins similar to those found on the generic microprocessor are the power pins (V_{CC} and V_{SS}) connected to a +5-V power supply.   The 8085 microprocessor has built-in clock circuitry with the X_1 and X_2 input pins typically connected to a crystal.   The MPU's internal frequency will be one-half the crystal frequency.

Several 8085 pins listed in Fig. 8-2 perform control functions similar to those observed on the generic microprocessor.   The read ($\overline{RD}$) and write ($\overline{WR}$) control outputs are used for informing the memory or I/O devices it is time to send or receive data via the data bus (actually the address/data bus in this unit).   The reset input ($\overline{RESET IN}$) acts like the generic MPU's reset in that the program counter is reset to 0000H.   The data and address busses and control lines are three-stated during a reset.   The contents of the internal registers may also be altered during a reset.   The RESET OUT pin is associated with the reset operation.   When the MPU is reset, the RESET OUT pin sends a signal to the peripherals that informs them that the system is being reset.

The clock (CLK) output from the 8085 microprocessor in Fig. 8-2 operates the same as the one on the generic MPU. The interrupt request input (*INTR*) to the 8085 is a general-purpose interrupt, as on the generic microprocessor. Unlike the generic microprocessor's interrupt, however, the 8085's *INTR* can be enabled or disabled by software instructions. Besides the regular interrupt request (*INTR*), the 8085 MPU has four other interrupt inputs. They are the *TRAP*, *RST 7.5*, *RST 6.5*, and *RST 5.5* input pins. The *TRAP* is the highest-priority interrupt, followed by the *RST 7.5*, *RST 6.5*, *RST 5.5*, and finally the lowest-priority interrupt, the *INTR*. The *TRAP* or any of the three restarts (*RST 7.5*, *RST 6.5*, *RST 5.5*) causes the MPU to jump to a subroutine at a specific call address. The restart interrupts can be enabled and disabled by software, while the *TRAP* interrupt cannot be disabled in this manner. The *INTR* interrupt jumps to an address dictated by a special instruction received from a peripheral device when the MPU's interrupt acknowledge ($\overline{INTA}$) output is activated.

The 8085 microprocessor has a primitive serial input and serial output. These are the *SID* (serial data input) and *SOD* (serial data output) pins shown in Fig. 8-2. The single bit of data on the *SID* input pin is loaded into the *MSB* position (bit 7) in the accumulator by the 8085's RIM instruction. The output pin *SOD* is set or reset as specified by the 8085's SIM instruction.

Consider the *READY* input to the 8085 microprocessor in Fig. 8-2. The *READY* input from a peripheral device informs the microprocessor that it is ready to send or receive data. If the *READY* input from the peripheral device is LOW during a read or write cycle, the MPU interprets this as a request to enter the *wait state*. The MPU will then wait until the peripheral signals that it is ready to transmit or receive data. The MPU will then proceed with the read or write cycle. The *READY* input is handy when using memories or peripherals that are too slow for the processing speed of the microprocessor.

Consider the *HOLD* input and *HLDA* (hold acknowledge) output pins on the 8085 MPU in Fig. 8-2. A *HOLD* input notifies the MPU that another device wants to use the address and data busses. This may occur during direct memory access operations. Upon receiving a *HOLD* input, the CPU will complete current data transfers on the busses. Then the 8085's address, data, $\overline{RD}$, $\overline{WR}$, and $IO/\overline{M}$ pins are three-stated so as not to interfere with data transfers on the busses. A *HLDA* output indicates to a peripheral that a hold request has been received and that the microprocessor will relinquish control of the busses in the next clock cycle.

8085 control signals			
$IO/\overline{M}$	S_1	S_0	Machine cycle status
0	0	1	Memory write
0	1	0	Memory read
1	0	1	I/O write
1	1	0	I/O read
0	1	1	Op code fetch
1	1	1	Interrupt acknowledge
*	0	0	Halt
*	×	×	Hold
*	×	×	Reset

* = three-state condition

× = unspecified

Fig. 8-3 The 8085 machine cycles

The $IO/\overline{M}$, S_0 and S_1 outputs are control signals that notify peripherals what type of machine cycle the MPU is performing. The machine cycle types are listed in the right column in Fig. 8-3. The appropriate combination of output signals at the $IO/\overline{M}$, S_0, and S_1 pins is detailed on the left.

With this brief overview of pin functions, the 8085 MPU appears to have several features not found on the generic microprocessor. Most of these features and some of their uses will be explored in later sections.

SOLVED PROBLEMS

8.1   The Intel 8085 is called a(n) _____ (number) -bit microprocessor because accumulator words are of this width.

   Solution:

   The Intel 8085 is called an 8-bit microprocessor because accumulator words are of this width.

8.2   The address/data bus is said to be _____ (decoded, multiplexed) because it alternately functions as an address bus and as a data bus.

   Solution:

   The address/data bus is said to be multiplexed because it alternately functions as an address bus and as a data bus.

8.3   Refer to Fig. 8-2.   The _____ output is used by the microprocessor to notify the peripherals when the address/data bus is being used as an address bus.

   Solution:

   The *ALE* (address latch enable) output is used by the 8085 microprocessor to notify the peripherals when the address/data bus is being used as an address bus.

8.4   Refer to Fig. 8-2.   The 8085 microprocessor uses a _____-V power supply.

   Solution:

   According to Fig. 8-2, the 8085 microprocessor uses a +5-V power supply.

8.5   Refer to Fig. 8-2.   If the $IO/\overline{M}$ and $\overline{WR}$ outputs were both LOW, the microprocessor would be _____ (reading out of, writing into) a(n) _____ (I/O port, memory location).

   Solution:

   If the $IO/\overline{M}$ and $\overline{WR}$ outputs were both LOW, the MPU would be writing into a memory location. The overbars indicate that a LOW activates the M, or memory, in the $IO/\overline{M}$ signal and a write on the $\overline{WR}$ output signal.

8.6   Refer to Fig. 8-2.   If the microprocessor were in a read cycle and the *READY* input went LOW, the CPU would _____ (immediately, go into the wait state until the peripheral device was ready and then) finish the read cycle.

   Solution:

   If the MPU were in a read cycle and the READY input went LOW, the CPU would go into the wait state until the peripheral device was ready and then finish the read cycle.

8.7   Refer to Fig. 8-3.   During an op code fetch machine cycle, control signals $S_0 = $ _____ (0, 1), $S_1 = $ _____ (0, 1), and $IO/\overline{M} = $ _____ (0, 1).

Solution:

According to Fig. 8-3, during an op code fetch machine cycle, control signals $S_0 = 1$, $S_1 = 1$, and $IO/\overline{M} = 0$.

8.8   Refer to Fig. 8-2.   List the input pins on the 8085 microprocessor IC that would be considered interrupts.

Solution:

The input pins on the 8085 MPU that are considered interrupts are the *INTR*, *TRAP*, *RST 7.5*, *RST 6.5*, and *RST 5.5*.   Some might also consider the *RESET IN* (reset) input to be an interrupt because it is caused by an external device and branches the program counter to a new program segment.

8.9   Refer to Fig. 8-2.   The serial I/O pins are labeled _____ and _____ on the 8085 microprocessor pin diagram.

Solution:

According to Fig. 8-2, the serial I/O pins are labeled *SID* and *SOD* on the 8085 microprocessor pin diagram.

8.3   THE 8085 ARCHITECTURE

The internal organization or architecture of the Intel 8085 microprocessor is reproduced in Fig. 8-4.   The 8085 has a 16-bit program counter and address latch which feed the dedicated address bus $(A_{15}-A_8)$ and the dual-purpose address/data bus (AD_7-AD_0).   Parallel data enters and leaves the MPU via the multiplexed address/data bus (AD_7-AD_0).   The address/data bus transmits an address when the *ALE* control line is HIGH and data when the *ALE* line is LOW.

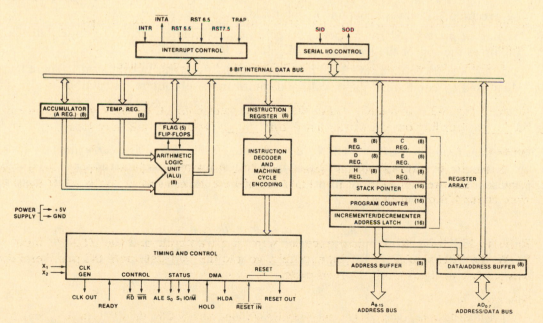

Fig. 8-4   Functional block diagram of 8085 MPU   (*Courtesy of Intel Corporation*)

The 8-bit internal data bus carries input or output data throughout the unit. The data can flow from the internal data bus to the 8-bit accumulator or temporary register, flags, instruction register, interrupt control unit, serial I/O control unit, any of the general-purpose registers (B, C, D, E, H, and L), 16-bit stack pointer, 16-bit program counter, or 8-bit data/address buffer. The serial inputs and outputs (SID and SOD) are shown in the upper right in Fig. 8-4. The interrupt inputs ($INTR$, $RST\ 5.5$, $RST\ 6.5$, $RST\ 7.5$, and $TRAP$) are shown at the upper left, with the $\overline{INTA}$ (interrupt acknowledge) output also illustrated. The arithmetic-logic unit (ALU) is being fed by two 8-bit registers (accumulator and temporary register) as in the generic microprocessor. The flag flip-flops have five status indicators instead of the two in the generic microprocessor.

The instruction register feeds the instruction decoder. The instruction decoder interprets the current instruction and determines the microprogram to be followed. The instruction decoder then instructs the timing and control section as to the sequence of events to be followed. The timing and control section coordinates actions of both the processor and the peripherals. The internal control lines are not shown in Fig. 8-4, but the control outputs and status outputs are shown. The $RESET$, $HOLD$, and $READY$ inputs are also shown entering the timing and control section of the 8085 microprocessor.

Registers

Like the generic microprocessor, the 8085 MPU uses both 8-bit and 16-bit registers. The 8085 has eight addressable 8-bit registers. Six of these can be used as 8-bit registers or 16-bit register pairs. In addition, the 8085 contains two more 16-bit registers. The 8085's registers are as follows:

1. The *accumulator* (A register) is the focus of all accumulator operations which include arithmetic, logic, load and store, and I/O instructions. It is an 8-bit register.

2. The *general-purpose* registers BC, DE, and HL may be used as six 8-bit or as three 16-bit registers depending on the instruction being executed. As in the generic microprocessor, the HL register pair (called a *data pointer* by Intel) can be used for address pointing. A few instructions use the BC and DE register pairs as address pointers, but normally they are used as general-purpose data registers.

3. The *program counter* (PC) always points to the memory location of the next instruction to be executed. It always contains a 16-bit address.

4. The *stack pointer* (SP) is a special-purpose address pointer (or data pointer) that always points to the top of the stack in RAM. It is a 16-bit register.

5. The *flag register* contains five 1-bit flags containing CPU status information. These flags are then used by conditional jump, call, and return from subroutine instructions.

Flags

The five flags found in the 8085's CPU are represented in Fig. 8-5. The *carry flag* (CY) is set or reset by arithmetic operations. Its status is then tested by program instructions. As with the generic microprocessor, an overflow from an 8-bit addition will result in the CY bit being set to

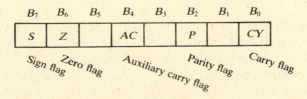

Fig. 8-5 Flags in the 8085's status register

1. In subtraction the *CY* flag acts as a "borrow" flag, indicating the minuend is less than the subtrahend if the flag is set.

The *zero flag* (*Z*) is set if the result of certain instructions is zero. The zero flag is cleared if the result is not zero. The action of the zero flag was observed on the generic microprocessor.

The *sign flag* (*S*) is set to the condition of the most significant bit of the accumulator following the execution of arithmetic or logical instructions. These instructions use the MSB of data to represent the sign of the number contained in the accumulator. A set sign flag represents a negative number, whereas a reset flag means a positive number.

The *auxiliary carry flag* (*AC*) indicates an overflow or carry out of bit 3 of the accumulator in the same manner a carry flag indicates an overflow from bit 7. This flag is commonly used in BCD (binary-coded-decimal) arithmetic.

The *parity flag* (*P*) tests for the number of 1 bits in the accumulator. If the accumulator holds an *even number* of 1s, it is said that even parity exists and the parity flag is set to 1. However, if the accumulator holds an odd number of 1s (called odd parity), the parity flag on the 8085 is reset to 0. For instance, if an ADD instruction resulted in leaving the sum 00110011_2 in the accumulator, the parity flag would be set to 1 because there is an even number (4) of 1s. If however, 10101110_2 were the sum, the *P* flag would be reset to 0 because there is an odd number (5) of 1s in the accumulator.

Stack Pointer

The *stack pointer* maintains the address of the last byte entered into the stack. The stack pointer can be initialized to use any portion of RAM as a stack. As on the generic microprocessor, the stack pointer is decremented each time data is pushed onto the stack and is incremented each time data is popped off the stack.

Arithmetic-Logic Unit

The ALU is closely associated with the accumulator, the flag register, and some temporary registers that are inaccessible to the programmer. Arithmetic, logic, and rotate operations are performed in the ALU. The results typically are deposited in the accumulator.

Instruction Register and Decoder

During an instruction fetch, the first byte of an instruction, the op code, is transferred to the 8-bit *instruction register*. The contents of the instruction register are, in turn, available to the *instruction decoder*. The output of the decoder, gated by timing signals, controls the registers, ALU, and data and address buffers. The outputs of the instruction decoder and internal clock generator produce the state and machine cycle timing signals.

Internal Clock Generator

The 8085 MPU incorporates a complete clock generator on its chip. It requires only the addition of a quartz crystal to establish timing for its operation. The 8085A can use a crystal up to 6.25 megahertz (MHz). The 8085A-2 version of the 8085 will operate with a crystal up to 10 MHz. The *CLK* output pin is a buffered clock output having a frequency of one-half the frequency of the crystal. The 8085AH, 8085AH-2, and 8085AH-1 clock inputs may also be driven with a 6-, 10-, or 12-MHz crystal.

Interrupts

The five *hardware interrupt* inputs are listed by priority in the left column in Fig. 8-6. The highest-priority interrupt is the *TRAP* input. Upon going HIGH for a time, the *TRAP* input will cause the 8085 to save the program counter contents in the stack and jump to memory location 0024H. The *TRAP* input cannot be disabled and is therefore called a *nonmaskable interrupt*.

Name	Priority	Address (1) Branched to when interrupt occurs	Type Trigger
TRAP	1	24H	Rising edge AND high level until sampled
RST 7.5	2	3CH	Rising edge (latched)
RST 6.5	3	34H	High level until sampled
RST 5.5	4	2CH	High level until sampled
INTR	5	(2)	High level until sampled

NOTES:
(1) In the case of TRAP and RST 5.5-7.5, the contents of the Program Counter are pushed onto the stack before the branch occurs.
(2) Depends on the instruction that is provided to the 8085A by the 8259 or other circuitry when the interrupt is acknowledged.

Fig. 8-6 Hardware interrupts on the 8085 MPU
(*Courtesy of Intel Corporation*)

The next three hardware interrupts listed in Fig. 8-6 are called restarts (to restart the program at a new location in memory). The *RST 7.5* interrupt causes the 8085 to save the contents of the program counter in the stack and jump to memory location 003CH. The next-highest-priority interrupt is the *RST 6.5*, which causes the 8085 to save the contents of the program counter in the stack and jump to memory location 0034H. The lower-priority *RST 5.5* interrupt causes the 8085 to save the contents of the program counter in the stack and jump to memory location 002CH.

The lowest-priority hardware interrupt is the *INTR* input, which causes the processor to fetch an instruction from a special external source. All the last four interrupts can be enabled and disabled by software.

Serial Input and Output

The *serial input* and *output* pins on the 8085 help minimize chip count in small systems by providing a serial interface port. The special 8085 RIM instruction transfers data from the serial input pin (*SID*) to bit 7 of the accumulator. This is illustrated in Fig. 8-7a. In the example in Fig. 8-7a, a HIGH is being transferred from the *SID* input to the MSB position in the accumulator.

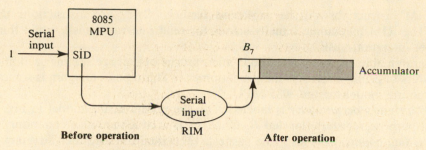

(a) 8085's RIM instruction for serial input

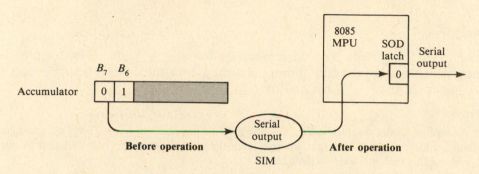

(b)   8085's SIM instruction for serial output

Fig. 8-7

A single serial bit may be output via the serial output (*SOD*) pin by using the special 8085 SIM instruction.   The serial output operation is diagramed in Fig. 8-7*b*.   A LOW is being output to the *SOD* pin in Fig. 8-7*b* via the serial output latch.   Note that the source of the data was bit 7 of the accumulator.   Bit 6 (B_6) of the accumulator must be set to 1 for the serial output to occur.

The serial input (*SID*) can also be used as a general purpose *TEST* input, while the serial output pin (*SOD*) can serve as a 1-bit control output.   In a later section on the 8085's instruction set the

Program status word
(flags)   Primary   accumulator

PSW	(8)	A	(8)	
B	(8)	C	(8)	Secondary accumulators/data counters
D	(8)	E	(8)	
H	(8)	L	(8)	
SP			(16)	Stack pointer
PC			(16)	Program counter

Fig. 8-8   Programming model of the 8085 microprocessor

RIM and SIM instructions will be explained further. They are instructions that have several purposes. The RIM mnemonic actually stands for *read interrupt mask*, while the SIM mnemonic stands for *set interrupt mask*.

The programmable registers of the 8085 microprocessor unit are summarized in Fig. 8-8. These are the registers of prime interest to the programmer. This type of diagram is sometimes referred to as a programming model for the 8085 MPU.

The 8-bit *primary accumulator* is labeled *A* in the programming model in Fig. 8-8. The other 8-bit general-purpose registers (labeled *B*, *C*, *D*, *E*, *H*, and *L*) are also commonly called *secondary accumulators/data counters*. This name suggests their dual use as either auxiliary accumulators or data counters (or address pointers). The 16-bit stack pointer (*SP*) and program counter (*PC*) are also shown on the programming model in Fig. 8-8.

SOLVED PROBLEMS

8.10 Refer to Fig. 8-4. The 8085 microprocessor has a _____ (number) -bit program counter which feeds the address latch. From the address latch the address is split in half and sent to peripherals via the _____ bus and the _____/_____ bus.

Solution:

According to the diagram in Fig. 8-4, the 8085 microprocessor has a 16-bit program counter which feeds the address latch. From the address latch the address is split in half and sent to peripherals via the address bus and the address/data bus.

8.11 Refer to Fig. 8-4. The *ALE* output control line will be _____ (HIGH, LOW) when the MPU is sending an address over the address/data bus.

Solution:

The *ALE* output control line will be HIGH when the MPU is sending an address over the address/data bus. When the *ALE* control line goes LOW, the address/data bus is converted to a bidirectional data bus.

8.12 Refer to Fig. 8-4. The *SID* and *SOD* pins on the 8085 microprocessor are most closely associated with the _____ (interrupt, serial I/O) control section.

Solution:

According to Fig. 8-4, the *SID* and *SOD* pins on the 8085 microprocessor are most closely associated with the serial I/O control section.

8.13 Besides the accumulator, list the six general-purpose 8-bit registers in an 8085 microprocessor.

Solution:

Besides the accumulator, the six general-purpose 8-bit registers are the *B*, *C*, *D*, *E*, *H*, and *L* registers. These can be used as register pairs (16-bit registers) during certain operations. The register pairs are *BC*, *DE*, and *HL*.

8.14 This 16-bit register always holds an address and points to the top of the stack in RAM.

Solution:

The stack pointer always holds an address and points to the top of the stack in RAM.

8.15 List the five status indicators in the flag register of the 8085 microprocessor.

Solution:

According to Fig. 8-5, the five flags, or status indicators, in the 8085 microprocessor are the sign flag, zero flag, auxiliary carry flag, parity flag, and carry flag.

8.16 The contents of the accumulator (the sum) in Fig. 8-9 after the add operation will be _____ (8 bits).

Solution:

Adding binary $11110000 + 00001111 = 1\,0000\,0111$. The contents of the accumulator in Fig. 8-9 after the add operation will be 00000111 (the least significant 8 bits of the sum).

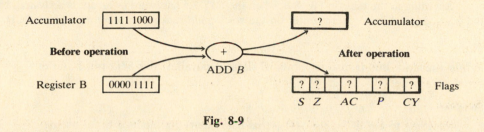

Fig. 8-9

8.17 The sign flag (S) will be _____ (reset to 0, set to 1) after the add operation in Fig. 8-9.

Solution:

The most significant bit (bit 7) in the accumulator is the sign bit. After the add operation the accumulator holds 00000111 in Fig. 8-9. Therefore the sign bit will be reset to 0.

8.18 The zero flag (Z) will be _____ (reset to 0, set to 1) after the add operation in Fig. 8-9.

Solution:

The contents of the accumulator after the add operation in Fig. 8-9 are 00000111. This is not zero; therefore the zero flag is reset to 0.

8.19 The auxiliary carry flag (AC) will be _____ (reset to 0, set to 1) after the add operation in Fig. 8-9.

Solution:

The B_3 position in the accumulator and register B both hold a 1 in Fig. 8-9. Binary $1 + 1 = 10_2$. This means there will be a carry out of the B_3 position to the B_4 position. Because of this carry, the auxiliary flag (AC) will be set to 1 after the add operation in Fig. 8-9.

8.20 The parity flag (P) will be _____ (reset to 0, set to 1) after the add operation in Fig. 8-9.

Solution:

After the add operation in Fig. 8-9, the accumulator will hold binary 00000111. This sum contains three 1s, which is *not even parity*, and therefore the parity flag will be reset to 0.

8.21 The carry flag (CY) will be _____ (reset to 0, set to 1) after the add operation in Fig. 8-9.

Solution:

Adding binary $11111000 + 00001111 = 1\,0000\,0111$. Because of the overflow beyond the accumulator's 8-bit limit, there is a carry out of the B_7 position. The carry flag (CY) will be set to 1 after the add operation in Fig. 8-9.

8.22   The highest-priority hardware interrupt on the 8085 microprocessor which cannot be disabled is called the _____ (*INTR*, *TRAP*).

Solution:

The highest-priority hardware interrupt on the 8085 microprocessor which cannot be disabled is called the *TRAP*.

8.23   Refer to Fig. 8-6.   When the *RST 7.5* hardware interrupt is activated, the CPU saves the contents of the _____ _____ on the stack and branches to memory address _____ (hex).

Solution:

According to the table in Fig. 8-6, when the *RST 7.5* hardware interrupt is activated, the CPU saves the contents of the program counter on the stack and branches to memory address 3CH.

8.24   While the data bus transfers 8 bits of data in parallel, the *SID* pin handles _____ (number) bit(s) at a time.

Solution:

According to Fig. 8-7*a*, the *SID* (serial data input) pin inputs 1 bit at a time.

8.4   ADDRESSING MODES

Like the generic microprocessor, the 8085 MPU uses five addressing modes.   These are:

1.   Implied addressing
2.   Register addressing
3.   Immediate addressing
4.   Direct addressing
5.   Register indirect addressing

Implied Addressing

The addressing mode of certain 8085 MPU instructions is *implied* by (or inherent in) the instruction's function.   For example, the STC (set carry flag) instruction deals with the carry flag only and no other registers or memory locations.

Register Addressing

Many 8085 MPU instructions use *register addressing*.   When using these instructions, the operation and the operand's source are specified.   Consider the execution of the ADD *C* instruction in Fig. 8-10.   In this example the operand from the source register (register *C* in this case) is being added to the operand located in the accumulator.   After the ADD *C* instruction is executed, the sum (00001111_2 in this example) is deposited in the accumulator.   As usual, the add operation also affects the flags in the status register.

The ADD *C* instruction illustrated in Fig. 8-10 used register addressing.   Both the operands were located in internal MPU registers (*A* and *C* registers).   Instructions using register addressing are very efficient in that they only use 1 byte of program memory space.   They are also executed very quickly because they do not have to fetch operands from memory.   Fetching from memory is a relatively slow operation.

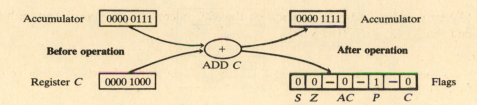

Fig. 8-10   The ADD *C* instruction (register addressing mode)

Immediate Addressing

Instructions that use *immediate addressing* have data immediately following the op code in program memory.   As an example, the 8085's ADI (add immediate) instruction is illustrated in Fig. 8-11.   The microprocessor fetches the op code (C6H in this example) from program memory.   After decoding, the MPU determines that this is an immediate addressing instruction.   It therefore finds the immediate data in the next consecutive program memory location after the op code.   This immediate data (00001000_2) is added to the contents of the accumulator (00001100_2).   After the add operation, the sum (00010100_2) is placed in the accumulator.

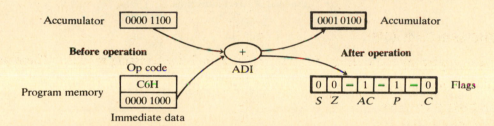

Fig. 8-11   The ADI instruction (immediate addressing mode)

All but two of the 8085 microprocessor's immediate instructions use the accumulator as an implied operand, as in the ADI operation shown in Fig. 8-11.   The 8085's MVI (move immediate) instruction can move immediate data to any register or memory location.   The 8085's LXI (load register pair immediate) instruction loads a register pair with a 16-bit value and therefore does not affect the accumulator.

Direct Addressing

Operations using *direct addressing* on the Intel 8085 MPU are specified using 3-byte instruction formats.   This format is represented in Fig. 8-12*a*.   Byte 1 contains the op code for the direct addressing instruction.   Byte 2 contains the low-order byte of the address of the operand.   Byte 3 of the instruction contains the high-order byte of the address of the operand.

The 8085's LDA (load *A* direct) instruction is being executed in Fig. 8-12*b*.   The 3-byte instruction is shown at the lower part of the diagram.   The op code for the LDA instruction is shown as 3AH.   The next 2 bytes of program memory are assembled within the microprocessor into a 16-bit address (0200H in this example).   This data memory address (0200H) is then accessed by the MPU.   The contents (11111111_2) of this address are then shown being loaded into the accumulator.

Instructions using direct addressing are sometimes avoided by microprocessor designers and programmers.   Direct addressing requires a lot of program memory space (3 bytes of program

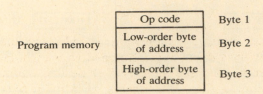

(a) Instruction format for direct addressing

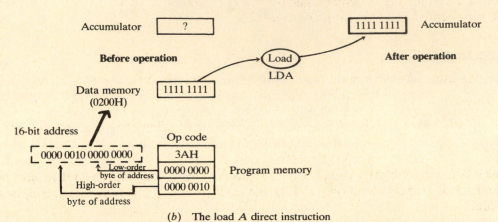

(b) The load *A* direct instruction

Fig. 8-12

memory for one instruction for the 8085 MPU). Direct addressing operations also require a relatively long execution time owing to the many memory accesses involved.

Register Indirect Addressing

Register indirect instructions reference memory using the contents of a register pair to point to the address of the operand. An example of a register indirect operation is illustrated in Fig. 8-13. The ADD *M* (add memory) instruction in Fig. 8-13 adds the contents of the accumulator to the contents of memory pointed to by the address in the *HL* register pair of the MPU. In this example, the *HL* register pair points to memory location 2050H. The operand in data memory location 2050H (00000001_2) is then added to the contents of the accumulator (11111111_2). The sum of binary $00000001 + 11111111 = 1\ 0000\ 0000$. The least significant 8 bits of the sum are deposited in the accumulator after the ADD *M* operation. The appropriate flags are also set and reset based on the add operation's result and are shown in Fig. 8-13.

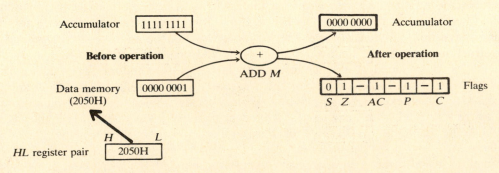

Fig. 8-13 An add register indirect instruction

Combined Addressing Modes

Some 8085 MPU instructions use a combination of addressing modes. A subroutine CALL instruction, for example, combines direct addressing and register indirect addressing. The direct address in a CALL instruction specifies the address of the desired subroutine. The register indirect address is that of the stack pointer. The CALL instruction first pushes the current contents of the program counter into the memory location specified by the stack pointer. Next the processor loads the direct address into the program counter. Finally, the MPU jumps to the subroutine whose address is now contained in the program counter.

SOLVED PROBLEMS

8.25 List the five addressing modes used by the Intel 8085 microprocessor.

Solution:

The Intel 8085 microprocessor uses the implied, register, immediate, direct, and register indirect addressing modes.

8.26 The CMC (complement carry) 8085 instruction affects only the carry flag and no other registers or memory locations. Therefore it uses the _____ (direct, implied) addressing mode.

Solution:

The CMC (complement carry) instruction uses the implied addressing mode because it affects only the carry flag and uses no other registers or memory locations.

8.27 The 8085's MOV *B,A* instruction (move *A* to *B*) transfers the contents of one register to another. The MOV *B,A* instruction therefore uses the _____ (immediate, register) addressing mode.

Solution:

The 8085's MOV *B,A* instruction (move *A* to *B*) executes a register-to-register operation and therefore uses the register addressing mode.

8.28 The 8085's MVI *A* instruction shown in Fig. 8-14 uses the _____ (implied, immediate) addressing mode.

Solution:

From Fig. 8-14 it is determined that data is moved from the second byte of program memory to the accumulator. This means that the 8085's MVI *A* (move immediate) instruction uses the immediate addressing mode.

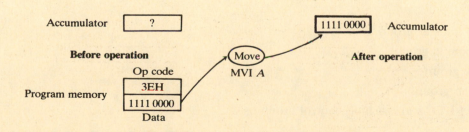

Fig. 8-14 A move immediate instruction

8.29 The 8085's SUB *M* instruction in Fig. 8-15 uses the _____ (register, register indirect) addressing mode.

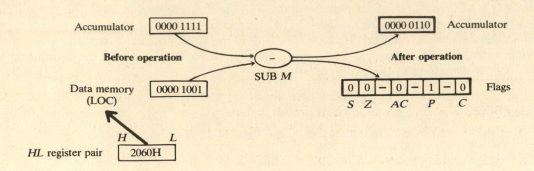

Fig. 8-15 The SUB *M* instruction

Solution:

From Fig. 8-15 it is determined that the subtrahend comes from a data memory location pointed to by the *HL* register pair. This means that the 8085's SUB *M* instruction uses the register indirect addressing mode.

8.30 In Fig. 8-15, the minuend is located in the accumulator while the subtrahend is found in data memory location _____ (hex).

Solution:

In Fig. 8-15, the minuend is located in the accumulator while the subtrahend is found in data memory location 2060H as pointed to by the *HL* register pair.

8.5   THE 8080/8085 INSTRUCTION SET

The Intel 8080 and 8085 microprocessors are used to form stored-program computers. The program instructions are stored as 8-bit bytes in a storage area(s) referred to as program memory. The Intel 8080/8085 microprocessor uses 1-, 2-, and 3-byte instructions. The first byte of the instruction is always the op code (operational code), which specifies which one of over 200 instructions the microprocessor should perform. The MPU recognizes these op codes when they are in 8-bit binary form. The set of instructions to which the 8080 and 8085 MPU will respond is permanently fixed in the design of the chips. The 8085 uses all the same op codes as the 8080 MPU. The 8085's instruction set also contains two extra instructions beyond the ones used by the 8080 MPU.

Intel Corporation groups the 8080/8085 microprocessor's instructions into the following functional categories:

1.   Data transfer group
2.   Arithmetic group
3.   Logic group
4.   Branch group
5.   Stack, I/O, and machine control group

The *data transfer group* of instructions moves data between registers or between memory locations and registers. Included are moves, loads, stores, and exchanges.

The *arithmetic group* of instructions performs adds, subtracts, increments, or decrements on data in registers or memory. The *logic group* of instructions performs ANDs, ORs, XORs, compares, rotates, or complements on data in registers or between memory and a register.

The *branch group* of instructions initiates conditional or unconditional jumps, calls, returns, and restarts. The *stack, I/O, and machine control group* includes instructions for maintaining the stack, reading from input ports, writing to output ports, setting and reading interrupt masks, and setting and clearing flags.

A summary of the *8080/8085* microprocessor's *instruction set* is detailed in Fig. 8-16. This is an alphabetical listing by mnemonic. Intel's copyrighted mnemonics are used along with the 8080/8085's unique op codes. The op codes are represented in hexadecimal notation in Fig. 8-16. A brief description is also given for each of the 239 microprocessor instructions. Two instructions are identified as being used exclusively by the 8085 MPU in Fig. 8-16. These are the RIM and SIM instructions.

The generic microprocessor's instruction set (Chap. 6) was a subset of the 8080/8085's and therefore used the same mnemonics and op codes. Because the 8080/8085 MPU has more registers and functions than the generic microprocessor, it will need more instructions. For instance, the generic microprocessor's instruction set lists four add instructions (see Fig. 6-4), whereas the first 18 instructions listed in Fig. 8-16 for the 8080/8085 MPU are add instructions. The 8080/8085 also has four more double add instructions (DAD *B*, DAD *D*, etc.) for a total of 22 add instructions. After using the generic microprocessor's instruction set, most students will have a fair understanding of the function of about half of the 8080/8085 instructions listed in Fig. 8-16. A more detailed study of the 8080/8085 MPU's instruction set will follow.

SOLVED PROBLEMS

8.31   Refer to Fig. 8-16. How many logical AND instructions do you find listed for the 8080/8085 microprocessor?

Solution:

The 8080/8085's instruction set summary in Fig. 8-16 listed nine different AND operations starting with ANA *A*.

8.32   Refer to Fig. 8-16. The generic microprocessor's instruction set contains one subroutine call instruction, whereas the 8080/8085 MPU can perform _____ (number) different call operations.

Solution:

The 8080/8085 MPU can perform nine different call operations starting with the CALL *aa* instruction in Fig. 8-16.

8.33   Refer to Fig. 8-16. The 8080/8085's instruction set lists _____ (number) different subtract operations.

Solution:

The 8080/8085's instruction set lists 18 different subtract operations starting with SUB *A* in Fig. 8-16. This does not include compare operations which use internal subtractions when comparing data.

8.34   Refer to Fig. 8-16. Some 8080/8085 mnemonics contain an added X such as in CDX *B*, INX *B*, LXI *B*, and STAX *B*. Each time the added X appears in these instructions, a _____ _____ (register pair, single register) is affected by the operation.

	Mnemonic	Op code (hex)	Description
A	ADD A	87	Add A to A (double A)
	ADD B	80	Add B to A
	ADD C	81	Add C to A
	ADD D	82	Add D to A
	ADD E	83	Add E to A
	ADD H	84	Add H to A
	ADD L	85	Add L to A
	ADD M	86	Add memory LOC (H & L) to A
	ADI v	C6	Add immediate data v to A
	ADC A	8F	Add A to A with carry (double A with carry)
	ADC B	88	Add B to A with carry
	ADC C	89	Add C to A with carry
	ADC D	8A	Add D to A with carry
	ADC E	8B	Add E to A with carry
	ADC H	8C	Add H to A with carry
	ADC L	8D	Add L to A with carry
	ADC M	8E	Add memory LOC (H & L) to A with carry
	ACI v	CE	Add immediate data v to A with carry
	ANA A	A7	Test A and clear carry
	ANA B	A0	AND B with A
	ANA C	A1	AND C with A
	ANA D	A2	AND D with A
	ANA E	A3	AND E with A
	ANA H	A4	AND H with A
	ANA L	A5	AND L with A
	ANA M	A6	AND memory LOC (H & L) with A
	ANI v	E6	AND immediate data v with A
C	CALL aa	CD	Call subroutine at address aa
	CZ aa	CC	If zero, CALL at address aa
	CNZ aa	C4	If not zero, CALL at address aa
	CP aa	F4	If plus, CALL at address aa
	CM aa	FC	If minus, CALL at address aa
	CC aa	DD	If carry, CALL at address aa
	CNC aa	D4	If no carry, CALL at address aa
	CPE aa	EC	If even parity, CALL at address aa
	CPO aa	E4	If odd parity, CALL at address aa
	CMA	2F	Complement A
	CMC	3F	Complement carry
	CMP A	BF	Set zero flag
	CMP B	B8	Compare A with B
	CMP C	B9	Compare A with C
	CMP D	BA	Compare A with D
	CMP E	BB	Compare A with E
	CMP H	BC	Compare A with H
	CMP L	BD	Compare A with L
	CMP M	BE	Compare A with memory LOC (H & L)
	CPI v	FE	Compare A with immediate data v
D	DAA	27	Decimal adjust A
	DAD B	09	Add B & C to H & L
	DAD D	19	Add D & E to H & L
	DAD H	29	Add H & L to H & L (double H & L)
	DAD SP	39	Add SP to H & L
	DCR A	3D	Decrement A
	DCR B	05	Decrement B
	DCR C	0D	Decrement C
	DCR D	15	Decrement D
	DCR E	1D	Decrement E
	DCR H	25	Decrement H
	DCR L	2D	Decrement L
	DCR M	35	Decrement memory LOC (H & L)
	DCX B	0B	Decrement B & C
	DCX D	1B	Decrement D & E
	DCX H	2B	Decrement H & L

Fig. 8-16 Instruction set summary for the 8080/8085 microprocessor (all mnemonics copyrighted © Intel Corporation, 1976)

226

	Mnemonic	Op code (hex)	Description
D	DCX *SP*	3B	Decrement *SP*
	DI	F3	Disable interrupts
E	EI	FB	Enable interrupts
H	HLT	76	Halt until interrupt
	IN *v*	DB	Input from device *v*
	INR *A*	3C	Increment *A*
	INR *B*	04	Increment *B*
	INR *C*	0C	Increment *C*
	INR *D*	14	Increment *D*
	INR *E*	1C	Increment *E*
	INR *H*	24	Increment *H*
	INR *L*	2C	Increment *L*
I	INR *M*	34	Increment memory LOC (*H & L*)
	INX *B*	03	Increment *B & C*
	INX *D*	13	Increment *D & E*
	INX *H*	23	Increment *H & L*
	INX *SP*	33	Increment *SP*
	JMP *aa*	C3	Jump to address *aa*
	JZ *aa*	CA	If zero, JMP to address *aa*
	JNZ *aa*	C2	If not zero, JMP to address *aa*
	JP *aa*	F2	If plus, JMP to address *aa*
J	JM *aa*	FA	If minus, JMP to address *aa*
	JC *aa*	DA	If carry, JMP to address *aa*
	JNC *aa*	D2	If no carry, JMP to address *aa*
	JPE *aa*	EA	If even parity, JMP to address *aa*
	JPO *aa*	E2	If odd parity, JMP to address *aa*
	LDA *aa*	3A	Load *A* from address *aa*
	LDAX *B*	0A	Load *A* from memory LOC (*B & C*)
L	LDAX *D*	1A	Load *A* from memory LOC (*D & E*)
	LHLD *aa*	2A	Load *H & L* from address *aa*
	LXI *B,vv*	01	Load *B & C* with immediate data *vv*
	LXI *D,vv*	11	Load *D & E* with immediate data *vv*
	LXI *H,vv*	21	Load *H & L* with immediate data *vv*
	LXI *SP,vv*	31	Load *SP* with immediate data *vv*
	MOV *A,B*	78	Move *B* to *A*
	MOV *A,C*	79	Move *C* to *A*
	MOV *A,D*	7A	Move *D* to *A*
	MOV *A,E*	7B	Move *E* to *A*
	MOV *A,H*	7C	Move *H* to *A*
	MOV *A,L*	7D	Move *L* to *A*
	MOV *A,M*	7E	Move memory LOC (*H & L*) to *A*
	MOV *B,A*	47	Move *A* to *B*
	MOV *B,C*	41	Move *C* to *B*
M	MOV *B,D*	42	Move *D* to *B*
	MOV *B,E*	43	Move *E* to *B*
	MOV *B,H*	44	Move *H* to *B*
	MOV *B,L*	45	Move *L* to *B*
	MOV *B,M*	46	Move memory LOC (*H & L*) to *B*
	MOV *C,A*	4F	Move *A* to *C*
	MOV *C,B*	48	Move *B* to *C*
	MOV *C,D*	4A	Move *D* to *C*
	MOV *C,E*	4B	Move *E* to *C*
	MOV *C,H*	4C	Move *H* to *C*
	MOV *C,L*	4D	Move *L* to *C*
	MOV *C,M*	4E	Move memory LOC (*H & L*) to *C*
	MOV *D,A*	57	Move *A* to *D*
	MOV *D,B*	50	Move *B* to *D*
	MOV *D,C*	51	Move *C* to *D*
	MOV *D,E*	53	Move *E* to *D*
	MOV *D,H*	54	Move *H* to *D*
	MOV *D,L*	55	Move *L* to *D*
	MOV *D,M*	56	Move memory LOC (*H & L*) to *D*

Fig. 8-16 (*cont.*)

	Mnemonic	Op code (hex)	Description
M	MOV E,A	5F	Move A to E
	MOV E,B	58	Move B to E
	MOV E,C	59	Move C to E
	MOV E,D	5A	Move D to E
	MOV E,H	5C	Move H to E
	MOV E,L	5D	Move L to E
	MOV E,M	5E	Move memory LOC (H & L) to E
	MOV H,A	67	Move A to H
	MOV H,B	60	Move B to H
	MOV H,C	61	Move C to H
	MOV H,D	62	Move D to H
	MOV H,E	63	Move E to H
	MOV H,L	65	Move L to H
	MOV H,M	66	Move memory LOC (H & L) to H
	MOV L,A	6F	Move A to L
	MOV L,B	68	Move B to L
	MOV L,C	69	Move C to L
	MOV L,D	6A	Move D to L
	MOV L,E	6B	Move E to L
	MOV L,H	6C	Move H to L
	MOV L,M	6E	Move memory LOC (H & L) to L
	MOV M,A	77	Move A to memory LOC (H & L)
	MOV M,B	70	Move B to memory LOC (H & L)
	MOV M,C	71	Move C to memory LOC (H & L)
	MOV M,D	72	Move D to memory LOC (H & L)
	MOV M,E	73	Move E to memory LOC (H & L)
	MOV M,H	74	Move H to memory LOC (H & L)
	MOV M,L	75	Move L to memory LOC (H & L)
	MVI A,v	3E	Move immediate data v to A
	MVI B,v	06	Move immediate data v to B
	MVI C,v	0E	Move immediate data v to C
	MVI D,v	16	Move immediate data v to D
	MVI E,v	1E	Move immediate data v to E
	MVI H,v	26	Move immediate data v to H
	MVI L,v	2E	Move immediate data v to L
	MVI M,v	36	Move immediate data v to memory LOC (H & L)
N	NOP	00	No operation
O	ORA A	B7	Test A and clear carry
	ORA B	B0	OR B with A
	ORA C	B1	OR C with A
	ORA D	B2	OR D with A
	ORA E	B3	OR E with A
	ORA H	B4	OR H with A
	ORA L	B5	OR L with A
	ORA M	B6	OR memory LOC (H & L) with A
	ORI v	F6	OR immediate data v with A
	OUT v	D3	Output A to device v
P	PCHL	E9	Jump to memory LOC contained in (H & L)
	POP B	C1	Pop B & C from stack
	POP D	D1	Pop D & E from stack
	POP H	E1	Pop H & L from stack
	POP PSW	F1	Pop A and flags from stack
	PUSH B	C5	Push B & C onto stack
	PUSH D	D5	Push D & E onto stack
	PUSH H	E5	Push H & L onto stack
	PUSH PSW	F5	Push A and flags onto stack
	RAL	17	Rotate CY + A left
	RAR	1F	Rotate CY + A right
	RLC	07	Rotate A left and into carry
	RRC	0F	Rotate A right and into carry
	RIM	20	Read interrupt mask (8085 only)
	RET	C9	Return from subroutine
R	RZ	C8	If zero, return from subroutine

Fig. 8-16 (cont.)

	Mnemonic	Op code (hex)	Description
R	RNZ	C0	If not zero, return from subroutine
	RP	F0	If plus, return from subroutine
	RM	F8	If minus, return from subroutine
	RC	D8	If carry, return from subroutine
	RNC	D0	If no carry, return from subroutine
	RPE	E8	If even parity, return from subroutine
	RPO	E0	If odd parity, return from subroutine
	RST 0	C7	Restart subroutine at address 00H
	RST 1	CF	Restart subroutine at address 08H
	RST 2	D7	Restart subroutine at address 10H
	RST 3	DF	Restart subroutine at address 18H
	RST 4	E7	Restart subroutine at address 20H
	RST 5	EF	Restart subroutine at address 28H
	RST 6	F7	Restart subroutine at address 30H
	RST 7	FF	Restart subroutine at address 38H
S	SIM	30	Set interrupt mask (8085 only)
	SPHL	F9	Load SP from H & L
	SHLD aa	22	Store H & L at memory LOC aa
	STA aa	32	Store A at memory LOC aa
	STAX B	02	Store A at memory LOC (B & C)
	STAX D	12	Store A at memory LOC (D & E)
	STC	37	Set carry flag
	SUB A	97	Clear A
	SUB B	90	Subtract B from A
	SUB C	91	Subtract C from A
	SUB D	92	Subtract D from A
	SUB E	93	Subtract E from A
	SUB H	94	Subtract H from A
	SUB L	95	Subtract L from A
	SUB M	96	Subtract contents of memory LOC (H & L) from A
	SUI v	D6	Subtract immediate data v from A
	SBB A	9F	Set A to minus carry
	SBB B	98	Subtract B from A with borrow
	SBB C	99	Subtract C from A with borrow
	SBB D	9A	Subtract D from A with borrow
	SBB E	9B	Subtract E from A with borrow
	SBB H	9C	Subtract H from A with borrow
	SBB L	9D	Subtract L from A with borrow
	SBB M	9E	Subtract memory LOC (H & L) from A with borrow
	SBI v	DE	Subtract immediate data v from A with borrow
X	XCHG	EB	Exchange D & E with H & L
	XTHL	E3	Exchange top of stack with H & L
	XRA A	AF	Clear A
	XRA B	A8	Exclusive OR B with A
	XRA C	A9	Exclusive OR C with A
	XRA D	AA	Exclusive OR D with A
	XRA E	AB	Exclusive OR E with A
	XRA H	AC	Exclusive OR H with A
	XRA L	AD	Exclusive OR L with A
	XRA M	AE	Exclusive OR memory LOC (H & L) with A
	XRI v	EE	Exclusive OR immediate data v with A

Fig. 8-16 (*cont.*)

Solution:

According to the descriptions in Fig. 8-16, each time the added X appears in instructions (such as CDX *B*, INX *B*, LXI *B*, and STAX *B*), a register pair is affected by the operation.

8.6   THE 8080/8085 DATA TRANSFER INSTRUCTIONS

A summary of the 8080/8085 microprocessor's data transfer instructions is shown in Fig. 8-17.   These instructions include move, exchange, load, and store operations.   Figure 8-17 gives only the mnemonic and hexadecimal op code for these 84 instructions.   Data transfer instructions are among the most widely used of all microprocessor instructions.

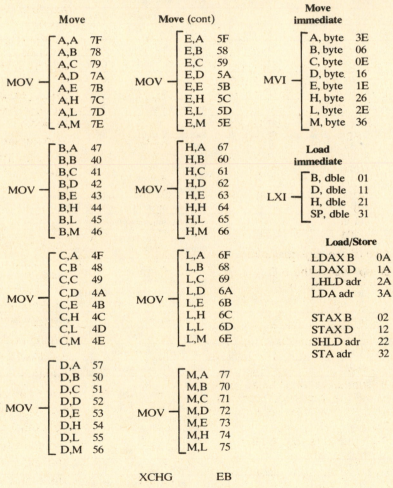

Fig. 8-17   Summary of 8080/8085 data transfer instructions (all mnemonics copyrighted © Intel Corporation, 1976)

The *data transfer group* of instructions on pp. 232–233 will be detailed using Intel Corporation's own format.   This group of instructions transfers data to and from registers and memory.   Condition flags are *not affected* by any instruction in this group.   Refer to Fig. 8-18 for the meanings of abbreviations (such as *r*1, DDD, SSS, etc.) used in the following descriptions from the Intel *User's Manual*.

SYMBOLS	MEANING
accumulator	Register A
addr	16-bit address quantity
data	8-bit quantity
data 16	16-bit data quantity
byte 2	The second byte of the instruc-tion
byte 3	The third byte of the instruc-tion
port	8-bit address of an I/O device
r,r1,r2	One of the registers A,B,C, D,E,H,L

RP	REGISTER PAIR
00	B-C
01	D-E
10	H-L
11	SP

rh	The first (high-order) register of a designated register pair.
rl	The second (low-order) register of a designated register pair.
PC	16-bit program counter register (PCH and PCL are used to refer to the high-order and low-order 8 bits respec-tively).
SP	16-bit stack pointer register (SPH and SPL are used to refer to the high-order and low-order 8 bits respectively).
r_m	Bit m of the register r (bits are number 7 through 0 from left to right).
LABEL	16-bit address of subroutine.

DDD,SSS — The bit pattern designating one of the registers A,B,C,D, E,H,L (DDD = destination, SSS = source):

DDD or SSS	REGISTER NAME
111	A
000	B
001	C
010	D
011	E
100	H
101	L

rp — One of the register pairs:

B represents the B,C pair with B as the high-order register and C as the low-order register;

D represents the D,E pair with D as the high-order register and E as the low-order register;

H represents the H,L pair with H as the high-order register and L as the low-order register;

SP represents the 16-bit stack pointer register.

RP — The bit pattern designating one of the register pairs B,D,H,SP:

	The condition flags:
Z	Zero
S	Sign
P	Parity
CY	Carry
AC	Auxiliary Carry
( )	The contents of the memory location or registers enclosed in the parentheses.
←	"Is transferred to"
$\wedge$	Logical AND
$\veebar$	Exclusive OR
$\vee$	Inclusive OR
+	Addition
−	Two's complement subtraction
*	Multiplication
↔	"Is exchanged with"
——	The one's complement (e.g., $\overline{(A)}$)
n	The restart number 0 through 7
NNN	The binary representation 000 through 111 for restart number 0 through 7 respectively.

Fig. 8-18 Abbreviations used with Intel Corporation's descriptions   (*Courtesy of Intel Corporation*)

Consider the 8080/8085 MOV *A,B* (op code = 78H) instruction. The MOV *A,B* would represent an instruction that moves data from register *B* to the accumulator (register *A*). This type of instruction is detailed on the next page in the "move register" (MOV *r1, r2*) section. Note that the first register (*A* in this example) is the destination of the transfer, while the second register (*B* in this example) is the source of data. The general op code pattern for this type of instruction is 01DDDSSS and can be completed using information from Fig. 8-18. The destination is the

MOV r1, r2   (Move Register)
  (r1) ← (r2)
  The content of register r2 is moved to register r1.

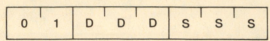

	Cycles:	1
	States:	4 (8085), 5 (8080)
	Addressing:	register
	Flags:	none

MOV r, M   (Move from memory)
  (r) ← ((H) (L))
  The content of the memory location, whose address is in registers H and L, is moved to register r.

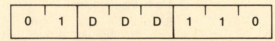

	Cycles:	2
	States:	7
	Addressing:	reg. indirect
	Flags:	none

MOV M, r   (Move to memory)
  ((H)) (L)) ← (r)
  The content of register r is moved to the memory location whose address is in registers H and L.

| 0 | 1 | 1 | 1 | 0 | S | S | S |

	Cycles:	2
	States:	7
	Addressing:	reg. indirect
	Flags:	none

MVI r, data   (Move Immediate)
  (r) ← (byte 2)
  The content of byte 2 of the instruction is moved to register r.

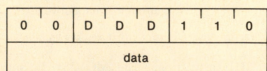

	Cycles:	2
	States:	7
	Addressing:	immediate
	Flags:	none

MVI M, data   (Move to memory immediate)
  ((H) (L)) ← (byte 2)
  The content of byte 2 of the instruction is moved to the memory location whose address is in registers H and L.

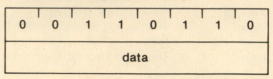

	Cycles:	3
	States:	10
	Addressing:	immed./reg. indirect
	Flags:	none

LXI rp, data 16 (Load register pair immediate)
  (rh) ← (byte 3),
  (rl) ← (byte 2)
  Byte 3 of the instruction is moved into the high-order register (rh) of the register pair rp. Byte 2 of the instruction is moved into the low-order register (rl) of the register pair rp.

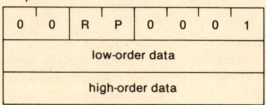

	Cycles:	3
	States:	10
	Addressing:	immediate
	Flags:	none

LDA addr   (Load Accumulator direct)
  (A) ← ((byte 3)(byte 2))
  The content of the memory location, whose address is specified in byte 2 and byte 3 of the instruction, is moved to register A.

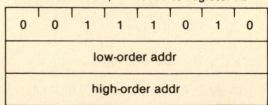

	Cycles:	4
	States:	13
	Addressing:	direct
	Flags:	none

STA addr   (Store Accumulator direct)
((byte 3)(byte 2)) ← (A)
The content of the accumulator is moved to the memory location whose address is specified in byte 2 and byte 3 of the instruction.

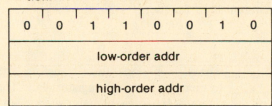

0	0	1	1	0	0	1	0

low-order addr

high-order addr

Cycles: 4
States: 13
Addressing: direct
Flags: none

LHLD addr   (Load H and L direct)
(L) ← ((byte 3)(byte 2))
(H) ← ((byte 3)(byte 2) + 1)
The content of the memory location, whose address is specified in byte 2 and byte 3 of the instruction, is moved to register L. The content of the memory location at the succeeding address is moved to register H.

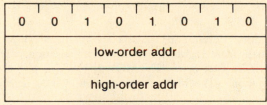

0	0	1	0	1	0	1	0

low-order addr

high-order addr

Cycles: 5
States: 16
Addressing: direct
Flags: none

SHLD addr   (Store H and L direct)
((byte 3)(byte 2)) ← (L)
((byte 3)(byte 2) + 1) ← (H)
The content of register L is moved to the memory location whose address is specified in byte 2 and byte 3. The content of register H is moved to the succeeding memory location.

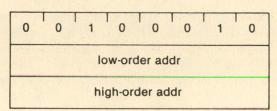

0	0	1	0	0	0	1	0

low-order addr

high-order addr

Cycles: 5
States: 16
Addressing: direct
Flags: none

LDAX rp   (Load accumulator indirect)
(A) ← ((rp))
The content of the memory location, whose address is in the register pair rp, is moved to register A. Note: only register pairs rp = B (registers B and C) or rp = D (registers D and E) may be specified.

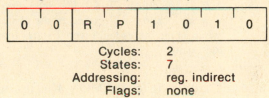

0	0	R	P	1	0	1	0

Cycles: 2
States: 7
Addressing: reg. indirect
Flags: none

STAX rp   (Store accumulator indirect)
((rp)) ← (A)
The content of register A is moved to the memory location whose address is in the register pair rp. Note: only register pairs rp = B (registers B and C) or rp = D (registers D and E) may be specified.

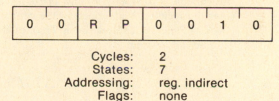

0	0	R	P	0	0	1	0

Cycles: 2
States: 7
Addressing: reg. indirect
Flags: none

XCHG   (Exchange H and L with D and E)
(H) ↔ (D)
(L) ↔ (E)
The contents of registers H and L are exchanged with the contents of registers D and E.

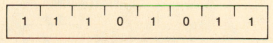

1	1	1	0	1	0	1	1

Cycles: 1
States: 4
Addressing: register
Flags: none

accumulator which uses the bit pattern 111, while the source is register B, which uses the bit pattern 000. The op code is then 01 111 000$_2$, or 78 in hexadecimal notation. According to previous Intel information the MOV A,B instruction uses one machine cycle to execute the data transfer. The 8085 machine cycle uses four T states. The MOV A,B instruction uses register addressing, and no flags are affected during the execution of this instruction. Each data transfer instruction in Fig. 8-17 fits one of the more general categories and can be analyzed as to function.

SOLVED PROBLEMS

8.35 The op code for the MOV A,M instruction is _____ (hex). This operation transfers data from _____ (a memory location, register A) to _____ (a memory location, register A). The memory location is identified by the contents of the _____ (HL register pair, second and third instruction bytes). The MOV A,M instruction uses _____ (number) machine cycles and _____ (number) T states. The MOV A,M instruction uses _____ (direct, register indirect) addressing.

Solution:

According to Fig. 8-17 and Intel's "move from memory" description, the op code for the MOV A,M instruction is 7EH. This operation transfers data from a memory location to register A. The memory location is identified by the contents of the HL register pair. The MOV A,M instruction uses two machine cycles and seven T states for execution. The MOV A,M instruction uses register indirect addressing.

8.36 The op code for the MOV M,C instruction is _____ (binary). This operation transfers data from _____ (a memory location, register C) to _____ (a memory location, register C). The memory location is identified by the contents of the _____ (HL register pair, second and third instruction bytes). The MOV M,C instruction uses _____ (number) machine cycles and _____ (number) T states. The MOV M,C instruction uses _____ (immediate, register indirect) addressing.

Solution:

According to Fig. 8-17 and Intel's "move to memory" description, the op code for the MOV M,C instruction is 01110001$_2$. This operation transfers data from register C to a memory location. The memory location is identified by the contents of the HL register pair. The MOV M,C instruction uses two machine cycles and seven T states during execution. The MOV M,C instruction uses register indirect addressing.

8.37 The 8085's op code for the MVI H instruction diagramed in Fig. 8-19 is _____ (binary).

Solution:

According to Fig. 8-17, the 8085's op code for the MVI H instruction diagramed in Fig. 8-19 is 00100110$_2$ or 26H.

Register H 1111 0000   ?   Register H

Before operation   Move   **After operation**

MVI H

Op code

Program memory   ? / 0000 0001

Data

Fig. 8-19

8.38   The contents of register H after the MVI H operation shown in Fig. 8-19 are _____ (8 bits).

Solution:

The MVI H instruction uses the immediate addressing mode.   The immediate data 00000001 from program memory is transferred to register H during this move operation.

8.39   The MVI H instruction shown in Fig. 8-19 uses _____ (number) machine cycles and _____ (number) T states to execute the data transfer.

Solution:

According to Intel's "move immediate" description, the MVI H instruction shown in Fig. 8-19 uses two machine cycles and seven T states to execute the data transfer.

8.40   The SHLD instruction shown in Fig. 8-20 uses the _____ (direct, immediate) addressing mode.

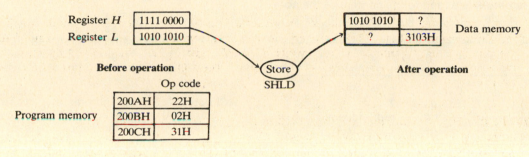

Fig. 8-20

Solution:

According to Intel's description, the SHLD instruction shown in Fig. 8-20 uses direct addressing.

8.41   After the store operation illustrated in Fig. 8-20, data memory location _____ (hex) contains 10101010_2, while location 3103H contains _____ (8 bits).

Solution:

The SHLD instruction uses direct addressing, so the 16-bit address is assembled from the second and third bytes of program memory.   Therefore, after the store operation illustrated in Fig. 8-20, data memory location 3103H contains 11110000_2, while location 3102H contains 10101010_2.

8.7   THE 8080/8085 ARITHMETIC INSTRUCTIONS

A summary of the 8080/8085 microprocessor's arithmetic instructions is shown in Fig. 8-21.   These instructions include add, add with carry, subtract, subtract with borrow, increment, decrement, and decimal adjust accumulator operations.   Only the mnemonic and op codes for the arithmetic instructions are given in Fig. 8-21 on p. 29.

As in the previous section, the *arithmetic group* of instructions will be detailed using Intel Corporation's own format.   This group of instructions performs arithmetic operations on data in registers and memory.   Unless indicated otherwise, all instructions in this group affect the zero (Z), sign (S), parity (P), carry (CY), and auxiliary carry (AC) flags.   All subtraction operations are performed via 2s complement arithmetic and set the carry flag to 1 to indicate a borrow and clear it to indicate no borrow.   Refer to Fig. 8-18 for meanings of abbreviations used in the following descriptions from the Intel *User's Manual*.

ADD r   (Add Register)

(A) ← (A) + (r)

The content of register r is added to the content of the accumulator. The result is placed in the accumulator.

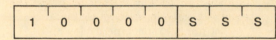

1	0	0	0	0	S	S	S

Cycles: 1
States: 4
Addressing: register
Flags: Z,S,P,CY,AC

ADD M   (Add memory)

(A) ← (A) + ((H) (L))

The content of the memory location whose address is contained in the H and L registers is added to the content of the accumulator. The result is placed in the accumulator.

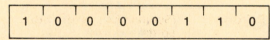

1	0	0	0	0	1	1	0

Cycles: 2
States: 7
Addressing: reg. indirect
Flags: Z,S,P,CY,AC

ADI data   (Add immediate)

(A) ← (A) + (byte 2)

The content of the second byte of the instruction is added to the content of the accumulator. The result is placed in the accumulator.

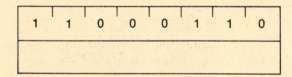

1	1	0	0	0	1	1	0
			data				

Cycles: 2
States: 7
Addressing: immediate
Flags: Z,S,P,CY,AC

ADC r   (Add Register with carry)

(A) ← (A) + (r) + (CY)

The content of register r and the content of the carry bit are added to the content of the accumulator. The result is placed in the accumulator.

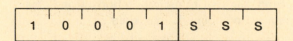

1	0	0	0	1	S	S	S

Cycles: 1
States: 4
Addressing: register
Flags: Z,S,P,CY,AC

ADC M   (Add memory with carry)

(A) ← (A) + ((H) (L)) + (CY)

The content of the memory location whose address is contained in the H and L registers and the content of the CY flag are added to the accumulator. The result is placed in the accumulator.

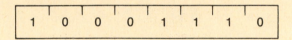

1	0	0	0	1	1	1	0

Cycles: 2
States: 7
Addressing: reg. indirect
Flags: Z,S,P,CY,AC

ACI data   (Add immediate with carry)

(A) ← (A) + (byte 2) + (CY)

The content of the second byte of the instruction and the content of the CY flag are added to the contents of the accumulator. The result is placed in the accumulator.

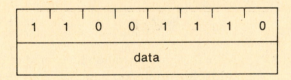

1	1	0	0	1	1	1	0
			data				

Cycles: 2
States: 7
Addressing: immediate
Flags: Z,S,P,CY,AC

SUB r   (Subtract Register)

(A) ← (A) − (r)

The content of register r is subtracted from the content of the accumulator. The result is placed in the accumulator.

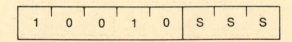

1	0	0	1	0	S	S	S

Cycles: 1
States: 4
Addressing: register
Flags: Z,S,P,CY,AC

SUB M   (Subtract memory)
$(A) \leftarrow (A) - ((H)(L))$
The content of the memory location whose address is contained in the H and L registers is subtracted from the content of the accumulator. The result is placed in the accumulator.

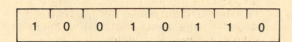

1	0	0	1	0	1	1	0

        Cycles: 2
        States: 7
    Addressing: reg. indirect
         Flags: Z,S,P,CY,AC

SUI data   (Subtract immediate)
$(A) \leftarrow (A) - (byte\ 2)$
The content of the second byte of the instruction is subtracted from the content of the accumulator. The result is placed in the accumulator.

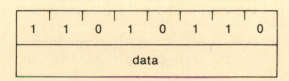

1	1	0	1	0	1	1	0
data								

        Cycles: 2
        States: 7
    Addressing: immediate
         Flags: Z,S,P,CY,AC

SBB r   (Subtract Register with borrow)
$(A) \leftarrow (A) - (r) - (CY)$
The content of register r and the content of the CY flag are both subtracted from the accumulator. The result is placed in the accumulator.

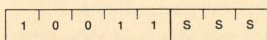

1	0	0	1	1	S	S	S

        Cycles: 1
        States: 4
    Addressing: register
         Flags: Z,S,P,CY,AC

SBB M   (Subtract memory with borrow)
$(A) \leftarrow (A) - ((H)(L)) - (CY)$
The content of the memory location whose address is contained in the H and L registers and the content of the CY flag are both subtracted from the accumulator. The result is placed in the accumulator.

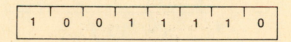

1	0	0	1	1	1	1	0

        Cycles: 2
        States: 7
    Addressing: reg. indirect
         Flags: Z,S,P,CY,AC

SBI data   (Subtract immediate with borrow)
$(A) \leftarrow (A) - (byte\ 2) - (CY)$
The contents of the second byte of the instruction and the contents of the CY flag are both subtracted from the accumulator. The result is placed in the accumulator.

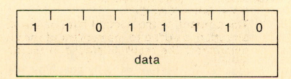

1	1	0	1	1	1	1	0
data								

        Cycles: 2
        States: 7
    Addressing: immediate
         Flags: Z,S,P,CY,AC

INR r   (Increment Register)
$(r) \leftarrow (r) + 1$
The content of register r is incremented by one. Note: All condition flags **except CY** are affected.

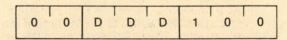

0	0	D	D	D	1	0	0

        Cycles: 1
        States: 4 (8085), 5 (8080)
    Addressing: register
         Flags: Z,S,P,AC

INR M   (Increment memory)
((H) (L) ← ((H) (L)) + 1
The content of the memory location whose address is contained in the H and L registers is incremented by one. Note: All condition flags **except CY** are affected.

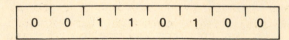

Cycles: 3
States: 10
Addressing: reg. indirect
Flags: Z,S,P,AC

DCR r   (Decrement Register)
(r) ← (r) − 1
The content of register r is decremented by one. Note: All condition flags **except CY** are affected.

Cycles: 1
States: 4 (8085), 5 (8080)
Addressing: register
Flags: Z,S,P,AC

DCR M   (Decrement memory)
((H) (L)) ← ((H) (L)) − 1
The content of the memory location whose address is contained in the H and L registers is decremented by one. Note: All condition flags **except CY** are affected.

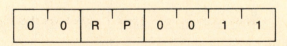

Cycles: 3
States: 10
Addressing: reg. indirect
Flags: Z,S,P,AC

INX rp   (Increment register pair)
(rh) (rl) ← (rh) (rl) + 1
The content of the register pair rp is incremented by one. Note: **No condition flags are affected.**

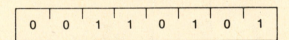

Cycles: 1
States: 6 (8085), 5 (8080)
Addressing: register
Flags: none

DCX rp   (Decrement register pair)
(rh) (rl) ← (rh) (rl) − 1
The content of the register pair rp is decremented by one. Note: **No condition flags are affected.**

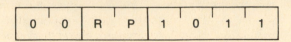

Cycles: 1
States: 6 (8085), 5 (8080)
Addressing: register
Flags: none

DAD rp   (Add register pair to H and L)
(H) (L) ← (H) (L) + (rh) (rl)
The content of the register pair rp is added to the content of the register pair H and L. The result is placed in the register pair H and L. Note: **Only the CY flag is affected.** It is set if there is a carry out of the double precision add; otherwise it is reset.

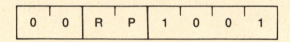

Cycles: 3
States: 10
Addressing: register
Flags: CY

DAA   (Decimal Adjust Accumulator)
The eight-bit number in the accumulator is adjusted to form two four-bit Binary-Coded-Decimal digits by the following process:

1. If the value of the lease significant 4 bits of the accumulator is greater than 9 **or** if the AC flag is set, 6 is added to the accumulator.

2. If the value of the most significant 4 bits of the accumulator is now greater than 9, **or** if the CY flag is set, 6 is added to the most significant 4 bits of the accumulator.

NOTE: All flags are affected.

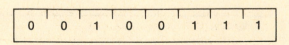

Cycles: 1
States: 4
Flags: Z,S,P,CY,AC

Consider the ADC B (add register B with carry) instruction listed in Fig. 8-21.   Its functioning is detailed in the ADC r (add register with carry) section.   Intel Corporation describes this instruction in symbol form as

$$(A) \leftarrow (A) + (r) + (CY)$$

This means that the content of r (register B in this example) and the content of the carry bit (CY) are added to the content of the accumulator (register A). The sum is deposited in the accumulator.   Intel's description shows that this operation uses a 1-byte instruction.   The description also shows that the ADC B instruction is executed in one machine cycle and four T states.   The register addressing mode is used, and all flags $(Z, S, P, CY,$ and $AC)$ are affected by the execution of this instruction.

Add*

ADD
A	87
B	80
C	81
D	82
E	83
H	84
L	85
M	86

ADC
A	8F
B	88
C	89
D	8A
E	8B
H	8C
L	8D
M	8E

Subtract*

SUB
A	97
B	90
C	91
D	92
E	93
H	94
L	95
M	96

SBB
A	9F
B	98
C	99
D	9A
E	9B
H	9C
L	9D
M	9E

Double Add†

DAD
B	09
D	19
H	29
SP	39

Increment**

INR
A	3C
B	04
C	0C
D	14
E	1C
H	24
L	2C
H	34

INX
B	03
O	13
H	23
SP	33

Decrement**

DCR
A	3D
B	05
C	0D
D	15
E	1D
H	25
L	2D
M	35

DCX
B	0B
D	1B
H	2B
SP	3B

Special

DAA*   27

Immediate

ADI byte	C6
ACI byte	CE
SUI byte	D6
SBI byte	DE

byte = constant or logical/arithmetic expression that evaluates to an 8-bit data quantity (second byte of 2-byte instructions)
* = all flags (C, Z, S, P, AC) affected
** = all flags except CARRY affected (exception: INX and DCX affect no flags)
† = only CARRY affected
All mnemonics copyright Intel Corporation 1976

Fig. 8-21 Summary of 8080/8085 arithmetic instructions

The ADC B (add register B with carry) instruction is being executed in Fig. 8-22.   The contents of register A (10000000 in this example) are being added to the contents of register B (10000000) and the contents of the carry bit (set to 1 in this example).   The problem might appear like this:

```
  1000 0000    register A
  1000 0000    register B
+          1    carry bit
1 0000 0001    sum
```

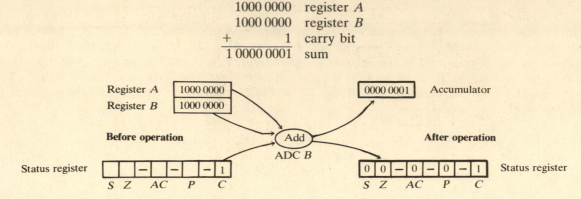

Fig. 8-22   The add with carry (ADC B) instruction

The sum equals 1 0000 0001.   The least significant 8 bits (0000 0001) are deposited in the accumulator.   This is shown in Fig. 8-22.   The overflow from the accumulator (the most significant bit of the sum) sets the carry flag (CY) to 1 after the operation.   The sign, zero, auxiliary carry, and even parity bits are reset to 0 after the ADC B instruction is executed in Fig. 8-22.

Next consider using the 8085's SBB M (subtract memory with borrow) instruction from the listing in Fig. 8-21.   Its functioning is detailed in the SBB M section.   Intel describes this instruction in symbol form as

$$(A) \leftarrow (A) - ((H)(L)) - (CY)$$

This means that the content of the memory location pointed to by the HL register is subtracted from the contents of the accumulator.   The carry bit (CY) in the status register is also subtracted from the contents of the accumulator.   The difference is deposited in the accumulator after the instruction is executed.   Intel Corporation also notes that SBB M is a 1-byte instruction using register indirect addressing.   It uses two machine cycles and seven T states for execution.   All flags are affected by the SBB M instruction.

The SBB M (subtract memory with borrow) instruction is being executed in Fig. 8-23b.   The accumulator holds 00000100, the carry bit is 1, and the data memory location pointed to by the HL register holds 00000010.   The operation of SBB M instruction on data is detailed in Fig. 8-23a.   The two subtrahends are first added (00000010 + 1 = 00000011).   The new combined subtrahend of 00000011 is then converted to its 2s complement form (11111101).   The minuend (00000100) is then added to the 2s complement of the subtrahend (11111101), yielding

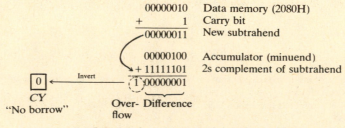

(a) Solution for subtract with borrow problem

Fig. 8-23

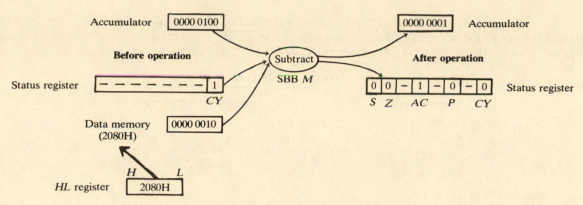

(b) The subtract with borrow (SBB M) instruction

Fig. 8-23 (cont.)

1 0000 0001.   The least significant 8 bits form the difference (00000001 in this example), while the overflow of 1 is inverted by the microprocessor resetting the carry flag (CY) to 0.   The reset carry flag means "no borrow" or that the minuend was larger than the combined subtrahends in this problem.

The add with carry and subtract with borrow instructions are not used with regular single-byte addition or subtraction.   These are special instructions used when adding or subtracting 2 or more bytes of data.   How to use these instructions in actual programming will be demonstrated in the chapter on programming.

SOLVED PROBLEMS

8.42   The op code for the ADD C instruction is _____ (hex).   This operation adds the contents of register _____ (letter) to the contents of the accumulator. The ADD C instruction uses _____ (register, register indirect) addressing.

Solution:

According to Fig. 8-21 and Intel's "add register" description, the op code for the ADD C instruction is 81H.   This operation adds the contents of register C to the contents of the accumulator. The ADD C instruction uses register addressing.

8.43   The op code for the INX H instruction is _____ (hex).   This operation _____ (decrements, increments) the _____ (BC, HL) register pair.   The INX H instruction affects _____ (all, no) flags.

Solution:

According to Fig. 8-21 and Intel's "increment register pair" description, the op code for the INX H instruction is 23H.   This operation increments the HL register pair.   The INX H instruction affects no flags.

8.44   The 8085's op code for the DAD B instruction diagramed in Fig. 8-24 is _____ (hex).

Solution:

According to Fig. 8-21, the op code for the DAD B instruction diagramed in Fig. 8-24 is 09H.

8.45   The DAD B instruction in Fig. 8-24 is adding the _____ (8, 16) -bit contents of the HL register pair to the contents of the _____ (two letters) register pair.

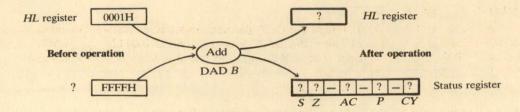

Fig. 8-24

Solution:

According to Intel's description, the DAD *B* instruction being used in Fig. 8-24 is adding the 16-bit contents of the *HL* register pair to the contents of the *BC* register pair.

8.46   After the DAD *B* operation in Fig. 8-24, the *HL* register pair will contain _____ (hex).

Solution:

Adding hexadecmial FFFF + 0001 = 1 0000H.   Therefore after the DAD *B* operation in Fig. 8-24, the *HL* register pair will contain 0000H.

8.47   List the condition of the flags in the status register after the DAD *B* instruction has been executed in Fig. 8-24.

Solution:

Only the carry flag is affected by the DAD *B* operation.   Therefore, the sign, zero, auxiliary carry, and even parity flag conditions in Fig. 8-24 are not predictable.   The carry flag (*CY*) will be set to 1 because of the overflow or carry during the addition (FFFF + 0001 = 1 0000H).

8.48   Refer to Fig. 8-25.   Is the number in the accumulator before the DAA operation a "legal" BCD (8421 binary-coded-decimal) number?

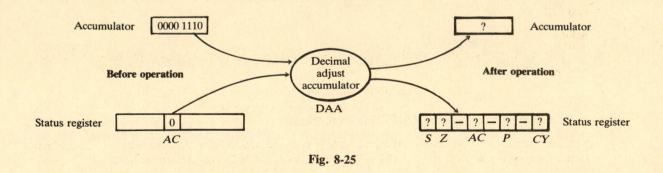

Fig. 8-25

Solution:

The number 0000 1110 is not a "legal" BCD number because the 1110 has no BCD equivalent.

8.49   The contents of the accumulator in Fig. 8-25 after the DAA operation will be _____ (BCD), which equals _____ in decimal.

Solution:

According to Intel's description of the DAA (decimal adjust accumulator) instruction, the contents of the accumulator in Fig. 8-25 after the DAA operation will be $0001\,0100_{BCD}$, which equals 14 in decimal.   Because 1110 is greater than 9, 0110 (6_{10}) was added to this "illegal" BCD number, yielding $0001\,0100_{BCD}$ (14_{10}).

8.50 List the condition of the flags in the status register after the DAA operation shown in Fig. 8-25.

Solution:

In Fig. 8-25 the DAA operation caused 0110 to be added to 0000 1110, yielding 0001 0100.   During this operation the flags were affected in the following manner:

Sign flag $(S) = 0$ Auxiliary carry flag $(AC) = 1$ Carry flag $(CY) = 0$
Zero flag $(Z) = 0$ Even parity flag $(P) = 1$

8.51 The SUB E instruction in Fig. 8-26 is subtracting the contents of register _____ (letter) from the contents of the accumulator.

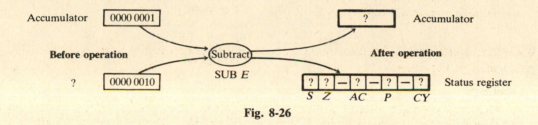

Fig. 8-26

Solution:

The SUB E instruction in Fig. 8-26 is subtracting the contents of register E from the contents of the accumulator.

8.52 After the SUB E instruction has been executed in Fig. 8-26, the contents of the accumulator will be _____ (8 bits).

Solution:

The MPU changes the subtrahend (00000010 in register E) to its 2s complement form (11111110) and adds as follows:

$$
\begin{array}{ll}
0000\,0001 & \text{minuend} \\
+\,1111\,1110 & \text{2s complement subtrahend} \\
\hline
0\,1111\,1111 & \text{difference}
\end{array}
$$

The least significant 8 bits of the difference (1111 1111) are deposited in the accumulator.   In decimal form, the problem is $1 - 2 = -1$.   The -1_{10} equals 1111 1111 in 2s complement notation.

8.53 Refer to Fig. 8-26.   List the condition of the flags in the status register after the SUB E instruction has been executed.

Solution:

After the SUB E operation in Fig. 8-26, the flags are in the following conditions:

Sign flag $(S) = 1$ Auxiliary carry flag $(AC) = 1$ Carry flag $(CY) = 1$
Zero flag $(Z) = 0$ Even parity flag $(P) = 1$

The MPU changes the subtrahend (00000010 in register E) to its 2s complement form (11111110) and adds as follows:

$$
\begin{array}{ll}
0000\ 0001 & \text{minuend} \\
+\ 1111\ 1110 & \text{2s complement subtrahend} \\
\hline
0\ 1111\ 1111 & \text{difference}
\end{array}
$$

$$\boxed{1} \xleftarrow{\text{invert}} $$
CY

Note that the overflow bit (most significant bit) in the difference is a 0 which is inverted and placed in the carry flag (CY) of the status register.   A set carry flag after a subtract operation means that the difference is a 2s complement number and that the subtrahend was greater than the minuend.

8.8   THE 8080/8085 LOGICAL INSTRUCTIONS

A summary of the 8080/8085 microprocessor's logical instructions is shown in Fig. 8-27.   These include AND, OR, XOR, compare, rotate, and complement instructions.   Only Intel's mnemonics and op codes are listed for each instruction in Fig. 8-27.

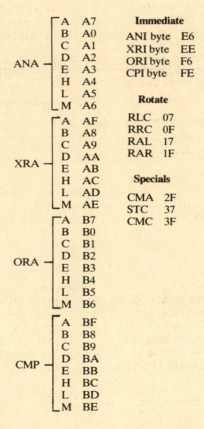

Immediate

ANI byte	E6
XRI byte	EE
ORI byte	F6
CPI byte	FE

Rotate

RLC	07
RRC	0F
RAL	17
RAR	1F

Specials

CMA	2F
STC	37
CMC	3F

Fig. 8-27   Summary of 8080/8085 logical instructions   (All mnemonics copyrighted © Intel Corporation, 1976)

As in the previous section, the *logical group* of instructions will be detailed using Intel Corporation's own format.   This group of instructions performs logical (Boolean) operations on data in registers and memory and on flags.   Refer to Fig. 8-18 for meanings of abbreviations used in the following descriptions from the Intel *User's Manual*.

ANA r   (AND Register)

$(A) \leftarrow (A) \wedge (r)$

The content of register r is logically ANDed with the content of the accumulator. The result is placed in the accumulator. **The CY flag is cleared and AC is set (8085). The CY flag is cleared and AC is set to the OR'ing of bits 3 of the operands (8080).**

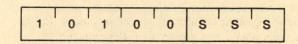

1	0	1	0	0	S	S	S

Cycles:	1
States:	4
Addressing:	register
Flags:	Z,S,P,CY,AC

ANA M   (AND memory)

$(A) \leftarrow (A) \wedge ((H)(L))$

The contents of the memory location whose address is contained in the H and L registers is logically ANDed with the content of the accumulator. The result is placed in the accumulator. **The CY flag is cleared and AC is set (8085). The CY flag is cleared and AC is set to the OR'ing of bits 3 of the operands (8080).**

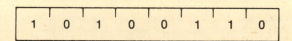

1	0	1	0	0	1	1	0

Cycles:	2
States:	7
Addressing:	reg. indirect
Flags:	Z,S,P,CY,AC

ANI data   (AND immediate)

$(A) \leftarrow (A) \wedge (byte\ 2)$

The content of the second byte of the instruction is logically ANDed with the contents of the accumulator. The result is placed in the accumulator. **The CY flag is cleared and AC is set (8085). The CY flag is cleared and AC is set to the OR'ing of bits 3 of the operands (8080).**

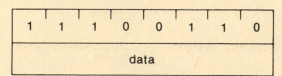

1	1	1	0	0	1	1	0
data							

Cycles:	2
States:	7
Addressing:	immediate
Flags:	Z,S,P,CY,AC

XRA r   (Exclusive OR Register)

$(A) \leftarrow (A) \veebar (r)$

The content of register r is exclusive-OR'd with the content of the accumulator. The result is placed in the accumulator. **The CY and AC flags are cleared.**

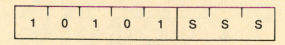

1	0	1	0	1	S	S	S

Cycles:	1
States:	4
Addressing:	register
Flags:	Z,S,P,CY,AC

XRA M   (Exclusive OR Memory)

$(A) \leftarrow (A) \veebar ((H)(L))$

The content of the memory location whose address is contained in the H and L registers is exclusive-OR'd with the content of the accumulator. The result is placed in the accumulator. **The CY and AC flags are cleared.**

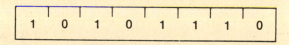

1	0	1	0	1	1	1	0

Cycles:	2
States:	7
Addressing:	reg. indirect
Flags:	Z,S,P,CY,AC

XRI data   (Exclusive OR immediate)

$(A) \leftarrow (A) \veebar (byte\ 2)$

The content of the second byte of the instruction is exclusive-OR'd with the content of the accumulator. The result is placed in the accumulator. **The CY and AC flags are cleared.**

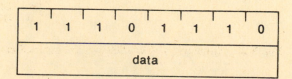

1	1	1	0	1	1	1	0
data							

Cycles:	2
States:	7
Addressing:	immediate
Flags:	Z,S,P,CY,AC

ORA r   (OR Register)

(A) ← (A) V (r)

The content of register r is inclusive-OR'd with the content of the accumulator. The result is placed in the accumulator. **The CY and AC flags are cleared.**

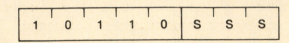

1	0	1	1	0	S	S	S

Cycles: 1
States: 4
Addressing: register
Flags: Z,S,P,CY,AC

CMP r   (Compare Register)

(A) − (r)

The content of register r is subtracted from the accumulator. The accumulator remains unchanged. The condition flags are set as a result of the subtraction. **The Z flag is set to 1 if (A) = (r). The CY flag is set to 1 if (A) < (r).**

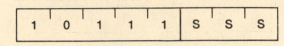

1	0	1	1	1	S	S	S

Cycles: 1
States: 4
Addressing: register
Flags: Z,S,P,CY,AC

ORA M   (OR memory)

(A) ← (A) V ((H) (L))

The content of the memory location whose address is contained in the H and L registers is inclusive-OR'd with the content of the accumulator. The result is placed in the accumulator. **The CY and AC flags are cleared.**

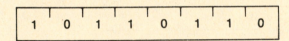

1	0	1	1	0	1	1	0

Cycles: 2
States: 7
Addressing: reg. indirect
Flags: Z,S,P,CY,AC

CMP M   (Compare memory)

(A) − ((H) (L))

The content of the memory location whose address is contained in the H and L registers is subtracted from the accumulator. The accumulator remains unchanged. The condition flags are set as a result of the subtraction. **The Z flag is set to 1 if (A) = ((H) (L)). The CY flag is set to 1 if (A) < ((H) (L)).**

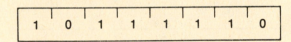

1	0	1	1	1	1	1	0

Cycles: 2
States: 7
Addressing: reg. indirect
Flags: Z,S,P,CY,AC

ORI data   (OR Immediate)

(A) ← (A) V (byte 2)

The content of the second byte of the instruction is inclusive-OR'd with the content of the accumulator. The result is placed in the accumulator. **The CY and AC flags are cleared..**

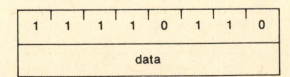

1	1	1	1	0	1	1	0
data							

Cycles: 2
States: 7
Addressing: immediate
Flags: Z,S,P,CY,AC

CPI data   (Compare immediate)

(A) − (byte 2)

The content of the second byte of the instruction is subtracted from the accumulator. The condition flags are set by the result of the subtraction. **The Z flag is set to 1 if (A) = (byte 2). The CY flag is set to 1 if (A) < (byte 2).**

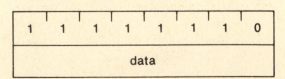

1	1	1	1	1	1	1	0
data							

Cycles: 2
States: 7
Addressing: immediate
Flags: Z,S,P,CY,AC

RLC   (Rotate left)

$(A_{n+1}) \leftarrow (A_n)$; $(A_0) \leftarrow (A_7)$

$(CY) \leftarrow (A_7)$

The content of the accumulator is rotated left one position. The low order bit and the CY flag are both set to the value shifted out of the high order bit position. **Only the CY flag is affected.**

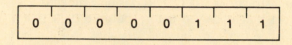

Cycles: 1
States: 4
Flags: CY

RRC   (Rotate right)

$(A_n) \leftarrow (A_{n+1})$; $(A_7) \leftarrow (A_0)$

$(CY) \leftarrow (A_0)$

The content of the accumulator is rotated right one position. The high order bit and the CY flag are both set to the value shifted out of the low order bit position. **Only the CY flag is affected.**

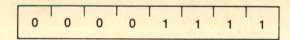

Cycles: 1
States: 4
Flags: CY

RAL   (Rotate left through carry)

$(A_{n+1}) \leftarrow (A_n)$; $(CY) \leftarrow (A_7)$

$(A_0) \leftarrow (CY)$

The content of the accumulator is rotated left one position through the CY flag. The low order bit is set equal to the CY flag and the CY flag is set to the value shifted out of the high order bit. **Only the CY flag is affected.**

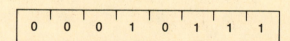

Cycles: 1
States: 4
Flags: CY

RAR   (Rotate right through carry)

$(A_n) \leftarrow (A_{n+1})$; $(CY) \leftarrow (A_0)$

$(A_7) \leftarrow (CY)$

The content of the accumulator is rotated right one position through the CY flag. The high order bit is set to the CY flag and the CY flag is set to the value shifted out of the low order bit. **Only the CY flag is affected.**

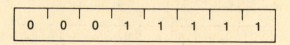

Cycles: 1
States: 4
Flags: CY

CMA   (Complement accumulator)

$(A) \leftarrow (\overline{A})$

The contents of the accumulator are complemented (zero bits become 1, one bits become 0). **No flags are affected.**

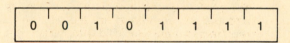

Cycles: 1
States: 4
Flags: none

CMC   (Complement carry)

$(CY) \leftarrow (\overline{CY})$

The CY flag is complemented. **No other flags are affected.**

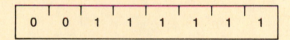

Cycles: 1
States: 4
Flags: CY

STC   (Set carry)

$(CY) \leftarrow 1$

The CY flag is set to 1. **No other flags are affected.**

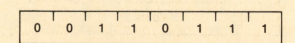

Cycles: 1
States: 4
Flags: CY

Note Intel's use of the ∧ symbol to symbolize logical AND in the ANA *r*, ANA *M*, and ANI data descriptions. In like manner, Intel uses the ∨ symbol to denote logical OR in the ORA *r*, ORA *M*, and ORI data descriptions. Furthermore, Intel uses the ⩝ symbol to stand for logical XOR (exclusive OR) in the XRA *r*, XRA *M*, and XRI data descriptions.

Consider the four 8080/8085 rotate instructions in Fig. 8-28. The action of the rotate left and right through carry instructions (RAL, RAR) is diagrammed in Fig. 8-28*a* and *b*. This rotating through carry action was observed while using the rotate instructions in the generic microprocessor.

The action of the rotate accumulator left and right instructions (RLC, RRC) is diagrammed in Fig. 8-28*c* and *d*. This action is somewhat different from that observed before because data is not rotated through the carry position.

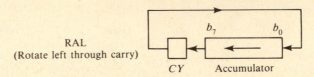

RAL
(Rotate left through carry)

CY   Accumulator

(*a*) Function of rotate left through carry instruction

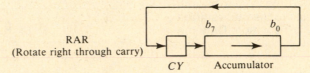

RAR
(Rotate right through carry)

CY   Accumulator

(*b*) Function of rotate right through carry instruction

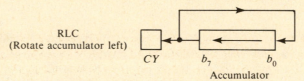

RLC
(Rotate accumulator left)

CY   Accumulator

(*c*) Function of rotate accumulator left instruction

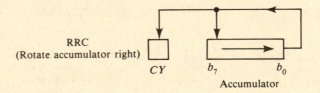

RRC
(Rotate accumulator right)

CY   Accumulator

(*d*) Function of rotate accumulator right instruction

Fig. 8-28

SOLVED PROBLEMS

8.54 The op code for the ANA *M* instruction is _____ (hex). This operation ANDs the contents of the accumulator with the contents of a _____ (data, program) memory location pointed to by the _____ (letters) register pair. This is a _____ (number) -byte instruction.

Solution:

According to Fig. 8-27 and Intel's "AND memory" description, the op code for the ANA *M* instruction is A6H. This operation ANDs the contents of the accumulator with the contents of a data memory location pointed to by the *HL* register pair. This is a 1-byte instruction.

8.55   The op code for the ORI instruction is _____ (hex). This is a _____ (number) -byte instruction which uses _____ (direct, immediate) addressing. The contents of the accumulator are ORed with the contents of _____ (data, program) memory.

Solution:

According to Fig. 8-27 and Intel's "OR immediate" description, the op code for the ORI instruction is F6H. This is a 2-byte instruction which uses immediate addressing. The contents of the accumulator are ORed with the contents of program memory.

8.56   The contents of the accumulator in Fig. 8-29 after the RLC operation will be _____ (8 bits).

Solution:

Based on the diagram in Fig. 8-28c, the contents of the accumulator in Fig. 8-29 after the RLC operation will be 00000001.

8.57   The carry flag will be _____ (reset to 0, set to 1) after the rotate left (RLC) operation shown in Fig. 8-29.

Solution:

The carry flag will be set to 1 after the rotate left (RLC) operation shown in Fig. 8-29.

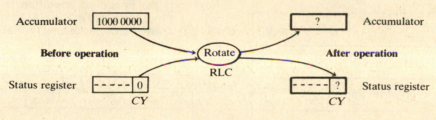

Fig. 8-29

8.9   THE 8080/8085 BRANCH INSTRUCTIONS

A summary of the 8080/8085 microprocessor's branch instructions is shown in Fig. 8-30 on p. 252. These include jump, call, return, and restart instructions. Only Intel's mnemonics and op codes are listed for each instruction in Fig. 8-30. A brief description of the mnemonics is given in the instruction set summary in Fig. 8-16.

As in the previous sections, the *branch group* of instructions will be detailed using Intel Corporation's own format. This group of instructions alters the normal sequential program flow. The two types of branch instructions are unconditional and conditional. Unconditional transfers simply perform the specified operation on the program counter. Conditional transfers examine the status of one of the four MPU flags to determine whether the specified branch is to be executed. The conditions that may be specified are listed in the Intel *User's Manual* as follows:

CONDITION	CCC
NZ — not zero (Z = 0)	000
Z — zero (Z = 1)	001
NC — no carry (CY = 0)	010
C — carry (CY = 1)	011
PO — parity odd (P = 0)	100
PE — parity even (P = 1)	101

P — plus (S = 0)   110
M — minus (S = 1)   111

JMP addr   (Jump)
(PC) ← (byte 3) (byte 2)
Control is transferred to the instruction whose address is specified in byte 3 and byte 2 of the current instruction.

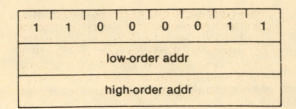

1	1	0	0	0	0	1	1
low-order addr							
high-order addr							

Cycles: 3
States: 10
Addressing: immediate
Flags: none

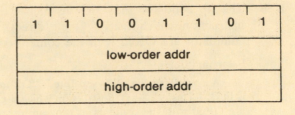

1	1	0	0	1	1	0	1
low-order addr							
high-order addr							

Cycles: 5
States: 18 (8085), 17 (8080)
Addressing: immediate/ reg. indirect
Flags: none

Jcondition addr (Conditional jump)
If (CCC),
(PC) ← (byte 3) (byte 2)
If the specified condition is true, control is transferred to the instruction whose address is specified in byte 3 and byte 2 of the current instruciton; otherwise, control continues sequentially.

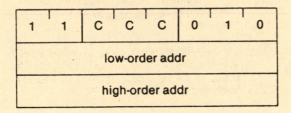

1	1	C	C	C	0	1	0
low-order addr							
high-order addr							

Cycles: 2/3 (8085), 3 (8080)
States: 7/10 (8085), 10 (8080)
Addressing: immediate
Flags: none

Ccondition addr (Condition call)
If (CCC),
((SP) − 1) ← (PCH)
((SP) − 2) ← (PCL)
(SP) ← (SP) − 2
(PC) ← (byte 3) (byte 2)
If the specified condition is true, the actions specified in the CALL instruction (see above) are performed; otherwise, control continues sequentially.

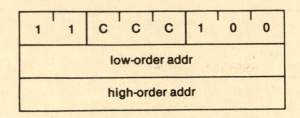

1	1	C	C	C	1	0	0
low-order addr							
high-order addr							

Cycles: 2/5 (8085), 3/5 (8080)
States: 9/18 (8085), 11/17 (8080)
Addressing: immediate/ reg. indirect
Flags: none

CALL addr (Call)
((SP) − 1) ← (PCH)
((SP) − 2) ← (PCL)
(SP) ← (SP) − 2
(PC) ← (byte 3) (byte 2)

The high-order eight bits of the next instruction address are moved to the memory location whose address is one less than the content of register SP. The low-order eight bits of the next instruction address are moved to the memory location whose address is two less than the content of register SP. The content of register SP is decremented by 2. Control is transferred to the instruction whose address is specified in byte 3 and byte 2 of the current instruction.

RET (Return)
(PCL) ← ((SP));
(PCH) ← ((SP) + 1);
(SP) ← (SP) + 2;
The content of the memory location whose address is specified in register SP is moved to the low-order eight bits of register PC. The content of the memory location whose address is one more than the content of register SP is moved to the high-order eight bits of register PC. The content of register SP is incremented by 2.

Cycles: 3
States: 10
Addressing: reg. indirect
Flags: none

Rcondition   (Conditional return)
If (CCC),
    (PCL) ← ((SP))
    (PCH) ← ((SP) + 1)
    (SP) ← (SP) + 2
If the specified condition is true, the actions specified in the RET instruction (see above) are performed; otherwise, control continues sequentially.

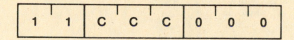

Cycles: 1/3
States: 6/12 (8085), 5/11 (8080)
Addressing: reg. indirect
Flags: none

RST n   (Restart)
    ((SP) − 1) ← (PCH)
    ((SP) − 2) ← (PCL)
    (SP) ← (SP) − 2
    (PC) ← 8 * (NNN)
The high-order eight bits of the next instruction address are moved to the memory location whose address is one less than the content of register SP. The

low-order eight bits of the next instruction address are moved to the memory location whose address is two less than the content of register SP. The content of register SP is decremented by two. Control is transferred to the instruction whose address is eight times the content of NNN.

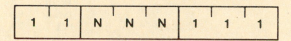

Cycles: 3
States: 12 (8085), 11 (8080)
Addressing: reg. indirect
Flags: none

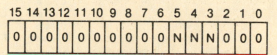

Program Counter After Restart

PCHL   (Jump H and L indirect —
                   move H and L to PC)
    (PCH) ← (H)
    (PCL) ← (L)
The content of register H is moved to the high-order eight bits of register PC. The content of register L is moved to the low-order eight bits of register PC.

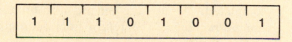

Cycles: 1
States: 6 (8085), 5 (8080)
Addressing: register
Flags: none

Consider the use of the conditional jump instruction in Fig. 8-31. The op code is listed as 11001010 in Fig. 8-31 for the JZ instruction. The 001 part of the op code (bits b_5, b_4, and b_3) specifies that the condition for the jump is that the zero flag be set ($Z = 1$). The zero flag does equal 1 in Fig. 8-31; therefore a new 16-bit address is transferred into the program counter (PC). The low-order address (00000000) is transferred, followed by the high-order address (00100001). The new address in the program counter then causes the MPU to jump to a new program location.

The CALL instruction is a special branch operation used for jumping from the main program to a subroutine. The CALL instruction combines the jump and push data on stack operations. As with the generic microprocessor, the 8080/8085's CALL instruction first pushes the 16-bit contents of the program counter (PC) on the stack. The CALL instruction then causes the 16-bit address of the subroutine to be transferred to the program counter. The microprocessor then jumps to the subroutine.

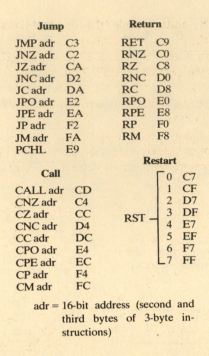

Jump		Return	
JMP adr	C3	RET	C9
JNZ adr	C2	RNZ	C0
JZ adr	CA	RZ	C8
JNC adr	D2	RNC	D0
JC adr	DA	RC	D8
JPO adr	E2	RPO	E0
JPE adr	EA	RPE	E8
JP adr	F2	RP	F0
JM adr	FA	RM	F8
PCHL	E9		

Restart

Call			RST		
CALL adr	CD			0	C7
CNZ adr	C4			1	CF
CZ adr	CC			2	D7
CNC adr	D4			3	DF
CC adr	DC			4	E7
CPO adr	E4			5	EF
CPE adr	EC			6	F7
CP adr	F4			7	FF
CM adr	FC				

adr = 16-bit address (second and
third bytes of 3-byte in-
structions)

Fig. 8-30 Summary of 8080/8085 branch instructions   (All mnemonics copyrighted © Intel Corporation, 1976)

Unlike the generic microprocessor, the 8080 and 8085 processors also have *conditional call instructions*.   The call operation as described earlier will be executed only if the specified condition is met.

As with the generic microprocessor, the 8080 and 8085 MPUs use return instructions.   Return instructions guide the processor back to the correct place in main program memory after a subroutine is completed.   Unlike the generic microprocessor, the 8080 and 8085 MPUs also have *conditional return instructions*.   The return from subroutine operation will be executed only if the specified condition is met.

Restart instructions are special-purpose call instructions designed primarily for use with interrupts.   Like the CALL, the restart instruction pushes the contents of the program counter on the stack and jumps to one of eight *predetermined addresses*.   This is different because a CALL instruction immediately specifies the address of the jump.   A 3-bit code (bits b_5, b_4, and b_3) in the op code of the RST instruction specifies the jump address.   For instance, a RST 2 instruction has an

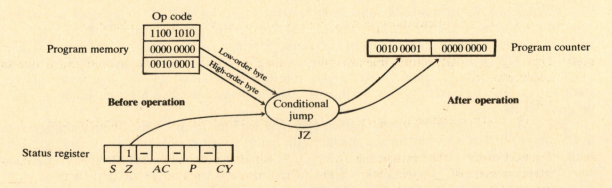

Fig. 8-31 Jump if zero instruction

op code of 11<u>010</u>111 (D7H).   The address code 010 (decimal 2) is multiplied by 8, yielding 16_{10}, or 10000_2.   This is the address of the jump ($0000\,0000\,0001\,0000_2$ in this example).

Consider the sample problem shown in Fig. 8-32 using the RST 7 instruction.   Note that the stack pointer is initialized at 2089H before the RST 7 operation.   The RST 7 instruction pushes the current program count onto the stack.   Then the predetermined address ($8 \times 7 = 56_{10} = 38H$) is transferred to the program counter (*PC*).   This causes the MPU to jump or restart at the new location of 0000 0000 0011 1000 (0038H).

The restart instruction is unique because it seldom appears in source code in application programs.   More often the peripheral devices seeking interrupt service pass this 1-byte instruction to the processor.   Restarts are therefore sometimes referred to as *software interrupts*.

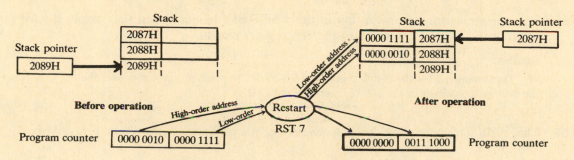

Fig. 8-32   Restart (RST 7) instruction

SOLVED PROBLEMS

8.58   The JMP instruction uses a _____ (number) -byte instruction and _____ (direct, immediate) addressing.   During execution of the JMP instruction, 2 bytes from program memory are transferred to the _____ (program counter, stack pointer).

Solution:

According to Intel's description, the JMP instruction uses a 3-byte instruction and immediate addressing.   During execution of the JMP instruction, 2 bytes from program memory are transferred to the program counter.

8.59   Call and _____ (restart, return) instructions are used in pairs to locate and return from subroutines.

Solution:

Call and return instructions are used in pairs to locate and return from subroutines.

8.60   The _____ (restart, return) operation is a special form of a call instruction used primarily with interrupts.

Solution:

The restart operation is a special form of a call instruction used primarily with interrupts.

8.61   The 8080/8085's JNC instruction is a _____ (conditional, unconditional) jump instruction whose op code is _____ in binary.   The jump if no carry operation is specified with a _____ (number) -byte instruction.   The JNC instruction uses the _____ (direct, immediate) addressing mode.

Solution:

According to Intel's description of the conditional jump, the JNC instruction is a conditional jump instruction whose op code is 11010010 in binary. The jump if no carry operation is specified with a 3-byte instruction. The JNC instruction uses the immediate addressing mode.

8.62 The mnemonic for the 1-byte instruction in the 8080/8085's branch group that causes the MPU to jump to memory location 0000H is _____.

Solution:

The mnemonic for the 1-byte instruction in the 8080/8085's branch group that causes the MPU to jump to memory location 0000H is RST 0.

8.63 The mnemonic for the instruction in the 8080/8085's branch group that causes the MPU to jump to the address contained in the *HL* register pair is _____.

Solution:

The mnemonic for the instruction in the 8080/8085's branch group that causes the MPU to jump to the address contained in the *HL* register pair is PCHL.

8.64 The 8080/8085 mnemonic for the conditional jump operation shown in Fig. 8-33 is_____.

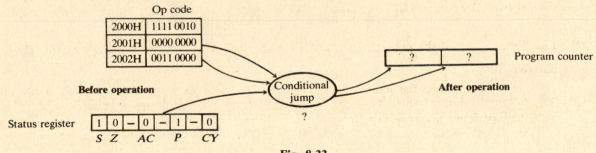

Fig. 8-33

Solution:

The 8080/8085 mnemonic for the conditional jump operation shown in Fig. 8-33 is JP, which stands for jump if plus.

8.65 Based on the status register in Fig. 8-33, the conditions _____ (are, are not) met for the conditional jump to occur.

Solution:

The sign flag equals 1 in Fig. 8-33, which means the previous number in the accumulator is minus. The plus condition does not exist, and therefore the jump to a new address does not occur.

8.66 The contents of the program counter after the conditional jump instruction in Fig. 8-33 has been executed are _____ (16 bits).

Solution:

The plus condition was not met ($S = 1$); therefore the program counter increments to the next sequential instruction at 2003H, or $0010\ 0000\ 0000\ 0011_2$.

8.67 The op code for the restart instruction used in Fig. 8-34 would be _____ in binary.

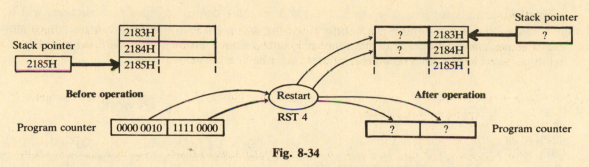

Fig. 8-34

Solution:

The op code for the RST 4 instruction used in Fig. 8-34 would be 11100111 in binary (E7 in hexadecimal).

8.68 List the contents of stack locations 2183H and 2184H after the restart operation shown in Fig. 8-34.

Solution:

The contents of the program counter are transferred to the stack in the following manner: First, stack location 2184H receives the high-order byte from the program counter; stack location 2184H then contains 00000010. Second, stack location 2183H receives the low-order byte from the program counter; stack location 2183H then contains 11110000.

8.69 List the contents of the program counter (*PC*) after the restart operation shown in Fig. 8-34.

Solution:

The MPU multiplies the restart number (decimal 4 in this example) by 8, yielding the address of 32_{10} (or 20H).   Binary 0000 0000 0010 0000 (0020H) is the new address in the program counter. The MPU then performs the jump to memory location 0020H.

8.10 THE 8080/8085 STACK, I/O, AND MACHINE CONTROL INSTRUCTIONS

A summary of the 8080/8085 microprocessor's stack, I/O, and machine control instructions is shown in Fig. 8-35.   These include push and pop, input and output, exchange, interrupt enables and disables, no operation and halts, and multiple-purpose read and set interrupt mask instructions.   Only Intel's mnemonics and op codes are listed for each instruction in Fig. 8-35.

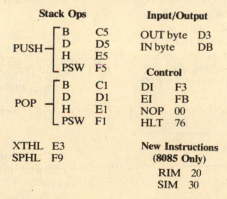

Fig. 8-35 Summary of 8080/8085 stack, I/O, and machine control instructions (All mnemonics copyrighted © Intel Corporation, 1976)

As in the previous sections, the *stack, I/O*, and *machine control group* of instructions will be detailed using Intel Corporation's own format. This group of instructions performs inputs and outputs, manipulates the stack, and alters internal control flags. Refer to Fig. 8-18 for meanings of abbreviations used in the following descriptions from the Intel *User's Manual*.

PUSH rp   (Push)

$((SP) - 1) \leftarrow (rh)$
$((SP) - 2) \leftarrow (rl)$
$((SP) \leftarrow (SP) - 2$

The content of the high-order register of register pair rp is moved to the memory location whose address is one less than the content of register SP. The content of the low-order register of register pair rp is moved to the memory location whose address is two less than the content of register SP. The content of register SP is decremented by 2. **Note: Register pair rp = SP may not be specified.**

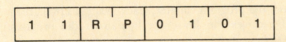

		R	P				
1	1	R	P	0	1	0	1

Cycles: 3
States: 12 (8085), 11 (8080)
Addressing: reg. indirect
Flags: none

PUSH PSW   (Push processor status word)

$((SP) - 1) \leftarrow (A)$
$((SP) - 2)_0 \leftarrow (CY), ((SP) - 2)_1 \leftarrow X$
$((SP) - 2)_2 \leftarrow (P), ((SP) - 2)_3 \leftarrow X$
$((SP) - 2)_4 \leftarrow (AC), ((SP) - 2)_5 \leftarrow X$
$((SP) - 2)_6 \leftarrow (Z), ((SP) - 2)_7 \leftarrow (S)$
$(SP) \leftarrow (SP) - 2$ X: Undefined.

The content of register A is moved to the memory location whose address is one less than register SP. The contents of the condition flags are assembled into a processor status word and the word is moved to the memory location whose address is two less than the content of register SP. The content of register SP is decremented by two.

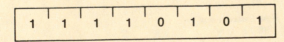

1	1	1	1	0	1	0	1

Cycles: 3
States: 12 (8085), 11 (8080)
Addressing: reg. indirect
Flags: none

FLAG WORD

D_7	D_6	D_5	D_4	D_3	D_2	D_1	D_0
S	Z	X	AC	X	P	X	CY

X: undefined

POP rp   (Pop)

$(rl) \leftarrow ((SP))$
$(rh) \leftarrow ((SP) + 1)$
$(SP) \leftarrow (SP) + 2$

The content of the memory location, whose address is specified by the content of register SP, is moved to the low-order register of register pair rp. The content of the memory location, whose address is one more than the content of register SP, is moved to the high-order register of register rp. The content of register SP is incremented by 2. **Note: Register pair rp = SP may not be specified.**

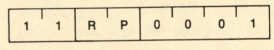

1	1	R	P	0	0	0	1

Cycles: 3
States: 10
Addressing: reg.indirect
Flags: none

POP PSW   (Pop processor status word)

$(CY) \leftarrow ((SP))_0$
$(P) \leftarrow ((SP))_2$
$(AC) \leftarrow ((SP))_4$
$(Z) \leftarrow ((SP))_6$
$(S) \leftarrow ((SP))_7$
$(A) \leftarrow ((SP) + 1)$
$(SP) \leftarrow (SP) + 2$

The content of the memory location whose address is specified by the content of register SP is used to restore the condition flags. The content of the memory location whose address is one more than the content of register SP is moved to register A.

The content of register SP is incremented by 2.

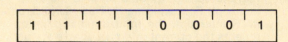

Cycles: 3
States: 10
Addressing: reg. indirect
Flags: Z,S,P,CY,AC

XTHL (Exchange stack top with H and L)

(L) ↔ ((SP))
(H) ↔ ((SP) + 1)

The content of the L register is exchanged with the content of the memory location whose address is specified by the content of register SP. The content of the H register is exchanged with the content of the memory location whose address is one more than the content of register SP.

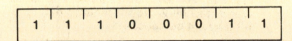

Cycles: 5
States: 16 (8085), 18 (8080)
Addressing: reg. indirect
Flags: none

SPHL (Move HL to SP)

(SP) ← (H) (L)

The contents of registers H and L (16 bits) are moved to register SP.

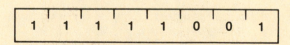

Cycles: 1
States: 6 (8085), 5 (8080)
Addressing: register
Flags: none

IN port (Input)

(A) ← (data)

The data placed on the eight bit bi-directional data bus by the specified port is moved to register A.

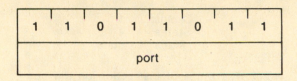

Cycles: 3
States: 10
Addressing: direct
Flags: none

OUT port (Output)

(data) ← (A)

The content of register A is placed on the eight bit bi-directional data bus for transmission to the specified port.

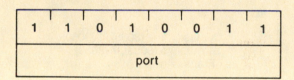

Cycles: 3
States: 10
Addressing: direct
Flags: none

EI (Enable interrupts)

The interrupt system is enabled following the execution of the next instruction. Interrupts are not recognized during the EI instruction.

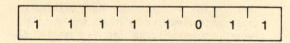

Cycles: 1
States: 4
Flags: none

NOTE: Placing an EI instruction on the bus in response to INTA during an INA cycle is prohibited. (8085)

DI (Disable interrupts)

The interrupt system is disabled immediately following the execution of the DI instruction. Interrupts are not recognized during the DI instruction.

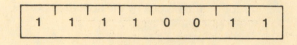

Cycles: 1
States: 4
Flags: none

NOTE: Placing a DI instruction on the bus in response to $\overline{INTA}$ during an INA cycle is prohibited. (8085)

HLT   (Halt)

The processor is stopped. The registers and flags are unaffected. (8080) A second ALE is generated during the execution of HLT to strobe out the Halt cycle status information. (8085)

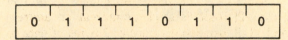

Cycles: 1+ (8085), 1 (8080)
States: 5 (8085), 7 (8080)
Flags: none

NOP   (No op)

No operation is performed. The registers and flags are unaffected.

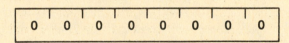

Cycles: 1
States: 4
Flags: none

RIM   (Read Interrupt Masks) (8085 only)

The RIM instruction loads data into the accumulator relating to interrupts and the serial input. This data contains the following information:

- Current interrupt mask status for the RST 5.5, 6.5, and 7.5 hardware interrupts (1 = mask disabled)
- Current interrupt enable flag status (1 = interrupts enabled) except immediately following a TRAP interrupt. (See below.)
- Hardware interrupts pending (i.e., signal received but not yet serviced), on the RST 5.5, 6.5, and 7.5 lines.
- Serial input data.

Immediately following a TRAP interrupt, the RIM instruction must be executed as a part of the service routine if you need to

retrieve current interrupt status later. Bit 3 of the accumulator is (in this special case only) loaded with the interrupt enable (IE) flag status that existed prior to the TRAP interrupt. Following an RST 5.5, 6.5, 7.5, or INTR interrupt, the interrupt flag flip-flop reflects the current interrupt enable status. Bit 6 of the accumulator (I7.5) is loaded with the status of the RST 7.5 flip-flop, which is always set (edge-triggered) by an input on the RST 7.5 input line, even when that interrupt has been previously masked. (See SIM Instruction.)

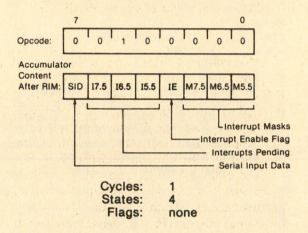

Cycles: 1
States: 4
Flags: none

SIM   (Set Interrupt Masks) (8085 only)

The execution of the SIM instruction uses the contents of the accumulator (which must be previously loaded) to perform the following functions:

- Program the interrupt mask for the RST 5.5, 6.5, and 7.5 hardware interrupts.
- Reset the edge-triggered RST 7.5 input latch.
- Load the SOD output latch.

To program the interrupt masks, first set accumulator bit 3 to 1 and set to 1 any bits 0, 1, and 2, which disable interrupts RST 5.5, 6.5, and 7.5, respectively. Then do a SIM instruction. If accumulator bit 3 is 0 when the SIM instruction is executed, the interrupt mask register will not change. If accumulator bit 4 is 1 when the SIM instruction is executed, the RST 7.5 latch is then reset. RST 7.5 is distinguished by the fact that its latch is always set by a rising edge on the RST 7.5 input pin, even if the jump to service routine is inhibited by masking. This latch remains high until cleared by a RESET IN, by a SIM Instruction with accumulator bit 4 high, or by an internal processor acknowledge to an RST 7.5 interrupt subsequent to the removal of the mask (by a SIM instruction). The RESET IN signal always sets all three RST mask bits.

If accumulator bit 6 is at the 1 level when the SIM instruction is executed, the state of accumulator bit 7 is loaded into the SOD latch and thus becomes available for interface to an external device. The SOD latch is unaffected by the SIM instruction if bit 6 is 0. SOD is always reset by the RESET IN signal.

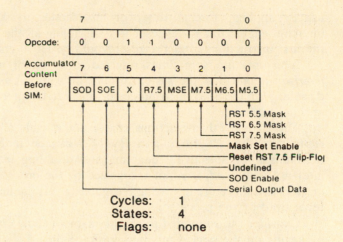

Cycles: 1
States: 4
Flags: none

This group contains instructions for pushing data onto or popping data off the stack. As with the generic microprocessor, the 8080/8085's stack is located off the microprocessor chip and in RAM. The top of the stack is defined by setting the 8080/8085's stack pointer at an address selected by the programmer. All 8080/8085 PUSH and POP instructions transfer 2 bytes of data to or from the stack using a single instruction. The PUSH *PSW* and POP *PSW* instructions transfer data from the *processor status word* to and from the stack. The processor status word is defined as the combined MPU status register (flags) and accumulator.

The 8080/8085's IN and OUT instructions function similar to those of the generic microprocessor. The IN operation inputs a byte of data from the port specified by the second byte of the instruction. In like manner, the OUT operation transfers a byte of data from the accumulator to the output port specified in the second byte of the instruction. As with the generic microprocessor, these instructions are used with an isolated I/O technique.

The XTHL operation is a 1-byte instruction for exchanging the top of the stack with the contents of the *HL* register pair. The SPHL operation is a data transfer instruction. It transfers the contents of the *HL* register pair to the microprocessor's stack pointer. This instruction can be used for initializing the stack pointer, thereby defining the top of the stack in RAM.

The NOP instruction performs no operation, as in the generic microprocessor. The NOP instruction is useful as a time delay in a timing loop.

The HLT instruction halts the processor. The program counter contains the address of the next sequential instruction. All other flags and registers are unchanged. Once in the halt state, the microprocessor can be restarted only by an external event, typically an interrupt. The HLT operation is used to stop the MPU when it is waiting for a peripheral device to finish its task and interrupt the processor.

Microprocessor actions can be initiated in one of two ways. First, microprocessor action can be initiated by an instruction from program memory. A second method of initiating MPU action is to use an external interrupt. Hardware interrupts on the 8080 or 8085 MPU can be controlled by two instructions. These are the enable interrupts (*EI*) and the disable interrupts (*DI*) instructions. When the EI instruction is executed, it will *set* an *interrupt-enable flip-flop* within the CPU. When the interrupt-enable flag (flip-flop) is set to 1 or enabled, the 8085 MPU will recognize and respond to any of the five possible hardware interrupts.

The DI (disable interrupts) instruction will cause the interrupt-enable flag (or flip-flop) to be reset to 0. When the interrupt-enable flag is reset to 0, the 8085 MPU will ignore all interrupts except the *TRAP* interrupt. The *TRAP* interrupt cannot be disabled by any 8085 program instruction.

The EI instruction is frequently used as part of a start-up sequence. When power is first turned on, the MPU begins trying to execute instructions from some unknown address. A *RESET* input is usually applied, forcing the program counter to 0000H. The $\overline{RESET}$ input also causes the interrupt-enable flag to be reset to 0, disabling all the 8085's interrupts except the *TRAP*. One of the first instructions after the reset would be EI to enable the interrupts.

Interrupts are sometimes referred to as either maskable or nonmaskable. A *nonmaskable interrupt* is one that the system cannot disable. A *maskable interrupt* is one that the system can disable. On the 8085 microprocessor, the *TRAP* interrupt is considered nonmaskable while the rest are maskable.

The EI and DI instructions enable and disable all the maskable interrupts as a group. Interrupts *RST 7.5*, *RST 6.5*, and *RST 5.5* can be individually enabled and disabled. The actual mechanism for selectively enabling and disabling interrupts is called an *interrupt mask*. If an interrupt is *masked*, it is not recognized by the processor (this is analogous to a bank robber being masked and therefore not being recognized). If the mask is removed, however, the interrupt will be recognized by the processor.

Consider the *simplified* interrupt example shown in Fig. 8-36. Follow the actions of the MPU by keying on the circled numbers in Fig. 8-36.

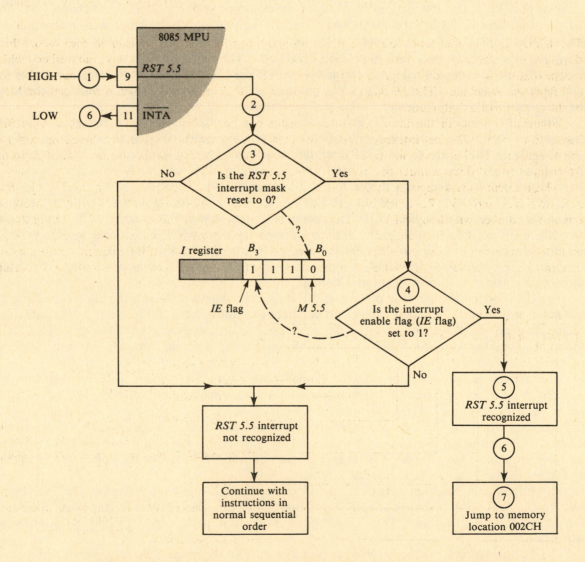

Fig. 8-36 Steps in processing an unmasked *RST 5.5* interrupt in the 8085 MPU

1. The *RST 5.5* input (pin 9) to the 8085 chip is activated with a HIGH signal.

2. To simplify the example, three things are assumed. They are:
   (*a*) The higher-priority *TRAP* interrupt is not activated.
   (*b*) The higher-priority *RST 7.5* interrupt pin is not activated or is masked.
   (*c*) The higher-priority *RST 6.5* interrupt pin is not activated or is masked.

3. The interrupt mask bit (B_0) of the *interrupt status register* is checked. It is reset to 0, or unmasked, which satisfies the first condition for the *RST 5.5* interrupt to be recognized by the MPU.

4. The interrupt-enable flag (B_3) of the interrupt status register is checked. It is set to 1, which means all interrupts are enabled.

5. The *RST 5.5* interrupt is recognized by the MPU. The processor then finishes its current instruction and stores the program counter contents in the stack.

6. The 8085 microprocessor chip issues an interrupt acknowledge ($\overline{INTA}$) signal to the peripherals.

7. The MPU then jumps to memory location 002CH. The restart memory location calculation is $5.5 \times 8 = 44_{10} = 2C_{16}$.

The MPU checked the condition of 2 bits within the interrupt status register in Fig. 8-36. First during step 3, the *5.5* mask bit (*M 5.5*) was checked. The *M 5.5* bit was 0, or unmasked, which meant that the MPU could recognize this interrupt. Second, during step 4, the interrupt-enable flag (*IE* flag) was checked. The *IE* flag in Fig. 8-36 was set to 1 (enabled), which meant that the MPU could recognize this interrupt.

Some of the bits in the interrupt status register can be changed using the 8085's unique SIM instruction. The SIM (set interrupt mask) instruction will place the contents of the accumulator in the *I* register. Earlier it was learned that the SIM instruction is also used to output a data bit to the *SOD* latch (serial data output) of the 8085 MPU (see Fig. 8-7*b*).

The interrupt mask register as set by the SIM instruction is diagramed in Fig. 8-37. The *RST 5.5*, *RST 6.5*, and *RST 7.5* mask bits can be set (masked) or reset (unmasked) if bit 3 (mask set enable) is enabled with a logical 1. A logical 1 in the bit 4 position will reset the *RST 7.5* flip-flop to 0. Bit 5 in Fig. 8-37 is undefined. Bits 6 and 7 in the interrupt mask register in Fig. 8-37 are associated with the processor's serial output (the *SOD* pin of the 8085 MPU). Enabling bit 6 with a 1 permits a transfer of data from bit 7 of the *I* register to the *SOD* latch at pin 4 of the 8085 chip.

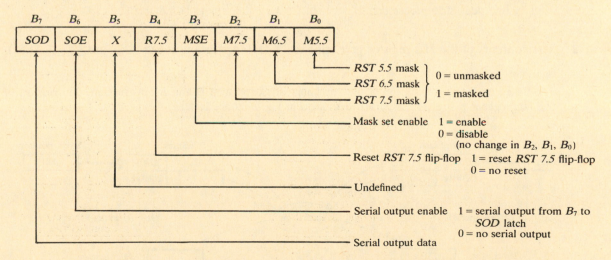

Fig. 8-37 Interrupt register organization as used by the 8085's SIM instruction

The interrupt status register as read by the RIM instruction is diagramed in Fig. 8-38.   The RIM instruction transfers the contents of the internal latches shown in Fig. 8-38 to the accumulator.   The RIM instruction was used earlier in Fig. 8-7a to input serial data from the *SID* pin of the 8085 MPU to bit 7 of the accumulator.   The status of various other latches is also displayed in the accumulator along with the serial input data.

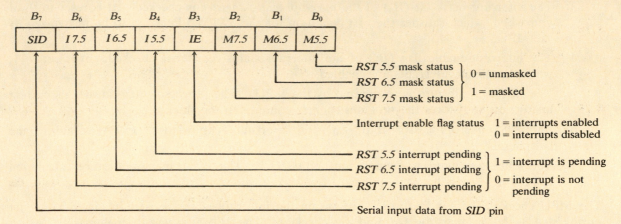

Fig. 8-38   Interrupt register organization as read by the 8085's RIM instruction

SOLVED PROBLEMS

8.70   List instructions from Fig. 8-35 that are associated with the stack.

Solution:

All the PUSH and POP instructions listed in Fig. 8-35 use the stack.   The XTHL and SPHL instructions are also associated with the stack in that they change the contents of the stack pointer.

8.71   List instructions from Fig. 8-35 that are used only by the 8085 microprocessor and not the older 8080 MPU.

Solution:

The RIM and SIM operations are the only new instructions used by the 8085 MPU that were not used by the older 8080 processor.

8.72   The contents of the *HL* register pair after the XTHL operation in Fig. 8-39 are _____ (hex).

Solution:

Based on Intel's description of the "exchange stack top with *H* and *L*" instruction, the contents of the *HL* register pair after the XTHL operation in Fig. 8-39 are 2000H.

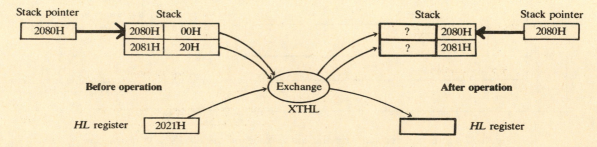

Fig. 8-39

8.73 What are the contents of stack locations 2080H and 2081H after the XTHL operation in Fig. 8-39?

Solution:

The contents of the stack after the XTHL operation in Fig. 8-39 are stack location 2080H = 21H and stack location 2081H = 20H.

8.74 The EI instruction will affect which bit in the interrupt status register shown in Fig. 8-38?

Solution:

The EI (enable interrupts) instruction will set B_3 (the interrupt-enable flag) to 1.

8.75 The HLT instruction has an op code of _____ (hex).   It affects _____ (all, no) flags.   Once in the halt state, the processor can be restarted only by an event such as a(n) _____ (interrupt, NOP instruction).

Solution:

The HLT instruction has an op code of 76H.   It affects no flags.   Once in the halt state, the processor can be restarted only by an external event such as an interrupt.

8.76 The OUT instruction uses the _____ (direct, register) addressing mode.   The address of the output port is found in _____ (data, program) memory.

Solution:

The OUT instruction uses the direct addressing mode.   The address of the output port is found in program memory.

8.77 The RIM instruction can be used to _____ (receive, send) serial data via the _____ (*SID*, *SOD*) pin of the 8085 microprocessor.   This single bit of data ends up in bit _____ (number) of the accumulator.

Solution:

Based on Intel's description of the "read interrupt masks" operation, the RIM instruction can be used to receive serial data via the *SID* pin of the 8085 microprocessor.   This single bit of data ends up in bit 7 of the accumulator.

8.78 If an input such as the *RST 6.5* interrupt is masked, it is _____ (disabled, enabled).

Solution:

If an input such as the *RST 6.5* interrupt is masked, it is disabled.

8.79 Refer to Fig. 8-40.   After the SIM operation, list the contents of each bit position in the *I* register.

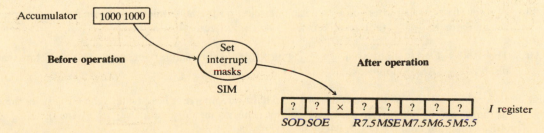

Fig. 8-40

Solution:

The *I* register in Fig. 8-40 will hold the following after the SIM operation:

SOD (serial output data) = 1   *MSE* (mask set enable) = 1   *M 5.5* (*RST 5.5* mask) = 0
SOE (serial output enable) = 0   *M 7.5* (*RST 7.5* mask) = 0
R 7.5 (reset *RST 7.5* flip-flop) = 0   *M 6.5* (*RST 6.5* mask) = 0

8.80 Refer to Fig. 8-40. Will the serial output data be latched into the *SOD* latch of the 8085 MPU?

Solution:

The serial output enable bit of the *I* register in Fig. 8-40 is disabled. Therefore the serial output data will not be transferred to and latched into the *SOD* latch of the 8085 MPU.

8.81 List the interrupts that will be left unmasked after the SIM instruction in Fig. 8-40.

Solution:

The *RST 7.5*, *RST 6.5*, and *RST 5.5* interrupts will be left unmasked after the SIM instruction in Fig. 8-40.

Supplementary Problems

8.82 Intel Corporation introduced the first microprocessor, the 4-bit 4004, in _____ (year).   *Ans.* 1971

8.83 Refer to Fig. 8-2. Pins 12 through 19 on the 8085 are dual-purpose _____/_____ bus lines.
Ans. address/data

8.84 Refer to Fig. 8-2. The *READY* input to the 8085 MPU is most closely associated with the _____ (halt, wait) state of the processor.   *Ans.* wait

8.85 Refer to Fig. 8-2. What two pins on the 8085 MPU (one input and one output) are most closely associated with a direct memory access?   *Ans.* *HOLD* input, *HLDA* (hold acknowledge) output

8.86 Refer to Fig. 8-3. The 8085's control signals are $IO/\bar{M} = 0$, $S_1 = 1$, and $S_2 = 0$. This means that the microprocessor is performing what type of machine cycle?   *Ans.* memory read (see Fig. 8-3)

8.87 This 16-bit 8085 register always holds an address and points to the next instruction to be executed.
Ans. program counter (*PC*)

8.88 A reset (0) sign flag after an arithmetic operation on the 8085 means the result in the accumulator is _____ (negative, positive).   *Ans.* positive

8.89 A reset (0) zero flag after an arithmetic operation on the 8085 microprocessor means the result in the accumulator is _____ (not zero, zero).   *Ans.* not zero

8.90 The 8085's *TRAP* input is a _____ (maskable, nonmaskable) interrupt and therefore cannot be disabled.   *Ans.* nonmaskable

8.91 Refer to Fig. 8-6. When the 8085's *RST 6.5* hardware interrupt is activated, the CPU saves the contents of the _____ _____ in the stack and branches to memory address _____ (hex).
Ans. program counter (*PC*), 34H

8.92   The 8085's secondary accumulators (*BC*, *DE*, and *HL*) can be used either as accumulators or as _____ _____.   *Ans.*   data counters (address pointers)

8.93   The 8085 microprocessor uses _____ (number) flags which contain status information.   *Ans.*   five

8.94   The 8085's MOV *A,L* instruction (move *L* to *A*) transfers the contents of one register to another.   It therefore uses the _____ addressing mode.   *Ans.*   register

8.95   The 8085's MVI *L* instruction moves data from the second byte of the instruction to register _____ (letter).   It uses the _____ addressing mode.   *Ans.*   *L*, immediate

8.96   Each of the 8085's register indirect addressing instructions uses _____ (1, 3) byte(s) of program memory.   *Ans.*   1

8.97   Each of the 8085's direct addressing instructions uses _____ (1, 2 or 3) byte(s) of program memory.   *Ans.*   2 or 3

8.98   Intel would classify an 8080/8085 "store *A* in memory" operation as a _____ (branch, data transfer) instruction.   *Ans.*   data transfer

8.99   Intel would classify an 8080/8085 "rotate" operation as a _____ (data transfer, logical) instruction.   *Ans.*   logical

8.100   Intel would classify an 8080/8085 "call" operation as a _____ (branch, logical) instruction.   *Ans.*   branch

8.101   Refer to Fig. 8-16.   Some 8080/8085 mnemonics contain an added I such as ADI *v*, ANI *v*, and MVI *A,v*.   Each time the added I appears in these instructions, it specifies the _____ addressing mode.   *Ans.*   immediate

8.102   Refer to Fig. 8-16.   List the mnemonics for two instructions used by the 8085 but not by the 8080 microprocessor.   *Ans.*   RIM, SIM

8.103   In the 8080/8085's MOV *D,E* instruction, register _____ (letter) is the source of data while register _____ (letter) is the destination.   *Ans.*   *E*, *D*

8.104   In the 8080/8085's MVI *A* instruction, the source of data is _____.   *Ans.*   second byte of the instruction found in program memory

8.105   The 8080/8085's MOV *B,M* instruction uses _____ addressing.   *Ans.*   register indirect

8.106   The 8080/8085's STA instruction uses _____ addressing.   *Ans.*   direct

8.107   The 8080/8085's MOV *A,L* instruction uses _____ addressing.   *Ans.*   register

8.108   The 8080/8085's ADD *M* instruction adds the contents of a memory location pointed to by the _____ (two letters) register pair to the contents of register _____ (letter).   The sum is deposited in register _____ (letter).   *Ans.*   *HL*, *A*, *A*

8.109   The op code for the INX *H* instruction shown in Fig. 8-41 is _____ (hex).   *Ans.*   23H

8.110   The INX *H* instruction being executed in Fig. 8-41 uses _____ addressing.   *Ans.*   register

8.111   List the contents of both registers *H* and *L* after the increment operation shown in Fig. 8-41.   *Ans.*   register *H* = 00000001, register *L* = 00000000

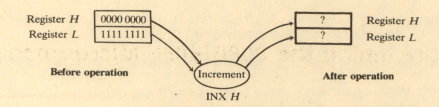

Fig. 8-41

8.112 The symbol ∨ is used by Intel to describe the logical _____ (AND, OR) operation.   *Ans.* OR

8.113 CALL instructions are most closely associated with subroutines, whereas restart instructions are closely associated with _____.   *Ans.* interrupts

8.114 The 8080/8085's JPE instruction is a _____ (conditional, unconditional) jump operation.
Ans. conditional

8.115 The 8080/8085's RNZ instruction checks the status of the _____ flag before executing the return operation.   *Ans.* zero (*Z*)

8.116 The 8080/8085's RP instruction shown in Fig. 8-42 is a _____ (number) -byte instruction with an op code of _____ (hex).   *Ans.* 1, F0

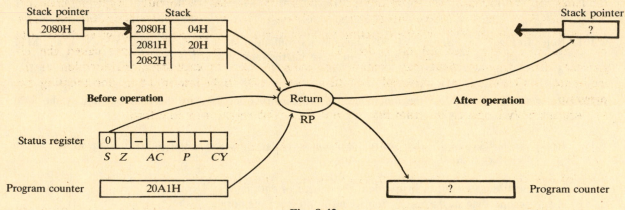

Fig. 8-42

8.117 The 8080/8085's program counter will contain _____ (hex) after the "return from subroutine if plus" operation illustrated in Fig. 8-42.   *Ans.* 2004H

8.118 The 8080/8085's stack pointer will contain _____ (hex) after the RP operation shown in Fig. 8-42.
Ans. 2082H

8.119 The 8080/8085's PUSH and POP operations are specified with _____ (1, 3) -byte instructions and use _____ addressing.   *Ans.* 1, register indirect

8.120 The 8080/8085's IN and OUT operations are specified with _____ (1, 2) -byte instructions and use _____ addressing.   *Ans.* 2, direct

8.121 Executing the 8085's DI instruction will disable which interrupts?
Ans. *INTR, RST 5.5, RST 6.5,* and *RST 7.5*

8.122 What three functions can be performed by the 8085's SIM instruction?
Ans. program the interrupt mask for the *RST 5.5, 6.5,* and *7.5* hardware interrupts; reset the edge-triggered *RST 7.5* interrupt latch; and load the *SOD* output latch

Chapter 9

Programming the 8080/8085 Microprocessor

9.1 INTRODUCTION

To the programmer, the 8080/8085-based microcomputer consists of the instruction set, memory, general-purpose registers, program counter, input/output ports, flags and stack pointer and stack. All these, except the memory and parallel inputs and outputs, are part of the microprocessor.

For convenience, the summary of the 8080/8085 microprocessor's instruction set is reprinted in Fig. 9-1. The instruction set was detailed in Chap. 8.

The 8080/8085's programming model is reproduced in Fig. 9-2a. It lists the registers that concern the programmer. The status register is shown in greater detail in Fig. 9-2b. A brief description of each of the five flags in the status register is also listed in Fig. 9-2b.

Source programs will be written in assembly language. The format used by Intel divides each assembly language line into the following fields:

Label   Op code   Operand   Comments

These fields are similar to those used in assembly language programming in Chap. 6. An entry in the *label field* is optional. The entry in the label field is the "name" of the line. Typically lines that are the target of jumps will have entries in the label field. The *op code field* contains the mnemonic operation code for the 8080/8085 instruction to be performed. The *operand field* gives the data to be operated on the specified op code. The operand field is also sometimes called the *argument*. The *comment field* may contain information useful in explaining the function of the instruction. Comments are optional, but their use is extremely important in documenting the program.

An assembly language program line for the 8080/8085 might look like this:

DATA   MOV   *A,M*   ; Input data to accumulator

Each of the four fields has an entry in this example. They are explained as follows:

1. Label field: Contains the entry DATA. This is the "name" of this line. It is probably the target of a later (or earlier) jump instruction.

2. Op code field: Contains the entry MOV. This tells the CPU that this is a data transfer instruction. The CPU then looks to the next operand field to find the source and destination of the data transfer.

3. Operand field: Contains the entry *A,M*. The *A* (accumulator) is the destination of the data while the memory (*M*) is the source. The memory location is pointed to by the *HL* register pair in this register indirect instruction.

4. Comment field: Contains the entry ; Input data to accumulator. This describes what happens when the instruction is executed. In this case, data is input to the accumulator from a memory location pointed to by the *HL* register pair. The semicolon (;) is used as a *delimiter* to separate the operand field from the comment field.

The op code and operand fields must be filled in, but the label and comment fields are optional. Some inherent instructions require an entry in the op code field and none in the operand field.

Recall from Chap. 6 that flowcharts, assembly language source programs, and assemblers are all aids in programming a microprocessor-based system. The assembled object program listing is the desired final result used by the microcomputer.

	Mnemonic	Op code (hex)	Description
A	ADD *A*	87	Add *A* to *A* (double *A*)
	ADD *B*	80	Add *B* to *A*
	ADD *C*	81	Add *C* to *A*
	ADD *D*	82	Add *D* to *A*
	ADD *E*	83	Add *E* to *A*
	ADD *H*	84	Add *H* to *A*
	ADD *L*	85	Add *L* to *A*
	ADD *M*	86	Add memory LOC (*H* & *L*) to *A*
	ADI *v*	C6	Add immediate data *v* to *A*
	ADC *A*	8F	Add *A* to *A* with carry (double *A* with carry)
	ADC *B*	88	Add *B* to *A* with carry
	ADC *C*	89	Add *C* to *A* with carry
	ADC *D*	8A	Add *D* to *A* with carry
	ADC *E*	8B	Add *E* to *A* with carry
	ADC *H*	8C	Add *H* to *A* with carry
	ADC *L*	8D	Add *L* to *A* with carry
	ADC *M*	8E	Add memory LOC (*H* & *L*) to *A* with carry
	ACI *v*	CE	Add immediate data *v* to *A* with carry
	ANA *A*	A7	Test *A* and clear carry
	ANA *B*	A0	AND *B* with *A*
	ANA *C*	A1	AND *C* with *A*
	ANA *D*	A2	AND *D* with *A*
	ANA *E*	A3	AND *E* with *A*
	ANA *H*	A4	AND *H* with *A*
	ANA *L*	A5	AND *L* with *A*
	ANA *M*	A6	AND memory LOC (*H* & *L*) with *A*
	ANI *v*	E6	AND immediate data *v* with *A*
C	CALL *aa*	CD	Call subroutine at address *aa*
	CZ *aa*	CC	If zero, CALL at address *aa*
	CNZ *aa*	C4	If not zero, CALL at address *aa*
	CP *aa*	F4	If plus, CALL at address *aa*
	CM *aa*	FC	If minus, CALL at address *aa*
	CC *aa*	DD	If carry, CALL at address *aa*
	CNC *aa*	D4	If no carry, CALL at address *aa*
	CPE *aa*	EC	If even parity, CALL at address *aa*
	CPO *aa*	E4	If odd parity, CALL at address *aa*
	CMA	2F	Complement *A*
	CMC	3F	Complement carry
	CMP *A*	BF	Set zero flag
	CMP *B*	B8	Compare *A* with *B*
	CMP *C*	B9	Compare *A* with *C*
	CMP *D*	BA	Compare *A* with *D*
	CMP *E*	BB	Compare *A* with *E*
	CMP *H*	BC	Compare *A* with *H*
	CMP *L*	BD	Compare *A* with *L*
	CMP *M*	BE	Compare *A* with memory LOC (*H* & *L*)
	CPI *v*	FE	Compare *A* with immediate data *v*
D	DAA	27	Decimal adjust *A*
	DAD *B*	09	Add *B* & *C* to *H* & *L*
	DAD *D*	19	Add *D* & *E* to *H* & *L*
	DAD *H*	29	Add *H* & *L* to *H* & *L* (double *H* & *L*)
	DAD *SP*	39	Add *SP* to *H* & *L*
	DCR *A*	3D	Decrement *A*
	DCR *B*	05	Decrement *B*
	DCR *C*	0D	Decrement *C*
	DCR *D*	15	Decrement *D*
	DCR *E*	1D	Decrement *E*
	DCR *H*	25	Decrement *H*
	DCR *L*	2D	Decrement *L*
	DCR *M*	35	Decrement memory LOC (*H* & *L*)
	DCX *B*	0B	Decrement *B* & *C*
	DCX *D*	1B	Decrement *D* & *E*
	DCX *H*	2B	Decrement *H* & *L*

Fig. 9-1 Instruction set summary for the 8080/8085 microprocessor (All mnemonics copyrighted © Intel Corporation, 1976)

	Mnemonic	Op code (hex)	Description
D	DCX SP	3B	Decrement SP
	DI	F3	Disable interrupts
E	EI	FB	Enable interrupts
H	HLT	76	Halt until interrupt
	IN v	DB	Input from device v
	INR A	3C	Increment A
	INR B	04	Increment B
	INR C	0C	Increment C
	INR D	14	Increment D
	INR E	1C	Increment E
	INR H	24	Increment H
	INR L	2C	Increment L
I	INR M	34	Increment memory LOC (H & L)
	INX B	03	Increment B & C
	INX D	13	Increment D & E
	INX H	23	Increment H & L
	INX SP	33	Increment SP
	JMP aa	C3	Jump to address aa
	JZ aa	CA	If zero, JMP to address aa
	JNZ aa	C2	If not zero, JMP to address aa
	JP aa	F2	If plus, JMP to address aa
J	JM aa	FA	If minus, JMP to address aa
	JC aa	DA	If carry, JMP to address aa
	JNC aa	D2	If no carry, JMP to address aa
	JPE aa	EA	If even parity, JMP to address aa
	JPO aa	E2	If odd parity, JMP to address aa
	LDA aa	3A	Load A from address aa
	LDAX B	0A	Load A from memory LOC (B & C)
L	LDAX D	1A	Load A from memory LOC (D & E)
	LHLD aa	2A	Load H & L from address aa
	LXI B,vv	01	Load B & C with immediate data vv
	LXI D,vv	11	Load D & E with immediate data vv
	LXI H,vv	21	Load H & L with immediate data vv
	LXI SP,vv	31	Load SP with immediate data vv
	MOV A,B	78	Move B to A
	MOV A,C	79	Move C to A
	MOV A,D	7A	Move D to A
	MOV A,E	7B	Move E to A
	MOV A,H	7C	Move H to A
	MOV A,L	7D	Move L to A
	MOV A,M	7E	Move memory LOC (H & L) to A
	MOV B,A	47	Move A to B
	MOV B,C	41	Move C to B
	MOV B,D	42	Move D to B
	MOV B,E	43	Move E to B
	MOV B,H	44	Move H to B
	MOV B,L	45	Move L to B
	MOV B,M	46	Move memory LOC (H & L) to B
M	MOV C,A	4F	Move A to C
	MOV C,B	48	Move B to C
	MOV C,D	4A	Move D to C
	MOV C,E	4B	Move E to C
	MOV C,H	4C	Move H to C
	MOV C,L	4D	Move L to C
	MOV C,M	4E	Move memory LOC (H & L) to C
	MOV D,A	57	Move A to D
	MOV D,B	50	Move B to D
	MOV D,C	51	Move C to D
	MOV D,E	53	Move E to D
	MOV D,H	54	Move H to D
	MOV D,L	55	Move L to D
	MOV D,M	56	Move memory LOC (H & L) to D

Fig. 9-1   (cont.)

	Mnemonic	Op code (hex)	Description
M	MOV E,A	5F	Move A to E
	MOV E,B	58	Move B to E
	MOV E,C	59	Move C to E
	MOV E,D	5A	Move D to E
	MOV E,H	5C	Move H to E
	MOV E,L	5D	Move L to E
	MOV E,M	5E	Move memory LOC (H & L) to E
	MOV H,A	67	Move A to H
	MOV H,B	60	Move B to H
	MOV H,C	61	Move C to H
	MOV H,D	62	Move D to H
	MOV H,E	63	Move E to H
	MOV H,L	65	Move L to H
	MOV H,M	66	Move memory LOC (H & L) to H
	MOV L,A	6F	Move A to L
	MOV L,B	68	Move B to L
	MOV L,C	69	Move C to L
	MOV L,D	6A	Move D to L
	MOV L,E	6B	Move E to L
	MOV L,H	6C	Move H to L
	MOV L,M	6E	Move memory LOC (H & L) to L
	MOV M,A	77	Move A to memory LOC (H & L)
	MOV M,B	70	Move B to memory LOC (H & L)
	MOV M,C	71	Move C to memory LOC (H & L)
	MOV M,D	72	Move D to memory LOC (H & L)
	MOV M,E	73	Move E to memory LOC (H & L)
	MOV M,H	74	Move H to memory LOC (H & L)
	MOV M,L	75	Move L to memory LOC (H & L)
	MVI A,v	3E	Move immediate data v to A
	MVI B,v	06	Move immediate data v to B
	MVI C,v	0E	Move immediate data v to C
	MVI D,v	16	Move immediate data v to D
	MVI E,v	1E	Move immediate data v to E
	MVI H,v	26	Move immediate data v to H
	MVI L,v	2E	Move immediate data v to L
	MVI M,v	36	Move immediate data v to memory LOC (H & L)
N	NOP	00	No operation
O	ORA A	B7	Test A and clear carry
	ORA B	B0	OR B with A
	ORA C	B1	OR C with A
	ORA D	B2	OR D with A
	ORA E	B3	OR E with A
	ORA H	B4	OR H with A
	ORA L	B5	OR L with A
	ORA M	B6	OR memory LOC (H & L) with A
	ORI v	F6	OR immediate data v with A
	OUT v	D3	Output A to device v
P	PCHL	E9	Jump to memory LOC contained in (H & L)
	POP B	C1	Pop B & C from stack
	POP D	D1	Pop D & E from stack
	POP H	E1	Pop H & L from stack
	POP PSW	F1	Pop A and flags from stack
	PUSH B	C5	Push B & C onto stack
	PUSH D	D5	Push D & E onto stack
	PUSH H	E5	Push H & L onto stack
	PUSH PSW	F5	Push A and flags onto stack
R	RAL	17	Rotate CY + A left
	RAR	1F	Rotate CY + A right
	RLC	07	Rotate A left and into carry
	RRC	0F	Rotate A right and into carry
	RIM	20	Read interrupt mask (8085 only)
	RET	C9	Return from subroutine
	RZ	C8	If zero, return from subroutine

Fig. 9-1 (*cont.*)

	Mnemonic	Op code (hex)	Description
R	RNZ	C0	If not zero, return from subroutine
	RP	F0	If plus, return from subroutine
	RM	F8	If minus, return from subroutine
	RC	D8	If carry, return from subroutine
	RNC	D0	If no carry, return from subroutine
	RPE	E8	If even parity, return from subroutine
	RPO	E0	If odd parity, return from subroutine
	RST 0	C7	Restart subroutine at address 00H
	RST 1	CF	Restart subroutine at address 08H
	RST 2	D7	Restart subroutine at address 10H
	RST 3	DF	Restart subroutine at address 18H
	RST 4	E7	Restart subroutine at address 20H
	RST 5	EF	Restart subroutine at address 28H
	RST 6	F7	Restart subroutine at address 30H
	RST 7	FF	Restart subroutine at address 38H
S	SIM	30	Set interrupt mask (8085 only)
	SPHL	F9	Load SP from H & L
	SHLD aa	22	Store H & L at memory LOC aa
	STA aa	32	Store A at memory LOC aa
	STAX B	02	Store A at memory LOC (B & C)
	STAX D	12	Store A at memory LOC (D & E)
	STC	37	Set carry flag
	SUB A	97	Clear A
	SUB B	90	Subtract B from A
	SUB C	91	Subtract C from A
	SUB D	92	Subtract D from A
	SUB E	93	Subtract E from A
	SUB H	94	Subtract H from A
	SUB L	95	Subtract L from A
	SUB M	96	Subtract contents of memory LOC (H & L) from A
	SUI v	D6	Subtract immediate data v from A
	SBB A	9F	Set A to minus carry
	SBB B	98	Subtract B from A with borrow
	SBB C	99	Subtract C from A with borrow
	SBB D	9A	Subtract D from A with borrow
	SBB E	9B	Subtract E from A with borrow
	SBB H	9C	Subtract H from A with borrow
	SBB L	9D	Subtract L from A with borrow
	SBB M	9E	Subtract memory LOC (H & L) from A with borrow
	SBI v	DE	Subtract immediate data v from A with borrow
X	XCHG	EB	Exchange D & E with H & L
	XTHL	E3	Exchange top of stack with H & L
	XRA A	AF	Clear A
	XRA B	A8	Exclusive OR B with A
	XRA C	A9	Exclusive OR C with A
	XRA D	AA	Exclusive OR D with A
	XRA E	AB	Exclusive OR E with A
	XRA H	AC	Exclusive OR H with A
	XRA L	AD	Exclusive OR L with A
	XRA M	AE	Exclusive OR memory LOC (H & L) with A
	XRI v	EE	Exclusive OR immediate data v with A

Fig. 9-1 (*cont.*)

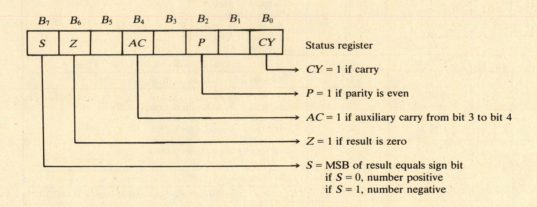

Flags	Status register (8)		A	(8)	Primary accumulator
	B	(8)	C	(8)	
	D	(8)	E	(8)	Secondary accumulators/data counters
	H	(8)	L	(8)	
	SP			(16)	Stack pointer
	PC			(16)	Program counter

(a) Programming model for the 8080 microprocessor

B_7 B_6 B_5 B_4 B_3 B_2 B_1 B_0

| S | Z | | AC | | P | | CY | Status register |

$CY = 1$ if carry

$P = 1$ if parity is even

$AC = 1$ if auxiliary carry from bit 3 to bit 4

$Z = 1$ if result is zero

$S = $ MSB of result equals sign bit
     if $S = 0$, number positive
     if $S = 1$, number negative

(b) Flags in the 8080/8085's status register

Fig. 9-2

9.2 STRAIGHT-LINE PROGRAMS

Consider the functional flowchart in Fig. 9-3a. It represents a *straight-line program* in that it contains no branches. The flowchart also represents a program that loads a binary number, converts it to its 2s complement form, and finally stores the 2s complement representation back in memory. Recall that functional flowcharts like the one in Fig. 9-3a are a general description of the problem solution.

A detailed flowchart for the same problem is shown in Fig. 9-3b. This flowchart was completed with the functions of a specific microprocessor in mind—the 8080/8085 MPU in this case. From the detailed flowchart in Fig. 9-3b, an assembly language program can be developed. Such a program is listed in Fig. 9-4a. Note that each program instruction has a comparable rectangular block on the

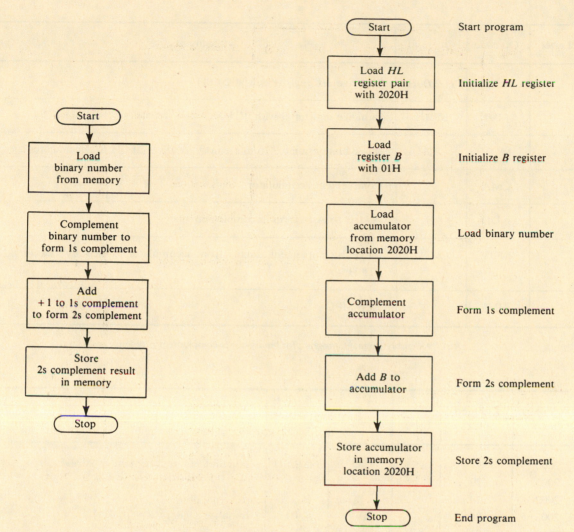

(a) Flowchart for binary–to–2s-complement program   (b) Detailed flowchart for binary–to–2s-complement program

Fig. 9-3

detailed flowchart in Fig. 9-3b.   As an example, the first rectangular block in Fig. 9-3b, which says "load *HL* register pair with 2020H," is satisfied with the "LXI *H*, 2020H" assembly program statement in Fig. 9-4.

The next step would be to translate the source assembly language program in Fig. 9-4a into its machine language equivalent.   This "assembly" or translation process can be done using a special computer program called an assembler or can be done by hand.   The instruction set in Fig. 9-1 can be used for hand translating of the assembly language program.   The program shown in Fig. 9-4b has the program memory address and the hexadecimal machine code listing for each instruction and operand.   The nonshaded section on the left in Fig. 9-4b represents the machine code as it might appear in program memory.

Note that the program listed in Fig. 9-4b contains no entries in the label field.   This is because labels are usually used to show the destination of a branching instruction.   The program in Fig. 9-4 represents a straight-line program and therefore contains no jumps.

Label	Op code	Operand	Comments
	LXI	H,2020H	; Initialize *HL* register pair at 2020H
	MVI	B,01H	; Initialize register *B* with 01H
	MOV	A,M	; Move binary number from memory location 2020H to accumulator
	CMA		; Complement accumulator
	ADD	B	; Add *B* to *A* to form 2s complement
	MOV	M,A	; Move 2s complement number from accumulator to memory location 2020H
	HLT		; Stop MPU

(a) Assembly language program for binary–to–2s-complement problem

Address (hex)	Contents (hex)	Label	Op code	Operand	Comments
2000	21		LXI	H,2020H	; Initialize *HL* register pair at 2020H
2001	20				
2002	20				
2003	06		MVI	B,01H	; Initialize register *B* with 01H
2004	01				
2005	7E		MOV	A,M	; Move binary number from memory location 2020H to accumulator
2006	2F		CMA		; Complement accumulator
2007	80		ADD		; Add *B* to *A* to form 2s complement
2008	77		MOV	M,A	; Move 2s complement number from accumulator to memory location 2020H
2009	76		HLT		; Stop MPU

(b) Object program for binary–to–2s-complement problem

Fig. 9-4

SOLVED PROBLEMS

9.1 The listing in Fig. 9-4 is an example of a _____ (branching, straight-line) program.

Solution:

The listing in Fig. 9-4 is an example of a straight-line program.

9.2 Refer to Fig. 9-5. The result found in data memory after running the program listed in Fig. 9-4 will be _____ (8 bits). This result will be the _____ (1s, 2s) complement representation of 00000010_2.

Solution:

The result found in data memory in Fig. 9-5 after running the program will be 11111110. This result will be the 2s complement representation of 00000010_2.

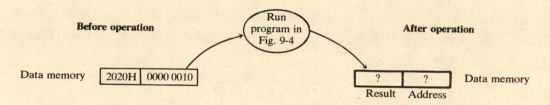

Fig. 9-5

9.3 Refer to Fig. 9-5. The address in data memory where the result will be deposited after running the program will be _____ (hex).

Solution:

The *HL* register pair will still point to memory location 2020H after the program. Therefore the address in data memory in Fig. 9-5 where the result will be deposited after running the program will be 2020H.

9.4 The flowchart in Fig. 9-6 represents a program segment that inputs an ASCII number and masks out the _____ (least, most) significant 4 bits. The result is the _____ (BCD, binary) equivalent of the ASCII number.

Solution:

The flowchart in Fig. 9-6 represents a program segment that inputs an ASCII number and masks out the most significant 4 bits. The result is the BCD equivalent of the ASCII number.

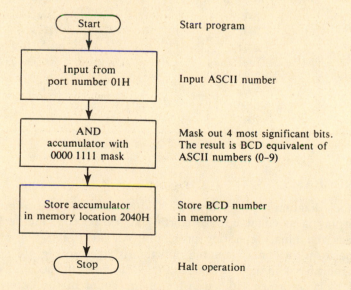

Fig. 9-6 Detailed flowchart of problem

9.5   Based on the detailed flowchart in Fig. 9-6, complete lines 2 and 3 of the 8080/8085 program segment shown below.

Label	Op code	Operand	Comments
LINE 1	IN	01H	; Input ASCII number from port 01H
LINE 2	____	____	; AND accu with 00001111 (0FH)
LINE 3	____	____	; Store accu at location 2040H
LINE 4	HLT		; Stop MPU

Solution:

One possible program segment that will perform the task detailed in Fig. 9-6 is as follows:

Label	Op code	Operand	Comments
LINE 1	IN	01H	; Input ASCII number from port 01H
LINE 2	ANI	0FH	; AND accu with 00001111 (0FH)
LINE 3	STA	2040H	; Store accu at location 2040H
LINE 4	HLT		; Stop MPU

9.6   List the hexadecimal 8080/8085 machine code required to execute the program from Prob. 9.5.   The program will start at memory location 2000H as follows:

Memory location (hex)	Contents (hex)
2000	BD ⎫
2001	01 ⎬ input instruction
2002	____
2003	____
2004	____
____	____
____	____

Solution:

Refer to the instruction set in Fig. 9-1 for op codes.   The following is an 8080/8085 machine code listing that will execute the program from Prob. 9.5:

Memory location (hex)	Contents (hex)
2000	BD
2001	01
2002	E6
2003	0F
2004	32
2005	40
2006	20
2007	76

9.3   LOOPING PROGRAMS

Consider the block diagram in Fig. 9-7a of an 8080/8085-based microcomputer system.   Assume the 8-bit binary display is to count upward starting at 00000000_2.   Figure 9-7b shows a detailed flowchart that solves the binary counting problem.   An 8080/8085 assembly language program segment that will perform the binary counting function is listed in Fig. 9-7c.

The first rectangular block in the flowchart in Fig. 9-7b shows the accumulator being initialized to 00H.   The second block represents the transfer of the count in the accumulator to output port 02H.   The third block shows the count being increased by 1 in the accumulator.   Next the program

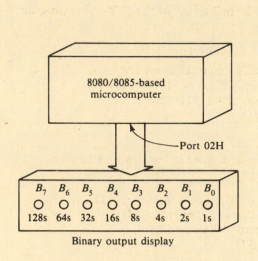

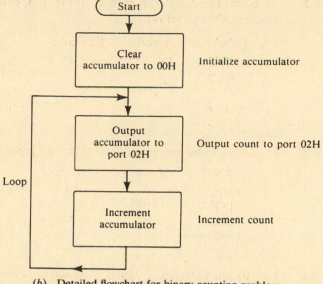

(a) Simplified block diagram of system for displaying binary counting

(b) Detailed flowchart for binary counting problem

Label	Op code	Operand	Comments
	XRA	A	; Clear accumulator
LOOP	OUT	02H	; Output accumulator to port 02H
	INR	A	; Increment accumulator
	JMP	LOOP	; Jump back to beginning of loop (symbolic address = LOOP)

(c) Assembly language program for the binary counting problem

Fig. 9-7

loops back to the output block.   The program would cause the output display to count upward in binary at a very high rate.

The 8080/8085 assembly language program in Fig. 9-7c will perform the binary counting function represented in the previous flowchart.   The XRA A instruction clears the accumulator.   The OUT instruction transfers the contents of the accumulator to output port 02H.   The count in the accumulator is increased by 1 using the INR A instruction.   The JMP instruction causes the MPU to branch back to the instruction with the symbolic label LOOP.   The program then continuously loops through the OUT, INR A, and JMP sequence.

In actual practice, the program represented in Fig. 9-7 would count much too fast for a person to observe.   Because of the fast sequencing, the binary output display lamps would appear to be lit continuously.   To slow down the counting process, it is typical to add a *time delay* in the program.   The flowchart in Fig. 9-8a represents a binary counting program that includes a time delay.

The detailed flowchart in Fig. 9-8b represents the binary counting program with a time

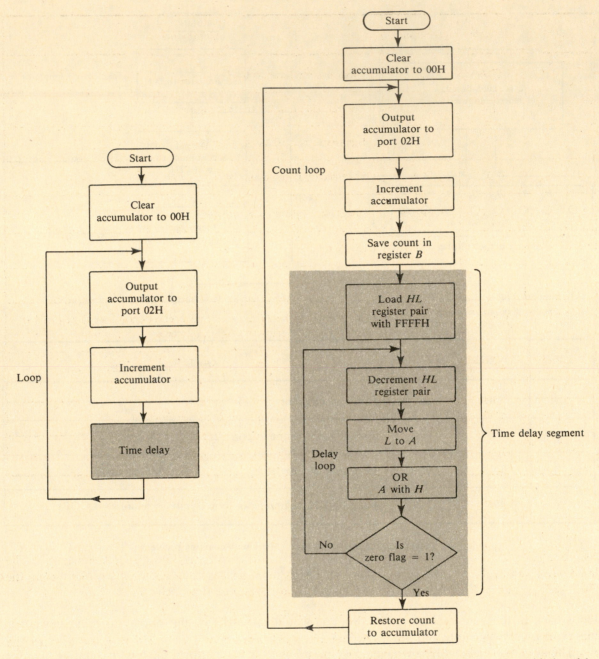

(a) Flowchart for binary counting
     problem with added time delay

(b) Detailed flowchart for binary counting problem with time delay

Fig. 9-8

delay. The five blocks near the bottom of the flowchart represent the time delay segment of the program. The time delay is being generated by repeating the delay loop 65,535 (FFFFH) times.

The assembly language program for the counting program with time delay is shown in Fig. 9-8c. Note that each block in the detailed flowchart (Fig. 9-8b) is implemented with a single assembly language instruction. The delay loop is given the symbolic address or label of DELAY in the program in Fig. 9-8c. The longer count loop is given the symbolic address of COUNT. The

Label	Op code	Operand	Comments
	XRA	A	; Clear accumulator to 00H
COUNT	OUT	02H	; Output accumulator to port number 02H
	INR	A	; Increment accumulator—increase count by one
	MOV	B,A	; Save accumulator count in register B
	LXI	H,FFFFH	; Load HL register pair with FFFFH
DELAY	DCX	H	; Decrement HL register pair
	MOV	A,L	; Move register L to accumulator for testing
	ORA	H	; Logically OR the H register with accumulator—set Z flag to 1 if both H and A register contain all zeros
	JNZ	DELAY	; If Z flag = 0, then jump to DELAY location (delay loop); otherwise continue
	MOV	A,B	; Restore count (move from B to accumulator)
	JMP	COUNT	; Jump to COUNT location (count loop)

(c)   Assembly language program for the binary counting problem with time delay

Fig. 9-8 (*cont.*)

program will cycle through the delay loop 65,536 times for each time through the count loop.   The DCX H, MOV A,L, ORA H, and JNZ instructions together consume about 24 μs when using the 8085 MPU.   Since the delay loop is repeated 65,536 times, the time delay is

$$24 \ \mu s \times 65,536 = 1,572,864 \ \mu s$$

The time delay segment of the program produces a delay of about 1.6 s.   The program displays the first count, delays 1.6 s, displays the second count, delays 1.6 s, etc.

The purpose of the MOV A,L and ORA H instructions in the assembly language program in Fig. 9-8c may not be immediately clear.   These two instructions are included to set the Z flag when the HL register pair is finally decremented to 0000H.   Unfortunately the previous "decrement HL register pair" operation (DCX H instruction) has *no effect on any of the flags*.   Therefore the MOV A,L and ORA H instructions have been added.

Time delay routines are commonly used in microcomputer programs.   They are based on the idea that each processor instruction uses a specific amount of time for execution.   Programming techniques are available for generating even longer time delays than the 1.6-s delay generated in the last example.

Consider the use of two loops in the program represented in Fig. 9-8b.   One loop is within the other loop.   This programming technique is called *nesting*.   The delay loop in Fig. 9-8b is said to be the nested, or inner, loop. The process of repeating instructions until a condition is met, as in the nested loop, is called *iteration*.

SOLVED PROBLEMS

9.7 The last instruction in the program in Fig. 9-7c is JMP. The program is directed to jump to what location by this instruction?

Solution:

The instruction "JMP LOOP" in Fig. 9-7c directed the processor to jump back to the symbolic address LOOP which happens to be the OUT (output) instruction in this example.

9.8 List the five instructions from Fig. 9-8c that form the time delay segment of the program.

Solution:

The LXI H; DCX H; MOV A,L; ORA H; and JNZ instructions in Fig. 9-8c form the time delay segment of the program. This segment is specifically identified in the detailed flowchart in Fig. 9-8b.

9.9 The time delay loop represented in the flowchart in Fig. 9-8b is called a(n) _____ (infinite, nested) loop by programmers.

Solution:

The time delay loop represented in the flowchart in Fig. 9-8b is called a nested loop.

9.10 Refer to Fig. 9-8c. The first time the JNZ instruction is encountered by the 8080/8085 processor in this program, the Z flag will be _____ (reset to 0, set to 1). Upon executing the JNZ instruction, the processor then jumps to the next instruction, which is _____.

Solution:

The first time the JNZ instruction is encountered in Fig. 9-8c, the Z flag will be reset to 0. The processor then jumps to the next instruction, which is DCX H (to the location with the symbolic address of DELAY).

9.11 Refer to Fig. 9-8c. When the *HL* register pair has been decremented to 0000H by the DCX H instruction, the Z flag is _____ (reset to 0, set to 1) by the ORA H operation. Based on this flag condition, the JNZ instruction is followed by the _____ operation.

Solution:

When the *HL* register pair in Fig. 9-8c has been decremented to 0000H by the DCX H instruction, the Z flag is set to 1 by the ORA H operation. Based on this flag condition, the JNZ instruction is followed by the MOV A,B operation.

9.12 List the hexadecimal 8080/8085 machine code required to execute the program in Fig. 9-8c. The program will start at memory location 2000H as follows:

Memory location (hex)	Contents (hex)	
2000	AF	clear accumulator
2001	____	
2002	____	
____	____	
____	____	

Solution:

Refer to the instruction set in Fig. 9-1. The following is an 8080/8085 machine code listing that will execute the program from Fig. 9-8c:

Memory location (hex)	Contents (hex)
2000	AF
2001	D3
2002	02
2003	3C
2004	47
2005	21
2006	FF
2007	FF
2008	2B
2009	7D
200A	B4
200B	C2
200C	08
200D	20
200E	78
200F	C3
2010	01
2011	20

9.4 MATHEMATICAL PROGRAMS

Consider the problem of adding the decimal numbers 1,110,527 and 192,514 using an 8080/8085-based system. Converting these numbers to hexadecimal, the manual solution to this addition problem might appear as in Fig. 9-9a. The hexadecimal sum of $10F1FF + 02F002 = 13E201_{16}$.

The 8080/8085 microprocessor's accumulator will handle only 8 bits of data (a byte) at a time. The processor could possibly handle this problem if the programmer divided the hexadecimal number into byte-length groups. Each smaller byte-length group would then be added separately. An example of this technique is shown in Fig. 9-9b. The least significant bytes in Fig. 9-9b are added ($FF + 02 = 01_{16}$ plus a carry). Next, the middle bytes are added (carry of $1 + F1 + F0 = E2_{16}$ plus a carry). Finally, the most significant bytes are added (carry of $1 + 10 + 02 = 13_{16}$). Note that on the last two adds, the carries from lesser significant bytes must be considered when calculating the sum. The 8080/8085 microprocessor has special "add with carry" instructions for this purpose.

The procedure for performing 24-bit addition (3-byte addition) might be as follows:

1. Add least significant byte of first number to least significant byte of second number.

2. Record the least significant partial sum.

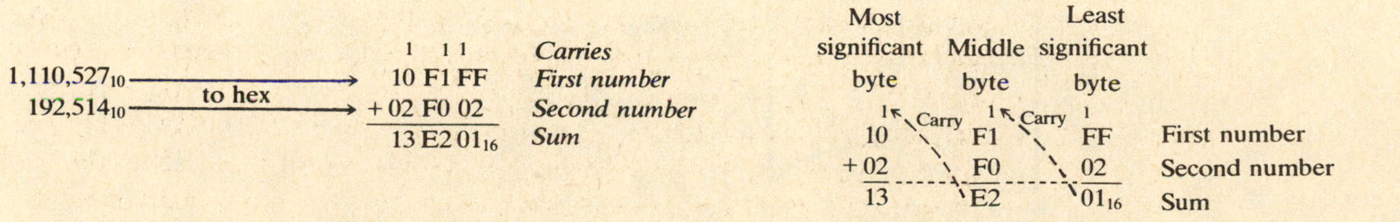

(a) Hexadecimal addition example

(b) 24-bit addition grouped in bytes as executed by an 8-bit microprocessor

Fig. 9-9

3. Add the carry from the previous addition, the middle byte of the first number, and the middle byte of the second number.

4. Record the middle partial sum.

5. Add the carry from the previous addition, the most significant byte of the first number, and the most significant byte of the second number.

6. Record the most significant partial sum.

In the addition problem, assume the first and second numbers are assigned memory locations as shown in Fig. 9-10*a*. The location of the result of the 24-bit addition is also detailed in the memory map in Fig. 9-10*a*. Using these data memory locations, the straight-line assembly language program in Fig. 9-10*b* was developed to solve the 3-byte addition problem. Note that the first ADD *M* instruction is an add without carry operation. However, the second and third ADC *M* instructions are add with carry operations.

The adding of larger numbers requires the use of multibyte addition. In this example the numbers added were 3 bytes long. This is also called *triple-precision addition*.

SOLVED PROBLEMS

9.13 The program listed in Fig. 9-10*b* is an example of _____ (double, triple) -precision addition.

Solution:

The program listed in Fig. 9-10*b* is an example of triple-precision addition.

Data memory

Address (hex)	Contents	
2020		Least significant byte of first number
2021		Least significant byte of second number
2022		Middle byte of first number
2023		Middle byte of second number
2024		Most significant byte of first number
2025		Most significant byte of second number
2026		Least significant byte
2027		Sum Middle byte
2028		Most significant byte

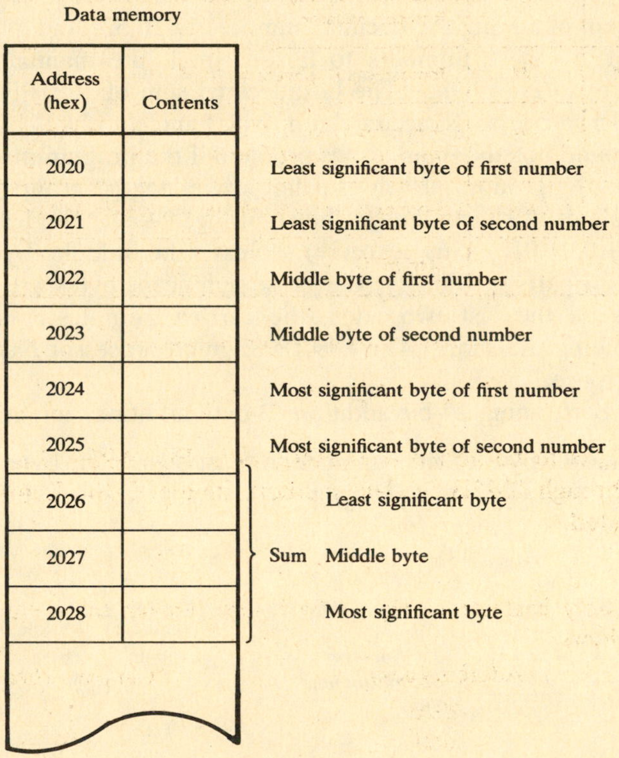

(*a*) Data memory map for 24-bit addition program

Fig. 9-10

Label	Op code	Operand	Comments
	LXI	H,2020H	; Initialize *HL* register pair at 2020H (*HL* register pair used as pointer)
	MOV	A,M	; Load least significant byte of first number from memory LOC 2020H into accumulator
	INX	H	; Increment *HL* pointer to 2021H
	ADD	M	; Add memory LOC 2021H to accumulator (add least significant bytes)
	STA	2026H	; Store least significant partial sum at memory LOC 2026H
	INX	H	; Increment *HL* pointer to 2022H
	MOV	A,M	; Load middle byte of first number from memory LOC 2022H into accumulator
	INX	H	; Increment *HL* pointer to 2023H
	ADC	M	; Add memory LOC 2023H, accumulator, and carry together (add middle bytes with carry)
	STA	2027H	; Store middle partial sum at memory LOC 2027H
	INX	H	; Increment *HL* pointer to 2024H
	MOV	A,M	; Load most significant byte of first number from memory LOC 2024H into accumulator
	INX	H	; Increment *HL* pointer to 2025H
	ADC	M	; Add memory LOC 2025H, accumulator, and carry together (add most significant bytes with carry)
	STA	2028H	; Store most significant partial sum at memory LOC 2028H
	HLT		; Stop MPU

(*b*) Assembly language program for 24-bit addition

Fig. 9-10   (*cont.*)

9.14   Assume $10F1FF_{16}$ is to be added to 02F002, as in Fig. 9-9*b*.   List the contents of memory locations 2020 through 2025H in data memory in Fig. 9-10*a* before the multibyte addition program is executed.

Solution:

The data memory contents in Fig. 9-10*a* before running the program for adding $10F1FF_{16} + 02F002_{16}$ are as follows:

Address (hex)	Contents (hex)
2020	FF
2021	02
2022	F1
2023	F0
2024	10
2025	02

9.15 List the contents of memory locations 2026H, 2027H, and 2028H in Fig. 9-10 after the program has been executed adding 10F1FF and 02F002.

Solution:

The "sum" data memory locations in Fig. 9-10 hold the following after the program has been executed ($10F1FF + 02F002 = 13E201_{16}$):

Address (hex)	Contents (hex)
2026	01 (least significant byte of sum)
2027	E2 (middle byte of sum)
2028	13 (most significant byte of sum)

9.16 Refer to Fig. 9-10*b*. The *HL* register pair is used as a _____ (general-purpose, pointer) register in this addition program.

Solution:

The *HL* register pair is used as an address pointer in the addition program in Fig. 9-10*b*.

9.17 The ADD *M* instruction shown in Fig. 9-10*b* is an _____ (add, add with carry) operation.

Solution:

The ADD *M* instruction shown in Fig. 9-10*b* is an add operation.

9.18 The STA 2027H instruction in Fig. 9-10*b* causes the contents of the _____ (*A*, *B*) register to be stored in memory location _____ (hex).

Solution:

The STA 2027H instruction in Fig. 9-10*b* causes the contents of the *A*, register (the accumulator) to be stored in memory location 2027H.

9.19 Refer to Fig. 9-11. The first number to be added is stored at what memory locations when using this program?

Solution:

According to the memory map in Fig. 9-11*a*, the first 4-byte number to be added is stored at memory locations 2020H through 2023H.

9.20 After the multibyte addition program in Fig. 9-11 is run, the sum is stored in what four memory locations?

Solution:

The STAX *D* instruction stores the partial sums at memory locations pointed to by the *DE* register pair. The sum is therefore stored at memory locations 2020H through 2023H after the program has been executed.

9.21 How must the MVI *C* instruction in Fig. 9-11*b* be changed to perform 24-bit instead of 32-bit addition?

Solution:

The instruction should read "MVI *C*,03H" if the program in Fig. 9-11*b*, is to perform 24-bit addition.   The operand for the MVI *C* instruction (03H in this case) is the number of bytes to be added.

9.22 Refer to Fig. 9-11. List the contents of the following memory locations when adding $12F0C3FF_{16}$ to $01B4D503_{16}$.

Memory location (hex)	Contents (hex)
2020	FF
2021	____
2022	____
2023	____
2030	____
2031	____
2032	____
2033	____

Solution:

Before adding $12F0C3FF_{16}$ to $01B4D503_{16}$, the data memory shown in Fig. 9-11 must be loaded with data as follows:

Memory location (hex)	Contents (hex)
2020	FF
2021	C3
2022	F0
2023	12
2030	03
2031	D5
2032	B4
2033	01

Data memory

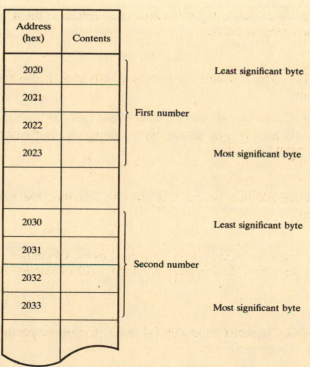

(a) Data memory map for 32-bit addition program

Fig. 9-11

Label	Op code	Operand	Comments
	MVI	C,04H	; Initialize C register with number of bytes to be added
	LXI	D,2020H	; Initialize DE pointer to location of least significant byte of first number
	LXI	H,2030H	; Initialize HL pointer to location of least significant byte of second number
	XRA	A	; Clear carry flag
LOOP	LDAX	D	; Load byte of first number into accumulator
	ADC	M	; Add byte of second number, accumulator, and carry bit together
	STAX	D	; Store partial sum in memory LOC pointed to by DE register
	DCR	C	; Decrement register C
	JZ	END	; If Z flag = 1, then jump to symbolic address labeled END
	INX	D	; Increment DE pointer
	INX	H	; Increment HL pointer
	JMP	LOOP	; Jump always to symbolic address labeled LOOP
END	HLT		; Stop MPU

(b) Assembly language program for sample problem

Fig. 9-11 (cont.)

9.23 What is the sum of adding $12F0C3FF_{16}$ and $01B4D503_{16}$? List the contents and locations where this multibyte sum will be stored after running the program in Fig. 9-11.

Solution:

Adding hexadecimal $12F0C3FF + 01B4D503 = 14A59902_{16}$. The result (sum) of the program in Fig. 9-11 will be stored as follows in data memory:

Memory location (hex)	Contents (hex)
2020	02 (least significant byte of sum)
2021	99
2022	A5
2033	14 (most significant byte of sum)

9.24 Refer to Fig. 9-11b. If the Z flag = 0, then the _____ instruction will be executed after the JZ instruction in this program.

Solution:

If the Z flag = 0 in Fig. 9-11b, then the INX D instruction will be executed after the JZ instruction in this program.

Supplementary Problems

9.25 To the programmer, the 8080/8085-based microcomputer consists of memory, input/output ports, flags, stack, stack pointer, _____ counter, _____ set, and general-purpose registers.
Ans. program, instruction

9.26 List the four fields in a typical assembly language instruction line.
Ans. label, op code (operation), operand, comments

9.27 The operand field is sometimes also called the _____.   *Ans.* argument

9.28 Assembly language statements usually contain entries in the _____ and _____ fields, whereas the label and comments are optional.   *Ans.* op code (operation), operand

9.29 The 8080/8085 program represented in Fig. 9-12 loads the ASCII numbers from memory locations _____ (hex) and _____ (hex), masks out the _____ (least, most) significant 4 bits, adds the numbers, decimal adjusts the sum, and stores the _____ (BCD, binary) sum at memory location 2032H.
Ans. 2030H, 2031H, most, BCD

9.30 The function represented by block 1 in Fig. 9-12*b* could be produced by what 8080/8085 instruction?
Ans. LXI *H*, 2030H

9.31 The function represented by block 2 in Fig. 9-12*b* could be produced by what 8080/8085 instruction?
Ans. MOV *A,M*

9.32 The function represented by block 3 in Fig. 9-12*b* could be produced by what 8080/8085 instruction?
Ans. ANI 0FH

9.33 The function represented by block 4 in Fig. 9-12*b* could be produced by what 8080/8085 instruction?
Ans. MOV *B,A*

9.34 The function represented by block 5 in Fig. 9-12*b* could be produced by what 8080/8085 instruction?
Ans. INX *H*

9.35 The function represented by block 8 in Fig. 9-12*b* could be produced by what 8080/8085 instruction?
Ans. ADD *B*

Data memory

Address (hex)	Contents (hex)	
2030	B5	ASCII representation of BCD number 5
2031	B9	ASCII representation of BCD number 9
2032		←BCD sum

(*a*) Data memory map for sample problem

Fig. 9-12

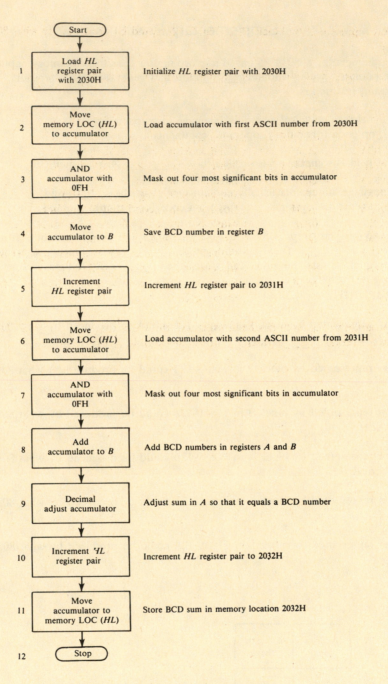

(b) Detailed flowchart for sample problem

Fig. 9-12 (*cont.*)

9.36 The function represented by block 9 in Fig. 9-12*b* could be produced by what 8080/8085 instruction? *Ans.* DAA

9.37 The function represented by block 11 in Fig. 9-12*b* could be produced by what 8080/8085 instruction? *Ans.* MOV *M,A*

9.38 The function represented by block 12 in Fig. 9-12b could be produced by what 8080/8085 instruction?
    Ans. HLT

9.39 Write an 8080/8085 assembly language program for the problem represented in Fig. 9-12.
    Ans.

Label	Op code	Operand	Comments
	LXI	*H*,2030H	; Initialize *HL* register
	MOV	*A,M*	; Load *A* with first ASCII number
	ANI	0FH	; Mask out most significant 4 bits in *A*
	MOV	*B,A*	; Save BCD number in *B*
	INX	*H*	; Increment *HL* register to 2031H
	MOV	*A,M*	; Load *A* with second ASCII number
	ANI	0FH	; Mask out most significant 4 bits in *A*
	ADD	*B*	; Add BCD numbers in *A* and *B*
	DAA		; Adjust sum in *A* so that it equals a BCD number
	INX	*H*	; Increment *HL* register to 2032H
	MOV	*M,A*	; Store BCD sum in memory location 2032H
	HLT		; Stop MPU

9.40 After the program in Fig. 9-12 has been executed, the BCD sum of _____ (BCD) will be deposited in data memory location _____ (hex).   *Ans.* $0001\ 0100_{BCD}$, 2032H

Chapter 10

The Motorola 6800 Microprocessor

10.1 INTRODUCTION

Motorola Corporation introduced its 6800 8-bit microprocessor in the mid-1970s. Motorola has since developed the "6800 family" with newer chips that generally are software- and to a lesser extent hardware-compatible with the 6800 MPU. The 6800, 6802 (6800 with internal clock and some RAM), and the more powerful 6809 are 8-bit microprocessors that are noted as being easy to use. Specialized versions of the 6800 family, such as the 6801, 6804, 68HC04, 6805, 68HC05, and 68HC11, are described as *single-chip computers*. They are called *microcomputer units* (MCUs) by the manufacturer. An MCU chip, such as the 68HC11, might include an 8-bit microprocessor unit (like the 6800), a timer, ROM, RAM, an A/D converter, an on-chip oscillator, programmable I/O lines, and even an EPROM. The 68HC11 would share the 6800's instruction set. Single-chip 8-bit MCUs are popular in low-cost dedicated computer systems.

In 1980, Motorola introduced its advanced 16-bit 68000 microprocessor. The 68000 was the first microprocessor to introduce a 32-bit internal architecture and large general-purpose register sets. Other members of the 68000 family are the 68HC000 (CMOS), 68008, 68010, 68020, and 68030 microprocessors. The 68000 MPU features a 32-bit internal architecture with a 16-bit external data bus, and it will address 16 megabytes (M bytes) of memory. The 68008 MPU has the same 32-bit internal architecture with a cost-saving 8-bit external data bus. The 68010 is an upgraded 16-bit external/32-bit internal virtual-memory MPU. The very popular 68020 is a 32-bit internal/32-bit external virtual-memory MPU. More recently, Motorola released its more powerful 68030 enhanced 32-bit microprocessor. The 68000 series' MPUs are *not compatible* with the older 8-bit 6800 family of microprocessors.

Virtual memory is a feature of advanced MPUs such as the 68010, 68020, and 68030. The term *virtual memory* means that a programmer can write programs as if memory capacity were unlimited. The virtual-memory technique permits programs to be larger than the capacity of main memory. The "extra" part of the program is stored on secondary storage (such as disks), but it is accessed as if it were in main memory.

The 6800 microprocessor is typically used in a microcomputer system. A minimum system configuration is illustrated in Fig. 10-1. The 6800 microprocessor requires a +5-V power supply and an external two-phase clock (no external clock is needed on the 6802 MPU). The restart input to the 6800 MPU shown in Fig. 10-1 is a hardware interrupt connected to the *RESET* pin of the chip and is used to initialize the system. The 6800 MPU has 16 address lines and 8 bidirectional data lines. The control lines are labeled as the control bus in Fig. 10-1. Added to the MPU in Fig. 10-1 is memory in the form of both ROM and RAM.

The interfacing between the MPU and the input/output devices in Fig. 10-1 is done with Motorola's special *6820 peripheral interface adapter* (PIA). Note that the 6820 PIA provides two 8-bit data paths which can be used as either input or output ports. The PIA also has 4 control lines between the PIA and the peripheral devices. The 6820 PIA has internal registers which make it programmable and provide temporary data storage to simplify the transfer of data. Note in Fig. 10-1 that interrupt pulses can be sent from the PIA via the control bus to the 6800 MPU. In summary, the 6820 PIA forms a two-way communication link and temporary storage device between the microprocessor and the peripheral devices.

Motorola also produces other special devices that are compatible with the 6800 microprocessor. A few of these are the *6850 asynchronous communications interface adapter* (ACIA) which is used for serial asynchronous data transmission, the *Motorola 6870 series clock chips* which can be used to provide the two-phase clock pulses required by the 6800 MPU, and the *6844 direct memory access controller* which provides 6800-based systems with logic to support four direct

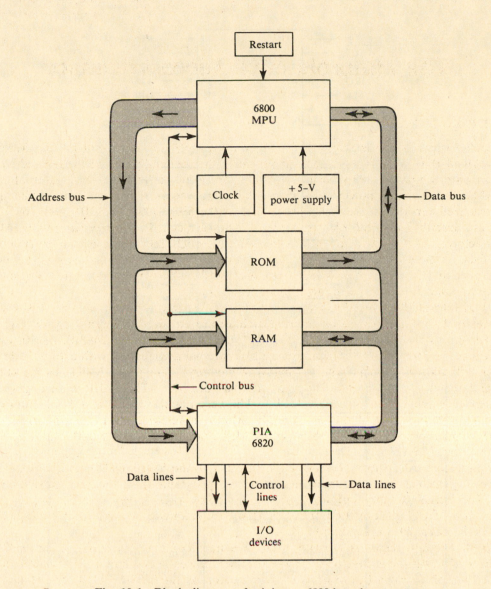

Fig. 10-1 Block diagram of minimum 6800-based system

memory access (DMA) channels.   Many other support chips are available for both the 6800 and 68000 series of microprocessors.

10.2 THE 6800 PIN DIAGRAM AND FUNCTIONS

The Motorola 6800 8-bit microprocessor is housed in a 40-pin dual-in-line package (DIP).   The pinout diagram for the 6800 MPU is illustrated in Fig. 10-2a. In Fig. 10-2b is a chart summarizing the pin names and descriptions.   The standard MC6800 MPU chip operates with a clock frequency of 1.0 MHz.   Faster versions of the 6800 MPU are available.   The MC68A00 is the same processor but operates with a clock frequency of 1.5 MHz, while the MC68B00 operates at 2.0 MHz.

The inputs and outputs on the 6800 MPU can be grouped as clock inputs, power inputs, data bus inputs/outputs, address bus outputs, and control inputs/outputs.   The arrows on the pin diagram in Fig. 10-2a show the direction of signal flow.

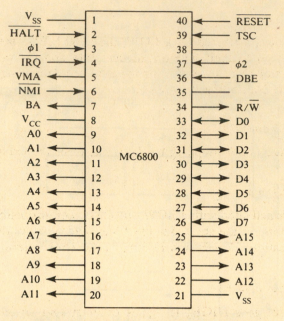

(a)   Pin diagram of 6800 MPU

Pin name	Description	Type
*A0–A15	Address lines	Tristate, output
*D0–D7	Data bus lines	Tristate, bidirectional
*$\overline{\text{HALT}}$	Halt	Input
*TSC	Three-state control	Input
*R/$\overline{\text{W}}$	Read/write	Tristate, output
*VMA	Valid memory address	Output
*DBE	Data bus enable	Input
*BA	Bus available	Output
*$\overline{\text{IRQ}}$	Interrupt request	Input
$\overline{\text{RESET}}$	Reset	Input
$\overline{\text{NMI}}$	Nonmaskable interrupt	Input
$\phi 1, \phi 2$	Clock signals	Input
V_{ss}, V_{cc}	Power	

*These signals connect to the System Bus.

(b)   Pin names and functions

Fig. 10-2

The function of each 6800 microprocessor pin is described briefly in the paragraphs that follow. In each paragraph, refer to Fig. 10-2 for location of each pin and a summary of functions.

Ground (V_{ss}) (pins 1 and 21)

These pins are connected to the negative side of the 5-V d.c. power supply.

Halt ($\overline{HALT}$) (pin 2)

When the $\overline{HALT}$ input is activated by a LOW, the 6800 MPU enters the *halt mode*. In this mode the three-state lines go to their high-impedance state and the processor stops. This input could be used for "single stepping" through a program in the debugging process. Many times the $\overline{HALT}$ input is disabled by connecting it to +5 V.

Clock ($\phi 1$ and $\phi 2$) (pins 3 and 37)

These input pins receive nonoverlapping clock signals from the external system clock circuitry.

Interrupt Request Line ($\overline{IRQ}$) (pin 4)

When the $\overline{IRQ}$ input is activated with a LOW, the 6800 microprocessor will complete the current instruction, push all registers on the stack, set the *I* flag, and jump to the interrupt service routine pointed to by memory locations FFF8H and FFF9H. The $\overline{IRQ}$ interrupt can be masked.

Valid memory address (VMA) (pin 5)

When the *VMA* output goes HIGH, it signals other system devices that the address on the address bus is valid.

Nonmaskable Interrupt ($\overline{NMI}$) (pin 6)

When the $\overline{NMI}$ input goes LOW, the response of the 6800 microprocessor is similar to its response when the $\overline{IRQ}$ goes LOW. The $\overline{NMI}$ interrupt is nonmaskable and its vectoring address is found in memory locations FFFCH and FFFDH. The contents of FFFCH and FFFDH then point to the start of the interrupt service routine.

Bus Available (BA) (pin 7)

When the *BA* output goes HIGH, it signals external devices that the 6800 microprocessor has stopped executing instructions. The 6800 MPU stops executing instructions because of a wait (WAI) instruction or a $\overline{HALT}$ hardware input. The *BA* control line provides a method of telling external devices that the 6800 MPU's data and address busses are three-stated and may be used for such things as DMA operations.

Power (V_{cc}) (pin 8)

The positive side of the 5-V d.c. power supply is connected to pin 8 of the 6800 microprocessor IC.

Address Lines (A_0-A_{15}) (pins 9–20, 22–25)

The 6800 MPU's 16 address outputs (A_0-A_{15}) are connected to the system's address bus. These lines are used for addressing devices such as ROMs, RAMs, and I/O devices.

Data Lines (D_0-D_7) (pins 26–33)

The 6800 MPU's eight data pins (D_0-D_7) are connected to the system's bidirectional data bus. These data bus lines are for transferring data to and from memory or I/O devices.

Read/Write ($R/\bar{W}$) Control (pin 34)

The $R/\bar{W}$ output is a control line that signals an external device (RAM, ROM, PIA, etc.) whether the 6800 MPU is reading or writing. A HIGH output from the $R/\bar{W}$ line signals a read, whereas a LOW output signals that a write operation is under way.

Data Bus Enable (DBE) (pin 36)

The *DBE* input controls the data bus drivers in the 6800 microprocessor. A HIGH input on the *DBE* pin enables the data lines, while a LOW input disables or three-states the data lines. Because data transfers to and from memory and I/O occur during the time the $\phi2$ clock is HIGH, the *DBE* pin is many times connected to the $\phi2$ line of the clock.

Three-State Control (TSC) (pin 39)

When the *TSC* input pin is driven HIGH by an external device, all address lines and the $R/\bar{W}$ line will be three-stated. The *TSC* line is used with DMA configurations. When DMA is not used, the *TSC* pin may be grounded.

Reset line ($\overline{RESET}$) (pin 40)

When the $\overline{RESET}$ pin is driven from HIGH to LOW, the 6800 microprocessor sets the *I* flag to 1 and jumps to the reset or restart interrupt service routine pointed to by FFFEH and FFFFH. The $\overline{RESET}$ input is typically used to initialize or restart the system.

SOLVED PROBLEMS

10.1 The Motorola 6800 is a(n) _____ (8, 16) -bit microprocessor.

Solution:

The Motorola 6800 is an 8-bit microprocessor. Its accumulator is 8 bits wide, and it transfers data in 8-bit groups via the data bus.

10.2 A single _____-V power supply is used to power the 6800 microprocessor. In Fig. 10-2*a*, the positive of the power supply is connected to the _____ pin, whereas the negative goes to the pins labeled _____.

Solution:

A single 5-V power supply is used to power the 6800 microprocessor. In Fig. 10-2*a*, the positive of the power supply is connected to the V_{cc} pin (pin 8), whereas the negative goes to the pins labeled V_{ss} (pins 1 and 21).

10.3 The 6800 microprocessor uses _____ (number) pins as address lines and _____ (number) pins as bidirectional data lines.

Solution:

The 6800 microprocessor uses 16 pins as address lines and 8 pins as bidirectional data lines.

10.4 The three hardware interrupts on the 6800 microprocessor are the $\overline{RESET}$, _____, and _____.

Solution:

The three hardware interrupts on the 6800 microprocessor are the $\overline{RESET}$, $\overline{NMI}$ (nonmaskable interrupt), and $\overline{IRQ}$ (interrupt request) inputs.

10.5 Activating the _____ input pin on the 6800 will cause the processor to stop and all three-state lines to go to their high-impedance state.

> **Solution:**
>
> Activating the $\overline{HALT}$ input pin on the 6800 will cause the processor to stop and all three-state lines to go to their high-impedance state.

10.6 The 6800 MPU uses a _____-phase nonoverlapping clock.

> **Solution:**
>
> The 6800 MPU uses a two-phase nonoverlapping clock.

10.7 Refer to Fig. 10-2a. Pin 34 on the 6800 MPU is labeled _____, which stands for _____/_____. When this control output is HIGH, the processor is _____ (reading, writing), whereas when this output is LOW, it is _____ (reading, writing).

> **Solution:**
>
> Based on information in Fig. 10-2 pin 34 on the 6800 MPU is labeled $R/\overline{W}$, which stands for read/write. When this control output is HIGH, the processor is reading, whereas when this output is LOW, it is writing.

10.8 Refer to Fig. 10-2a. Pin 5 on the 6800 MPU is labeled _____, which stands for _____ _____ _____.

> **Solution:**
>
> Based on information in Fig. 10-2, pin 5 on the 6800 MPU is labeled VMA, which stands for valid memory address.

10.3 THE 6800 ARCHITECTURE

A block diagram of the internal organization of the Motorola 6800 microprocessor unit is shown in Fig. 10-3. The 6800 has an 8-bit three-state buffered data bus (D_0–D_7). The numbers near each input or output in Fig. 10-3 are pin numbers. Across the top in Fig. 10-3 is the 16-bit buffered address bus (A_{15}–A_0). The 6800 MPU contains a 16-bit program counter, a 16-bit stack pointer, a 16-bit index register, two 8-bit accumulators (A and B), and an 8-bit condition code register. The nine control signals are shown at the left in Fig. 10-3. They are the reset, nonmaskable interrupt, go/halt, interrupt request, three-state control, and data bus enable inputs, and the bus available, valid memory address, and read/write outputs. The $\phi 1$ and $\phi 2$ clock inputs are also shown at the left in Fig. 10-3.

The arithmetic-logic unit (ALU) section performs the arithmetic and logic operations, while the associated condition code register contains the six flags. The instruction register feeds the instruction decoder and control block. The instruction decoder interprets the current instruction and determines the procedure to be followed to execute the instruction. The instruction decoder directs the control to generate the appropriate internal and external signals to complete the instruction. The internal control lines which coordinate the microprocessor's operation are not shown in Fig. 10-3.

Registers

The block diagram of the 6800 MPU in Fig. 10-3 makes it appear simpler than the 8085 unit. This is primarily due to the use of only two accumulators. The 6800 MPU is sometimes thought of as a memory-oriented processor because it typically makes many transfers to and from

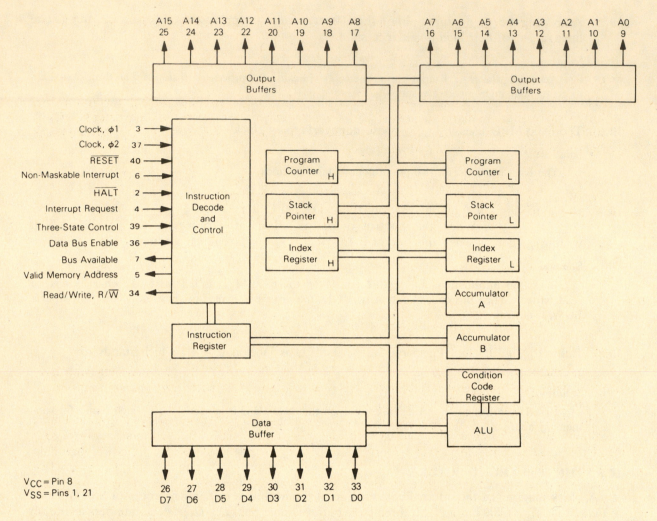

Fig. 10-3 Functional block diagram of 6800 MPU (*Courtesy of Motorola, Inc.*)

memory. The 6800 also uses memory-mapped I/O. The inputs and outputs are treated as memory locations.

The 6800 microprocessor's registers are as follows:

1. The two 8-bit *accumulators* (*ACCA* and *ACCB*) are the focus of a large share of the microprocessor's operations. Accumulator operations include arithmetic, logic, load and store, input and output, and others. The second accumulator (*ACCB*) is not just a general-purpose register but a real accumulator in that all operations that can be performed in accumulator *A* can also be performed in accumulator *B*.

2. The *program counter* (*PC*) is a 16-bit register that always holds the address of the next instruction to be executed. It serves the same purpose as the program counter in the generic, 8080, and 8085 microprocessors.

3. The *stack pointer* (*SP*) is a 16-bit special-purpose register. The stack pointer contents form a 16-bit address which defines the top of the stack in RAM. Both the generic and the 8080/8085 MPUs also contain stack pointers.

4. The *index register* (*IX*) is a 16-bit special-purpose register. Its primary use is to point to and modify addresses.

5. The *condition code register* (*CCR*) is an 8-bit register that contains the six flags used by the 6800 MPU.

Flags

The 6800 MPU uses six condition code bits or flags. These six flags are represented in Fig. 10-4. These flags are grouped into a single 8-bit register called the condition code register (*CCR*) by Motorola. As in other microprocessors, the branch instructions then test the flags to determine whether a branch or no branch condition exists.

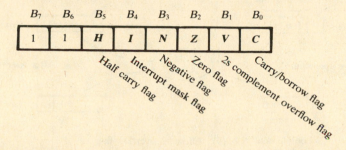

Fig. 10-4 Flags in the 6800's condition code register

As on the generic, 8080, and 8085 microprocessors, the *carry flag* (*C*) is set to 1 whenever a carry (or "borrow") is generated out of the MSB of the accumulator. A sum larger than the capacity of the 8-bit accumulator then sets the *C* flag to 1.

The *overflow flag* (*V*) in the condition code register of the 6800 MPU indicates a 2s complement overflow. When dealing with signed numbers in the 6800, the MSB (B_7) of the accumulator(s) is the sign bit. The remaining 7 bits are written in 2s complement form. These 7 bits will then hold numbers equivalent to $+127_{10}$ to -128_{10}. This is the range of signed numbers. If the result of an arithmetic operation exceeds this range, the overflow flag (*V*) is set to 1. This warns the user that an error has been produced.

Consider adding the positive numbers 79_{10} and 64_{10}. Decimal $+79$ equals 01001111 in 2s complement notation. Decimal $+64$ equals 01000000 in 2s complement. These 2s complement numbers are being added in Fig. 10-5a. Owing to the carry that occurs from the B_6 to B_7 positions, the sign bit of the result has been changed to 1, or to a negative. This is an error. The 6800 processor in Fig. 10-5b is being used to add the same positive numbers (in 2s complement notation) using the *A* and *B* accumulators. The sum (10001111 in this example) is deposited in accumulator *A* after the add operation. The overflow flag (*V*) is set to 1, indicating that the sum is larger than $+127_{10}$ (sum = $79_{10} + 64_{10} = 143_{10}$ in this example).

Consider adding two negative numbers such as -79_{10} and -64_{10}. Decimal -79 equals 10110001 in 2s complement notation. Decimal -64 equals 11000000 in 2s complement. Since the most significant bits of both 2s complement numbers are 1, they represent negative numbers between -1 and -128. These 2s complement numbers are being added in Fig. 10-6a. The result is 1 0111 0001. The sign bit should remain at 1 (for negative), but it has been changed. The result is an error because it exceeded the range limit of -128_{10}.

The task of adding the negative numbers -79_{10} (10110001 in 2s complement) and -64_{10} (11000000 in 2s complement) using the 6800 MPU is shown in Fig. 10-6b. The 2s complement numbers are held in the *A* and *B* accumulators. The sum is to appear in accumulator *A* after the add operation. The sum is in error because of an overflow problem. The overflow flag (*V*) is set to 1, warning the user that the range of the 6800 processor was exceeded. The carry flag (*C*) is also set to 1, indicating the carry out from the B_7 position. This is shown in Fig. 10-6a.

The *zero flag* (*Z*) in the condition code register of the 6800 MPU is set to 1 whenever the

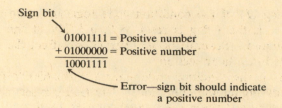

Sign bit

$$01001111 = \text{Positive number}$$
$$+\ 01000000 = \text{Positive number}$$
$$10001111$$

Error—sign bit should indicate
a positive number

(a)   2s complement addition showing effect on sign bit

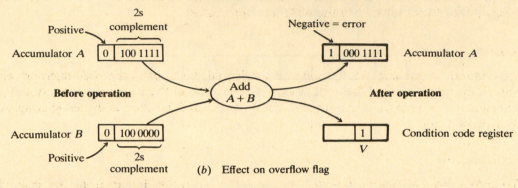

(b)   Effect on overflow flag

Fig. 10-5

accumulator becomes zero as the result of an operation or data transfer.   If the zero flag is reset to 0, this means that the accumulator *does not* contain a zero.

The *negative flag* (N) in the condition code register of the 6800 MPU is used to indicate a negative result.   It serves the same purpose as the sign flag in the 8080/8085 processor.   The sign bit is B_7 in the accumulator.   If the result of the last arithmetic, logical, or data transfer operation was negative, the N flag will be set to 1.   If the result was positive, however, the N flag will be reset to 0.   The N flag will be the same as the MSB of the accumulator.

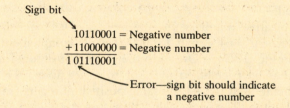

Sign bit

$$10110001 = \text{Negative number}$$
$$+\ 11000000 = \text{Negative number}$$
$$1\ 01110001$$

Error—sign bit should indicate
a negative number

(a)   2s complement addition showing effect on sign bit

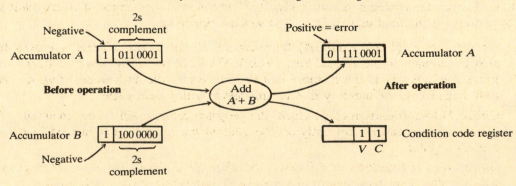

(b)   Effect on overflow flag

Fig. 10-6

The *interrupt mask flag* (I) of the condition code register in the 6800 MPU inhibits all $\overline{IRQ}$ interrupts when set to 1. If the I flag is reset to 0, a LOW at the $\overline{IRQ}$ input pin of the 6800 processor chip will be honored. Several special instructions affect the interrupt mask flag. These instructions will be detailed in a later section.

The *half carry flag* (H) in the condition code register of the 6800 MPU indicates a carry from B_3 to B_4 of the accumulator during an add operation. The H flag is set to 1 if there is a carry from B_3 to B_4. The H flag is reset to 0 if there is no carry from B_3 to B_4.

The two most significant bits of the condition code register shown in Fig. 10-4 are not used as flags. They are always set to 1 in the 6800 microprocessor.

Arithmetic-Logic Unit

The *arithmetic-logic unit* (ALU) might be considered the heart of the 6800 microprocessor. It performs all the arithmetic and logic operations. The results of these operations are stored in one of the accumulators. The ALU performs such operations as adding, subtracting, comparing, ANDing, ORing, and XORing.

Instruction Decoder

The *instruction decoder* represented in Fig. 10-3 interprets inputs from the instruction register. Based on these inputs, the instruction decoder directs the control section to execute the current instruction.

System Clock

The 6800 microprocessor requires a two-phase nonoverlapping clock. The clock circuitry is located off the 6800 chip and feeds the clock $\phi1$ and $\phi2$ input pins shown in Fig. 10-3. The clock synchronizes the internal operations of the microprocessor. It also synchronizes the external devices. Clock waveforms are shown in Fig. 10-7. A single *clock cycle* is identified in Fig. 10-7a. The cycle time duration may range from 1 to 10 μs for the standard 6800 microprocessor. The clock time cannot be slowed down below 10 μs per cycle. If operated too slowly, some of the dynamic internal registers may lose their data. Notice in Fig. 10-7a that when phase 1 ($\phi1$) is HIGH, phase 2 ($\phi2$) is always LOW. The opposite is also true.

Consider the timing of a single instruction when using the 6800 MPU. To execute an instruction, any microprocessor goes through three steps: (1) op code fetch, (2) decode, and (3) execute instruction. The example diagramed in Fig. 10-7b is for the "load accumulator A immediate" instruction. During the first cycle shown in Fig. 10-7b, the 6800 MPU will perform the op code fetch and decoding of the instruction. During the second cycle, the instruction will be executed. Key on the circled numbers in Fig. 10-7b to follow the sequence of events while the 6800 MPU is performing the *load accumulator A immediate* operation.

1. On the L-to-H (LOW-to-HIGH) transition of $\phi1$ clock, the address is moved from the program counter to the address bus. The 6800's VMA and $R/\bar{W}$ pins go HIGH. A HIGH VMA line indicates to the memory that the address on the address bus is valid. A HIGH $R/\bar{W}$ line signals the memory that the processor is in a read cycle.

2. On the H-to-L transition of $\phi1$ clock, the program counter will be incremented. This will not change the address currently on the address bus because it is latched in the memory address register.

3. On the L-to-H transition of $\phi2$ clock, the 6800 MPU signals the memory to place the op code for the "load accumulator A immediate" instruction on the data bus.

4. On the H-to-L transition of $\phi2$ clock, the MPU accepts the op code from the data bus, transfers it to the instruction register, and decodes the instruction. After decoding, the

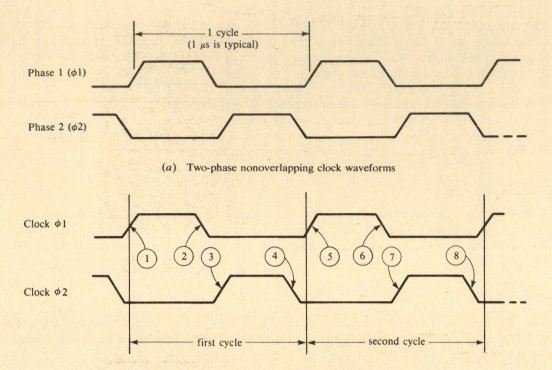

(a)   Two-phase nonoverlapping clock waveforms

(b)   Timing of the "load accumulator A immediate" instruction

Fig. 10-7

processor now has determined that the "load accumulator A immediate" instruction is to be executed during the second cycle.   During the first MPU cycle the op code was read from memory (fetched) and decoded.

5.   On the L-to-H transition of $\phi1$ clock, the address of the operand is moved from the program counter to the memory address register and address bus.

6.   On the H-to-L transition of $\phi1$ clock, the program counter is incremented.

7.   On the L-to-H transition of $\phi2$ clock, the processor signals the memory to place the operand (data to be loaded into accumulator A) on the data bus.

8.   On the H-to-L transition of $\phi2$ clock, the 6800 MPU accepts the operand off the data bus and transfers it to accumulator A.

The previous eight steps typically occur in $2\,\mu s$ when using a standard 6800 microprocessor.   Note that events that occur during $\phi1$ clock are within the 6800 MPU itself whereas the $\phi2$ clock is applied to the external devices.   The $\phi2$ clock is used in controlling memory operations in this example.

Interrupts

The 6800 microprocessor has three types of *hardware interrupts*.   They are the reset, nonmaskable interrupt, and interrupt request.   The 6800 MPU also has a single *software* interrupt (SWI) instruction.

When the $\overline{RESET}$ interrupt pin on the 6800 MPU is held LOW for a time and then goes HIGH, the processor automatically jumps to a special *reset interrupt sequence*.   This sequence is detailed in Fig. 10-8a.   The interrupt mask flag (I) is first set to 1, and then the program counter is loaded with the address contained at memory locations FFFEH and FFFFH.   These two memory locations are reserved for the *reset vector*.   The reset vector is nothing more than an address of the program that

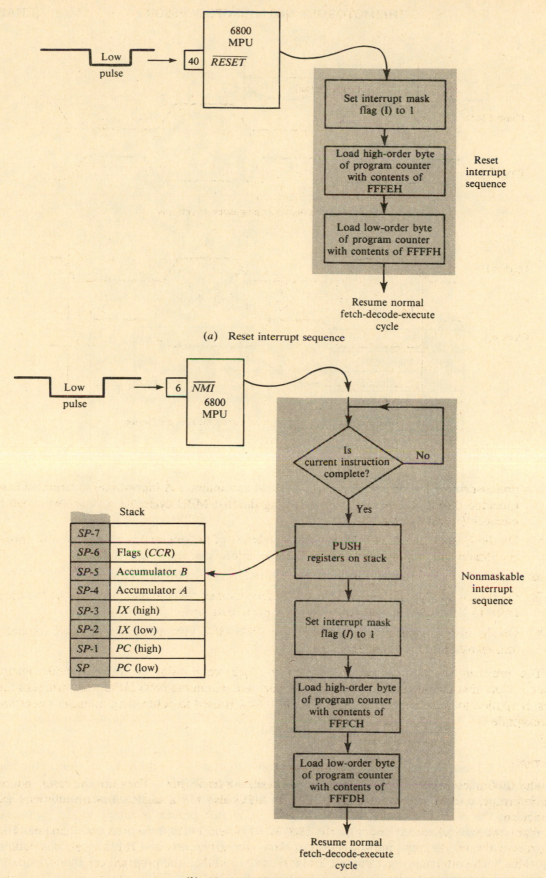

(a) Reset interrupt sequence

(b) Nonmaskable interrupt sequence

Fig. 10-8

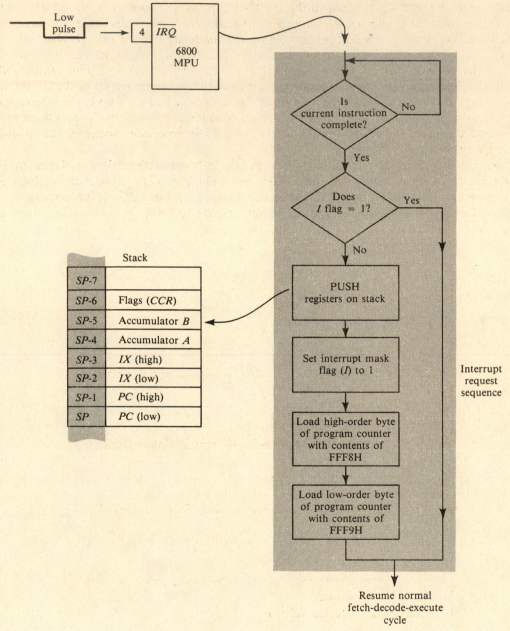

(c)   Interrupt request sequence

Fig. 10-8 (*cont.*)

will service the reset input.   It is typical in the 6800 MPU for the ROM to be located at the highest memory addresses, while the RAM usually starts at address 0000H.

The *nonmaskable interrupt* ($\overline{NMI}$) input to the 6800 MPU is being activated in Fig. 10-8*b*.   When the $\overline{NMI}$ pin of the 6800 MPU goes LOW, the processor jumps to the *nonmaskable interrupt sequence* shown at the right in Fig. 10-8*b*.   The current instruction is completed, the contents of the 6800's registers saved on the stack, the *I* flag set, and the nonmaskable interrupt vector fetched from memory locations FFFCH and FFFDH.   The MPU will then jump to the nonmaskable interrupt service routine.

The *interrupt request* ($\overline{IRQ}$) input to the 6800 MPU is being activated in Fig. 10-8c.   When the $\overline{IRQ}$ pin of the 6800 MPU goes LOW, the processor jumps to the *interrupt request sequence* detailed at the right in Fig. 10-8c.   The current instruction is completed and the *I* flag is checked.   If the *I* flag is set to 1, the processor ignores the interrupt request and continues with the regular program.   The interrupt request input is maskable and thereby has a lower priority than either the $\overline{RESET}$ or the $\overline{NMI}$ inputs.   If the *I* flag were reset to 0, the processor would next push the contents of the registers on the stack in the order shown in Fig. 10-8c.   The next step in the interrupt request sequence is to set the *I* flag to 1.   Next the program counter is loaded with the interrupt request vector located at memory locations FFF8H and FFF9H.   The processor then jumps to the address of the interrupt request service routine.

The interrupt vector memory assignments in all 6800-based systems are shown in Fig. 10-9.   These are reserved memory locations.   The addresses placed in these memory locations will cause the processor to jump to the location of the appropriate interrupt service routine.

The 6800 microprocessor's SWI and associated instructions will be covered in a later section.

ROM		
Address	Contents	
FFF8	High byte	Interrupt request vector (address)
FFF9	Low byte	
FFFA	High byte	Software interrupt vector (address)
FFFB	Low byte	
FFFC	High byte	Nonmaskable interrupt vector (address)
FFFD	Low byte	
FFFE	High byte	Reset vector (address)
FFFF	Low byte	

Fig. 10-9   Interrupt vector memory locations in 6800-based systems

SOLVED PROBLEMS

10.9   The 6800 MPU has _____ (number) 8-bit accumulator(s), a 16-bit program counter, a _____ (number) -bit stack pointer, a 16-bit _____ register, an instruction register, and a _____ _____ register containing six flags.

Solution:

According to Fig. 10-3, the 6800 MPU has two 8-bit accumulators, a 16-bit program counter, a 16-bit stack pointer, a 16-bit index register, an instruction register, and a condition code register containing six flags.

10.10 The 6800 MPU has a(n) _____ (number) -bit three-state buffered address bus and an 8-bit three-state buffered _____ bus.

Solution:

According to Fig. 10-3, the 6800 MPU has a 16-bit three-state buffered address bus and an 8-bit three-state buffered data bus.

10.11 The 6800's condition code register contains six flags. List them.

Solution:

According to Fig. 10-4, the 6800's condition code register contains a half carry flag (H), interrupt mask flag (I), negative flag (N), zero flag (Z), 2s complement overflow flag (V), and carry/borrow flag (C).

10.12 Refer to Fig. 10-10.   The contents of accumulator A after the add operation are _____ (8 bits).

Solution:

Adding the 2s complement numbers $01000011 + 10000011 = 10000011$. The contents of accumulator A after the add operation are 10000011.   Unfortunately an error has occurred owing to an overflow from the B_6 to the B_7 position.

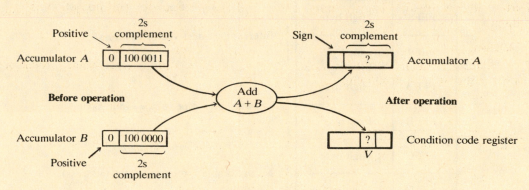

Fig. 10-10

10.13 Refer to Fig. 10-10.   The overflow flag (V) is _____ (reset to 0, set to 1) after the add operation.

Solution:

Adding the 2s complement numbers $01000011 + 01000000 = 10000011$ (decimal $+67$ plus $+64 = +131$).   The V flag is set to 1, indicating that a 2s complement overflow has caused a range error.   The "sum" in the accumulator after the add operation is therefore not the correct 2s complement sum.

10.14 Refer to Fig. 10-11.   The contents of accumulator A after the subtract operation are _____ (binary).

Solution:

Subtracting binary $00001111 - 00000001 = 00001110$ (decimal $15 - 1 = 14$).   The contents of accumulator A after the subtract operation are 00001110_2.

10.15 Refer to Fig. 10-11.   The Z flag is _____ (reset to 0, set to 1) after the subtract operation.

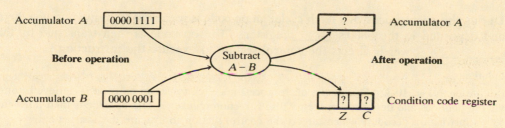

Fig. 10-11

Solution:

Subtracting binary $00001111 - 00000001 = 00001110$.   The Z flag is reset to 0 after the subtract operation in Fig. 10-11 because the difference is not zero.

10.16 Refer to Fig. 10-11.   The C flag is _____ (reset to 0, set to 1) after the subtract operation.

Solution:

Due to no borrow, the C flag is reset to 0 after the subtract operation in Fig. 10-11.   The reset C flag indicates that the number in accumulator A is larger than the number in accumulator B.

10.17 Refer to Fig. 10-12.   The contents of the accumulator after the add operation are _____ (8 bits).

Solution:

Adding $10001001 + 10001001 = 1\,0001\,0010_2$.   The contents of the accumulator after the add operation in Fig. 10-12 are 00010010.

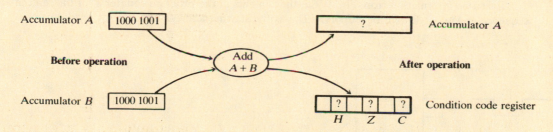

Fig. 10-12

10.18 Refer to Fig. 10-12.   The H flag is _____ (reset to 0, set to 1) after the add operation.

Solution:

Adding $10001001 + 10001001 = 1\,0001\,0010$.   The H flag is set to 1 after the add operation in Fig. 10-12 because there was a carry from the B_3 to the B_4 position in the accumulator.

10.19 Refer to Fig. 10-12.   The Z flag is _____ (reset to 0, set to 1) after the add operation, whereas the C flag is _____ (reset to 0, set to 1).

Solution:

Adding $10001001 + 10001001 = 1\,0001\,0010$.   The Z flag is reset to 0, whereas the C flag is set to 1 after the add operation in Fig. 10-12.

10.20 During the microprocessor's fetch cycle, an op code is retrieved from memory via the data bus and deposited in the 6800's _____ register.   The op code is then translated by the 6800's _____ _____, which directs the control section to execute the instruction.

Solution:

Refer to Fig. 10-3.   During the microprocessor's fetch cycle, an op code is retrieved from memory via the data bus and deposited in the 6800's instruction register.   The op code is then translated by the 6800's instruction decoder, which directs the control section to execute the instruction.

10.21 The 6800 MPU uses a _____-phase _____ (nonoverlapping, overlapping) clock.   Generally, phase 1 of the clock synchronizes _____ (internal, external) processor operations, while the $\phi 2$ clock pulses synchronize both internal operations and external devices.

Solution:

Refer to Fig. 10-7.   The 6800 MPU uses a two-phase nonoverlapping clock.   Generally, phase 1 of the clock synchronizes internal processor operations, while the $\phi 2$ clock pulses synchronize both internal operations and external devices.

10.22 Refer to Fig. 10-13.   The interrupt mask flag (I) will be _____ (reset to 0, set to 1) after the reset interrupt sequence shown in this example.

Solution:

Based on information from Fig. 10-8a, the interrupt mask flag (I) in Fig. 10-13 will be set to 1 after the reset interrupt sequence.

10.23 Refer to Fig. 10-13.   The contents of the program counter after the reset interrupt sequence will be _____ (hex).   This is the starting address of the _____ _____ routine.

Solution:

Based on information from Fig. 10-8a, the contents of the program counter after the reset interrupt sequence in Fig. 10-13 will be FC00H.   This is the starting address of the reset service routine.

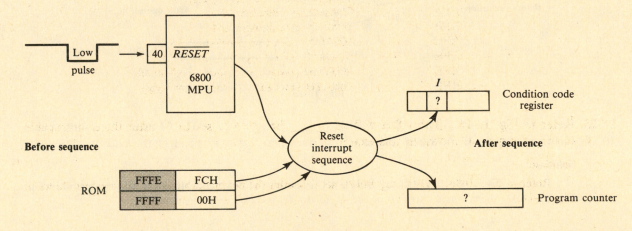

Fig. 10-13

10.24 Refer to Fig. 10-14.   List the contents of the stack after the nonmaskable interrupt sequence shown in this example.

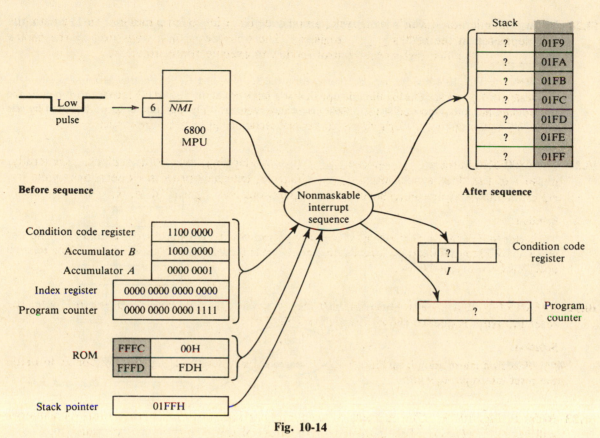

Fig. 10-14

Solution:

Refer to the procedure shown in Fig. 10-8b. The contents of the stack in Fig. 10-14 after the nonmaskable interrupt sequence are as follows:

Stack location (hex)	Contents
01F9	11000000 (condition code register)
01FA	10000000 (accumulator B)
01FB	00000001 (accumulator A)
01FC	00000000 (index register—high byte)
01FD	00000000 (index register—low byte)
01FE	00000000 (program counter—high byte)
01FF	00001111 (program counter—low byte)

10.25 Refer to Fig. 10-14. The I flag will be _____ (reset to 0, set to 1) after the nonmaskable interrupt sequence shown in this example.

Solution:

Refer to Fig. 10-8b. The I flag will be set to 1 after the nonmaskable interrupt sequence shown in Fig. 10-14.

10.26 Refer to Fig. 10-14. The contents of the program counter after the nonmaskable interrupt sequence will be _____ (hex).

Solution:

Refer to Fig. 10-8b. The contents of the program counter after the nonmaskable interrupt sequence in Fig. 10-14 will be 00FDH. This is the address of the nonmaskable interrupt service routine.

10.27 Refer to Fig. 10-15.   The interrupt request flag (*I*) is _____ (reset to 0, set to 1) *before* the interrupt request sequence.

Solution:

Refer to Fig. 10-4 for the flag locations within the *CCR*.   The *CCR* contains 11001000 before the sequence shown in Fig. 10-15.   This means that the interrupt request flag (*I*) is reset to 0 before the interrupt request sequence.   This will have the effect of permitting $\overline{IRQ}$ inputs to be honored by the 6800 MPU.

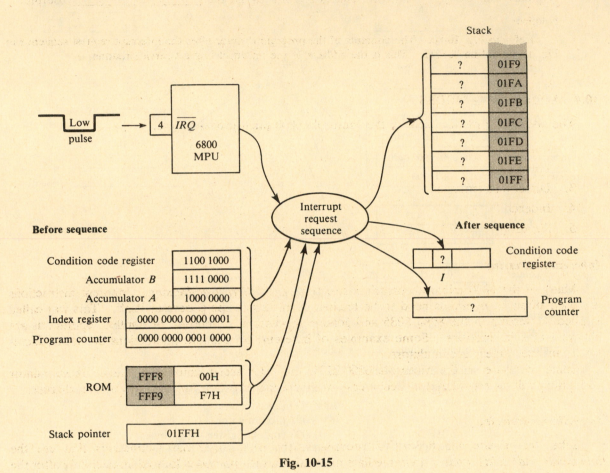

Fig. 10-15

10.28 Refer to Fig. 10-15.   List the contents of the stack after the interrupt request sequence.

Solution:

Refer to Fig. 10-8*c*.   The contents of the stack in Fig. 10-15 after the interrupt request sequence will be as follows:

Stack location (hex)	Contents
01F9	11001000 (condition code register)
01FA	11110000 (accumulator *B*)
01FB	10000000 (accumulator *A*)
01FC	00000000 (index register—high byte)
01FD	00000001 (index register—low byte)
01FE	00000000 (program counter—high byte)
01FF	00010000 (program counter—low byte)

10.29 Refer to Fig. 10-15.   The *I* flag will be _____ (reset to 0, set to 1) after the interrupt request sequence shown in this example.

> **Solution:**
>
> Refer to Fig. 10-8*c*.   The *I* flag will be set to 1 after the interrupt request sequence in Fig. 10-15.

10.30 Refer to Fig. 10-15.   The contents of the program counter after the interrupt request sequence will be _____ (hex).   This is the address of the _____ _____ _____ routine.

> **Solution:**
>
> Refer to Fig. 10-8*c*.   The contents of the program counter after the interrupt request sequence in Fig. 10-15 will be 00F7H.   This is the address of the interrupt request service routine.

10.4 ADDRESSING MODES

The addressing modes used by the Motorola 6800 microprocessor are:

1. Inherent (implied)
2. Immediate
3. Direct and extended
4. Indexed
5. Relative

Inherent Addressing

Many of the 6800 microprocessor's instructions use *inherent addressing*.   Inherent instructions are used when no operands need to be fetched from outside the processor itself.   This was called implied addressing in the 8080/8085 and generic processors.   Inherent, or implied, operations are always 1-byte instructions.   Some examples of inherent, or implied, instructions are clear, increment, and decrement accumulators.

Some literature on the Motorola 6800 MPU mentions accumulator addressing.   Accumulator addressing will be considered a special case of inherent addressing for purposes of this chapter.

Immediate Addressing

Like the generic and 8080/8085 processors, the 6800 MPU has instructions that use the *immediate addressing mode*.   In immediate instructions, the operand is located immediately after the op code in program memory.

The "load accumulator *A* immediate" instruction is being executed in Fig. 10-16*a*.   In this example, the 6800's op code for the "load accumulator *A* immediate" instruction is shown as 86H in Fig. 10-16*a*.   The data to be loaded (11111111 in this example) is shown as the second byte of the instruction in program memory.   The immediate data is then loaded into accumulator *A*.

Most 6800 immediate operations are 2-byte instructions.   However, a few are 3-byte instructions.   An example of a 3-byte immediate instruction being executed is shown in Fig. 10-16*b*.   In this example, the "load stack pointer immediate" instruction is being executed.   Note that the second byte of the instruction is the high byte (00000011 in this example), whereas the third byte is the low byte (11111111 in this case).

Direct and Extended Addressing

Operations using *direct addressing* on the 6800 MPU are specified using 2-byte instruction formats.   This format is represented in Fig. 10-17*a*.   Byte 1 contains the op code for the direct

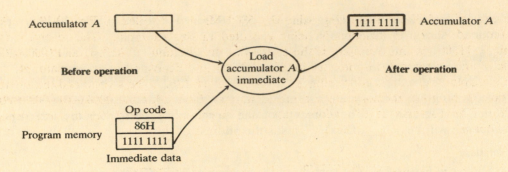

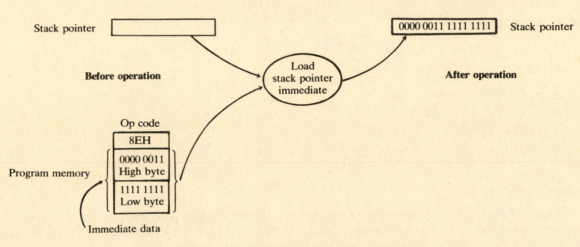

(a) 2-byte instruction with immediate addressing

(b) 3-byte instruction with immediate addressing

Fig. 10-16

addressing instruction. Byte 2 contains the *address* of the operand. Because the address is only 8 bits wide, the range of addresses available is limited to the first 256_{10} memory locations. Motorola's direct addressing is similar to base page or zero page addressing on other processors (like the 6502).

Operations using *extended addressing* on the 6800 MPU are specified using 3-byte instruction formats. This is the same as direct addressing on the generic, 8080, and 8085 microprocessors. The 6800 instruction format for extended addressing is represented in Fig. 10-17b. Byte 1 contains the op code for the extended addressing instruction. Byte 2 contains the high-order byte of the operand's address. Byte 3 contains the low-order byte of the operand's address. With extended addressing, the entire range of $65,536_{10}$ memory locations can be addressed.

(a) Instruction format for 6800's direct addressing   (b) Instruction format for 6800's extended addressing

Fig. 10-17

An example of direct addressing using the 6800 MPU is detailed in Fig. 10-18a. The "load accumulator A direct" instruction is being executed in this example. The second byte in the program (11110000 in this example) is the address of the operand. The operand (00000100 in this example) is then fetched from memory location 00F0H and deposited in accumulator A.

An example of extended addressing is shown in Fig. 10-18b. The second and third bytes of the instruction in program memory are assembled into a 16-bit address (0000 0001 0000 0000 in this example). The contents of this address are then fetched from data memory and deposited in accumulator A.

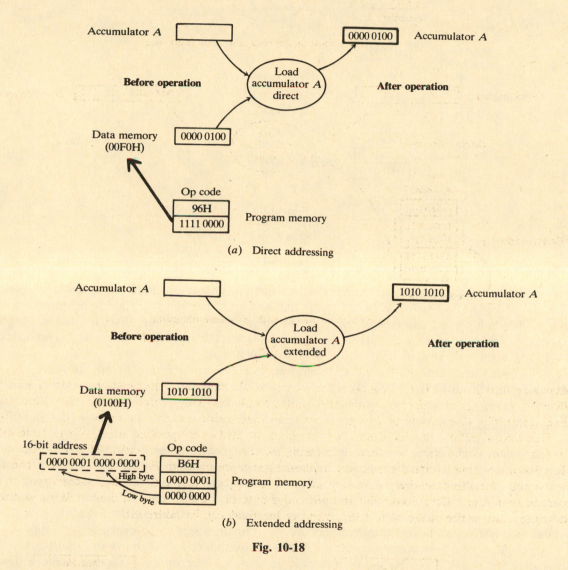

(a) Direct addressing

(b) Extended addressing

Fig. 10-18

Indexed Addressing

The 6800 microprocessor contains a 16-bit index register (*IX*) which is used in *indexed addressing*. The indexed mode of addressing requires the use of a 2-byte instruction. The format of the instruction is shown in Fig. 10-19a. The first byte contains the customary op code for the indexed instruction. The second byte contains the *offset*. The *offset is added to the contents of the index register* to determine the address of the operand.

An example of an instruction using the indexed addressing mode is detailed in Fig. 10-

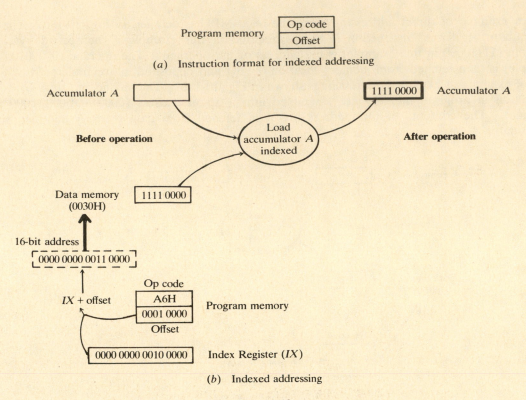

(a)   Instruction format for indexed addressing

(b)   Indexed addressing

Fig. 10-19

19*b*.   Here the "load accumulator *A* indexed" instruction is being executed.   Indexed addressing is a lot like extended addressing in that a 16-bit address is generated.   The address of the operand is generated by adding the contents of the 16-bit index register (*IX*) to the offset located in program memory.   This new address (0030H in this example) is the location of the operand.   The operand (11110000 in this example) is then loaded into accumulator *A*.

The offset value retrieved from the second byte of the instruction may be any unsigned number ranging from 00H to FFH ($0–255_{10}$).

Relative Addressing

The *relative addressing mode* is used with most of the branching instructions on the 6800 microprocessor.   The format of relative addressing instructions is shown in Fig. 10-20*a*.   The first byte of the instruction is the op code.   The second byte of the instruction is called the *offset*.   The offset is interpreted as a *signed 7-bit number*.   If the MSB of the offset is 0, the number is positive, and this means a forward jump or branch is to be executed.   If the MSB of the offset is 1, the number is negative, and this means a backward jump or branch is to be executed.

An example of a *forward jump* using the 6800's relative addressing is shown in Fig. 10-20*b*.   The program counter (*PC*) before the operation is at 0009H.   The op code for the "branch always relative" instruction (20H) is fetched from location 0009H in program memory.   The program counter is incremented to 000AH, and the offset (00000100) is fetched.   The program counter was incremented to the address of the next instruction (000BH) just before the actual operand fetch.   The 6800 processor internally adds the offset (04H) to the current contents of the program counter (000BH).   The new address in the program counter after the "branch always relative" operation will then be $000B + 04 = 000FH$ ($0000\ 0000\ 0000\ 1111_2$).   The processor would then jump to this new address and fetch an instruction from location 000FH.   Note that the offset's MSB is a 0.   This means a positive offset, causing a forward jump or branch.

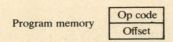

(a)   Instruction format for relative addressing

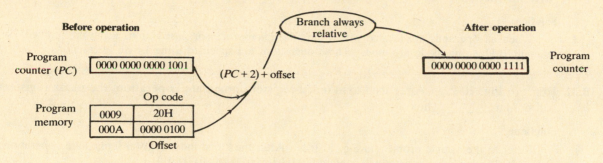

(b)   Relative addressing—branching forward

Fig. 10-20

An example of a *backward jump* using relative addressing is illustrated in Fig. 10-21. The program counter (PC) before the operation is at 001DH. The op code for the "branch always relative" instruction is shown as 20H in program memory location 001DH. The offset in program memory location 001EH is the 2s complement number 11111010 (equal to −06H). The negative offset means that the branch will be backward. The destination address of the "branch always relative" operation is calculated in two steps. First, add +2 to the program counter.

$$
\begin{array}{lll}
PC & 0000\ 0000\ 0001\ 1101 & 001DH \\
+2 & +\ 0010 & +\ 2H \\
\hline
   & 0000\ 0000\ 0001\ 1111 & 001FH
\end{array}
$$

Second, add the offset to the partial sum.

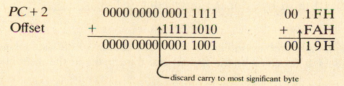

The new address is then 0019H. The program counter in Fig. 10-21 contains the new address of 0000 0000 0001 1001$_2$ after the backward "branch always relative" operation.

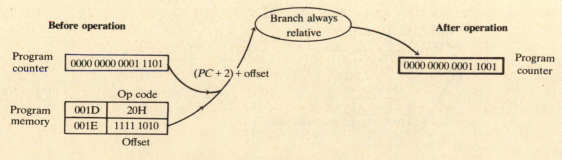

Fig. 10-21   Relative addressing–branching backward

SOLVED PROBLEMS

10.31 When all operands are located within the 6800 microprocessor, instructions using the implied, or _____, addressing mode are used.   These operations are specified using _____ (number) -byte instructions.

Solution:

When all operands are located within the 6800 microprocessor, instructions using the implied, or inherent, addressing mode are used.   These operations are specified using 1-byte instructions.

10.32 Refer to Fig. 10-22.   After the "load index register immediate" operation, the index register will contain _____ (hex).

Solution:

Refer to the sample problem in Fig. 10-16b.   After the "load index register immediate" operation in Fig. 10-22, the index register will contain 0011H ($0000\,0000\,0001\,0001_2$).

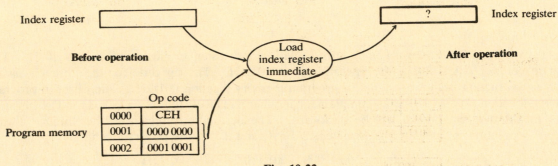

Fig. 10-22

10.33 Refer to Fig. 10-23.   The address of the data memory at the left is _____ (hex) as specified by the second and third bytes of the instruction in _____ _____.

Solution:

Refer to the sample problem in Fig. 10-18b.   The address of the data memory location at the left in Fig. 10-23 is 0180H as specified by the second and third bytes of the instruction in program memory.

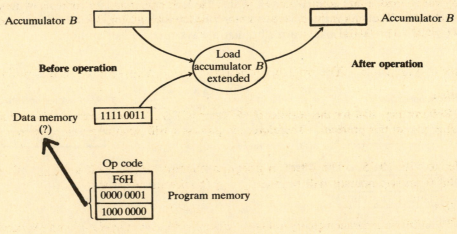

Fig. 10-23

10.34 Refer to Fig. 10-23.   The contents of accumulator *B* after the "load accumulator *B* extended" operation will be _____ (8 bits).

Solution:

The contents of accumulator *B* after the "load accumulator *B* extended" operation in Fig. 10-23 will be 11110011.

10.35 Refer to Fig. 10-24.   The op code E6H specifies the "_____ _____ _____ _____" instruction.

Solution:

The op code E6H in Fig. 10-24 specifies the "load accumulator *B* indexed" instruction.

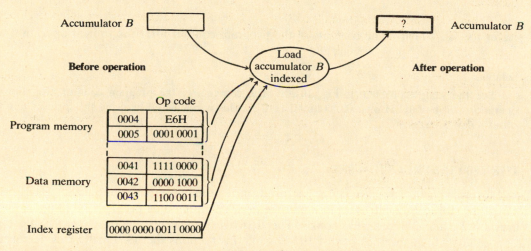

Fig. 10-24

10.36 Refer to Fig. 10-24.   The contents of data memory location _____ (hex) will be loaded into accumulator *B*.   After the load operation, the contents of accumulator *B* will be _____ (8 bits).

Solution:

Refer to the sample problem in Fig. 10-19.   The contents of data memory location 0041H in Fig. 10-24 will be loaded into accumulator *B*.   After the load operation, the contents of accumulator *B* will be 11110000.   The data memory location was calculated by adding the index register contents to the offset (0030 + 11 = 0041H).

10.37 Refer to Fig. 10-25.   The branch condition is _____ (false, true) in this problem.

Solution:

Refer to Fig. 10-4 for the position of the carry (*C*) flag.   The branch condition (branch if carry is clear) is true in this problem.   Therefore, the processor will jump to a new location.

10.38 Refer to Fig. 10-25.   The offset in program memory begins with a _____ (0, 1); therefore, the 6800 microprocessor will branch _____ (backward, forward).

Solution:

The offset in program memory in Fig. 10-25 begins with a 0; therefore, the 6800 microprocessor will branch forward.

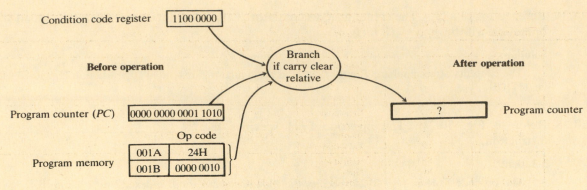

Fig. 10-25

10.39 Refer to Fig. 10-25. The contents of the program counter after the branch operation will be
_____ (hex) or _____ (binary).

Solution:

See the sample problem in Fig. 10-20. The contents of the program counter after the branch operation will be 001EH or $0000\ 0000\ 0001\ 1110_2$. This is calculated by using the formula $(PC + 2) +$ offset = new address.

10.5 THE 6800 INSTRUCTION SET

The Motorola 6800 microprocessor is used in stored program computers. The program instructions are stored as 8-bit bytes in a storage area referred to as program memory. The 6800 MPU uses 1-, 2-, and 3-byte instructions. The first byte of the instruction is always the op code (operation code), which specifies one of 197 possible instructions the 6800 MPU can perform. As with most general-purpose microprocessors, the set of instructions is permanently fixed in the design of the 6800 chip.

Motorola groups the 6800 microprocessor's instructions into the following groups:

1. Accumulator and memory instructions

2. Index register and stack pointer instructions

3. Jump and branch instructions

4. Condition code register instructions

Each of these groups will be covered in greater detail in subsequent sections of this chapter.

A summary of the *6800 MPU instruction set* is detailed in Fig. 10-26. This is an alphabetical listing by mnemonic. Motorola's mnemonics are used along with the 197 unique op codes. The op codes are represented in hexadecimal notation in this summary. A brief description is also given for each of the 6800 mnemonics. Unlike the 8080/8085 and generic processors, the 6800 MPU does not use a unique mnemonic for each op code. Some mnemonics have as many as four possible op codes, depending on the addressing modes. Because of this, the addressing mode is also given for each of the 6800 instructions in Fig. 10-26.

Consider the first instruction in Fig. 10-26. The "add accumulator *B* to accumulator *A*" instruction uses the mnemonic ABA and a hexadecimal op code of 1BH. According to Fig. 10-26, it uses inherent addressing. The ABA instruction's operation is summarized as

$$\text{Add } A \text{ to } B \rightarrow A$$

This means to add accumulator *A* to accumulator *B* with the result being deposited in accumulator *A*.

	Mnemonic	Op code (hex)	Addressing mode	Description
A	ABA	1B	Inherent	Add A to $B \rightarrow A$
	ADC A	89 99 A9 B9	Immediate Direct Indexed Extended	Add A to M with carry $\rightarrow A$
	ADC B	C9 D9 E9 F9	Immediate Direct Indexed Extended	Add B to M with carry $\rightarrow B$
	ADD A	8B 9B AB BB	Immediate Direct Indexed Extended	Add A to $M \rightarrow A$
	ADD B	CB DB EB FB	Immediate Direct Indexed Extended	Add B to $M \rightarrow B$
	AND A	84 94 A4 B4	Immediate Direct Indexed Extended	AND A with $M \rightarrow A$
	AND B	C4 D4 E4 F4	Immediate Direct Indexed Extended	AND B with $M \rightarrow B$
	ASL	68 78	Indexed Extended	Arithmetic shift M left into carry
	ASL A	48	Inherent	Arithmetic shift A left into carry
	ASL B	58	Inherent	Arithmetic shift B left into carry
	ASR	67 77	Indexed Extended	Arithmetic shift M right into carry
	ASR A	47	Inherent	Arithmetic shift A right into carry
	ASR B	57	Inherent	Arithmetic shift B right into carry
B	BCC	24	Relative	If C flag $= 0$, then branch
	BCS	25	Relative	If C flag $= 1$, then branch
	BEQ	27	Relative	If Z flag $= 1$, then branch
	BGE	2C	Relative	If 2s complement number ≥ 0, then branch
	BGT	2E	Relative	If 2s complement number > 0, then branch
	BHI	22	Relative	If minuend $>$ subtrahend, then branch
	BIT A	85 95 A5 B5	Immediate Direct Indexed Extended	AND A with M, flags affected (A and M unchanged)
	BIT B	C5 D5 E5 F5	Immediate Direct Indexed Extended	AND B with M, flags affected (B and M unchanged)
	BLE	2F	Relative	If 2s complement number ≤ 0, then branch
	BLS	23	Relative	If subtrahend $\geq$ minuend, then branch
	BLT	2D	Relative	If 2s complement number < 0, then branch
	BMI	2B	Relative	If minus ($N = 1$), then branch
	BNE	26	Relative	If not equal zero ($Z = 0$), then branch
	BPL	2A	Relative	If plus ($N = 0$), then branch
	BRA	20	Relative	Branch always
	BSR	8D	Relative	Branch to subroutine (PC to stack)
	BVC	28	Relative	If overflow clear ($V = 0$), then branch
	BVS	29	Relative	If overflow set ($V = 1$), then branch
C	CBA	11	Inherent	Compare A with B ($A - B$)

Fig. 10-26   Instruction set summary for the 6800 microprocessor

	Mnemonic	Op code (hex)	Addressing mode	Description
C	CLC	0C	Inherent	Clear C flag
	CLI	0E	Inherent	Clear I flag
	CLR	6F 7F	Indexed Extended	Clear memory location
	CLR A	4F	Inherent	Clear A
	CLR B	5F	Inherent	Clear B
	CLV	0A	Inherent	Clear V flag
	CMP A	81 91 A1 B1	Immediate Direct Indexed Extended	Compare A with M $(A - M)$
	CMP B	C1 D1 E1 F1	Immediate Direct Indexed Extended	Compare B with M $(B - M)$
	COM	63 73	Indexed Extended	Complement M (1s complement)
	COM A	43	Inherent	Complement A (1s complement)
	COM B	53	Inherent	Complement B (1s complement)
	CPX	8C 9C AC BC	Immediate Direct Indexed Extended	Compare index register with M $(X_H/X_L) - (M/M + 1)$
D	DA A	19	Inherent	Decimal adjust A (converts binary addition of BCD characters into BCD format)
	DEC	6A 7A	Indexed Extended	Decrement M
	DEC A	4A	Inherent	Decrement A
	DEC B	5A	Inherent	Decrement B
	DES	34	Inherent	Decrement stack pointer
	DEX	09	Inherent	Decrement index register
E	EOR A	88 98 A8 B8	Immediate Direct Indexed Extended	Exclusive OR A with $M \rightarrow A$
	EOR B	C8 D8 E8 F8	Immediate Direct Indexed Extended	Exclusive OR B with $M \rightarrow B$
I	INC	6C 7C	Indexed Extended	Increment M
	INC A	4C	Inherent	Increment A
	INC B	5C	Inherent	Increment B
	INS	31	Inherent	Increment stack pointer
	INX	08	Inherent	Increment index register
J	JMP	6E 7E	Indexed Extended	Jump to address
	JSR	AD BD	Indexed Extended	Jump to subroutine (PC on stack)
L	LDA A	86 96 A6 B6	Immediate Direct Indexed Extended	Load M into A
	LDA B	C6 D6 E6 F6	Immediate Direct Indexed Extended	Load M into B
	LDS	8E 9E	Immediate Direct	Load M into SP, $M \rightarrow SP_H$, $(M + 1) \rightarrow SP_L$

Fig. 10-26 (*cont.*)

	Mnemonic	Op code (hex)	Addressing mode	Description
L	LDS	AE BE	Indexed Extended	Load M into SP, $M \rightarrow SP_H$, $(M+1) \rightarrow SP_L$
	LDX	CE DE EE FE	Immediate Direct Indexed Extended	Load M into index register, $M \rightarrow X_H$, $(M+1) \rightarrow X_L$
	LSR	64 74	Indexed Extended	Logic shift M right into carry
	LSR A	44	Inherent	Logic shift A right into carry
	LSR B	54	Inherent	Logic shift B right into carry
N	NEG	60 70	Indexed Extended	2s complement of $M \rightarrow M$
	NEG A	40	Inherent	2s complement of $A \rightarrow A$
	NEG B	50	Inherent	2s complement of $B \rightarrow B$
	NOP	01	Inherent	No operation (2 cycles used)
O	ORA A	8A 9A AA BA	Immediate Direct Indexed Extended	OR A with $M \rightarrow A$
	ORA B	CA DA EA FA	Immediate Direct Indexed Extended	OR B with $M \rightarrow B$
P	PSH A	36	Inherent	Push A on stack
	PSH B	37	Inherent	Push B on stack
	PUL A	32	Inherent	Pull A from stack
	PUL B	33	Inherent	Pull B from stack
R	ROL	69 79	Indexed Extended	Rotate M left through carry
	ROL A	49	Inherent	Rotate A left through carry
	ROL B	59	Inherent	Rotate B left through carry
	ROR	66 76	Indexed Extended	Rotate M right through carry
	ROR A	46	Inherent	Rotate A right through carry
	ROR B	56	Inherent	Rotate B right through carry
	RTI	3B	Inherent	Return from interrupt (Flags, A, B, X, PC pulled from stack)
	RTS	39	Inherent	Return from subroutine (PC pulled from stack)
S	SBA	10	Inherent	Subtract B from $A \rightarrow A$
	SBC A	82 92 A2 B2	Immediate Direct Indexed Extended	Subtract M from A with carry ($A - M - C \rightarrow A$)
	SBC B	C2 D2 E2 F2	Immediate Direct Indexed Extended	Subtract M from B with carry ($B - M - C \rightarrow B$)
	SEC	0D	Inherent	Set C flag to 1
	SEI	0F	Inherent	Set I flag to 1 (set interrupt mask)
	SEV	0B	Inherent	Set V flag to 1
	STA A	97 A7 B7	Direct Indexed Extended	Store A in M
	STA B	D7 E7 F7	Direct Indexed Extended	Store B in M
	STS	9F AF BF	Direct Indexed Extended	Store SP in M, $SP_H \rightarrow M$, $SP_L \rightarrow (M+1)$

Fig. 10-26 (*cont.*)

	Mnemonic	Op code (hex)	Addressing mode	Description
S	STX	DF EF FF	Direct Indexed Extended	Store X in M, $X_H \rightarrow M$, $X_L \rightarrow (M+1)$
	SUB A	80 90 A0 B0	Immediate Direct Indexed Extended	Subtract M from $A \rightarrow A$
	SUB B	C0 D0 E0 F0	Immediate Direct Indexed Extended	Subtract M from $B \rightarrow B$
	SWI	3F	Inherent	Software interrupt
T	TAB	16	Inherent	Transfer A to B
	TAP	06	Inherent	Transfer A to processor CCR
	TBA	17	Inherent	Transfer B to A
	TPA	07	Inherent	Transfer processor CCR to A
	TST	6D 7D	Indexed Extended	Test M by $(M) - 00$ (N and Z flags set or reset)
	TST A	4D	Inherent	Test A by $(A) - 00$ (N and Z flags set or reset)
	TST B	5D	Inherent	Test B by $(B) - 00$ (N and Z flags set or reset)
	TSX	30	Inherent	Transfer $SP + 1 \rightarrow X$
	TXS	35	Inherent	Transfer $X - 1 \rightarrow SP$
W	WAI	3E	Inherent	Wait for interrupt (PC, I, A, B, CCR pushed on stack)

Fig. 10-26 (*cont.*)

The 6800 instruction set summary in Fig. 10-26 does not give detail on flags, clock cycles, or the number of instruction memory bytes used by each instruction. It does, however, give the programmer a quick overview of the operations available using Motorola's 6800 microprocessor.

SOLVED PROBLEMS

10.40 Motorola subdivides the 6800 microprocessor's instructions into four groups. List them.

Solution:

Motorola subdivides the 6800 microprocessor's instructions into accumulator and memory instructions, index register and stack pointer instructions, jump and branch instructions, and condition code register instructions.

10.41 Refer to Fig. 10-26. The ADD A instruction can be used in one of _____ (number) addressing modes. The ADD A instruction adds the contents of accumulator _____ (A, B) to the contents of a _____ location. The results are placed in _____ _____.

Solution:

The ADD A instruction listed in Fig. 10-26 can be used in one of four addressing modes. The ADD A instruction adds the contents of accumulator A to the contents of a memory location. The results are placed in accumulator A.

10.42 Refer to Fig. 10-27. The op code for the 6800's ADD B instruction used in this example is _____ (hex). This op code specifies the "add B to M" instruction using the _____ addressing mode.

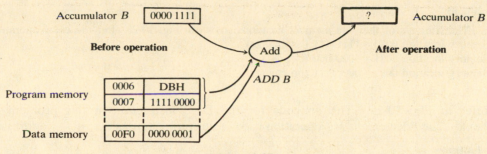

Fig. 10-27

Solution:

See the ADD *B* instruction in Fig. 10-26.   The op code for the 6800's ADD *B* instruction used in the example in Fig. 10-27 is DBH.   This op code specifies the "add *B* to *M*" instruction using the direct addressing mode.

10.43 Refer to Fig. 10-27.   The contents of accumulator *B* after the add operation will be _____.

Solution:

Adding binary $00001111 + 00000001 = 00010000$.   Therefore the contents of accumulator *B* after the add operation in Fig. 10-27 will be 00010000_2.

10.44 Refer to Fig. 10-28.   The clear operation in this example uses the op code _____ (hex). This instruction uses the _____ addressing mode.

Solution:

See the CLR instruction in Fig. 10-26.   The clear operation shown in Fig. 10-28 uses the op code 7FH.   This instruction uses the extended addressing mode.

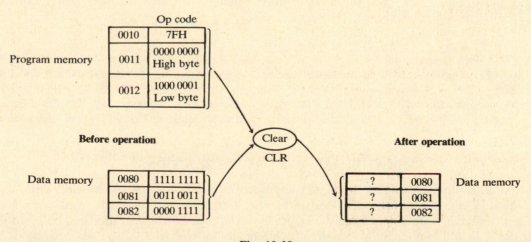

Fig. 10-28

10.45 Refer to Fig. 10-28.   List the contents of data memory locations 0080H, 0081H, and 0082H after the clear operation.

Solution:

The contents of the data memory locations shown in Fig. 10-28 after the clear operation will be:
Memory location 0080 = 11111111 (no change)
Memory location 0081 = 00000000 (cleared)
Memory location 0082 = 00001111 (no change)

10.46 Refer to Fig. 10-29. The op code for the DEC instruction in this problem is _____ (hex). The "decrement M" operation used in this problem uses the _____ addressing mode.

Solution:

See the DEC instruction in Fig. 10-26. The op code for the DEC instruction used in Fig. 10-29 is 6AH. The "decrement M" operation used in this problem uses the indexed addressing mode.

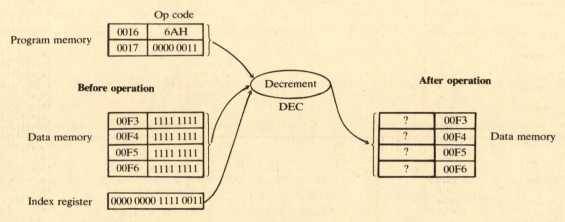

Fig. 10-29

10.47 Refer to Fig. 10-29. List the contents of data memory locations 00F3H, 00F4H, 00F5H, and 00F6H after the "decrement M" operation.

Solution:

Using indexed addressing, the new address pointed to in data memory is 00F3 + 3 = 00F6H. Therefore, the contents of the data memory locations after the "decrement M" operation will be:

Memory location 00F3 = 11111111 (no change)   Memory location 00F5 = 11111111 (no change)
Memory location 00F4 = 11111111 (no change)   Memory location 00F6 = 11111110 (decremented)

10.6 THE 6800 ACCUMULATOR AND MEMORY INSTRUCTIONS

Motorola's summary of just the 6800 microprocessor's *accumulator and memory instructions* is reproduced in Fig. 10-30. These include arithmetic, logic, data test, and data transfer instructions.

Consider the first operation listed in Fig. 10-30. The regular add operation can be performed in either the A or B accumulator. Therefore, two mnemonics are listed for the add operation. They are ADD A and ADD B. Note that the ADD A operation can be performed using immediate, direct, indexed, or extended addressing. The op code for the ADD A immediate instruction will be 8BH, while ADD A direct uses the unique op code of 9BH, etc. It can also be determined from Fig. 10-30 that the ADD A immediate operation is specified with a 2-byte instruction (note the 2 under the # sign). Also, the ADD A immediate operation uses two clock or machine cycles for execution (note the 2 under the ~ sign).

OPERATIONS	MNEMONIC	IMMED OP	~	=	DIRECT OP	~	=	INDEX OP	~	=	EXTND OP	~	=	IMPLIED OP	~	=	BOOLEAN/ARITHMETIC OPERATION (All register labels refer to contents)	5 H	4 I	3 N	2 Z	1 V	0 C
Add	ADDA	8B	2	2	9B	3	2	AB	5	2	BB	4	3				$A + M \rightarrow A$	↕	●	↕	↕	↕	↕
	ADDB	CB	2	2	DB	3	2	EB	5	2	FB	4	3				$B + M \rightarrow B$	↕	●	↕	↕	↕	↕
Add Acmltrs	ABA													1B	2	1	$A + B \rightarrow A$	↕	●	↕	↕	↕	↕
Add with Carry	ADCA	89	2	2	99	3	2	A9	5	2	B9	4	3				$A + M + C \rightarrow A$	↕	●	↕	↕	↕	↕
	ADCB	C9	2	2	D9	3	2	E9	5	2	F9	4	3				$B + M + C \rightarrow B$	↕	●	↕	↕	↕	↕
And	ANDA	84	2	2	94	3	2	A4	5	2	B4	4	3				$A \cdot M \rightarrow A$	●	●	↕	↕	R	●
	ANDB	C4	2	2	D4	3	2	E4	5	2	F4	4	3				$B \cdot M \rightarrow B$	●	●	↕	↕	R	●
Bit Test	BITA	85	2	2	95	3	2	A5	5	2	B5	4	3				$A \cdot M$	●	●	↕	↕	R	●
	BITB	C5	2	2	D5	3	2	E5	5	2	F5	4	3				$B \cdot M$	●	●	↕	↕	R	●
Clear	CLR							6F	7	2	7F	6	3				$00 \rightarrow M$	●	●	R	S	R	R
	CLRA													4F	2	1	$00 \rightarrow A$	●	●	R	S	R	R
	CLRB													5F	2	1	$00 \rightarrow B$	●	●	R	S	R	R
Compare	CMPA	81	2	2	91	3	2	A1	5	2	B1	4	3				$A - M$	●	●	↕	↕	↕	↕
	CMPB	C1	2	2	D1	3	2	E1	5	2	F1	4	3				$B - M$	●	●	↕	↕	↕	↕
Compare Acmltrs	CBA													11	2	1	$A - B$	●	●	↕	↕	↕	↕
Complement, 1's	COM							63	7	2	73	6	3				$\overline{M} \rightarrow M$	●	●	↕	↕	R	S
	COMA													43	2	1	$\overline{A} \rightarrow A$	●	●	↕	↕	R	S
	COMB													53	2	1	$\overline{B} \rightarrow B$	●	●	↕	↕	R	S
Complement, 2's	NEG							60	7	2	70	6	3				$00 - M \rightarrow M$	●	●	↕	↕	①	②
(Negate)	NEGA													40	2	1	$00 - A \rightarrow A$	●	●	↕	↕	①	②
	NEGB													50	2	1	$00 - B \rightarrow B$	●	●	↕	↕	①	②
Decimal Adjust, A	DAA													19	2	1	Converts Binary Add. of BCD Characters into BCD Format	●	●	↕	↕	↕	③
Decrement	DEC							6A	7	2	7A	6	3				$M - 1 \rightarrow M$	●	●	↕	↕	④	●
	DECA													4A	2	1	$A - 1 \rightarrow A$	●	●	↕	↕	④	●
	DECB													5A	2	1	$B - 1 \rightarrow B$	●	●	↕	↕	④	●
Exclusive OR	EORA	88	2	2	98	3	2	A8	5	2	B8	4	3				$A \oplus M \rightarrow A$	●	●	↕	↕	R	●
	EORB	C8	2	2	D8	3	2	E8	5	2	F8	4	3				$B \oplus M \rightarrow B$	●	●	↕	↕	R	●
Increment	INC							6C	7	2	7C	6	3				$M + 1 \rightarrow M$	●	●	↕	↕	⑤	●
	INCA													4C	2	1	$A + 1 \rightarrow A$	●	●	↕	↕	⑤	●
	INCB													5C	2	1	$B + 1 \rightarrow B$	●	●	↕	↕	⑤	●
Load Acmltr	LDAA	86	2	2	96	3	2	A6	5	2	B6	4	3				$M \rightarrow A$	●	●	↕	↕	R	●
	LDAB	C6	2	2	D6	3	2	E6	5	2	F6	4	3				$M \rightarrow B$	●	●	↕	↕	R	●
Or, Inclusive	ORAA	8A	2	2	9A	3	2	AA	5	2	BA	4	3				$A + M \rightarrow A$	●	●	↕	↕	R	●
	ORAB	CA	2	2	DA	3	2	EA	5	2	FA	4	3				$B + M \rightarrow B$	●	●	↕	↕	R	●
Push Data	PSHA													36	4	1	$A \rightarrow M_{SP}, SP - 1 \rightarrow SP$	●	●	●	●	●	●
	PSHB													37	4	1	$B \rightarrow M_{SP}, SP - 1 \rightarrow SP$	●	●	●	●	●	●
Pull Data	PULA													32	4	1	$SP + 1 \rightarrow SP, M_{SP} \rightarrow A$	●	●	●	●	●	●
	PULB													33	4	1	$SP + 1 \rightarrow SP, M_{SP} \rightarrow B$	●	●	●	●	●	●
Rotate Left	ROL							69	7	2	79	6	3				M	●	●	↕	↕	⑥	↕
	ROLA													49	2	1	A	●	●	↕	↕	⑥	↕
	ROLB													59	2	1	B	●	●	↕	↕	⑥	↕
Rotate Right	ROR							66	7	2	76	6	3				M	●	●	↕	↕	⑥	↕
	RORA													46	2	1	A	●	●	↕	↕	⑥	↕
	RORB													56	2	1	B	●	●	↕	↕	⑥	↕
Shift Left, Arithmetic	ASL							68	7	2	78	6	3				M	●	●	↕	↕	⑥	↕
	ASLA													48	2	1	A	●	●	↕	↕	⑥	↕
	ASLB													58	2	1	B	●	●	↕	↕	⑥	↕
Shift Right, Arithmetic	ASR							67	7	2	77	6	3				M	●	●	↕	↕	⑥	↕
	ASRA													47	2	1	A	●	●	↕	↕	⑥	↕
	ASRB													57	2	1	B	●	●	↕	↕	⑥	↕
Shift Right, Logic	LSR							64	7	2	74	6	3				M	●	●	R	↕	⑥	↕
	LSRA													44	2	1	A	●	●	R	↕	⑥	↕
	LSRB													54	2	1	B	●	●	R	↕	⑥	↕
Store Acmltr.	STAA				97	4	2	A7	6	2	B7	5	3				$A \rightarrow M$	●	●	↕	↕	R	●
	STAB				D7	4	2	E7	6	2	F7	5	3				$B \rightarrow M$	●	●	↕	↕	R	●
Subtract	SUBA	80	2	2	90	3	2	A0	5	2	B0	4	3				$A - M \rightarrow A$	●	●	↕	↕	↕	↕
	SUBB	C0	2	2	D0	3	2	E0	5	2	F0	4	3				$B - M \rightarrow B$	●	●	↕	↕	↕	↕
Subtract Acmltrs.	SBA													10	2	1	$A - B \rightarrow A$	●	●	↕	↕	↕	↕
Subtr. with Carry	SBCA	82	2	2	92	3	2	A2	5	2	B2	4	3				$A - M - C \rightarrow A$	●	●	↕	↕	↕	↕
	SBCB	C2	2	2	D2	3	2	E2	5	2	F2	4	3				$B - M - C \rightarrow B$	●	●	↕	↕	↕	↕
Transfer Acmltrs	TAB													16	2	1	$A \rightarrow B$	●	●	↕	↕	R	●
	TBA													17	2	1	$B \rightarrow A$	●	●	↕	↕	R	●
Test, Zero or Minus	TST							6D	7	2	7D	6	3				$M - 00$	●	●	↕	↕	R	R
	TSTA													4D	2	1	$A - 00$	●	●	↕	↕	R	R
	TSTB													5D	2	1	$B - 00$	●	●	↕	↕	R	R

LEGEND:

OP Operation Code (Hexadecimal);
~ Number of MPU Cycles;
# Number of Program Bytes;
+ Arithmetic Plus;
− Arithmetic Minus;
· Boolean AND;
M_{SP} Contents of memory location pointed to be Stack Pointer;

+ Boolean Inclusive OR;
⊕ Boolean Exclusive OR;
M Complement of M;
→ Transfer Into;
0 Bit = Zero;
00 Byte = Zero;

Note — Accumulator addressing mode instructions are included in the column for IMPLIED addressing

Fig. 10-30 Accumulator and memory instructions (*Courtesy of Motorola, Inc.*)

CONDITION CODE SYMBOLS:

H	Half-carry from bit 3;
I	Interrupt mask
N	Negative (sign bit)
Z	Zero (byte)
V	Overflow, 2's complement
C	Carry from bit 7
R	Reset Always
S	Set Always
↕	Test and set if true, cleared otherwise
●	Not Affected

CONDITION CODE REGISTER NOTES:

(Bit set if test is true and cleared otherwise)

①	(Bit V)	Test: Result = 10000000?
②	(Bit C)	Test: Result ≠ 00000000?
③	(Bit C)	Test: Decimal value of most significant BCD Character greater than nine?
		(Not cleared if previously set.)
④	(Bit V)	Test: Operand = 10000000 prior to execution?
⑤	(Bit V)	Test: Operand = 01111111 prior to execution?
⑥	(Bit V)	Test: Set equal to result of N⊕C after shift has occurred.

Fig. 10-30 Accumulator and memory instructions (*cont.*)

The symbolic operation of the ADD A instruction is listed as $A + M \rightarrow A$ in Fig. 10-30. This means that the contents of accumulator A are added to the contents of memory location M. The result of the operation (the sum in this case) is placed in accumulator A, as denoted by the arrow.

The right columns in Fig. 10-30 indicate that the H, N, Z, V, and C flags are affected by the ADD A operation. However, the I flag is not affected by this instruction. A special legend and notes are placed at the end of the table in Fig. 10-30 to explain many of the symbols.

SOLVED PROBLEMS

10.48 Refer to Fig. 10-30. The LDA B instruction transfers the contents of a _____ location to accumulator _____. The _____, _____, and _____ flags are affected by the LDA B operation.

Solution:

See the LDA B instruction in Fig. 10-30. The LDA B instruction transfers the contents of a memory location (M) to accumulator B. The N, Z, and V flags are affected by the LDA B operation. The V flag is always reset (see the R in Fig. 10-30) by the LDA B operation.

10.49 Refer to Fig. 10-31. The LDA B 3-byte instruction used in this problem has an op code of _____ (hex). This instruction uses _____ addressing.

Solution:

See the LDA B instruction in Fig. 10-30. The LDA B instruction used in Fig. 10-31 has an op code of F6H. This instruction uses extended addressing.

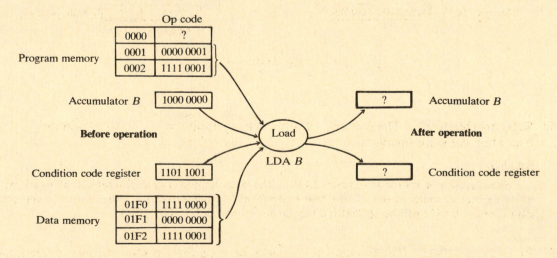

Fig. 10-31

10.50 Refer to Fig. 10-31.   The contents of accumulator *B* after the load operation will be _____ (8 bits).

> **Solution:**
>
> Extended addressing is used by the LDA *B* instruction in Fig. 10-31, which means data will be copied out of data memory location 01F1H.   Therefore, the contents of accumulator *B* after the load operation will be 00000000.

10.51 Refer to Fig. 10-31.   The contents of the condition code register after the load operation will be _____ (8 bits).

> **Solution:**
>
> See the LDA *B* instruction in Fig. 10-30.   The contents of the condition code register after the load operation in Fig. 10-31 will be 11010101.   Only the *N* and *Z* flags have been changed during the load operation.

10.52 Refer to Fig. 10-32.   The "store accumulator *A*" instruction used in this problem uses _____ addressing.

> **Solution:**
>
> See the STA *A* instruction in Fig. 10-30.   The op code A7H used in Fig. 10-32 represents the "store accumulator *A*" instruction and uses indexed addressing.

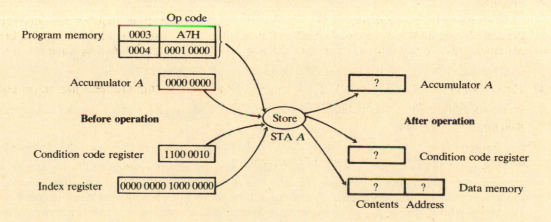

Fig. 10-32

10.53 Refer to Fig. 10-32.   The contents of data memory location _____ (hex) will be _____ (8 bits) after the store operation.

> **Solution:**
>
> See the STA *A* instruction in Fig. 10-30.   The data memory location is calculated by adding the index register contents to the offset (0080 + 10 = 0090H in this example).   Therefore, the contents of data memory 0090H will be 00000000 after the store operation in Fig. 10-32.

10.54 Refer to Fig. 10-32.   The contents of the condition code register after the store operation will be _____ (8 bits).

Solution:

The *N*, *Z*, and *V* flags are affected by the STA *A* operation according to the table in Fig. 10-30. The contents of the condition code register after the store operation in Fig. 10-32 will be 11000100.

10.55 Refer to Fig. 10-33.   The op code for the TST *A* instruction is _____ (hex).   This "test *A*" instruction uses _____ addressing.

Solution:

See the TST *A* instruction in Fig. 10-30. The op code for the TST *A* instruction is 4DH. This "test *A*" instruction uses inherent, or implied, addressing.

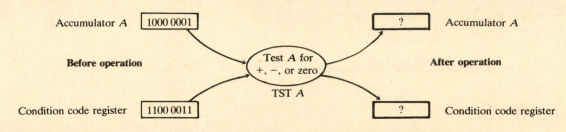

Fig. 10-33

10.56 Refer to Fig. 10-33.   The contents of accumulator *A* after the TST *A* operation will be _____ (8 bits).

Solution:

The test operation does not change the value in accumulator *A*. Therefore, the contents of accumulator *A* in Fig. 10-33 after the TST *A* operation will be 10000001.

10.57 Refer to Fig. 10-33.   The contents of the condition code register after the TST *A* operation will be _____ (8 bits).

Solution:

According to Fig. 10-33, only the *N*, *Z*, *V*, and *C* flags are affected by the TST *A* instruction. The contents of the condition code register after the TST *A* operation will be 11001000. The *V* and *C* flags are always reset by this operation. The *N* flag will be set to 1, indicating that accumulator *A* holds a negative number. The *Z* flag will be reset to 0, indicating that accumulator *A* does not contain a zero.

10.7   THE 6800 INDEX REGISTER AND STACK POINTER INSTRUCTIONS

The next group of 6800 microprocessor operations is the *index register and stack pointer instructions*, detailed in Fig. 10-34. These include increment and decrement, load and store, and transfer instructions used with the index register and stack pointer. Recall that the 6800's 16-bit index register is used when executing instructions in the indexed addressing mode. The 16-bit stack pointer is used to locate the top of the stack in RAM.

Consider the "compare index register" instruction in the first line of the table in Fig. 10-34. The mnemonic is CPX. The CPX instruction can access memory using immediate, direct, indexed, or extended addressing. Compare instructions are essentially subtract operations with the registers and memory locations left unchanged. The *Z* flag is either set or reset and can be used for later conditional branching. The *N* and *V* flags are also affected but are not intended for conditional branching after this operation.

POINTER OPERATIONS	MNEMONIC	IMMED			DIRECT			INDEX			EXTND			IMPLIED			BOOLEAN/ARITHMETIC OPERATION	COND. CODE REG.					
		OP	~	#	OP	~	#	OP	~	#	OP	~	#	OP	~	#		5 H	4 I	3 N	2 Z	1 V	0 C
Compare Index Reg	CPX	8C	3	3	9C	4	2	AC	6	2	BC	5	3				$X_H - M, X_L - (M + 1)$	●	●	①	↕	②	●
Decrement Index Reg	DEX													09	4	1	$X - 1 \rightarrow X$	●	●	●	↕	●	●
Decrement Stack Pntr	DES													34	4	1	$SP - 1 \rightarrow SP$	●	●	●	●	●	●
Increment Index Reg	INX													08	4	1	$X + 1 \rightarrow X$	●	●	●	↕	●	●
Increment Stack Pntr	INS													31	4	1	$SP + 1 \rightarrow SP$	●	●	●	●	●	●
Load Index Reg	LDX	CE	3	3	DE	4	2	EE	6	2	FE	5	3				$M \rightarrow X_H, (M + 1) \rightarrow X_L$	●	●	③	↕	R	●
Load Stack Pntr	LDS	8E	3	3	9E	4	2	AE	6	2	BE	5	3				$M \rightarrow SP_H, (M + 1) \rightarrow SP_L$	●	●	③	↕	R	●
Store Index Reg	STX				DF	5	2	EF	7	2	FF	6	3				$X_H \rightarrow M, X_L \rightarrow (M + 1)$	●	●	③	↕	R	●
Store Stack Pntr	STS				9F	5	2	AF	7	2	BF	6	3				$SP_H \rightarrow M, SP_L \rightarrow (M + 1)$	●	●	③	↕	R	●
Indx Reg → Stack Pntr	TXS													35	4	1	$X - 1 \rightarrow SP$	●	●	●	●	●	●
Stack Pntr → Indx Reg	TSX													30	4	1	$SP + 1 \rightarrow X$	●	●	●	●	●	●

① (Bit N) Test: Sign bit of most significant (MS) byte of result = 1?
② (Bit V) Test: 2's complement overflow from subtraction of ms bytes?
③ (Bit N) Test: Result less than zero? (Bit 15 = 1)

Fig. 10-34 Index register and stack pointer instructions (*Courtesy of Motorola, Inc.*)

SOLVED PROBLEMS

10.58 Refer to Fig. 10-35. The LDX operation shown in this example uses an op code of _____ (hex). This instruction uses _____ addressing.

Solution:

The LDX operation in Fig. 10-35 uses an op code of CEH. This instruction uses immediate addressing.

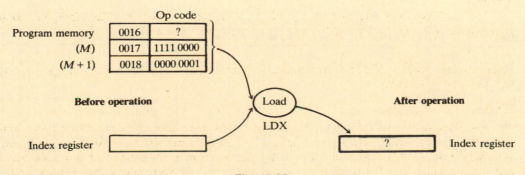

Fig. 10-35

10.59 Refer to Fig. 10-35. The contents of the index register after the load operation will be _____ (hex).

Solution:

See the LDX instruction in Fig. 10-34. The contents of the index register in Fig. 10-35 after the load operation will be F001H.

10.60 Refer to Fig. 10-36. Program memory location 001CH should contain the op code _____ (hex) to specify the "load stack pointer extended" operation.

Solution:

See the LDS instruction in Fig. 10-34. Program memory location 001CH in Fig. 10-36 should contain the op code BEH to specify the "load stack pointer extended" operation.

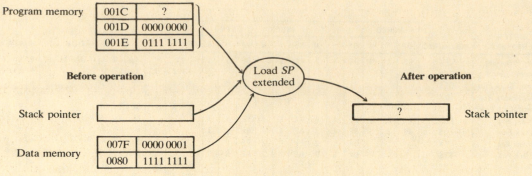

Fig. 10-36

10.61 Refer to Fig. 10-36.   The contents of the stack pointer after the load operation will be _____ (hex).

Solution:

See the LDS instruction in Fig. 10-34.   The contents of the stack pointer after the load operation in Fig. 10-36 will be 01FFH.

10.8   THE 6800 JUMP AND BRANCH INSTRUCTIONS

The *jump and branch instructions* for the 6800 microprocessor are detailed in Fig. 10-37.   These instructions are used to control the transfer of operation from one point to another in the program.   Note that all branch operations use the relative addressing mode.   The "no operation"

		RELATIVE			INDEX			EXTND			IMPLIED				COND. CODE REG.					
																5	4	3	2	1	0
OPERATIONS	MNEMONIC	OP	~	#	OP	~	#	OP	~	#	OP	~	#	BRANCH TEST		H	I	N	Z	V	C
Branch Always	BRA	20	4	2										None		•	•	•	•	•	•
Branch If Carry Clear	BCC	24	4	2										C = 0		•	•	•	•	•	•
Branch If Carry Set	BCS	25	4	2										C = 1		•	•	•	•	•	•
Branch If = Zero	BEQ	27	4	2										Z = 1		•	•	•	•	•	•
Branch If ⩾ Zero	BGE	2C	4	2										N ⊕ V = 0		•	•	•	•	•	•
Branch If > Zero	BGT	2E	4	2										Z + (N ⊕ V) = 0		•	•	•	•	•	•
Branch If Higher	BHI	22	4	2										C + Z = 0		•	•	•	•	•	•
Branch If ⩽ Zero	BLE	2F	4	2										Z + (N ⊕ V) = 1		•	•	•	•	•	•
Branch If Lower Or Same	BLS	23	4	2										C + Z = 1		•	•	•	•	•	•
Branch If < Zero	BLT	2D	4	2										N ⊕ V = 1		•	•	•	•	•	•
Branch If Minus	BMI	2B	4	2										N = 1		•	•	•	•	•	•
Branch If Not Equal Zero	BNE	26	4	2										Z = 0		•	•	•	•	•	•
Branch If Overflow Clear	BVC	28	4	2										V = 0		•	•	•	•	•	•
Branch If Overflow Set	BVS	29	4	2										V = 1		•	•	•	•	•	•
Branch If Plus	BPL	2A	4	2										N = 0		•	•	•	•	•	•
Branch To Subroutine	BSR	8D	8	2												•	•	•	•	•	•
Jump	JMP				6E	4	2	7E	3	3				See Special Operations		•	•	•	•	•	•
Jump To Subroutine	JSR				AD	8	2	BD	9	3						•	•	•	•	•	•
No Operation	NOP										01	2	1	Advances Prog. Cntr. Only		•	•	•	•	•	•
Return From Interrupt	RTI										3B	10	1					①			
Return From Subroutine	RTS										39	5	1			•	•	•	•	•	•
Software Interrupt	SWI										3F	12	1	See Special Operations		•	•	•	•	•	•
Wait for Interrupt *	WAI										3E	9	1			•	②	•	•	•	•

*WAI puts Address Bus, R/W, and Data Bus in the three-state mode while VMA is held low.

① (All)   Load Condition Code Register from Stack. (See Special Operations)
② (Bit 1) Set when interrupt occurs. If previously set, a Non-Maskable Interrupt
              is required to exit the wait state.

Fig. 10-37 Jump and branch instructions (*Courtesy of Motorola, Inc.*)

(NOP) instruction only advances the program counter by one and has no other effect on flags, registers, or memory locations.

Consider the "jump to subroutine" (JSR) instruction listed in Fig. 10-37. The JSR instruction uses either indexed or extended addressing. Details of the JSR's operation are given in Fig. 10-38. The "branch to subroutine" (BSR) instruction has the same function as the JSR operation. It, however, uses the relative addressing. The "branch to subroutine" instruction is also explained in greater detail in Fig. 10-38.

Jump (JMP) and "return from subroutine" (RTS) instructions are listed in the table in Fig. 10-37. Greater detail on their functioning is given in Fig. 10-38. The "software interrupt" (SWI) and "wait for interrupt" (WAI) instructions are also listed in the table in Fig. 10-37. Again, greater detail is given on those two instructions under interrupts in Fig. 10-38. Finally, the "return from interrupt" (RTI) instruction is listed and detailed in both Figs. 10-37 and 10-38. The RTS instruction is used as the last instruction in a subroutine, while the RTI instruction serves the same purpose in an interrupt service routine.

The WAI is a commonly used instruction. It is used at the end of a program much like the halt (HLT) instruction on the 8080/8085 MPU. According to Fig. 10-38, the WAI instruction first places the contents of the processor registers on the stack. Then it enters a "do nothing" *wait loop*. The 6800 MPU continues in this loop until a hardware interrupt ($\overline{IRQ}$, $\overline{NMI}$, $\overline{RESET}$) is received by the processor.

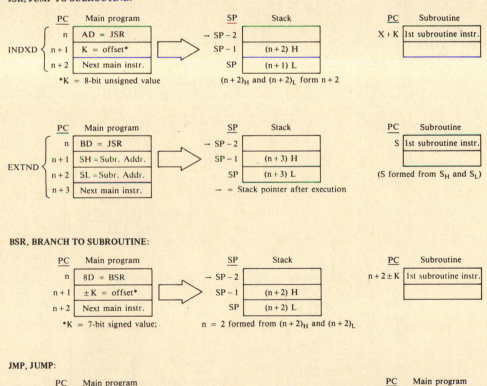

Fig. 10-38 Explanation of jump and branch special operations

RTS, RETURN FORM SUBROUTINE:

PC	Subroutine
S	39 = RTS

SP	Stack
SP	
SP + 1	N_H
→ SP + 2	N_L

PC	Main program
n	Next main instr.

INTERRUPTS:

Software interrupt
Main program

n	3F = SWI
n + 1	Next main instr.

Wait for interrupt
Main program

n	3E = WAI
n + 1	Next main instr.

Hardware interrupt or nonmaskable interrupt (NMI)
Main program

n	Last prog. byte

NMI ? — Yes / No

Int mask set? (CCR 4) — No / Yes

Continue main prog.

n + 1	Next main instr.

SP	Stack
→ SP – 7	
SP – 6	Condition code
SP – 5	Accumulator B
SP – 4	Accumulator A
SP – 3	Index register (X_H)
SP – 2	Index register (X_L)
SP – 1	(n + 1) H
SP	(n + 1) L

Stack MPU register contents

SWI   HDWR INT   WAI   NMI   Restart

Int. Mask set? (CCR 4) — Yes / No

Hdwr. int. req.

Wait loop   NMI

FFFA FFFB   FFF8 FFF9   FFFC FFFD   FFFE FFFF

Interrupt memory assignment 1

FFF8	Constant, hardware	MS
FFF9	Constant, hardware	LS
FFFA	Software	MS
FFFB	Software	LS
FFFC	Nonmaskable instr.	MS
FFFD	Nonmaskable instr.	LS
FFFE	Restart	MS
FFFF	Restart	LS

NOTE: MS = Most significant address byte
      LS = Least significant address byte

1. Memory location responding to the indicated addresses should be reserved for interrupt vectors

First instruction address formed by fetching 2-bytes from performed memory assignment

Set interrupt mask (CCR 4)

Load interrupt vector into program counter

Interrupt program

1	1st interrupt instr.

Fig. 10-38 (*cont.*)

RTI, RETURN FROM INTERRUPT:

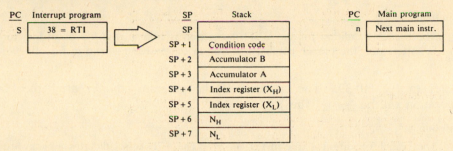

Fig. 10-38 (*cont.*)

SOLVED PROBLEMS

10.62 All the 6800 MPU branch instructions use the _____ addressing mode.

Solution:

According to Fig. 10-37, all the 6800 MPU branch instructions use the relative addressing mode.

10.63 All the 6800 MPU branch operations are specified with _____ (number) -byte instructions. The first byte of the instruction is always the _____ _____. The second byte of the instruction is called the _____.

Solution:

According to Fig. 10-37, all the 6800 MPU branch operations are specified with 2-byte instructions. The first byte of the instruction is always the op code. The second byte of the instruction is called the offset, or sometimes the displacement.

10.64 Refer to Fig. 10-39. The op code for the "branch if zero" operation is _____ (hex). The contents of program memory location 0028H equal the _____ (address, offset), which is _____ (−, +) 7H.

Solution:

See the BEQ instruction in the table in Fig. 10-37. The op code for the "branch if zero" operation in Fig. 10-39 is 27H. The contents of program memory location 0028H equal the offset, which is −7H. The −7H offset suggests a backward branch.

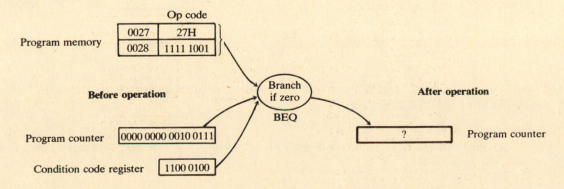

Fig. 10-39

10.65 Refer to Fig. 10-39. The branch condition is _____ (false, true) in this problem.

Solution:

The branch condition for the BEQ instruction is branch if $Z = 1$ according to the table in Fig. 10-37. Therefore, the branch condition is true in the problem shown in Fig. 10-39.

10.66 Refer to Fig. 10-39. The contents of the program counter after the "branch if zero" operation will be _____ (hex).

Solution:

The branch condition is true in Fig. 10-39. The $-7H$ offset dictates a backward branch. Therefore, the contents of the program counter after the "branch if zero" operation in Fig. 10-39 will be 0022H $[(0027 + 2) - 7 = 0022H]$.

10.67 Refer to Fig. 10-40. The "jump to subroutine" operation in this problem is specified by the op code _____ (hex). This operation uses _____ addressing.

Solution:

See the JSR instruction in Fig. 10-37. The "jump to subroutine" operation in Fig. 10-40 is specified by the op code BDH. This operation uses extended addressing.

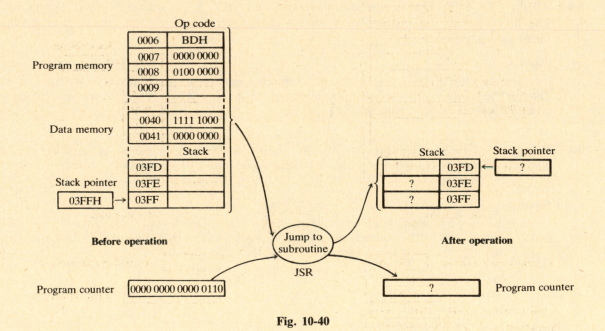

Fig. 10-40

10.68 Refer to Fig. 10-40. List the contents of the stack pointer and stack locations 03FEH and 03FFH after the JSR operation.

Solution:

See the "JSR extended" details in Fig. 10-38. After the "JSR extended" operation shown in Fig. 10-40, the contents are:
Stack pointer = 03FDH
Stack location 03FEH = 00000000 (PC_H)
Stack location 03FFH = 00001001 (PC_L) $(PC + 3)$

10.69 Refer to Fig. 10-40. The contents of the program counter after the JSR operation will be
_____ (hex).   This is the address of the _____.

Solution:

See the "JSR extended" details in Fig. 10-38.   The contents of the program counter in Fig. 10-40
after the JSR operation will be F800H.   This is the address of the subroutine.

10.70 Refer to Fig. 10-41.   The op code for the SWI instruction is _____ (hex).   SWI stands for
the _____ _____ operation.

Solution:

See the SWI instruction in Fig. 10-37.   The op code for the SWI instruction in Fig. 10-41 is
3FH.   SWI stands for the software interrupt operation.

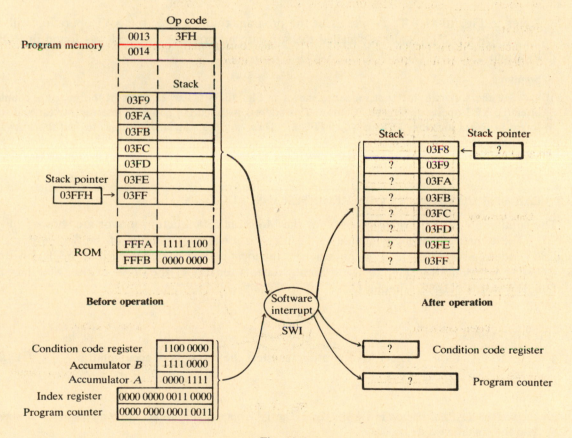

Fig. 10-41

10.71 Refer to Fig. 10-41.   List the contents of the stack pointer and stack after the software
interrupt operation.

Solution:

After the SWI operation in Fig. 10-41, the contents of the stack pointer are 03F8H, and the contents
of the stack are as follows:

Stack location (hex)	Contents
03F9	11000000 (condition code register)
03FA	11100000 (accumulator *B*)
03FB	00001111 (accumulator *A*)
03FC	00000000 (index register—high byte)
03FD	00110000 (index register—low byte)
03FE	00000000 (*PC*—high byte)
03FF	00010100 (*PC*—low byte) (*PC* + 1)

10.72 Refer to Fig. 10-41.   The contents of the condition code register after the SWI operation will be _____ (8 bits).

Solution:

See the software interrupt sequence shown in Fig. 10-38.   The *I* flag will be set.   Therefore, the contents of the condition code register in Fig. 10-41 after the SWI operation will be 11010000.

10.73 Refer to Fig. 10-41.   The contents of the program counter after the SWI operation will be _____ (hex).   This address is called the software interrupt _____ and was found in ROM locations _____ (hex) and _____ (hex).

Solution:

See the software interrupt sequence shown in Fig. 10-38.   The contents of the program counter after the SWI operation will be FC00H.   This address is called the software interrupt vector and was found in ROM locations FFFAH and FFFBH.   These are the standard locations to find the software interrupt vector in a 6800 system.

10.9   THE 6800 CONDITION CODE REGISTER INSTRUCTIONS

The *condition code register instructions* for the Motorola 6800 microprocessor are shown in Fig. 10-42*a*.   These instructions are available to the user for *direct* manipulation of the flags within the condition code register (*CCR*).   For convenience, the location and names of each of the flags within the *CCR* are reproduced in Fig. 10-42*b*.   Some students remember the order of the 6800 flags by recalling the words "HINZ Vitamin C."

SOLVED PROBLEMS

10.74 Refer to Fig. 10-43.   The TAP operation transfers the contents of accumulator _____ (*A*, *B*) to the _____ _____ _____.

Solution:

See the TAP instruction in Fig. 10-42*a*.   The TAP operation transfers the contents of accumulator *A* to the condition code register.

10.75 Refer to Fig. 10-43.   List the flag conditions in the *CCR* after the TAP operation.

Solution:

The flag conditions after the TAP operation in Fig. 10-43 are:
H flag = 0   *N* flag = 0   *V* flag = 1
 I flag = 1   *Z* flag = 1   *C* flag = 1

10.76 List the mnemonics for the instructions that are used to set and reset the interrupt mask flag.

| OPERATIONS | MNEMONIC | IMPLIED | | | BOOLEAN OPERATION | COND. CODE REG. | | | | | |
| | | OP | ~ | # | | 5 | 4 | 3 | 2 | 1 | 0 |
						H	I	N	Z	V	C
Clear Carry	CLC	0C	2	1	0 → C	●	●	●	●	●	R
Clear Interrupt Mask	CLI	0E	2	1	0 → I	●	R	●	●	●	●
Clear Overflow	CLV	0A	2	1	0 → V	●	●	●	●	R	●
Set Carry	SEC	0D	2	1	1 → C	●	●	●	●	●	S
Set Interrupt Mask	SEI	0F	2	1	1 → I	●	S	●	●	●	●
Set Overflow	SEV	0B	2	1	1 → V	●	●	●	●	S	●
Acmltr A → CCR	TAP	06	2	1	A → CCR	①					
CCR → Acmltr A	TPA	07	2	1	CCR → A	●	●	●	●	●	●

① (ALL) Set according to the contents of Accumulator A.

LEGEND:

OP	Operation Code (Hexadecimal);
~	Number of MPU Cycles;
#	Number of Program Bytes;
+	Arithmetic Plus;
−	Arithmetic Minus;
·	Boolean AND;
M$_{SP}$	Contents of memory location pointed to be Stack Pointer;

+	Boolean Inclusive OR;
⊙	Boolean Exclusive OR;
M̄	Complement of M;
→	Transfer Into;
0	Bit = Zero;
00	Byte = Zero;

CONDITION CODE SYMBOLS:

H	Half-carry from bit 3;
I	Interrupt mask
N	Negative (sign bit)
Z	Zero (byte)
V	Overflow, 2's complement
C	Carry from bit 7
R	Reset Always
S	Set Always
‡	Test and set if true, cleared otherwise
●	Not Affected

Note – Accumulator addressing mode instructions are included in the column for IMPLIED addressing

(a) Condition code register instructions

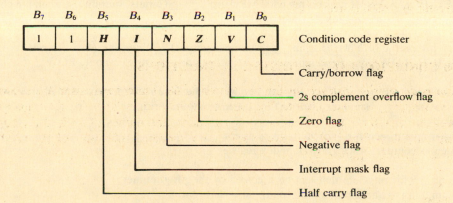

(b) Flags in the condition code register

Fig. 10-42 (*Courtesy of Motorola, Inc.*)

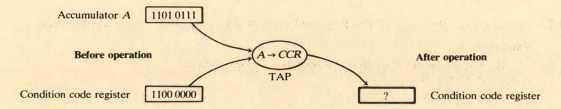

Fig. 10-43

Solution:

See Fig. 10-42*a*. The mnemonics used to set and reset the interrupt (*I*) mask flag are SEI and CLI.

10.77 The "clear carry" instruction uses the mnemonic _____, the op code _____ (hex), _____ addressing, and _____ (number) clock cycles for execution. It _____ (resets, sets) the _____ flag in the _____ _____ _____.

Solution:

See the "clear carry" instruction in Fig. 10-42. The "clear carry" instruction uses the mnemonic CLC, the op code 0CH, implied (or inherent) addressing, and two clock cycles for execution. It resets the *C* flag in the condition code register.

Supplementary Problems

10.78 The 6800 microprocessor was introduced by Motorola in _____ (1968, 1974).   *Ans.* 1974

10.79 A minimum 6800 microcomputer system might include the 6800 MPU, clock, power supply, restart switch, both _____ and _____ memories, and a 6820 _____ to interface with I/O devices.
Ans. RAM, ROM, PIA (peripheral interface adapter)

10.80 The $\overline{RESET}$, $\overline{IRQ}$, and $\overline{NMI}$ pins on the 6800 MPU are _____ (inputs, outputs), and all are classified as hardware _____.   *Ans.* inputs, interrupts

10.81 The $\overline{HALT}$ pin on the 6800 MPU is an _____ (input, output). When the $\overline{HALT}$ pin is activated by a _____ (HIGH, LOW), the processor enters the halt mode.   *Ans.* input, LOW

10.82 The 6800 MPU's $R/\overline{W}$ is an _____ (input, output). When the $R/\overline{W}$ pin goes LOW, it is a signal that the processor is _____ (reading, writing).   *Ans.* output, writing

10.83 List the 6800 microprocessor's three 16-bit registers.
Ans. program counter, stack pointer, index register

10.84 List three 6800 8-bit registers that can be accessed by the programmer.
Ans. accumulator *A*, accumulator *B*, condition code register

10.85 The 6800 MPU uses _____-_____ I/O in that inputs and outputs are treated like memory locations. The 6800 MPU _____ (does, does not) use special IN and OUT instructions for I/O operations.   *Ans.* memory-mapped, does not

10.86 In 6800 MPU-based systems, the _____ (RAM, ROM) is usually located at the low addresses starting at 0000H, while the _____ (RAM, ROM) is located at the high addresses ending with FFFFH.
Ans. RAM, ROM

10.87 Interrupt vectors are located in the _____ (highest, lowest) memory locations in 6800-based systems.
Ans. highest (located at FFF8 through FFFFH)

10.88 Only the _____ ($\overline{IRQ}$, $\overline{NMI}$, $\overline{RESET}$) hardware interrupt is maskable.   *Ans.* $\overline{IRQ}$

10.89 The reset interrupt sequence detailed in Fig. 10-8*a* causes the _____ flag to be set, and the reset interrupt vector is found at memory locations _____ (hex) and _____ (hex).
Ans. *I*, FFFEH, FFFFH

10.90 According to Fig. 10-9, ROM locations FFF8H and FFF9H in 6800-based systems are always reserved for the _____ _____ _____.   *Ans.* interrupt request vector (address)

10.91 List the six memory addressing modes used by 6800 MPU instructions.
Ans. inherent (or implied), immediate, direct, extended, indexed, and relative addressing

10.92 In immediate addressing, the operand is found in _____ (data, program) memory.   *Ans.* program

10.93 The 6800 microprocessor's direct addressing operations are specified using _____ (number) -byte instructions.   *Ans.* 2

10.94 The 6800 microprocessor's extended addressing operations are specified using _____ (number) -byte instructions.   *Ans.* 3

10.95 In 6800 indexed addressing, the operand's address is calculated by adding the value of the _____ found in the second byte of the instruction to the contents of the _____ register.   *Ans.* offset, index

10.96 In 6800 relative addressing, the destination address of the branch is calculated by adding _____ (number) to the contents of the program counter and then adding the value of the _____ in program memory.   *Ans.* 2, offset

10.97 In 6800 relative addressing, an offset of 11111100 indicates a _____ (backward, forward) branch.
Ans. backward (MSB = 1)

10.98 The AND *A* instruction in Fig. 10-26 can be used in one of _____ (number) addressing modes. The AND *A* instruction ANDs the contents of _____ _____ with the contents of a _____ location. The results of the ANDing are placed in _____ _____.
Ans. four, accumulator *A*, memory (*M*), accumulator *A*

10.99 While all the branch instructions use _____ addressing, the jump instructions use _____ and _____ addressing.   *Ans.* relative, indexed, extended

10.100 The COM *B* instruction in Fig. 10-26 causes the content of accumulator _____ to be changed to its _____ complement form, while the NEG *B* instruction causes the content of _____ _____ to be changed to its _____ _____ form.   *Ans.* B, 1s, accumulator B, 2s complement

10.101 Refer to Fig. 10-44. The op code for the ROL *A* instruction is _____ (hex).   *Ans.* 49H

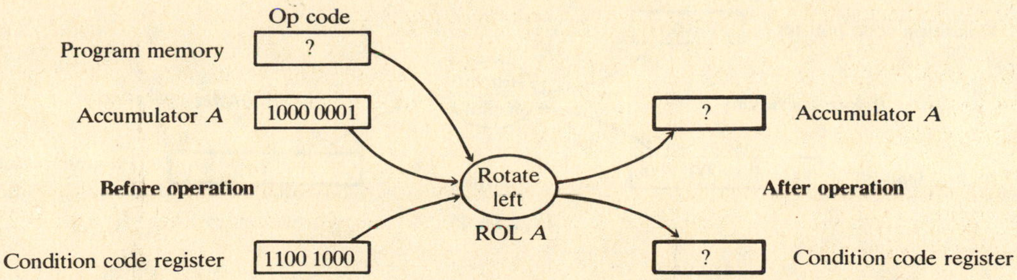

Fig. 10-44

10.102 Refer to Fig. 10-44. The contents of accumulator *A* after the ROL *A* operation will be _____ (8 bits).
Ans. 00000010

10.103 Refer to Fig. 10-44. The contents of the condition code register after the ROL *A* operation will be _____ (8 bits).   *Ans.* 11000011

10.104 Refer to Fig. 10-45. The op code for the SBA instruction is _____ (hex). This 1-byte instruction uses _____ addressing.   *Ans.*   10H, inherent (or implied)

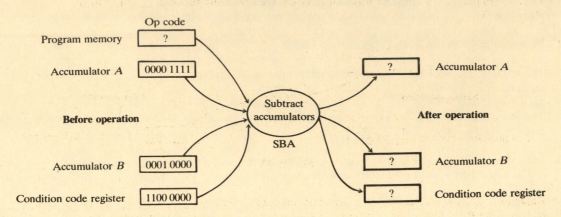

Fig. 10-45

10.105 Refer to Fig. 10-45. The contents of accumulator *A* after the SBA operation will be _____ (8 bits). *Ans.*   11111111 (2s complement representation of −1)

10.106 Refer to Fig. 10-45. The contents of the *CCR* after the "subtract accumulators" operation will be _____ (8 bits).   *Ans.*   11001001 (*N* and *C* flags changed)

10.107 The "return from subroutine" instruction is specified with the op code _____ (hex) or the mnemonic _____. This instruction is used at the end of all _____.   *Ans.*   39H, RTS, subroutines

10.108 Refer to Fig. 10-46. The "branch if plus" operation is specified with the op code 2AH or the mnemonic _____. The branch operation uses _____ addressing.   *Ans.*   BPL, relative

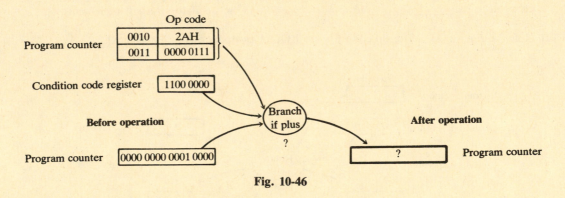

Fig. 10-46

10.109 Refer to Fig. 10-46. The "branch if plus" condition is _____ (false, true), based on the flag conditions.   *Ans.*   true (*N* = 0)

10.110 Refer to Fig. 10-46. The contents of the program counter after the "branch if plus" operation will be _____ (hex).   *Ans.*   0019H [(0010 + 2) + 7 = 0019H]

10.111 The offset in the indexed instruction is an 8-bit _____ value. However, the offset in the relative instruction is a _____ (number) -bit signed value.   *Ans.*   unsigned, 7

10.112 The WAI instruction in Fig. 10-38 pushes all the processor registers on the _____ and then enters the _____ loop.   *Ans.*   stack, wait

10.113 Refer to Fig. 10-47.   The CLI instruction is specified with the op code _____ (hex).
   Ans.   0EH

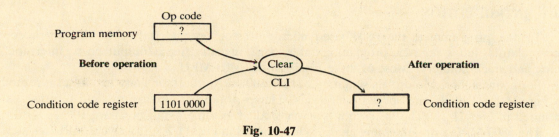

Fig. 10-47

10.114 Refer to Fig. 10-47.   The CLI instruction specifies the "clear _____ _____" operation.   It _____ (resets, sets) the *I* flag in the condition code register.   *Ans.*   interrupt mask, resets

10.115 Refer to Fig. 10-47.   The contents of the condition code register after the CLI operation will be _____ (8 bits).   *Ans.*   11000000 (*I* flag cleared)

Chapter 11

Programming the 6800 Microprocessor

11.1 INTRODUCTION

To the programmer, the 6800-based microprocessor system consists of the instruction set, accumulators, index register, program counter, flags, memory, input/output ports, interrupts, and stack and stack pointer. Most of these reside in the 6800 MPU.

For convenience, Motorola's summary of the 6800 microprocessor's instruction set is reproduced in Fig. 11-1. Details on "special operations" (jumps, branches, interrupts, and returns) are also included in Fig. 11-1. The instruction set was studied in some detail in Chap. 10.

The 6800 MPU's programming model is reproduced in Fig. 11-2. It lists the MPU registers that concern the programmer. The condition code register is also shown in some detail in Fig. 11-2.

The 6800-based system's memory map that will be used in this chapter is shown in Fig. 11-3. The lowest 512_{10} addresses (0000H through 01FFH) are reserved for user programs and data. In real applications, some of these RAM locations may be reserved for special purposes. The highest 1024_{10} addresses (FC00H through FFFFH) are for ROM. The ROM would contain a monitor program for initializing the system. It would also contain interrupt vectors in memory locations FFF8H through FFFFH. The ROM would also hold many other valuable user subroutines. The 6800 system uses memory-mapped I/O. To the programmer, accessing a peripheral device is a matter of "storing the accumulator to memory location 5002H" for output. Accessing an input device in this 6800 system is a matter of "loading the accumulator from location 5000H." Input and output ports are treated as if they were memory locations.

The steps in developing any program for a microprocessor system were summarized in Chap. 6: (1) define and analyze the problem, (2) flowchart the problem solution, (3) write the assembly language program, (4) write or generate the machine language version of the program, (5) debug the program, and (6) document the program. All techniques used with the generic and 8080/8085 processors can be used with a 6800-based system. The changes will be in the assembly language format and the actual mnemonics and op codes. Mnemonics and op codes are not standard from processor to processor.

The six fields shown in Fig. 11-4 will be used in this chapter when dealing with object and source programs for the 6800-based system. The machine code or object program is listed at the left in Fig. 11-4. The *address field* will contain the program memory address in hexadecimal. The *contents field* will hold the op codes and operands (also in hexadecimal). This field is also sometimes called the object code field.

The source program or assembly language part of the 6800 instruction format is shown at the right in Fig. 11-4. The *label field* may or may not contain a "title" for the line. The *mnemonic field* is sometimes called the operator field. It contains the 6800's mnemonics which specify an operation. The *operand field* contains information on the addressing mode and holds the operand. The operand is a value, address, or label that references one of them. The *comment field* is used to help explain what each line of the program is doing.

Several unique 6800 assembly language conventions are illustrated in Fig. 11-5. Each assembly language line in this example represents a "load accumulator A" instruction. Therefore, each line starts with the same mnemonic of LDA A. However, the addressing mode used in each line is different.

The first assembly language line in Fig. 11-5 represents the "load accumulator A immediate" operation. The # sign in the operand field means immediate addressing. The $ sign means that the number following is in hexadecimal.

The second and third lines in Fig. 11-5 represent the "load accumulator A" operation in the direct and extended addressing modes. No special symbol is used for either. If the operand

ADDRESSING MODES / BOOLEAN/ARITHMETIC OPERATION / COND. CODE REG.

OPERATIONS	MNEMONIC	IMMED OP	~	=	DIRECT OP	~	=	INDEX OP	~	=	EXTND OP	~	=	IMPLIED OP	~	=	BOOLEAN/ARITHMETIC OPERATION (All register labels refer to contents)	H (5)	I (4)	N (3)	Z (2)	V (1)	C (0)
Add	ADDA	8B	2	2	9B	3	2	AB	5	2	BB	4	3				A + M → A	↕	•	↕	↕	↕	↕
	ADDB	CB	2	2	DB	3	2	EB	5	2	FB	4	3				B + M → B	↕	•	↕	↕	↕	↕
Add Acmltrs	ABA													1B	2	1	A + B → A	↕	•	↕	↕	↕	↕
Add with Carry	ADCA	89	2	2	99	3	2	A9	5	2	B9	4	3				A + M + C → A	↕	•	↕	↕	↕	↕
	ADCB	C9	2	2	D9	3	2	E9	5	2	F9	4	3				B + M + C → B	↕	•	↕	↕	↕	↕
And	ANDA	84	2	2	94	3	2	A4	5	2	B4	4	3				A · M → A	•	•	↕	↕	R	•
	ANDB	C4	2	2	D4	3	2	E4	5	2	F4	4	3				B · M → B	•	•	↕	↕	R	•
Bit Test	BITA	85	2	2	95	3	2	A5	5	2	B5	4	3				A · M	•	•	↕	↕	R	•
	BITB	C5	2	2	D5	3	2	E5	5	2	F5	4	3				B · M	•	•	↕	↕	R	•
Clear	CLR							6F	7	2	7F	6	3				00 → M	•	•	R	S	R	R
	CLRA													4F	2	1	00 → A	•	•	R	S	R	R
	CLRB													5F	2	1	00 → B	•	•	R	S	R	R
Compare	CMPA	81	2	2	91	3	2	A1	5	2	B1	4	3				A − M	•	•	↕	↕	↕	↕
	CMPB	C1	2	2	D1	3	2	E1	5	2	F1	4	3				B − M	•	•	↕	↕	↕	↕
Compare Acmltrs	CBA													11	2	1	A − B	•	•	↕	↕	↕	↕
Complement, 1's	COM							63	7	2	73	6	3				$\overline{M}$ → M	•	•	↕	↕	R	S
	COMA													43	2	1	$\overline{A}$ → A	•	•	↕	↕	R	S
	COMB													53	2	1	$\overline{B}$ → B	•	•	↕	↕	R	S
Complement, 2's (Negate)	NEG							60	7	2	70	6	3				00 − M → M	•	•	↕	↕	①	②
	NEGA													40	2	1	00 − A → A	•	•	↕	↕	①	②
	NEGB													50	2	1	00 − B → B	•	•	↕	↕	①	②
Decimal Adjust, A	DAA													19	2	1	Converts Binary Add. of BCD Characters into BCD Format	•	•	↕	↕	↕	③
Decrement	DEC							6A	7	2	7A	6	3				M − 1 → M	•	•	↕	↕	④	•
	DECA													4A	2	1	A − 1 → A	•	•	↕	↕	④	•
	DECB													5A	2	1	B − 1 → B	•	•	↕	↕	④	•
Exclusive OR	EORA	88	2	2	98	3	2	A8	5	2	B8	4	3				A ⊕ M → A	•	•	↕	↕	R	•
	EORB	C8	2	2	D8	3	2	E8	5	2	F8	4	3				B ⊕ M → B	•	•	↕	↕	R	•
Increment	INC							6C	7	2	7C	6	3				M + 1 → M	•	•	↕	↕	⑤	•
	INCA													4C	2	1	A + 1 → A	•	•	↕	↕	⑤	•
	INCB													5C	2	1	B + 1 → B	•	•	↕	↕	⑤	•
Load Acmltr	LDAA	86	2	2	96	3	2	A6	5	2	B6	4	3				M → A	•	•	↕	↕	R	•
	LDAB	C6	2	2	D6	3	2	E6	5	2	F6	4	3				M → B	•	•	↕	↕	R	•
Or, Inclusive	ORAA	8A	2	2	9A	3	2	AA	5	2	BA	4	3				A + M → A	•	•	↕	↕	R	•
	ORAB	CA	2	2	DA	3	2	EA	5	2	FA	4	3				B + M → B	•	•	↕	↕	R	•
Push Data	PSHA													36	4	1	A → M$_{SP}$, SP − 1 → SP	•	•	•	•	•	•
	PSHB													37	4	1	B → M$_{SP}$, SP − 1 → SP	•	•	•	•	•	•
Pull Data	PULA													32	4	1	SP + 1 → SP, M$_{SP}$ → A	•	•	•	•	•	•
	PULB													33	4	1	SP + 1 → SP, M$_{SP}$ → B	•	•	•	•	•	•
Rotate Left	ROL							69	7	2	79	6	3				M	•	•	↕	↕	⑥	↕
	ROLA													49	2	1	A	•	•	↕	↕	⑥	↕
	ROLB													59	2	1	B	•	•	↕	↕	⑥	↕
Rotate Right	ROR							66	7	2	76	6	3				M	•	•	↕	↕	⑥	↕
	RORA													46	2	1	A	•	•	↕	↕	⑥	↕
	RORB													56	2	1	B	•	•	↕	↕	⑥	↕
Shift Left, Arithmetic	ASL							68	7	2	78	6	3				M	•	•	↕	↕	⑥	↕
	ASLA													48	2	1	A	•	•	↕	↕	⑥	↕
	ASLB													58	2	1	B	•	•	↕	↕	⑥	↕
Shift Right, Arithmetic	ASR							67	7	2	77	6	3				M	•	•	↕	↕	⑥	↕
	ASRA													47	2	1	A	•	•	↕	↕	⑥	↕
	ASRB													57	2	1	B	•	•	↕	↕	⑥	↕
Shift Right, Logic	LSR							64	7	2	74	6	3				M	•	•	R	↕	⑥	↕
	LSRA													44	2	1	A	•	•	R	↕	⑥	↕
	LSRB													54	2	1	B	•	•	R	↕	⑥	↕
Store Acmltr.	STAA				97	4	2	A7	6	2	B7	5	3				A → M	•	•	↕	↕	R	•
	STAB				D7	4	2	E7	6	2	F7	5	3				B → M	•	•	↕	↕	R	•
Subtract	SUBA	80	2	2	90	3	2	A0	5	2	B0	4	3				A − M → A	•	•	↕	↕	↕	↕
	SUBB	C0	2	2	D0	3	2	E0	5	2	F0	4	3				B − M → B	•	•	↕	↕	↕	↕
Subtract Acmltrs.	SBA													10	2	1	A − B → A	•	•	↕	↕	↕	↕
Subtr. with Carry	SBCA	82	2	2	92	3	2	A2	5	2	B2	4	3				A − M − C → A	•	•	↕	↕	↕	↕
	SBCB	C2	2	2	D2	3	2	E2	5	2	F2	4	3				B − M − C → B	•	•	↕	↕	↕	↕
Transfer Acmltrs	TAB													16	2	1	A → B	•	•	↕	↕	R	•
	TBA													17	2	1	B → A	•	•	↕	↕	R	•
Test, Zero or Minus	TST							6D	7	2	7D	6	3				M − 00	•	•	↕	↕	R	R
	TSTA													4D	2	1	A − 00	•	•	↕	↕	R	R
	TSTB													5D	2	1	B − 00	•	•	↕	↕	R	R

Condition Code Register columns: H I N Z V C

LEGEND:

OP	Operation Code (Hexadecimal);	M$_{SP}$	Contents of memory location pointed to be Stack Pointer;	00	Byte = Zero;	R Reset Always
~	Number of MPU Cycles;	+	Boolean Inclusive OR;	H	Half-carry from bit 3;	S Set Always
#	Number of Program Bytes;	⊕	Boolean Exclusive OR;	I	Interrupt mask	↕ Test and set if true, cleared otherwise
+	Arithmetic Plus;	M	Complement of M;	N	Negative (sign bit)	• Not Affected
−	Arithmetic Minus;	→	Transfer Into;	Z	Zero (byte)	CCR Condition Code Register
·	Boolean AND;	0	Bit = Zero;	V	Overflow, 2's complement	LS Least Significant
				C	Carry from bit 7	MS Most Significant

(a) Accumulator and memory instructions

Fig. 11-1 The 6800 MPU's instruction set (*Courtesy of Motorola, Inc.*)

POINTER OPERATIONS	MNEMONIC	IMMED OP	~	#	DIRECT OP	~	#	INDEX OP	~	#	EXTND OP	~	#	IMPLIED OP	~	#	BOOLEAN/ARITHMETIC OPERATION	5 H	4 I	3 N	2 Z	1 V	0 C
Compare Index Reg	CPX	8C	3	3	9C	4	2	AC	6	2	BC	5	3				$X_H - M, X_L - (M + 1)$	•	•	①	↕	②	•
Decrement Index Reg	DEX													09	4	1	$X - 1 \rightarrow X$	•	•	•	↕	•	•
Decrement Stack Pntr	DES													34	4	1	$SP - 1 \rightarrow SP$	•	•	•	•	•	•
Increment Index Reg	INX													08	4	1	$X + 1 \rightarrow X$	•	•	•	↕	•	•
Increment Stack Pntr	INS													31	4	1	$SP + 1 \rightarrow SP$	•	•	•	•	•	•
Load Index Reg	LDX	CE	3	3	DE	4	2	EE	6	2	FE	5	3				$M \rightarrow X_H, (M + 1) \rightarrow X_L$	•	•	③	↕	R	•
Load Stack Pntr	LDS	8E	3	3	9E	4	2	AE	6	2	BE	5	3				$M \rightarrow SP_H, (M + 1) \rightarrow SP_L$	•	•	③	↕	R	•
Store Index Reg	STX				DF	5	2	EF	7	2	FF	6	3				$X_H \rightarrow M, X_L \rightarrow (M + 1)$	•	•	③	↕	R	•
Store Stack Pntr	STS				9F	5	2	AF	7	2	BF	6	3				$SP_H \rightarrow M, SP_L \rightarrow (M + 1)$	•	•	③	↕	R	•
Indx Reg → Stack Pntr	TXS													35	4	1	$X - 1 \rightarrow SP$	•	•	•	•	•	•
Stack Pntr → Indx Reg	TSX													30	4	1	$SP + 1 \rightarrow X$	•	•	•	•	•	•

(b)   Index register and stack manipulation instructions

OPERATIONS	MNEMONIC	RELATIVE OP	~	#	INDEX OP	~	#	EXTND OP	~	#	IMPLIED OP	~	#	BRANCH TEST	5 H	4 I	3 N	2 Z	1 V	0 C
Branch Always	BRA	20	4	2										None	•	•	•	•	•	•
Branch If Carry Clear	BCC	24	4	2										$C = 0$	•	•	•	•	•	•
Branch If Carry Set	BCS	25	4	2										$C = 1$	•	•	•	•	•	•
Branch If = Zero	BEQ	27	4	2										$Z = 1$	•	•	•	•	•	•
Branch If ⩾ Zero	BGE	2C	4	2										$N \oplus V = 0$	•	•	•	•	•	•
Branch If > Zero	BGT	2E	4	2										$Z + (N \oplus V) = 0$	•	•	•	•	•	•
Branch If Higher	BHI	22	4	2										$C + Z = 0$	•	•	•	•	•	•
Branch If ⩽ Zero	BLE	2F	4	2										$Z + (N \oplus V) = 1$	•	•	•	•	•	•
Branch If Lower Or Same	BLS	23	4	2										$C + Z = 1$	•	•	•	•	•	•
Branch If < Zero	BLT	2D	4	2										$N \oplus V = 1$	•	•	•	•	•	•
Branch If Minus	BMI	2B	4	2										$N = 1$	•	•	•	•	•	•
Branch If Not Equal Zero	BNE	26	4	2										$Z = 0$	•	•	•	•	•	•
Branch If Overflow Clear	BVC	28	4	2										$V = 0$	•	•	•	•	•	•
Branch If Overflow Set	BVS	29	4	2										$V = 1$	•	•	•	•	•	•
Branch If Plus	BPL	2A	4	2										$N = 0$	•	•	•	•	•	•
Branch To Subroutine	BSR	8D	8	2										} See Special Operations	•	•	•	•	•	•
Jump	JMP				6E	4	2	7E	3	3				} See Special Operations	•	•	•	•	•	•
Jump To Subroutine	JSR				AD	8	2	BD	9	3				}	•	•	•	•	•	•
No Operation	NOP										01	2	1	Advances Prog. Cntr. Only	•	•	•	•	•	•
Return From Interrupt	RTI										3B	10	1		—	①	—	—	—	—
Return From Subroutine	RTS										39	5	1	}	•	•	•	•	•	•
Software Interrupt	SWI										3F	12	1	} See Special Operations	•	•	•	•	•	•
Wait for Interrupt*	WAI										3E	9	1	}	•	②	•	•	•	•

(c)   Jump and branch instructions

OPERATIONS	MNEMONIC	IMPLIED OP	~	#	BOOLEAN OPERATION	5 H	4 I	3 N	2 Z	1 V	0 C
Clear Carry	CLC	0C	2	1	$0 \rightarrow C$	•	•	•	•	•	R
Clear Interrupt Mask	CLI	0E	2	1	$0 \rightarrow I$	•	R	•	•	•	•
Clear Overflow	CLV	0A	2	1	$0 \rightarrow V$	•	•	•	•	R	•
Set Carry	SEC	0D	2	1	$1 \rightarrow C$	•	•	•	•	•	S
Set Interrupt Mask	SEI	0F	2	1	$1 \rightarrow I$	•	S	•	•	•	•
Set Overflow	SEV	0B	2	1	$1 \rightarrow V$	•	•	•	•	S	•
Acmltr A → CCR	TAP	06	2	1	$A \rightarrow CCR$	—	—	①	—	—	—
CCR → Acmltr A	TPA	07	2	1	$CCR \rightarrow A$	•	•	•	•	•	•

CONDITION CODE REGISTER NOTES:

(Bit set if test is true and cleared otherwise)

①   (Bit V)   Test: Result = 10000000?

②   (Bit C)   Test: Result ≠ 00000000?

③   (Bit C)   Test: Decimal value of most significant BCD Character greater than nine? (Not cleared if previously set.)

④   (Bit V)   Test: Operand = 10000000 prior to execution?

⑤   (Bit V)   Test: Operand = 01111111 prior to execution?

⑥   (Bit V)   Test: Set equal to result of $N \oplus C$ after shift has occurred.

⑦   (Bit N)   Test: Sign bit of most significant (MS) byte of result = 1?

⑧   (Bit V)   Test: 2's complement overflow from subtraction of MS bytes?

⑨   (Bit N)   Test: Result less than zero? (Bit 15 = 1)

⑩   (All)   Load Condition Code Register from Stack. (See Special Operations)

⑪   (Bit I)   Set when interrupt occurs if previously set a Nonmaskable interrupt is required to exit the wait state.

⑫   (ALL)   Set according to the contents of Accumulator A.

(d)   Condition code register manipulation instructions

Fig. 11-1 (cont.)

JSR, JUMP TO SUBROUTINE:

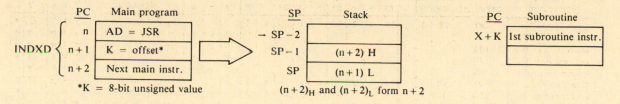

BSR, BRANCH TO SUBROUTINE:

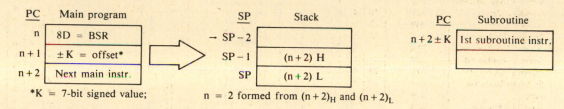

JMP, JUMP:

RTS, RETURN FROM SUBROUTINE:

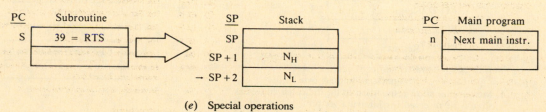

(e) Special operations

Fig. 11-1 (cont.)

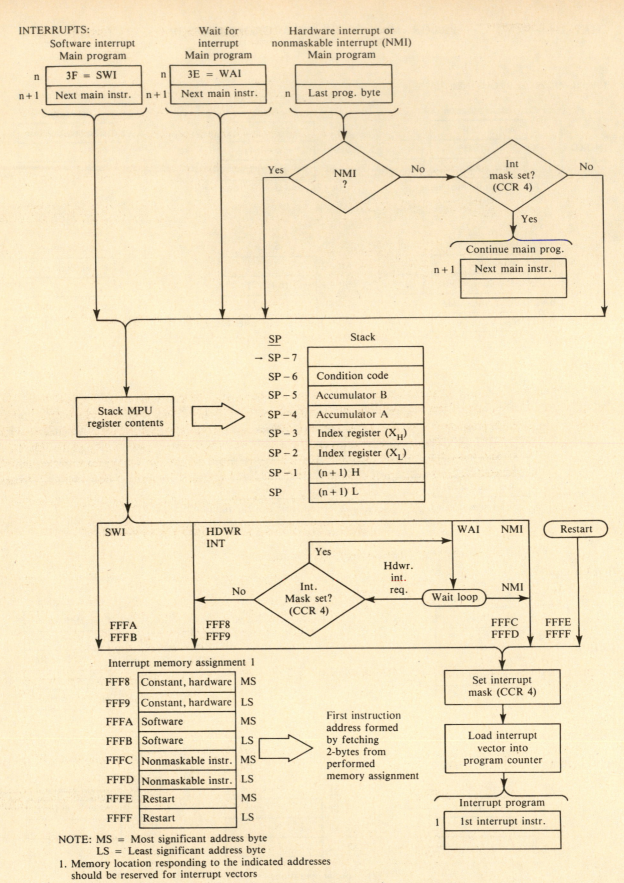

INTERRUPTS:

| | | Software interrupt Main program | | | Wait for interrupt Main program | | | Hardware interrupt or nonmaskable interrupt (NMI) Main program |

n | 3F = SWI

n+1 | Next main instr.

n | 3E = WAI

n+1 | Next main instr.

n | Last prog. byte

NMI ?

Yes → No → Int mask set? (CCR 4) → No

Yes

Continue main prog.

n+1 | Next main instr.

Stack MPU register contents

SP	Stack
→ SP – 7	
SP – 6	Condition code
SP – 5	Accumulator B
SP – 4	Accumulator A
SP – 3	Index register (X_H)
SP – 2	Index register (X_L)
SP – 1	(n + 1) H
SP	(n + 1) L

SWI   HDWR INT   WAI   NMI   Restart

Yes

Hdwr. int. req.

No ← Int. Mask set? (CCR 4)

Wait loop   NMI

FFFA   FFF8   FFFC   FFFE
FFFB   FFF9   FFFD   FFFF

Interrupt memory assignment 1

FFF8	Constant, hardware	MS
FFF9	Constant, hardware	LS
FFFA	Software	MS
FFFB	Software	LS
FFFC	Nonmaskable instr.	MS
FFFD	Nonmaskable instr.	LS
FFFE	Restart	MS
FFFF	Restart	LS

First instruction address formed by fetching 2-bytes from performed memory assignment

Set interrupt mask (CCR 4)

Load interrupt vector into program counter

Interrupt program

1 | 1st interrupt instr.

NOTE: MS = Most significant address byte
LS = Least significant address byte
1. Memory location responding to the indicated addresses
should be reserved for interrupt vectors

(e) Special operations (cont.)

Fig. 11-1 (cont.)

RTI, RETURN FROM INTERRUPT:

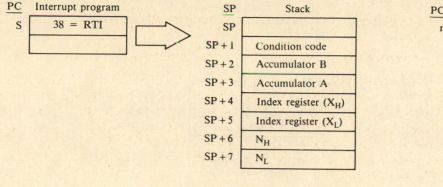

(e)   Special operations (cont.)

Fig. 11-1 (cont.)

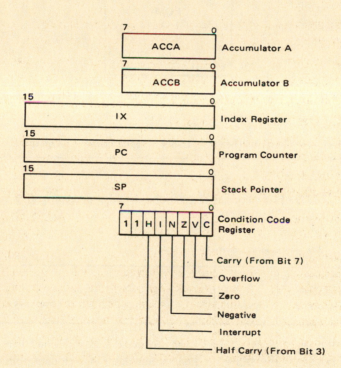

Fig. 11-2   The programming model of the 6800 MPU (*Courtesy of Motorola, Inc.*)

(address) is FFH or less, the assembler automatically assigns the "load accumulator *A* direct" op code.   If, however, the operand (address) is greater than FFH, the assembler assigns the "load accumulator *A* extended" op code.

The last assembly language line in Fig. 11-5 represents the "load accumulator *A* indexed" operation.   The number 3 in the operand field represents the offset.   The *X* means the instruction uses indexed addressing.

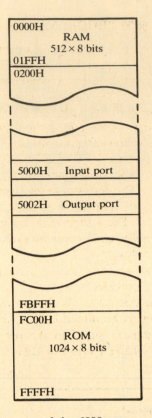

Fig. 11-3 Memory map of the 6800 system used in this chapter

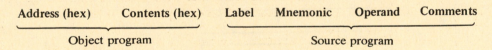

Fig. 11-4 Format of 6800 object and source programs

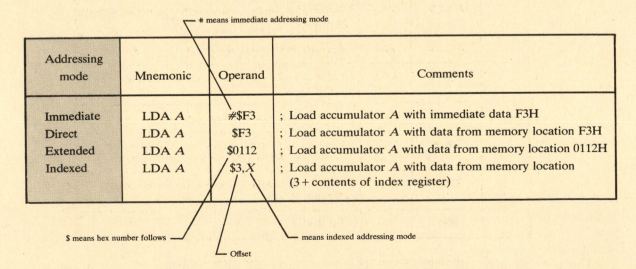

Fig. 11-5 Some conventional practices used in 6800 assembly language statements

11.2 INTERPRETING A SIMPLE 6800 PROGRAM

A simple 6800 MPU program segment will be interpreted in this section. The program is detailed in Fig. 11-6.   The task of the program segment is to add three hexadecimal numbers located at memory locations 0020H, 0030H, and 0040H.   The 2-byte sum will be stored in two consecutive memory locations (0050H and 0051H).   The 6800 source or assembly language program to complete this task is listed in Fig. 11-6a.   The memory map in Fig. 11-6b locates the program memory, the memory locations of the three numbers to be added, and the locations used for storing the 2-byte sum.   The memory map in Fig. 11-6b shows that the numbers to be added in this example are FFH, 04H, and FEH.   The sample addition of FF + 04 + FE = 0201H.

The first three instructions in the program segment in Fig. 11-6a are used to initialize the index register and accumulators A and B.   The index register is initialized to 0020H by the "load index register immediate" instruction.   Recall that the # symbol in the LDX #$0020 instruction represents the immediate addressing mode.   The $ symbol in this instruction means the following number (0020 in this example) is in hexadecimal notation.   Accumulators A and B are cleared to 00H by the inherent CLR A and CLR B instructions.

The ADD B $00,X instruction in line 4 in Fig. 11-6a represents an "add memory contents to accumulator B" operation.   The X shows that this instruction uses indexed addressing.   The offset is 00H, as noted by the $00 part of the operand.   With the index register initialized at 0020H and the offset equal to 00H, the first number to be added comes from memory location 0020H (0020H + offset of 00H = 0020H).   In like manner, line 5 in the program segment in Fig. 11-6a adds the contents of memory location 0030H (0020H + offset of 10H = 0030H) to the contents of accumulator B.

	Label	Mnemonic	Operand	Comments
1		LDX	#$0020	; Initialize index register to 0020H
2		CLR A		; Clear accumulator A
3		CLR B		; Clear accumulator B
4		ADD B	$00,X	; Add first number from memory location (X + offset of 00H) to accumulator B
5		ADD B	$10,X	; Add second number from memory location (X + offset of 10H) to accumulator B
6		ADC A	#$00	; Add 00H and carry to accumulator A
7		ADD B	$20,X	; Add third number from memory location (X + offset of 20H) to accumulator B
8		ADC A	#$00	; Add 00H and carry to accumulator A
9		STA A	$30,X	; Store most significant byte of sum in memory location (X + offset of 30H)
10		STA B	$31,X	; Store least significant byte of sum in memory location (X + offset of 31H)
11		WAI		; Halt MPU

(a) Assembly language program to add numbers from three memory locations

Fig. 11-6

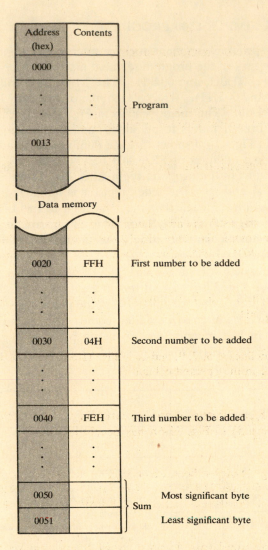

(b) Memory map used to add numbers from three memory locations program

Fig. 11-6 (*cont.*)

The ADC *A* #$00 instruction in line 6 of Fig. 11-6*a* represents an "add with carry immediate" operation. In effect, this instruction adds the contents of the carry flag to accumulator *A*. The carry flag was set or reset by the last ADD *B* instruction in line 5.

The ADD *B* $20,*X* instruction in line 7 of Fig. 11-6*a* adds the third number from data memory to the partial sum in accumulator *B*. The third number's memory location is 0040H (0020H + offset of 20H = 0040H). Next, the ADC *A* #$00 instruction in line 8 adds any carry to accumulator *A*. The accumulated carries are now located in accumulator *A*. This is the most significant byte of the sum. The least significant byte of the sum is now located in accumulator *B*.

The STA *A* $30,*X* instruction in line 9 in Fig. 11-6*a* represents the "store accumulator *A* indexed" instruction. It stores the contents of accumulator *A* in memory location 0050H (0020 + offset of 30H = 0050H). This is the most significant byte of the sum. In like manner, the least significant byte of the sum is stored in memory location 0051H (0020H + offset of 31H = 0051H) by the STA *B* $31,*X* in line 10. Finally, the WAI instruction in line 11 in Fig. 11-6*a* halts the microprocessor unit.

SOLVED PROBLEMS

11.1 List the three instructions from the program segment in Fig. 11-6a that use inherent, or implied, addressing.

Solution:

Inherent instructions do not need an operand.   Therefore, the three instructions in Fig. 11-6a that do not have an operand and use inherent, or implied, addressing are CLR A, CLR B, and WAI.

11.2 List the three instructions from the program segment in Fig. 11-6a that use immediate addressing.

Solution:

The # symbol in the 6800 assembly language listing means the instruction uses the immediate addressing mode.   Therefore, the three instructions in Fig. 11-6a that use immediate addressing are LDX #$0020 (line 1), ADC A #$00 (line 6), and ADC A #$00 (line 8).

11.3 The instructions on lines 4, 5, 7, 9, and 10 of the program segment in Fig. 11-6a all use the _____ addressing mode.

Solution:

The instructions on lines 4, 5, 7, 9, and 10 in Fig. 11-6a all use the indexed addressing mode.   This is symbolized by the X in the operand column.

11.4 List the contents of accumulators A and B, carry flag, and index register just after the ADD B $10,X instruction (line 5) in Fig. 11-6a has been executed.

Solution:

After line 5 in Fig. 11-6a has been executed, the register contents will be as follows:
Accumulator A = 00H (cleared in line 2)   Carry flag = set to 1 (because of carry in line 5)
Accumulator B = 03H (FF + 04 = 1 03H)   Index register = 0020H (loaded in line 1)

11.5 List the contents of accumulators A and B, carry flag, and index register just after the ADD B $20,X, instruction (line 7) in Fig. 11-6a has been executed.

Solution:

After line 7 in Fig. 11-6a has been executed, the register contents will be as follows:
Accumulator A = 01H (carry added in line 6)   Carry flag = set to 1 (because of carry in line 7)
Accumulator B = 01H (FF + 04 + FE = 201H)   Index register = 0020H (loaded in line 1)

11.6 List the contents of accumulators A and B just after the ADC A #$00 instruction in line 8 in Fig. 11-6a has been executed.

Solution:

After line 8 in Fig. 11-6a, accumulator A contains the most significant byte of the sum, while accumulator B holds the least significant byte.   Solving the hexadecimal addition in Fig. 11-6 yields FF + 04 + FE = 201H.   Therefore, accumulator A contains 02H after line 8 in the program segment, while accumulator B holds 01H.

11.7 List the contents of memory locations 0050H and 0051H in Fig. 11-6 after the entire program segment has been executed.

Solution:

After the program segment in Fig. 11-6a has been executed, the contents of the "sum" data memory locations in Fig. 11-6b will be:

Memory location 0050H = 02H (high-order byte)
Memory location 0051H = 01H (low-order byte)

11.8   Using the 6800 instruction set, give the object program (machine code) for the program segment in Fig. 11-6a.   Use program memory locations 0000H through 0013H.

Solution:

Refer to the 6800 instruction set in Fig. 11-1.   The object program or machine code for the program segment in Fig. 11-6a may be assembled as follows:

Address (hex)	Contents (hex)
0000	CE
0001	00
0002	20
0003	4F
0004	5F
0005	EB
0006	00
0007	EB
0008	10
0009	89
000A	00
000B	EB
000C	20
000D	89
000E	00
000F	A7
0010	30
0011	E7
0012	31
0013	3E

11.9   Draw a detailed flowchart for the program segment shown in Fig. 11-6a.

Solution:

See one possible solution in Fig. 11-7.

11.3   USING THE INDEX REGISTER

The 6800's index register is used in conjunction with the indexed mode of addressing.   Indexed addressing is often referred to as the most powerful mode of addressing available to the 6800 MPU.   The index register is often used when a program must deal with data in table form.   The simple program segment detailed in this section will be used to illustrate the use of simple tables and the index register.   Forward and backward branches will also be illustrated in the example that follows.

Consider the source or assembly language program listed for the 6800 MPU in Fig. 11-8a.   It will add numbers from the augend and addend tables in Fig. 11-8b and place the sum in the table at the bottom of this memory map.   For instance, the program will first add 01 + 02, placing the sum of 03H in the "sums table" at memory location 0040H.   Then it will repeat the action by adding 03 + 04, placing the sum of 07H in the "sums table" at memory location 0041H, etc.   The program

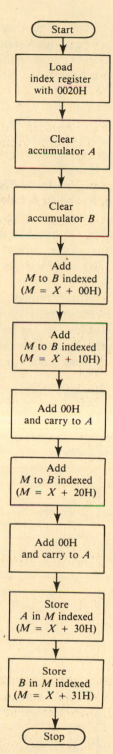

Fig. 11-7 Detailed flowchart for the adding program

in Fig. 11-8a also has a feature that will terminate the program if the sum of the numbers exceeds FFH.

The first instruction in the program segment listed in Fig. 11-8a will initialize the index register to 0020H. The second instruction (see line 2 in Fig. 11-8a) is a "load accumulator A indexed" operation.   The LDA *A* $00,*X* instruction loads a number from the augend table in data memory into accumulator *A*.   The very first number to be loaded in this example will be 01H from memory location 0020H (0020H + offset of 00H = 0020H).   Note that the instruction in line 2 has a label of LOOP and is the target of a backward branch from the BNE LOOP operation near the bottom of the program segment.

The ADD *A* $10,*X* instruction (see line 3 in Fig. 11-8*a*) adds the addend in data memory to the augend which is in accumulator *A*.   The addend's memory location will be 0030H (0020H + offset of 10H = 0030H) on the first pass through the program segment.

The fourth instruction (BCS STOP) in Fig. 11-8*a* checks whether the carry flag is set to 1.   If not, the program will continue normally.   If the *C* flag = 1, an error will occur if the contents of the accumulator are stored.   Because an error is about to occur, the processor is directed to branch forward to the end of the program segment by the BCS instruction.   The final wait or halt operation uses the symbolic address of STOP in this example.

Assuming no carry, the program continues to line 5 of the program segment in Fig. 11-8*a*.   The STA *A* $20,*X* instruction causes the sum in accumulator *A* to be stored in the sum table.   On the first pass through the program segment, the sum will be stored at data memory location 0040H (0020H + offset of 20H = 0040H).

The INX instruction on line 6 in Fig. 11-8*a* increments the contents of the index register.   The CPX #$0025 instruction on line 7 compares the current contents of the index register with one higher than the last address in the tables.   If the index register has not reached this address (0025H in this example), the *Z* flag is reset to 0 and the branch condition for the BNE LOOP instruction is met.   Recall that a compare instruction is a subtract operation that is used to set or reset the *Z*

	Label	Mnemonic	Operand	Comments
1		LDX	#$0020	; Initialize index register at 0020H
2	LOOP	LDA *A*	$00,*X*	; Load augend from first table in memory (*X* + offset of 00H) into accumulator *A*
3		ADD *A*	$10,*X*	; Add addend from second table in memory (*X* + offset of 10H) to accumulator *A*
4		BCS	STOP	; If *C* flag = 1, then branch forward to STOP (stop program if any sum is greater than FFH)
5		STA *A*	$20,*X*	; Store accumulator *A* (sum) in third table in memory (*X* + offset of 20H)
6		INX		; Increment contents of index register
7		CPX	#$0025	; Compare index register with 0025H (subtract 0025H from contents of index register)
8		BNE	LOOP	; If *Z* flag = 0, then branch back to symbolic address called LOOP
9	STOP	WAI		; Halt MPU

(*a*) Assembly language program for adding from tables

Fig. 11-8

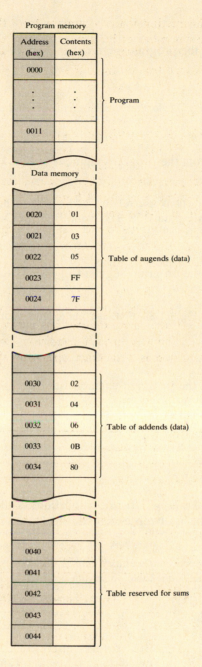

(b) Memory map used for adding-from-tables program

Fig. 11-8 (*cont.*)

flag.   The BNE LOOP instruction in line 8 in Fig. 11-8*a* checks the *Z* flag.   If the *Z* flag = 0, the branch test is true for the BNE instruction and the processor branches back to the symbolic address LOOP (line 2).   When the index register has been incremented to 0025H, the compare operation will cause the *Z* flag to be set to 1.   The branch test for the BNE instruction will be false, and the processor will not branch but continue to the next sequential operation.   The final instruction is the WAI operation, which halts the microprocessor unit.

SOLVED PROBLEMS

11.10 List the instructions from the program segment in Fig. 11-8a that use inherent, or implied, addressing.

Solution:

The two instructions in Fig. 11-8a that use inherent, or implied, addressing are INX and WAI.

11.11 List the two instructions from the program segment in Fig. 11-8a that use relative addressing.

Solution:

The 6800 branching instructions use relative addressing. Therefore, the two instructions in Fig. 11-8a that use relative addressing are BCS STOP and BNE LOOP.

11.12 List the instructions from the program segment in Fig. 11-8a that use immediate addressing.

Solution:

The two instructions in Fig. 11-8a that use immediate addressing are LDX #$0020 and CPX #$0025.

11.13 List the instructions from the program segment in Fig. 11-8a that use indexed addressing.

Solution:

The three instructions in Fig. 11-8a that use indexed addressing are LDA A $00,X; ADD A $10,X; and STA A $20X.

11.14 List the contents of the "sums table" (memory locations 0040–0044H) shown in Fig. 11-8 after the entire program segment has been executed.

Solution:

Refer to the program segment and memory map in Fig. 11-8. Also use the 6800 instruction set in Fig. 11-1. The contents of the "sums table" after the program segment in Fig. 11-8 is complete will be:

Address (hex)	Contents (hex)
0040	03H (01 + 02 = 03H)
0041	07H (03 + 04 = 07H)
0042	0BH (05 + 06 = 0BH)
0043	unpredictable (FF + 0B = 10AH)
	C flag = 1, branch to STOP
0044	unpredictable (program exited loop and did not store sum in this memory location)

11.15 Using the 6800 instruction set, give the object program (machine code) for the program segment in Fig. 11-8a. Use program memory locations 0000H through 0011H.

Solution:

Refer to the 6800 instruction set in Fig. 11-1. The object program (machine code) for the program segment in Fig. 11-8a may be assembled as follows:

Address (hex)	Contents (hex)
0000	CE
0001	00
0002	20
0003	A6
0004	00
0005	AB
0006	10
0007	25
0008	08
0009	A7
000A	20
000B	08
000C	8C
000D	00
000E	25
000F	26
0010	F2
0011	3E

11.16 Draw a detailed flowchart for the program segment in Fig. 11-8.

Solution:

See one possible solution in Fig. 11-9.

11.17 Which instruction in the program segment in Fig. 11-8a must be changed to extend the length of the tables?

Solution:

The CPX #$0025 instruction in Fig. 11-8a must be changed to extend the length of the tables.   For instance, if the tables were 10 bytes long (augend table would range from 0020 to 0029H), this instruction would read CPX #$002A.   The immediate data in the instruction would be one higher than the highest address in the first table.

11.4 A 6800 PROGRAM USING A LOOK-UP TABLE

The index register can be used in programs for converting one code to another.   The codes are many times placed in *look-up tables*.   In this section a program will be developed that gives the sine of a given angle.   This same type of program could be developed for other trigonometric conversions.

The detailed flowchart in Fig. 11-10a outlines how any angle from 1 to 89° can be converted into its sine.   The memory map for this program is drawn in Fig. 11-10b.   Of special interest in the memory map is the use of a look-up table in sequential memory locations from 0021H through 0079H.   The contents of this table are in BCD format and must be written into memory before executing the program.   The angle in question is stored in location 0015H (angle = 4° in this example).

The idea of the program is to use the input data (the angle) added to one less than the first address in the look-up table to point to the correct address in the table.   The BCD data stored at that look-up table location will finally be retrieved and stored at the memory location reserved for output data.   The output data will be the sine of the input angle.   The input data must be in hexadecimal, while the output sine of the angle will be in BCD format.

Consider block 1 in the detailed flowchart in Fig. 11-10a. This block represents the "load accumulator *A* direct" operation. The angle will be loaded from a memory location reserved for input data. According to Fig. 11-10b, input data will be loaded from memory location 0015H. In this example, the angle of 4° is loaded into accumulator *A* of the processor.

Block 2 in the flowchart represents the "add accumulator *A* immediate" operation. The immediate data is a number one less than the low-order byte of the starting address of the look-up

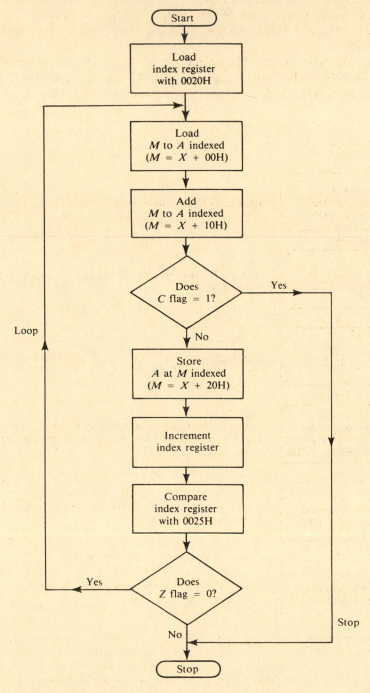

Fig. 11-9 Detailed flowchart for the adding-from-tables program

table. In this example, 0021H is the starting address of the look-up table. Therefore, 20H is the immediate data that must be added in block 2 of the flowchart.

Block 3 of the flowchart in Fig. 11-10a represents the "store accumulator A direct" operation. The sum in accumulator A is being temporarily stored at data memory location 0011H. Data memory locations 0010H and 0011H now hold the address that contains the sine of the angle.

Block 4 of the flowchart represents the "load index register direct" operation. The high-order byte of the index register is loaded from memory location 0010H. The high-order byte of the address is 00H. The low-order byte of the index register is loaded from memory location 0011H. In this example, 24H (20H + 04H = 24H) is loaded into the low-order byte of the index register.

Block 5 of the flowchart in Fig. 11-10a represents the "load accumulator B indexed" operation. The offset is 00H. The sine of the angle (in BCD format) is loaded into accumulator B from the memory address in the look-up table. In this example, the index register points to memory

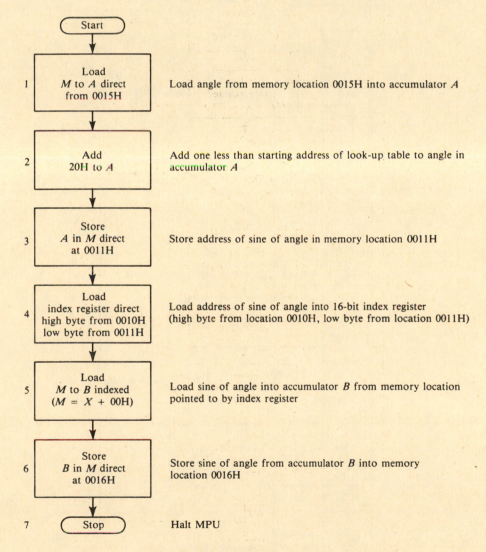

(a) Detailed flowchart for the sine-of-an-angle program

Fig. 11-10

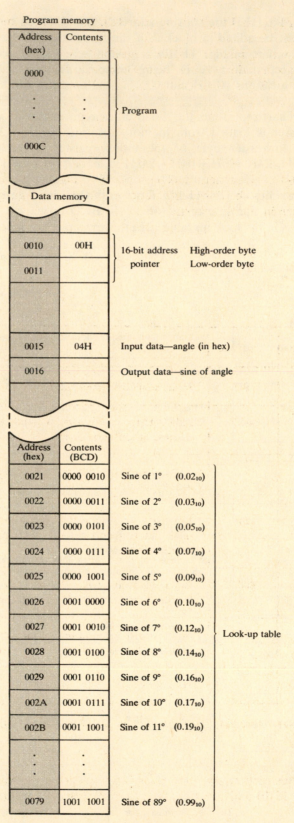

(*b*) Memory map for the sine-of-an-angle program

Fig. 11-10 (*cont.*)

location 0024H. According to Fig. 11-10*b*, the BCD contents of memory location 0024H are $0000\,0111_{BCD}$, which represents 0.07_{10}.

Block 6 of the flowchart represents the "store accumulator *B* direct" operation. The sine of the angle is stored in memory location 0016H, which has been reserved for output data. The output data in this case will be the sine of 4°, or $0000\,0111_{BCD}$. Block 7 in Fig. 11-10*a* represents the halt or wait operation.

SOLVED PROBLEMS

11.18 Refer to Fig. 11-10. Complete a 6800 assembly language version of the sine-of-an-angle program represented by the flowchart. Use one assembly language statement for each of the seven lower blocks in the flowchart.

Solution:

Refer to the 6800 instruction set in Fig. 11-1 and the flowchart and memory map in Fig. 11-10. One possible solution is shown in Fig. 11-11.

Label	Mnemonic	Operand	Comments
	LDA *A*	$15	; Input angle into accumulator *A* from memory location 0015H
	ADD *A*	#$20	; Add 20H to accumulator *A* (Add one less than beginning address of look-up table)
	STA *A*	$11	; Store *A* (address of sine of angle) in memory location 0011H
	LDX	$10	; Load address of sine of angle into index register (high-order byte from location 0010H, low-order byte from location 0011H)
	LDA *B*	$00,*X*	; Load accumulator B with sine of angle from memory location pointed to by index register
	STA *B*	$16	; Store sine of angle in output location (memory location 0016H)
	WAI		; Halt MPU

Fig. 11-11 Assembly language version of the sine-of-an-angle program

11.19 Using the 6800 instruction set, give the object program (machine code) for the program segment in Figs. 11-10 and 11-11. Use program memory locations 0000H through 000CH.

Solution:

Refer to the 6800 instruction set in Fig. 11-1. The object program (machine code) for the segment in Fig. 11-11 may be assembled as follows:

Address (hex)	Contents (hex)
0000	96
0001	15
0002	8B
0003	20
0004	97
0005	11
0006	DE
0007	10
0008	E6
0009	00
000A	D7
000B	16
000C	3E

11.20 Refer to Fig. 11-10. To find the sine of the angle 9°, memory location 0015H would be loaded with _____ (hex).

Solution:

See the memory map in Fig. 11-10*b*. Memory location 0015H would be loaded with 09H to find the sine of the angle 9°.

11.21 Refer to Fig. 11-12. The contents of data memory location 0016H after the execution of the program in Fig. 11-11 will be _____ (8 bits). This is the _____ (BCD, hexadecimal) representation of the sine of 9°, which is _____ (number in hundredths).

Solution:

See Fig. 11-10. The contents of data memory location 0016H in Fig. 11-12 after the execution of the program will be 0001 0110. This is the BCD representation of the sine of 9°, which is 0.16.

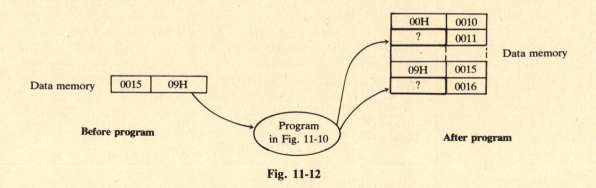

Fig. 11-12

11.22 Refer to Fig. 11-12. The contents of data memory location 0011H after the execution of the program in Fig. 11-11 will be _____ (hex). This is the low-order byte of the address in the _____-_____ _____ that contains the sine of 9°.

Solution:

The contents of data memory location 0011H after the execution of the program in Fig. 11-11 will be 29H (20H + 09H = 29H). This is the low-order byte of the address in the look-up table that contains the sine of 9°.

Supplementary Problems

11.23 To the programmer, a 6800-based microcomputer consists of the _____ set, accumulators A and B, _____ register, program _____, flags, memory, _____/_____ ports, interrupts, and stack and stack pointer. *Ans.* instruction, index, counter, input/output

11.24 According to the memory map in Fig. 11-3, address 00FFH is a _____ (RAM, ROM) location, while FFFFH is located in _____. Address 5002H in this system is the location of an _____ _____. *Ans.* RAM, ROM, output port

11.25 Refer to Fig. 11-6a. The first three instructions in this program segment are used to initialize the _____ register to _____ (hex), accumulator A to _____ (hex), and accumulator B to _____ (hex). *Ans.* index, 0020H, 00H, 00H

11.26 Refer to Fig. 11-6a. The ADC A #$00 instruction in line 6 represents the "add accumulator A with carry _____ (addressing mode)" operation. The carry flag [which is _____ (0, 1) in this example] is added to accumulator A. After executing line 6 in Fig. 11-6a, accumulator A contains _____ (hex). *Ans.* immediate, 1, 01H

11.27 Most programmers consider _____ addressing to be the 6800 microprocessor's most powerful mode of addressing. *Ans.* indexed

11.28 The 6800 microprocessor's _____ instructions use the relative addressing mode. *Ans.* branch

11.29 Assume that the program in Fig. 11-8a is run with the data shown in Fig. 11-13. List the contents of the sums table after the program has been executed.

Data memory

Address (hex)	Contents (hex)	
0020	06	
0021	03	
0022	CE	Table of augends (data)
0023	C2	
0024	1E	

Address (hex)	Contents (hex)	
0030	07	
0031	10	
0032	31	Table of addends (data)
0033	2C	
0034	02	

Fig. 11-13 New data for adding-from-tables program

Ans.

Address (hex)	Contents (hex)
0040	0D
0041	13
0042	FF
0043	EE
0044	20

11.30 Assume that the program in Fig. 11-8*a* is run with the data shown in Fig. 11-13.   When the program is complete, the index register will contain _____ (hex) and accumulator *A* will contain _____ (hex). *Ans.* 0025H, 20H

11.31 Refer to Fig. 11-11.   The LDA *B* $00,*X* instruction in this program segment represents the "load accumulator *B* _____ (addressing mode)" operation.   The offset is _____ (hex). *Ans.* indexed, 00H

11.32 Refer to Fig. 11-14.   The contents of data memory location 0016H after the execution of the program in Fig. 11-11 will be _____ (8 bits).   This is the BCD representation of the sine of _____°, which is _____ (number in hundredths).   *Ans.*   0001 1001, 0BH° (11_{10}°), 0.19

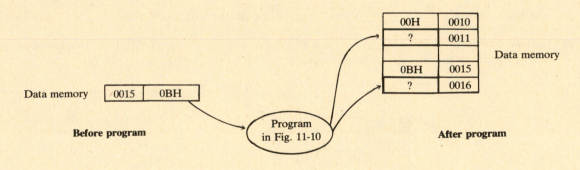

Fig. 11-14

11.33 Refer to Fig. 11-14.   The contents of data memory location 0011H after the execution of the program in Fig. 11-11 will be _____ (hex).   This is the _____ (high, low) -order byte of the address in the look-up table that contains the sine of 11_{10}° (0BH°).   *Ans.* 2BH, low

11.34 Refer to Fig. 11-15.   The 6800 assembly language statement in line 1 of the program segment is the "load accumulator *A* _____ (addressing mode)" instruction.   In this program it represents an _____ (input, output) operation from the port with the address of _____ (hex). *Ans.* extended, input, 5000H

11.35 Refer to Fig. 11-15.   The statement in line 2 of the program segment represents the "_____ accumulator *A* _____ (addressing mode)" operation.   *Ans.* store, direct

11.36 Refer to Fig. 11-15.   The statement in line 3 of the program segment represents the "_____ accumulator *A* _____" operation.   *Ans.* AND, immediate

11.37 Refer to Fig. 11-15.   The 6800 assembly language statement in line 4 of the program segment represents an _____ (input, output) operation to the port at address _____ (hex).   *Ans.* output, 5002H

	Label	Mnemonic	Operand	Comments
1		LDA A	$5000	; Load ASCII number from input port with address of 5000H to accumulator A
2		STA A	$80	; Store ASCII number in accumulator A at memory location 0080H
3		AND A	#$0F	; Mask out four MSBs by ANDing accumulator A with 0FH; a BCD number will remain in accumulator A
4		STA A	$5002	; Store BCD number in accumulator A at output port with address of 5002H
5		WAI		; Stop MPU

Fig. 11-15 Assembly language version of input–store–convert-to-BCD–output program

Chapter 12

The 6502 Microprocessor

12.1 INTRODUCTION

In 1975, MOS Technology introduced the inexpensive 6502 microprocessor. It is considered to be an enhanced version of the earlier 6800 MPU. The registers and instruction set of the 6502 resemble those of the 6800 MPU. However, the 6502 features more advanced addressing modes and an on-chip clock. MOS Technology was absorbed by Commodore which no longer is listed as a supplier of the 6502 MPU. In recent times companies like Rockwell International, NCR, GTE Microcircuits, Hyundai, and Western Design Center are the suppliers of the 6500 series of microprocessors.

The 6502 MPU is one of many microprocessors in the 6500 series. Other versions of the basic NMOS 6502 are the 6503, 6504, 6505, 6506, 6507, 6512, 6513, 6514, 6515, and the 6500/1 one-chip microcomputer. The 6500/1 MCU contains an 8-bit processor, clock, ROM, a small RAM, timer, and four 8-bit I/O ports. CMOS versions of the 6502 were introduced in the early 1980s. These are the 65C02 microprocessors. The 65C02 MPUs are compatible with the older NMOS versions but also have a few added features. There are also several versions of the 65C02 MPU available. Western Design Center enhanced the 6500 series in the mid-1980s by developing the 16-bit 65802 and 65816 microprocessors. The 65802 and 65816 MPUs are compatible in that they can emulate the original 6502 and 65C02 microprocessors. William Mensch of Western Design Center claims that work is in progress on a 32-bit processor called the "65832." It will be compatible with all of the previous members of the 6500 series.

Like other microprocessors, the 6502 functions as part of a system. One minimum system configuration featuring the 6502 MPU is illustrated in Fig. 12-1. The 8-bit 6502 microprocessor is the heart of the system and the center of all data transfers. The system features a small keypad for input and a simple output display using several seven-segment LEDs. A special interface chip, the *6520 peripheral interface adapter* (PIA), is used for handling the data transfers to and from the 6502 MPU. The 6520 PIA is pin-for-pin compatible with the 6820 PIA chip from Motorola. The 6520 can handle two 8-bit channels of either input or output. In this example, one channel is for input (from the keypad), while the other is used for output to the display. The 6520 PIA contains the proper buffers and control registers for storing and transferring inputs and outputs. It can also handle interrupts and relay them to the 6502 MPU via the control bus. All the chips in the system use a common +5-V power supply. The 6502 MPU features an 8-bit data bus for transferring data to and from the PIA, RAM, or ROM. The 6502 has 16 address lines forming the address bus in Fig. 12-1. Some of the address lines are decoded in Fig. 12-1 to generate the chip select signals for the memory (ROM and RAM) and input/output (PIA). Control lines coordinate action between the 6502 MPU and the memory and PIA. The reset block in Fig. 12-1 connects directly to the $\overline{RES}$ input to the 6502 as well as to the $\overline{RES}$ input to the 6520 PIA.

The very popular 6502 and its close relatives may be the first microprocessors studied by many students. They are used in some of the most popular home computers such as the Apple II series and several low-cost Commodore and Atari units. They are also featured in some popular microprocessor trainers used in technical and vocational education.

12.2 THE 6502 PIN DIAGRAM AND FUNCTIONS

The 6502 8-bit microprocessor may be purchased in a dual-in-line package (DIP). The pin diagram for the 6502 MPU is illustrated in Fig. 12-2*a*. Some manufacturers now merchandise upgraded versions of the 6502 (like 65C02) in square 44-pin plastic chip carrier (PLCC) packages. With the proper leads, the PLCC package is used when surface mounting of ICs is required. A

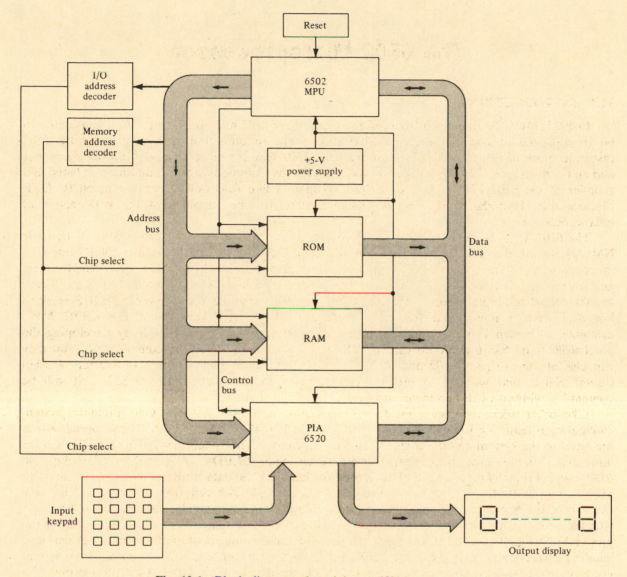

Fig. 12-1 Block diagram of a minimum 6502-based system

chart summarizing the pin names and descriptions follows the pin diagram in Fig. 12-2*b*. The standard 6502 MPU operates on either a 1- or 2-MHz clock.   The newer 65C02 comes in 2-, 4-, 6-, or 8-MHz versions.

The inputs and outputs on the 6502 MPU can be grouped as clock inputs/outputs, power connections, data bus inputs/outputs, address bus outputs, and control inputs/outputs.   The arrows on the pin diagram in Fig. 12-2*a* show the direction of signal flow.

The function of each 6502 microprocessor pin is described briefly in the paragraphs that follow.   In each paragraph, refer to Fig. 12-2 for the location of the pin on the DIP IC and a summary of functions.

Ground (V_{ss}) (*pins 1 and 21*)

These pins are connected to the negative side of the 5-V power supply.

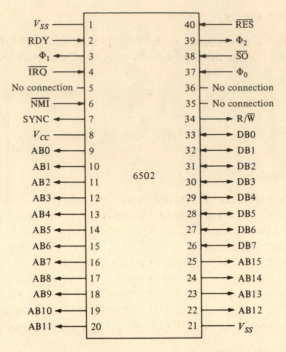

(a) Pin diagram of 6502 MPU DIP IC

Pin name	Description	Type
$AB0-AB15$	Address bus	Output
$DB0-DB7$	Data bus	Tristate, bidirectional
RDY	Ready control	Input
$\phi 1, \phi 2$	Clock (to system)	Output
$\overline{IRQ}$	Interrupt request	Input
$SYNC$	Identify op code fetch cycle	Output
$R/\bar{W}$	Read/write	Output
$\phi 0$	CPU clock	Input
$\overline{SO}$	Set overflow flag	Input
$\overline{RES}$	Reset	Input
$\overline{NMI}$	Nonmaskable interrupt	Input
V_{cc}, V_{ss}	Power	

(b) Pin names and functions

Fig. 12-2

Ready (RDY) (pin 2)

This input signal allows the user to single-cycle the microprocessor on all cycles except write cycles. A negative transition to the LOW state during phase 1 ($\phi 1$) will halt the MPU with the output address lines reflecting the current address being fetched. This condition will remain throughout the subsequent phase 2 ($\phi 2$) in which the RDY signal is LOW. This feature allows microprocessor interfacing with slow PROMs as well as providing for fast direct memory access (DMA). If the RDY signal is LOW during a write cycle, it is ignored until the following read operation.

Clock (φ0 and φ2) (pins 37 and 39)

The 6502 MPU requires a two-phase, nonoverlapping clock. The 6502 has an internal clock generator, but the frequency is controlled externally. A crystal should feed pins 37 and 39 to set the frequency of the oscillator.

Clock (φ1) (pin 3)

This pin outputs phase 1 of the clock signal for synchronizing events in an MPU-based system.

Interrupt request ($\overline{IRQ}$) (pin 4)

A LOW at this input requests that an interrupt sequence begin within the microprocessor. The MPU will complete the current instruction being executed before recognizing the request. At that time, the interrupt mask bit in the status code register will be examined. If the interrupt mask flag is not set, the microprocessor will begin an interrupt sequence. The program counter and processor status register are stored on the stack. The microprocessor will then set the interrupt mask flag to 1 so that no further interrupts may occur. At the end of this cycle, the program counter will be loaded with the data from memory locations FFFEH and FFFFH (low-order byte from FFFE and high-order byte from FFFF). This will transfer control to the memory vector located at these addresses. The RDY input must be HIGH for any interrupt to be recognized.

Nonmaskable Interrupt ($\overline{NMI}$) (pin 6)

A negative-going edge on this input requests that a nonmaskable interrupt sequence be generated within the microprocessor. The $\overline{NMI}$ is an unconditional interrupt. The program counter and processor status register are stored on the stack. The MPU will then set the interrupt mask flag to 1 so that no further interrupts may occur. At the end of this cycle, the program counter will be loaded with the data from memory locations FFFAH and FFFBH (low-order byte in FFFA and high-order byte in FFFB). The instructions loaded at these locations cause the microprocessor to jump to a nonmaskable interrupt routine in memory.

SYNC (pin 7)

This output line is provided to identify those cycles during which the microprocessor is doing an op code fetch. The SYNC line goes HIGH during φ1 of an op code fetch and stays HIGH for the remainder of that cycle. If the RDY line is pulled LOW during the φ1 clock pulse in which the SYNC line went HIGH, the processor will stop in its current state and will remain there until the RDY line goes HIGH. In this manner, the SYNC signal can be used to control RDY to cause single-instruction execution.

Power (V_{cc}) (pin 8)

The positive side of the 5-V power supply is connected to pin 8 of the 6502 DIP IC.

Address Lines (AB_0–AB_{15}) (pins 9–20, 22–25)

The 6502 MPU's 16 address outputs (AB_0–AB_{15}) are connected to the system's address bus. These lines are used to address devices such as ROMs, RAMs, and I/O devices.

Data Lines (DB_0–DB_7) (pins 26–33)

The 6502 MPU's eight data pins (DB_0–DB_7) are connected directly to the system's bidirectional data bus. These data bus lines are for transferring data to and from memory and I/O devices.

Read/Write Control (R/W̄) (pin 34)

The $R/\bar{W}$ output is a control line that signals an external device (RAM, ROM, PIA, etc.) as to whether the 6502 MPU is reading or writing. A HIGH output from the $R/\bar{W}$ line signals a read, whereas a LOW output signals that a write operation is under way.

Set Overflow Flag (S̄Ō) (pin 38)

A negative-going edge on this input sets the overflow bit (flag) in the status code register.

Reset (R̄ĒS̄) (pin 48)

This input is used to reset or restart the microprocessor from a power-down condition. During the time that this line is held LOW, writing to or reading from the MPU is inhibited. After a system initialization time of six clock cycles, the mask interrupt flag will be set and the microprocessor will load the program counter from memory vector locations FFFCH (low-order byte) and FFFDH (high-order byte). This is the starting location of the reset or restart program.

SOLVED PROBLEMS

12.1 The 6502 is a(n) _____ (8, 16)-bit microprocessor having _____ (8, 16) data bus pins and _____ (8, 16) address pins and can directly address up to _____K of memory.

Solution:

The 6502 is an 8-bit MPU having 8 data pins and 16 address pins and can access 64K of memory ($2^{16} = 65,536 = 64K$ of memory).

12.2 List three inputs that can be used as hardware interrupts on the 6502 microprocessor.

Solution:

The three hardware interrupts on the 6502 MPU are the $\overline{RES}$ (reset), $\overline{NMI}$ (nonmaskable interrupt), and $\overline{IRQ}$ (interrupt request) inputs.

12.3 The original 6502 uses an _____ (external, internal) _____ (one, two)-phase nonoverlapping clock.

Solution:

The 6502 uses an internal two-phase nonoverlapping clock.

12.4 Refer to Fig. 12-2a. Pin 40 on the 6502 DIP IC is labeled _____ which stands for restart or _____. Pin 40 is an active _____ (HIGH, LOW) input.

Solution:

Pin 40 on the 6502 DIP IC is labeled $\overline{RES}$ which stands for restart or reset. It is an active LOW input.

12.5 Pin 34 on the 6502 DIP IC is labeled $R/\bar{W}$ which stands for _____/_____. When this control _____ (input, output) is HIGH, the processor is reading, whereas when this pin is LOW, it is _____ (reading from, writing to) memory.

Solution:

Pin 34 on the 6502 is labeled $R/\bar{W}$ which stands for read/write. When this control output pin is HIGH, the MPU is reading, whereas when this pin is LOW, it is writing to memory.

12.6 A single _____-V power supply is used to power the 6502 microprocessor.   In Fig. 12-2*a*, the positive of the power supply is connected to the _____ pin, whereas the negative goes to the pins labeled _____.

Solution:

A single 5-V power supply is used to power the 6502 MPU.   In Fig. 12-2*a*, the positive of the power supply is connected to the V_{cc} pin (pin 8), whereas the negative goes to the pins labeled V_{ss} (pins 1 and 21).

12.7 The _____ input signal allows for the 6502 MPU to interface with slower memory chips (PROMs, RAMs, etc.), as well as providing for direct memory access.

Solution:

The *RDY* (ready) input signal allows for the 6502 MPU to interface with slower memory chips, as well as providing for direct memory access.

12.3   THE 6502 ARCHITECTURE

A block diagram of the internal organization of the 6502 microprocessor unit is sketched in Fig. 12-3.   The 6502 has an 8-bit, three-state buffered data bus (DB_0–DB_7).   At the left in Fig. 12-3 are 16 buffered address outputs (AB_0–AB_{15}) which connect to the system address bus.   The 6502 contains a 16-bit program counter (*PCH* and *PCL*), two 8-bit index registers (*X* and *Y*), and an 8-bit accumulator (*A*).   The 6502 also has an 8-bit processor status register (*PS* register) which contains seven flags.

The 6502 has eight control signals.   The input control signals are reset, interrupt request, nonmaskable interrupt, ready, and set overflow flag.   The output control signals are the sync, clock, and read/write.

The arithmetic-logic unit (ALU) section of the 6502 MPU performs the arithmetic and logic operations.   The processor status (*PS*) register consists of seven individual flags that can be individually set or reset.   The instruction register feeds the instruction decode block in Fig. 12-3.   The instruction decode logic determines the exact procedure (microprogram) to be followed in the execution of the instruction.   The instruction decode logic generates the appropriate internal and external signals to complete the instruction.   Only some of the internal control lines are shown in Fig. 12-3.

The stack point register found in the 6502 microprocessor is unusual.   The stack pointer in both the 8080/8085 and 6800 is a 16-bit register that can locate the stack anywhere in the first 64K of memory.   The stack point register in the 6502 MPU is detailed in the programming model in Fig. 12-4.   Notice that it is a 16-bit register with the high-order byte *permanently* set to 01H.   Only the low-order byte can be changed by the programmer to any number from 00 to FFH.   This means that the stack will be on page 01H in memory in 6502-based systems.   The top of the stack is commonly set at 01FFH in 6502-based systems.

Registers

The model in Fig. 12-4 summarizes the registers used by the programmer.   It makes the 6502 microprocessor appear simpler than either the 8080/8085 or 6800 MPUs.   The 6502, like the 6800, is a memory-oriented microprocessor in that it has few internal registers and must access memory constantly.   In comparison, the 8080/8085 MPU is sometimes classified as a register-oriented unit because of its many internal general-purpose registers.   The 6502, like the 6800, uses memory-mapped I/O.   The inputs and outputs are treated as memory locations.

The 6502 microprocessor's registers are as follows:

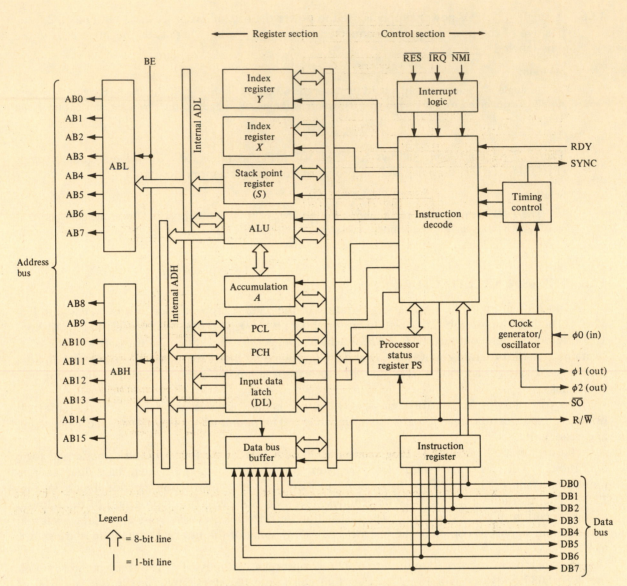

Fig. 12-3 Functional block diagram of 6502 MPU (*Courtesy of Western Design Center, Inc.*)

1. A single 8-bit *accumulator* (*A*) is the focus of many of the microprocessor's operations. The accumulator is also associated in Fig. 12-3 with the ALU. Results of arithmetic and logical operations are transferred to the accumulator or *A* register. Accumulators are common to all microprocessors.

2. The *program counter* (*PC*) is a 16-bit register that always holds the address of the next instruction to be executed. It serves the same purpose as the *PC* in the generic, 8080/8085, and 6800 microprocessors.

3. The two *index registers* (*X* and *Y*) are 8-bit special-purpose registers. They may be used to count program steps or to provide an index value in calculating effective addresses.

4. The *stack point register* (*S*) is an 8-bit register used to define the top of the stack in RAM. Figure 12-4 shows that the high-order byte of this register is always set to 01H. The generic, 8080/8085, and 6800 MPUs had 16-bit stack pointers which gave them more flexibility in defining the location and length of the stack.

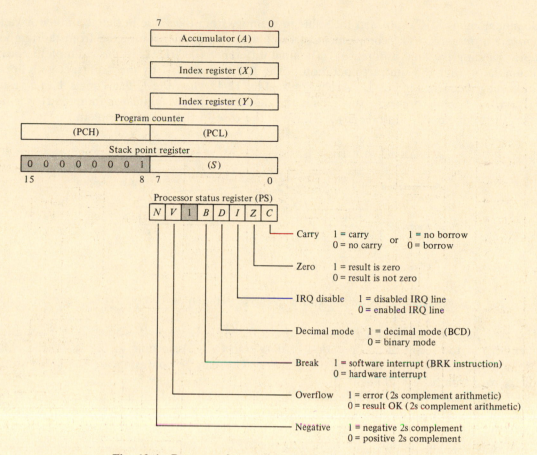

Fig. 12-4 Programming model with flags for the 6502 MPU

5. The *processor status register* (*PS*) is an 8-bit register that contains the seven flags used by the 6502 microprocessor. The 6800 calls this the condition code register. All microprocessors have a register that contains flags.

Flags

The seven flags contained in the *PS* register of the 6502 MPU are detailed in Fig. 12-4. As with other microprocessors, the branch instructions test the status of the flags to determine whether branch or no branch conditions exist. Two of the flags (*D* and *I*) on the 6502 MPU indicate the mode of operation of the processor.

The *carry flag* (*C*) is set to 1 if a carry is generated by the last add instruction. It is reset to 0 if no carry is generated. Unlike other MPUs, the 6502 only has an "add with carry" ($A + M + C \rightarrow A$) instruction, so the carry flag is always added to the addend and augend. For this reason, the *C* flag must be cleared to 0 at the beginning of an addition program.

The *C* flag is also used in subtraction as a "borrow" indicator. Its operation is *different* from most other MPUs in that if a borrow occurred during the last subtraction, the *C* flag is *cleared to B*. If no borrow occurred during the last subtraction, the *C* flag is set to 1. This is summarized in Fig. 12-4. Unlike other MPUs, the 6502 only has a "subtract with borrow" ($A - M - \bar{C} \rightarrow A$) instruction. The *C* flag must be *set to 1* at the beginning of a subtraction program.

A sample binary subtraction problem using the 6502 MPU is illustrated in Fig. 12-5. In this example, 00010000_2 from program memory is subtracted from 00011111_2 in the accumulator yielding a difference of 00001111_2 (appears in the accumulator). The "subtract with borrow" operation (whose mnemonic is SBC) subtracts the value in memory from the value in the accumulator yielding a *temporary difference*. The complement of the C flag ($\bar{C}$) is then subtracted from the temporary difference yielding the final difference. The final difference (00001111_2 in this example) appears in the accumulator after the subtract operation. The C flag is set to 1 by the "subtract with borrow" operation diagramed in Fig. 12-5. According to Fig. 12-4, when the C flag equals 1 as a result of subtraction, *no borrow occurs*. This means the number in the accumulator (minuend) was larger than that in the memory (subtrahend). This was the case in the sample problem in Fig. 12-5.

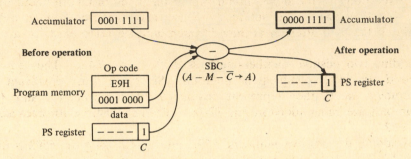

Fig. 12-5 Effect of subtract with carry operation on C (borrow) flag

The *zero flag* (Z) in the *PS* register of the 6502 MPU is set to 1 whenever the accumulator becomes zero as the result of an operation or data transfer. According to Fig. 12-4, the Z flag is reset to 0 if the accumulator *does not equal zero*. This can be confusing for beginning students. All microprocessors have a Z flag.

The *I flag* is the $\overline{IRQ}$ disable indicator. According to Fig. 12-4, if the I flag equals 1, it means the interrupt request input to the chip is disabled and will not be honored. If the I flag is cleared to 0, a LOW at the $\overline{IRQ}$ pin to the 6502 microprocessor chip would be acted upon. Microprocessors that have more than one method of interrupting the MPU will have an I flag (or something like it) to determine which interrupt comes first when several are activated at the same time.

The *D flag* indicates if the 6502 is in its native binary or alternate *decimal (BCD) arithmetic mode*. If the D flag is set to 1, the 6502 MPU will interpret the operands as BCD numbers when adding and subtracting. Remember that BCD notations are direct representations of decimal numbers. If the D flag is reset to 0, the 6502 MPU assumes the operands are binary numbers.

Consider the sample problem diagramed in Fig. 12-6. Two BCD numbers are being added ($0010\,1001 + 0010\,0110 = 0101\,0101_{BCD}$ or $29 + 26 = 55_{10}$). Notice in Fig. 12-6 that the D flag is set to 1 before the add operation. This means that the 6502 MPU interprets the operands from the accumulator ($0010\,1001$) and memory ($0010\,0110$) as BCD numbers. The BCD sum appears in the accumulator after the "add with carry" operation. Also note that the C flag was purposely cleared to 0 before the "add with carry" operation. In this example, if the 6502 MPU were in the binary mode, the operands 29H and 26H would add up to 4FH.

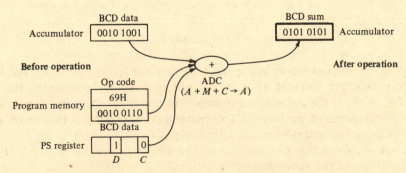

Fig. 12-6 BCD addition—effect of D flag

The *break flag* (B) of the 6502 MPU is set to 1 if the last interrupt was caused by the BRK instruction.   This is called a software interrupt.   The B flag is reset to 0 after a hardware interrupt (such as $\overline{NMI}$, $\overline{IRQ}$, or $\overline{RES}$).   The contents of the B flag are summarized in Fig. 12-4.

The *overflow flag* (V) in the 6502 MPU indicates a 2s complement overflow.   It operates in the same way as the V flag on the 6800 microprocessor.   When dealing with signed numbers on the 6502, the MSB (B_7) of the accumulator is the sign bit.   The remaining 7 bits are written in 2s complement form.   These 7 bits (B_6–B_0) will then hold a number equivalent to +127 to -128_{10}.   This is the range of the signed numbers.   If the result of an arithmetic operation exceeds this range, the overflow flag (V) is set to 1.   This warns the user that an overflow error has occurred.   If the V flag is 0 after an arithmetic operation, no error exists in the resulting signed number.

Consider adding two positive numbers such as $+79_{10}$ and $+64_{10}$.   They equal 01001111 and 01000000, respectively, in 2s complement notation.   Since the most significant bits in both 2s complement numbers are 0, they represent positive numbers between 0 and +127.   These 2s complement numbers are being added in Fig. 12-7a.   The result is in error because it exceeded the upper limit of $+127_{10}$.

The task of adding the positive numbers $+79_{10}$ and $+64_{10}$ using the 6502 is illustrated in Fig. 12-7b.   The 6502 MPU's "add with carry" instruction generates a result of 10001111 which appears in the accumulator after the add operation.   The *sum is in error* because of an overflow problem.   This error is indicated in Fig. 12-7b by the overflow flag (V) being set to 1 as a result of the add operation.

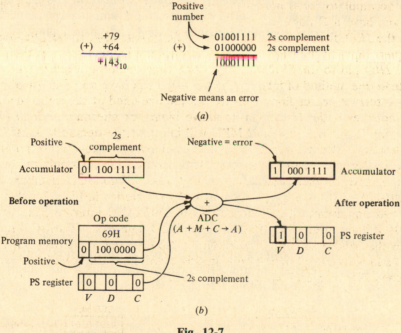

Fig. 12-7

When studying the add operation in Fig. 12-7, some students may observe that the D flag is reset to 0.   This means that the 6502 MPU is in the binary mode.   Technically, the 10001111 in the accumulator in Fig. 12-7b is the correct binary sum.   However, it is not the correct signed number as represented in 2s complement notation.   The programmer controls whether or not the numbers being added are binary, 2s complement, or decimal (BCD).

The *negative flag* (N) in the processor status register of the 6502 MPU is used to indicate a negative result.   It serves the same purpose as the N flag in the 6800 and the sign (S) flag in the 8080/8085 MPU.   The sign bit is the MSB or B_7 in the accumulator.   If the result of the last arithmetic, logical, or data transfer operation was negative, the N flag will be set to 1. If the result is positive, however, the N flag will be reset to 0. The N flag will be the same as the MSB of the result in the accumulator.

Arithmetic-Logic Unit

The *arithmetic-logic unit* (ALU) is the section of the 6502 MPU that performs arithmetic and logic operations. These include adding, subtracting, incrementing, decrementing, ORing, and XORing.

Instruction Register and Decoding Logic

Recall that microprocessors cycle through a fetch-decode-execute sequence. During the fetch stage an op code is latched into the *instruction register* shown in Fig. 12-3. The op code is then decoded by the instruction decoding section which generates the appropriate internal and external control signals. Observe in Fig. 12-3 that the *instruction decode logic* responds not only to the op code of the current instruction but also to timing signals flowing in from the *timing-control* block and also to any hardware interrupt.

System Clock

The 6502 MPU's internal clock generates a two-phase nonoverlapping clock signal. Typical clock waveforms are shown in Fig. 12-8. The clock feeds the timing-control block which synchronizes the microprocessor's internal operations. Both phase 1 and phase 2 clock signals are available to external devices through output pins 3 ($\phi 1$) and 39 ($\phi 2$).

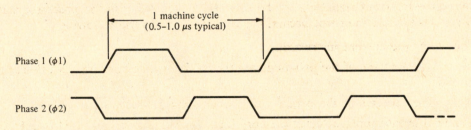

Fig. 12-8 Two-phase nonoverlapping clock waveforms

A single machine cycle is identified in Fig. 12-8. Notice that when phase 1 ($\phi 1$) is HIGH, phase 2 ($\phi 2$) is always LOW. The opposite is also true. Program instructions on the 6502 MPU take from two to seven machine cycles to execute. If a machine cycle had a time duration of 0.5 μs, then single instructions could be executed within 1 to 3.5 μs.

Interrupts

The 6502 microprocessor has three types of *hardware interrupts*. They are the reset, nonmaskable interrupt, and interrupt request. The 6502 also has a single *software interrupt* called the BRK instruction. For comparison, the 6800 MPU has the same three hardware interrupts and a single software interrupt (SWI) instruction. However, be cautious because the 6502 interrupts do not operate exactly like those on the 6800 microprocessor.

To review, a hardware interrupt is caused by an external device (such as a PIA) sending a LOW signal to one of three pins on the 6502 chip. Generally, this causes the MPU to jump to a special program called an interrupt service routine. After servicing the interrupt, the regular program continues.

In case two or more interrupts are activated at the same time, the 6502 MPU has a priority system. The table in Fig. 12-9 shows that the reset ($\overline{RES}$) is the highest priority interrupt, while the interrupt request ($\overline{IRQ}$) is the lowest priority interrupt.

Priority	Interrupt source	Interrupt vector (address of interrupt service routine)	
		High-order byte	Low-order byte
Highest	$\overline{RES}$ (reset)	FFFDH	FFFCH
	$\overline{NMI}$ (nonmaskable interrupt)	FFFBH	FFFAH
	BRK instruction (software interrupt)	FFFFH	FFFEH
Lowest	$\overline{IRQ}$ (interrupt request)	FFFFH	FFFEH

Fig. 12-9 Interrupts on the 6502 MPU

The *reset* ($\overline{RES}$) input is used to initialize the 6502 microprocessor when power is first turned on or to restart the microprocessor using a push-button switch after power is on. During power-up time the $\overline{RES}$ pin is held LOW and writing from the MPU is inhibited. After the $\overline{RES}$ pin goes HIGH, the MPU will delay six machine cycles and fetch the interrupt vector from memory location FFFDH (high-order byte) and FFFCH (low-order byte). The *interrupt vector* stored at these memory locations is the *address* of the program that initializes the system. It is the task of the system programmer to locate this program in memory and to write this program. Initializing routines are commonly stored in ROM in microcomputer systems.

The *nonmaskable interrupt* ($\overline{NMI}$) is an edge-sensitive pin and responds to an H-to-L transition of the input signal. The H-to-L transition will cause only a single interrupt to occur. The response to a nonmaskable interrupt signal cannot be disabled by the *I* flag in the processor status register.

When a nonmaskable interrupt occurs, the 6502 MPU does the following:

1. Completes the current instruction.

2. Pushes the contents of the program counter on the stack (*PCH* on stack first, *PCL* on stack second).

3. Pushes the contents of the processor status register on the stack.

4. Locates the interrupt vector at memory location FFFBH and FFFAH (see Fig. 12-9).

5. Sets the *I* (interrupt disable) flag to 1.

6. Loads the program counter with the starting address of the interrupt service routine (high-order byte from address FFFBH, low-order byte from address FFFAH).

7. Runs the nonmaskable interrupt service routine.

8. Executes the RTI (return from interrupt) instruction causing the original contents of the processor status register and then the program counter to be pulled off the stack.

9. Returns control to the program that was interrupted. Notice that the flags (including the *I* flag) are restored to the same values they had before the interrupt.

The *break* (BRK) is a software interrupt. Observe in Fig. 12-9 that it is third in the priority listing. When executed, the BRK instruction does the following:

1. Sets the *B* (break) flag in the processor status register to 1. This indicates that the interrupt was caused by a BRK instruction and not a hardware interrupt such as $\overline{IRQ}$.

2. Pushes the contents of the program counter on the stack (*PCH* on stack first, *PCL* on stack second).

3. Pushes the contents of the processor status register on the stack.

4. Sets the *I* (interrupt disable) flag to 1. This disables the 6502's ability to service the lower priority $\overline{IRQ}$ interrupt.

5. Locates the interrupt vector at memory locations FFFFH and FFFEH (see chart in Fig. 12-9).

6. Loads program counter with the starting address of the break interrupt processing routine.

After the break interrupt processing routine is run, the RTI instruction causes the original contents of the processor status register and the program counter to be pulled off the stack. Finally, control is returned to the program that was interrupted. Notice that the flags (including the *I* and *B* flags) are restored to the same values they had before the interrupt.

The *interrupt request* ($\overline{IRQ}$) is a level-sensitive input pin on the 6502 MPU. Notice from Fig. 12-9 that the interrupt request has the lowest priority. When an interrupt request occurs, the 6502 MPU does the following:

1. Completes the current instruction.

2. Checks if the interrupt disable (*I*) flag is set to 1. If the *I* flag is set to 1, the interrupt is disregarded and the regular program continues. However, if the *I* flag equals 0, the interrupt will be honored.

3. Sets the *I* flag to 1 so that a second $\overline{IRQ}$ signal does not cause a second interrupt request to be honored.

4. Pushes the contents of the program counter on the stack (*PCH* on the stack first, *PCL* on the stack second).

5. Pushes the contents of the processor status register on the stack.

6. Locates the interrupt vector at memory location FFFFH and FFFEH (see Fig. 12-9).

7. Loads the program counter with the starting address of the interrupt request service routine.

8. Runs the interrupt request service routine.

9. Executes the RTI instruction causing the original contents of the processor status register and then the program counter to be pulled off the stack.

10. Returns control to the program that was interrupted. Notice that the flags (including the *I* flag) are restored to the same values they were before the interrupt.

Some students will be bothered by several problems in the 6502's interrupt system. Two problems with possible solutions are as follows:

1. *First problem.* Only the contents of the program counter and the processor status register are automatically saved on the stack during an interrupt. The contents of the accumulator and *X* and *Y* registers may be lost when the interrupt service routine is executed. It is common to use the "push accumulator on stack" instruction near the beginning of the interrupt service routine to save the contents of the 6502's internal registers.

2. *Second problem.* The interrupt vector for the BRK instruction and the $\overline{IRQ}$ hardware interrupt are the same (see chart in Fig. 12-9). A short routine near the beginning of the interrupt service routine could cause a branch either to the break processing routine if the *B* (break) flag is set to 1 or to the interrupt request service routine if the *B* flag is cleared to 0.

SOLVED PROBLEMS

12.8 The 6500 microprocessor contains a(n)_____-bit accumulator, a 16-bit _____ counter, a stack _____ register, and two 8-bit _____ registers. The 6500 also contains an instruction register and decoder, interrupt logic, an internal clock, timing-control section, _____ (three letters), and seven flags in the _____ _____ register.

Solution:

The 6500 MPU contains an 8-bit accumulator, a 16-bit program counter, a stack point register, and two 8-bit index registers (X and Y). It also contains an instruction register and decoder, interrupt logic, an internal clock, timing-control section, ALU, and seven flags in the processor status register.

12.9 The 6500's processor status register (PS) contains seven flags. List them.

Solution:

According to Fig. 12-4, the 6500's processor status register contains a negative flag (N), overflow flag (V), break flag (B), decimal mode flag (D), $\overline{IRQ}$ disable flag (I), zero flag (Z), and carry flag (C).

12.10 Refer to Fig. 12-10. The 8-bit accumulator will contain _____ in _____ (BCD, binary) after the "add with carry" operation.

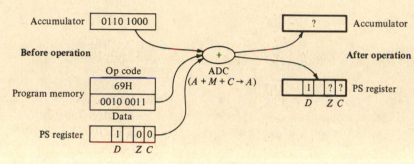

Fig. 12-10

Solution:

Adding $0110\ 1000 + 0010\ 0011 = 1001\ 0001_{BCD}$ ($68 + 23 = 91_{10}$). The accumulator will contain 1001 0001 in BCD after the add instruction in Fig. 12-10.

12.11 Refer to Fig. 12-10. The C flag will be _____ (reset to 0, set to 1) after the add operation indicating that _____ (a carry, no carry) occurred.

Solution:

The carry flag (C) in Fig. 12-10 will be reset to 0 after the add operation indicating that no carry occurred.

12.12 Refer to Fig. 12-10. The zero flag (Z) in Fig. 12-10 will be _____ (reset to 0, set to 1) after the add operation indicating that the accumulator _____ (does, does not) contain a zero.

Solution:

The zero flag (Z) in Fig. 12-10 will be reset to 0 after the add operation indicating that the accumulator does not contain a zero.

12.13 Refer to Fig. 12-10. *Before* the add operation, the D flag is _____ (reset to 0, set to 1) indicating the 6502 MPU is in the _____ (binary, decimal) mode.

Solution:

The D flag in Fig. 12-10 is set to 1 before the add operation indicating the 6502 MPU is in the decimal (BCD) mode.

12.14 Refer to Fig. 12-11. The contents of the accumulator after the subtract operation are _____ (8 bits).

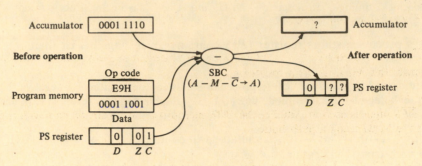

Fig. 12-11

Solution:

Subtracting $00011110 - 00011001 = 00000101$ ($30 - 25 = 5_{10}$). The accumulator in Fig. 12-11 will hold the difference of 00000101_2 (5_{10}) after the subtraction of binary numbers.

12.15 Refer to Fig. 12-11. The Z flag will be _____ (reset to 0, set to 1) after the subtract operation. The C flag will be _____ (reset to 0, set to 1) after the subtract operation which indicates _____ (a borrow, no borrow).

Solution:

The Z flag in Fig. 12-11 will be reset to 0 meaning the accumulator does not contain a zero. The C flag will be set to 1 after the subtract operation which indicates no borrow. This is different from most microprocessors.

12.16 The stack must be located on page _____ (hex) in memory in a 6502-based system. The stack point register has its high-order byte permanently set to _____ (hex), while the low-order byte can be set from 00H to _____H.

Solution:

The stack must be located on page 01H in memory in a 6502 system. The stack point register has its high-order byte permanently set to 01H, while the low-order byte can be set anywhere in a range from 00H to FFH. The top of the stack is set at 01FFH in many 6502-based systems.

12.17 The 6502, like the 6800 MPU, uses _____ (isolated, memory-mapped) I/O.

Solution:

The 6502 uses memory-mapped I/O.

12.18 During the microprocessor's fetch cycle, an _____ (op code, operand) is retrieved from memory via the data bus and deposited in the 6502's _____ register. The instruction is then translated by the 6502's _____ _____ logic, which generates the appropriate internal and external control signals to execute the instruction.

Solution:

Refer to Fig. 12-3. During the microprocessor's fetch cycle, an op code is retrieved from memory via the data bus and deposited in the 6502's instruction register. The op code is then translated by the 6502's instruction decode logic, which generates the appropriate internal and external control signals.

12.19 List the three hardware interrupts and one software interrupt available on the 6502 MPU from highest to lowest priority.

>   **Solution:**
>
>   See Fig. 12-9 for the listing.

12.20 The $\overline{RES}$ input is used to _____ the 6502 microprocessor system when power is first turned on or to restart the MPU using a push button.

>   **Solution:**
>
>   The $\overline{RES}$ input is used to initialize the 6502 microprocessor system when power is first turned on or to restart the MPU using a push button.

12.21 Refer to Fig. 12-12.   List the contents of the stack after the nonmaskable interrupt sequence.

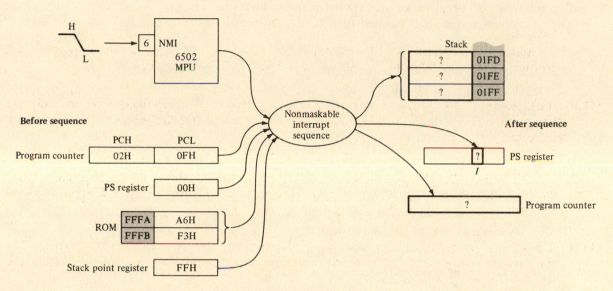

Fig. 12-12

>   **Solution:**
>
>   The contents of the stack in Fig. 12-12 after the nonmaskable interrupt sequence will be as follows:
>
> | Stack location (hex) | Contents |
> |---|---|
> | 01FD | 00 (*P* register) |
> | 01FE | 0F (*PC*—low-byte) |
> | 01FF | 02 (*PC*—high-byte) |

12.22 Refer to Fig. 12-12.   The *I* flag will be _____ (reset to 0, set to 1) after the interrupt request sequence (before an RTI instruction).

>   **Solution:**
>
>   The $\overline{IRQ}$ disable (*I*) flag will be set to 1 after the interrupt request sequence in Fig. 12-12.

12.23 Refer to Fig. 12-12.   The contents of the program counter after the nonmaskable interrupt sequence will be _____ (hex).   This is the address of the _____ interrupt service routine.

Solution:

The contents of the program counter after the interrupt in Fig. 12-12 will be F3A6H.   This is the address of the nonmaskable interrupt service routine.

12.4 SIMPLE ADDRESSING MODES

The programming model studied in Fig. 12-4 made the 6502 microprocessor appear to have a very limited set of registers.   This is true, but the 6502 gains its power from its varied addressing modes.   The 6502 microprocessor has from 9 to 14 addressing modes depending on how they are defined.   This is far more than either the generic, 8080/8085, or 6800 microprocessors have.   The 8080/8085 had five, while the 6800 MPU had six addressing modes.   The 65C02 MPU adds two more addressing modes, and the 16-bit 65816 microprocessor adds nine more addressing modes.

Recall that the term *addressing mode* refers to the technique used to locate and fetch an operand from an internal MPU register or an external memory location.

The 14 addressing modes listed for the 6502 microprocessor from one source are as follows:

1. Implied
2. Accumulator (also listed as implied)
3. Stack (also listed as implied)
4. Immediate
5. Absolute
6. Zero page
7. Relative
8. Absolute X (absolute indexed with X)
9. Absolute Y (absolute indexed with Y)
10. Zero page X (zero page indexed with X)
11. Zero page Y (zero page indexed with Y)
12. Indirect (absolute indirect)
13. (IND), Y (indirect Y) [zero page indirect indexed with Y (postindexed)]
14. (IND, X) (indirect X) [zero page indexed indirect with X (preindexed)]

Most manufacturer's have fewer addressing modes listed since they group several of these modes under a single title.   However, this listing is helpful in explaining how each addressing mode works.

The first six addressing modes from the list above will be featured in this section.   The final eight more complex addressing modes will be considered in Sec. 12.5.

Implied Addressing

In the *implied addressing* mode, the address or register containing the operand is implicitly stated in the op code of the instruction.   These are therefore 1-byte instructions.   This addressing may be called inherent addressing by other MPU manufacturers.

The 6502 microprocessor has many instructions using implied addressing.   One example is detailed in Fig. 12-13.   Here the "transfer index register X to accumulator" is the instruction being executed.   It is a single-byte instruction which transfers data (00H in this example) from the X register to the accumulator.   Notice that two flags are affected.   The N flag is reset to 0.   The Z flag is set to 1 in Fig. 12-13 indicating the accumulator holds a zero as the result of the most recent data transfer.

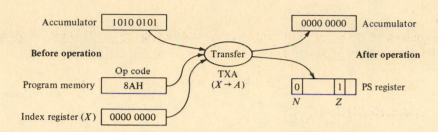

Fig. 12-13   Implied addressing (1-byte instruction)

Accumulator Addressing

The *accumulator addressing* mode suggests an operation on the contents of the accumulator. Instructions in this group may be classified as having *implied* addressing by some manufacturers. Accumulator instructions are represented by a 1-byte instruction. An example of an instruction using accumulator addressing is illustrated in Fig. 12-14. The single-byte instruction shifts the data in the accumulator one bit to the left as symbolized in Fig. 12-14. A zero is shifted into the LSB of the accumulator, while the MSB is shifted into the carry flag. The effect of the "arithmetic shift left" operation is to multiply the binary value in the accumulator by 2 (03H × 2 = 06H in this example). Notice that three flags are affected by the ASL *A* operation. Note that the operand (00000011 in the accumulator) is modified and returned to the accumulator as 00000110.

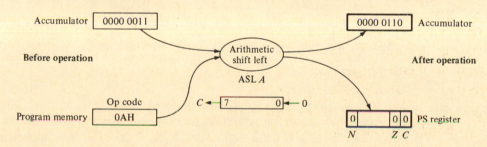

Fig. 12-14   Accumulator or implied addressing (1-byte instruction)

Stack Addressing

Stack addressing is used by the 6502's stack instructions (push and pull). These instructions are also commonly classified as using *implied* addressing. These instructions are for "pushing" the contents of registers on the stack or for "pulling" data off the stack. These instructions find the top of the stack using the address stored in the stack point register. These stack operations are 1-byte instructions.

One example of stack addressing is shown in Fig. 12-15. The "push accumulator on stack" operation places the contents of the accumulator (00110011 in this example) on the top of the stack (memory location 01FFH in this example). The stack point (*SP*) register is then decremented so that it is pointing at the new top of the stack.

Immediate Addressing

In the *immediate addressing* mode, the operand is the second byte of the instruction. These are 2-byte instructions used to store constant data. The generic, 8080/8085, and 6800 MPUs all made use of immediate addressing.

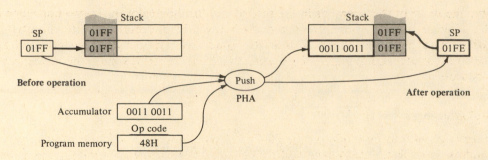

Fig. 12-15 Stack or implied addressing (1-byte instruction)

An example of an instruction using the immediate addressing mode is detailed in Fig. 12-16. Here the "load index register X" instruction is being executed. In this example, 11110000 is loaded from the memory location *immediately following* the op code into the index register X. Note that both the N and Z flags are affected by this load index register X immediate instruction.

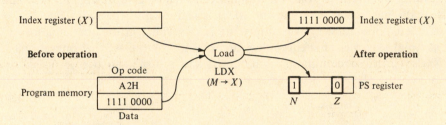

Fig. 12-16 Immediate addressing (2-byte instruction)

Absolute Addressing

In the *absolute addressing* mode, the exact location in memory to be accessed is specified in the instruction. After the op code, the second byte of the instruction specifies the low-order byte of the effective address while the third byte gives the high-order byte. The absolute addressing mode allows access to the 6502 MPU's entire 64K bytes of memory. The disadvantage with using absolute addressing is that it is a 3-byte instruction which takes more time to execute than some other addressing modes.

A simple example using absolute addressing is illustrated in Fig. 12-17. The "store accumulator in memory" instruction is being executed. The second and third bytes of the instruction are assembled into the effective address (0300H in this example). The data from the accumulator (00110011 in this example) is then stored in location 0300H in RAM.

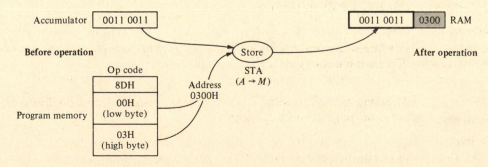

Fig. 12-17 Absolute addressing (3-byte instruction)

Observe the *order* of the operands in the second and third bytes of the instruction when using the 6502 MPU. The second byte holds the low-order byte of the address, while the third byte contains the high-order byte of the address. This is the same order used by the generic and 8080/8085 microprocessors (direct addressing). However, the 6800 MPU reverses this order when using extended addressing.

Zero Page Addressing

The *zero page addressing* mode on the 6502 MPU is almost like absolute addressing in that the effective address is known. Zero page addressing instructions allow for shorter code and execution times because only the second byte of the instruction is fetched and the high-order address byte is assumed to be zero (00H). Zero page addressing might also be called *direct page addressing* and operates like direct addressing on the 6800 microprocessor.

An example of zero page addressing is diagramed in Fig. 12-18. The "decrement memory by one" instruction is being executed. The contents of a known memory location (0055H in this example) is decremented. Because the memory location is on page zero (00H) of memory, the more efficient zero page addressing may be used instead of absolute addressing. Notice that the N and Z flags are affected. The Z flag is set to 1 which means the result of the decrement operation yielded a zero.

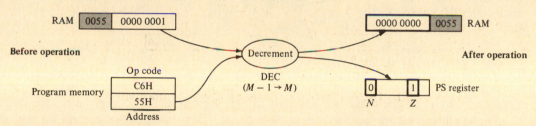

Fig. 12-18 Zero page addressing (2-byte instruction)

SOLVED PROBLEMS

12.24 In the _____ addressing mode, the address or register containing the operand is implicitly stated in the op code of the instruction. This is also referred to as inherent addressing.

Solution:

In the implied addressing mode, the address or register containing the operand is implicitly stated in the op code of the instruction.

12.25 In the _____ addressing mode, the second and third bytes of the instruction are used to form the effective address of a known memory location.

Solution:

In the absolute addressing mode, the second and third bytes of the instruction are used to form the effective address of a known memory location.

12.26 In the _____ addressing mode, the second byte of the instruction forms the low-order byte of the effective address on page zero in memory.

Solution:

In the zero page (also sometimes called direct page) addressing mode, the second byte of the instruction forms the low-order byte of the effective address on page zero in memory.

12.27 In the _____ addressing mode, the operand to be acted upon is in the accumulator. The instruction is 1-byte long and is considered by some manufacturers to use implied addressing.

> **Solution:**
>
> In the accumulator addressing mode, the operand to be acted upon is in the accumulator. The instruction is 1-byte long and is considered by some manufacturers to use implied addressing.

12.28 In the _____ addressing mode, the operand is contained in the second byte of the instruction. These are 2-byte instructions.

> **Solution:**
>
> In the immediate addressing mode, the operand is contained in the second byte of the instruction. These are 2-byte instructions.

12.29 Specialized instructions dealing with the LIFO (last-in–first-out) memory on page 01 of the 6502-based system use the _____ (stack, zero page) addressing mode. Some classify this group as using implied addressing because they are _____ (1, 2, 3)-byte instructions.

> **Solution:**
>
> Specialized instructions dealing with the LIFO memory on page 01 of the 6502-based system use the stack addressing mode. Some classify this group as using implied addressing because they are 1-byte instructions.

12.5 MORE 6502 ADDRESSING MODES

This section will detail some of the more complex addressing modes used by the 6502 microprocessor. Most of these have less straightforward methods of locating effective addresses than the simple addressing modes studied in Sect. 12.4. Beginning programmers on any microprocessor spend a lot of time learning exactly how each addressing mode works.

The addressing modes detailed in this section are as follows:

1. Relative addressing
2. Absolute X addressing
3. Absolute Y addressing
4. Zero page X addressing
5. Zero page Y addressing
6. Indirect addressing (absolute indirect)
7. (IND, X) addressing (indirect X)
8. (IND), Y addressing (indirect Y)

Relative Addressing

The *relative addressing* mode is used only with branch instructions on the 6502 microprocessor. They operate like the relative addressing instructions used by the 6800 MPU. The task of relative addressing is to calculate a destination for a conditional branch. Branches using relative addressing make use of 2-byte instructions. After the op code, the second byte of the instruction is the operand which is the *offset*. The MPU calculates the effective address (destination of the branch) by adding the offset to the contents of the low-order byte (PCL) of the program counter. The range of the offset is a signed 2s complement number from -128 to $+127_{10}$. A positive offset means a branch forward, while a negative offset means a branch backward.

An example of a branch instruction using relative addressing is illustrated in Fig. 12-19.   The program counter before the operation contains 0005H.   The op code for the "branch on result of zero" instruction is fetched from location 0005H in program memory.   After decoding, the 6502 MPU checks the Z (zero) flag.   It is set to 1 in this example, and the condition is met to continue the branch operation.   The PC is incremented to 0006H, and the offset (00001111) is fetched.   The program counter is incremented to the next address (0007H) just before the actual operand fetch.   The microprocessor internally adds the offset (0FH) to the current contents of the PCL (07H).   The next address in the PC after the "branch on result of zero" operation is the destination address (07H + 0FH = 0016H or $0000\,0000\,0001\,0110_2$) of the branch.   The 6502 MPU will then jump to this new address and fetch an instruction from memory location 0016H.   Observe that the MSB of the offset in this example is 0.   This means a positive offset ($+15_{10}$ in this example).   A positive offset means a forward branch.

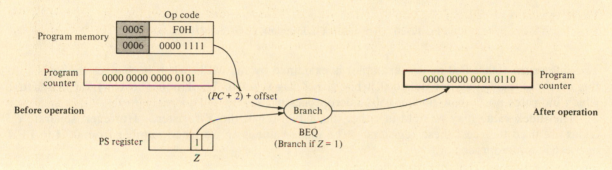

Fig. 12-19   Relative addressing—used with branch instructions (2-byte instruction)

Absolute X and Absolute Y Addressing

The 6502 contains two 8-bit index registers which are used with the several *indexed addressing* modes available on this microprocessor.   By comparison, the 6800 MPU contains only a single index register.   The index registers in the 6502 microprocessor are labeled X and Y.   Indexed addressing is very useful when using tabular material or arrays.

In the *absolute X* (*absolute indexed with X*) *addressing* mode, the effective address is formed by adding the contents of the index register (X) to the address contained in the second and third bytes of the instruction.   The instruction is said to contain the *base address*, while the index register contains the *index* or count.

The effective addresses using the *absolute Y* (*absolute indexed with Y*) *addressing* mode are calculated in the same manner as in absolute X addressing.   The index from the Y register is added to the base address found in the second and third bytes of the instruction.   Observe that *absolute X* and *absolute Y* are listed as two different addressing modes even though their operations are nearly identical.

An example of an instruction that uses the absolute X addressing mode is detailed in Fig. 12-20.   Here the "compare memory and accumulator" instruction is being executed.   The compare instruction directs the MPU to subtract the value in a memory location from that in the accumulator.   Only the N, Z, and C flags are affected, while the value in the accumulator remains unchanged even after the subtract operation.

The effective address in data memory must be calculated by the 6502 MPU when using the absolute X addressing mode.   The method used is diagramed on the left in Fig. 12-20.   The base address is assembled from the second and third bytes of the instruction.   The value in the index register (X) is added to the base address yielding the effective address (03H + 0200H = 0203H in this example).   The value from memory location 0203H is subtracted from the value in the accumulator.

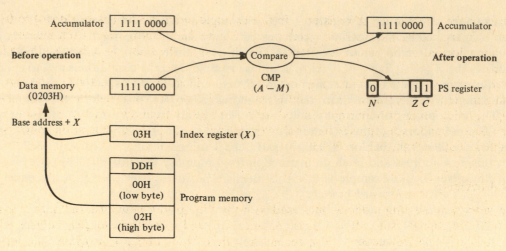

Fig. 12-20   Absolute *X* addressing (3-byte instruction)

The difference (00000000 in this example) is examined by the MPU when it changes the flags.   In this example the *N* flag is reset to 0, while the *Z* flag is set to 1.   The *C* (borrow) flag is set to 1 which indicates no borrow on the 6502 microprocessor.

The index value may be held in either the *X* register or the *Y* register.   However, separate op codes are used to access these registers.   The index value is an unsigned number from 00H to FFH in the 6502 microprocessor.

Zero Page X and Zero Page Y Addressing

The *zero page X* and *zero page Y* addressing modes operate very much like the absolute *X* and *Y* modes.   However, arrays being accessed using indexed addressing must be on page zero in memory when using these new addressing modes.   The zero page *X* addressing mode is sometimes also called either the *zero page indexed with X* or the *direct page X* addressing mode.   In like manner, the zero page *Y* addressing mode is sometimes also called the *zero page indexed with Y* or the *direct page Y* addressing mode.

An example of an instruction using the zero page *X* addressing mode is diagramed in Fig. 12-21.   Here the "load accumulator with memory" instruction is being executed.   The effective address is calculated by the 6502 MPU by adding the *base address* in the second byte of the

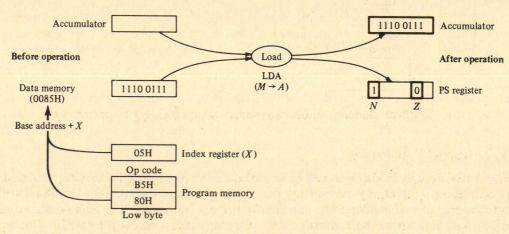

Fig. 12-21   Zero page *X* addressing (2-byte instruction)

instruction to the index in the X register.   In this example, adding 80H (base address) to 05 (index) yields an effective address of 85H on page zero.   Figure 12-21 shows data from memory location 0085H being loaded into the accumulator.   The N and Z flags are also being affected by this operation.

When using zero page X addressing, the entire array must be on page zero.   The zero page X addressing mode is full-featured with 16 different op codes on the 6502 microprocessor.   However, zero page Y addressing only permits limited load and store operations.   Observe from Fig. 12-21 that zero page X addressing makes use of 2-byte instructions.   The number in the index register is an unsigned number from 00H to FFH.

Indirect Addressing

The *indirect addressing* mode is only used with the "jump to a new location" (JMP) instruction by the 6502 microprocessor.   It is also sometimes referred to as the *absolute indirect addressing* mode.   It is a 3-byte instruction.   The second and third bytes of the instruction hold an address.   However, this is *not the effective address*.   This address is a "pointer" that points to the location of the effective address.   The 6502 MPU has several other advanced addressing modes that also use indirect addressing.

An example of the indirect addressing mode is illustrated in Fig. 12-22.   The "jump to new location" instruction is being executed.   The second and third bytes of the instruction are assembled into an address that acts as a pointer.   It points to address 0422H in memory.   At this address (0422H) and the next address (0423H), the two parts of the effective address are located.   The JMP instruction causes the high and low bytes of the effective address to be assembled and placed in the program counter.

There are two addresses generated when using the indirect addressing mode.   The first address can be thought of as a "pointer."   The second address is the effective address.

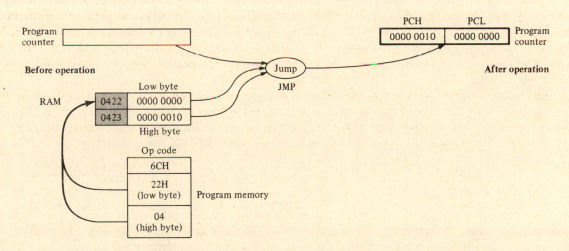

Fig. 12-22   Indirect or absolute indirect addressing (3-byte instruction)

(IND, X) or Indirect X Addressing

(IND, X) addressing is also referred to as *indirect X* or more exactly *zero page indexed indirect with X addressing*.   (IND, X) addressing uses a 2-byte instruction.   The second byte of the instruction (base address) is added to the index from the X register.   The sum points to a memory location on page zero where the low-order byte of the effective address is located.   The high-order byte of the effective address is stored in the next higher memory location.

An example of the (IND, X) addressing mode is diagramed in Fig. 12-23. The "AND memory with accumulator" instruction is being executed. Both *indexing* and *indirection* techniques are being used in this type of addressing. The second byte of the instruction is the base address. Next the index from the X register is added to the base address (70H + 06H = 76H in this example). This is the location on page zero of the low-order byte of the effective address. In Fig. 12-23, the effective address (0362H) is found on page zero stored in consecutive memory locations 0076H and 0077H. The effective address of the data to be ANDed is assembled from these zero page locations. Finally, the data from the accumulator is ANDed with that from memory location 0362H. ANDing 11111100 with 01111111 (bit by bit) results in 01111100 which appears in the accumulator after the operation. The N and Z flags are both reset to 0 by the AND operation.

The (IND, X) addressing mode may seem overly complicated. However, it is useful because you can access double-byte arrays of absolute memory addresses located on page zero. Observe in Fig. 12-23 that the index is added to the base address *first* and then the indirect address is accessed. This is called *preindexing*. It is also possible to use postindexing where the indirection occurs first and then indexing. The next indexing mode uses postindexing.

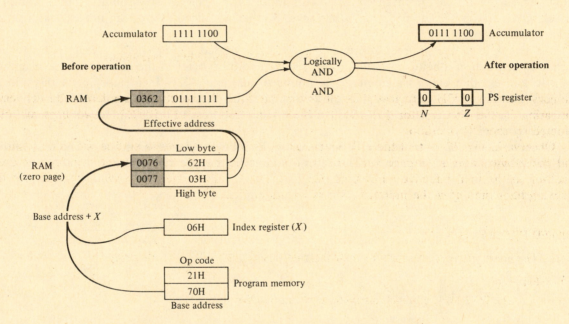

Fig. 12-23   (Ind, X) or indirect X addressing (2-byte instruction)

(*IND*), *Y or Indirect Y Addressing*

(*IND*), *Y addressing* is also referred to as *indirect Y* or more exactly as *zero page indirect indexed with Y addressing*. (IND), Y addressing uses a 2-byte instruction. The second byte of the instruction points to a zero page memory location. This location holds the low-order byte of the indirect address, while the next zero page location holds the high-order byte. The 16-bit indirect address is finally added to the index stored in the Y register. The sum is the final effective address.

An example of the (IND), Y addressing mode is detailed in Fig. 12-24. The "OR memory with accumulator" instruction is being executed. Again, both *indirection* and *indexing* techniques are being used in addressing. The second byte of the instruction using (IND), Y addressing points to a location on page zero in memory (0088H in this example). This is the location of the low-order byte of the indirect address. The high-order byte is located in the next consecutive memory location (0089H in this example). The indirect address is assembled, and the index from the Y register is added yielding the effective address (0253H + 04H = 0257H in this example). The data from

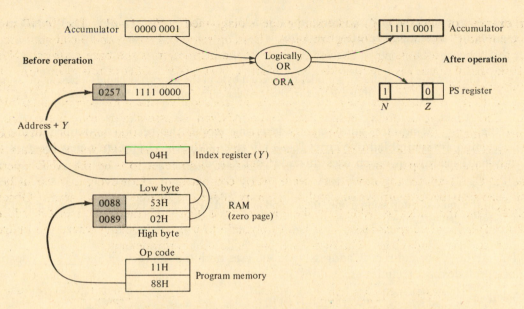

Fig. 12-24   (Ind), Y or indirect Y addressing (2-byte instruction)

memory location 0257H is logically ORed (bit by bit) with that in the accumulator with the result appearing in the accumulator (11110000 ORed with 00000001 = 11110001). Two flags are also affected by the OR operation.

Observe in Fig. 12-24 that the OR operation using (IND), Y addressing first uses indirection to find the 2-byte address on page zero of RAM. Then indexing is applied to the indirect address resulting in the final effective address of 0257H. This is an example of *postindexing* because the indexing happened *after* the indirect address was assembled.

SOLVED PROBLEMS

12.30 The 6502 microprocessor's branch instructions all use _____ addressing.

Solution:

The 6502 MPU's branch instructions all use relative addressing.

12.31 When using relative addressing, the second byte of the instruction contains a signed 2s complement number called an _____ (address, offset).

Solution:

When using relative addressing, the second byte of the instruction contains a signed 2s complement number called an offset.

12.32 In the _____ (absolute, zero page) X addressing mode, the second and third bytes in the instruction hold a base address which is added to the index found in the _____ register to calculate the effective address.

Solution:

In the absolute X addressing mode, the second and third bytes in the instruction hold a base address which is added to the index found in the X register to calculate the effective address.

12.33 In the _____ (absolute, zero page) X addressing mode, the second byte in the instruction holds a base address on page zero which is added to the _____ (index, flag) found in the X register in calculating the effective address.

Solution:

In the zero page X addressing mode, the second byte in the instruction holds a base address on page zero which is added to the index found in the X register in calculating the effective address.

12.34 In the _____ (indirect, zero page) addressing mode, the second and third bytes in the instruction are assembled to form a 16-bit effective address. Jump (to a new location) is the only 6502 instruction which uses this addressing mode.

Solution:

In the indirect addressing mode, the second and third bytes in the instruction are assembled to form a 16-bit effective address.

12.35 The (IND, X) or indirect X addressing mode uses both the indirection and _____ (postindexing, preindexing) techniques.

Solution:

The (IND, X) or indirect X addressing mode uses both indirection and the preindexing techniques.

12.36 The (IND), Y or indirect Y addressing mode first finds the indirect address on page _____ (zero, one) of memory. The index from the _____ register is added to the indirect address to calculate the effective address. This addressing mode uses _____ (postindexing, pre-indexing).

Solution:

The (IND), Y or indirect Y addressing mode first finds the indirect address on page zero of memory. The index from the Y register is added to the indirect address to calculate the effective address. This addressing mode uses postindexing.

12.37 The "branch if minus" instruction (BMI) would use the _____ addressing mode. The first byte of the instruction contains the _____ (index, op code), while the second would contain the offset.

Solution:

The "branch if minus" instruction would use the relative addressing mode. The first byte of the instruction contains the op code, while the second byte contains the offset.

12.38 The "load accumulator with memory" (LDA) operation using absolute X addressing would require a _____ (1, 2, 3)-byte instruction. It would use the _____ register to hold the index.

Solution:

The load accumulator operation using absolute X addressing would require a 3-byte instruction. It would use the X register to hold the index.

12.6 THE 6502 INSTRUCTION SET

A summary of the 6502 instruction set is given in Fig. 12-25. Included in the chart are the mnemonics, op codes, addressing modes, and brief descriptions of the instructions. The 6502 microprocessor has 151 unique instructions (op codes). Also included in Fig. 12-25 for reference are

	Mnemonic	Op code	Addressing mode	Description
A	ADC	69 6D 65 61 71 75 7D 79 72*	Immediate Absolute Zero page (Ind, X) (Ind), Y Zero page X Absolute X Absolute Y Indirect	Add M to A with carry → A
	AND	29 2D 25 21 31 35 3D 39 32*	Immediate Absolute Zero page (Ind, X) (Ind), Y Zero page X Absolute X Absolute Y Indirect	AND M with A → A
	ASL	0E 06 0A 16 1E	Absolute Zero page Implied Zero page X Absolute X	Shift left one bit (memory or accumulator)
B	BCC	90	Relative	Branch on carry clear ($C = 0$)
	BCS	B0	Relative	Branch on carry set ($C = 1$)
	BEQ	F0	Relative	Branch on result zero ($Z = 1$)
	BIT	89* 2C 24 34* 3C*	Immediate Absolute Zero page Zero page X Absolute X	Test bits in memory with accumulator
	BMI	30	Relative	Branch on result minus ($N = 1$)
	BNE	D0	Relative	Branch on result not zero ($Z = 0$)
	BPL	10	Relative	Branch on result plus ($N = 0$)
	BRA*	80	Relative	Branch always
	BRK	00	Implied	Break
	BVC	50	Relative	Branch on overflow clear ($V = 0$)
	BVS	70	Relative	Branch on overflow set ($V = 1$)
C	CLC	18	Implied	Clear carry flag
	CLD	D8	Implied	Clear decimal mode
	CLI	58	Implied	Clear interrupt disable bit
	CLV	B8	Implied	Clear overflow flag
	CMP	C9 CD C5 C1 D1 D5 DD D9 D2*	Immediate Absolute Zero page (Ind. X) (Ind), Y Zero page X Absolute X Absolute Y Indirect	Compare A with N ($A - N$)
	CPX	E0 EC E4	Immediate Absolute Zero page	Compare index X with N ($X - N$)
	CPY	C0 CC C4	Immediate Absolute Zero page	Compare index Y with N ($Y - N$)
D	DEC	CE C6 3A* D6 DE	Absolute Zero page Implied Zero page X Absolute X	Decrement memory by one
	DEX	CA	Implied	Decrement index X by one
	DEY	88	Implied	Decrement index Y by one

Fig. 12-25 Instruction set summary for the 6502 and 65C02 microprocessors

	Mnemonic	Op code	Addressing mode	Description
E	EOR	49 4D 45 41 51 55 5D 59 52*	Immediate Absolute Zero page (Ind. X) (Ind), Y Zero page X Absolute X Absolute Y Indirect	Exclusive OR M with $A \rightarrow A$
I	INC	EE E6 1A* F6 FE	Absolute Zero page Implied Zero page X Absolute X	Increment memory by one
	INX	E8	Implied	Increment index X by one
	INY	C8	Implied	Increment index Y by one
J	JMP	4C 7C* 6C	Absolute (Ind, X) Indirect	Jump to new location
	JSR	20	Absolute	Jump to new location saving return add
L	LDA	A9 AD A5 A1 B1 B5 BD B9 B2*	Immediate Absolute Zero page (Ind, X) (Ind), Y Zero page X Absolute X Absolute Y Indirect	Load M into A
	LDX	A2 AE A6 BE B6	Immediate Absolute Zero page Absolute Y Zero page Y	Load M into index X
	LDY	A0 AC A4 B4 BC	Immediate Absolute Zero page Zero page X Absolute X	Load M into index Y
	LSR	4E 46 4A 56 5E	Absolute Zero page Implied Zero page X Absolute X	Shift right one bit (memory or accumulator)
N	NOP	EA	Implied	No operation
O	ORA	09 0D 05 01 11 15 1D 19 12*	Immediate Absolute Zero page (Ind, X) (Ind), Y Zero page X Absolute X Absolute Y Indirect	OR A with $M \rightarrow A$
P	PHA	48	Implied	Push accumulator on stack
	PHP	08	Implied	Push processor status on stack
	PHX*	DA	Implied	Push index X on stack
	PHY*	5A	Implied	Push index Y on stack
	PLA	68	Implied	Pull accumulator from stack
	PLP	28	Implied	Pull processor status from stack
	PLX*	FA	Implied	Pull index X from stack
	PLY*	7A	Implied	Pull index Y from stack
R	ROL	2E 26 2A 36 3E	Absolute Zero page Implied Zero page X Absolute X	Rotate one bit left (memory or accumulator)

Fig. 12-25   (*cont.*)

	Mnemonic	Op code	Addressing mode	Description
R	ROR	6E 66 6A 76 7E	Absolute Zero page Implied Zero page *X* Absolute *X*	Rotate one bit right (memory or accumulator)
	RTI	40	Implied	Return from interrupt
	RTS	60	Implied	Return from subroutine
S	SBC	E9 ED E5 E1 F1 F5 FD F9 F2*	Immediate Absolute Zero page (Ind, *X*) (Ind), *Y* Zero page *X* Absolute *X* Absolute *Y* Indirect	Subtract *M* from *A* with borrow
	SEC	38	Implied	Set carry flag
	SED	F8	Implied	Set decimal mode
	SEI	78	Implied	Set interrupt disable status
	STA	8D 85 81 91 95 9D 99 92*	Absolute Zero page (Ind, *X*) (Ind), *Y* Zero page *X* Absolute *X* Absolute *Y* Indirect	Store accumulator in memory
	STP†	DB	Implied	Stop
	STX	8E 86 96	Absolute Zero page Zero page *Y*	Store index *X* in memory
	STY	8C 84 94	Absolute Zero page Zero page *X*	Store index *Y* in memory
	STZ*	9C 64 74 9E	Absolute Zero page Zero page *X* Absolute *X*	Store zero in memory
T	TAX	AA	Implied	Transfer accumulator to index *X*
	TAY	A8	Implied	Transfer accumulator to index *Y*
	TRB*	1C 14	Absolute Zero page	Test and reset memory bits with accumulator
	TSB*	0C 04	Absolute Zero page	Test and set memory bits with accumulator
	TSX	BA	Implied	Transfer stack pointer to index *X*
	TXA	8A	Implied	Transfer index *X* to accumulator
	TXS	9A	Implied	Transfer index *X* to stack pointer
	TYA	98	Implied	Transfer index *Y* to accumulator
W	WAI†	CB	Implied	Wait for interrupt

*Found on 65C02 and succeeding microprocessors in the 65xxx series of microprocessors.
†Found on 65C02 by Western Design Center, Inc. and succeeding microprocessors in the 65xxx series.

Fig. 12-25 *(cont.)*

several "new" mnemonics and op codes added by Western Design Center, Inc. in the upgraded 65C02 MPU. The 65C02 is a CMOS version of the 6502. Western Design Center's 65C02 adds 27 new op codes and two new addressing modes. However, the 65C02 and the 6502 have the same architecture. It is said that the instruction set of 65C02 is a *superset* of the 6502. The 65C02 can be used as a plug-in replacement for the older 6502 NMOS microprocessor. For instance, all newer versions of the popular Apple *IIe* microcomputer come with the CMOS 65C02 chip instead of the original 6502 chip.

Rockwell International Corporation also designed and produces a 65C02 microprocessor which is an enhanced version of the 6502 MPU. Rockwell's 65C02 chip is different than Western Design Center's version of the 65C02. Rockwell's version of the 65C02 has even more enhancements than Western Design Center's upgrade. The "added" instructions in Fig. 12-25 are *not* those of Rockwell's 65C02 microprocessor. The Rockwell 65C02 MPU's instruction set is a superset of the 6502.

Like the generic, 8080/8085, and 6800 MPUs, the 6502 is used in stored program microcomputers. Also the program instructions are stored as 8-bit bytes in program memory. The 6502 microprocessor uses 1-, 2-, and 3-byte instructions. The first byte of the instruction is always the op code (operational code) which specifies 1 of over 150 instructions the microprocessor can perform. The MPU recognizes these op codes when they are coded in 8-bit binary form. The set of instructions to which the 6502 MPU will respond is permanently fixed in the design of the chips. The 6502's instruction set is a *subset* of the 65C02, 16-bit 65802, 16-bit 65816, and the future 32-bit 65832 microprocessors.

The 6502 microprocessor's instructions will be grouped into the following functional categories:

1. Data transfer group

2. Flow of control group

3. Arithmetic group

4. Logic and bit manipulation group

5. Interrupts and system control group

The *data transfer* group of instructions moves data between MPU registers, or between memory locations (I/O) and processor registers, or between processor registers and the stack. Included in this group are load, store, push, pull, and transfer instructions.

The *flow of control* group deals with instructions that *alter* the normal straight-line execution of a program. These include branch, jump, jump to subroutine, and return from subroutine instructions. The important and powerful programming techniques of looping, selection among options, and subroutines can be implemented using instructions from this group.

The *arithmetic* group of instructions performs adds and subtracts, and increments or decrements data in registers or memory. This group also contains the compare instructions.

The *logic and bit manipulation* group of instructions performs logical AND, OR, and XOR operations on data. It also includes shift, rotate, and bit test instructions.

The *interrupts and system control* group includes those instructions dealing with interrupts and the processor status register. Also included are the no operation (NOP) and decimal mode instructions.

Consider the very first instruction in Fig. 12-25. The "add memory to accumulator with carry" instruction uses the mnemonic of ADC and has an op code of 69H. According to Fig. 12-25, the first instruction uses immediate addressing. All the nine possible op codes for the ADC instruction share the following description:

$$\text{Add } M \text{ to } A \text{ with carry} \rightarrow A$$

This means to add the contents of a memory location (M) to that in the accumulator (A) plus the carry. The result will be deposited in the accumulator (A) after the add with carry operation is complete.

The summary of the 6502 and 65C02's instruction set in Fig. 12-25 does not give details on flags, clock cycles, the number of machine cycles, or the number of instruction memory bytes used by each instruction. It does, however, give the programmer a quick overview of the operations available when using the 6502 and the 65C02 microprocessors.

A second useful chart is reproduced in Fig. 12-26. This is an alphabetical listing of the 6502 and 65C02 microprocessors' mnemonics with their meanings. This chart will give the programmer insight into the function of each instruction.

Mnemonic	Meaning	Mnemonic	Meaning
ADC	Add memory to accumulator with carry	NOP	No operation
AND	"AND" memory with accumulator	ORA*	"OR" memory with accumulator
ASL	Shift one bit left	PHA	Push accumulator on stack
BCC	Branch on carry clear	PHP	Push processor status on stack
BCS	Branch on carry set	PHX†	Push index X on stack
BEQ	Branch on result zero	PHY†	Push index Y on stack
BIT*	Test memory bits with accumulator	PLA	Pull accumulator from stack
BMI	Branch on result minus	PLP	Pull processor status from stack
BNE	Branch on result not zero	PLX†	Pull index X from stack
BPL	Branch on result plus	PLY†	Pull index Y from stack
BRA†	Branch always	ROL	Rotate one bit left
BRK	Force break	ROR	Rotate one bit right
BVC	Branch on overflow clear	RTI	Return from interrupt
BVS	Branch on overflow set	RTS*	Return from subroutine
CLC	Clear carry flag	SBC*	Subtract memory from accumulator with borrow
CLD	Clear decimal mode	SEC	Set carry flag
CLI	Clear interrupt disable bit	SED	Set decimal mode
CLV	Clear overflow flag	SEI	Set interrupt disable bit
CMP*	Compare memory and accumulator	STA*	Store accumulator in memory
CPX	Compare memory and index X	STP†	Stop the clock
CPY	Compare memory and index Y	STX	Store index X in memory
DEC	Decrement by 1	STY	Store index Y in memory
DEX	Decrement index X by 1	STZ†	Store zero in memory
DEY	Decrement index Y by 1	TAX	Transfer accumulator to index X
EOR*	"Exclusive-or" memory with accumulator	TAY	Transfer accumulator to index Y
INC*	Increment by 1	TRB†	Test and reset memory bits with accumulator
INX	Increment index X by 1	TSB†	Test and set memory bits with accumulator
INY	Increment index Y by 1	TSC	Transfer stack pointer register to accumulator
JMP*	Jump to new location	TSX	Transfer stack pointer to index X
JSR	Jump to new location saving return address	TXA	Transfer index X to accumulator
LDA*	Load accumulator with memory	TXS	Transfer index X to stack pointer
LDX	Load index X with memory	TYA	Transfer index Y to accumulator
LDY	Load index Y with memory	WAI†	Wait for interrupt
LSR	Shift one bit right		

*Old instruction with new addressing mode on 65C02.
†New instruction on 65C02.

Fig. 12-26 Meaning of 6502 and 65C02 mnemonics (*Courtesy of Western Design Center, Inc.*)

SOLVED PROBLEMS

12.39 Refer to Fig. 12-25. The AND instruction for the 6502 MPU can be used in one of _____ (number) addressing modes. The AND instruction logically ANDs (bit by bit) the contents of a _____ location with the contents of the _____ inside the MPU. After the AND operation, the result is placed in the _____.

Solution:

According to the chart in Fig. 12-25, the 6502's AND instruction can be used in one of eight addressing modes. The instruction logically ANDs the contents of a memory location with the contents of the accumulator. The result is placed in the accumulator.

12.40 Refer to Fig. 12-25. The BIT instruction using immediate addressing is available on the _____ (6502, 65C02, both the 6502 and 65C02) microprocessor(s).

Solution:

According to the chart in Fig. 12-25, the BIT instruction using immediate addressing is available on the 65C02 microprocessor.

12.41 Refer to Fig. 12-27. The "store A in M" instruction being executed has an op code of _____ and uses _____ addressing.

Solution:

Refer to the chart in Fig. 12-25. The "store A in M" instruction in Fig. 12-27 has an op code of 85H and uses zero page addressing.

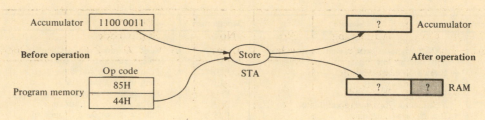

Fig. 12-27

12.42 Refer to Fig. 12-27. After the "store *A* in *M*" operation, the contents of the accumulator will be _____. The binary value _____ will be stored in RAM memory location _____ (hex).

Solution:

After the store operation in Fig. 12-27, the contents of the accumulator will be 11000011. The binary value 11000011 will be stored in RAM memory location 0044H.

12.43 Refer to Fig. 12-28. This "exclusive-OR accumulator with memory" operation uses an op code of _____ and employs the _____ addressing mode. The operands in program memory are _____ (hex) in memory location 0011H and _____ (hex) in 0012H.

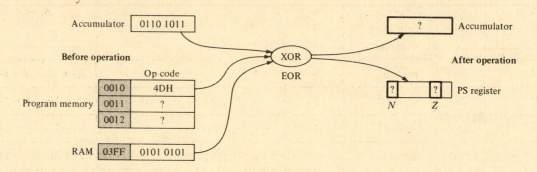

Fig. 12-28

Solution:

The XOR operation in Fig. 12-28 uses an op code of 4DH and employs the absolute addressing mode. The operands in program memory are FF in 0011H (low-order byte) and 03H in memory location 0012H (high-order byte).

12.44 Refer to Fig. 12-28. After the XOR operation, the accumulator contains _____ (binary). The *N* flag is _____ (reset to 0, set to 1), and the *Z* flag is _____ (reset to 0, set to 1) by the operation.

Solution:

After the XOR operation in Fig. 12-28, the accumulator contains 00111110. Both the *N* and *Z* flags are reset to 0 by the operation.

12.7 THE 6502 DATA TRANSFER INSTRUCTIONS

A summary of just the 6502 and 65C02 microprocessors' data transfer instructions is illustrated in Fig. 12-29. This summary includes data load, store, push, pull, and transfer instructions.

Mnemonic	Op code	Addressing mode	No. cycles	No. bytes	Processor Status code $N\ V\ B\ D\ I\ Z\ C$		Operation
LDA	A9	Immediate	2	2			
	AD	Absolute	4	3			
	A5	Zero page	3	2			
	A1	(Ind, X)	6	2			
	B1	(Ind), $Y^\dagger$	5	2	$N\ -\ -\ -\ -\ Z\ -$		$M \rightarrow A$
	B5	Zero page X	4	2			
	BD	Absolute $X^\dagger$	4	3			
	B9	Absolute $Y^\dagger$	4	3			
	B2*	Indirect	5	2			
LDX	A2	Immediate	2	2			
	AE	Absolute	4	3			
	A6	Zero page	3	2	$N\ -\ -\ -\ -\ Z\ -$		$M \rightarrow A$
	BE	Absolute $Y^\dagger$	4	3			
	B6	Zero page Y	4	2			
LDY	A0	Immediate	2	2			
	AC	Absolute	4	3			
	A4	Zero page	3	2	$N\ -\ -\ -\ -\ Z\ -$		$M \rightarrow A$
	B4	Zero page X	4	2			
	BC	Absolute $X^\dagger$	4	3			
PHA	48	Implied‡	3	1	$-\ -\ -\ -\ -\ -\ -$		$A \rightarrow Ms \quad S-1 \rightarrow S$
PHP	08	Implied‡	3	1	$-\ -\ -\ -\ -\ -\ -$		$P \rightarrow Ms \quad S-1 \rightarrow S$
PHX*	DA	Implied‡	3	1	$-\ -\ -\ -\ -\ -\ -$		$X \rightarrow Ms \quad S-1 \rightarrow S$
PHY*	5A	Implied‡	3	1	$-\ -\ -\ -\ -\ -\ -$		$Y \rightarrow Ms \quad S-1 \rightarrow S$
PLA	68	Implied‡	4	1	$N\ -\ -\ -\ -\ Z\ -$		$S+1 \rightarrow S \quad Ms \rightarrow A$
PLP	28	Implied‡	4	1	$N\ V\ 1\ D\ I\ Z\ C$		$S+1 \rightarrow S \quad Ms \rightarrow P$
PLX*	FA	Implied‡	4	1	$N\ -\ -\ -\ -\ Z\ -$		$S+1 \rightarrow S \quad Ms \rightarrow X$
PLY*	7A	Implied‡	4	1	$N\ -\ -\ -\ -\ Z\ -$		$S+1 \rightarrow S \quad Ms \rightarrow Y$
STA	8D	Absolute	4	3			
	85	Zero page	3	3			
	81	(Ind, X)	6	2			
	91	(Ind), $Y^\dagger$	6	2	$-\ -\ -\ -\ -\ -\ -$		$A \rightarrow M$
	95	Zero page X	4	2			
	9D	Absolute $X^\dagger$	5	3			
	99	Absolute $Y^\dagger$	5	3			
	92*	Indirect	5	2			
STX	8E	Absolute	4	3			
	86	Zero page	3	2	$-\ -\ -\ -\ -\ -\ -$		$X \rightarrow M$
	96	Zero page Y	4	2			

Fig. 12-29 Data transfer instructions for the 6502 and 65C02 MPU

Mnemonic	Op code	Addressing mode	No. cycles	No. bytes	Processor Status code N V B D I Z C	Operation
STY	8C	Absolute	4	3		
	84	Zero page	3	2	− − − − − − −	$Y \rightarrow M$
	94	Zero page X	4	2		
STZ*	9C	Absolute	4	3		
	64	Zero page	3	2	− − − − − − −	$00 \rightarrow M$
	74	Zero page X	4	2		
	9E	Absolute X†	5	3		
TAX	AA	Implied‡	2	1	N − − − − Z −	$A \rightarrow X$
TAY	A8	Implied‡	2	1	N − − − − Z −	$A \rightarrow Y$
TSX	BA	Implied‡	2	1	N − − − − Z −	$S \rightarrow X$
TXA	8A	Implied‡	2	1	N − − − − Z −	$X \rightarrow A$
TXS	9A	Implied‡	2	1	− − − − − − −	$X \rightarrow S$
TYA	98	Implied‡	2	1	N − − − − Z −	$Y \rightarrow A$

*Found on 65C02 and succeeding microprocessors in the 65xxx series.
†Add 1 to "n" if page boundary is crossed, except STA and STZ.
‡Accumulator address is included in Implied address.
Note: X = index X, Y = index Y, A = accumulator, $+$ = add, $-$ = subtract; M = memory per effective address, Ms = memory per stack pointer. P = processor status register, S = stack point register, n = number of cycles.

Fig. 12-29 (*cont.*)

Consider the first instruction listed in Fig. 12-29. The LDA (load accumulator from memory) instruction has nine possible op codes listed. The last op code (B2H) is only available on the upgraded 65C02 microprocessor. Each hexadecimal op code in the LDA group represents the same basic operation. The difference between them is in the addressing mode. For instance, op code A9H represents the LDA operation using immediate addressing. However, the op code ADH represents the LDA operation using absolute addressing.

The chart in Fig. 12-29 also gives the number of machine cycles needed for each operation. This specification gives the relative length of time it takes for each instruction to be executed. For instance, the LDA immediate instruction (op code = A9H) is executed in only two machine cycles. This instruction also requires a 2-byte instruction. It also affects only the N and Z flags. The operation is shown in symbolic form as $M \rightarrow A$. This means the data in memory location (M) is loaded into the accumulator (A).

Observe the note at the bottom of the chart in Fig. 12-29. This note explains the special symbols used in the chart.

SOLVED PROBLEMS

12.45 Refer to Fig. 12-29. The LDY instruction transfers the contents of a _____ location to the _____ index register. The _____ and _____ flags are affected by the load operation.

Solution:

According to the chart in Fig. 12-29, the LDY instruction transfers the contents of a memory location to the Y index register. The N (negative) and Z (zero) flags are affected by the load operation.

12.46 Refer to Fig. 12-29. The STZ instruction transfers a(n) _____ to a memory location. The STZ instruction affects _____ (all, no) flags and is only available on the _____ (6502, 65C02) microprocessor.

Solution:

According to the chart in Fig. 12-29, the STZ instruction transfers a zero (00H) to a memory location. The STZ instruction affects no flags and is only available on the 65C02 microprocessor.

12.47 Refer to Fig. 12-30. What is the task of the TXS instruction?

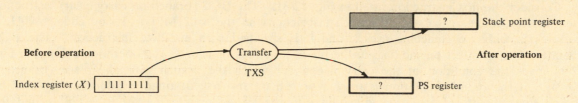

Fig. 12-30

Solution:

According to Fig. 12-26, TXS stands for "transfer index X to stack pointer." In Fig. 12-29, this data transfer is shown in symbolic form as $X \rightarrow S$.

12.48 Refer to Fig. 12-30. After the TXS operation, the stack point register holds _____ (8 bits). This sets the address of the top of the stack in _____ (PIA, RAM) at _____ (4 hex digits). The TXS operation affects _____ (all, none) of the flags in the processor status register.

Solution:

After the TXS operation in Fig. 12-30, the stack pointer holds 11111111_2. This sets the address of the top of the stack in RAM at 01FFH. Remember that the stack is always located on page 01H of RAM in 6502-based systems. According to the chart in Fig. 12-29, the TXS operation affects no flags.

12.49 Refer to Fig. 12-30. The TXS operation employs an op code of _____ and uses _____ addressing. It requires a _____ (1, 2, 3)-byte instruction and consumes _____ (number) machine cycle(s) when executed.

Solution:

The TXS operation in Fig. 12-30 uses an op code of 9AH and employs implied addressing. It requires a 1-byte instruction and consumes two machine cycles when executed.

12.50 Describe the action of the PLA instruction on the 6502 microprocessor.

Solution:

According to Fig. 12-26, PLA is the "pull accumulator from stack" operation. The chart in Fig. 12-29 shows two actions that take place when the PLA instruction is executed. They are (1) the stack pointer is incremented, and (2) the contents of the new top of the stack in memory is transferred to the accumulator.

12.51 Refer to Fig. 12-29. When the PHA instruction is executed on the 6502 MPU, the stack pointer is _____ (decremented, incremented) _____ (after, before) the data from the accumulator is pushed on the stack.

Solution:

According to the operation column in Fig. 12-29, when the PHA instruction is executed, the stack pointer is decremented after the data from the accumulator is pushed on the stack.

12.8   THE 6502 FLOW OF CONTROL INSTRUCTIONS

A summary of just the 6502 and 65C02 microprocessors' flow of control instructions is detailed in Fig. 12-31. This summary includes the branch, jump, jump to subroutine, and return from subroutine instructions.

Consider the first instruction listed in Fig. 12-31. The BCC (branch on carry clear) instruction uses relative addressing as do all branch instructions on the 6502 MPU. Its op code is 90H, it executes in only two machine cycles, and it is specified with a 2-byte instruction. The BCC operation has no effect on the flags in the processor status register. The operation column in Fig. 12-31 gives the condition of the carry flag under which the branch will take place (branch if $C = 0$). If the branch condition is true, a branch occurs to a destination address calculated by adding the contents of the program counter to the signed number ($+127$ to -128) called the offset. If however, the branch condition is false, then the MPU will simply fetch the next instruction in the program listing.

Mnemonic	Op code	Addressing mode	No. cycles	No. bytes	Processor status code N V B D I Z C	Operation
BCC	90	Relative[†]	2	2	– – – – – – –	Branch if $C = 0$
BCS	B0	Relative[†]	2	2	– – – – – – –	Branch if $C = 1$
BEQ	F0	Relative[†]	2	2	– – – – – – –	Branch if $Z = 1$
BMI	30	Relative[†]	2	2	– – – – – – –	Branch if $N = 1$
BNE	D0	Relative[†]	2	2	– – – – – – –	Branch if $Z = 0$
BPL	10	Relative[†]	2	2	– – – – – – –	Branch if $N = 0$
BRA*	80	Relative[†]	2	2	– – – – – – –	Branch always
BVC	50	Relative[†]	2	2	– – – – – – –	Branch if $V = 0$
BVS	70	Relative[†]	2	2	– – – – – – –	Branch if $V = 1$
JMP	4C 7C* 6C	Absolute (Ind, X) Indirect	3 6 6	3 3 3	– – – – – – –	Jump to new location
JSR	20	Absolute	6	3	– – – – – – –	Jump to subroutine
RTS	60	Implied[‡]	6	1	– – – – – – –	Return from subroutine

*Found on 65C02 and succeeding microprocessors in the 65xxx series.
[†]Add 1 to "n" if branch occurs to same page.   Add 2 to "n" if branch occurs to different page.
[‡]Accumulator address is included in implied address.
n = number of cycles.

Fig. 12-31   Flow of control instructions for the 6502 and 65C02 MPU

Notice in Fig. 12-31 that the carry (C), zero (Z), negative (N), and overflow (V) flags can be tested by various branch instructions.

The JSR and RTS instructions deal with *jumping to* and *returning from subroutines*. Their operation is somewhat different from those on the 6800 MPU. The following paragraphs will detail how the 6502 microprocessor executes the JSR and RTS instructions.

The JSR mnemonic means "*jump to a new location saving the return address.*" The JSR is specified with a 3-byte instruction using absolute addressing. When executed, the JSR instruction causes the following actions:

1. MPU fetches op code for JSR and increments *PC*.
2. MPU decodes op code for JSR, fetches low-order byte of new address (*ADL*), and increments *PC*.
3. MPU stores *ADL* internally.
4. High-order byte of current address (*PCH*) is pushed on top of stack (usually 01FFH), and stack pointer is decremented from 01FFH to 01FEH.
5. Low-order byte of current address (*PCL*) is pushed on top of stack, and stack pointer is decremented.
6. MPU fetches high-order byte of new address (*ADH*) from program memory.
7. MPU transfers new address (*ADL* and *ADH*) to program counter.

After the JSR operation is complete, the old address is stored on the stack in RAM and the new address (starting address of the subroutine) is stored in the program counter. The old address that is stored on the stack is thought of as the return address on most microprocessors. However, on the 6502 the old address that is stored on the stack is actually *one less than the return address*. This is usually not too important because the RTS instruction used to end a subroutine increments the program counter to the return address *before* the MPU fetches the next instruction in the main program.

The RTS mnemonic means "return from subroutine." The RTS instruction is specified with a 1-byte instruction using implied addressing. The instruction loads the low-order and high-order bytes of the "old address" into the program counter and increments the program counter to the correct return address. The return address points at the instruction that follows the JSR instruction in the main program. The stack pointer is incremented twice as the two addresses are pulled off the stack.

SOLVED PROBLEMS

12.52 All the 6502 MPU branch instructions use _____ addressing. The branch operations are all specified using _____ (1, 2, 3)-byte instructions. The first byte in an instruction is always the _____, while the second is a signed 2s complement number called the _____.

Solution:

Branch instructions use relative addressing. Branch operations are all specified using 2-byte instructions. The first byte is always the op code, while the second byte is the offset.

12.53 Refer to Fig. 12-32. The JSR instruction means "jump to new location saving the _____ address." It is commonly used for jumping to a _____ (branch, subroutine).

Solution:

According to Fig. 12-26, the JSR instruction means "jump to a new location saving the return address." It is commonly used for jumping to a subroutine.

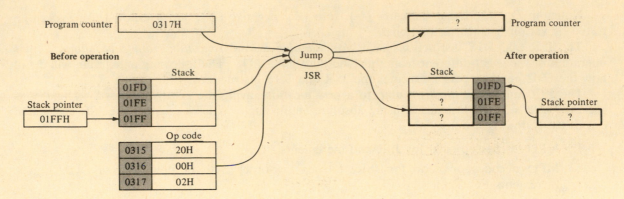

Fig. 12-32

12.54 Refer to Fig. 12-32. The task of the JSR instruction is to first save the high- and low-order bytes of the program counter on the _____. Then it loads the second and third bytes of the instruction into the _____ _____.

Solution:

The function of the JSR instruction is to first save the high- and low-order bytes of the program counter on the stack. Then it loads the second and third bytes of the instruction into the program counter.

12.55 Refer to Fig. 12-32. List the contents of the stack pointer, stack, and program counter after the JSR instruction has been executed.

Solution:

The contents of the stack pointer, stack, and program counter after the JSR operation has been executed are as follows:

$$\text{Stack pointer} = \text{01FDH (new top of stack)}$$
$$\text{Stack (01FEH)} = \text{17H (low-byte—old address)}$$
$$\text{Stack (01FFH)} = \text{03H (high-byte—old address)}$$
$$\text{Program counter} = \text{0200H (new address)}$$

12.56 Refer to Fig. 12-33. Before the RTS operation, the stack holds one less than the _____ address.

Solution:

Before the RTS operation in Fig. 12-33, the stack holds one less than the return address. This address will be transferred to the program counter. The program counter will then be incremented by 1.

12.57 Refer to Fig. 12-33. List the contents of the program counter and stack point register (stack pointer) after the RTS operation.

Solution:

The contents of the *PC* and *SP* after the RTS operation in Fig. 12-33 are as follows:
Program counter = 0318H (0317H from stack plus 1 equals 0318H)
Stack pointer = 01FFH (01FDH + 2 = 01FFH)

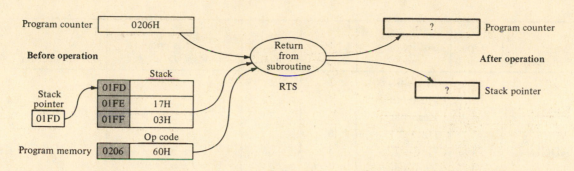

Fig. 12-33

12.9 THE 6502 ARITHMETIC INSTRUCTIONS

A summary of just the 6502 and 65C02 microprocessors' arithmetic instructions is detailed in Fig. 12-34. This summary includes the add, subtract, compare, increment, and decrement instructions.

Consider the first mnemonic listed in Fig. 12-34. The ADC mnemonic stands for the "add memory to accumulator with carry" operation. The ADC instruction has nine different op codes depending on the addressing mode. Observe that the last op code (72H) is only available on the enhanced 65C02 MPU. Each instruction also has listed the number of machine cycles required to complete the operation. Next is listed the number of bytes needed to specify that instruction in program memory. Observe from Fig. 12-34 that four flags are affected by ADC instructions. The "operation" column in the chart gives a brief description of the operation. In the case of the ADC instruction, the add operation is shown in symbolic form as $A + M + C \rightarrow A$. This means that the contents of the accumulator (A) are added to the contents of a selected memory location (M) plus the contents of the carry flag (C). After the operation, the sum is placed in the accumulator.

You are reminded that the 6502 microprocessor has only add with carry (ADC) and subtract with borrow (SBC) instructions. Therefore, the programmer must be careful to clear the carry flag to 0 using the CLC instruction *before adding*. In like manner, the programmer must set the C (borrow) flag to 1 using the SEC instruction *before subtracting*. The meaning of the C flag during subtraction is also somewhat confusing on the 6502 MPU. The meaning of these flags may be reviewed in Fig. 12-4. For instance, if the C flag is reset to 0 after a subtract operation, this means that a borrow occurred and that the number in memory (M) is larger than that in the accumulator (A).

Also recall that the 6502 microprocessor can perform addition and subtraction on either binary or decimal (BCD) numbers. The D flag in the processor status register defines the current mode of the MPU. If $D = 0$, the 6502 is in the binary mode. However if $D = 1$, the processor is in the decimal (BCD) mode.

The programmer may define numbers to be added or subtracted as signed numbers using the MSB as the sign bit. Recall that a 0 sign bit means the number is positive, while a 1 sign bit signifies a negative number. Remember that signed numbers are in 2s complement notation.

SOLVED PROBLEMS

12.58 Refer to Fig. 12-34. The DEC instruction using _____ addressing has an op code of C6H. It is specified with a _____ (1, 2, 3)-byte instruction which requires _____ machine cycles to execute. Both the _____ and _____ flags are affected. The mnemonic DEC stands for _____.

Solution:

See Fig. 12-34. The DEC instruction using zero page addressing has an op code of C6H. It is specified with a 2-byte instruction and requires five machine cycles for execution. Both the N and Z flags are affected. The mnemonic DEC stands for decrement.

Mnemonic	Op code	Addressing mode	No. cycles	No. bytes	Processor status code $N\ V\ B\ D\ I\ Z\ C$	Operation
ADC[‡]	69	Immediate	2	2		
	6D	Absolute	4	3		
	65	Zero page	3	2		
	61	(Ind, X)	6	2		
	71	(Ind), $Y^{\dagger}$	5	2	$N\ V\ -\ -\ -\ Z\ C$	$A + M + C \rightarrow A$
	75	Zero page X	4	2		
	7D	Absolute X	4	3		
	79	Absolute $Y^{\dagger}$	4	3		
	72*	Indirect	5	2		
CMP	C9	Immediate	2	2		
	CD	Absolute	4	3		
	C5	Zero page	3	2		
	C1	(Ind, X)	6	2		
	D1	(Ind), $Y^{\dagger}$	5	2	$N\ -\ -\ -\ -\ Z\ C$	$A - M$
	D5	Zero page X	4	2		
	DD	Absolute $X^{\dagger}$	4	3		
	D9	Absolute $Y^{\dagger}$	4	3		
	D2*	Indirect	5	2		
CPX	E0	Immediate	2	2		
	EC	Absolute	4	3	$N\ -\ -\ -\ -\ Z\ C$	$X - M$
	E4	Zero page	2	2		
CPY	C0	Immediate	2	2		
	CC	Absolute	4	3	$N\ -\ -\ -\ -\ Z\ C$	$Y - M$
	C4	Zero page	3	2		
DEC	CE	Absolute	6	3		
	C6	Zero page	5	2		
	3A*	Implied[§]	2	1	$N\ -\ -\ -\ -\ Z\ -$	Decrement
	D6	Zero page X	6	2		
	DE	Absolute $X^{\dagger}$	6	3		
DEX	CA	Implied[§]	2	1	$N\ -\ -\ -\ -\ Z\ -$	$X - 1 \rightarrow X$
DEY	88	Implied[§]	2	1	$N\ -\ -\ -\ -\ Z\ -$	$Y - 1 \rightarrow Y$
INC[‡]	EE	Absolute	6	3		
	E6	Zero page	5	2		
	1A*	Implied[§]	2	1	$N\ -\ -\ -\ -\ Z\ -$	Increment
	F6	Zero page X	6	2		
	FE	Absolute $X^{\dagger}$	6	3		
INX	E8	Implied[§]	2	1	$N\ -\ -\ -\ -\ Z\ -$	$X + 1 \rightarrow X$
INY	C8	Implied[§]	2	1	$N\ -\ -\ -\ -\ Z\ -$	$Y + 1 \rightarrow Y$

Fig. 12-34 Arithmetic instructions for the 6502 and 65C02 MPU

Mnemonic	Op code	Addressing mode	No. cycles	No. bytes	Processor status code $N\ V\ B\ D\ I\ Z\ C$	Operation
SBC‡	E9	Immediate	2	2		
	ED	Absolute	4	3		
	E5	Zero page	3	2		
	E1	(Ind, X)	6	2		
	F1	(Ind), $Y^{\dagger}$	5	2	$N\ V\ -\ -\ -\ Z\ C$	$A - M - \bar{C} \rightarrow A$
	F5	Zero page X	4	2		
	FD	Absolute $X^{\dagger}$	4	3		
	F9	Absolute $Y^{\dagger}$	4	3		
	F2*	Indirect	5	2		

*Found on 65C02 and succeeding microprocessors in the 65xxx series.
†Add 1 to "n" if page boundary is crossed, except STA and STZ.
‡Add 1 to "n" if decimal mode.
§Accumulator address is included in implied address.
Note: X = index X, Y = index Y, A = accumulator, + = add, − = subtract, and M = memory per effective address, n = number of cycles.

Fig. 12-34 (*cont.*)

12.59 Refer to Fig. 12-34. The CMP instruction using _____ addressing has an op code of C1H. It is specified with a _____ (1, 2, 3)-byte instruction which requires _____ machine cycles to execute. The _____, _____, and _____ flags are affected. The mnemonic CMP stands for _____. The CMP operation is symbolized by the expression _____.

Solution:

    See Fig. 12-34. The CMP instruction using index X addressing has an op code of C1H. It is specified with a 2-byte instruction which requires six machine cycles to execute. The N, Z, and C flags are affected. The mnemonic CMP stands for compare. The CMP operation is symbolized by the expression $A - M$. Observe that this is a subtract operation, but the resulting difference is discarded instead of being left in the accumulator.

12.60 Refer to Fig. 12-35. The ADC instruction in this problem uses an op code of _____ and employs _____ addressing. The 6502 MPU is in its _____ (binary, decimal) arithmetic mode.

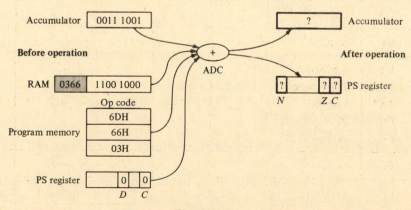

Fig. 12-35

Solution:

The ADC instruction in Fig. 12-35 uses an op code of 6DH and employs absolute addressing. The 6502 MPU is in its binary arithmetic mode.

12.61 Refer to Fig. 12-35. List the contents of the accumulator and the condition of the Z and C flags after the ADC operation.

Solution:

The contents of the accumulator and flags after the ADC operation in Fig. 12-35 are as follows:
Accumulator = 01H (39H + C8H + 00H = 101)
Z flag = 0 (result of ADC was not a zero)
C flag = 1 (result of ADC produced a carry)

12.62 Refer to Fig. 12-36. The SBC (subtract with carry) instruction in this problem uses an op code of _____ and employs _____ addressing. The operation is symbolized by the expression _____. The 6502 MPU is in the _____ (binary, decimal) arithmetic mode during this operation.

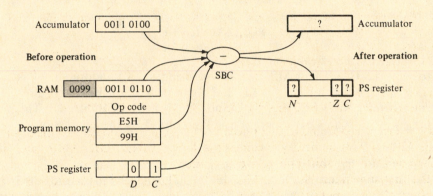

Fig. 12-36

Solution:

The SBC instruction in this problem uses an op code of E5H and employs zero page addressing. The operation is symbolized by the expression $A - M - \bar{C} \rightarrow A$. From the expression, observe that the minuend is held in the accumulator (A) and the subtrahend is held in memory (M). The *complement of the C flag* is subtracted from the difference between A and M. The 6502 MPU is in the binary arithmetic mode during this operation.

12.63 Refer to Fig. 12-36. List the contents of the accumulator and flags after the SBC operation.

Solution:

The contents of the accumulator and flags after the SBC operation in Fig. 12-36 are as follows:
Accumulator = FEH (34H − 36H − 00H = FEH or $52_{10} - 54_{10} - 0_{10} = -2_{10}$)
N flag = 1 (result is negative number)
Z flag = 0 (result is not zero)
C flag = 0 (borrow occurred, $M > A$, and result is a negative number and is in 2s complement notation)

12.64 Refer to Fig. 12-37. The SBC instruction in this problem uses an op code of _____ and employs immediate addressing. The 6502 is in the _____ (binary, decimal) mode. The operation is symbolized by the expression _____.

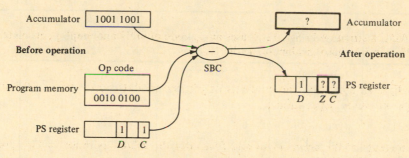

Fig. 12-37

Solution:

The SBC instruction in Fig. 12-37 uses an op code of E9H and employs immediate addressing. The 6502 is in the decimal mode. The operation is symbolized by the expression $A - M - \bar{C} \rightarrow A$.

12.65 Refer to Fig. 12-37. List the contents of the accumulator and flags after the SBC operation.

Solution:

The contents of the accumulator and flags after the SBC operation in Fig. 12-37 are as follows:
Accumulator $= 75_{10}$ ($99_{10} - 24_{10} - 0_{10} = 75_{10}$)
Z flag $= 0$ (result is not zero)
C flag $= 1$ (no borrow occurred and $A \geq M$)

12.10 THE 6502 LOGIC AND BIT MANIPULATION INSTRUCTIONS

A summary of just the 6502 and 65C02 microprocessors' logic and bit manipulation instructions is detailed in Fig. 12-38. This summary includes the logical AND, OR, XOR, and bit test instructions. Also included are the shift and rotate operations.

Consider the first mnemonic listed in Fig. 12-38. The AND mnemonic stands for the "AND memory with accumulator" operation. The AND instruction has nine different op codes depending on the addressing mode. Observe that the last op code (32H) is only available on the enhanced 65C02 MPU. For each instruction in the chart in Fig. 12-38, the number of machine cycles required to complete the operation is given. Next is given the number of bytes needed to specify that instruction in program memory. Observe from Fig. 12-38 that only two flags are affected by the AND instructions. The "operation" column in the chart gives a brief description of the operation. In the case of the AND instruction, the logical AND operation is shown in symbolic form as $A \wedge M \rightarrow A$. This means that the contents of the accumulator (A) are logically ANDed (bit by bit) with the contents of a selected memory location (M). The result is placed in the accumulator (A).

Observe that the manufacturer of the 6502 microprocessor uses the $\wedge$ symbol for AND, the $\vee$ symbol for OR, and the $\forall$ symbol for exclusive-OR (XOR). These are different symbols than those used in Chap. 3 when logic gates were studied. Logical AND instructions are used to *selectively reset* individual bits. In like manner, logical OR instructions are used to *selectively set* individual bits. Finally, logical XOR instructions are used to *selectively complement* individual bits.

The BIT instruction stands for the "test memory bits with accumulator" operation. This instruction performs an AND between a memory location and the accumulator but does not store the result in the accumulator. Its purpose is to set or reset flags to be examined later by a conditional branch instruction. The BIT instruction is symbolized in Fig. 12-38 as $A \wedge M$. The N and V flags are affected by the BIT instruction in an unusual manner. The BIT instruction affects the N flag with N being set to the value of the MSB (bit 7) of the memory being tested. Likewise, the V flag is set equal to bit 6 of the memory being tested. The Z flag is set to 1 only if the result of the AND operation yields a zero. The content of the accumulator is not affected. The BIT instruction

Mnemonic	Op code	Addressing mode	No. cycles	No. bytes	Processor status code N V B D I Z C	Operation
AND	29	Immediate	2	2		
	2D	Absolute	4	3		
	25	Zero page	3	2		
	21	(Ind, X)	6	2		
	31	(Ind), $Y^{\dagger}$	5	2	N – – – – Z –	$A \wedge M \rightarrow A$
	35	Zero page X	4	2		
	3D	Absolute $X^{\dagger}$	4	3		
	39	Absolute $Y^{\dagger}$	4	3		
	32*	Indirect	5	2		
ASL	0E	Absolute	6	3		
	06	Zero page	5	2		
	0A	Implied‡	2	1	N – – – – Z C	$C \leftarrow \boxed{7\ 0} \leftarrow 0$
	16	Zero page X	6	2		
	1E	Absolute $X^{\dagger}$	6	3		
BIT§	89*	Immediate	2	2		
	2C	Absolute	4	3		
	24	Zero page	3	2	$M7$ $M6$ – – – Z –	$A \wedge M$
	34*	Zero page X	4	2		
	3C*	Absolute $X^{\dagger}$	4	3		
EOR	49	Immediate	2	2		
	4D	Absolute	4	3		
	45	Zero page	3	2		
	41	(Ind, X)	6	2		
	51	(Ind), $Y^{\dagger}$	5	2	N – – – Z –	$A \veebar M \rightarrow A$
	55	Zero page X	4	2		
	5D	Absolute $X^{\dagger}$	4	3		
	59	Absolute $Y^{\dagger}$	4	3		
	52*	Indirect	5	2		
LSR	4E	Absolute	6	3		
	46	Zero page	5	2		
	4A	Implied‡	2	1	0 – – – – Z C	$0 \rightarrow \boxed{7\ 0} \rightarrow C$
	56	Zero page X	6	2		
	5E	Absolute $X^{\dagger}$	6	3		
ORA	09	Immediate	2	2		
	0D	Absolute	4	3		
	05	Zero page	3	2		
	01	(Ind, X)	6	2		
	11	(Ind), $Y^{\dagger}$	5	2	N – – – – Z –	$A \vee M \rightarrow A$
	15	Zero page X	4	2		
	1D	Absolute $X^{\dagger}$	4	3		
	19	Absolute $Y^{\dagger}$	4	3		
	12*	Indirect	5	2		

Fig. 12-38 Logic and bit manipulation instructions for the 6502 and 65C02 MPU

Mnemonic	Op code	Addressing mode	No. cycles	No. bytes	Processor status code N V B D I Z C	Operation
ROL	2E 26 2A 36 3E	Absolute Zero page Implied‡ Zero page X Absolute $X^†$	6 5 2 6 6	3 2 1 2 3	N – – – – Z C	
ROR	6E 66 6A 76 7E	Absolute Zero page Implied‡ Zero page X Absolute $X^†$	6 5 2 6 6	3 2 1 2 3	N – – – – Z C	
TRB*§§	1C 14	Absolute Zero page	6 5	3 2	– – – – – Z –	$\bar{A} \wedge M \rightarrow M$
TSB*§§	0C 04	Absolute Zero page	6 5	3 2	– – – – – Z –	$A \vee M \rightarrow M$

*Found on 65C02 and succeeding microprocessors in the 65xxx series.
†Add 1 to "n" if page boundary is crossed, except STA and STZ.
‡Accumulator address is included in implied address.
§N and V flags are unchanged in immediate mode.
§§Z flag indicates $A \wedge N$ result (same as BIT instruction).
Note: X = index X, Y = index Y, A = accumulator, $\vee$ = or, $\veebar$ = exclusive or, $\wedge$ = and, M = memory per effective address, $M6$ = memory bit no. 6, and $M7$ = memory bit no 7.

Fig. 12-38 (*cont.*)

allows for examination of an individual bit (using a mask) without disturbing the value in the accumulator.

SOLVED PROBLEMS

12.66 Refer to Fig. 12-38. The ROL instruction using _____ addressing has an op code of 3EH. It is specified with a _____ (1, 2, 3)-byte instruction which requires _____ machine cycles to execute. The mnemonic ROL stands for _____. During the rotate, the C flag is shifted into bit _____ (0, 7) position in the accumulator, while the MSB is shifted into the _____ flag.

  Solution:

  See Figs. 12-26 and 12-38. The ROL instruction using absolute X addressing has an op code of 3EH. It is specified with a 3-byte instruction which requires six machine cycles to execute. The mnemonic ROL stands for "rotate one bit left." During the rotate, the C flag is shifted into bit 0 of the accumulator, while the MSB is shifted into the C flag.

12.67 Refer to Fig. 12-39. The EOR instruction in this problem uses an op code of _____ and employs _____ addressing. The contents of the accumulator are exclusively _____ (ANDed, ORed) with the contents of memory location 0322H.

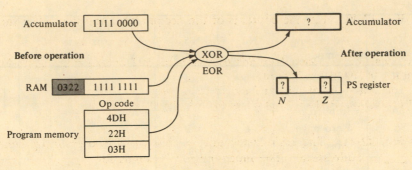

Fig. 12-39

Solution:

The EOR instruction in Fig. 12-39 uses an op code of 4DH and employs absolute addressing. The contents of the accumulator are exclusively ORed (bit by bit) with the contents of memory location 0322H.

12.68 Refer to Fig. 12-39. List the contents of the accumulator and flags after the EOR operation.

Solution:

The contents of the accumulator and flags after the EOR operation in Fig. 12-39 are as follows:
Accumulator = 00001111 ($11110000_2 \veebar 11111111_2 \rightarrow 00001111_2$)
N flag = 0 (MSB of result is 0)
Z flag = 0 (result is not 0)

12.69 Exclusively ORing a binary number with 11111111 yields the _____ (1s, 2s) complement of the number.

Solution:

Exclusively ORing a binary number with 11111111 yields the 1s complement of the number.

12.70 Refer to Fig. 12-40. The BIT instruction in this problem uses the op code of _____ and employs _____ addressing. The mnemonic BIT stands for _____. The BIT instruction is essentially a logical _____ (AND, OR) operation.

Solution:

The BIT instruction in Fig. 12-40 uses the op code of 24H and employs zero page addressing. The mnemonic BIT stands for "test memory bits with accumulator." The BIT instruction is essentially a logical AND operation.

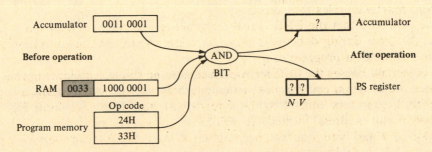

Fig. 12-40

12.71 Refer to Fig. 12-40.   List the contents of the accumulator and flags after the BIT operation.

Solution:

The contents of the accumulator and flags after the BIT operation in Fig. 12-40 are as follows:
Accumulator = 00110001 (unchanged)
N flag = 1 (bit 7 from RAM = 1, bit 7 moved to N flag)
V flag = 0 (bit 6 from RAM = 0, bit 6 moved to V flag)

12.72 Refer to Fig. 12-41.   The LSR instruction in this problem uses an op code of _____ and employs _____ addressing.   The mnemonic LSR stands for _____.

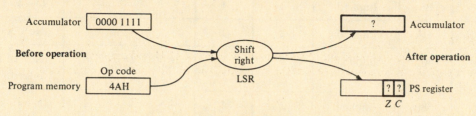

Fig. 12-41

Solution:

The LSR instruction in Fig. 12-41 uses an op code of 4AH and employs implied addressing.   The mnemonic LSR stands for logical shift right or shift one bit right.

12.73 Refer to Fig. 12-41.   List the contents of the accumulator and flags after the LSR operation.

Solution:

The contents of the accumulator and flags after the LSR operation in Fig. 12-41 are as follows:
Accumulator = 00000111
Z flag = 0 (result is not 0)
C flag = 1 (LSB is shifted into C flag)

12.11   THE 6502 INTERRUPTS AND SYSTEM CONTROL INSTRUCTIONS

A summary of just the 6502 and 65C02 microprocessors' interrupt and system control instructions is detailed in Fig. 12-42.   This summary includes the flag set and reset operations.   Also included are break, return from interrupt, and no operation instructions.

Observe in Fig. 12-42 that all instructions in this group use implied addressing and are specified with simple 1-byte instructions.   Most of the flag set and reset instructions are simple operations that execute in only two machine cycles.   A few instructions, like BRK and RTI, are more complex and take six or seven machine cycles to execute.

Recall from Sec. 12-3 that the BRK (break) instruction is a *software interrupt*.   It is commonly inserted into a program during debugging to analyze the contents of many registers and memory locations in the middle of a program run.

The BRK command causes the 6502 microprocessor to go through an interrupt sequence.   During this sequence the program counter and processor status register are automatically pushed on the stack and the MPU transfers control to the interrupt vector.   Observe from Fig. 12-9 that the interrupt vector is an address located at FFFEH (low-order byte) and FFFFH (high-order byte).   The address stored here transfers the program to the break interrupt servicing routine.   This service routine usually includes saving the contents of other registers and checking the B (break) flag.   If the B flag is set, the MPU branches to the break interrupt service routine.   Observe from

Mnemonic	Op code	Addressing mode†	No. cycles	No. bytes	Processor Status code N V B D I Z C	Operation
BRK	00	Implied	7	1	– – 1 0 1 – –	Break
CLC	18	Implied	2	1	– – – – – – 0	0 → C
CLD	D8	Implied	2	1	– – – 0 – – –	0 → D
CLI	58	Implied	2	1	– – – – 0 – –	0 → I
CLV	B8	Implied	2	1	– 0 – – – – –	0 → V
NOP	EA	Implied	2	1	– – – – – – –	No operation
RTI	40	Implied	6	1	N V 1 D I Z C	Return from interrupt
SEC	38	Implied	2	1	– – – – – – 1	1 → C
SED	F8	Implied	2	1	– – – 1 – – –	1 → D
SEI	78	Implied	2	1	– – – – 1 – –	1 → I
STP*	DB	Implied	3	1	– – – – – – –	Stop
WAI*	CB	Implied	3	1	– – – – – – –	0 → RDY

*Found on 65C02 by Western Design Center, Inc. and succeeding microprocessors in the 65xxx series.
†Accumulator address is included in implied address.

Fig. 12-42 Interrupt and system control instructions for the 6502 and 65C02 MPU

Fig. 12-42 that the *B* and *I* (interrupt disable) flags are both set when the BRK instruction is executed. Also the *D* (decimal) flag is reset to 0.

RTI is the "return from interrupt" instruction used to end an interrupt service routine. The RTI instruction pulls the contents of the processor status register and program counter off the stack. This reinitializes the 6502 MPU to the same state as when it was interrupted. Notice that all flags are affected by the operation because they are reinitialized to their preinterrupt state.

The NOP (no operation) instruction does nothing except increment the program counter and use up two machine cycles of time. It is typically used in debugging to substitute for unwanted code or to leave a "hole" for a later patch. It is also commonly used in timing loops.

SOLVED PROBLEMS

12.74 Refer to Fig. 12-42. The SEC instruction uses an op code of _____ and employs _____ addressing. The mnemonic SEC stands for _____.

Solution:
Refer to Figs. 12-26 and 12-42. The SEC instruction uses an op code of 38H and employs implied addressing. The mnemonic SEC stands for "set carry flag."

12.75 Refer to Fig. 12-42. The _____ instruction would be used to return the 6502 MPU to the binary mode after doing BCD decimal calculations.

Solution:

The CLD (clear decimal mode) instruction would be used to return the 6502 MPU to the binary mode (*D* flag reset to 0).

12.76 Refer to Fig. 12-43. The BRK instruction uses an op code of _____ and employs _____ addressing. The BRK instruction is a software _____.

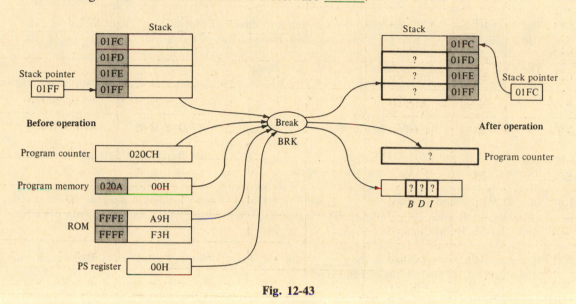

Fig. 12-43

Solution:

The BRK instruction in Fig. 12-43 uses an op code of 00H and employs implied addressing. The BRK instruction is a software interrupt.

12.77 Refer to Fig. 12-43. List the contents of the stack, program counter, and flags after the BRK instruction has been executed.

Solution:

The stack, *PC*, and *PS* register contents after the BRK instruction in Fig. 12-43 are as follows:
Stack address 01FDH = 00H (*PS* register contents stored here)
Stack address 01FEH = 0CH (*PCL* from program counter stored here)
Stack address 01FFH = 02H (*PCH* from program counter stored here)
Program counter = F3A9H (interrupt vector from FFFEH and FFFFH in ROM)
B flag = 1 (set to 1 by BRK instruction)
D flag = 0 (reset to 0 by BRK instruction)
I flag = 1 (set to 1 by BRK instruction)

Supplementary Problems

12.78 The 6502 microprocessor was introduced in _____ (1975, 1983) by MOS Technology. It is considered to be an enhancement of the _____ (6800, 8080) microprocessor. *Ans.* 1975, 6800

12.79 The 8-bit CMOS version of the 6502 microprocessor is the _____. Two 16-bit enhancements of the 6502 are the _____ and _____. *Ans.* 65C02, 65802, 65816

12.80   The 6502 microprocessor is available in a _____-pin DIP IC.   For surface mounting, some manufacturers produce the 65C02, 65802, and 65816 chips in the 44-pin square _____ package.
Ans.   40, PLCC (plastic chip carrier)

12.81   The 6502 MPU pins labeled *Vcc* are connected to the _____-V of the power supply.   *Ans.*   +5

12.82   The 6502 IC has three hardware interrupt input pins.   Name them.   *Ans.* $\overline{IRQ}$, $\overline{NMI}$, $\overline{RES}$

12.83   The 6502 IC has _____ address pins allowing it to directly address _____K of memory.   The 6502 also has eight _____ pins for transferring data into and out of the MPU.   *Ans.*   16, 64, data

12.84   The 6502 chip contains five 8-bit registers.   List them.
Ans.   accumulator (*A*), index registers (*X* and *Y*), stack pointer register (*S*), processor status register (*PS*)

12.85   The *PS* register of the 6502 microprocessor contains _____ (number) flags.   *Ans.*   seven

12.86   Like the 6800, the 6502 MPU uses _____-_____ I/O in that inputs and outputs are treated like memory locations.   *Ans.*   memory-mapped

12.87   In 6502 MPU-based systems, the _____ (RAM, ROM) is usually located at the low addresses starting at 0000H, while the _____ (RAM, ROM) is located at the high addresses ending with FFFFH.
Ans.   RAM, ROM

12.88   Interrupt vectors are located in the _____ (highest, lowest) memory locations in 6502-based systems.
Ans.   highest (FFFAH through FFFFH)

12.89   Only the _____ hardware interrupt is maskable on the 6502 microprocessor.   *Ans.* $\overline{IRQ}$

12.90   On a 6502-based system, the stack is always located on page _____ in RAM.
Ans.   01H (high-order byte of stack point register is permanently set to 01H)

12.91   The 6502 microprocessor's implied addressing operations are specified using _____ (1, 2, 3)-byte instructions.   *Ans.*   1

12.92   The 6502 microprocessor's absolute addressing operations are specified using _____ (1, 2, 3)-byte instructions.   *Ans.*   3

12.93   In 6502 zero page addressing, the second byte in the instruction contains an _____ (address, offset) on page _____ (hex) in memory.   *Ans.*   address, 00H

12.94   Relative addressing is only used with the 6502's _____ instructions.   *Ans.*   branch

12.95   This form of addressing is specified with a 1-byte instruction, and it implies an operation on the accumulator.   Shift and rotate instructions are in this group.
Ans.   accumulator (or implied on some lists)

12.96   In _____ addressing on the 6502 MPU the effective address is formed by adding the index in register *X* to the base address contained in the second and third bytes of the instruction.
Ans.   absolute *X*

12.97   In _____ addressing, the second byte of the instruction is the operand.   *Ans.*   immediate

12.98   The _____ hardware interrupt has the highest priority if more than one interrupt occurs at the same time on the 6502 MPU.   *Ans.* $\overline{RES}$ (reset or restart)

12.99 The 6502's JSR instruction has an op code of _____ and employs _____ addressing. The mnemonic JSR stands for _____.
Ans. 20H, absolute, "jump to subroutine" or "jump to new location saving return address"

12.100 The 6502's SBC instruction can use _____ (number) different addressing modes. The mnemonic SBC stands for _____. The SBC operation is described symbolically as _____.
Ans. 8, "subtract memory from accumulator with borrow," $A - M - \bar{C} \rightarrow A$

12.101 Before adding using the ADC instruction, the programmer should use the _____ (mnemonic) instruction to clear the carry flag to 0. *Ans*. CLC

12.102 Before subtracting using the SBC instruction, the programmer should use the SEC instruction to _____. *Ans*. set the carry flag to 1

12.103 The newer 65C02 MPU uses CMOS, while the older 6502 microprocessor uses _____ (NMOS, DMOS) technology. *Ans*. NMOS

12.104 The _____ (mnemonic) instruction is referred to as a software interrupt. *Ans*. BRK

12.105 The RTI instruction uses an op code of _____ and employs _____ addressing. RTI is used as the last instruction in a(n)_____ 40H, implied, (interrupt service routine, subroutine).
Ans. 40H, implied, interrupt service routine

12.106 Setting the *D* flag to 1 places the 6502 MPU in the _____ (binary, decimal) mode. It will then perform _____ (BCD, binary) arithmetic. *Ans*. decimal, BCD

12.107 What four flags can be tested by the conditional branch instructions in the 6502 microprocessor? *Ans* C, Z, N, V

Chapter 13

Programming the 6502 Microprocessor

13.1 INTRODUCTION

To the programmer, the 6502-based microprocessor system consists of the instruction set, accumulator, two index registers (X and Y), program counter, flags, memory, input/output ports, interrupts, stack, and stack point register.   Many of these are contained within the 6502 chip.

A summary from Rockwell International of the 6502 microprocessor's instruction set is reproduced in Fig. 13-1.   The instruction set was studied in some detail in Chap. 12.

For convenience, the 6502 MPU programming model is reproduced in Fig. 13-2.   It lists the MPU registers that concern the programmer.   The processor status register is shown in Fig. 13-2 with the individual flags detailed.

A memory map of the simple 6502-based system that will be used in this chapter is drawn in Fig. 13-3.   The lowest 1024_{10} addresses (0000H through 03FFH) are reserved for user programs, the stack, and data.   In real applications, some of the RAM locations (especially on page zero) may be reserved for special purposes.   The highest 4096_{10} addresses (F000H through FFFFH) are used by ROM.   The ROM would contain a monitor program for initializing the system, would contain interrupt vectors in memory locations FFFAH through FFFFH, and also would permanently store other valuable subroutines such as interrupt service routines.   This simple system contains only 1K of RAM and 4K of ROM.   This is far less than the 64K of memory that the 6502 MPU is capable of addressing.

The 6502 system uses memory-mapped I/O.   To the programmer, access to a peripheral device is a matter of storing to or loading from a memory location.   On this simple system, memory locations 0400H through 0403H will be used for input and output.   The design of the *I/O address decoder* (see Fig. 12-1) determines the addresses used to access input and output ports.   Input and output is typically accomplished via special peripheral interface adapter ICs such as the PIA shown in Fig. 12-1.

The steps in developing any program for a microprocessor system were summarized in Chap. 6: (1) Define and analyze the problem, (2) flowchart the problem solution, (3) write the assembly language program, (4) write or generate the machine language version of the program, (5) debug the program, and (6) document the program.   All techniques used with the generic, 8080/8085, and 6800 processors can be used with a 6502-based system.   The changes will be in the assembly language format and the actual mnemonics, op codes, and addressing modes which are not standard from processor to processor.   While some addressing modes are used on almost all microprocessors (i.e., implied, immediate, zero page, absolute), they may be named differently by the various manufacturers.

The six fields shown in Fig. 13-4 will be used in this chapter when dealing with object and source programs for the 6502-based system.   These are standard fields which are used with most assembler programs.   The machine code or object code program format is listed at the left in Fig. 13-4.   The *memory address field* will contain the program memory address in hexadecimal.   The *memory contents field* will hold the op codes, operands, and addresses in hexadecimal.

The source program or assembly language part of the 6502 instruction format is shown at the right in Fig. 13-4.   The *label field* may or may not contain a "title" for the line.   The *mnemonic field* contains one of the 6502's mnemonics listed on the left and right edges in Fig. 13-1.   This is commonly the first field filled in by the programmer because it specifies the fundamental action to be taken (i.e., ADC for add, STA for store, LDA for load).   The *operand field* contains information on the addressing mode, the address or operand, and the type of numbers specified (binary, hexadecimal, or decimal).   Some instructions do not require an entry in the operand column.   An example would be 1-byte implied instructions.   The *comments field* is used to help explain what each line or section of the program is doing. Entries in the comments field are not required but are highly recommended for good documentation.

Several 6502 assembly language conventions are illustrated in Fig. 13-5. Each assembly language line in this example represents a "load index register X from memory" instruction. Therefore, each line starts with the same mnemonic of LDX. However, the addressing mode used in each line is different.

The first assembly language line in Fig. 13-5 represents the "load index register X immediate" operation. The # sign in the operand field means immediate addressing. The *lack of a symbol*, such as a $ (meaning hex) or % (meaning binary), before the number 99 means it is a decimal number.

The second and third lines in Fig. 13-5 represent the "load index register X" in the zero page and absolute addressing modes. No special symbol is used before or after either. If the operand (address in this case) is FFH or less, the assembler automatically assigns the "load index register X zero page" op code. If, however, the operand (address) is greater than FFH, the assembler assigns the "load index register X absolute" op code. The $ symbol means that the number that follows is a hexadecimal number. In this case, $6A means that 6A is a hexadecimal number.

The fourth line in Fig. 13-5 represents the "load index register X" operation using zero page Y addressing. The operand of $AA,$Y$ means that the effective address of the data to be loaded must be calculated. The base address (AAH) is added to the contents of the Y register yielding the effective address.

The fifth line in Fig. 13-5 represents the "load index register X" using absolute Y addressing. The operand of $BB00,$Y$ means that the effective address of the data to be loaded must be calculated. The effective address is calculated by adding the base address (BB00H) to the contents of Y yielding the effective address.

13.2 INTERPRETING A BCD ADDITION PROGRAM

A 6502 MPU program will be interpreted in this section. The program is detailed in Fig. 13-6. The task of the program is to add multibyte BCD (decimal) numbers stored in memory. The multibyte BCD sum will be stored in consecutive memory locations. The memory map in Fig. 13-6a locates the program memory, the memory location of the BCD numbers to be added, and the location used for storing the multibyte sum. A sample problem used for testing is shown in Fig. 13-6a ($608752_{10} + 513945_{10} = 1122697_{10}$). The 6502 source or assembly language program to perform this addition is listed in Fig. 13-6b.

The first three instructions in the program in Fig. 13-6b are used to initialize the D and C flags and index register Y. The SED instruction changes the 6502 MPU to its decimal mode. The CLC instruction clears the carry flag to 0 in preparation for addition. The LDY absolute instruction loads index register Y with the number of bytes in the addition problem. In the example shown in Fig. 13-6a, the number 03H would be loaded into the Y register from memory location 0200H.

The next three instructions (lines 4–6 in Fig. 13-6b) load the augend, add the addend, and store the sum in memory, respectively. The LDA absolute Y instruction loads the BCD number from the augend area of memory (memory locations 0211–0213 in this example) into the accumulator. The ADC absolute Y instruction adds the contents of the accumulator (augend) to the addend (from memory locations 0221–0223 in this example). The sum will appear in the accumulator with any carry setting the C flag to 1. The STA absolute Y instruction will store the sum (without carry) in the sum area of memory (memory locations 0231–0234 in this example).

The DEY instruction (line 7 in Fig. 13-6b) decrements the contents of index register Y. The BNE (line 8) instruction checks the Z flag. The Z flag was set or reset by the last DEY operation. If $Z = 0$, the BNE instruction causes a *branch back to* the symbolic address of ADD. The label ADD shows the beginning of the add and store procedure. However, if the Z flag equals 1, the BNE instruction will allow the program to continue to line 9 of the program.

Instructions		Immediate			Absolute			Zero page			Accum.			Implied			(IND, X)		
Mnemonic	Operation	Op	n	#	Op	n	#	Op	n	#	Op	n	#	Op	n	#	Op	n	#
ADC	$A+M+C \rightarrow A^{*§}$	69	2	2	6D	4	3	65	3	2							61	6	2
AND	$A \wedge M \rightarrow A^{*}$	29	2	2	2D	4	3	25	3	2							21	6	2
ASL	$C \leftarrow \boxed{7\ 0} \leftarrow 0$				0E	6	3	06	5	2	0A	2	1						
BCC	Branch on $C=0^{†}$																		
BCS	Branch on $C=1^{†}$																		
BEQ	Branch on $Z=1^{†}$																		
BIT	$A \wedge M$				2C	4	3	24	3	2									
BMI	Branch on $N=1^{†}$																		
BNE	Branch on $Z=0^{†}$																		
BPL	Branch on $N=0^{†}$																		
BRK	Break													00	7	1			
BVC	Branch on $V=0^{†}$																		
BVS	Branch on $V=1^{†}$																		
CLC	$0 \rightarrow C$													18	2	1			
CLD	$0 \rightarrow D$													D8	2	1			
CLI	$0 \rightarrow 1$													58	2	1			
CLV	$0 \rightarrow V$													B8	2	1			
CMP	$A - M$	C9	2	2	CD	4	3	C5	3	2							C1	6	2
CPX	$X - M$	E0	2	2	EC	4	3	E4	3	2									
CPY	$Y - M$	C0	2	2	CC	4	3	C4	3	2									
DEC	$M - 1 \rightarrow M$				CE	6	3	C6	5	2									
DEX	$X - 1 \rightarrow X$													CA	2	1			
DEY	$Y - 1 \rightarrow Y$													88	2	1			
EOR	$A \forall M \rightarrow A^{*}$	49	2	2	4D	4	3	45	3	2							41	6	2
INC	$M + 1 \rightarrow M$				EE	6	3	E6	5	2									
INX	$X + 1 \rightarrow X$													E8	2	1			
INY	$Y + 1 \rightarrow Y$													C8	2	1			
JMP	Jump to new loc.				4C	3	3												
JSR	Jump sub.				20	6	3												
LDA	$M \rightarrow A^{*}$	A9	2	2	AD	4	3	A5	3	2							A1	6	2
LDX	$M \rightarrow X^{*}$	A2	2	2	AE	4	3	A6	3	2									
LDY	$M \rightarrow Y^{*}$	A0	2	2	AC	4	3	A4	3	2									
LSR	$0 \rightarrow \boxed{7\ 0} \rightarrow C$				4E	6	3	46	5	2	4A	2	1						
NOP	No operation													EA	2	1			
ORA	$A \vee M \rightarrow A$	09	2	2	0D	4	3	05	3	2							01	6	2
PHA	$A \rightarrow Ms \quad S-1 \rightarrow S$													48	3	1			
PHP	$P \rightarrow Ms \quad S-1 \rightarrow S$													08	3	1			
PLA	$S+1 \rightarrow S \quad Ms \rightarrow A$													68	4	1			
PLP	$S+1 \rightarrow S \quad Ms \rightarrow P$													28	4	1			
ROL	$\boxed{7\ 0} \leftarrow \boxed{C} \leftarrow$				2E	6	3	26	5	2	2A	2	1						
ROR	$\rightarrow \boxed{C} \rightarrow \boxed{7\ 0}$				6E	6	3	66	5	2	6A	2	1						
RTI	RTRN int													40	6	1			
RTS	RTRN sub													60	6	1			
SBC	$A - M - \bar{C} \rightarrow A^{*}$	E9	2	2	ED	4	3	E5	3	2							E1	6	2
SEC	$1 \rightarrow C$													38	2	1			
SED	$1 \rightarrow D$													F8	2	1			
SEI	$1 \rightarrow I$													78	2	1			
STA	$A \rightarrow M$				8D	4	3	85	3	2							81	6	2
STX	$X \rightarrow M$				8E	4	3	86	3	2									
STY	$Y \rightarrow M$				8C	4	3	84	3	2									
TAX	$A \rightarrow X$													AA	2	1			
TAY	$A \rightarrow Y$													A8	2	1			
TSX	$S \rightarrow X$													BA	2	1			
TXA	$X \rightarrow A$													8A	2	1			
TXS	$X \rightarrow S$													9A	2	1			
TYA	$Y \rightarrow A$													98	2	1			

Fig. 13-1 The 6502 MPU's instruction set (*Courtesy of Rockwell International Corp.*)

(IND), Y			Z page, X			ABS, X			ABS, Y			Relative			Indirect			Z page, Y			Processor status codes	Mnemonic
Op	n	#	Op	n	#	Op	n	#	Op	n	#	Op	n	#	Op	n	#	Op	n	#	7 6 5 4 3 2 1 0 / N V − B D I Z C	
71	5	2	75	4	2	7D	4	3	79	4	3										N V − − − − Z C	ADC
31	5	2	35	4	2	3D	4	3	39	4	3										N − − − − − Z −	AND
			16	6	2	1E	7	3													N − − − − − Z C	ASL
												90	2	2							− − − − − − − −	BCC
												B0	2	2							− − − − − − − −	BCS
												F0	2	2							− − − − − − − −	BEQ
																					M₇ M₆ − − − − Z −	BIT
												30	2	2							− − − − − − − −	BMI
												D0	2	2							− − − − − − − −	BNE
												10	2	2							− − − − − − − −	BPL
																					− − 1 − 1 − − −	BRK
												50	2	2							− − − − − − − −	BVC
												70	2	2							− − − − − − − −	BVS
																					− − − − − − − 0	CLC
																					− − − − 0 − − −	CLD
																					− − − − − 0 − −	CLI
																					− 0 − − − − − −	CLV
D1	5	2	D5	4	2	DD	4	3	D9	4	3										N − − − − − Z C	CMP
																					N − − − − − Z C	CPX
																					N − − − − − Z C	CPY
			D6	6	2	DE	7	3													N − − − − − Z −	DEC
																					N − − − − − Z −	DEX
																					N − − − − − Z −	DEY
51	5	2	55	4	2	5D	4	3	59	4	3										N − − − − − Z −	EOR
			F6	6	2	FE	7	3													N − − − − − Z −	INC
																					N − − − − − Z −	INX
																					N − − − − − Z −	INY
															6C	5	3				− − − − − − − −	JMP
																					− − − − − − − −	JSR
B1	5	2	B5	4	2	BD	4	3	B9	4	3										N − − − − − Z −	LDA
									BE	4	3							B6	4	2	N − − − − − Z −	LDX
			B4	4	2	BC	4	3													N − − − − − Z −	LDY
			56	6	2	5E	7	3													0 − − − − − Z C	LSR
																					− − − − − − − −	NOP
11	5	2	15	4	2	1D	4	3	19	4	3										N − − − − − Z −	ORA
																					− − − − − − − −	PHA
																					− − − − − − − −	PHP
																					N − − − − − Z −	PLA
																					(Restored)	PLP
			36	6	2	3E	7	3													N − − − − − Z C	ROL
			76	6	2	7E	7	3													N − − − − − Z C	ROR
																					(Restored)	RTI
																					− − − − − − − −	RTS
F1	5	2	F5	4	2	FD	4	3	F9	4	3										N V − − − − Z ‡	SBC
																					− − − − − − − 1	SEC
																					− − − − 1 − − −	SED
																					− − − − − 1 − −	SEI
91	6	2	95	4	2	9D	5	3	99	5	3										− − − − − − − −	STA
																		96	4	2	− − − − − − − −	STX
			94	4	2																− − − − − − − −	STY
																					N − − − − − Z −	TAX
																					N − − − − − Z −	TAY
																					N − − − − − Z −	TSX
																					N − − − − − Z −	TXA
																					− − − − − − − −	TXS
																					N − − − − − Z −	TYA

*Add 1 to N if page boundary is crossed.

†Add 1 to N if branch occurs to same page. Add 2 to N if branch occurs to different page.

§If in decimal mode, Z flag is invalid. Accumulator must be checked for zero result.

X = index X, Y = index Y, A = Accumulator, M = memory per effective address, Ms = memory per stack pointer, + = add, − = subtract, ∧ = and, ∨ = or, ∀ = exclusive-or, M_7 = memory bit 7, M_6 = memory bit 6, n = no cycles, # = no bytes, OP = op code, S = stack pointer, P = processor status register.

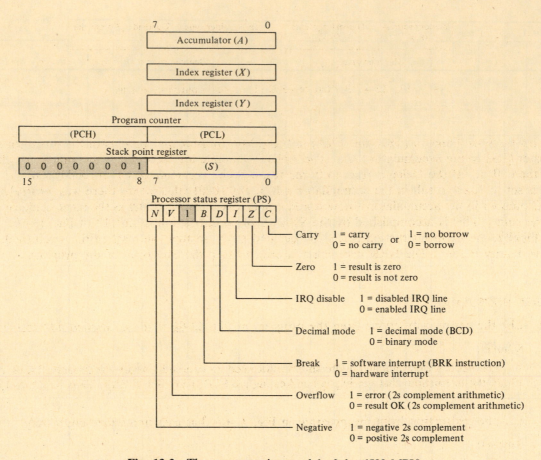

Fig. 13-2 The programming model of the 6502 MPU

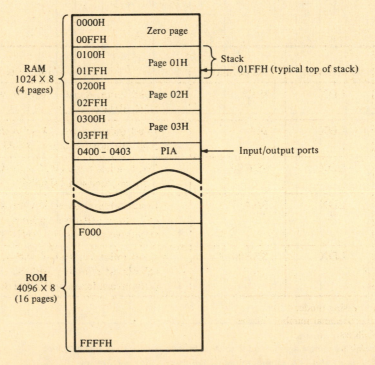

Fig. 13-3 Memory map of the 6502 system used in this chapter

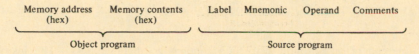

Fig. 13-4 Format of 6502 object and source programs

Instructions 9 and 10 (TSX and TXA) in Fig. 13-6b transfer the contents of the processor status register (*PS*) to the accumulator (*A*).   The AND immediate instruction (line 11) masks out all flags but the *C* flag.   If the *C* flag is reset to 0, the result in the accumulator will be 0000 0000.   If the *C* flag is set to 1, the result in the accumulator will be 0000 0001 (this means there was a carry).   The BCD number in the accumulator is now stored in memory location 0230H as the most significant byte of the sum.   This is accomplished by the STA absolute instruction in line 12 of Fig. 13-6b.

Finally, the CLD instruction clears the decimal mode so that the 6502 MPU is returned to its native binary mode.   The BRK instruction is used to stop the execution of the program.

SOLVED PROBLEMS

13.1   List the seven instructions from the program in Fig. 13-6b that use implied addressing.

Solution:

Instructions using implied addressing do not need an operand.   From the program listing in Fig. 13-6b, the instructions that use implied addressing are SED, CLC, DEY, TSX, TXA, CLD, and BRK.

13.2   List the instruction from the program in Fig. 13-6b that uses immediate addressing.

Solution:

The operand of an immediate instruction starts with the # symbol.   The single instruction that uses immediate addressing is AND (from Fig. 13-6b).

Addressing mode	Mnemonic	Operand	Comments
Immediate	LDX	# 99	; Load index register *X* with immediate BCD data of 99_{10}
Zero page	LDX	$6A	; Load index register *X* with data from zero page memory location 006AH
Absolute	LDX	$DD00	; Load index register *X* with data from memory location DD00H
Zero page, *Y*	LDX	$AA,*Y*	; Load index register *X* with data from calculated effective address (effective address = AAH + *Y*)
Absolute, *Y*	LDX	$BB00,*Y*	; Load index register *X* with data from calculated effective address (effective address = BB00H + *Y*)

means immediate addressing mode.
No % or $ symbol means decimal number follows.
$ means hex number follows.
Y means index in *Y* register.

Fig. 13-5 Some conventional practices used in 6502 assembly language statements

13.3 List the two instructions from the program in Fig. 13-6*b* that use absolute addressing.

Solution:

The operand of an absolute instruction contains a 2-byte address. The instructions from the program in Fig. 13-6*b* that use absolute addressing are LDY $0200 and STA $0230. Observe that the 2-byte addresses are given as hexadecimal numbers ($ symbol means hex).

13.4 List the instruction from the program in Fig. 13-6*b* that uses relative addressing.

Solution:

Only branch instructions use relative addressing. Therefore, BNE is the only instruction in the program that uses relative addressing.

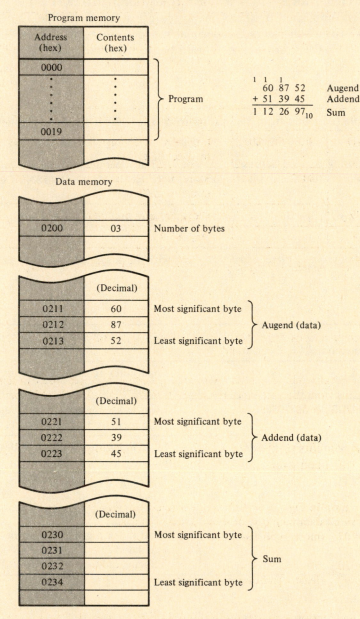

(*a*) Memory map for BCD addition problem

Fig. 13-6

	Label	Mnemonic	Operand	Comments
1		SED		; Set decimal mode (D flag = 1)
2		CLC		; Clear carry flag
3		LDY	$0200	; Load index register Y from memory location 0200H
4	ADD	LDA	$0210, Y	; Load accumulator from memory location (0210H + Y)
5		ADC	$0220, Y	; Add accumulator to memory (0220H + Y) and place sum in A
6		STA	$0230, Y	; Store accumulator in memory location (0230H + Y)
7		DEY		; Decrement index in register Y by 1
8		BNE	ADD	; If Z flag = 0, then branch back to symbolic address called ADD
9		TSX		; Transfer processor status register (S) to X register
10		TXA		; Transfer X register to accumulator (A)
11		AND	#%0000 0001	; Logically AND flags in (A) with mask of 0000 0001$_2$ to check if C flag is at 1 or 0
12		STA	$0230	; Store most significant byte of sum in memory location 0230H
13		CLD		; Clear decimal mode (D flag = 0)
14	STOP	BRK		; Halt MPU

(b) Assembly language program for BCD addition problem

Fig. 13-6 (cont.)

13.5 List the three instructions from the program in Fig. 13-6b that use absolute Y addressing.

Solution:

The operand of absolute Y instructions would contain a 2-byte address followed by the letter Y. The instructions from the program in Fig. 13-6b that use absolute Y addressing are LDA $0210, Y$; ADC $0220, Y$; and STA $0230, Y$.

13.6 What would the contents of memory locations 0230H through 0233H in Fig. 13-6 be after the entire program has been executed?

Solution:

After the program in Fig. 13-6b has been executed using the data shown in the memory map, the contents of the "sum" data memory locations are as follows:
Memory 0230H = 01_{10} (most significant byte of sum)
Memory 0231H = 12_{10}
Memory 0232H = 26_{10}
Memory 0233H = 97_{10} (least significant byte of sum)

13.7 Using the 6502 instruction set, assemble the object program (machine code) from the program in Fig. 13-6. Use program memory locations 0000H through 0019H as shown in the memory map.

Solution:

Refer to the 6502 instruction set in Fig. 13-1. The object program or machine code for the program in Fig. 13-6 may be assembled as follows:

Address (hex)	Contents (hex)
0000	F8
0001	18
0002	AC
0003	00
0004	02
0005	B9
0006	10
0007	02
0008	79
0009	20
000A	02
000B	99
000C	30
000D	02
000E	88
000F	D0
0010	F4
0011	BA
0012	8A
0013	29
0014	01
0015	8D
0016	30
0017	02
0018	D8
0019	00

13.8   Draw a detailed flowchart of the multibyte BCD addition problem shown in Fig. 13-6.

Solution:

One possible solution is shown in Fig. 13-7.

13.3   BINARY MULTIPLICATION

The fundamentals of binary multiplication were introduced in Chap. 2.   The instruction set of the 6502 MPU only contains add and subtract instructions.   It is common to use the add instruction along with shift, rotate, and branch instructions when programming multiplication routines on simple 8-bit microprocessors.   The technique that will be used for binary multiplication is called the *shift and add* or add and shift method.   It is also possible to program the microprocessor to perform multiplication using the repeated addition method.   Many larger 16- and 32-bit microprocessors have multiply instructions in their instruction set.

Consider the simple multiplication problem copied in Fig. 13-8a.   The sample problem is worked out in decimal, hexadecimal, and binary.   Observe in the binary problem that the multiplicand is *added to the partial product only when a 1 appears* in the multiplier.   If a 0 appears in the multiplier, nothing is added into the partial product, but the partial product is shifted one place to the left.

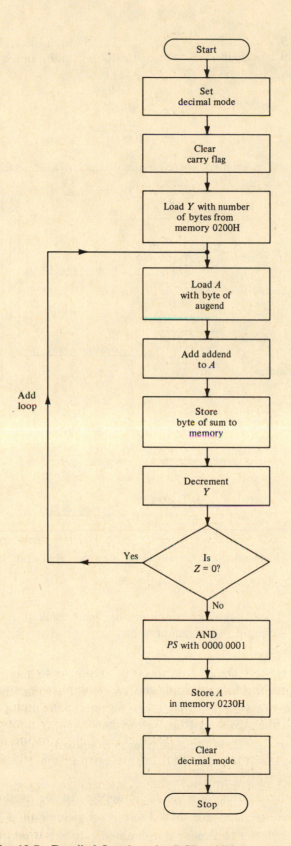

Fig. 13-7 Detailed flowchart for BCD addition problem

$$
\begin{array}{ccc}
15 & 0F & \begin{aligned} 1111 & \quad \text{multiplicand} \\ \times\, 1001 & \quad \text{multiplier} \end{aligned} \\
\underline{\times\ 9} & \underline{\times\ 09} & \begin{aligned} \overline{1111} \\ 0000 \\ 0000 \\ \underline{1111\quad} \\ \overline{10000111_{2}} \end{aligned} \\
135_{10} & 87_{16} &
\end{array}
$$

(a) Multiplication problem worked out in decimal, hexadecimal, and binary

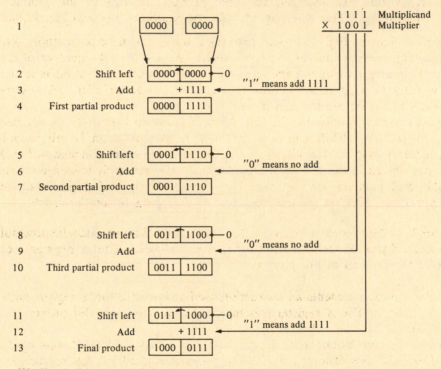

(b) Simple binary multiplication problem using the "shift and add" technique

Fig. 13-8

The diagram in Fig. 13-8b helps explain how the "shift and add" method of multiplication works. To simplify the example, 4-bit numbers and registers have been used. Follow the line numbers on the left.

Line 1   Product registers are cleared to 0000. Observe that the product register must be twice the width of the multiplicand and multiplier registers.

Line 2   The product registers are shifted one bit to the left.   This could be done on the 6502 MPU with the ASL and ROL instructions.

Line 3   The left bit (8s bit) in the multiplier is examined.   This could be done on the 6502 microprocessor using the ASL instruction.   It is a 1 so the multiplicand (1111) is added to the product registers.

Line 4   The first partial product (0000 1111) appears in the product registers.

Line 5   The product registers are shifted left again yielding 0001 1110.

Line 6   The 4s bit in the multiplier is examined.   It is a 0 which means that no addition occurs or that 0000 is added.

Line 7   The second partial product remains at 0001 1110.

Line 8   The third shift left is executed yielding 0011 1100.

Line 9   The 2s bit in the multiplier is examined.   It is a 0 which means that no addition occurs.

Line 10   The third partial product remains at 0011 1100.

Line 11   The final shift left is executed yielding 0111 1000.

Line 12   The 1s bit of the multiplier is examined.   It is a 1 which means that the multiplicand (1111) must be added to the current contents of the product registers (0111 1000).

Line 13   After the last addition, the final product appears in the product registers as $1000\,0111_2$.   This result agrees with the solutions found in Fig. 13-8a.

The sample problem in Fig. 13-8 demonstrates a technique used to multiply binary numbers using an 8-bit microprocessor such as the 6502 MPU.   Notice that the number of shifts and adds corresponds to the number of bits in the multiplier and multiplicand.   Also note that the binary product may be twice as wide as the multiplier and multiplicand registers.   Also observe that the shift left operation comes before the add in this procedure.

A *binary multiplication* routine for the 6502 MPU is shown in Fig. 13-9.   A detailed flowchart is drawn in Fig. 13-9a.   The "shift and add" method of multiplication is being employed in this flowchart.   A memory map for the binary multiplication program is sketched in Fig. 13-9b.

Generally, each block in the flowchart represents a single assembly language statement.   Refer to the flowchart and memory map in Fig. 13-9 during the following discussion of the binary multiplication program.   Key on the numbers next to the boxes in the flowchart.

Blocks 1 and 2.   These blocks represent three instructions that initialize the accumulator and the low- and high-order bytes of the product storage area to 00H.   The A register accumulates the low-order byte of the product in this program.

Block 3.   This block represents an instruction used to initialize the X register with the number of bits in the multiplier.   The X register is being used as a counter in this program.

Blocks 4 and 5.   These blocks represent two instructions that shift the "16-bit product registers" left one bit.   First, the low-order byte of the product is shifted left (A register).   Second, the high-order byte of the product (memory location 0231H) is rotated left.   It is important that any carry from the low-order byte be shifted into the LSB position in the high-order byte of the product.   Using first the 6502 ASL and then the ROL instructions will take care of the carry from low- to high-order byte of the product registers.

Block 6.   This block is used to determine if the MSB in the multiplier is a 0 or a 1.   An arithmetic shift left instruction will move the MSB of the multiplier into the carry flag.   The carry flag is then examined by the next branch instruction.

Block 7.   This branch instruction must ask the question: Is $C = 0$?   If the carry flag is reset to 0, then the multiplicand *will not* be added to the partial product in the accumulator and the program branches directly to block 12.   However, if the carry flag is set to 1, the multiplicand *will* be added to the partial product (blocks 8–11).

Blocks 8 and 9.   These blocks represent instructions that first clear the carry flag and then add the multiplicand from memory location 0210H to the partial product in the accumulator.

Blocks 10 and 11.   The branch instruction in block 10 must ask the question: Does $C = 0$?   If the carry flag was set to 1 by the previous addition, then the carry must be added to the high-order

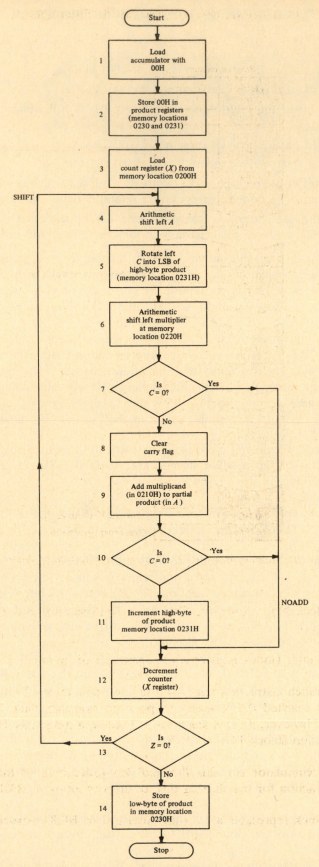

(a) Detailed flowchart for binary multiplication routine using the "shift and add" technique

Fig. 13-9

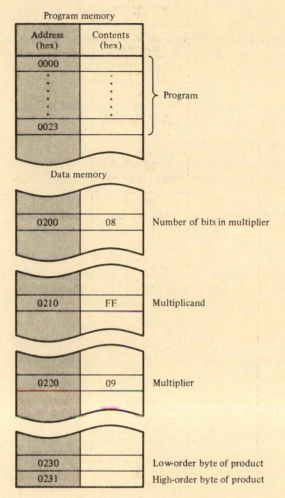

(b) Memory map for the binary multiplication problem

Fig. 13-9 (cont.)

byte of the product (block 11).   However, if the carry flag was reset to 0, the program branches to block 12 on the flowchart.

Block *12*.   The counter (index register X) is decremented by one.

Block *13*.   This branch instruction must ask the question: Does $Z = 0$?   If the Z flag is reset to 0 (counter has not reached 00H), then the program branches back to the "shift and add" procedure (block 4).   However, if the Z flag is set to 1 (counter has reached 00H), then the program exits to the last instruction (block 14).

Block *14*.   The accumulator contains the final low-order byte of the product.   This block represents a store instruction for transferring this to memory location 0230H.

Block *15*.   This block represents a software interrupt or BRK instruction on the 6502 MPU.

SOLVED PROBLEMS

13.9   The instruction sets of most 8-bit microprocessors such as the 6502, 8085, and 6800 _____ (do, do not) contain multiply or divide instructions.

Solution:

The instruction sets of most 8-bit microprocessors do not contain multiply or divide instructions. To perform multiplication and division with these processors, a multiply or divide routine must be programmed.

13.10 The _____ method of binary multiplication represented in Fig. 13-8*b* follows the procedure used when doing this calculation by hand.

Solution:

The "shift and add" (or "add and shift") method of binary multiplication represented in Fig. 13-8*b* follows the procedure used when doing this calculation by hand.

13.11 If the multiplicand and multipliers are 8-bit binary numbers, the product registers must be _____-bits wide.

Solution:

When using the "shift and add" method of binary multiplication, the product register must be twice the width of the multiplicand and multiplier registers. Therefore, when using 8-bit multipliers and multiplicands, a 16-bit produce register would be needed.

13.12 Using the 6502 instruction set in Fig. 13-1 and the flowchart and memory map in Fig. 13-9, write an assembly language program for multiplying two binary numbers.

Solution:

An assembly language program for multiplying two binary numbers using the procedure and memory map in Fig. 13-9 is written on the right (unshaded) side in Fig. 13-10. This is one of several correct solutions.

13.13 Using the 6502 instruction set, assemble the object program (machine code) for the binary multiplication problem detailed in Fig. 13-9. Use program memory locations 0000H through 0023H as shown in the memory map.

Solution:

Refer to the 6502 instruction set in Fig. 13-1. The object program or machine code for the program is shown at the left (shaded area) in Fig. 13-10.

13.4 HEX–TO–SEVEN-SEGMENT DECODING

Seven-segment decoders in IC form and their use in driving seven-segment displays were introduced in Chap. 3. Recall that the segments on the display are labeled with letters *a* through *g*. The standard labeling for seven-segment displays is reproduced in Fig. 13-11*a*. The top section of Fig. 13-11*b* illustrates a common method of forming the hexadecimal numbers 0 through F on a seven-segment display. Particularly note that B_{16} is formed as a lowercase letter *b* and D_{16} is formed as a lowercase letter *d*.

The task in this section is to write a 6502 program that will act as a *hexadecimal–to–seven-segment decoder*. Figure 13-11*c* shows that bit 0 through bit 6 will have a specific meaning in our arbitrary decoding scheme. Observe that a 1 in the B_0 (bit 0) position will *turn on* segment *a* of a seven-segment display. Note also that a 0 in any position means the corresponding segment is *turned off*. The codes used to represent various hexadecimal characters are shown below the numerals in Fig. 13-11*b*. For example, to form the number 7_{16}, the binary code required to turn on just segments *a*, *b*, and *c* would be 0111 0000 or 70H. You will see the code 70H directly below the

Address (hex)	Contents (hex)	Label	Mnemonic	Operand	Comments
0000	A9 00		LDA	#$00	; Load accumulator immediate with 00H
0002	8D 30 02		STA	$0230	; Store 00H in memory location 0230H (clear low byte of product register)
0005	8D 31 02		STA	$0231	; Store 00H in memory location 0231H (clear high byte of product register)
0008	AE 00 02		LDX	$0200	; Load number of bits in multiplier from memory location 0200H to X register
000B	0A	SHIFT	ASL	A	; Arithmetic shift left accumulator (shifts low byte of product 1 bit left)
000C	2E 31 02		ROL	$0231	; Rotate memory location 0220 left (rotate high byte of product left 1 bit)
000F	0E 20 02		ASL	$0220	; Arithmetic shift left memory location 0220H (shifts multiplier left 1 bit)
0012	90 09		BCC	NOADD	; If $C = 0$, then branch to symbolic address of NOADD
0014	18		CLC		; Clear carry flag
0015	6D 10 02		ADC	$0210	; Add multiplicand (location 0201) to low byte of product (in accumulator)
0018	90 03		BCC	NOADD	; If $C = 0$, then branch to symbolic address of NOADD
001A	EE 31 02		INC	$0231	; Add 1 to high byte of product (location 0231H) if $C = 1$
001D	CA	NOADD	DEX		; Decrement counter (X register)
001E	D0 EB		BNE	SHIFT	; If $Z = 0$, then branch backward to symbolic address SHIFT
0020	8D 30 02		STA	$0230	; Store low byte of product in memory location 0230H
0023	00	STOP	BRK		; Halt MPU

Fig. 13-10 Assembly language and machine code for binary multiplication problem

seven-segment display of 7 in Fig. 13-11b. These codes will be used when the hex–to–seven-segment decoder is programmed.

A table will be used to store the codes for hexadecimal numbers when the hex–to–seven-segment decoder is programmed. This lookup table is shown on the memory map in Fig. 13-12b. In this example, the codes are stored at the beginning of page zero in memory. The program is stored on page 2, and the hex number to be decoded and the resulting seven-segment

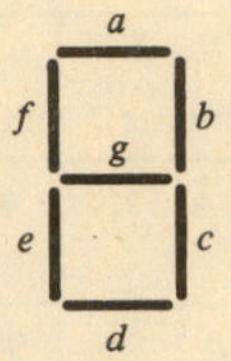

(a) Standard segment identification on seven-segment display (such as seven-segment LED display)

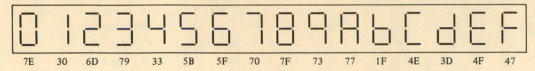

| 7E | 30 | 6D | 79 | 33 | 5B | 5F | 70 | 7F | 73 | 77 | 1F | 4E | 3D | 4F | 47 |

(b) Hexadecimal character set using a seven-segment display with nonstandard hex codes (below each number)

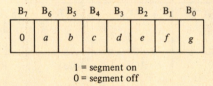

B_7	B_6	B_5	B_4	B_3	B_2	B_1	B_0
0	a	b	c	d	e	f	g

1 = segment on
0 = segment off

(c) Meaning of individual bits when developing code for hex seven-segment characters

Fig. 13-11

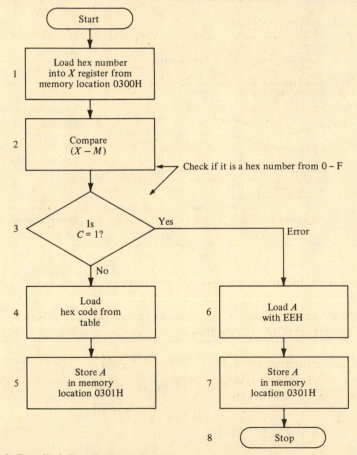

(a) Detailed flowchart for hex–to–seven-segment decoder problem

Fig. 13-12

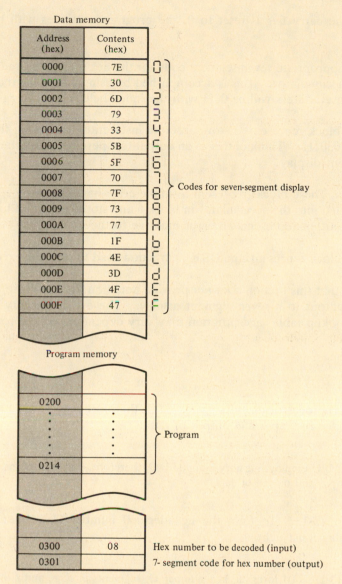

Data memory

Address (hex)	Contents (hex)
0000	7E
0001	30
0002	6D
0003	79
0004	33
0005	5B
0006	5F
0007	70
0008	7F
0009	73
000A	77
000B	1F
000C	4E
000D	3D
000E	4F
000F	47

Codes for seven-segment display

Program memory

0200	
⋮	⋮
0214	

Program

0300	08	Hex number to be decoded (input)
0301		7- segment code for hex number (output)

(b) Memory map for hex–to–seven-segment decoder problem

Fig. 13-12 (*cont.*)

code is output into storage locations on page 3 of memory. The specific memory locations are shown in Fig. 13-12*b*.

A detailed flowchart of the hex–to–seven-segment decoding program is drawn in Fig. 13-12*a*. Key on the numbers next to the flowchart blocks during the brief explanation that follows.

Block 1. Load the hexadecimal number to be decoded into the *X* register. This would be similar to an input from a peripheral device such as a hex keypad. Remember that the 6502 MPU uses memory-mapped I/O, so a load operation would be used to input data.

Blocks 2 and 3. These blocks check to make sure that the input is a legal hexadecimal number from 0 through F. A compare instruction may be used to reset the carry (*C*) flag to 0 if the input is a legal hex number. However, it sets the carry (*C*) flag to 1 if the number input is greater than or equal to 10H. If the carry flag is set to 1, an error has occurred and the program branches to the error routine. If the carry flag is reset to 0, the program continues with blocks 4 and 5 on the flowchart.

Block 4. The appropriate seven-segment code for the hex number stored in the *X* register must be loaded into the accumulator. This is accomplished by using a load instruction with zero page *X* addressing. The base address will be 00H with the index held in the *X* register.

Block 5. This block represents a store absolute instruction for storing the seven-segment code in memory location 0301H. Think of this as an output to a peripheral interface adapter which might drive a seven-segment display.

Blocks 6 and 7. These blocks represent a simple error-handling routine. In this example, the number EEH is loaded into the accumulator in block 6 and stored at output location 0301H by block 7. The EE at the output represents an error message to the operator.

Block 8. This block represents the BRK instruction used to stop the execution of the program.

You will notice that this section *does not* provide detail on the hardware requirements for input from a keypad or output to a seven-segment display. The actual memory locations used for the input and output, lookup table, and program may vary depending on the 6502 system.

SOLVED PROBLEMS

13.14 The 6502 microprocessor employs _____ I/O; therefore, simple load and _____ instructions may be used for the input and output of data.

Solution:

The 6502 MPU employs memory-mapped I/O; therefore, simple load and store instructions may be used for the input and output of data.

13.15 Refer to Fig. 13-11. To form the hexadecimal number C, segments _____ of a seven-segment display must light.

Solution:

See Fig. 13-11. To form the hex number C, segments *a*, *d*, *e*, and *f* of a seven-segment display must light or be activated.

13.16 Using the 6502 instruction set in Fig. 13-1 and the flowchart and memory map in Fig. 13-12, write an assembly language program for a hex–to–seven-segment decoder.

Solution:

One possible assembly language hex–to–seven-segment decoder program is written at the right (unshaded portion) in Fig. 13-13.

13.17 Using the 6502 instruction set, assemble the object program (machine code) for the hex–to–seven-segment decoder program detailed in Fig. 13-12. Use program memory locations 0200H through 0214H as shown on the memory map.

Solution:

Refer to the 6502 instruction set in Fig. 13-1. The object program or machine code for the hex–to–seven-segment decoder program is shown at the left (shaded area) in Fig. 13-13.

Address (hex)	Contents (hex)	Label	Mnemonic	Operand	Comments
0200	AE 00 03		LDX	$0300	; Load hex number (0–F) into X register from memory location 0300H
0203	E0 10		CPX	#$10	; Compare ($X - M$)
0205	B0 08		BCS	ERROR	; If $C = 1$, then branch to error routine at symbolic address ERROR
0207	B5 00		LDA	$00,X	; Load A with data (hex code) from address calculated as 00H + X
0209	8D 01 03		STA	$0301	; Store hex code in memory location $0301H
020C	4C 14 02		JMP	STOP	; Jump to memory location with symbolic address of STOP
020F	A9 EE	ERROR	LDA	#$EE	; Load accumulator with EEH immediate
0211	8D 01 03		STA	#0301	; Store EEH in memory location 0301H
0214	00	STOP	BRK		; Halt MPU

Fig. 13-13   Assembly language and machine code for hex–to–seven-segment decoder problem

13.18 Refer to Fig. 13-12a. The compare instruction in block 2 is essentially a _____ (add, subtract) operation. Its purpose is to either _____ (reset, set) the carry flag if the input is a legal hex number or to _____ (reset, set) the C flag if the hex number is $\geq$10H.

Solution:

The compare instruction in block 2 of Fig. 13-12a is essentially a subtract operation. Its purpose is to either reset the C flag to 0 if the input is a legal hex number or to set the C flag to 1 if the hex number is $\geq$10H. If the C flag is set to 1, it means the number is too large and an error has occurred.

13.5   USING SUBROUTINES

The concept of a *subroutine* as a subprogram that performs a specific task has been introduced in several previous sections. The transfer of control from the main program to the subroutine is accomplished by the 6502 MPU's *jump to subroutine* (JSR) instruction. The reverse, or transfer of control from the subroutine back to the main program, is performed by the 6502's *return from subroutine* (RTS) instruction. The stack is automatically used during the jump to and return from subroutines to store the contents of the program counter. Therefore, the stack point register must be initialized (usually with 01FFH on 6502-based systems). Also, the *push* and *pull* instructions are commonly used as part of a subroutine to save the values in the processor status register and/or accumulator. Recall that the generic and 8080/8085 microprocessors were a little different in that they used the CALL and RET instructions to access subroutines. However, both the 6800 and 6502 MPUs use the JSR and RTS instructions to jump to and return from subroutines.

A flowchart for a sample program is sketched in Fig. 13-14a. The task of the program is to (1) select and store the lowest number from a list, (2) select and store the highest number from a list, and (3) subtract the smallest number from the largest and store the difference in a reserved memory location.

A memory map for the sample problem is drawn in Fig. 13-14b.   Notice that the main routine and two subroutines are located at the beginning of page zero.   Data memory contains the address of the list of numbers (0060H and 0061H) for indirect addressing.   The number of elements in the list is given at memory location 0070H.   The list of numbers is stored starting at memory location 0080H.   Storage locations are reserved for the highest number, lowest number, and the difference between the two at memory locations 0090H through 0092H.

The main routine of the sample program is fairly short as suggested by the flowchart in Fig. 13-14a.   Key on the numbers next to the flowchart blocks during the brief explanation that follows.

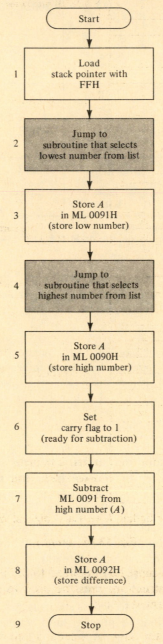

(a) Flow chart for main routine of finding lowest and highest numbers problem

Fig. 13-14

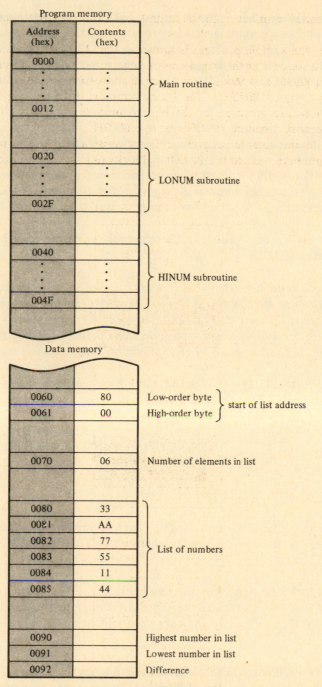

Program memory

Address (hex)	Contents (hex)	
0000		
⋮	⋮	Main routine
0012		
0020		
⋮	⋮	LONUM subroutine
002F		
0040		
⋮	⋮	HINUM subroutine
004F		

Data memory

Address	Contents	
0060	80	Low-order byte } start of list address
0061	00	High-order byte
0070	06	Number of elements in list
0080	33	
0081	AA	
0082	77	List of numbers
0083	55	
0084	11	
0085	44	
0090		Highest number in list
0091		Lowest number in list
0092		Difference

(b) Memory map for finding lowest and highest numbers problem

Fig. 13-14 (*cont.*)

Block 1. The stack point register must be initialized to 01FFH. The 6502 does not have a load stack pointer operation, so several instructions must be used to do the job. A combination of the LDX and TXS instructions will perform the task.

Block 2. This block represents the task of selecting the smallest number from a list. The subprogram that will do this job is found in a separate subroutine titled LONUM (for lowest number).

Block 3. The lowest number is held in the 6502's accumulator after the LONUM subroutine. It is stored in the appropriate memory location by this store instruction.

Block 4. This block represents the task of selecting the highest number from the list. The subprogram that will perform this job is found in a separate subroutine called HINUM (for highest number).

Block 5. The highest number is held in the 6502's accumulator after the HINUM subroutine. It is stored in the appropriate memory location by this store instruction.

Blocks 6 and 7. The C flag is set to 1 in preparation for subtraction. Block 7 represents a subtract operation (lowest number subtracted from the highest number). Observe that the highest number is in the accumulator, while the low number is stored in memory location 0091H.

Block 8. The difference now resides in the accumulator of the 6502 MPU. It is stored in its reserved memory location 0092H.

Block 9. This block represents the BRK instruction used to stop the execution of the program. Detailed flowcharts for the LONUM (select lowest number) and HINUM (select highest number) subroutines are diagrammed in Figs. 13-15 and 13-16, respectively. These two routines are almost identical, so only the LONUM subroutine will be detailed. Key on the numbers next to the flowchart blocks in Fig. 3-15 during the brief explanation that follows.

Block 2.1. Initialize the Y register with the number of elements in the list of numbers. In this example the number is 06H. The Y register will be used as a counter in this subroutine.

Block 2.2. Initialize the accumulator with the first number (FFH). The first of the "lower numbers" from the list will be compared with this number and will replace it in the accumulator during the program.

Block 2.3. Decrement the counter (Y register).

Block 2.4. Push the processor status register on the top of the stack. This is a method of saving the flags that exist after the decrement operation. The flags will be pulled from the stack later in the subroutine.

Block 2.5. This block represents the compare operation. The compare instruction's purpose is to set or reset the C flag by subtracting the current number in the list from the number in the accumulator $(A - M)$. If $A < M$, then the carry flag will be reset to 0. However, if $A \geq M$, the carry flag will be set to 1.

Block 2.6. A "branch if carry clear" instruction examines the C flag. If $C = 0$, then the lowest number is already in the accumulator and a branch occurs skipping the change of numbers (see block 2.7 in Fig. 13-15). However, if $C = 1$, then the number in the accumulator is larger and must be discarded and replaced by the lower number from memory (see block 2.7 in Fig. 13-15).

Block 2.8. The flags are restored by the "pull processor status register off stack" operation. This is required because block 2.9 will look at the Z flag which was affected by the decrement Y operation back in block 2.3.

Block 2.9. The "branch if not equal to zero" instruction examines the Z flag. If $Z = 0$, then the program will branch back to block 2.3 and compare another number from the list with that in the accumulator. If $Z = 1$, the program will continue on to block 2.10 to complete the subroutine.

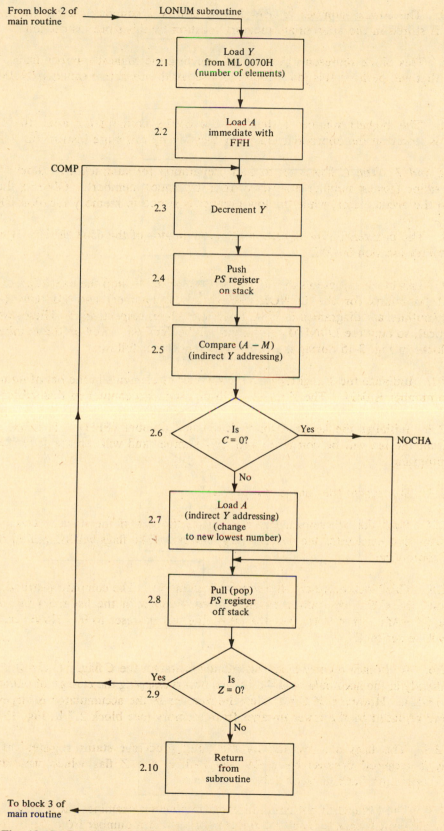

Fig. 13-15 Detailed flowchart for LONUM (finding lowest number) subroutine

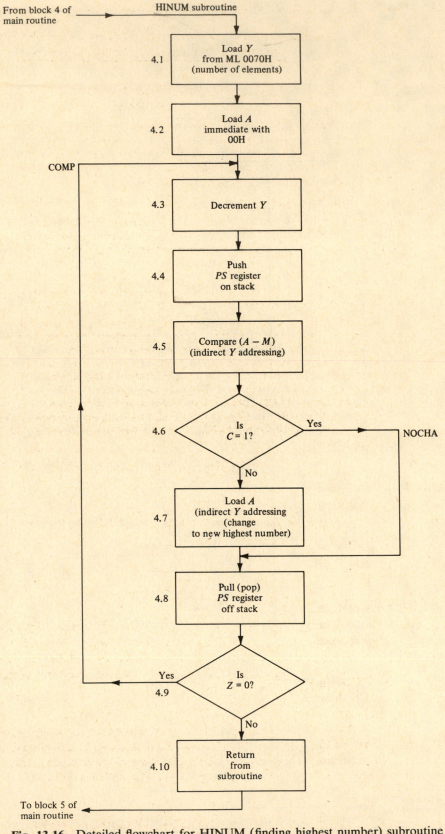

Fig. 13-16 Detailed flowchart for HINUM (finding highest number) subroutine

Block 2.10. This block represents the RTS instruction which restores the program counter to the correct return address (pulled off stack) in the main routine and returns control to the main program.

A detailed flowchart for the second subroutine (HINUM) which selects the highest number from the list is reproduced in Fig. 13-16. It is almost identical to the LONUM subroutine except for blocks 4.2, 4.6, and 4.7.

SOLVED PROBLEMS

13.19 Refer to Fig. 13-14. The top of the stack is set to _____ (hex) in this program.

Solution:

See Fig. 13-14a. The top of the stack is set to 01FFH by block 1 of this program. This is accomplished by loading FFH into the stack point register. The high-order byte of the stack pointer is permanently set to 01H on the 6502 microprocessor.

13.20 Block 2 in Fig. 13-14a represents a _____ (group of, single) instruction(s) that selects the _____ (highest, lowest) number from a list of numbers in memory.

Solution:

Block 2 in Fig. 13-14a represents a group of instructions (called a subroutine) that selects the lowest number from a list in memory.

13.21 What is the purpose of the operation represented by block 6 of the flowchart in Fig. 13-14a?

Solution:

On the 6502 microprocessor, the *C* flag must be set to 1 before performing a subtraction problem.

13.22 Using the flowchart and memory map from Fig. 13-14 as well as the 6502 instruction set, write an assembly language program for just the main routine of this problem.

Solution:

One possible assembly language program for the main routine outlined in Fig. 13-14 is written at the right (unshaded portion) in Fig. 13-17.

13.23 Using the 6502 instruction set, assemble the object program (machine code) for the main routine of the problem detailed in Fig. 13-14. Use program memory locations 0000H through 0012H as shown on the memory map.

Solution:

Refer to the 6502 instruction set in Fig. 13-1. The object program or machine code for the program in Fig. 13-14 is shown at the left (shaded area) in Fig. 13-17.

13.24 Using the flowchart from Fig. 13-15 and the memory map from Fig. 13-14b as well as the 6502 instruction set, write an assembly language program for just the LONUM subroutine of this problem.

Solution:

One possible assembly language program for the LONUM subroutine outlined in Fig. 13-15 is written at the right (unshaded portion) in Fig. 13-18.

Address (hex)	Content (hex)	Label	Mnemonic	Operand	Comments
0000	A2 FF		LDX	#$FF	; Load X immediate with FFH
0002	9A		TXS		; Transfer FFH to SP (set SP to 01FFH)
0003	20 20 00		JSR	LONUM	; Jump to subroutine with symbolic address LONUM (find lowest number from list)
0006	85 91		STA	$91	; Store A in memory location 0091H (store low number)
0008	20 40 00		JSR	HINUM	; Jump to subroutine with symbolic address HINUM (find highest number from list)
000B	85 90		STA	$90	; Store A in memory location 0090H (store high number)
0000	38		SEC		; Set $C = 1$ (ready for subtraction problem)
000E	E5 91		SBC	$91	; Subtract $(A - M \rightarrow A)$ (subtract low number from high number)
0010	85 92		STA	$92	; Store A in memory location 0092H (store difference)
0012	00	STOP	BRK		; Halt MPU

Fig. 13-17 Assembly language and machine code for main routine of finding lowest and highest number problem

13.25 Using the 6502 instruction set, assemble the object program (machine code) for the LONUM subroutine of the problem detailed in Fig. 13-15. Use program memory locations 0020H through 002FH as shown on the memory map.

Solution:

Refer to the 6502 instruction set in Fig. 13-1. The object program or machine code for the program in Fig. 13-15 is shown at the left (shaded area) in Fig. 13-18.

Supplementary Problems

13.26 To the programmer, the 6502-based system consists of the _____ set, accumulator, two index registers (_____ and _____), program _____, flags, memory, I/O ports, _____ (in RAM), and stack point register.   *Ans.* instruction, X, Y, counter, stack

13.27 List the four fields in a typical 6502 assembly language instruction line.
Ans. label, mnemonic (op code or operation), operand, comments

13.28 Assembly language statements must contain an entry in the _____ field, whereas entries in the other fields are optional.   *Ans.* mnemonic

Address (hex)	Content (hex)	Label	Mnemonic	Operand	Comments
0020	A4 70	LONUM	LDY	$70	; Load Y with # of elements in list stored at memory location 0070H
0022	A9 FF		LDA	#$FF	; Load A with FFH (assume lowest number is FFH)
0024	88	COMP	DEY		; Decrement Y (Y register is counter)
0025	08		PHP		; Push PS register on stack (save flags)
0026	D1 60		CMP	($60), Y	; Compare $(A - M)$ set $C = 1$ if $A \geq M$ reset $C = 0$ if $A < M$ (indirect Y addressing)
0028	90 02		BCC	NOCHA	; If $C = 0$, then branch to symbolic address NOCHA
002A	B1 60		LDA	($60), Y	; Load A with new lowest number from list (use indirect Y addressing)
002C	28	NOCHA	PLP		; Pull PS register off stack (restore flags)
002D	D0 F5		BNE	COMP	; If $Z = 0$, then branch back to symbolic address COMP
002F	60		RTS		; Return from subroutine

Fig. 13-18 Assembly language and machine code for LONUM (finding lowest number) subroutine

13.29 The stack is always located on page _____ (hex) in 6502-based systems.   *Ans.*   01H

13.30 The 6502 MPU employs _____ I/O.   *Ans.*   memory-mapped

13.31 When writing an assembly language program for a 6502-based system, _____ (all, most) instructions require an entry in the operand column.   *Ans.*   most

13.32 When writing an assembly language program, entries in the _____ field are not required but are considered very desirable for good documentation.   *Ans.*   comments

13.33 A $ symbol in the operand column of a 6502 assembly language program means the data that follows is a _____ number.   *Ans.*   hexadecimal

13.34 A # symbol in the operand column of a 6502 assembly language program means the instruction is employing _____ addressing.   *Ans.*   immediate

13.35 Refer to Fig. 13-18.   The "LDY $70" instruction uses _____ addressing.   *Ans.*   zero page

13.36 Refer to Fig. 13-18.   The DEY instruction uses _____ addressing.   *Ans.*   implied

13.37 Refer to Fig. 13-18.   The "CMP ($60), Y" instruction uses _____ addressing.
Ans.   indirect Y or (IND), Y

13.38 Refer to Fig. 13-18. The "BCC NOCHA" instruction uses _____ addressing.   *Ans.* relative

13.39 Refer to Fig. 13-18. In the "BNE COMP" instruction, the title COMP is called a(n) _____ address.   *Ans.* symbolic

13.40 Refer to Fig. 13-18. Program line 002AH is executed only when the new number in the list (in memory) is _____ (higher, lower) than the number in the accumulator.   *Ans.* lower

13.41 Refer to Fig. 13-18. The RTS instruction will only be executed after the counter (*Y* register) is decremented to _____ (hex).   *Ans.* 00H

13.42 Using the flowchart from Fig. 13-16 and the memory map from Fig. 13-14*b* as well as the 6502 instruction set, write an assembly language program for just the HINUM subroutine of this problem.   *Ans.* see right side (unshaded portion) of Fig. 13-19

Address (hex)	Contents (hex)	Label	Mnemonic	Operand	Comments
0040	A4 70	HINUM	LDY	$70	; Load *Y* from memory location 0070H (load # of elements in list)
0042	A9 00		LDA	#$00	; Load *A* with 00H immediate (assume highest number is 00H)
0044	88	COMP	DEY		; Decrement *Y* (*Y* register is counter)
0045	08		PHP		; Push *PS* register on stack (save flags)
0046	D1 60		CMP	($60),*Y*	; Compare (*A* − *M*) set *C* = 1 if *A* ≥ *M* reset *C* = 0 if *A* < *M* (indirect *Y* addressing)
0048	B0, 02		BCS	NOCHA	; If *C* = 1, then branch to symbolic address NOCHA
004A	B1 60		LDA	($60),*Y*	; Load *A* with new highest number from list (use indirect *Y* addressing)
004C	28	NOCHA	PLP		; Pull *PS* register off stack (restore flags)
004D	D0 F5		BNE	COMP	; If *Z* = 0, then branch back to symbolic address COMP
004F	60		RTS		; Return from subroutine

Fig. 13-19 Assembly language and machine code for HINUM (finding highest number) subroutine

13.43 Using the 6502's instruction set, assemble the object program (machine code) for the HINUM subroutine of the problem detailed in Fig. 13-16. Use program memory locations 0040H through 004FH as shown on the memory map in Fig. 13-14*b*.   *Ans.* see left side (shaded area) of Fig. 13-19

Chapter 14

Some 16-Bit and 32-Bit Microprocessors

14.1 INTRODUCTION

Most widely used microprocessors are divided into two groups based on their origin. Some label these groups as the 6's and the 8's. The 6's group traces its origin back to the original 6800 microprocessor designed by Motorola. A "family tree" of the 6's group of MPUs is illustrated on the left in Fig. 14-1. Likewise, the 8's group "family tree" is drawn on the right side in Fig. 14-1. The 8's group traces its origin back to Intel's 8080 microprocessor. The "family trees" in Fig. 14-1 are not meant to include all the variations of processors but only outline the major MPUs. One source recently listed hundreds of variations of these and other microprocessors.

Observe that the trend, as you progress upward on the "family tree," is toward greater and greater complexity. Complexity is noted in Fig. 14-1 in terms of the *bit size* of the internal registers (either accumulator or general-purpose). The bit size shown in Fig. 14-1 may or may not be the same as the width of the data bus. For instance, the complexity of the Intel 80386 is listed in Fig. 14-1 as 32 bits. Another measure of complexity might be the number of parts integrated on the chip. The Intel 80386 MPU is reported to have over 275,000 transistors integrated on a single silicon chip. Also note that each branch in Fig. 14-1 is labeled near the top with the manufacturer responsible for its development. The 6500-series branch has several major developers listed.

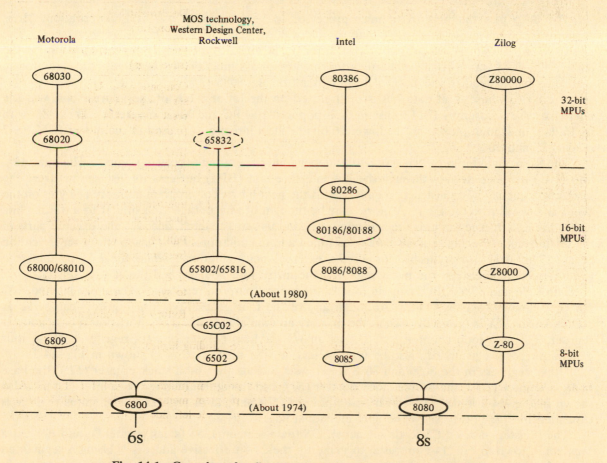

Fig. 14-1 Genealogy for 6's group and 8's group of microprocessors

A development date is listed as approximately 1974 for the original 6800 and 8080 micro-processors.   The 16-bit MPUs entered the marketplace in the late 1970s and early 1980s.   A 65832 MPU is listed in Fig. 14-1 in the 6500-series column.   According to Western Design Center, this 32-bit microprocessor is now under development.

In terms of popular microcomputers, MPUs from the 8's group are found in all the IBM microcomputers (such as the PC, PC Jr., PC-XT, PC-AT) and clones.   The newer IBM Personal System/2 models (such as model 25, 30, 50, 60, and 80) also use microprocessors from the 8's group.   On the other hand, Apple Computer has used microprocessors from the 6's group.   The 6502 and 65C02 MPUs have been used in the Apple II, II+, IIc, and IIe microcomputers.   The 65816 processor is used in the Apple II$_{GS}$ computer.   The 68000 MPUs are used in the Apple Macintosh, Commodore Amiga, and Atari ST series microcomputers.   The 6502 has also been used in many other older machines such as the Commodore Pet, VIC-20, and Commodore-64. Generally, Radio Shack has used chips from the 8's group, but the 6809 chip was used in the popular Radio Shack Color Computer.   Heath/Zenith microcomputers typically use the 8's group of MPUs in their machines.   Compaq microcomputers (such as the Compaq Deskpro 386) are generally IBM compatible and use chips from the 8's group of MPUs.

Not all microprocessors fit neatly into the 6's and 8's groupings outlined in Fig. 14-1.   A few other powerful processors that are not listed include the Texas Instruments 9900 series, the National Semiconductor 8900 and 32000 series, and AT & T's WE32100 MPU.

14.2   INTEL 8086 AND 8088

The 8086 was the first 16-bit microprocessor to be introduced by Intel Corporation.   It is designed to be upwardly compatible with the older 8080/8085 series of 8-bit microprocessors.   The upward compatibility allows programs written for the 8080/8085 to be easily converted to run on the 8086.   The 8088 was introduced shortly after the 8086 and is functionally the same, but it features an 8-bit data bus instead of the 16-bit data bus found on the 8086.

The 8088, whose 8-bit data bus is multiplexed on the lower 8 bits of the address bus, was the microprocessor chosen by IBM to use in their popular IBM PC and XT computers.   The 8086, with its 16 data lines multiplexed on the lower 16 bits of the address bus, is used in the newer IBM PS/2 models 25 and 30.

The 8086 is made up of two separate, independently operating processing units.   The execution unit (EU) accesses devices through the bus interface unit (BIU) but gets its instructions from the instruction queue.   The instruction queue holds the next 6 bytes of program memory (4 bytes on the 8088) and sends it to the EU.   A *queue* may be thought of as a storage area similar to a waiting line where the first instruction in is the first one out.   In this way the fetch, decode, and execute parts of the fetch-decode-execute sequence are overlapped and the microprocessor has much faster execution times.   The BIU is responsible for all the external bus operations, while the EU contains the general-purpose registers, the index registers, the instruction pointer, and the status register.

The 8086 and 8088 MPUs contain four 16-bit general-purpose registers.   These are labeled *AX*, *BX*, *CX*, and *DX* in Fig. 14-2.   Although any of the four general-purpose registers can serve as accumulators, *AX* is generally used as the primary accumulator.   *BX* is often used as a base address register, *CX* as a loop counter, and *DX* as an I/O address pointer or data register.   These four general-purpose registers can also be used as sets of 8-bit register pairs as shown in Fig. 14-2.

Other registers in the 8086 and 8088 register set include the 16-bit stack pointer (*SP*), the base address pointer (*BP*), the source index pointer (*SI*), and the destination index pointer (*DI*).   Also shown in Fig. 14-2 is the 16-bit instruction pointer (*IP*) and status register.   The status register is expanded in Fig. 14-2 to show the nine individual flags.

The registers labeled *CS* (code segment), *DS* (data segment), *SS* (stack segment), and *ES* (extra segment) shown in Fig. 14-2 are used to make up the 20-bit effective address.   Using a segmented memory scheme, the 8086 and 8088 can access up to 1 megabyte (Mbyte) of memory.

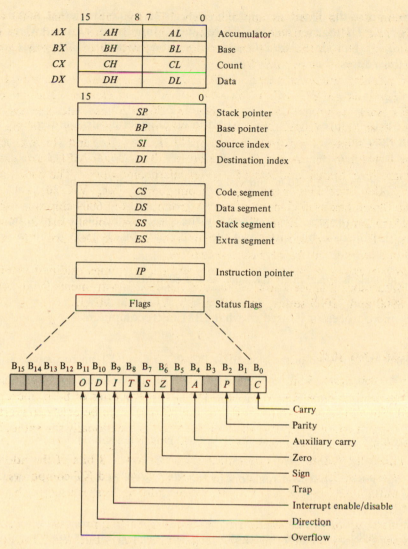

Fig. 14-2 Programming model for the Intel 8086 and 8088 microprocessors (*Courtesy of Intel Corporation*)

The 8086 and 8088 use nine addressing modes to perform operations on data, memory, and I/O devices. In the *immediate mode*, the operand immediately follows the op code in program memory. *Register addressing* is fast in that the operand can be in any of the four general-purpose registers. In *direct addressing* the operand's address in memory is given immediately after the op code in program memory. *Register indirect addressing* names which register (*BX, BP, SI,* or *DI*) contains the address of the operand. In *based addressing* the operand address is found by taking the contents of either the *BX* or *BP* register and adding the displacement that follows the op code in the program to them. Use of the *BX* register implies indexing through the data segment, while use of the *BP* register implies indexing through the stack segment. *Indexed addressing* is similar to based addressing except that the displacement is added to the contents of the *SI* or *DI* registers, and it always implies the use of the data segment. Adding the contents of the *BX* or *BP* register, the contents of the *SI* or *DI* register, and the displacement following the op code to find the operand address is called *based indexed addressing*. *String addressing* is a mode that is used when operations are performed on data strings. Two addresses, a source address and a destination address, are found using the *SI* and *DI* registers along with the *DS* and *ES* registers. The source address is found by adding the contents of the *SI* register and the *DS* register, while the destination address is the sum of the contents of the *DI* register and the *ES* register. Input and output devices can be accessed using the *I/O addressing* mode. The I/O addressing mode uses the *DX* register to output a 16-bit I/O address on the address bus.

SOLVED PROBLEMS

14.1 The 8086 MPU features _____ (8, 16)-bit internal general-purpose registers and a(n) _____ (8, 16)-bit data bus.

Solution:

The 8086 MPU features 16-bit internal registers and a 16-bit data bus.

14.2 The Intel _____ (number) is functionally the same as the 8086 MPU, but it features a(n) _____ (8, 32)-bit data bus instead of the 16-bit data bus found on the 8086.

Solution:

The Intel 8088 is functionally the same as the 8086 MPU but features a narrower 8-bit data bus.

14.3 The 8088 microprocessor is used in what IBM microcomputers?

Solution:

The 8088 MPU is used in the older IBM PC, PC Jr., and XT microcomputers.

14.4 The 8086 microprocessor is used in what IBM microcomputers?

Solution:

The 8086 MPU is used in the newer IBM PS/2 models 25 and 30.

14.5 List the four general-purpose registers in the 8086/8088 microprocessor and give their usual functions.

Solution:

The 8086/8088 general-purpose registers are shown in Fig. 14-2 as follows:

AX—used as accumulator   *CX*—used as loop counter
BX—used as base address register   *DX*—used as I/O address pointer or data register

14.6 Name the two separate processing units in the 8086/8088 microprocessor.

Solution:

The 8086/8088 MPU contains two separate processing units called the execution unit (EU) and the bus interface unit (BIU).

14.3 INTEL 80186, 80188, AND 80286

The *Intel 16-bit 80186 microprocessor* is fundamentally an 8086 chip with many added features. The 80186 MPU combines 15 to 20 of the most common 8086 system components into one highly integrated package. The 80186 is faster than the 8086 MPU. The 80186 is upward compatible with 8086 and 8088 software but adds 10 new instruction types to the existing 8086/8088 instruction set. A few of the added features include a clock generator, two independent high-speed DMA (direct memory access) channels, a programmable interrupt controller, three programmable 16-bit timers, and programmable chip-select logic.

Because of all the added features, the 80186 microprocessor comes in a large 68-pin PLCC (plastic chip carrier) package while the 8086 comes in the smaller 40-pin DIP (dual-in-line package) form. The 80186 microprocessor uses exactly the same register set and flags as the 8086/8088. These were drawn in Fig. 14-2. Like the 8086, the 80186 MPU can directly access 1 Mbyte of memory.

The *Intel 8-bit 80188* has the same features as the 80186 except it only has an 8-bit data bus like its close relative the 8088 microprocessor. The 80188 MPU features the same 16-bit internal registers (see Fig. 14-2), the expanded instruction set, the greater speed, and the integrated extra system components that were available on the 80186 microprocessor. Because of its many features, the 80188 is available in the same 68-pin PLCC package used by the 80186 IC. The 80188 is a full-featured version of the 8088 microprocessor. System designers would probably consider the 80186 and 80188 as replacements for the 8086 and 8088 in *new* designs. However, because of the added features and extra pins on the ICs (80186 and 80188), they are not direct plug-in replacements for the older 8086 and 8088 ICs.

The *Intel 16-bit 80286* is a more sophisticated 16-bit microprocessor closely related to the 8086 and the 80186 MPUs. The 80286 chip is well known because it is used as the central processor in the IBM PS/2 models 50 and 60 and in the Compaq 286 microcomputers. The 80286 adds features that make it useful for multiple-user and multitasking systems. The 80286 MPU adds 16 more instructions beyond those used by the 80186. The 80286 can access up to 16 Mbytes of physical memory or 1 gigabyte [1 gigabyte (Gbyte) = 1 billion bytes] of virtual memory per task. The 80286 is a high-performance MPU with processing power approximately 6 times greater than that of the 8086. Because of its many functions, the 80286 (like the 80186) is available in the large 68-pin PLCC package. The 80286 is upwardly software compatible with the older 8086, 8088, 80186, and 80188 microprocessors.

The 80286 MPU operates in two modes. One is the *real address* mode which can be thought of as emulating the 8086 and 80186 MPUs. In this mode the 80286 can access up to 1 Mbyte of memory just like the less sophisticated 8086 and 80186 microprocessors. The real power of the 80286 is in the other mode, the *protected virtual-address* mode which is also called the *protected* mode. In the protected mode, the 80286 MPU maps 1 Gbyte of virtual addresses per task into a 16-Mbyte real address space. The protected mode is named as such because it provides memory protection to isolate the individual task's programs and data. This provides for multitasking and easier networking of microcomputers.

The 80286 register set is reproduced in Fig. 14-3*a*. Observe that almost all the registers are the same as those used on the 8086/8088 and 80186/80188 MPUs. The 80286's *flag register* shown in Fig. 14-3*b* has two added fields: the nested task flag and the I/O privilege level. Comparing the register set in Fig. 14-2 with the one in Fig. 14-3 you will observe that the 80286 processor contains

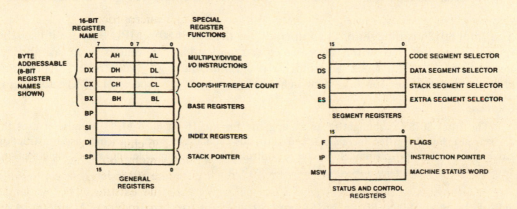

(*a*) Register set for 80286 microprocessor (*Courtesy of Intel Corporation*)

Fig. 14-3

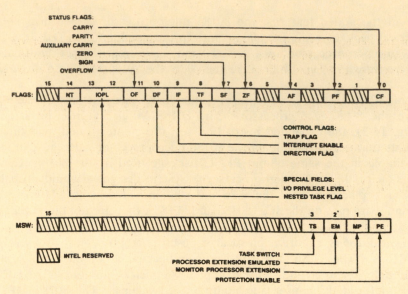

(b)   Status (flags) and control register bit functions for the 80286 microprocessor
(*Courtesy of Intel Corporation*)

Fig. 14-3   (*cont.*)

an additional *machine status word* (*MSW*) register.   Bit 0 of the MSW register controls whether the 80286 is in the real address mode or in the protected mode.

SOLVED PROBLEMS

14.7   The Intel_____ (80186, 80286) has exactly the same register set as the 8086 MPU.

   Solution:

   The Intel 80186 has exactly the same register set as the 8086 MPU.

14.8   The 8088 and the _____ (number) microprocessors both have the same register set and 8-bit data busses.

   Solution:

   The 8088 and the 80188 MPUs both have the same register set (see Fig. 14-2) and 8-bit data busses.

14.9   The Intel 80186 is thought of as an upgrade for the 16-bit 8086 MPU because it uses the same register set, but the 80186 increases speed and adds capabilities such as an increased instruction _____, a clock generator, a programmable _____ controller, a programmable chip-_____ logic section, and a two-channel _____ _____ access (DMA) subsystem.

   Solution:

   The Intel 80186 is thought of as an upgrade for the 16-bit 8086 MPU because it uses the same register set, but the 80186 increases speed and adds capabilities such as an increased instruction set, a clock generator, a programmable interrupt controller, a programmable chip-select logic section, and a two-channel direct memory access (DMA) subsystem.

14.10   All of the 8086, 8088, 80186, 80188, and 80286 chips can access _____ Mbyte(s) of memory directly.   However, the 80286 can be switched to the protected virtual address mode (or protected mode) where it can access _____ Mbyte(s) of physical memory and _____ Gbyte(s) of virtual memory per task.

Solution:

All of the 8086, 8088, 80186, 80188, and 80286 chips can access 1 Mbyte of memory directly. However, the 80286 can be switched to the protected virtual address mode (or protected mode) where it can access 16 Mbytes of physical memory and 1 Gbyte of virtual memory per task.

14.11 All the 8086, 8088, 80186, and 80188 chips _____ (share, do not share) the same register set.

Solution:

All the 8086, 8088, 80186, and 80188 chips share the same register set.

14.12 The 80286 MPU is the processor used in what two IBM microcomputers?

Solution:

The 80286 MPU serves as the CPU in both models 50 and 60 of IBM's PS/2 microcomputers.

14.4 INTEL 80386

The *Intel 32-bit 80386 microprocessor* is a very advanced microprocessor especially adapted for multitask operating systems. The 80386 is manufactured using high-speed CMOS (CHMOS) technology. The 80386 was selected as the processor in the powerful IBM PS/2 model 80 and the Compaq 386 microcomputers.

The 80386 features 32-bit internal registers and a 32-bit data bus. The 80386 MPU can address up to 4 Gbytes of physical memory and 64 terabytes [1 terabyte (Tbyte) = 1 trillion bytes] of virtual memory. The 80386 microprocessor's registers and instruction set are a superset of the earlier 8086, 80186, and 80286 microprocessors. The 80386 chip is housed in a very large (132-pin) pin-grid array (PGA) package. A pin diagram of the 80386 IC is illustrated in Fig. 14-4. The area of the ceramic 132-pin PGA package is approximately 1.5-in^2, and the thickness is less than 0.25 in. Note the

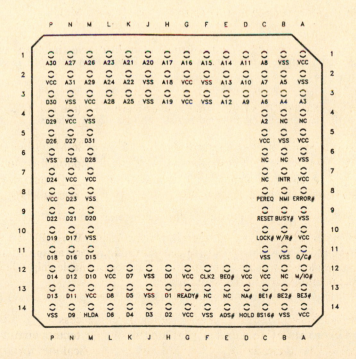

Fig. 14-4 Pin diagram for 80386 microprocessor packaged in a 132-pin PGA (pin-grid array) IC

somewhat unusual numbering system used in Fig. 14-4 for the pins on the 80386 IC.   For instance, the A18 (address line 18) pin is numbered as pin H2.

The Intel 80386 MPU consists of a central processing unit, a memory management unit, and a bus interface unit.   The 80386 has two modes of operation: the real address mode (real mode) and the protected virtual-address mode (protected mode).   In the real mode, the 80386 operates like a very fast 8086 microprocessor.   The protected mode provides access to the memory management, paging, and privilege capabilities of the MPU.

To ensure high performance, the 80386 bus interface offers address pipelining, dynamic data bus sizing, and direct byte-enable signals for each byte of the data bus.   It is reported that the 80386 can execute over three million instructions per second.

The 80386 MPU contains 32 registers in the following categories:

1.   General-purpose registers
2.   Segment registers
3.   Instruction pointer and flags
4.   Control registers
5.   System address registers
6.   Debug registers
7.   Test registers

The 32-bit general-purpose registers, 16-bit segment selector registers, and instruction pointer and flags are shown in Fig. 14-5.   The 80386's registers are a superset of those in the 80286, 80186, 80188, 8086, and 8088.   The special *EFLAGS* register is shown in more detail in Fig. 14-5.

The other types of registers (control, system address, debug, and test) are used mostly by system software.   For instance, the *MSW* register in the 80286 is part of the control register in the 80386 MPU.

The 80386 microprocessor supports a multitude of data types.   Some of these are bit, bit field, bit string, byte, integer, long integer, signed quad word, string, BCD, and packed BCD.   When the 80386 is connected to a 80387 numerics coprocessor, signed floating-point numbers are supported.

SOLVED PROBLEMS

14.13 The Intel 80386 microprocessor features _____ (16, 32)-bit internal registers and a _____ (16, 32)-bit data bus.

Solution:

The 80386 MPU features 32-bit internal registers and a 32-bit data bus.

14.14 The Intel 80386 MPU can address 4 _____ (Gbytes, Mbytes) of physical memory and 64 _____ (Mbytes, Tbytes) of virtual memory.

Solution:

The 80386 MPU can address 4 Gbytes of physical memory and 64 Tbytes of virtual memory.

14.15 The 80386 MPU chip is typically housed in a _____-pin _____ package.

Solution:

The 80386 MPU chip is typically housed in a 132-pin PGA (pin-grid array) package by Intel.

14.16 The 80386 MPU consists of a central _____ unit, a _____ management unit, and a _____ interface unit.

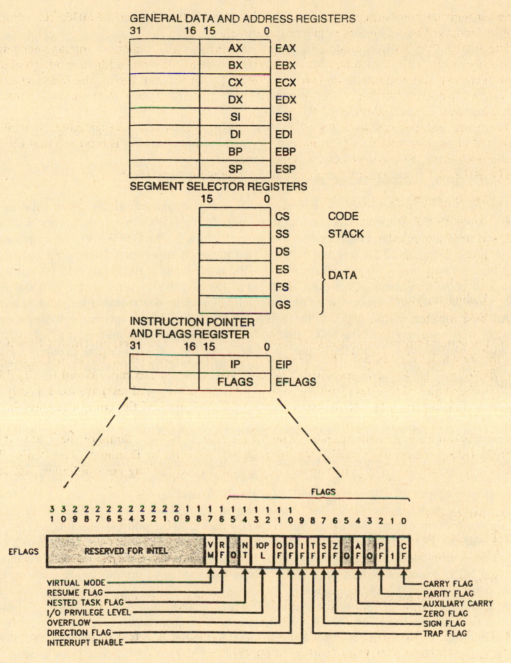

Fig. 14-5   Register set and EFLAGS register for the Intel 80386 microprocessor   (*Courtesy of Intel Corporation*)

Solution:

The 80386 MPU consists of a central processing unit, a memory management unit, and a bus interface unit.

14.17   The 80386's instruction and register sets are supersets of those found on what other Intel microprocessors?

Solution:

The Intel 80386's instruction and register sets are supersets of those found on the 80286, 80186, 80188, 8086, and 8088 microprocessors.

14.18 The 80386 microprocessor is used in what IBM computer?

Solution:

The 80386 microprocessor is used in the powerful IBM PS/2 model 80 computer.

14.5 MOTOROLA 68000, 68008, 68010, AND 68012

The 68000 microprocessor was first developed and marketed by Motorola in the late 1970s. Since 1979, Motorola has continued to upgrade the 68000-series microprocessor family with faster and more complex microprocessors and support chips. The 68000 MPU is sometimes referred to as a 16-bit external/32-bit internal MPU. This means it supports a 16-bit data bus, while it has 32-bit internal registers. However, the 68000 MPU is generally classified as a 16-bit unit. A newer high-speed version of the 68000 is the CMOS 68HC000 microprocessor. The 68000 was selected by Apple Computer as the processor in the original Macintosh, Macintosh Plus, and Macintosh SE.

An 8-bit version of the 68000 is the 68008 8-bit external/32-bit internal microprocessor. The 16-bit 68010 is an upgrade of the 68000 that adds virtual-memory capabilities, multiple-vector tables, and added instructions. The 68010 uses a 16-bit data bus, 32-bit internal registers, and a 24-bit address bus. The 68012 MPU is an enhancement of the 68010 and uses a 16-bit data bus, 32-bit internal registers, and a 30-bit address bus.

The 68000 chip is available in a large 64-pin dual-in-line package (DIP) IC. The pin diagram for the 68000 IC is illustrated in Fig. 14-6a. Notice that the 68000 MPU uses separate IC pins for the data bus and address bus. Many Intel products multiplex these lines. The 68000 MPU can access 16 Mbytes of memory. The A_0 pin is not required on the 68000 because instructions and data are accessed from even-number addresses. The high-order bytes are accessed from the even address, and the low-order bytes are accessed from the odd address. The 68000 MPU is also available in a 68-pin PLCC package and a 68-pin PGA package.

A pin diagram for the 68008 MPU is drawn in Fig. 14-6b. The smaller 48-pin dual-in-line package supports a narrow 8-bit data bus (D_0-D_7) and a 20-bit address bus (A_0-A_{19}).

The 68000 MPU can operate in one of two modes: the *user* mode or the *supervisor* mode. The user mode is employed when user applications programs are running. The supervisor mode is used when the MPU executes system programs. These two modes of operation are used on the 68000, 68008, 68010, and 68012 microprocessors.

A *user programming model* for the 68000 MPU is reproduced in Fig. 14-7. These are the registers available on the 68000, 68008, 68010, and 68012 microprocessors when they are operating in the user mode. Observe in Fig. 14-7 that the 68000 has eight data registers. The data registers can handle single-bit data, 8-bit data (bytes), 16-bit data (words), or 32-bit data (long words). Data in byte form would occupy bits 7 through 0.

The 68000 processors have seven general-purpose address registers as shown in Fig. 14-7. These address registers might hold addresses of operands, addresses of pointers to operands, indexes, or base addresses depending on the addressing mode. The 68000 and 68008 MPUs have 56 powerful instruction types and 14 addressing modes. For added speed, all the processors in the 68000 family use varying degrees of pipelining. *Pipelining* is the process of fetching and executing instructions at the same time instead of first fetching a single instruction, decoding the instruction, and finally executing the instruction in a linear fashion. The 68000, 68008, 68010, and 68012 all use a two-word instruction prefetch to speed up the processor. They all use memory-mapped I/O and can perform operations on five main data types. Earlier models of the 68000 family are compatible with the more complex later models. The program counter and user stack pointer registers are also

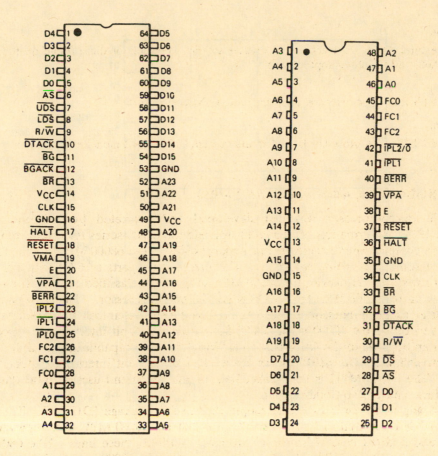

(a)   Pin diagram for the 68000 microprocessor   (b)   Pin diagram for the 68008 microprocessor

Fig. 14-6   (*Courtesy of Motorola, Inc.*)

shown.   The user mode part of the condition code register (*CCR*) or status register is also shown in Fig. 14-7.   The individual flags are detailed near the bottom in Fig. 14-7.

The fundamental registers shown in Fig. 14-7 are common to all models in the 68000 series of microprocessors.   When a 68000-series MPU enters the supervisor mode, other registers are available.   The number and type of supervisor mode registers vary from model to model within the 68000 family of MPUs.   The 68000 and 68008 microprocessors use register A7 (see Fig. 14-7) as a system stack pointer (*SSP*) when they are in the supervisor mode.   This adds several useful bits to the status register.   The more complicated 68010 and 68012 MPUs use the same system stack pointer (*SSP*) as the 68000 as well as an extended status register.   The 68010 and 68012 also have a 32-bit vector base register (*VBR*), a 3-bit source function code register (*SFC*), and a 3-bit destination function code register (*DFC*).

SOLVED PROBLEMS

14.19   Both the 68000 and 68008 MPUs use 32-bit _____ registers.   The 68000 MPU employs a(n) _____ (8, 16, 32)-bit data bus, while the 68008 processor uses an 8-bit _____ bus.

   Solution:

   Both the 68000 and 68008 MPUs use 32-bit internal registers.   The 68000 MPU employs a 16-bit data bus, while the 68008 processor uses an 8-bit data bus.

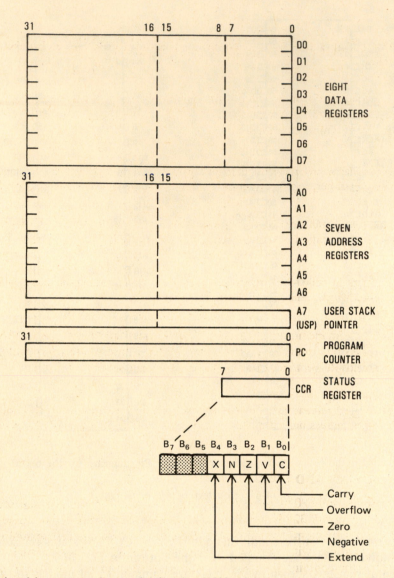

Fig. 14-7 User (mode) programming model for the 68000 microprocessor (*Courtesy of Motorola, Inc.*)

14.20 The 68000 uses 23 address lines, the 68008 uses _____ address lines, the 68010 uses _____ address lines, and the 68012 MPU employs _____ address lines.

Solution:

The 68000 uses 23 address lines, the 68008 uses 20 address lines, the 68010 uses 24 address lines, and the 68012 MPU employs 30 address lines.

14.21 The 68000 uses _____ (multiplexed, separate) pins for the data and address pins on the microprocessor IC.

Solution:

The 68000 uses separate pins for the data and address pins on the microprocessor IC.

14.22 List the name of the two modes of operation for the 68000 MPU.

Solution:

   The two modes of operation employed by the 68000 MPU are called the user mode and the supervisor mode.

14.23 All 68000-series microprocessors contain eight 32-bit _____ registers, _____ (number) 32-bit address registers, a 32-bit user _____ _____, a _____ counter, and a status register containing _____ (number) flags.

Solution:

   All 68000-series microprocessors contain eight 32-bit data registers, seven 32-bit address registers, a 32-bit user stack pointer, a program counter, and a status register containing five flags.

14.24 Data registers in 68000-series microprocessors can handle single-bit data, 8-bit data called _____, 16-bit data called _____, and 32-bit data called _____ words.

Solution:

   Data registers in 68000-series microprocessors can handle single-bit data, 8-bit data called bytes, 16-bit data called words, and 32-bit data called long words.

14.25 The 68010 is an enhancement of the 68000 MPU that employs a _____ (16, 32)-bit data bus, _____ (16, 32)-bit internal registers, a 24-bit address bus, and adds _____-memory capabilities, multiple-vector tables, and added instructions.

Solution:

   The 68010 is an enhancement of the 68000 MPU that employs a 16-bit data bus, 32-bit internal registers, a 24-bit address bus, and adds virtual-memory capabilities, mutliple-vector tables, and added instructions.

14.6 MOTOROLA 68020 AND 68030

   The Motorola 68020 and 68030 are very high-performance 32-bit microprocessors. Both feature 32-bit internal registers, a full 32-bit data bus, and an extremely wide 32-bit address bus. Each can directly access 4 Gbytes of memory. Both the 68020 and 68030 support virtual memory, and both are object-code–compatible with earlier members of the 68000 family (such as the 68000 and 68010). Each processor contains the basic register set shown in Fig. 14-7 (also used by the 68000, 68008, 68010, and 68012). This register set is employed when the 68000-series processor is in the *user mode* of operation. This basic register set includes eight data registers, seven address registers, a user stack pointer, a program counter, and a condition code register. Both microprocessors are implemented using Motorola's HCMOS technology which allows CMOS and HMOS (high-density NMOS) gates to be combined on one chip for maximum speed, low-power consumption, and small die (chip) size. Apple Computer selected the 68020 as the processor for the powerful Macintosh II microcomputer.

   Both the 68020 and 68030 MPUs use enhanced addressing modes to support high-level languages. On-chip instruction caches increase the speed or throughput of the processors. The *throughput* of a computer is the rate at which information can be processed by a system. The 68030 adds an on-chip data cache as well as an instruction cache. Processor speeds range from 12.5 to 25 MHz. Both processors feature pipelined architecture with internal parallelism allowing multiple instructions to be executed at one time. The 68030 increases this internal parallelism which allows accesses from internal caches to occur in parallel with bus transfers and multiple instructions to be executed concurrently. Generally, computer system throughput can be increased by increasing the speed of the CPU or by adding parallel information paths. The 68020 and 68030 have used both methods to increase their throughput or productivity.

The most obvious differences between the 68020 and 68030 is in their throughput and in the number of "other" registers added to the basic register set shown in Fig. 14-7. The supervisor programming model for the 68020 MPU is shown in Fig. 14-8a. Also shown is the status register used by both the 68020 and 68030 MPUs with the individual bits detailed in Fig. 14-8c. The more complicated supervisor programming model for the 68030 microprocessor is reproduced in Fig. 14-8b. The 68030 has both a high-speed 256-byte *instruction cache* and a high-speed 256-byte *data cache* that can be accessed at the same time. The reasons for using on-chip high-speed cache memories were to cut down on data bus activity, to allow the 68030 to interface with somewhat slower memory chips, and to increase CPU throughput. The 68030 also has several enhancements that make it well suited for graphics applications.

SOLVED PROBLEMS

14.26 Both the 68020 and 68030 MPUs are classified as _____ (16, 32)-bit microprocessors.   They both feature 32-bit _____ registers and _____ (16, 32)-bit data busses.

>   **Solution:**
>
>   Both the 68020 and 68030 MPUs are classified as 32-bit microprocessors. They both feature 32-bit internal registers and 32-bit data busses.

14.27 Both the 68020 and 68030 MPUs can directly access 4 _____ (Gbytes, Mbytes) of memory using _____ (16, 32)-bit address busses.

>   **Solution:**
>
>   Both the 68020 and 68030 MPUs can directly access 4 Gbytes of memory using 32-bit address busses.

14.28 When in the user mode of operation, the 68020 employs the register set shown in Fig. _____ (14-7, 14-8a).

>   **Solution:**
>
>   When in the user mode of operation, the 68020 employs the register set shown in Fig. 14-7.

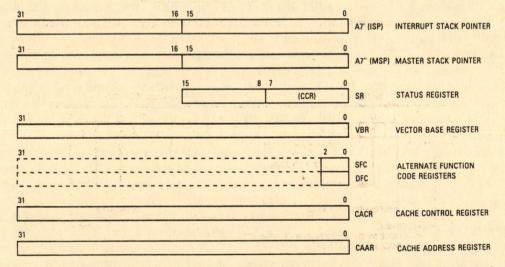

(a)   Supervisor (mode) programming model for the 68020 microprocessor (*Courtesy of Motorola, Inc.*)

Fig. 14-8

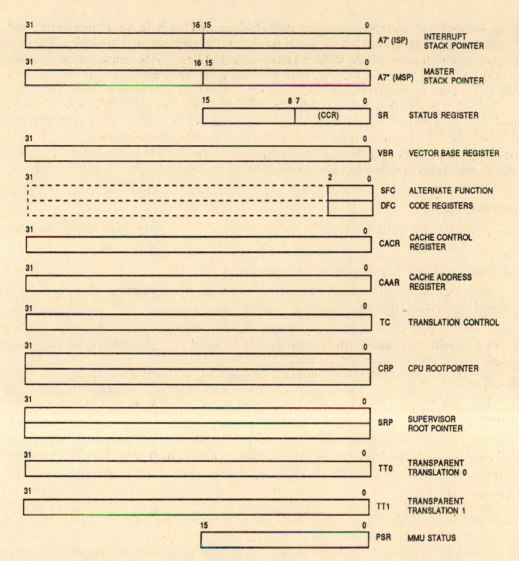

(b)   Supervisor (mode) programming model for the 68030 microprocessor (*Courtesy of Motorola, Inc.*)

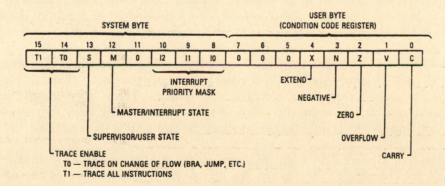

(c)   Detail of the status register for the 68020 and 68030 microprocessors (*Courtesy of Motorola, Inc.*)

Fig. 14-8   (*cont.*)

14.29 The reasons for using on-chip instruction caches and cache data memories on the _____ (68020, 68030) MPU were to cut down on _____ bus activity, to allow the MPU to interface with _____ (faster, slower) memory chips, and to _____ (decrease, increase) throughput.

Solution:

The reasons for using on-chip instruction caches and cache data memories on the 68030 MPU were to cut down on data bus activity, to allow the MPU to interface with slower memory chips, and to increase throughput.

14.30 The 68020 was the microprocessor chosen to be used in the Apple Macintosh _____ computer.

Solution:

The 68020 was the microprocessor chosen to be used in the Apple Macintosh II computer.

14.7 WESTERN DESIGN CENTER 65802 AND 65816

Unlike Intel and Motorola, Western Design Center (WDC) took the approach of designing their CMOS 65802 and 65816 16-bit microprocessors to be fully upward compatible with the older 6502 and 65C02 microprocessors. Both were introduced in 1985, and the 65816 MPU became well known when Apple Computer, Inc. introduced the Apple II_{GS} computer which employs this microprocessor.

Both the 65802 and 65816 are 16-bit internal and 8-bit external microprocessors. They both feature 16-bit accumulators and 8-bit data busses. The 65802 has 16 address lines which allows addressing of 64K bytes of memory. The 65816 employs 24 address lines which allows addressing of 16 Mbytes of physical memory. The 65802 is pin-to-pin compatible with the 6502. The 65802 and 65816 MPUs are both available in either a 40-pin DIP package or a 44-pin PLCC IC package.

Both microprocessors feature a relocatable direct page (formally page zero on the 6502 and 65C02), nine new addressing modes, and 28 new operations. They also have two modes of operation. In *native* mode the registers can be used for either 8-bit or 16-bit operations. In *6502 emulation* mode the 6502's register set and instruction timings are emulated exactly (with corrections of a few bugs found on the 6502). The 65802 and 65816 are both powered-up into emulation mode and can be set into either mode through software.

The programming model in Fig. 14-9 shows the 16-bit accumulator, the 16-bit stack register, the two 16-bit index registers (X and Y), the 16-bit program counter, the 16-bit direct register, the 8-bit data bank register, and the 8-bit program bank register. The direct register is used to relocate the direct page, while the 8-bit data bank (DBR) and program bank (PBR) registers are used in 24-bit addressing to specify the bank in which memory transfers and instruction fetches are made. In emulation mode, both microprocessors also add a second, hidden, 8-bit accumulator (known as the B register) to the 6502's emulated register set. In native mode, the accumulator and index registers can be set to either 8- or 16-bits by using the M and X bits in the status register, as shown in Fig. 14-9. Also notice in Fig. 14-9, that the X bit replaces the B flag in the status register in the native mode. Since the 65802 and 65816 both add separate interrupt vectors, shown in Fig. 14-10, for software and hardware interrupts, the B flag is not needed. The E (emulation) bit is called a *phantom* bit because it cannot be directly tested, set, or cleared. The carry flag is overlayed with the emulation bit, and the XCE instruction exchanges the two so that the emulation bit can then be set or reset.

Coprocessors are supported by both microprocessors through a new COP instruction and its corresponding interrupt vector. The 65816 and the 44-pin PLCC version of the 65802 support multiprocessor systems with the memory lock ($\overline{ML}$) pin. The vector pull ($\overline{VP}$) pin of the 65816 and 44-pin PLCC 65802 allows implementation of vectored interrupt design. Found only on the 65816 are the valid data address (VDA), valid program address (VPA), and abort ($\overline{ABORT}$) pins. The

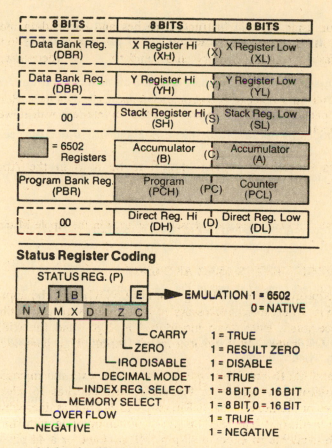

Fig. 14-9 Programming model for the 65816 microprocessor (*Courtesy of Western Design Center, Inc.*)

Name	Source	Emulation (E = 1)	Native (E = 0)	Priority Level
ABORT	Hardware	00FFF8,9	00FFE8,9	2
BRK	Software	00FFFE,F	00FFE6,7	N/A
COP	Software	00FFF4,5	00FFE4,5	N/A
IRQ	Hardware	00FFFE,F	00FFEE,F	4
NMI	Hardware	00FFFA,B	00FFEA,B	3
RES	Hardware	00FFFC,D	00FFFC,D (1 → E)	1

Fig. 14-10 Vector locations for the 65802 and 65816 microprocessors (*Courtesy of GTE Microcircuits.*)

VDA and *VPA* pins are used to implement dual cache and DMA cycle stealing. *Cycle stealing* is a method of DMA where a block of data is transferred 1 byte at a time. The $\overline{ABORT}$ input pin and corresponding interrupt vector gives support to virtual-memory system design.

SOLVED PROBLEMS

14.31 The 65816 and 65802 MPUs are _____ (fully, partially) compatible with the earlier 6502 microprocessor.

Solution:

The 65816 and 65802 MPUs are fully compatible with the earlier 6502 microprocessor.

14.32 The 65816 has _____ (16, 32)-bit internal registers and a(n) _____ (8, 16)-bit data bus. It can address up to 16_____ (Kbytes, Mbytes) of physical memory.

Solution:

       The 65816 has 16-bit internal registers and an 8-bit data bus. It can address up to 16 Mbytes of physical memory.

14.33 List the two modes of operation for the 65802 and 65816 microprocessors.

Solution:

       The two modes of operation for the 65802 and 65816 MPUs are the native mode and the 6502 emulation mode.

14.34 The 65816's direct register shown in Fig. 14-9 is used to _____ (relocate, stop) the direct page (formerly called _____ page on the 6502) in memory.

Solution:

       The 65816's direct register shown in Fig. 14-9 is used to relocate the direct page (formerly called zero page on the 6502) in memory.

14.35 The _____ input pin on the 65816 and the corresponding interrupt vector lend support to virtual-memory system design.

Solution:

       The $\overline{ABORT}$ input pin on the 65816 and the corresponding interrupt vector lend support to virtual-memory system design.

Supplementary Problems

14.36 The _____ (number) was the first 16-bit microprocessor introduced by Intel Corporation. *Ans.* 8086

14.37 The 6's group of microprocessors traces its origin back to the Motorola _____ (number) MPU. *Ans.* 6800

14.38 Refer to Fig. 14-1. Generally, 16-bit and 32-bit microprocessors are _____ (less, more) complex than 8-bit MPUs. *Ans.* more

14.39 Refer to Fig. 14-1. Generally, Apple Computer, Inc. has used chips from the _____ group while IBM's microcomputers use MPUs from the _____ group. *Ans.* 6's, 8's

14.40 The Intel 8086 chip features _____ (8, 16)-bit internal registers and a(n) _____ (8, 16)-bit data bus. The 8086 MPU can address _____ Mbyte(s) of memory. *Ans.* 16, 16, 1

14.41 The Intel _____ (number) MPU was used in the popular IBM PC microcomputer. *Ans.* 8088

14.42 The Intel _____ (80186, 80188) can be thought of as a faster upgraded version of the 8088 MPU. It _____ (is, is not) a plug-in replacement for the 8088 IC. *Ans.* 80188, is not

14.43 The Intel 80386 is a very advanced _____ (16, 32)-bit MPU especially adapted for multitask operating systems. It is used in the IBM _____ microcomputer. *Ans.* 32, PS/2 model 80

14.44 The Intel 80386 MPU features _____ (16, 32)-bit internal registers and a _____ (16, 32)-bit data bus. It can address _____ of physical memory.   *Ans.* 32, 32, 4 Gbytes

14.45 The Motorola 68000 is referred to as a _____ (16, 32)-bit external/_____ (16, 32)-bit internal MPU. This means it has a _____-bit data bus and _____-bit internal registers.
Ans. 16, 32, 16, 32

14.46 The 68000 MPU is used in what popular Apple microcomputer(s)?
Ans. original Macintosh, Macintosh Plus, and Macintosh SE

14.47 The 68000 MPU is available from Motorola in what three types of IC packages?
Ans. 64-pin DIP, 68-pin PLCC, 68-pin PGA

14.48 List the two modes of operation used by Motorola 68000-series microprocessors.
Ans. user mode, supervisor mode

14.49 The _____ (endurance, throughput) of a computer is the rate at which information can be processed by the system.   *Ans.* throughput

14.50 Generally, the throughput of a computer system can be increased by increasing the _____ of the MPU or by adding _____ information paths in the processor.   *Ans.* speed, parallel

14.51 Both the 68020 and 68030 MPUs employ a(n) _____-bit address bus capable of addressing _____ of memory.   *Ans.* 32, 4 Gbytes

14.52 The 65816 MPU is used in what Apple microcomputer?   *Ans.* Apple II$_{GS}$

14.53 The 65816 microprocessor was developed by _____ and employs _____ (8, 16)-bit internal registers and a(n) _____ (8, 16)-bit data bus.   *Ans.* Western Design Center, Inc.; 16; 8

14.54 List the two modes of operation used by the 65816 and 65802 microprocessors.
Ans. native mode, 6502 emulation mode

Index